RETAIL MANAGEMENT

A GLOBAL PERSPECTIVE

Text and Cases

RETAIL MANAGEMENT

A GLOBAL PERSPECTIVE

Text and Cases

Dr. Harjit Singh

MFC (Gold Medalist), MBA (Dual), M.Phil (Commerce)

S Chand And Company Limited

(ISO 9001 Certified Company)

S. Chand And Company Limited

(ISO 9001 Certified Company)

Head Office: D-92, Sector–2, Noida – 201301, U.P. (India), Ph. 91-120-4682700

Registered Office: A-27, 2nd Floor, Mohan Co-operative Industrial Estate, New Delhi – 110 044, Phone: 011-49731800

www.**schandpublishing.com;** e-mail: **info@schandpublishing.com**

Marketing Offices:

Chennai	:	Ph: 23632120; chennai@schandpublishing.com
Guwahati	:	Ph: 2738811, 2735640; guwahati@schandpublishing.com
Hyderabad	:	Ph: 40186018; hyderabad@schandpublishing.com
Jalandhar	:	Ph: 4645630; jalandhar@schandpublishing.com
Kolkata	:	Ph: 23357458, 23353914; kolkata@schandpublishing.com
Lucknow	:	Ph: 4003633; lucknow@schandpublishing.com
Mumbai	:	Ph: 25000297; mumbai@schandpublishing.com
Patna	:	Ph: 2260011; patna@schandpublishing.com

First Edition 2009
Second Revised Edition 2011
Third Revised Edition 2014; Reprints 2018, 2020 (Twice), 2022 (Twice), 2024

Reprint 2025

ISBN: 978-81-219-3207-3 **Product Code:** H8RMT60BMGT10ENAC14O

PRINTED IN INDIA

By Vikas Publishing House Private Limited, Plot 20/4, Site-IV, Industrial Area Sahibabad, Ghaziabad – 201 010 and Published by S Chand And Company Limited, A-27, 2nd Floor, Mohan Co-operative Industrial Estate, New Delhi – 110 044.

DEDICATION

"This book is dedicated to my wife Prabhjot, son Avneet and daughter Ms. Reet without their inspiration and tireless efforts this book would not have been possible."

PREFACE TO THE SECOND EDITION

I dare not lengthen this book much more,
lest it be out of moderation and should
stir up men's apathy because of its size.

Anonymous

I'm encouraged by the widespread response from India as well as abroad to the previous edition of the book. This new edition is a major revision of the book that brings it fully up to date, expands the coverage, and includes numerous improvements to the original material. The changes reflect my own experiences in using the book, as well as suggestions received from readers. As such no new chapter has been introduced but this revised edition contains retail in detail.

In revising the book I took the opportunity to rewrite and rearrange material especially in chapter 5: Retail Marketing Segmentation, Chapter 11: Managing a Retail Brand (*earlier called Branding Strategies*) and in Chapter 16: Supply Chain Management.

As expected, the book has been written in simple language with clear-cut explanation and suitable examples. The key aspects are presented in boxes or in annexures to make the concept crystal clear. I'm sure like previous one, this edition will not only be appreciated but also will be of greater use to the readers.

Author is grateful to the entire team of Management, Editorial and DTP staff of S. Chand & Company Ltd., New Delhi for their sincere cooperation and bringing out the second edition in such less time.

Dr. Harjit Singh

PREFACE TO THE FIRST EDITION

Driven by changing lifestyles, rising income levels, favourable demographic patterns and by the entry of corporate sector, Indian retail is growing like never before. Mall space, from a meager one million square feet in 2002 has touched over 50 million square feet by end-2008 and is estimated to cover 100 million plus square feet by 2010. Besides this, Indian cities are also witnessing a paradigm shift from traditional forms of *kirana* retailing to well organized self service sector. This is also evidenced by AT Kearney's Annual Global Retail Development Index (GRDI) 2007 that has ranked India on the top in terms of Market saturation and time pressure as compared to Russia and China. Though the market has been dominated by unorganized players, the entry of national and international organized players is set to change the scenario. Organized retail segment has been growing at a blistering pace, leaving all previous national and international estimates. Bangaluru, Delhi, Noida, Chennai, and Hyderabad have become major retail hubs. Large conglomerates like Tata, Birla, ITC, RPG, Reliance, and Raheja have initiated huge investment in retailing. Oil giants like IOC, BPCL and HPCL are also expanding from fuel retailing to grocery & food retailing. Foreign collaborations are exploding and triggering the rapidly growing Indian middle class.

However, the success of retail industry would depend on how efficiently retail stores perform their day-to-day operations. The store operations play very important role in the profitability and long-term survival. The rate at which new and new stores are coming up and are getting out of the competition is a serious issue for Indian retail industry. It seems that these retail stores are coming in the market without proper homework. The approach, a store has towards merchandising placement, the visual aspects, the customers and team work, affects the store's bottomline. The store staff doesn't know how to attend the customers wisely? How to implement new techniques of selling and sales promotion? Even store manger is not effective in training and development parts of employees. Money is being spent on training and development of store's employees still retail staff hesitate in experimenting new in their selling behaviour. With the increasing competition, they necessitate to be updated when it comes to cost cutting techniques and managing store's day-to-day activities.

This book, in its present form is an icy shower in the hinterland of retail world and is intended to provide a comprehensive text to cover this much talked but less understood issue in the global perspective and is essential reading for anyone who wants to know the nuts and bolts of retailing, its present status and interested in knowing how it is affecting the life of common men. The global context has been kept in view throughout the book and the basic ideas are supported by empirical findings and media reports.

The book is divided into six sections. Section I introduces the reader to basic concepts and theories of retailing, various retail formats, essence for strategic planning in retailing, retailing in India and across the globe and sets the tone for strategic retailing. Further, reasons for retail growth, global retailing trends and various aspects of consumer behaviour are mentioned.

Section II deals with Retailing Strategy, Store Location, Retail Marketing Segmentation, Strategic Planning in Retail, Financial Strategy and Inventory Control. The reader is also exposed to managerial issues associated with merchandise optimization, forecasting, emerging opportunities and threats in retail selling.

Section III which is Merchandise Management explains how effectively merchandise is planned and managed. Further it comprises of planning as to what to buy, from where to buy, how much to buy, how to negotiate, how to pay, how to receive, stock and reorder. Critical issues like negotiation, acquisition, evaluation, legal and ethical aspects related to merchandise management are expressed.

Section IV is devoted to Store Management that describes administrative, management, security, supply chain management and loss prevention issues. Appropriateness of training store employees, various methods of employees' training are also explained in detail.

Section V deals with the essence, role and methods of communicating to store employees. The concept of customer service, how to promote retail sales effectively and the issue of building customer relationships and competitive advantage has been studied in detail.

Finally Section VI discusses the various inferences drawn from previous chapters and presents the future of retailing. How internet retailing is becoming popular, what are the career opportunities in retailing and Indian Government's policy towards FDI in retailing is discussed.

Though, primarily targeted for postgraduate students, **Retail Management: Text and Cases** would be useful to the graduates, retail executives, academicians and practicing managers too. I will appreciate and gratefully acknowledge the suggestions and comments from the readers and fellow teachers of the subject to further improve the book.

Author can be reached at author_retail@rediffmail.com.

Dr. Harjit Singh

ACKNOWLEDGEMENTS

Preparing an acknowledgement is one of the most pleasant tasks in textbook script, as on one side you fight the final deadlines and on other side plan for the launch party of your dream work. Despite this, no one should be so selfish that he forgets those who inspired and kept him on track during text writing and this should be acknowledged.

In the light of the foregoing, I offer my deep sense of appreciation to my mentor, Dr. S.D.Vashishtha, Professor and Head, Department of Commerce, M.D.University and my friend Vinay Dutta, Senior Professor, Fore School of Management, New Delhi who have been a continuous source of inspiration in carrying out this book.

This trifle work of mine would have been a zygote, if not have achieved the support, co-operation and blessings of few people without whom I would not have been able to turn up. Therefore, I would like to put my heartfelt thanks to Dr. Sanjay Jain, Dr. Arun Julka, Dr. Mahajan, Dr. V.K. Garg, Dr. Harish Handa, Delhi University, Prof. R.Vinayak, Prof. S.S. Chahal, and Prof. M.S. Malik from M.D. University, Rohtak and Prof. K.K. Uppal of Punjabi University, Patiala.

Tradition asks me to send 'thanks' to my significant others, children, friends, relatives, and so on and Who are we to break the custom? I respect my legacy, I am indebted to my beloved parents, brother and in-laws who deserve nothing short of honour. I thank them for their love, affection and sincere hand for assisting me and creating an ambience where I could put my best into this book.

Friends are nature's souvenirs, and I'm gifted with tons of friends who have gone to edges to support my efforts, my deeds and helped me in various ways for successful completion of this book. My kind indebtness to other works has been duly acknowledged at the relevant places.

As this book was to a large extent written during weekends; which encroached upon the time normally meant for my family and social obligations, I would be remiss if I failed to thank my dear wife Prabhjot, who gave up so much of her time to support me writing this book and my son *Avneet* (Sidak) & daughter *Reet* for having provided enormous support inspite of bearing the brunt of elongated study hours. Really they are gracious enough to forgive me for a lots of times I rejected their proposal for sight seeing and having weekends outside. I now promise to spend more time with them in the future.

Finally, I would like to thank you, the reader, for reading/buying this book. Agreed that I wrote this book by putting myself into readers' shoes, it's the least I could do to personally thank you for the support you're showing by reading the preface. It's the small things that make the biggest difference in life, and I would like to express my earnest thanks to you for the effort you've put in to read my book.

Dr. Harjit Singh

LIST OF ABBREVIATIONS

ABC	Always Best Control
AIDA	Awareness, Interest, Desire and Action
APMCA	Agricultural Produce Marketing Committee Act
ATM	Automatic Teller Machine
BCG	Boston Consulting Group
B2B	Business to Business
B2C	Business to Consumer
BEP	Break Even Point
BOGOF	Buy One Get One Free
BOM	Beginning of the Month
BPCL	Bharat Petroleum Corporation Limited
CAGR	Compound Annual Growth Rate
CCTV	Close Circuit Television Camera
CD	Cross Docking
CEO	Chief Executive Officer
COD	Channel of Distribution
CONCOR	Container Cooperation of India Ltd
CPFR	Collaborative Planning, Forecasting & Replenishment
CRM	Customer Relationship Management
CSL	Customer Satisfaction Level
EAS	Electronic Article Surveillance
ECR	Efficient Customer Response
EDI	Electronic Data Interchange
EDLP	Every Day Low Prices
EOM	End of the Month
EOQ	Economic Order Quantity
EOU	Export Oriented Units
FAQ	Frequently Asked Questions
FIPB	Foreign Investment Promotion Board
FMCG	Fast Moving Capital Goods
FTP	File Transfer Protocol
FSI	Free Standing Insert
FSN	Fast, Slow, Non-Moving
FTZ	Free Trade Zones
GOI	Government of India
GRDI	Global Retail Development Index
HML	High, Medium, Low
HPCL	Hindustan Petroleum Corporation Ltd
HUDCO	Housing and Development Corporation Limited
ICICI	Industrial Credit and Investment Corporation of India
ICT	Information and Communication Technology
IHDP	International Home Deco Park

IMC	Integrated Marketing Communication
IOC	Indian Oil Corporation
IP	Intellectual Property
IPO	Initial Public Offer
IT	Information Technology
JIT	Just in Time
LP	Loss Prevention
LPG	Liberalization, Privatization and Globalization
MBP	Merchandise Budget Plan
MCFT	Modular Curved Frame Technology
MCPU	Manufacturing Cost per Unit
MNC	Multi National Company
MRP	Materials Requirement Planning
MRP	Maximum Retail Price
MSE	Madras Stock Exchange
M&S	Marks and Spencer
NBFC	Non Banking Finance Company
NCR	National Capital Region
NRF	National Retail Federation
OMS	Operations Master Schedule
OTB	Open to Buy
POG	Plan-o-gram
POP	Point-of-Purchase
POS	Point-of-Service
QR	Quick Response
R&D	Research and Development
RM	Retail Management
Rs.	Rupee
SEBI	Securities and Exchange Board of India
SEZ	Special Economy Zones
SPH	Sales per Hour
SIM	Selective Inventory Management
SKU	Store Keeping Unit
SWOT	Strength, Weakness, Opportunity and Threat
TCPO	Transport Cost per Unit
TQM	Total Quality Management
USP	Unique Selling Preposition
UMP	Unique Marketing Preposition
VED	Vital, Essential, Desirable
VICS	Voluntary Inter-industry Commerce Standards Committee
VM	Visual Merchandising
VMI	Vendor Managed Inventory
WWW	World Wide Web
WAP	Wireless Application Protocol
XML	Extensible Markup Language
ZI	Zero Inventory

BRIEF CONTENTS

DETAILED CONTENTS

SECTION-I: RETAILING INTRODUCTION

SECTION-III: MANAGING MERCHANDISE

SECTION-V: RETAIL COMMUNICATION

SECTION-VI: FUTURE OF RETAILING

LIST OF EXHIBITS

List of Figures

RETAILING INTRODUCTION

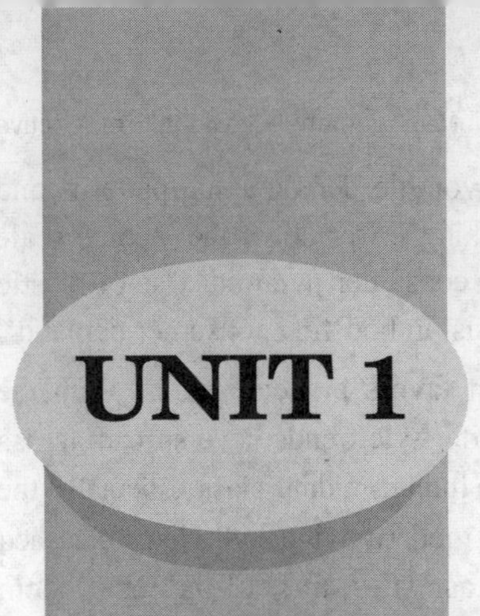

INTRODUCTION TO RETAILING

LEARNING OBJECTIVES

- Understanding how retailing originated in India
- Knowing the functions a retailer has to perform in his day to day routine
- Describing the status of retailing in India and abroad
- Explaining the present scenario and future of traditional *kirana* stores
- Identifying the essence of productivity in modern retailing

"An implicit confession is almost as bad as an implicit faith; wicked men commonly confess their sins by wholesale, we are all sinners; but the true penitent confesses his sins by retail"

Thomas Brooks

INTRODUCTION

Liberalized financial and political environment in India has prompted a wave of large number of entrants into the country's rapidly growing retail industry during the past few years, without doubt, the retail industry in India is in the throes of radical restructuring. The fundamental drivers of change are increasing per capita income, growing GDP, availability of consumer finance and therefore irreversible. Retailing in general sense consists of business activities that are involved in buying and selling of goods and services to ultimate consumers for their own use – ranging from Bread butter to automobiles to apparels to airline tickets. In India, after agriculture, the retail is the second largest sector that provides enough employment to Indian workforce. But retailing in India is at cross roads on the one side, retail sales are making new heights year after year and on the other side, traditional Indian retailers (*Kirana* stores) face numerous challenges.

Experts believe that retail expansion in the coming five to seven years is expected to be stronger than our Indian GDP growth, driven by changing lifestyles and by strong income growth, which in turn will be supported by favorable demographic patterns and the extent to which organized retailers succeed in reaching lower down the income scale to reach potential consumers towards the bottom of the consumer pyramid. Use of plastic money, easy availability of consumer credit will also assist in boosting consumer demand[1].

Today, a vast majority of India's young population favors branded goods. With the spread of satellite televisions and visual media, urban life style trends have spread across the rural areas also. The shopping extravaganza of the Indian middle class especially the young population for clothing, eating outside and lust for modern living styles has unleashed new possibilities for retail growth even in the rural areas. Thus, 85% of the retail boom which was focussed only in the metros has started to infiltrate towards smaller cities and towns. Tier-II cities are already receiving focussed attention of retailers and the other smaller towns and even villages are likely to join in the coming years. This is a positive trend, and the contribution of these tier-II cities to total organized retailing sales is expected to grow to 20-25%[2]. One of the principal reasons behind the explosion of retail and its fragmented nature in the country is the fact that retailing is probably the primary form of disguised unemployment/underemployment in the country. Given the already over-crowded agriculture sector, and the stagnating manufacturing sector, and the hard nature and relatively low wages of jobs in both, many million Indians are virtually forced into the services sector[3].

In this chapter, attempt has been made to understand much talked but less understood issue of retailing. The chapter begins with the concept of retail and examines its significance to the economy and the reasons why to study retailing and how it's gaining worldwide acceptance. This chapter also discusses the principles and various functions of retailing.

MEANING AND DEFINITION

To better understand the role of retail format in an economy and its significance, let us first try to understand what actually retail is? And how it is different from wholesale business?

RETAILING

Provides

- time utility
- place utility
- possession utility

Through

- Store location
- Store environment
- Merchandise selection
- Salespersons

Retailing consists of selling merchandise from a permanent location (a retail store) in small quantities directly to the consumers. These consumers may be individual buyers or corporate. In the world of Trade and Commerce, a retailer purchases goods or merchandise in bulk from manufacturers directly and then sells in small quantities are known as Retail stores or shops. Shops may be located in residential areas, colony streets, community

1 *www.researchandmarkets.com*

2 *http://www.fibre2fashion.com*

3 *www.idiafdiwatch.org*

centers or in modern shopping arcades/ malls. In fact, any organization selling merchandise to final consumers –whether a producer, wholesaler or a retailer –is doing retail business. It does not take into account how the merchandise is being sold. While on the other hand, retail format is a blend of product range, pricing, marketing and the way the items are displayed. A retail-format will be suitable for a retailer does not depend upon market practice but upon retailer's budget, merchandise and the need of the locality. A good format draws more footfalls and helps retailer a platform to succeed and earn name and fame.

CHARACTERISTICS OF RETAILING

Retailing is different from other forms of business in the following ways:

(i) It offers direct interaction with customers/end consumers.
(ii) Sale volume is comparatively large in quantities but less in monetary value as compared to exporting/manufacturing.
(iii) Customer service plays a vital role in the success of retail business.
(iv) Sales promotions are offered at this point only.
(v) In almost all countries, retail outlets are more than any other form of business.
(vi) Location and layout are critical factors in retail business.
(vii) It offers employment opportunity to all age groups irrespective of age and gender, qualification or religion etc.

EVOLUTION OF RETAILING IN INDIA

The beginning of retail business in India can be traced back to the emergence of Weekly Bazaars and Rural Fairs (Melas). These weekly bazaars, used to be big attraction to both urban and rural people by catering their day to day requirements of grocery, utensils, spices, grain, clothing, live stock, wooden/hand made items, hand made candles, fruits etc. besides serving source of entertainment. In comparison to weekly markets, village fairs usually were bigger in size with a wide variety of goods sold from handmade items, food, clothing, cosmetics and small consumer durables. Then the traditional age saw the emergence of the neighborhood 'kirana' store (usually known as Convenience stores or Mom-and-pop store) to cater to convenience of the Indian consumers as shown in figure 1.1.

Ultimately the government came forward and supported the rural retail and many local franchise stores. They came to nation's main commerce stream with the financial and marketing support of Khadi & Village Industries Commission (KVIC). Today KVIC has a nationwide chain of more than 7000 stores in India. This phase also eyewitnesses the emergence of multi level shopping stores with parking facility. Then with the opening up of economy in 1980s, the retailing in India saw huge change in terms of its size and functioning. S Kumar's, Bombay Dyeing and Raymonds were among few companies to come up with retail chains in textile sector.

Ancient Retailing

The business of retail flourished in the past because some were having surplus of one good and shortage of another good and vice versa. According to records, earlier traders were cretans who sailed the Mediterranean and started the retailing business with the people of thatarca. They continued for roughly 2000 years and distributed goods to Egypt and Babylonia.

Carthage, Sidon and Tyre used to be the main trading goods. Later on this group was ultimately taken over by the Romans. The Romans set up a very sophisticated form of retailing, in the major commercial areas especially urban one. The concepts of shops (outlets) in fact originated in Rome. The ancient ruins even confirm that first of all departments store originated in Rome but with the fall of Rome Empire, retailing disintegrated and spreaded to the remaining part of the world.

Later Titan (a Tata Product) launched retail showrooms in various parts of the country under organized form of retailing. As time passed, the new retail players moved on from manufacturing to pure retailing. Retail outlets such as Food world in FMCG, Crossword in books, Music World and Planet M in Music, entered the market during mid 1995 . Malls emerged in metros and big cities like Hyderabad giving a world-class experience to the customers under one roof. Supermarkets and Hypermarkets started emerging with the continuous improvement in the distribution channels, supply chain management, back-end and technology operations, etc. Today India has a host of both small and large formats with exclusive stores having national and international brands under one roof catering to all sections of the society. These new retail formats such as super markets and hyper markets are constantly trying to provide the customer with the 3 V's. (Variety, Value, and Volume). Over the last couple of years, Indian retail industry has witnessed a ridiculous growth rate due to the entry of various international quality formats to suit the Indian middle class, by offering affordable merchandise under great width and depth. Today Indian retail industry is the second largest employer in the country with almost over 12 million retail stores in India. Although the retail sector is still dominated by unorganized retail sector, organized retailing is growing fast at almost 25-30% per annum and is believed to touch a figure of Rs. 2,00,000 crore by 2010 . The Indian economy is projected to grow between 10-11 % in 2011-12 having grown at a stable rate of around 6-7% over the last decade.

Figure 1.1

Evolution of Indian retail

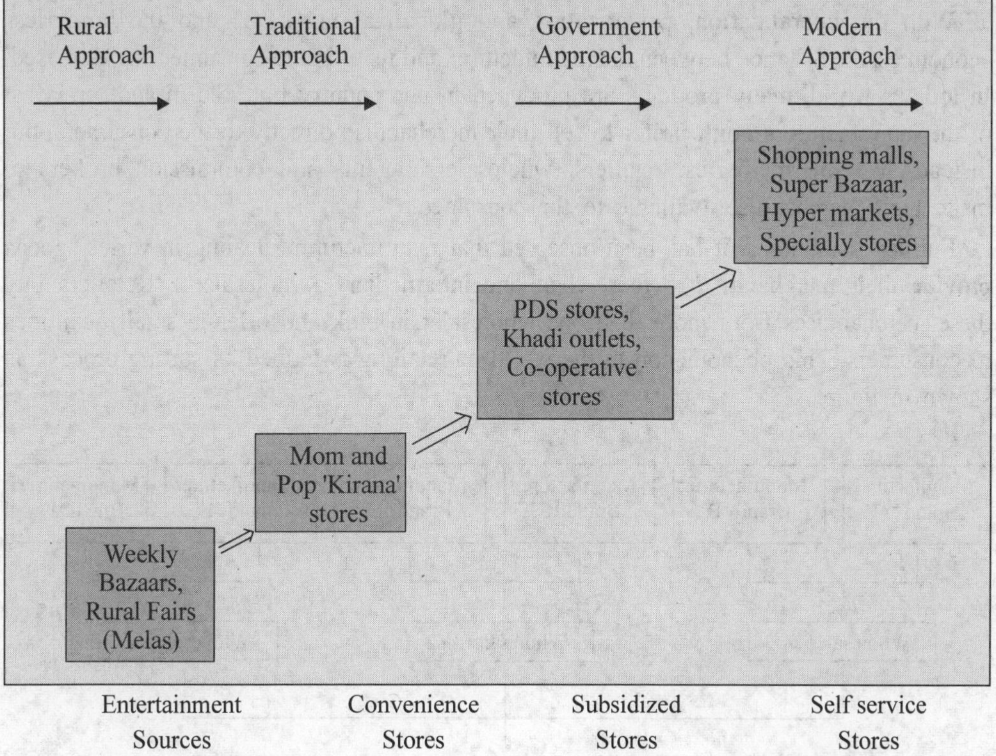

Rural Approach
Traditional Approach
Government Approach
Modern Approach
Shopping malls, Super Bazaar, Hyper markets, Specially stores
PDS stores, Khadi outlets, Co-operative stores
Mom and Pop 'Kirana' stores
Weekly Bazaars, Rural Fairs (Melas)
Entertainment Sources
Convenience Stores
Subsidized Stores
Self service Stores

FUNCTIONS OF A RETAILER

Retailing is the last stage in a channel of distribution, which consists of all the trades and people involved in the physical movement and transfer of ownership of goods and services from manufacturer to ultimate consumer as is shown in figure 1.2:

Manufacturer
Wholesaler
Retailer
Final Consumer

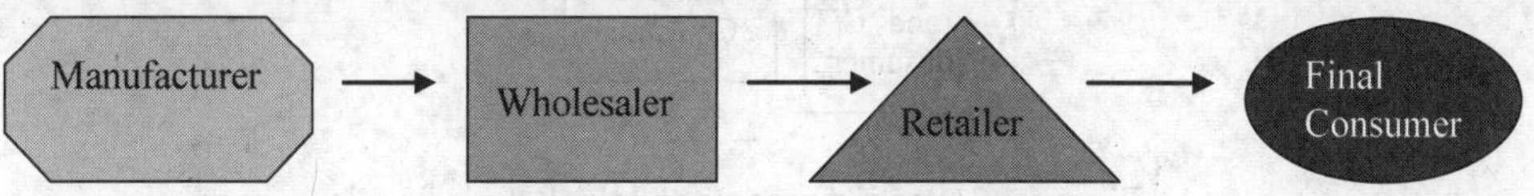

Figure 1.2: Channel of distribution

If we analyze the distribution process we find that the retailer plays a key role as the contact between manufactures, wholesalers and the ultimate consumers. Retailers are the gate keepers to the market for all other members of the sales distribution process while on the other hand wholesaling is an intermediate stage in the distribution channel during which merchandise (both goods and services) are sold to business customers not to ultimate consumers. Business customers here are wholesalers, exporters and retailers who buy for resale or to run their business. One thing in this regard should be noted that wholesaling excludes producers and farmers because their task is to produce the goods. Therefore, the best way of understanding the relationship between wholesalers and retailers is to look at it from the manufacturer's point of view that provides the clear picture of the sales distribution process.

With the liberalization, privatization and globalization (LPG) and the borderless economies, the distance between the manufacturer and its ultimate consumer has increased. In today's world, many products are produced in one country but sold in another. Most of the manufacturers don't prefer to sell their merchandise directly to the consumers, but instead, like intermediaries, retailers, wholesalers, agents and commission brokers to make their merchandise available to the consumer.

Further, sometimes, it has been observed that manufacturers dealing in variety goods provide their merchandise to more than one intermediary (wholesalers). Retailers buy these merchandises from more than one wholesaler in bulk and offer in small quantities to consumers. This phenomenon in the world of retailing is termed as sorting process as shown in figure 1.3:

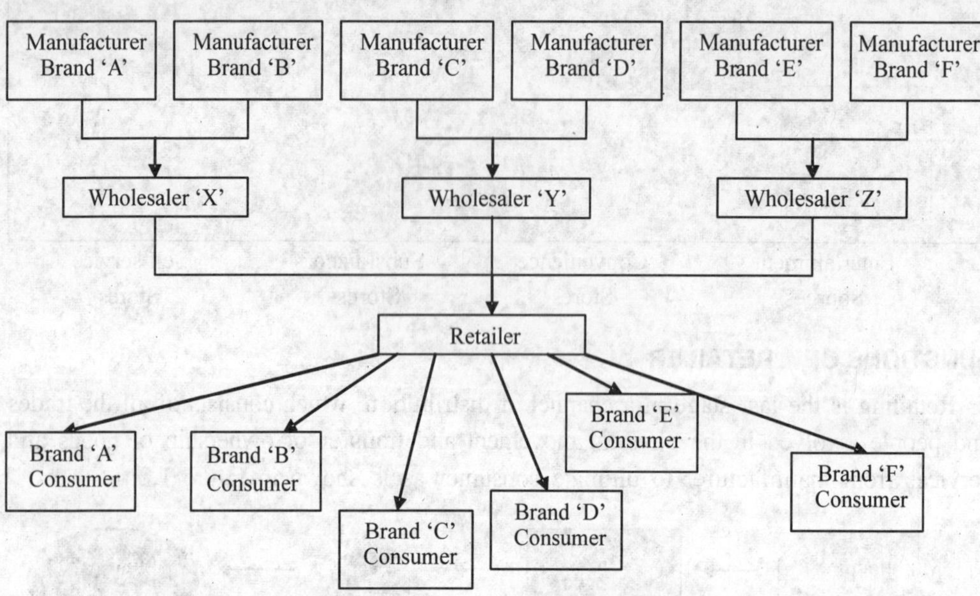

Figure 1.3: Sorting process and the Retailer's role

The benefit of sorting process is that according to the variety of merchandise and business complexity, it can change different shapes, consequently, manufacturer becomes more effective and ultimately consumers find this comfortable and convenient as they get different goods and services under one roof and in as much quantity as they need. Otherwise, it becomes difficult for the consumer to visit one source to another to collect and assortment of goods and services. Further, wholesalers enjoy selling the goods and services in bulk rather than attending individual consumers, as their invested amount is more and therefore, want quick return on their investments.

Retailing Functions

Retailers are the last and vital members in the channel of distribution. The retailer serves the manufacturer by providing his goods and services to the consumers and creates a channel of information where customers' feedback, their expectations and points of dissatisfaction (if any) are shared with the manufacturer. From customer's point of view, the retailer's main function is to provide merchandise in the right quality, quantity, price, time, and at the right place. This objective is achieved through following perspectives:

1. **Identifying Consumer Demands**: The first task that a retailer has to perform is to identify the consumer needs and wants. The retailer does not provide raw materials, but offers finished goods and services in a ready-to-use form that the consumers want. For this, from time-to-time, retailer gathers information about consumers' liking, disliking, tastes and preferences.
2. **Management of Merchandise**: The second task that a retailer performs is the management of merchandise. The retailer performs the function of storing the merchandise and provides as and when required by the customer.
3. **Convenience of timing**: The retailer creates time utility by keeping the store open and ready for sale according to consumers' convenience. The new trend in retailing to longer trade hours reflects the socio-cultural changes where over one in ten people work outside normal hours resulting in changing trading hours and panacea for small retailers against the cheaper prices of the super stores and other retail chains. By being available at a location that has easy access and convenient to shop, retailer creates place utility. Finally, when selected and bought by customers, retailers create ownership utility.

In short, retailers are not only the final link between the consumers and the manufacturers but a vital part of modern business world. In the absence of retailing, one can easily imaging how difficult and costly for a consumer to approach a manufacturer for various things every time he wants. Retailers do not sell things in small quantities but make their shopping convenient and less risky. Retailers have floor staff to answer their queries regarding how to use effectively and safely, guide them what to buy according to individual preferences and budget and give demonstration or display products so that the consumers should have a feel of the merchandise before buying. The successful retailer focuses its activities on meeting these objectives through effective marketing.

RETAILING PRINCIPLES

In order to be sound and effective, an organization must be governed by the following basic principles:

1. Clear definition of objectives and policies

According to this principle of retail organization, each employee must understand the objectives and policies of the store. If the objectives are not clearly defined, the employees in the retail organization shall not be in a position to understand what is expected from them and in what type of activities the organization engage itself.

2. Duties and Responsibilities

According to this principle, the duties and responsibilities of each and every employee, working at various levels in the retail store should be clearly defined. The line of authority must be clear from the highest to the lowest positions. All employees must be well informed of their respective position, responsibilities in the retail organization and the persons to whom they are answerable and who reports to them.

3. Unity of Command

According to this principle, one employee working at junior level should be responsible to one direct supervisor. The purpose is to avoid any conflict regarding responsibilities of employees receiving orders from more than one supervisor.

4. Supervision and Control

According to this principle, even after delegating the authority, the supervisor still will be responsible for a manager's or employees' mistakes. He cannot get rid of the mistake done by his juniors or those who are to achieve the goal.

5. Interest in employees

According to this principle, the retail organization should show continuous interest in its employees, job promotion, employees' participation in management, internal promotion, efforts/job recommendation, job enrichment, induction and so on; improve employee's morale and efficiency.

6. Monitoring of Human Resource

According to this principle, issues related to employees like attendance, employee turnover, punctuality and absenteeism should be regularly monitored otherwise they can create problems for the whole organization.

7. Rule of Simplicity

According to this principle, simplicity in all sorts of operations is must for running a retail organization properly. There should be a limit to the number of employees a manager could directly supervise.

8. Responsibility and Authority

According to this principle, assigning duties without any authority will not work in a retail organization. Therefore, responsibilities should be associated with proper authority. An employee who is responsible to achieve some retail organization's objectives needs the power to achieve it.

9. Division of Labour

According to this principle, in order to achieve organizational objectives, the work should be divided among subordinates properly. It means dividing the retail organization's work in various departments into various components and then assigning the same to each employee of the organization. It enables the management to fix up the responsibilities on each employee concerned.

RETAIL SALES GOALS

Retail Sales measures the gross receipts of a retail store by selling durable and non-durable goods. The main components of retail sales are grocery, food & clothing and shoe retailing. In India, consumer spending roughly accounts for over 60% of GDP and is therefore, a vital element in the country's economic growth. Any change in retail sales pattern is important and is seen as the timeliest indicator of wide consumption patterns.

Retail sales may have short term and long term goals in nature. Short term retail sales goals are supposed to support and merge into long term goals. The goals of retail sales irrespective of a country's profile are:

(i) to serve a link between the manufacturer and end consumers
(ii) to improve communication with retail customers
(iii) to improve sales target
(iv) to provide efficient customer service knowing the power of mouth advertisement
(v) to build image among general public
(vi) to improve social responsibility
(vii) to serve different markets
(viii) to get quick feedback about the merchandise sold and consumer services offered
(ix) to convert visitors to buyers
(x) Optimum utilization of fixed cost related expenses.

RETAILING IN INDIA

India is known as the 'nation of shops'. After agriculture, retailing is the second largest employer in India. Approximately, over 12 million shops exist in various parts of the country. These shops are totally unorganized, independent, owned-managed outlets. Presence of unorganized/traditional retailing is highly prominent in small towns and cities with main presence of neighborhood "*kirana*" stores, push-cart vendors, "*melas*" and "*mandis*". Organized formats are only in the initial stages of adoption in these regions. Leading retail players in the industry are beginning to explore these markets and the rural consumers are slowly beginning to embrace the newer organized retail formats.

The changing Urban Consumer

- Inclined to international styles
- Inclined to acquiring property
- More demanding and discerning
- High level of education
- Ready to spend on shopping
- Shopping is a family fun

Figure 1.4
Retail Sales in India

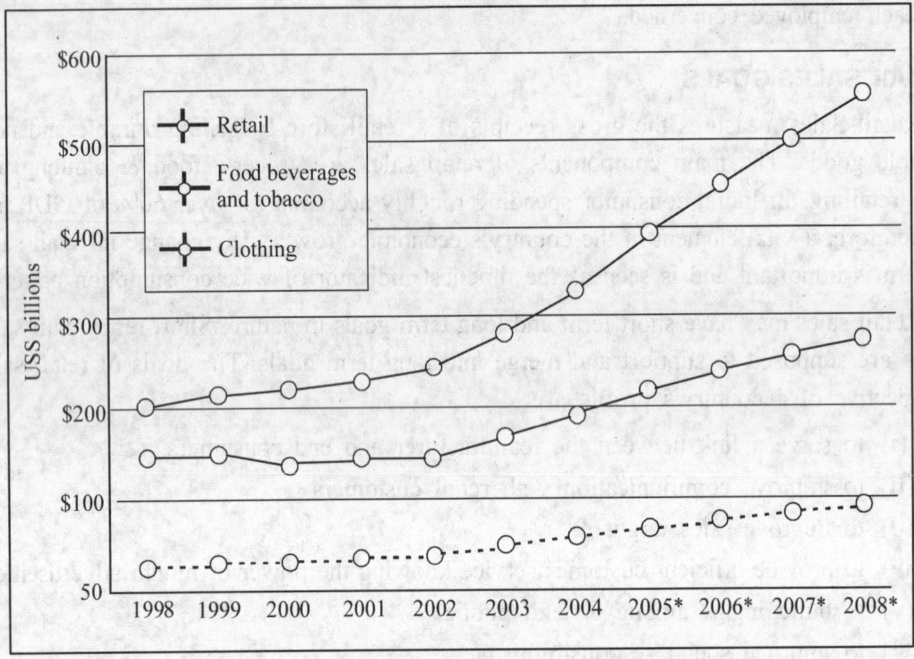

Sources : *Economist Intellegence Unit and A.T. Kerney analysis* * *Data for 2005-2008 is based on estimates*

Due to rising per capita income and fast emerging middle-class has made India the favorable destination for retailing. New and new malls are coming up in the urban parts of the country. Franchisee' outlets are mushrooming. More and more business houses are venturing into the retail industry. New retail formats are emerging and even changing the traditional face of jewellery shops, furniture shops, book stores and pharmacy shops. People are spending their major portion of income on food and clothing. The share was 72.8% in 2006, worth approximately 9861.4 billion; while non-food and clothing sales was worth 3476.8 billion and this trend seems to continue in the years to come. The Indian retail industry is broadly divided into two segments:

(i) Organized retailing, and
(ii) Unorganized retailing.

Top players:

1. Pantaloon Retail
2. K Raheja Group
3. Tata group
4. RPG group
5. Landmark group
6. Piramal Group
7. Vishal
8. Bharti-Walmart
9. Reliance
10. AV Birla Group

Organized Retailing

In India, traditional forms of independent owned small business and co-operatives have lost their earlier charm. Though the arrival of organized retail in India is a bit late but it is increasing by leaps and bounds. In 2010, the retail industry in India was amounted to Rs 20,000 billion is expected to cross Rs 50,000 billion by 2015 in which organized sector will cross 3,000 million. The most significant period of growth for the sector was between years 2000 and 2006, when the sector revenues increased by about 93.5 per cent translating to an average annual growth of 13.3 per cent. The sector's growth was partly a reflection of the impressive Indian economic growth and overall rise in income levels of consumers. Hence it is believed that organized retail in India is expected to scale up to meet global standards over the next five years[4].

Figure 1.5
Indian organized Retail Market

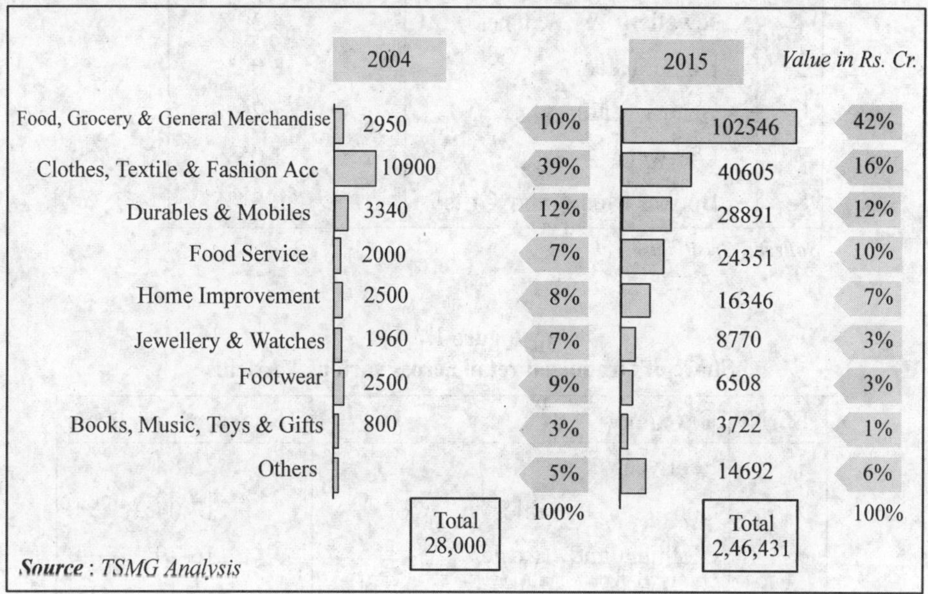

Retail Growth Across Segments

Unlike Europe, Indian Retailing is mainly classified by the type of products retailed, as opposed to the different retail formats in operation. If we study these retail verticals, one may find that the Food and Beverages vertical only accounts nearly 75 (as shown in figure1.6 while figure 1.7 depicts share of organized retail under various retail verticals) per cent of the total retail market. Amongst all the present groups, this category has the highest consumer demand across all income levels with food, grocery and allied products largely purchased from the local stores or push-cart vendors.

Next comes 'apparels and consumer durables' being the fastest growing verticals in the retail sector. Cell phones as a product category has witnessed the highest growth in consumer demand amongst all retail product offerings, with increasing penetration of telecommunications in towns and villages. The Telecommunications sector has been adding on an average 5 million new users every month. The other product categories are gaining atraction predominantly in the urban areas and emerging cities, with increasing average income and spending power of young urban India.

Figure 1.6
Share of Verticals across Various Segments

Sl. No	Category	Share of Verticals
1	Food & Beverages	74.41%
2	Clothing and Textiles	9.31%
3	Consumer Durables	4.87%
4	Jewellery & Watches	4.30%
5	Home Décor	3.04%
6	Beauty Care	2.20%
7	Footwear	1.05%
8	Books, Music and Gifts	0.84%

Source: *Crisil Research*

Figure 1.7
Share of Organized retail across various Verticals

Sl. No	Category	Share of Verticals
1	Footwear	32.84
2	Consumer Durables	17.04
3	Clothing and Textiles	16.39
4	Food & Beverages	13.08
5	Home Décor and Furnish	8.76
6	Jewellery & Watches	6.19
7	Beauty Care	3.56
8	Books, Music and Gifts	0.98

Source: *Crisil Research*

Organized retailing in India is mainly present in metro cities only. But few players are now eyeing Tier II and Tier III cities to explore the opportunities. According to India Retail Report, 2007, the Indian retail industry is valued at $270 billion with organized retailing contributing 4.5 percent and is expected to see a growth at a CAGR of 37 % as shown in figure 1.8) while figure 1.10 represents the organized retail growth from 2002-2007.

4 *www.ibef.org.*

Figure 1.8

Sectors contributing organized retail

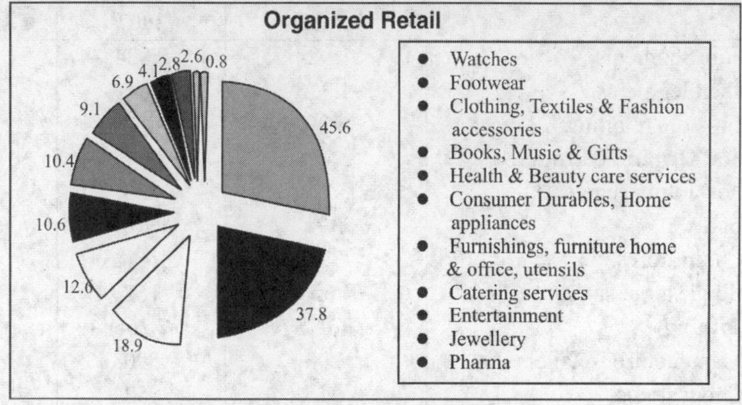

Source: *India Retail Report*

Figure: 1.9

Organized Retailing Surging High: Up-beating Middle Class

As India surges high with its earning middle class, the retail sector in the country is bound to come across opportunities like never before. Till a few years back, the retail sector in India was more of an unorganized one with petty vendors dominating the chunk of the industry but now the scenario has fast been changing. Finally, the sector is converting into what we call as organized retailing. To avail this opportunity, not only Indian corporate majors like Reliance, Tata, ITC and Pantaloon have entered into the segment but more and more foreign players are also showing interest in USD 500 billion Indian retail markets. Today, if one turn around he will find giant shopping malls and multiplexes all the way. Perhaps that's why the retail revolution is said to be spearheading the real estate boom in India.

Figure 1.10

Estimated Growth in Organized Retail $(mn)

	2002	2007	CARG (%)
Large Segments	1,924	5,024	21%
Other Segments	1,315	2,645	15%
Non-store retailing	239	422	12%
Total Organized retail	**3,478**	**8,091**	**18%**
The 4 Large segments			
Food	**391**	**1,624**	**33%**
- Chain stores	326	1,462	35%
- Single large stores	65	162	20%
Clothing	**1,075**	**2,266**	**16%**
- Manufacturer retailers	293	590	15%
- Chain stores	315	852	22%
- Single large stores	467	824	12%
Consumer durables	**359**	**822**	**18%**
- Manufacturer retailers	141	284	15%
- Chain stores	98	298	25%
- Single large stores	120	240	15%
Books & Music	**97**	**310**	**26%**
- Chain stores	54	202	30%
- Single large stores	43	108	20%

Source : *Economics Times Retail Knowledge Series*

The growth in Indian organized retail sector is mainly because of shift in consumer behavior. This change has come due to the following reasons:

1. Rapidly increasing income level
2. Changes in lifestyle
3. Favorable pattern of geography
4. Retail offers one-roof shopping experience
5. Emergence of nuclear family concept
6. Improved purchasing power of Indian middle class
7. Presence of domestic and foreign players
8. Expansion of family owned businesses
9. Effect of LPG (Liberalization, Privatization and Globalization)
10. Building chains around brands
11. Mass inflow of FDI in Indian retail sectors
12. Liberalization of the Indian economy which has led to the opening up of the market for consumer

Large Indian Retailers

Department store
Lifestyle
Pantaloons
Piramyds
Shoppers Stop
Trent

Hypermarket
Big Bazaar
Giants
Shoprite
Star

Entertainment
Fame Adlabs
Fun Republic
Inox
PVR

goods has helped the MNC brands like Kellogg, Unilever, Nestle, etc. to make significant inroads into the vast consumer market by offering a wide range of choices to the Indian consumers[5].

13. Emergence of new business sectors like ICT, engineering firms, outsourcing etc

Facts about Indian Retailing

Retail industry is one of the largest contributors to Indian GDP. The study at Tata Strategic Management Group (TSMG) indicates that over the next decade, the Indian retail industry is likely to grow at a compounded annual growth rate (CAGR) of 5.5% (at constant prices) to USD 374 billion (Rs 16,77,000 crore) in 2015. The organized retail market is expected to grow much faster, at a GAGR of 21.8% to USD 55 billion (Rs 2,46,000 crore) in the same time frame. The success story of wal-mart in the small and remote areas of USA has further tempted Indian retailers to focus on smaller towns and rural parts of the country. It presents a tremendous opportunity for Indian retail industry (especially organized retail) to grow and prosper.

Unorganized Retailing

Traditional retailing continues to be the backbone of the Indian retail industry, with traditional/unorganized retailing contributing to over 95 per cent of total retail revenues. The prototypical '*baniya*' outlets or the corner store formats comprise a key part of Indian retail store formats mostly run as small family businesses. The unorganized retailing comprises of '*mom and pop*' stores or '*kirana*' stores. These are very small shops located near the residential areas, popularly known as '*baniya shops*'. The **UMP** (Unique Marketing Preposition) of these stores is location advantage. These shop owners in order to retain their customers can even go to their customers' houses to get orders. Trading hours are flexible and the retailer to consumer ratio is very low due to the presence of several '*kirana*' stores in the locality. Credit facility varies from store to store and customer to customer. Customers' reliability and relation with the shopkeeper is enough to avail credit facility. Branding is not the criterion to attract the customers, as customers prefer low-priced products. Further retailer's suggestion and recommendation regarding any product or service plays a significant role in the customer's purchase decision.

Traditionally, retailers procure merchandise from wholesalers in bulk and sell in small quantities to the ultimate consumers. Figure 1.11 depicts the percentage of organized and unorganized retail across the world among leading economies. It is very clear from the picture that the gap between organized and unorganized retailing is very large. Organized retailing in India holds only 3 % share in the total retail business while China 20%, Indonesia 30%, Thailand 40%, Taiwan 81% and US 85%.

[5] *www.ibef.org*

Figure 1.11

Percentage of Organized Retail Across the World

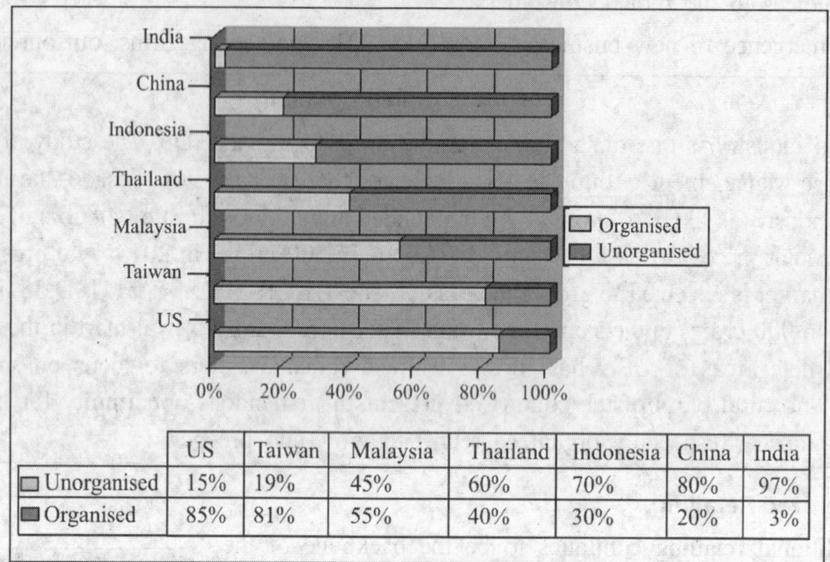

	US	Taiwan	Malaysia	Thailand	Indonesia	China	India
Unorganised	15%	19%	45%	60%	70%	80%	97%
Organised	85%	81%	55%	40%	30%	20%	3%

Figure 1.12

Various Segments in the Indian Retail Industry

Segment	Percentage of the overall retail pie	Penetration percentage of organised retail
Food and grocery	66	1
Apparel (clothing and footwear)	7	24
Medical & health services	10	1
Jewelry and watches	5	5
Durables	5	14
Personal care and effects	3	4
Others	2	3
Sports and leisure	2	9

Source: *AT Kearney, India*

Figure 1.13

Retail Trade in India & South East Asia

Countries	Organized Retail (%)	Unorganized Retail (%)
India	2	98
China	20	80
South Korea	15	85
Indonesia	25	75
Philippines	35	65
Thailand	40	60
Malaysia	50	50

RETAILING ACROSS THE GLOBE

Since 2005, Indian retail industry has been hot sector of the Indian economy. The rapidly increasing middle class is catching eyes of biggies like Birla, Reliance, Wal-Mart, Bharti, and so on. The modern retail Industry in BRICs (Brazil, Russia, India and China) is seen as having the maximum potential on growth worldwide. It grew by almost 30% in India and 13% in China and Russia last year. As the developed markets are becoming mature, retailers are eyeing new growth opportunities in upcoming economies.

According to A.T Kearney report, 2007 India holds 1st position successively for the second year. In this landmark report, the ***growth prospects*** of thirty leading economies are considered. The ranking criteria have four broad categories:

(i) Country Risk

(ii) Market Attractiveness

(iii) Market Saturation and

(iv) Time pressure for a new entrant to start retail business

The report has ranked India on the top in terms of Market saturation and time pressure as compared to Russia and China. India has got aggregated score of 92, followed by Russia at 89 (Second) and China with 86 (Third).

Figure 1.14

India's Ranking & Performance Against World's Leading Economies

2007 Rank	Country	Region Weight	Country Risk 25%	Market attracti-veness 25%	Market Satur-ation 30%	Time pressure score 20%	GRD I
1	India	Asia	67	42	80	74	92
2	Russia	Eastern Europe	62	52	53	90	69
3	China	Asia	75	46	46	84	68
4	Vietnam	Asia	57	34	76	59	74
5	Ukraine	Eastern Europe	41	43	44	88	69
6	Chile	S. America	80	51	42	43	69
7	Latvia	Eastern Europe	77	32	21	86	68
8	Malaysia	Asia	70	44	46	54	68
9	Mexico	S. America	83	58	33	33	64
10	Saudi Arabia	Mid. East / N. Africa	65	40	66	35	64
11	Tunisia	Mid. East / N. Africa	60	33	77	37	64
12	Bulgaria	Eastern Europe	62	32	42	68	63

13	Turkey	Mid. East / N. Africa	52	50	57	43	62
14	Egypt	Mid. East / N. Africa	43	37	85	35	61
15	Morocco	Mid. East / N. Africa	59	33	70	37	60
16	Thailand	Asia	71	39	30	55	59
17	Slovenia	Eastern Europe	100	33	13	47	58
18	United Arab Emirates	Mid. East / N. Africa	100	35	33	24	57
19	Croatia	Eastern Europe	73	38	10	70	56
20	Brazil	S. America	53	61	59	18	56
21	Uruguay	S. America	35	41	65	49	56
22	Peru	S. America	42	34	79	34	55
23	Philippines	Asia	41	48	63	37	54
24	Indonesia	Asia	36	40	70	37	52
25	Algeria	Mid. East / N. Africa	25	30	90	35	51
26	Hungary	Eastern Europe	98	38	2	48	51
27	Romania	Eastern Europe	60	31	22	66	50
28	Lithuania	Eastern Europe	75	33	17	54	50
29	Argentina	S. America	31	50	43	54	50
30	Columbia	S. America	44	50	52	26	47

Source: *Idea taken from www.atkearney.com*

Key to Rank:

On the Radar Screen

To Consider

Low Priority

Legend

For Country Risk	Market Attractiveness	Market Saturation	Time Pressure
0 – high Risk 100 – low Risk	0 – low Attractiveness 100 – high attractiveness	0 – saturated 100 – not saturated	0 – no time pressure 100 –urgency to enter

Figure 1.15
Top 15 Global Markets by Opportunity

Rank 2007	Rank2006	Country	Region
1	1	China	Asia-Pacific
2	4	Russia	Central/Oriental Europe
3	2	U.S.A.	North America
4	5	United Kingdom	Western Europe
5	6	Malaysia	Asia-Pacific
6	3	India	Asia-Pacific
7	13	South Africa	Africa
8	8	Australia	Asia-Pacific
9	9	Canada	North America
10	7	Japan	Asia-Pacific
11	30	Nigeria	Africa
12	12	Turkey	Central/Oriental Europe
13	11	Philippines	Asia-Pacific
14	10	Spain	Western Europe
15	15	France	West Europe

Source: *TNS Retail Forward*

Figure 1.16
Top 10 Chinese Retailers

Rank	Company	Sector	Sales (in US $ bn)	Sales Growth (%)	Store Number
1	Gome	Consumer Electronics	14.60	18	1020
2	Bailian	Food	12.48	13	6454
3	Suning	Consumer Electronics	12.24	40	632
4	Vanguard	Food	7.20	33	2539
5	Dashang	Food	7.19	39	145
6	Carrefour	Food	4.24	24	112
7	Wu-mart	Food	4.00	21	718
8	RT-Mart	Food	3.68	31	85
9	Chongqing Shangshe	Food	3.17	23	263
10	NGS	Consumer Electronics	3.16	13	322

Source: *Chain Chain Store& Franchise Association*

GLOBAL RETAILING TRENDS

No doubt that organized retailing in developed world is far ahead than in India. According to estimates, over 80% of all retail sales in the USA is accounted for by the organized retailers while in Europe, this figure accounts to 70%, 40% in Brazil and Argentina and nearly 35% in Taiwan and Korea. According to U.S. Department of labour, more than 22.5 million Americans are employed in the retailing industry in over 2 million retail stores. Retailers throughout the globe now have understood that sustainable competitive advantage can be achieved only by those retailing firms that integrate consumer demand directly into their merchandising and supply chain planning workflows. Global retailers know that if they have to stay ahead of changing consumer shopping habits and increasing merchandise choices, committed ethical behavior, community involvement, innovative promotions and pace with new technology is essential. Besides this, in the recent years following trends in global retailing have been observed:

1. Going Internationalization

As the domestic markets are becoming saturated, retailers have started looking to overseas markets for business growth, economies of scale, especially in Asia. Similarly staples and Nike are entering the Indian and Chinese markets. Target and Dollar stores (US based) also continue to grow their geographic presence aggressively in Asian countries. Further, geopolitical developments, including Tie-ups, joint ventures, trade pacts within the regions is facilitating movements of goods and services across frontiers. The North American Free Trade Agreement (NAFTA) – and its likely extension to include some additional central and South American nations in the coming years, - the European Union (EU) and future alliances will gradually but steadily abolish traditional geographical and political borders.

Global Retailing Opportunities

Malaysia, Australia, USA and United Kingdom are the most attractive destinations to invest in retail sector. Russia and China have been attracting global players by their fast growth, ease of setting up retail business factor and rapidly increasing middle class purchasing power but these two countries have a higher level of business risks than other nations. This group does not comprise India as its growth lowed down under inflation mull over. The USA despite economic slowdowns and other factors, still remain highly attractive destination. In Western Europe, if global prospects remain steady, most countries will stagnate except for UK, Sweden and Spain.

2. Value driven retailer to *values* driven retailer

Value retailers like Wal-Mart, Costco and Target which previously were recognized as the destination for the monthly stock-up trip now continue to improve "shopability," by providing more convenient store layouts and shopping experiences that make the customers buying quicker and easier. This trend focuses on programs designed to meet consumer lifestyles and needs based on money, time, family size and type, and personal and social obligations. Timberland (figure 1.17) provides "***nutritional label***" on their products detailing the energy used in making the shoes, the portion that is renewable, and the factory's labor record to show their impact on environment.

Figure 1.17

About Timberland & its Nutritional Value Concept

Timberland is a trademark for a number of lines of outdoors wear, primarily boots designed for hiking and mountain climbing; they are popular as a primary element of fashion, originating from their popularity with African-American and Latin youths in New York City, New Jersey, and Connecticut areas. The Timberland Company also has many items for sale in the apparel market including watches, leather goods, eye-ware and other goods.

As a part of its Corporate Social Responsibility, timberland provides '***nutritional label***' for all shoes like labels on food stuffs which aims to provide consumers information "about the product they are purchasing, including where it was manufactured, how it was produced, and its effect on the environment."
Specifically, it offers data on two aspects of Timberland's environmental impact – the energy used to produce the shoe and the company's purchases of renewable energy — and three aspects of its community impact — the number of hours served by Timberland employees in community service, the percentage of its factories "assessed against a code of conduct," and the child labor employed in making the shoe. It also tells where in the world the shoe was manufactured as shown in the picture.

Our Footprint Notre Empreinte	
Environmental Impact Impact sur l'environnement	
Energy to Produce: (per pair)*	3.1 kWh
Énergie utilisée (par paire)*	3.1 kWh
Renewable energy (Timberland-owned facilities):	5%
L'energie renouvelable (sites appartenant à Timberland) :	5%
Community Impact Impact sur la communauté	
Hours served in our communities:	119,776
Nombre total d'heures données :	119,776
% of factories assessed against code of conduct:*	100%
% d'usines évaluées pour leur conformité au code de conduite :*	100%
Child labor:*	0%
Main-d'oeuvre enfantine :*	0%
Manufactured Fabriqué à	
OSI Vietnam, Vietnam OSI Vietnam, Vietnam	
* metrics based on global footwear production for 2005	
* informations fondées sur production totale de chaussures en 2005	
FOR MORE INFORMATION VISIT WWW.TIMBERLAND.COM/CSRREPORT	
POUR PLUS D'INFORMATIONS : WWW.TIMBERLAND.COM/CSRREPORT	

Another example is of book stores; for centuries, bookshops have been associated with library-style presentation with sections signposted accordingly. Considering sea change in the consumer services, Amazon and Kindle world (famous booksellers) cannot afford to look stale. In Manchester, Waterstone's has opened a store that features graphics rather than words to guide shoppers around. For instance, to find a crime novel, shoppers can look for the overhead picture of a misdemeanor about to be committed. The substitution of pictures for words is a trend that has been taking place for some time, but it is at its most obvious in a context where the primacy of print has rarely been in dispute. Singapore's Page One follows a similar path with an interior that imitates the pages of a book and features asymmetric bookshelves[6].

3. Enhancing service offerings

Walgreen's, for instance, has built a superior brand proposition around pharmacy authority and convenience. Walgreen's capital spending, organizational energy, and

6 *http://www.cnbceb.com/Articles/2008/July/44/shelf-life-10-retail-trends.aspx*

marketing dollars all focus on delivering convenience at every level, through real estate strategy, quick in-and-out convenience, layout, assortment and micro-merchandising. Best Buy[7] has had a lot of achievements with its Geek Squad offering repair, support and installation services at all stores; PetSmart[8], the largest US pet supplies retailer, besides selling pets, is also providing pet services like Doggie Day Camp, grooming, training and boarding facilities. A number of retailers associated with PetSmart, believe that since launching these services, they've seen a jump in both retail revenues as well as traffic to stores, which has boosted consumer loyalty.

Futuristic stores are increasingly seeking to interact with customers. In Nokia's London store, customers removing a handset from its display can view product information that appears on the walls above. And upstairs, a lounge washed in blue-light provides a hyper-modern retail environment. Across the street, the Apple store offers free email access, a 'genius' bar and a 'learn-how-to' theatre. It's also worth noting Bangkok's SpaceGal – a Star Trek-style lingerie store that subverts expectations about how the retail segment should appear and encourages interaction[9].

4. Expanding Private Brands

To increase margins and draw increase awareness to store developed private brands as compared to well established or third party brands, retailers now are introducing their own store brands. Retail firms believe that these own or private labels have evolved from 'cheap and nasty substitutes' to the real thing though 'copycat' private labels still remain a strong strategy for retailers. However, the copycat no longer depends on the price advantage to fight the branded product; it has improved on quality and offers a value proposition to the consumer. For example, Wal-Mart, casts the net wider on private labels to create a 'house of brands'. The only caution for retailers is that there should be a well thought-out blend of private labels and other brands. Manufacturers should also fight back by innovating: changing the way they look at consumers, seeking out early adapters for ideas, using sound marketing techniques and adopting a thorough product development process.

---

7 *Best Buy Co., Inc. is a Fortune 100 company and the largest specialty retailer of consumer electronics in the United States and Canada. The company's subsidiaries include Geek Squad, Magnolia Audio Video, Pacific Sales, and, in Canada the Best Buy Canada subsidiary operates most stores under the Future Shop label. Together these operate more than 1,150 stores in the United States, Puerto Rico, Canada, China, Mexico and Turkey. The company's corporate headquarters are located in Richfield, Minnesota, USA (near Minneapolis).*

8 *PetSmart, Inc. is a US and Canada based retail chain engaged in the sale of specialty pet supplies and services such as grooming and dog training, cat boarding facilities, Doggie Day Care and sale of Bird, fish, horse and small animal products. In August 2005, the company announced that it was rebranding its name from PetsMart to PetSmart. This move is designed to emphasize its evolution from a pet supply store to a solutions-oriented company.*

9 *http://www.cnbceb.com*

About Wal-Mart's Private Brands

According to Wal-Mart sources, about forty percent of merchandise sold in Wal-Mart are private label store brands, or products offered by Wal-Mart and produced through contracts with manufacturers. Wal-Mart began offering private label brands in 1991 with the launch of Sam's Choice, a brand of drinks produced by Cott Beverages exclusively for Wal-Mart. Sam's Choice quickly became popular, and by 1993 was the third beverage brand in the United States. Other Wal-Mart brands include Great Value and Equate in the USA and Canada, and Smart Price in Britain. Some of its private brands are more acknowledged than the global well established brands.

In India, Nestle (a well renowned Swiss MNC) popularized the coffee kiosk concept in India, where it offers various flavors through its vending machines installed at public places and places of high traffic such as PVRs, shopping plazas, food centers and office premises. These vending machines come in different sizes and styles to meet varied needs of consumers at various locations. For instance, its high capacity multitask vending machines provides coffees with snacks, drinks, confectionary items and packed foods. Similarly Cadbury India, with the tie-ups of telecommunications companies like E-Cuba India and BPL Mobile has launched chocolate vending machines activated by mobile handsets in select corporate and congregation points in Mumbai.

5. Migration of retail format

Over the past few decades, due to competition and entry of world's largest companies in this sector, retail formats have been changing radically. The co-operatives and basic department stores of the early 20th century have given entry to mass merchandisers (Wal-Mart), warehouse clubs (Marko, Sam's Club), hypermarkets (Carrefour), discounters (Aidi), convenience stores (7-Eleven), and category killers (Toys 'R' Us, Sports Authority). UK's Tesco Group operates supermarkets, hypermarkets, departmental stores, convenience stores, neighborhood stores, mail order, and like most others recently cyber retailing (on-line retailing/e-stores). The most important business philosophy for various old, emerging and new retailing formats is convenience in terms of 'under-one roof', 'one-stop location', 'time saving or ease of shopping, making consumers 'king' in real sense.

Figure 1.18
About Walgreen

Walgreen (one of the biggest US based drugstore) is a leading pharmacy chain, mail service, and pharmacy benefit manager, with specialty pharmacy operations. It also operates worksite health centers, home care facilities and specialty, institutional and mail service pharmacies. Its Take Care Health Systems subsidiary manages 220 convenient care clinics at Walgreen drugstores. Walgreen states that it serves more than 5 million customers per day, filled 583 million prescriptions in fiscal 2007, and expects to have 7,000 stores by 2010.

(A typical view of Walgreen Pharmacy)

It was founded in Chicago, Illinois, in 1901 and has since expanded throughout the United States of America. Its headquarters is located in Deerfield, Illinois. A typical Walgreen store is about 14,500 square feet (1,350 m^2) with 11,000 square feet (1,000 m^2) of sales area. They offer nearly 25,000 items for sale and usually staff between 25 and 30 people per store. On average, one store pulls in $8.5 million in annual sales. Most stores include a pharmacy, a photo lab, a cosmetics counter, and a general merchandise area.

6. Consolidation

Since the dawn of 21st century, there has been a substantial re-structuring of the retailing in globe especially in Europe. The implications extend afar Europe but they have had largely impact within European countries. This corporate restructuring not only involves changes in existing horizontal competitive relationships amongst retailers but also involves new forms of relationship with manufacturers, vendors and wholesalers. For instance, Home Depot (an American retailer of home improvement and construction products and services), acquired 12 stores in China from Home Way (a Chinese retailer) in the year 2006. Similarly Best Buy (a Fortune 100 company and the largest specialty retailer of consumer electronics in the United States and Canada, accounting for 21% of the market) acquired 75% stake in Jiangsu Five Star Appliance (China's third largest consumer electronic retailer).

Highlights of Consolidations in Indian Scenario

- Apple Inc has entered into an exclusive marketing and distribution deal with Reliance Retail through "iStore by Reliance Digital".
- British retailer Marks & Spencer's has tied with Reliance Retail and plans to open at least 50 new stores in India over the next five years, with an initial investment of up to US$ 58 million.
- German sportswear and Apparel Company, Adidas is going in for a major expansion across India, and plans to have a total of about 450 franchisee outlets in the country.
- Microsoft's first shop-in-shop pilot has been launched with the Tata Group subsidiary Infiniti Retail's multi-brand consumer durables retail format, Croma.

- The UK-based international coffee chain, Costa Coffee, plans to double the number of retail outlets by the end of 2008.
- The Walt Disney Company, consumer product retailing arm of global animation giant, will soon add 135 new stores to its existing 15 stores.
- UK's largest home textile retail chain, Rosebys, which was acquired by Gujarat Heavy Chemicals in 2006, is set to foray into the domestic market this year with a slew of stores.
- Wal-Mart, the world's biggest retailer, has tied-up with Sunil Mittal's Bharti Enterprises for entering into Indian retail market.
- World's leading coffee chain, Starbucks' enters India through a tie-up with the country's leading multiplex operator PVR Limited.

REASONS FOR RETAIL GROWTH

Following are the reasons to explain the popularity and growth of retail industry in India.

1. Organized retail versus unorganized retail

Growth of organized retailing in India reveals the success of retail sector in India over the past five years. The rapidly increasing middle class in India seek more value in terms of improved assortments and quality, one-shop experience, financing options, payment flexibility, return and exchange policies, trial rooms for clothing products and competitive prices. This has fueled the scope for organized retailing (see figure 1.19) to tap recent rich market. Further, change in the taste, lifestyle and shopping attitude are the reasons for the growth of organized retailing in India.

Figure 1.19

Rapidly Increasing Indian Retail Sales

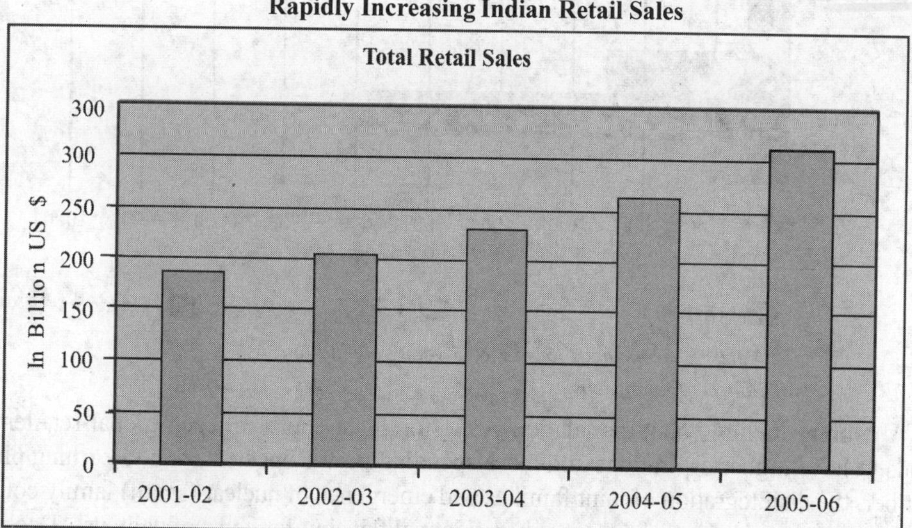

2. Emergence of nuclear family concept and changing age profile

India has witnessed a change in the age and income pattern over the last decade, which is likely to continue in the years to come. India is believed to have more young population as compared to US and China. Two-thirds of Indian population is under 35, with the median age of 23 years, as opposed to the world median age of 33. India is home to 20 per cent of the global population under 25 years of age. This trend is projected to continue for the next decade, with the share set to reach its maximum in 2010. The large proportion of the working-age population translates to a lucrative consumer base vis-à-vis other economies of the world, placing India on the radar as one of the most promising retail destinations of the world[10].

Figure 1.20

Growing Indian Young Population

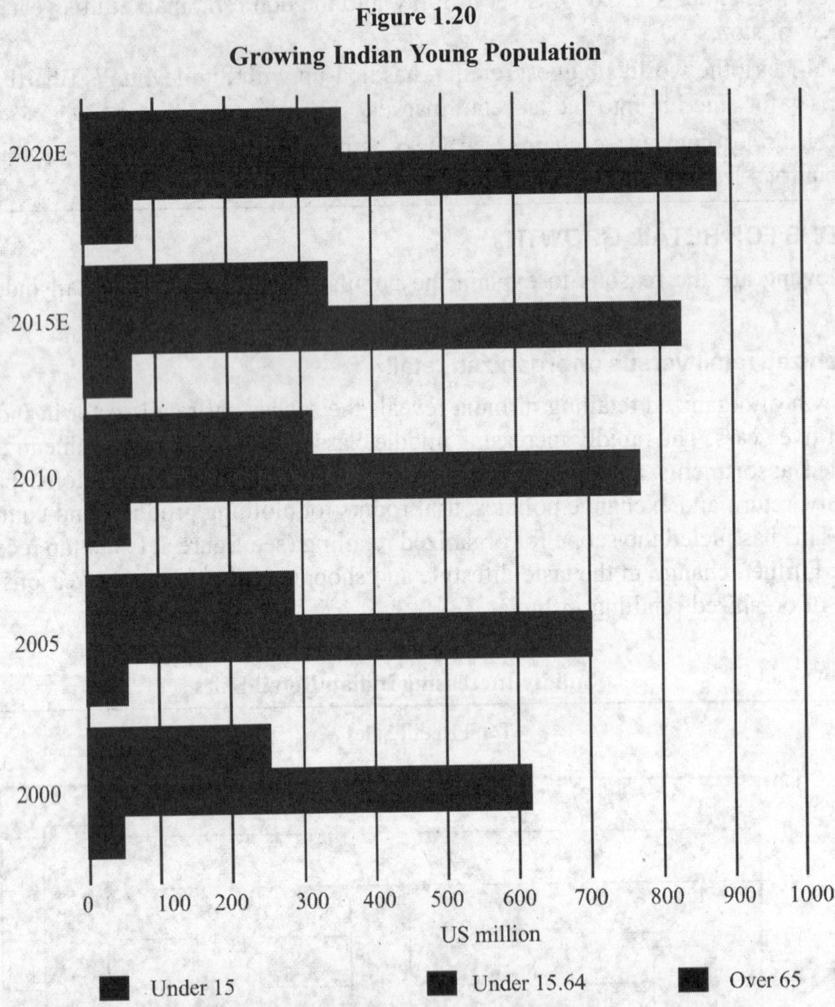

Note: *'E' here stands for expected young population*

Source: *Indian Census*

A country having young population is the foremost choice of each global retailer and tends to have higher aspirations and more spending power once entering to earning phase. Further, the disintegration of joint families and emergence of nuclear (small) family concept has led to increased demand for not only residential flats but for items of daily use. Declining interest rates and decreased dependence on loans, has led to retail industry to grow.

---

10 *www.ibef.org*

3. Increased disposable Income

With the growth of income levels and more than one earning members households, the Indian average disposable income is growing fast resulting in enhance demand for goods and services. Energized by ranking as the fourth largest economy in terms of Purchasing Power Parity (PPP), next only to United States, Japan and China, India is expected to outpace Japan by the year 2010 to become world's third largest economy. Further, with 54 per cent of the Indians aged below 25, the young Indian consumer is buying big to look good and feel good. These changes are visible in the consumption growth of consumer durables. To quote live examples, the number of household having cars, dish TV/cable TV subscribers, cell phone users, airline travelers has increased considerably over the last decade.

Figure 1.21

Rapidly Increasing Indian GDP

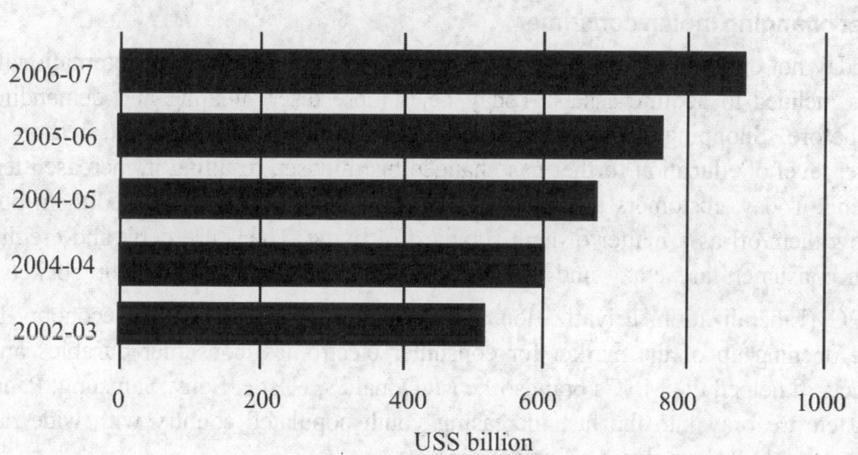

***Source:** RBI Website*

Purchasing power of Indian urban consumer towards Apparels, Cosmetics, Shoes, Food, Watches, Jewellery, and Beverages, is not only growing but are slowly becoming lifestyle products that are widely accepted by the urban masses. Hence Indian retailers need to leverage this opportunity and should aim to grow by diversifying and introduce new formats.

4. New business opportunities

With the rise of upcoming business sectors like IT, BPOs, LPOs, KPOs and engineering firms, medical tourism etc, employment opportunities are increasing resulting in increased purchasing power and demand for goods and services. With a fitting combination of a low-cost and highly skilled labour force, today India is considered as one of the ideal outsourcing destinations of the world. Due to overwhelming response from throughout the world, the Information Technology (IT) / Information Technology Enabled Service (ITES) sector accounts for 3% of the GDP, and is still growing at 30 to 35% annually. Also, with cost competitiveness, availability of skilled manpower, and a high level of service maturity, India is set to reorganize, from being an ideal business process outsourcing (BPO) destination to an ideal knowledge process outsourcing (KPO) destination. Including the services sector, India is gaining critical mass in manufacturing as well. It is attracting MNCs for raising sourcing activities from India largely retailing, auto/engineering, consumer electronics and textiles.

5. FDI in retail

The heavy influx of FDI in the retail industry has resulted in mall revolution, development of infrastructure and emergence of new retail formats. As foreign players can not enter into Indian retail industry independently, tie-ups between Indian and foreign players is on the rise. Bharti-Walmart joint venture is one such example in this series. FDI has enabled many Indian corporate to enter at large scale in the country. Due to boom in Indian economy and increasing FDI inflow, World Bank estimates, India to be the world's second largest economic nation after China by the year 2050, ahead of US.

6. Fast changing Indian consumer

Today not only the urban but rural customer is becoming aware of international styles and is inclined to acquire assets. Today he is more discriminating and demanding than ever before. Shopping is not need-based but a family experience and reason to joy. Greater level of education further has changed his mindset, resulting in increased tendency to spend. Today, customers buy most of the things not because they need them but want to show them off as a matter of high standard of living. Thanks to debit and credit cards, Indian consumers are crazy and are prepared to even spend out of their pockets.

LPG (Liberalization, Privatization and Globalization) of the Indian economy has led to the opening up of the market for consumer electronics, consumer durables and food products. It helped the MNCs brands like McDonald's, Nestle, Sony, Samsung, Panasonic, Nokia etc to foray into the fast increasing youth populated country with wide range of assortments and alternatives to consumers.

7. Availability of Skilled Labour

Plentiful raw material, low cost skilled labour, presence across the value chain and a large and growing domestic market presents the strengths of the Indian retail industry. India today, has an enormous resource of talent and skilled labour. Over 38.5 million students were enrolled in about 150,000 pre-college institutes and over 11.7 million in 14,500 higher education institutions in 2010-11. With ***English*** being the language for business in India, the language skills of the Indian workforce score higher than that of emerging economies.

8. Low cost of Operations

One of the biggest advantages of MNCs presence in India is low cost of operations. According to the Boston Consulting Group (BCG), access to the large talent pool and higher employee satisfaction translates into better employee performance (and cost savings on recruitment and training). This leads to a productivity increase of over 30 percent in

---

11 *http://www.sabslab.com/images/Advantages-of-Offshoring-to-India.pdf*

India. Indians also produce superior quality of work and even the error rates in accounting is reduced by 60 percent after transferring outsourcing work to India[11]. Global retail giants are also increasingly turning to Tier II and Tier III cities for retail establishments and for manpower sourcing. With well-educated small town graduates turning to the urban cities for employment, these graduates are ideal candidates for sales and marketing executive roles in modern organized retail formats. Figure 1.22 depicts the details of the growth of population in India and its urbanization.

Figure 1.22
Urbanization of India

Growth of Population and Urbanization	1981	1991	2001
Population Growth	24.70%	23.80%	21.30%
Urban Population as % of total	23.30%	25.70%	33.40%
Percentage of population in Class I cities	60.40%	65.20%	73.70%

Source: Census India

9. E-Commerce

The increasing use of computers and World Wide Web in most of the business spheres are making the Indian shoppers more accessible to the growing influences of national and international retail chains. Reach of Dish TV channels has helped in creating awareness about local and global products. About forty eight percent of Indian population is young and below 20 and is expected to increase by fifty five percent by 2015. This young population is eager to learn computers, watch more than sixty TV channels and present the largest tendency to spend is undoubtedly contributing to the retail success in the country.

Figure 1.23
Trends in E-Commerce

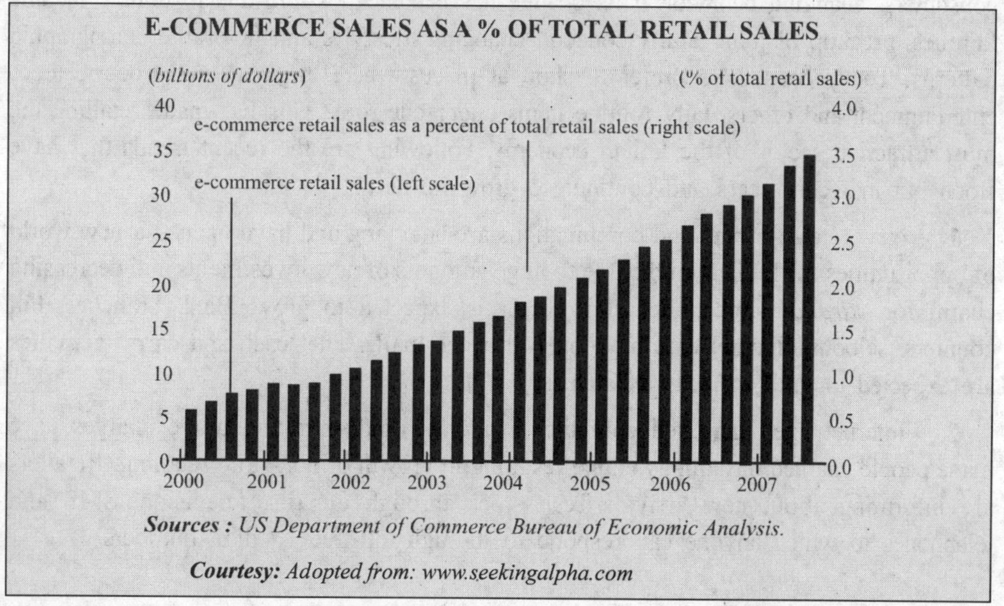

Sources : *US Department of Commerce Bureau of Economic Analysis.*

Courtesy: *Adopted from: www.seekingalpha.com*

Figure 1.24

Labour Cost per Worker Across Asian Countries

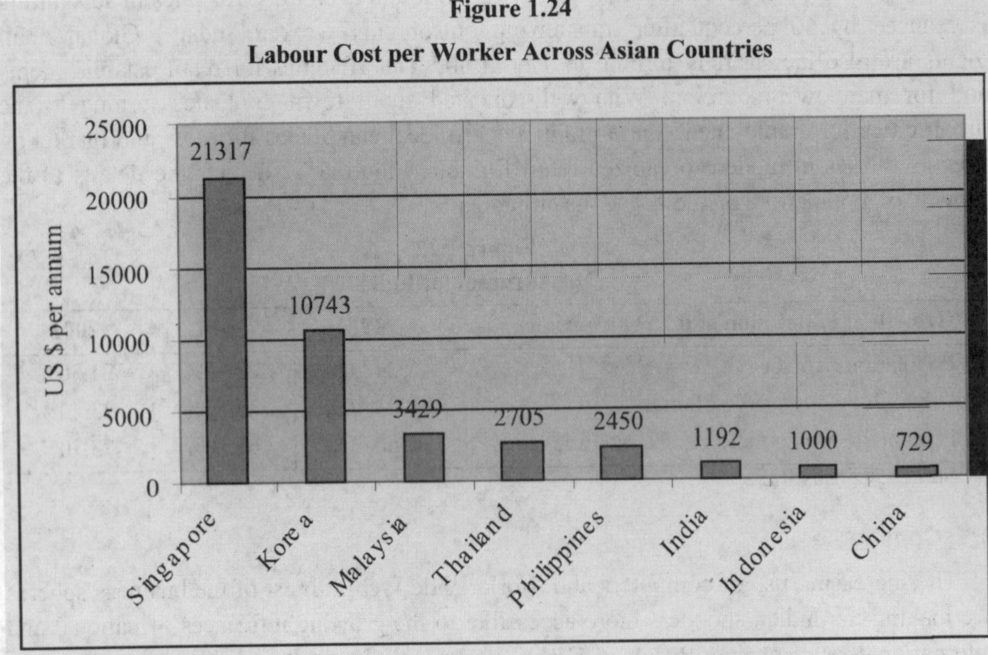

Source: *Department of Industrial Policy & Promotion*

EMERGING TRENDS IN RETAILING

Retailing today is the fastest growing sectors in the global economy and is under transition phase; not only in South Asian countries like India and China but throughout the world. The increased popularity of organized retailing is mainly because of the consumers' changing behavior. This change has become possible due to double income families, breakup of joint family concept, changing lifestyles and favorable demographic patterns. Today consumers prefer to shop at places where they can get grocery, food, entertainment and others daily routine items under one roof. This has made retailing the most attractive sector of the Indian economy. Following are the recent trends that have stood out in recent years and continue to grow further:

1. New retail formats and combinations are emerging and have opened a new world of opportunities for Indian youth. Due to huge amounts of new investments and decreasing charm for '*kirana*' stores, the retail sector is expected to grow. Bank branches, bill counters, saloons, internet café have opened in the malls. The 'cash and carry' activities are expected to grab majority of attention.

2. Internet age, increased computer awareness and shrinking usage charges have made people enabled buy things online resulting in growth of non-store retailing. Retailers are informing about new arrivals/fresh stock through e-mails, television, SMS and telephones to which anyone can respond to through toll-free 16 digit numbers.

3. Specialty stores like 'Reliance Digital', 'Music World' 'Metal Junctions', 'Nokia World' and 'Pantaloons' have their presence in most of the malls in the country. Departmental stores have given way to malls, having a mixture of large and small retailers offering varied brands for each and every section of the society.

4. Sales promotion channels are increasingly becoming professional and targeting differently to different lifestyle groups. Newer and newer promotional techniques are emerging. Event managers are hired and visual merchandising professionals are consulted. Today retailers are not sticking to traditional methods of promoting a sale but personal selling, door-to-door selling, free home delivery and payment through plastic money have emerged and is being widely used. Use of advanced technology is not the matter of affordability but is the reason for survival. Retailers are using computers, electronic devices, check out scanning systems, tag guns, vending machines, money counters and digital signage to enhance store's productivity. CCTVs, cameras, sensors and theft alarms are being used to prevent store theft.

5. Today retail organizations are not only targeting big cities but are considering tier II and tier III cities like Jaipur, Pune, Shimla, Karnal, Panipat, Coimbatore, Baroda, Chandigarh etc also. The South Indian states are one step ahead when it comes to shopping in the supermarkets for day-to-day needs and also have been influencing other states where supermarkets are being established. However, the main center of organized retailing is undeniably Chennai, which once was considered as a 'conservative', 'traditional' and cost-sensitive' market. The success of Chennai as retail hub has surprised all but list of factors contributed to its success. Reasonable real estate prices, double household income, increased presence of MNCs and industrial boom has led to the emergence of new residential societies resulting in increased purchasing power and demands for day-to-day goods under one roof.

6. Use of Plastic Money

Use of credit and debit cards for buying merchandise is relatively a new phenomenon but is gaining popularity immensely. Credit and debit cards are commonly known as 'plastic money'. Today, especially in metros, retail spending is mainly done by plastic cards, accounting for over 45 percent and is likely to touch 65 percent over the next five years.

7. Distance – No bar

Thanks to increased public transportation, better roads, highways and an overall improvement in the transportation infrastructure that has enabled customers to visit from one place to another smoothly than ever before. Now for want of quality goods, a customer can travel several kilometers to reach a particular store.

---

[12] *www.indiaretailbiz.com, visited on July 3, 2008.*

8. Partnerships and tie-ups among retailers, real estate developers, brands, franchisees, and financers have become the fashion of the day to spread risk related to huge investments and uncertainty.

9. The government infrastructure support, relaxation on foreign direct investments further has accelerated the growth of Indian organized retail sector. Consequently, the shopping malls are coming up throughout the country in a big way.

10. Sophisticated customers: Due to Internet revolution, customers are becoming conversant about the products they are interested in buying. For example, over thirty percent of Indian consumers collect information from the Internet about prices, features, guarantee/warranty options before visiting any store for the actual purchase. This is particularly true in case of automobiles, cell phones, consumer electronics, hotel bookings, travel packages etc. This suggested the retailers that they need to respond to varying consumer needs and growing assortment.

11. The gap between organized and unorganized (traditional '*kirana*' shopping) retailing is coming close due to mall revolution and increasing Indian middle class in terms of size and income. According to a study conducted by 'Deloitte Haskins and Sells[12]', one of the four largest accounting firms in the world, Indian retailing is growing at a faster pace as was expected from it and could constitute 25% of the total retail sector by 2011. The study further reveals that new malls, increased disposable income and easy access to credit facilities have led to organized retailing to record all time high rate of growth of 50% per annum in 2007. The traditional '*kirana*' stores by introducing modern retailing concepts such as self service, free home delivery system, credit facility and other value added services have been trying to reshape themselves.

12. Need for retailing skills: Undoubtedly, retailing in India is still in nascent stage. The success of organized retailing is yet to be proved. The success will be felt once an equitable stage is achieved. This requires enough store size, traffic flow, and revenue earned, but besides these factors, retailers have started concentrating on recruiting qualified and trained retail staff. Following are the areas where specialized skills are increasingly felt:

(a) Managing Merchandise: inventory management, vendor selection, presenting merchandise, pricing the merchandise, planning and implementing merchandise assortments.

(b) Store operations and management: Layout, inventory management, buying, store keeping, customer relationship, objections handling, visual merchandising.

(c) Strategic management: Strategic planning, targeting, positioning marketing, site location, building and creating sustainable advantage.

(d) Administration: Marketing, finance, human resource and so on.

---

12 *www.indiaretailbiz.com, visited on July 3, 2008.*

SUMMARY

Retailing is the fastest growing sector of Indian economy and second largest employment sector after agriculture. Organized retailing has only 3-5% share of the total Indian retailing. The local '*kirana*' stores play important role and has been well acknowledged among customers and marketers, but the way malls are coming up in tier II and tier III cities, it seems the gap between organized and unorganized retailing will reduce. Not only Indian business houses but also foreign players are entering into the Indian retail industry. FDI in retailing has been relaxed and has made India the second largest consumer market in the world.

REVIEW QUESTIONS

True and False Questions

1. Use of plastic money, easy availability of consumer credit may assist in boosting consumer demand.
2. One of the principal reasons behind the explosion of retail and its fragmented nature in the country is the fact that retailing is probably the primary form of disguised unemployment/underemployment in the country.
3. Retailing consists of selling merchandise from a permanent location (a retail store) in large quantities directly to the consumers.
4. Retailing offers employment opportunity to all groups irrespective of age and gender, qualification or religion etc.
5. Retailing is the last stage in a channel of distribution, which consists of all the trades and people involved in the physical movement and transfer of ownership of goods and services from manufacturer to ultimate consumer.
6. According to principal of Unity of Command, one employee working at junior level should be responsible to many supervisors.
7. After manufacturing, retailing is the second largest employer in India. Approximately, over 12 million shops exist in various parts of the country.
8. Organized retailing in India is mainly present in Tier II and Tier III cities only. But few players are now eyeing to explore the opportunities in metros too.
9. According to A.T Kearney report, 2007 India holds 3rd position successively for the second year.
10. Global retailers know that if they have to stay ahead of changing consumer shopping habits and increasing merchandise choices, committed ethical behavior, community involvement, innovative promotions and pace with new technology is essential.
11. Retailers throughout the globe now understand that sustainable competitive advantage can be achieved only by those retailing firms that integrate consumer demand directly into their merchandising and supply chain planning workflows.

12. Wal-Mart, the world's biggest retailer, has tied-up with Sunil Mittal's Bharti Enterprises for entering into Indian retail market.
13. World's leading coffee chain, Starbucks' enters India through a tie-up with the country's leading multiplex operator PVR Limited.
14. A country having old population is the foremost choice of each global retailer and tends to have higher aspirations and more spending power once entering to earning phase.
15. Today, customers buy most of the things not because they need them but want to show them off as a matter of high standard of living.

Answers:

1. True	2. True	3. False	4. True
5. False	6. False	7. False	8. False
9. False	10. True	11. True	12. True
13. True	14. False	15. True	

Multiple Choice Questions

1. LPG stands for :-
   (*a*) Liberalisation, Public, and Government.
   (*b*) Liberalisation, Privatisation and Government.
   (*c*) Liberalisation, Privatisation and Globalisation.
   (*d*) Legal, Public and Government.
2. Retailing provides three utilities homely.
   (*a*) time, place and price (*b*) time, popularity and possession
   (*c*) time, money and price (*d*) time, place and possession
3. Retailing offers direct interaction with
   (*a*) End consumers (*b*) Wholesalers
   (*c*) Marketers (*d*) Media
4. KVIC means
   (*a*) Khadi and Village Industries Commission.
   (*b*) Kuteer Village Industries Corporation.
   (*c*) Khadi Vikas Industries Commission.
   (*d*) Kuteer Vikas Industries Corporation.
5. FMCG means
   (*a*) Fast moving customer goods.
   (*b*) Fast moving consumer goods.
   (*c*) Final merchandise consumer goods.
   (*d*) Fast melting consumer goods.

6. Wholesaler is a link between
   (*a*) Retailer and final consumer (*b*) Manufacturer and retialer
   (*c*) Manufacturer and Public (*d*) Manufacturer and suppliers
7. Indian retailing is dominated by
   (*a*) Organised retail (*b*) Unorganised retail
   (*c*) Both of above (*d*) None of above
8. Which is the fastest growing retail vertical
   (*a*) Pharmaceutical retail
   (*b*) Airport retial
   (*c*) Apparels and Consumer durables
   (*d*) Entertainment retail
9. Which of the followings is the slowest growing retail vertical :
   (*a*) Books, Music and Gifts (*b*) Beauty care
   (*c*) Food & Beverages (*d*) Consumer Durables
10. CAGR stands for
    (*a*) Compound annual growth rate
    (*b*) Company annual growth rate
    (*c*) Calculated annual growth rate
    (*d*) Computed annual growth rate
11. How many approximate retail shops. India has
    (*a*) 3 million (*b*) 12 million
    (*c*) 17 million (*d*) 21 million
12. Private Label brands are also known as :
    (*a*) Third party brands (*b*) Store's own brands
    (*c*) Manufacturer's brands (*d*) Imported brands
13. Walgreen store is into :
    (*a*) Luxury goods (*b*) Entertainment goods
    (*c*) Furniture (*d*) Pharmaceuticals
14. Nestle is an :
    (*a*) Swiss MNC (*b*) Indian MNC
    (*c*) United Kingdom MNC (*d*) American MNC
15. Toys 'R' Us and Sports Authority belong to which retail format :
    (*a*) Warehouse clubs (*b*) Hyper markets
    (*c*) Category killers (*d*) Super market
16. Wal Mart has tie-up with :
    (*a*) Bharti Enterprises (*b*) Reliance retail
    (*c*) Aditya Birla's More (*d*) Spencers

17. The primary reason for mall revolution and emergence of new retail formats is :
    (*a*) Government subsidies (*b*) Heavy influx of FDI
    (*c*) Entry of foreign retailers (*d*) India's growing population
18. BCG is a :
    (*a*) Consultancy group (*b*) Retailer
    (*c*) Wholesaler (*d*) American rating agency
19. Disposable Income, In general means :
    (*a*) Individual's capacity to spend
    (*b*) Individual's capacity to borrow money
    (*c*) Individual's capacity to save
    (*d*) Individual's capacity to earn
20. What are future prospects of Indian retail :
    (*a*) Organised retail will decline
    (*b*) Both organised and Unorganised retail forms will abolish
    (*c*) Organised retail will grow and Unorganised retail will decline
    (*d*) Organised retail will grow and Unorganised retail will be the trend of past

Answers

1. c	2. d	3. a	4. a
5. b	6. b	7. b	8. c
9. a	10. a	11. b	12. b
13. d	14. a	15. c	16. a
17. b	18. a	19. a	20. c.

Check your progress

1. What is CAGR?
2. What is UMP?
3. What do you mean by Wholesaler?
4. Who is retailer?
5. Who is end consumer?
6. What is organized retail?
7. What is merchandise?
8. Who is a manufacturer?
9. Who is wholesaler?
10. What does plastic money mean?
11. What is private brand?
12. What comes under grocery?
13. What is BCG?
14. What is KVIC?
15. What is LPG?

Short-Answer Questions

1. Write a short note on origin of retailing in India?
2. Explain the principle of 'Unity of Command'?
3. Why supervision and control are required in retail sector?
4. Why a retail firm should show interest in its employees?
5. Explain the relationship between authority and responsibility?
6. Differentiate between organized and unorganized retailing?
7. Briefly explain retail sales goals?
8. How ancient retailing is different from modern retailing?
9. What functions are expected from a retailer?
10. Briefly criticize the impact of organized retail over unorganized retail?
11. Explain some main features of Retail business?
12. Explain the Indian organized retail market?
13. What opportunities exist in retailing?
14. Discuss the retailing across the globe?
15. Why retailing in India is said to be a buzzword today?

Long-Answer Questions

1. What do you mean by retail business? What are its basic principles? And explain the role/functions of a retailer in a competitive business environment with suitable examples wherever necessary?
2. Critically describe the goals and objectives of a retail organisation by giving relevant examples?
3. Explain in detail the emerging trends in Indian retail? What impact you expect it will have on traditional *kirana* stores?
4. Suppose after getting management degree, you decide to open a retail business. What points you would like to consider with regard to store location, competition, impact of emerging trends, and government attitude towards organised retail?
5. Being a management graduate, what remedial measures you would suggest to unorganised retailers (*that account for 12 million*) to stay in competition and increase sales turnover and profit thereof?

APPENDIX

Exhibit 1.1: Retail Players across Verticals in India

FOOD AND GROCERY

- Aditya Birla Group
- Apna Bazaar
- Barista
- Bikano
- BJN Group
- Café Coffee Day
- FabMall
- Godrej
- Haldiram's
- Hindustan Unilever Limited
- ITC
- Magna
- Mc Donald's
- NF
- Rameshwar
- Spar

CLOTHING AND TEXTILES

- Biba
- Ebony
- FabIndia
- Kappa
- Lee
- Lee Cooper
- Levi's
- Bombay Dying
- Mango
- Nalli
- Pepe Jeans
- Peter England
- Pyramid
- Raymonds

FOOTWEAR

- Adidas
- Liberty
- Action
- New Balance
- Reebok
- UMBRO
- Woodland
- Paragon

HOME DECOR AND FURNISHINGS

- Bombay Dyeing
- Carmicheal house
- Durian
- Gautier
- Lifestyle
- Nilkamal
- Pantaloon
- Raymond

ELECTRONICS

- 21 RETAIl
- BPL
- Croma
- Godrej
- Hitachi
- LG
- Next
- Onida
- Microsoft
- Philips
- Samsung
- Nokia
- Sony
- Videocon
- Whirlpool

BEAUTY CARE

- Amway
- Biotiue
- Health Glow
- Himalaya
- L'orreal
- Lakme
- Maybelline
- Revlon

BOOKS AND MUSIC

- Crossword
- Depot
- Hallmark
- Music World
- Planet M

Exhibit 1.2: Typical Indian Retail Stores

Building Material Stores	Ladies Stores
CDs/VCDs/DVDs Stores	Garden Care Stores
Confectionary Stores	Stationery Stores
Consumer Electronic Stores	Infants' Stores
Curtain, Drapery and Upholstery Stores	Handicraft Stores
Drug/Pharmaceutical Stores	Liquor Stores
Dry-cleaning Stores	Pet Animal Stores
Fast food stores	Optical Stores
Fish Aquarium Stores	Cell Phone Stores
Floor Decoration Store	Bakery Stores
Florists	Luggage and Baggage Stores
Fruit and Juices Stores	Hardware Stores
Fuel Stores	Book Stores
Gasoline Service Stations	Furniture Stores
Gents Wear Stores	Family Wear Stores
Grocery Stores	Musical Instrument Stores
Home Décor Stores	Export Item Stores
Household appliance stores	Photoshop Stores
Kids Wear Stores	Gift, Souvenir and Novelty Stores
Ladies Wear Stores	Apparel Stores
Milk Dairy Product Stores	Video Games Stores
Motor Vehicle Stores	Two Wheeler Dealer Stores
Paint/Wallpaper Stores	Non Veg. Stores
Shoe Stores	Khadi Stores
Tobacco Stores	Jewelry Stores
Travel Accessories Stores	Automobile Stores
Variety Stores	Toys and Games Stores

Exhibit 1.3: Global Brands in India

Adidas	Tupper Ware
Arrow	Tommy Hilfiger
Debenhams	Levis
Dollarstore	Pizza Hut
Giordan	Subway
Kenstar	KFC
LG	Lacoste
Canon	Landmark Group
Nokia	Lasenza

Levi's	Planet Sports
Mango	Promod
Marcoricci Italy	Red Earth
Marks & Spencer	Reebok
Marrybrown	Royal Sporting House
Mc Donalds	Ruby Tuesday
Metro	Samsonite
Movenopick	Shoprite
Nike	Subway
Nine West	TGI Friday's
Pepe Jeans	Tissot
Pizza	United Colors of Benetton

Exhibit 1.4: Global Luxury Brands in India

Bose	John Balliano
BVLGARI	Longines
Canali	Louis Vuitton
Cartier	Mango
Cerruti	Mont Blanc
Chanel	Morgan
Chopard	Omega
Denon	Prada
Dior	Rado
Do Daks	SA
Dolce & Gabbana	Swarovski
Donna Karan	The Samile Row
Er Manegildo Zegna	Tiffany & Co.
Fendi	Tommy Hilfiger
Florsheim	UBL
GUCCI	Vacheron Constantin
Harman kardon	Versace
Hugo Boss	Vertu

Exhibit 1.5: Leading Players in Multiplexes Market

Adlabs Cinemas	PVR Ltd
Cinemax	Prasad IMAX
DT Cinema	Pyramid Saimira
E-City Ventures	Shringar
Inox Leisure Ltd	Waves Cinemas
M2K Cinemas	

Source: *CB Richard Ellis*

Exhibit 1.6: Future of organized Retail in India

There is no magic answer to this question. However, one can make some educated guesses based on established best practices and how Indian conditions will modify or replace conventional wisdom. Let's consider some of the factors that could affect the future of organized Retail in India.

Consumers – Who understands the Indian consumer the best will win in the end. What do we mean by the Indian consumer? Is it the teenager in Mumbai who commutes by local train, buys fashionable clothes from Linking Road and watches movies at the multiplex? Or is it the housewife who buys vegetables from the *sabzi mandi* and saves up money for chicken on Sundays. Or is it the fisherman out at sea who uses a cell phone to communicate his catch to the market on the shore? The Indian consumer is hard to pin down. As someone wisely said, the Indian consumer shifts loyalties with every 25 kilometers and with every 10 Rupees. The dimensions to deal with include class, education, language, caste and local customs in addition to the standard marketing dimensions used in the West.

Merchandising – Merchandising is what retailers do. This aspect has not received much media attention in India. However, this is often what differentiates a successful retailer from a flash in the pan retailer. Examples that come to mind include Zara, 7-Eleven and Walmart. Put simply, merchandising is the art-science of deciding what to sell where, at what price and when. The retailers that understand the Indian consumers and provide the right products at the right price will beat the competition.

Talent – This is already becoming a bottleneck for several Indian retailers. Experienced corporate professionals as well as fresh talent at the store level are hard to come by. The retailers that are able to retain their talent and provide them with growth opportunities could easily gain an upper hand in running a successful operation in India.

Real Estate – This is a huge concern in India where quality real estate has become too expensive for many retailers to run a successful operation in cities. This is especially true for mass merchandise/discount retailers who operate on razor-thin margins. The acquisition of cheap leases in prime areas could decide whether a retailer becomes profitable at all or not. Another strategy is to expand in smaller towns and villages where real estate is still affordable and purchasing power is not as bad as one might think.

Supply Chain – This often quoted but not-so-often understood term basically refers to the back-end operations of a retailer. This includes the entire network of suppliers, warehouses, distribution centers and logistics operations. Effectively getting products to the right place at the right time is a lot tougher than it sounds when there are thousands of items and hundreds of stores involved. The supply chain infrastructure needs to be built from the ground up in India. This could easily affect the balance sheet of any retailer planning to start operations in India.

Policy – Although most people agree that FDI in Retail is just a matter of time, what this means is that till FDI is allowed, we will see our domestic players like The Future Group and Reliance Retail leading the way. What will happen when FDI is eventually allowed is anyone's guess. If the examples of Brazil or China are taken into account, we will see a lot of consolidation with a few (6-8) large players remaining and several smaller niche players. Retail is a highly localized business (local preferences, local talent), so there is no guarantee that a foreign player will do better than an Indian player, as evidenced by Wal-Mart's failures in Germany and Korea. Surely, there are interesting times ahead!

Source: *Adapted from India Retail News. (http://www.indiaretailnews.com) Visited on October 27, 2008*

Exhibit 1.7: Emerging Retail Hubs in India

High Growth Cities	Emerging Cities	Potential Cities
Ahmedabad	Agra	Allahabad
Chandigarh	Amritsar	Aurangabad
Jaipur	Bhubaneshwar	Bhopal
Kochi	Coimbatore	Guwahati
Lucknow	Goa	Jamnagar
Ludhiana	Indore	Jodhpur
Pune	Jalandhar	Madurai
Gurgaon	Jamshedpur	Patna
Vadodara	Thiruvananthapuram	Rajkot
	Kanpur	Ranchi
	Mangalore	Rohtak
	Mysore	Sonepat
	Nagpur	Srinagar
	Nashik	Varanasi
	Surat	Meerut
	Vishakhapatnam	Vijayawada

UNIT 2

RETAILING FORMATS

LEARNING OBJECTIVES

- Understanding how retailing originated in India
- Understanding various existing and emerging retail formats in India
- Explaining why franchising and leased formats are growing fast.
- Understanding the types of store and non store based retail sales mix and explaining what trends are shaping today's retailers.
- Examining a wide variety of food based retailers involved with store based strategy mixes.
- Describing and differentiating between the characteristics of direct marketing and direct selling.
- Explaining various non-store based retail formats and understanding how World Wide Web retail format is becoming popular throughout the globe.

"We are seeing pioneers moving out to the Internet, banks that are taking transactions, retail shopping on the Internet, and although it's going to take most of a decade before most adults are turning to the Internet for a high percentage of their act"

Bill Gates

INTRODUCTION

Retailing in India is a buzzword and is growing very fast. According to one estimate, one third of the one million or so new businesses created each year belong to retail industry. It represents an amazing conglomerate of independent *'kirana'* stores, departmental stores, convenience stores, specialty store, factory outlets, convenience stores, kiosk stores, category killers, and cooperative stores. Over the last five years due to mall revolution and westernized impact, various new retail formats have emerged. Same item of merchandise, a retailer can buy from a wider variety of retailers. Some retailers not only provide physical buying but 'on-line' and order on telephone' is being provided. This chapter deals with various types of retail formats that coexist with traditional '*kirana*' stores that are changing themselves in a big way. Each type of retail formats offer a different set of features and has its own merits and demerits over others. Usually these retail formats are classified under three categories as under:

A. On the basis of ownership
B. On the basis of merchandise offered and
C. Non-store retailing

Figure 2.1
Classification of Retail Formats

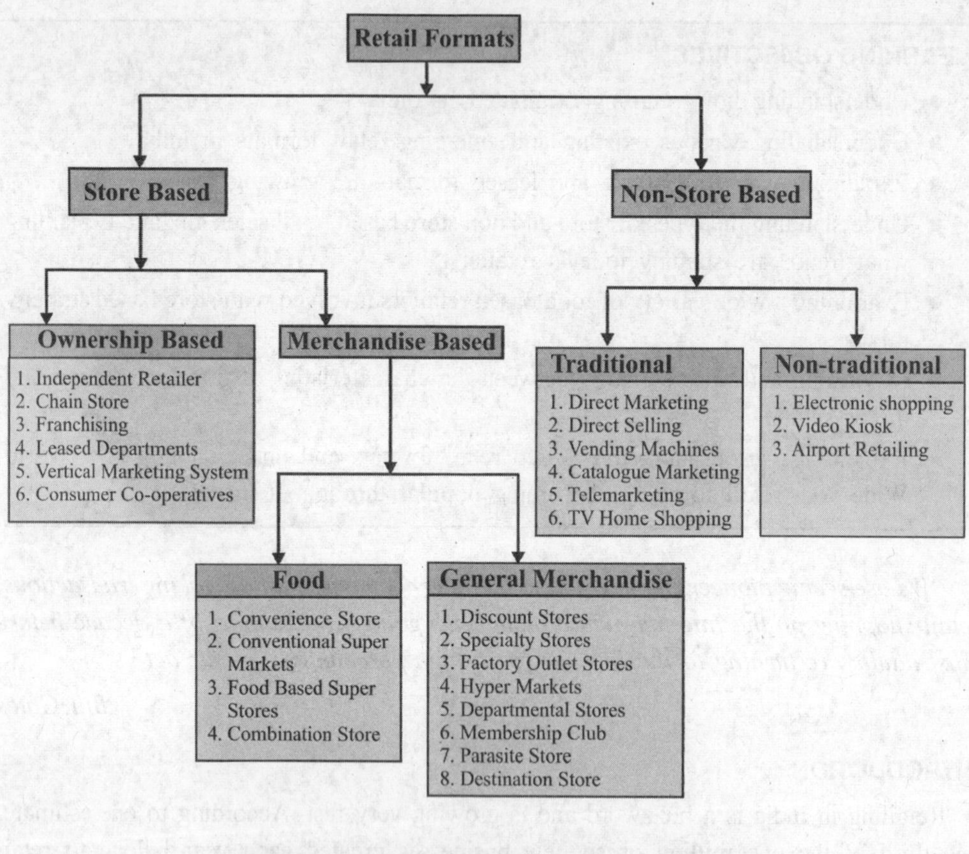

PART (A) STORE BASED RETAIL FORMAT

RETAIL STORES ON THE BASIS OF OWNERSHIP

The term '***retail sales by ownership***' refers to the basic system or basic format of doing business. In India, around 12 million retail outlets are covered under this format. Under this format, proprietor is responsible for the success and failure of the store. It is a type of format, which legally has no separate existence from its owner. Opportunities in retail ownership are in plenty. From market positioning and operating perspectives, each ownership format serves a particular market and has its own advantages and disadvantages.

Over Ninty percent retail firms / outlets in India are independent and hence unorganized. With the globalization and borderless economies, this percentage is coming down but still unorganized stores (mom and pop stores) are in plenty. This number may be because of ease of entry. Ownership pattern has its own competitive advantages and disadvantages. Among independent competitive advantages, main are flexibility, low investments, less interference, quick decisions, direct strategic control, image, consistency, personal attention and entrepreneurial spirit. Among disadvantages, common are limited finance, less bargaining power, labor intensity, reduced media access, few economies of scale, less expertise, over-dependence on the owner, excess workload and limited planning and supervision due to individual's limitations. The retail sale by ownership is classified as under:

(1) Independent Retailer
(2) Chain stores
(3) Franchising
(4) Leased department stores
(5) Vertical Marketing system
(6) Consumer co-operatives

(1) INDEPENDENT RETAILER

An Independent Retailer usually is a small retailer (always not true) and is found in all lines of trade and in all communities. He may be a young man, fresh graduate just starting his own business or he may be a man of advanced years with many of them spent in the field of retailing. In India, many of the independent stores tend to be passed on from one generation to another. In either case he has a business of his own. He is independent infact as well as in name. The high numbers of independent retailers is associated with the 'ease of entry' into the market place. The entry and growth of independent retailers in India is a big reason in the high rate of new retail outlets failure.

Merchandising Philosophy

It sets the guiding principles for all the merchandise decisions that a retailer makes. The advantages of such a philosophy are:

- To have smooth chain of commands
- The buyer's expertise is used in selling
- Enables a retailer to reach its goals.

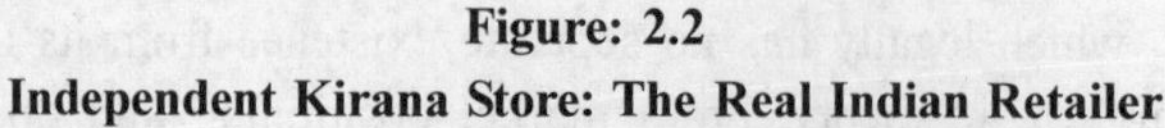

Figure: 2.2
Independent Kirana Store: The Real Indian Retailer

The Independent Retailer: The real *kirana* store has no restrictions on who, how or where a business to set up. The freedom to do what one wants to do make an independent retailer the real retailer.
Courtesy: *The Mail Today*

Merits

1. The independent retailer has no restrictions on who, how or where the business to be set up. He is free to do what he wants and to select a convenient location.
2. The independent retailer takes all decisions related to the store functioning. It drastically saves the time that usually exist between decision-making and the implementation process. Therefore, an independent retailer can respond quickly to the environmental changes and adopt proper strategies.
3. The independent retailer can concentrate on a local area to achieve its business goals.
4. To serve the local demand, a retailer can decide the trading hours, merchandise to be sold / removed and prices as and when desired.
5. It avoids duplication of work, ambiguity of role and excess stock due to clarity of role, thus resulting in increased productivity and time utilization.
6. To start an independent store is comparatively an easy task as it requires low investment, modest fixtures and merchandise.
7. The independent store by providing limited but deep merchandise can act as a specialized store to serve a particular consumer segment.

Demerits

1. Due to limited exposure and small investments, in most of the cases, they don't stand in competition with the emergence of giant retailers and international store outlets.
2. As independent stores are dependent on labor intensive techniques, they find themselves difficult to improve store-productivity when it comes to stock-keeping, ordering, merchandising, displays, accounting and dispatching.
3. Undoubtedly, the bargaining power of independent retailers is comparatively less as they offer limited merchandise. On the other hand, big retailers (like supermarkets, hypermarkets and chain stores) due to bulk buying, negotiate vendors effectively and offer less prices, better quality goods and great service at short notice or in small lots create problem for independent stores.
4. Due to limited operations, less working capital, improper logistic arrangements, retailers are not able to have benefits of economies of scale.
5. Independent retailers due to limited funds cannot go for mass sales promotion programs resulting in limited target market and geographical coverage.

(2) CHAIN STORE/CHAIN RETAILER

A chain retailer or a chain store is a group of two or more outlets carrying the same sort of merchandise assortment, owned and controlled jointly and usually supplied from one or more central warehouses. The main advantage of such a retail format is to make retailer enable to bargain well with the suppliers. Another advantage is cost effectiveness in advertising and sales promotions. Thus, a very small number of stores constitute a chain-store system.

> A distinguishing characteristic of a chain store system is that it is centrally managed and is usually engaged in some level of common purchasing and decision-making. According to one estimate, US has around 1 lakh retail chains that operate nearly 7 lakhs outlets.

Merits of Chain stores

- Good bargaining power with suppliers
- Cost effectiveness due to centralized operations
- Ease of managing store operations
- Use of advanced technology increases their working efficiency
- Experts hiring allow close monitoring of environmental changes

Demerits of Chain stores

- The establishment cost to set up such chain of outlets requires huge money and expertise.
- Difficulty in managerial control due to geographically dispersed branches/outlets
- Due to centralized decision-making, some outlets may have difficulty in adapting to local needs.
- Due to huge network of outlets, it is difficult for management to monitor their day to day activities resulting in communication gap, inefficiencies, and delay in decision making.
- Expense on safety stock remains high.

Leading Chain stores in India

1. Archies
2. Big Bazaar
3. Food Bazaar
4. Lifestyle store
5. Mc Donald's
6. Mobile Store
7. NIIT
8. Pantaloons
9. Pizza Hut
10. KFC
11. Spencers
12. Spinach
13. Vishal Mega Mart
14. Westside
15. Cafe Coffee Day

Chain Store Merchandising Principles

Chain store merchandising is termed as large scale merchandising or mass merchandising and is based on following principles:

I. Merchandising suitable for distribution by chain stores must be highly standardized.

II. Merchandise that requires a relatively high degree of technical or professional knowledge is not well suited for the chain store distribution.

III. A sound system of merchandise control and supervision is essential.

IV. A product that requires fitting service or proper installation must be avoided for chain store merchandising.

(3) FRANCHISING

A Franchise is a contractual agreement between the franchiser and the franchisee that allows the franchisee the right to supply its brand (goods and services) exclusively within a defined area, as per a particular format for a specified period of time. In return, franchisee pays a fixed fee in advance and a monthly percentage of gross sales made by him under franchiser name and fame in the form of royalty. In India, franchising business is becoming very popular and growing rapidly. The small businesses find it convenient by being a part of large, multinational firm because franchiser provides great assistance to franchisee for locating and constructing the retail store (including interiors, and exteriors), developing the goods and services for selling, hiring employees, training, advertising and administering the store effectively.

Franchising

Franchising is a form of licensing in which franchiser provides the exclusive rights to sell its products and/or services for a specified period of time in a specified geographical area. Franchising actually is a French word that means *honesty* or *freedom*.

Key franchisers in India

- Aptech
- Chabbra 555
- Coke
- Domino's Pizza
- Koutons
- McDonald's
- NIIT
- Pepsi
- Pizza's Hut
- Priknit
- Reliance Fresh
- Sagar Ratna's
- Store 99
- Vishal Mega Mart

Types of Franchising

In commerce, franchising structure can vary according to the goods and services provided. In most of the agreements, the franchisee is prohibited from selling goods and/or services of other brands from the same retail outlet in any circumstances. The franchising may be of two categories:

***(a)* Product or a trademark franchising**: In this sort of franchising, a franchisee with mutual consent acquires the name and identity of the franchiser by agreeing to sell the franchiser's goods and services exclusively made and supplied by him under his name. In actual, under such an arrangement, franchisee use the franchiser's business methods, selling techniques, standardized product lines and advertising on co-operative basis. Although, franchisee adheres to certain operating rules and regulations, but still is independent in their day-to-day operations. In consultation with the franchiser, franchisee can decide the store hours according to the locality needs. Archies Gallery, Hallmark stores, which are spread all over India, is the best suitable examples of a product/trademark franchisee.

***(b)* Business Format Franchising**: In business format franchising, there is a more synergetic relationship between a franchiser and the franchisee. The franchisee receives assistance on the issue of site location, building the store, quality control, accounting practices, training to store employees, and the problems faced in conducting the store. Besides these services, a franchisee enjoys the benefits of prototype stores, standardized product lines, selling and presenting skills and co-operative advertising. McDonald's outlets, Domino's, Pizza Hut are the best suited examples of business format franchising. In India, since 2000, most growth has been observed under this type of franchising format.

(c) Area Development Franchising System: In an area development franchisee system, the franchiser grants development rights of a particular area to the franchisee in turn for a front-end development fee. The franchisee on his part is responsible for developing a certain number of units within a given period of time. Excel Infotech EIIT has adopted this unique mode of franchising[1].

Franchising At a Glance

Merits of Franchising to Franchisee:

- Individual franchisee can own and run a retail store with relatively small investment at relatively low risks.
- Franchisees acquire well established and successful brands that require very less or no time to produce customers.
- In franchising, due to franchiser's name and fame, franchisee may be successful much faster than if they try to start and run a business from scratch.
- Under such agreement, a franchisee usually has monopoly position as he obtains exclusive rights for a specified geographical location. For example, sector 18 of Noida or a particular block/colony.
- As franchisee is the owner of the outlet, they take personal care and due attention.

Demerits of Franchising to Franchisee:

- Due to presence of more than one retail outlets of the same brand, the problem of over-saturation may occur, resulting in low sales and division of profits among each other.
- Under contractual agreement, franchisee may be restrict/bind to make purchases through franchisor or through some approved suppliers as listed/provided by them
- Under some industries, franchisee agreements are of short duration which require yearly/continuous renewal upon expiry. If renewal is not made, the whole investment made by the franchisee will go waste.
- Charging royalty over gross sales rather than franchisee' profit is another big disadvantage.

AN EXAMPLE OF FRANCHISEE OPPORTUNITY

A Case of Bigshoebazaar.com

Bigshoebazaar.com is India's largest online shoe store, retailing shoes and accessories made by some of India's best footwear and accessory brands. The company is based out of Delhi and operates through its website and retail network. Shoes sold on Bigshoebazaar are 100% authentic branded products sourced directly from manufacturers and sold with their consent.

---
[1] *www.Indianmba.com*

How do they sell?

A Bigshoebazaar shoe store has 3 unique abilities that no other store has:

(1) They sell shoes made by 45 brands

(2) They sell shoes from Rs 100 Rs to Rs 8000

(3) Their area of operation is 16 sq kms

It is almost impossible that once a customer visits a Bigshoebazaar store, he will ever go out empty handed. Because when a customer visits Bigshoebazaar, he has a choice to choose from more than 500 designs made by 45 brands, neatly displayed on the wall.

- 500 top selling designs in his area, all displayed according to brand and category. If he still wants something else, he can choose from more than 4000 designs from the website.
- So a customer gets much more choice at Bigshoebazaar and at fixed prices and huge discounts.
- They have upto 40% off on branded shoes and almost 500 designs are always on sale.
- If a customer chooses a shoe which they have in stock, he pays cash and takes the shoes like a normal transaction.
- If a customer chooses shoes which are not in stock with them, then he places the order on the website and they dispatch the shoes immediately from their Delhi warehouse.
- Customers collect a token amount of 15% from them and the remaining payment would be taken at the time of delivery

Within 3 days, they deliver the shoes either at your shop or at the customers home. Throughout this period you can check the status of the order and update the customer.

To know more please call Mr. Harish Kumar Pathak at 09212169601 or email them at head_operation@bigshoebazaar.com

Why Bigshoebazaar.com?

Basis of Differentiation	Bigshoebazaar.com	Other shoe store
Investment	Minimum 5-8 lac rupees	Minimum 30-50 lac rupees
Space	Minimum 600 sq ft	Minimum 900 sq ft
Stock	800 to 1000 pairs	3000-4000 pairs
Variety	45 brands | 4000+ designs	1-2 brands | 40-50 designs
Area of operations	16 sq kms	One market
Average Sales	8 to 10 lacs per month	2 to 4 lacs per month
Average Net profit	90000 to 110000 per month	40000 to 80000 per month

4. LEASED DEPARTMENT STORES

A leased department which is also known as shop-in-shops or store-in-store, is a section of a department in a retail store in the form of speciality/discount store given to any outside party on monthly rental basis. The person who provides the store space to outside party is known as lessor, and the person who takes the shop/store space is known as lessee. The payment made by lessee to lessor for the use of store space is decided in a contract in the form of monthly rent. The lessee (the proprietor) is usually responsible for all aspects of business such as managing fixtures and furniture. In order to maintain the overall consistency and co-ordination, the store has some operating and administrative restrictions for each lessee in a uniform manner.

For a lessee (retailer), the main reason to have rented premises is the property price that usually is so high that buying the premises is beyond the reach of the retailer.

Tips for locating a suitable landlord (for retailers)

Before locating and finalizing a landlord, a retailer should consider these issues as leased agreement which is usually a long-term contract and involves huge investments.

These are:

- Are the other tenants (if any) are comfortable with the said leased department. If no, why?
- What sought of businesses other retailers are into and from how much time?
- Collect viewpoints of some retailers whether associated or not with the business line a retailer is entering into?
- What sought of services is provided and hindrances (if any) are created by the landlord?
- Interacting with the present tenants provides the best picture to a retailer, whether he should forward with the lease agreement or not?

Leased Departments in India

In India, leased departments are an emerging trend in the field of retail business. Most of the renowned retail chain stores set up their outlets or extension counters in commercial complexes of residential areas, malls, PVR multiplexes, public places like bus terminals, railway stations, metro stations, airports and on national highways. The reason behind their popularity is the business and marketing philosophy of the retail chains that insures the availability of their brands to the consumers near their place of work or home.

Advantages and disadvantages of leased departments

Following are the advantages of having leased departments from stores' point of view:

- It provides one-stop shopping experience.
- Leased stores pay for property, personnel and other expenses resulting in fewer burdens on lessor.

- Lessor gets regular monthly income in the form of rent.
- Employees' management, merchandise displays and arrangement, reordering of items, complaint handling and so on are handled by individual lessees.

Disadvantages:

- Operating hours may vary form store to store on the basis of goods and /or services sold.
- Items sold /business lines are restricted.
- If lessees are performing well, the store owner may increase the rent or lessees themselves can create problems by changing /not obeying agreements' rules and regulations.
- The bad image of one lessee can spoil the image of entire store.

Product (Goods) Vs services

In business world, be it retail or wholesale, products belong to either goods or services. Goods are intengible products that move from raw material stage to work-in progress (WIP) stage to the finished goods. Finished goods and their by-products then can stay in warehouses or at the point of display until customers buy them. When customers visit stores, they think of displayed goods as per their requirements, if convinced, they pay the money to buy it, which involves transfer of ownership from a retailer to customer.

On the other hand, services are intangible in nature and therefore, cannot be stored in inventory. Service is something that someone performs for the customer, like giving customer a haircut or offering medical aid or even teaching students retail management. Like goods, a customer will not get something to use like a pen drive, notebook and spectacles but customer get what he/she wanted.

The basic difference between a product and service is its tangibility. A product is something a customer can touch, feel, see and hold in his/her hand (provided it is something huge like a motorcycle or a house). A Service is any activity of benefit that a retailer can offer to its customers and they do not result in transfer of ownership.

5. VERTICAL MARKETING SYSTEM

A Vertical Marketing System (VMS) is a system in which almost all the members of distribution channel such as manufacturers, wholesalers and retailers work together to satisfy human needs and wants by facilitating the smooth flow of goods and services from manufacturer to ultimate consumer.

In traditional marketing system, manufacturers, wholesalers and retailers are separate entities that try to maximize their own profits. The philosophy behind developing vertical marketing system is that when one member of distribution channel tries to maximize its profits on the expense of rest of the members, it will create conflicts resulting in decline in profits for the whole channel of distribution. To avoid these conflicts, now retail firms have started forming vertical marketing systems. Three types of VMS are in existence through which goods and services are usually distributed to customers. These are:

(*i*) Independent firm VMS

(*ii*) Partially integrated VMS

(*iii*) Fully integrated VMS

(*i*) Independent firm VMS is a marketing system where manufacturers play vital role to provide goods and services to customers. This is the case where retailers are very small and therefore, manufacturers have to reach the whole market. Also when firm's financial resources are limited and channel members are not in a position to share risks and expenses, therefore, they want manufacturer to come forward and lead the retailing efforts. Independent retailers on the other hand, target their customer base and build loyality by becoming friendly retailer and mouth advertisement.

Examples:

- Campbell
- Coke
- GE
- JC Penney
- Kellog
- McKesson Corp
- P&G
- Pepsi
- Toys R Us
- Wal Mart

(*ii*) Partially integrated VMS is a marketing system in which two independent, financially strong firms along a channel of distribution perform all manufacturing and distribution functions without the involvement of any intermediary. This is the case where involvement of wholesalers may be expensive and/or unaffordable. The example of such system is where manufacturers and retailers divide all the retailing activities like production, storage and distribution without any independent wholesalers. Partially integrated VMS is most suitable where (i) wholesalers are costly to afford, (ii) company has ample resources, (iii) both manufacturers and retailers are large, (iv) unit sales are moderate, and (v) strict control over channel is required.

(*iii*) Fully integrated VMS is a system where one member of the distribution channel for say manufacturer performs all production, storage and distribution functions without the involvement of any channel member. This is the case where manufacturer being resource sound wants direct interaction with its customers. Earlier throughout the globe, this system was usually employed by manufacturers of repute but now due to ease of finance facilities and retailing being a significant contributor to any nation's economy, retailers are also moving upward in the chain. Vishal Mega Mart and Reliance Fresh work on the principle of integrated marketing system and provide efficient customer service, wider assortment without increasing the price of commodities. In short, fully integrated system is based on the concept of 'manufacturing to retailing'. Other examples are:

- Banana Republic
- Gallo
- Giant Foods
- Hallmark
- Oil Companies
- Sears
- Sherwin Williams
- The Gap

6. CONSUMER COOPERATIVES

Consumer Cooperatives are retail outlets owned and managed by its customer members. A group of interested customers (members) start retail operations by investing money, receive stock certificates, elect members to run day to day activities and share the profits on the basis of investment made or certificates held.

The reason to setup consumer cooperative is that local retailers are not able to satisfy consumers' needs (whatever the reason may be). Therefore, consumers are left with no option but to open their own store. Examples of cooperatives in India are the 'Kendriya Bhandaars', owned and managed by government, 'Apna Bazaar' shops in Mumbai and 'Super Bazaar' stores in Delhi. In some cases, these stores are run by the local residents of society/colony/apartment residents.

Figure 2.3

Apna Bazar: Biggest Chain of Supermarkets in India

An outside and inside view of Apna Bazar Super Market, Ashok Nagar, Mumbai

About Apna Bazar

Apna Bazar is the biggest chain of supermarkets in India operating with more than 500 outlets throughout the Mumbai, selling more than 6,000 essential commodities. It is the only biggest supermarket chain that keeps in view the development of consumer association, indirectly cooperates with every activity and supports consumer rights to acquire quality products without compromising on quality. It also possesses one of the best and biggest warehouse facilities and provides direct employment to more than 1,000 volunteers and indirect employment to more than 10,000 people. In this way it has been a good job creator and sustainer. Their outlets are well spaced to display the vast range of products at easy view angles, with ample room for people's movements. Each and every outlet covers an average plinth area which is said to be a better space for this sort of retailing format.

Courtesy: *Company Website (www.apnabazar.org)*

State Consumer Cooperative Organizations

In a few States, where the central stores and the local traditional stores have not made much progress, the State Federations have come forward to provide merchandise by establishing supermarkets. Assam, Madhya Pradesh, Karnataka and Assam are the leading states having such kind of cooperatives stores. Janata Bazar owned and run by Karnataka Federation with an annual sale of more than one crore rupee is one of the biggest retailers of the Karnataka state. Similarly in Madhya Pradesh, Pridarshani super market at Bhopal is the leading retailer of Madhaya Pradesh with an annual turnover of rupee five crore. Some of the leading State Consumer Co-operatives are:

1. Karnataka Cooperative Consumers Federation Ltd
2. Maharashtra State Cooperative Consumers Federation Ltd.
3. Gujarat State Cooperative Consumers Federation Ltd. and
4. Pondicherry State Cooperative Consumers Federation Ltd. (CONFED).

Characteristics

1. Limited expansion
2. Profit is shared by its members
3. They sell usually essential commodities at reasonable price
4. Main purpose is social service not to earn profit, and
5. Average customer service

Note: *In India, consumer cooperatives are not popular and therefore are limited in number because members (consumers) are not expert in buying, marketing and handling goods and services. But some cooperatives have gone ahead and have emerged into leading retail chain, for instance, '**Mother Diary**' in Delhi and '**Parag**' in Lucknow. Indian government in order to save Indian art and helping artisans and small and medium sized industries open stores and provide marketing assistance from time to time. **KVIC** stores throughout the country and State Handloom Emporiums in big cities are example of such retail format.*

RETAIL STORES ON THE BASIS OF MERCHANDISE OFFERED

Under this category, retailers are broadly divided into two categories:

(A). Food Based Retailers and

(B). General Merchandise Retailers

(A). FOOD BASED RETAILERS

After the launch of New Industrial Policy, 1991 the Indian economy has re-energized itself in terms of capital invested and number of new ventures started. One such development that has become topic of each debate and conferences is the ***organized food retailing***. India is not only the country of '*kirana*' stores but has a biggest population of working middle class. For every thirty families, there is a store – no matter big or small, grocery or soft drink corner. But this trend is not to continue in the years to come as big business houses like Reliance, Tesco, Walmart-Bharti, and Birla are opening shops throughout the country. This would replace the traditional '*kirana*' or department store. This already has created fears in the mind of unorganized '*kirana*' stores and small type shop keepers. Food stores are becoming popular as even better quality goods (when compared to local stores) they are offering in low cost under hygienic and attractive ambience outlets with dining arrangements. Food stores in India are divided into four categories as under:

1. Convenience Store
2. Conventional Super Markets
3. Food Based Super Stores
4. Combination Store

1. CONVENIENCE STORES

There are small retailers that offer a limited variety of merchandise at small scale but convenient locations ranging from 2,000 – 3,000 sq. ft. These outlets /stores are modern versions of the traditional '*kirana*' stores. The future of this category is better as they enable shoppers to shop quickly with a speedy checkout. The convenience stores are becoming popular in metro cities where generally both husband and wife are employed and have no spare time to shop. Secondly, convenience stores as per their name are located alongside busy roads, parking areas or at petrol filling stations. In metros, one can find these outlets at railway stations, bus stands and near residential areas. These stores usually have long shopping hours and are spreading near densely populated colonies and residential societies. As compared to other types of stores like supermarket, convenience stores usually charge higher prices.

Convenience stores at a Glance

Positive Aspects

- Quick shopping
- Less checkout time
- Self service level
- Long shopping hours

Negative Aspects

- Limited product range
- High pricing
- Small stores

Assortment: An assortment is the selection of merchandise a retailer carries to sell in his retail outlet. Assortment includes both the breadth of product categories and the variety within each category.

Width of Assortment: Width of assortment refers to the number of distinct goods/services categories that a retailer has purchased and displayed for retail selling in his outlet.

Breadth of Assortment: It refers to the variety in a particular product/service.

Micro Merchandising: It refers to a strategy whereby a retailer adjusts its shell space allocations to respond to the customers and other differences (if any) among local markets.

2. CONVENTIONAL SUPER MARKET

A conventional supermarket is a departmentalized grocery store with a wide range of dairy products and household items such as soft and hard drinks (wherever allowed to be sold), household cleaning products, shampoos, soaps, clothes, medicines and plastic items. A supermarket offers a large retail facility with huge range of merchandise under same roof at low prices by shrinking margins. Supermarkets usually rely on high inventory turnover and built either near a residential area or on the outskirt of the city. Customers in supermarkets use 'trolleys' or 'baskets' for collecting their desired products and pay for the same at the checkout counters (billing sections) near exits. Due to cost effective and consumer savvy, conventional supermarkets are facing intense competition from traditional '*kirana*' stores and other types of food outlets.

Supermarket at a Glance

A conventional supermarket is relatively large, low-priced, low-margin, high-volume, self-service operation designed to serve variety needs for food and household items. Other benefits include convenient shopping hours and space for parking.

Features:

Location	:	Near/edge of town
Size	:	Large
Product range	:	Vast range, deep and broad
Pricing policy	:	Low pricing
Selling theme	:	Every Day low Pricing **(EDLP)**
Target market	:	Mass
Atmosphere	:	Busy and well organized
Service level	:	Self service

Supermarket in India is one of the fast growing segments but so far there is no standard criterion that makes a supermarket format. Even many traditional '*kirana*' stores are refurbishing their shops/retail outlets and advertising themselves as supermarkets. They use Every Day Low pricing (EDLP) selling policy to build store traffic and provide a one-stop shopping.

3. FOOD BASED SUPERSTORES

In India, food retailing is the buzzword today. There is a large variety of food stores operating in food retailing. This is not surprising as the Indian middle class income is increasing rapidly and therefore they prefer to shop at supermarkets for its hygienic environment, convenience and attractive ambience. This 'value' and 'feel good' perspective offered by food retailers stimulate customers to try new and different things. Though food retailing in India is becoming popular very fast but with a population of more than one billion and a middle class population of over four hundred millions, food retailing is still in its nascent stage.

With the entry of corporate houses like Bharti, Walmart, Reliance Fresh, Vishal Mega Mart, Aditya Birla group, and the existing Big Bazaar, Spencer, and Food Mart outlets are making foray in the so called untapped market. The pace with which these food companies are spreading throughout the country, the net of the organized retail outlets is going to reach soon the small populations towns of one lacs to over five lacs after covering all small, medium and big cities.

A view of Aditya Birla group owned 'More' outlet

Superstores are usually large supermarkets that have space area ranges from 20,000 to 50,000 sq. ft. These stores as the very name implies, sell grocery items and offer customers the ability to buy fill-in general merchandise.

Features

(i) Offer one-stop shopping experience
(ii) Stimulate impulse purchase
(iii) The concept of EDLP (Everyday Low Price) is usually followed
(iv) Large, low margin and self service stores

Advantage

It is easy to convert super markets into food-based stores than combination stores.

Food Retailing: Sizing up the Challengers

India is well and truly on its way to becoming a fast food nation, with virtually every chain worth its ketchup and fries making a beeline for our shores. As McDonald's talks about introducing its famous breakfast offerings and adding 40 new outlets in 2008, let's see what the competition is up to.

Taco Bell: After two years of exploratory talks and an extensive survey, the US-based Tex-Mex chain has said it would start its India innings by the end of this year. Through the chain, which is a subsidiary of Yum! Brands (the same entity that owns Pizza Hut and KFC), foresee its growth primarily in Tier II cities, it plans an 11-city launch, starting with Delhi, Mumbai, Hyderabad, Bangalore and Agra.

Burger King: The world's second-largest burger chain, which is owned by a clutch of private equity players, is also eyeing the India as part of its Asian expansion plans. It has given Kotak Mahindra the responsibility of finding an Indian partner, so the market is rife with speculation that the burger behemoth is in talks with Pepsi bottler and KFC franchisee Ravi Jaipuria, the Future Group and DLF.

KFC: Media reports suggest the chain plans to invest US$50-75 million (Rs 2,200 crore toRs 3,300 crore) on expanding its operations by raising the number of outlets from 34 to 100 by the end of 2010-end. Look out for 16 new KFC outlets by the end of this year.

Domino's: The pizza major has finalized plans to invest Rs 10,000 crore in India over the next two-three years and add 70 new stores around the country in 2008-09, lifting its store count to 250. In June, incidentally, Domino's made its foray into Kerela. The brand aims at having 500 stores by 2010 and a little birdie tells us they may come out with their own brand of burgers.

Pizza Hut: From its 139 restaurants, and still counting, Pizza Hut serves around 300,000 guests in 36 cities around the country every week. The company, which has been in India for as long as McDonald's (since 1996, when it opened its first dine-in restaurant in Bangalore), plans to scale up to 175 restaurants by 2010.

Subway: Five years after its launch, the submarine sandwich maker today has a network of 123 franchisee-run restaurants in India and a tie-up with Nestle and Pepsi, which is established when it entered the market with a store in South Delhi neighbourhood of Saket in 2001.

Nirula's: Synonymous with 'hamburger steaks' since 1928, the Delhi-based fast food restaurant chain, which was bought from Lalit and Deepak Nirula in 2006 by its managing director, Samir Kuckreja, and the Malaysian equity firm, Navis Capital Partners, has rolled out a Rs 150-crore plan for expansion across the country. In the next three years, the chain will have about 150 outlets across the country, and by 2012-13, it plans to have a footprint in 20 international locations.

Source: *Mail Today, Vol.1, No. 268, Cover Story Pg. 4, August 10, 2008*

4. COMBINATION STORES/SUPER CENTRES

Combination stores basically are food-based retailers that combine their supermarket and general merchandise sales at one place. While in India, there is as such no standardization on the parameters of what makes a supermarket, is one of the fastest growing retail formats. In a combination store, general merchandise sales usually accounts for 30-40% of total store sales. As economies of scale are higher in a combination store, therefore, these stores offer low pricing policy and make profits on account of impulse sales.

Super Centre

A super center is a combination of supermarket and a discount retail store. Super centers usually have average size of about 1,50,000 sq.ft and allot 30-40% of their retail space to grocery items and remaining to discounted general merchandise, presenting threat to traditional supermarkets.

Combination stores provide one-stop shopping experience, and therefore, customers do not consider distance factor to come to these stores.

(B). GENERAL MERCHANDISE RETAILERS

General merchandise retailers usually sell all non-food items such as house wares, furniture, consumer electronics, toiletries, toys, greeting cards, plastic wares, hardware, Jewelry items, shoes, kitchen appliances, clothes, readymade garments, bakery, music world, gift items, cell phones, home appliances, cooking wares, furniture, sports and food courts. The retailers under General Merchandise category are classifed as under:-

1. Discount Stores
2. Specialty Stores
3. Factory Outlet Store
4. Hyper Markets
5. Departmental Stores
6. Membership Club
7. Parasite Store
8. Destination Store

1. DISCOUNT STORES / DISCOUNTERS

Discount stores include:

(1) Limited line Discount Store: Limited line discount stores sell limited lines of merchandise at low prices but the brands offered are well reputed. Due to limited line, stores may change their stock according to buying opportunities and change in customer liking and disliking very frequently. Limited line discount stores may be located near the residential areas, out of city or edge of city to take advantage of suburban site like easier access and lower rent.

(2) Full line Discount Store: A full line discount store offers broad merchandise assortment in high volume but at low cost. As the name implies, besides carrying the general product line expected at departmental store, it includes house wares, kitchen wares, gardening, sports accessories, and auto accessories with centralized check out service system. The reasons for the success of such retail formats are many. The important among them are:

(a) low pricing
(b) average to good quality merchandise
(c) good facilities
(d) well managed standardized retail outlets.

These stores face strong competition from other retailers like category killers and other low priced discounters.

(3) Off-price store: Off price retailers usually buy merchandise at less than regular wholesale prices (normally between one-fifth to one-third of the original wholesale price) and sell them at less than retail prices. Off price stores often buy leftover merchandise, overruns, and irregulars obtained at low prices direct from the manufacturers or big retailers. These stores offer an inconsistent merchandise assortment, latest fashion goods at reduced prices. The reason for making them enable to purchase at lower prices is that these stores/retailers don't claim/ask suppliers for any advertising and sales promotion allowances and any delayed payments.

In India over the last few years, the sales graph of off-price stores has declined with the increasing popularity of departmental and supermarkets. Consequently, now off-price retailers have changed their modus operandi and are buying latest merchandise and also carry the manufacturer's surplus, discounted or irregular goods. In India, these stores are usually run by the parent company to increase the business under retailing format. Pantaloon factory outlets, Levi's factory outlets and Liberty factory outlets are the examples of this category.

Discount stores at a Glance

Discounters typically operate with very low pricing policy by strictly controlling operating costs such as expenses incurred on store layout, cost of land, e-retailing and by offering limited/very few services to their shoppers. Due to bulk buying, discounters typically offer 20-40% below supermarket and discount store prices but don't accept credit cards and make no home delivery.

Features:

Location	:	Near/Far
Store size	:	Medium
Merchandise assortment	:	Limited

Pricing policy	:	Low (very low)
Service level	:	Self
Promotion emphasis	:	Advertising
Target Market	:	Mass
Product category	:	General

2. SPECIALITY STORE

A specialty store concentrate on a narrow product line, with a deep assortment in that product line, such as apparel and accessories, furniture, consumer electronics etc. The specialty stores have very clearly defined target market and therefore provide a top level of consumer service and sales expertise in the concerned category. These stores operate in an area typically not more than 8,000 sq. ft. in contrast to a mass marketing approach, specialty stores offer limited variety but full range of merchandise. These stores generally have discounted competitive pricing strategy.

Key Specialty Stores of India

- Adidas
- Apollo Tyres
- Aquaguard
- Bata
- Bausch and Lomb
- Food Bazaar
- Gautier Furniture
- Haldiram Bhujiwala
- Inalsa
- KC Das
- Khadims
- Music World
- Nokia World
- Pantaloons
- Proline Fitness Station
- Reynolds
- Sify Way
- Sony World

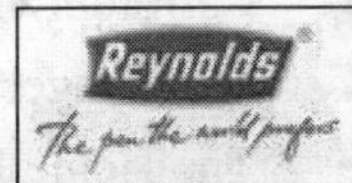

Specialty Stores

Narrow product line with a deep assortment, such as apparel stores, jewelry, sporting goods, furniture and bookstores. A clothing store would be single-line store; a women's clothing store would be a limited-line store; and a men's custom shirt store would be a super specialty store.

Features:

- Personal care
- Excellent customer service
- Impressive store ambience
- Low pricing

A **Category Killer** or a **Power Retailer** is basically a large category specialist. Most category killer use a self service practice and kills the category of merchandise (for say Interiors) for other small retailers of the same line by offering complete assortment in the concerned category. They stock deep variety, for instance, Toys "R" Us offers more than 10,000 items in their stores.

Due to declining interest in traditional apparel shops, a new sort of speciality retailer is emerging very fast in the country especially in metros with the names of *category specialists* or *category killers*. A category killer is a discount store that offers a very large selection in the concerned product category at affordable prices. 'Chhabra 555', 'Bombay Selection', 'P.P.Designer Estate' in Delhi and 'Nalli's' in Chennai can be termed as cetgory killer in Sarees. 'The Lift' in Mumbai is a footwear killer spread in an area of 15,000 sq. ft. Drug stores, mobile stores are also speciality stores or category killers that are becoming very popular in the country. They concentrate on health and telephony instruments. Of the Top-200 Global Retailers, 21% of retailers fall in the specialty stores category, followed by 18% in supermarket, 12% in department and 9% each in hypermarket and discount stores[2].

MBOs

Category killers outlets, also known as multi brands outlets (MBOs), offer several brands across a single product category. These usually do well in busy market places, community centers and Metros.

Figure 2.4

Top Retailers Globally

Rank	Name of the Retailer	Country of Origin
1	Wal-mart Stores	USA
2	Carrefour Group	France
3	The Kroger Company	USA
4	The Home Depot	USA
5	Metro	Germany

Source: *Retail Association of India (RAI website)*

[2] *www.coolavenues.com*

3. FACTORY OUTLET STORES

A Factory retail outlet is a retail store, owned and managed by a retail firm (usually manufacturer) for the purpose of selling defected items, close outs, irregular, cancelled orders and season-end items. These are off-price retail stores and are commonly known as factory outlets. In India, they are usually found at the outskirts of the city, reducing storing, operational and distribution expenses. They usually create threat to existing retailers by offering heavy discounts. Some of the factory outlets are in permanent covered sheds/locations and offer additional facilities such as parking, restaurant, and recreational facilities.

The manufacturer has following reasons to have a Factory Outlet:

(i) It is the means to dispose off surplus, cancelled, out of fashion and defected stock.

(ii) As these are located outside the town, besides increasing firm's revenues, do not affect the sales at manufacturers' department and specialty stores.

Features

(i) Open seven days a week

(ii) Long working hours

(iii) Limited consumer service

(iv) Less marketing efforts

(v) Out of the way location

4. HYPERMARKET

In commerce, hypermarkets are characterized by large store size, low running costs and margins, low prices and very large range of merchandise. A hypermarket usually is a very large retail unit offering merchandise at low prices and combines various department stores. In India, hypermarkets have a floor area of more than 50,000 sq. ft. These have their own multi-level spacious car parking facility for their customers and employees. In fact, hypermarkets are giants that offer long range of merchandise in varied quantity and quality under one roof.

Big Bazaar and Reliance Retail are two major hypermarket chain stores. Big Bazaar - a hypermarket opened its first store in April 2002 at Phoenix Mills premises in Mumbai with an area of 50,000 sq. ft. According to Pantaloon Retail (India) Ltd, owner of Big Bazaar outlets in India, Big Bazaar offers over 1,70,000 items in over 20 product categories. In short, in Big Bazaar there is something for everyone. But there is nothing wrong in saying that even after eight years since 2002, hypermarkets are still in the experimental stage in India. Reliance retail and Bharti-Wal-Mart are the new entrants in this category.

The first choice places for Hypermarkets

- Ahmedabad
- Bangalore
- Chandigarh
- Delhi
- Gurgaon
- Hyderabad
- Noida

Hypermarket

Selling area	:	> 50,000 sq. ft
Cash Counters	:	20 – 60
Numbers of items sold	:	Thousands to lakhs
Number of Employees	:	Hundred to thousands
Covered Area	:	Upto 60%
Pricing Policy	:	Special (discounted)
Discount	:	4 –40%
Central Theme	:	Is Se Sasta Kahin Nahi
Service Level	:	Self service
Payment Mode	:	Cash/debit/Credit cards
Ownership structure	:	Corporate chain

Positive Aspects

- Low pricing
- Convenience shopping
- Comfort
- Right quality, quantity and price
- Excellent service
- Good parking facility
- Wide product range

Negative Aspects

- Far away from the city (only)

Items Sold

In hypermarket, usually groceries account for about 60% of total sales, the store also sell a large number of other items like garments, consumer durables, fruits, vegetables, plastic items, electronic items, jewelry etc. In fact, apart from the wide product range, hypermarkets have their own outlets of bakery, music world, gift items, cell phones, home appliances, cooking wares, furniture, sports and food courts.

5. DEPARTMENTAL STORES

A department store (Traditional Departmental Store) is a large retail outlet that offers a large variety and deep assortment and is organized into separate departments for the purpose of selling, display and promotion, customer service and control. Each department sells unique products and has its own selling, accounts, packaging and security staff. Not only in India, but this type of format is popular and well appreciated in many parts of the world. To be defined as a department store, usually it follows following conditions:

(1) It must employ minimum 50 people as store staff.

(2) Most selling goods relate to FMCG and daily used items.

(3) It should have proper balance between home furniture, consumer electronics, apparel and food.

(4) All the departments should generate balance contribution towards sales. For instance, not more than 80% of annual sales can come from single product line.

In India, apparel and furnishing are two common categories in most of the department stores. The major Indian department stores like Ebony, Shopper's Stop, Westside, Music World, Globus and Lifestyle deal in women's, men's, kids' clothing, furniture, jewelry, kitchenware and furnishing.

Department Stores at a Glance

- C3 (Cost, Comfort and Convenience)
- Food World
- Marks & Spencer
- More….. – A Aditya Birla Group
- Pantaloons
- Reliance Fresh
- Shopper's Stop
- Six to Ten
- Spencer's
- Spinach
- Vishal Mega Mart
- Gokul Mega Mart
- Pocket Friendly Mega Mart

Department store merely is a large general store. A department store, however, is to be distinguished from a general store in that departments and groups of departments operate it, whereas a general store is not.

Traditional Department Stores

A traditional department store offers several product lines – typically clothing, household goods, jewelry and home furnishings. Each department within the store has separate line, managed by specialist buyers or merchandisers and offer mid-to-high quality products.

Features:

Size	:	20,000 – 40,000 sq. ft
Pricing	:	Moderate to above average
Customer service	:	High level
Product category	:	General
Ownership structure	:	Corporate chain
Pricing Strategy	:	Competitive
Keeping pace with technology	:	Yes

6. MEMBERSHIP CLUB RETAILING

Warehouse club stores usually sell merchandise in fixed quantities at low prices. These stores require that their customers should take their membership and visit their stores. The products offered are food items, grocery, and clothing with an array of consumer electronic items that vary from season to season. Customer service is nominal due to low price policy.

7. PARASITE STORE

A parasite store is a small store/outlet, which neither has its own floor area nor its own customer traffic. The size, nature and timing of these stores, depend on people/ visitors who are drawn to that location for their own reason. The reason for their visit may be to meet government officials, attending a Seminar or Conference in a Hotel, or Railway/Airline booking. A Coffee Parlour in a Shopping Centre, a Magazine and Newspaper Stall in a Hotel Lobby and a Hair Saloon/Beauty Parlour in a PVR Cinema Complex, all are examples of Parasites. The purpose for using the term 'parasite' is to convey the sense that customers visit these locations not because of their presence but patronize these stores while they are there.

Why Parasite?

In medical terms, parasite is an animal or plant that lives in a close relationship with another organism for its life functions. The parasite has its identity only because of its host. Living with the host, parasites grows, lives and multiplies itself and seldom destroy its hosts.

Parasite store depends on existing traffic flow of a shopping centre or retail business area. In actual, as such, it has no identity of its own and standing in the line of retail business. Customers visit these stores not because of its sales promotion efforts, customer service, store image and merchandising efforts, but the circumstantial visits made by the customers to these hosts (shopping complexes, malls, hotels, government offices, public places or railway/Metro stations).

Characteristics:

- It does not have its own trading area.
- It does not have its own customer traffic flow.
- Its activities are dependent on the main host;
- It usually has less/no competition within the host area.
- It has limited product range.

8. DESTINATION STORE

The destination store, as the name implies, is the retail store where customers make a special visit for the purpose of shopping. The main philosophy behind the destination store lies because of its uniqueness in terms of merchandise assortment, way of presentation, ambience, pricing and customer service. For a retail store, it is not easy to become 'a destination store' in the eyes of the customers.

How to become a Destination Store?

The key to become a destination store lies in the following considerations:

1. Retail location: Once a new-comer retailer asked from a successful retailer "what is the secret of your success?" He answered that the most important consideration is the 'location'. No doubt, some locations are better than others in some aspects. It includes convenience, cleanliness, proximity to residential area, quality, selection, customer service and handling the customers. For instance, to have a franchisee of 'Agarwal Sweet Corner' in NCR, Delhi, requires you to have a corner shop located either at the end of the road or street.

2. **Service that attracts**: Somebody said, today is the world of retailing, it is not the product but the customer service that gives you the profit. A product is available in different types of stores or shops but if the customer prefers to go to a particular store then the answer is simple – it's the welcome and way of handling that attracts the customer to visit a particular store. If all retailing factors are equal and same like quality, price, presentation and selection of goods displayed between your retail store and other nearby stores, then you will find it is 'customer service' that makes your store a dream (destination)store. Here is a list that can be beneficial to make your store customer savvy:

- Proximity to your store;
- Does your store meet what is publicized and presented within the store?
- Does your store invite strangers or casual shoppers from outside?
- Are your windows neatly cleaned and displays kept up regularly?
- Do you have enough parking place;
- Have you heard customers talking about your customer service;
- Convenience.

Each retailer is not fortunate enough to have a good location. Sometimes, you have no shortage of funds and human resources but suitable location is not available in the area where you have planned to open a retail store. Here you have nothing to do about a bad location except make it convenient to the customers. Convenience here implies 'can a shopper get in and out of the store quickly and easily?' For a retailer, it means, blend of full and self-service system, variety of merchandise assortments, regular fill up of racks and provision of customer complaint handling.

3. **Unique Signage:** Signage is a non-living thing that speaks much and have long lasting impact on the customers' memory, whatever people have opinion about McDonald's Restaurants, one can find their signage a kilometer away and those golden arches speak enough to kids and compel their parents to visit without questioning. In retail competition, nothing is less important in a destination store than badly presented signs in the stores, signs and windows that are never cleaned, falling apart or otherwise ignored. This is not to be considered in case of a single store but is important if you are planning to open more than one outlet. If you can create a unique identity that shoppers believe and relate to, it will help you (retailer) to a large extent in case of multiple outlets.

Figure 2.5

Retail Summary Chart

Format Type	Variety	Assort-ment	Pricing Policy Nature	Service	Size (000 sq.ft.)	SKUs (in 000)	Location
Hyper Stores	Broad	Very	Low to Deep	Low	100-300	100 plus Neighbourhood	
Specialty Store	Narrow	Deep	High	High	4-12	5	Malls
Department Store	Broad	Broad	Average to High	Average to High	100-200	100	Malls
Discount Stores	Average	Average	Low	Low	20-30	50	Companies' outlets n malls
Factory outlet	Narrow	Very Deep	Low	Low	50-120	10	stand-alone strip center shopping area
Parasite Store	Narrow	Average to Shallow	High	High	Not Fixed usually very small	5-10	Malls
Destination Store	Average	Average to Shallow	Average to High	High	Not fixed	3-5	stand-alone center shopping area
Membership Club	Average	Limited	Average	Low	Vary from club to club	Depending upon members requirement	members store/in Institutional areas

Figure 2.6

Retailing Formats Adopted by Key Players

Retailer	Original formats	Later formats
RPG Retail	Supermaker (Footworld)	Hypermaket (Spencer's) Specialty store (Health & Glow)
Piramal's	Department store (Piramyd Megastore)	Discount store (TruMart)
Pantaloon Retail	Small format outlets (Shoppe) Department store (Pantaloon)	Supermarket (Food Bazaar) Hypermaket (Big Bazaar) Mall (Central)
K Raheja Group	Department store (Shopper' Stop) Specialty store (Crossword)	Supermarket (TBA) Hypermarket (TBA)
Tata/Trent	Department store (Westside)	Hypermarket (Star India Bazaar)
Landmark Group	Department store (Lifestyle)	Hypermarket (TBA)
Others	Discount store (Subhiksha, Margin Free, Apna Bazaar), Supermarket (Nilgiri's), Specialty Electronics (Vivek's Vijay Sales)	

Source : *KPMG in India analysis 2005*

PART (B) NON-STORE BASED (TRADITIONAL) RETAIL MIX & NON-TRADITIONAL SELLING

The first part of this section explains the store based i.e. bricks-and-mortar retail format. This part discusses various types of retail formats that work mostly in non-store retail environments. The main types of retailers under this category are:

(A) TRADITIONAL RETAILING

1. DIRECT MARKETING/DIRECT RESPONSE MARKETING

It is the branch of marketing by which an organization directly communicates to its customers to generate revenue producing response, transaction or sale through leaflets, pamphlets, brochures, print ads mailed or catalogs distributed directly to its existing and potential consumers. In other words, direct marketing is a form of retailing under which a potential customer is first exposed to a product or service through any form of non-personal communication and then orders by phone, fax, courier or email.

According to Direct Marketing Association[3] "Direct marketing is an interactive system of marketing that uses one or more advertising media to affect a measurable response at any location." The response can be in the form of:

- an order (direct order)
- an inquiry (lead generation)
- a visit to a store or other place of business for purchase of a specific product (s) or service(s) traffic generation)
- Most important, it usually results in the creation of a DATABASE of respondents.

Direct order includes all direct response advertising communications — trough any medium (mail, print, TV, radio, electronic media (such as the Internet) —that are specifically designed to solicit and close a sale. All of the information necessary for the prospective buyer to make a decision to purchase and complete the transaction (product description, price, a response mechanism (phone number, toll free number, or order form) is provided in the advertisement[4].

Lead Generation includes all direct response advertising communications (through any medium) that are designed to generate interest in product or a service and provide the prospective buyer with a means to request and receive additional information about the product or service. The advertising message prompts the customer to follow-up to get further information (from a phone number or address information) or qualify as a lead.

---

[3] *Established in 1917, DMA is the USA based leading global trade association of business and NGOs using and supporting direct marketing tools and techniques. It advocates industry standards for responsible marketing, promotes relevance as the key to reaching consumers with desirable offers, and provides cutting-edge research, education, and networking opportunities to improve results throughout the entire direct marketing process. Today it has more than 3,600 members from the US and 46 other nations, including the majority of companies listed on the Fortune 100. (www.the-dma.org)*

[4] *Source: www.dmasc.org and www.the-dma.org*

Traffic Generation includes all direct response advertising communications conducted (through any medium) that are designed to motivate the prospective buyer to visit a store, or other business establishment to buy an advertised product or service. The advertising message includes pricing and product information, information about a particular sale, local store location, hours of operation, sometimes a telephone number or coupon, but usually not an order form.

A direct relationship with the consumer is the basis of direct marketing. In direct marketing, customers become aware of the products/services offered through a non-personal medium like TV, internet, mail, phone or catalogue etc. These are discussed as follows:

(i) Catalogue/Mail Order Retailing: It is a form of retailing in which retail outlets communicate about their merchandise through a catalogue. This retail format is comparatively new to Indian retail industry. On the other hand, mail order retailing is a retail format in which retailers communicate with their customers using mails/letters or brochures.

(ii) Television Shopping: In India, Asian Sky Shop was among the first few retailers who introduced the concept of television shopping. In this form of retailing, a product is advertised on television with its demonstration and features followed by opinions of those who have used the same product and are satisfied with its performance. Other aspects like mode of payment, delivery time, guarantee and warranty are also discussed. For each city, phone numbers are continuously displayed. The buyer can call in and place the order by giving address details. The product is then delivered at home through courier/VPP(Value Paid on Postage).

(iii) Electronic Shopping/Electronic Retailing: Today, most of the big size retailers have their own website, which allows a retailer to conduct a targeted business twenty four hours a day and seven days a week. Providing retail business offers the retailer not only a modern way of getting business but also cost effectiveness. This one time small investment in creating and registering the website on World Wide Web is accessible to everyone irrespective of location, time zone, income level or computer system. The internet also provides the fuel and information about the goods and services through digital images, visual and audio effects. Electronic brochures provide three-dimensional aspects of the goods and services which a shopper can explore any time before having buying decision.

One of the well known and oldest examples is Amazonbooks.com. Amazon is the largest and the maximum accessible bookshop in the world. According to Amazon sources, today, 30% of its sales come from cyber retailing only. Dell, a well known computer company, claims to sell more than $ 1 million of its personal computers everyday on the internet. The distinguishing feature of these retailers is that they sell their products through internet and as such do not have any physical store. Under retailing through internet concept, customer visits a website of the store, checks the shown items with regard to its size, colour and related features. Having convinced with some items, customer fill up the form and after entering credit/debit card details and postal address completes the transaction. Once the transaction is complete, the goods are delivered directly to the customer at his/her doorstep.

Electronic Shopping/Electronic Retailing

Electronic Shopping is variously referred to as virtual retailing or e-tailing. Due to ease of access and lower operating costs, the internet is revolutionizing retailing in many fundamental ways like eliminating wholesalers/intermediaries after the concept of manufacturing to retailing.

Merits of Electronic Retailing:

- Low operating cost
- Time saving
- No effect of time, distance and income group
- No need to visit the store
- Easy access

Demerits of Electronic Retailing:

- The cost of delivery is passed on to the customer
- Sometimes difficult to judge about displayed products
- Misuse of credit cards
- Possibility of tempering by courier or delivery agencies
- No examination and feel of goods before buying.

2. DIRECT SELLING

It is a retail format where salesperson makes a personal contact with the ultimate consumers at his home or at his/her place of work. In this format, usually salesperson invites some friends or neighbours at his home, office or club and demonstrates the product after formal lecture/briefing. Buying and selling is done on the spot. In India, direct selling concept came in mid 1990s with the entry of so-called Modicare and went through a bad phase before attaining a significant contribution to Indian economy for worth Rs. 2000 crore today.

Features

(i) Mainly handled by housewives comprising up to 70% of total sales people in India.

(ii) Highly interactive in nature

(iii) Sales depend on communication and way of demonstration

(iv) Non-store retail format

(v) Absence of intermediaries

Reasons for increasing popularity

(i) This system is free from long checkout lines
(ii) Ease of payment facility
(iii) Salesperson is known to customer
(iv) People have no time to shop everything
(v) Free from traffic congestion, parking problems etc
(vi) It may appoint other people to work with/ for them as distributors. The master distributor earns a commission on the basis of quantity sold and through recruiting other distributors and receiving a portion of the income earned by these distributors because of their own efforts.

Advantages of direct selling approach:

Following are the advantages of the direct selling approach:

(i) reduction in marketing cost
(ii) reduced cost for seller
(iii) lower prices for buyer
(iv) source of earning
(v) convenience for customers
(vi) free from business formalities

3. VENDING MACHINES

Vending machines are automatic machines that serve the purpose of selling general merchandise like soft drinks, burgers, snacks etc. to customers in the absence of any retailer. The concept of vending machine is very popular in European countries like USA. In India, it is of recent origin and is found in areas of high traffic to sell newspapers, magazines, beverages etc. The objective behind use of vending machines is that it reduces cost on human resources. It is believed that the very first vending machine was designed and implemented by Hero of Alexandria, which used to accept a coin and then dispense a fixed quantity of 'holy water'.

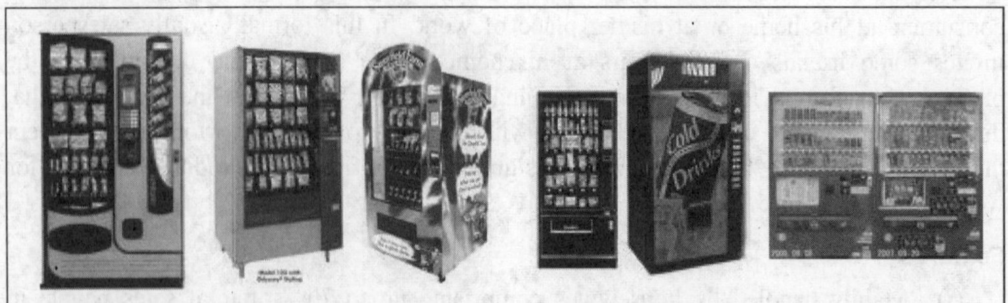

A View of vending machines used throughout the globe

Vending machines work either on the basis of inserting metal coins or card swipes. Some vending machines have inbuilt refrigeration units or heating outlet to keep the eatables ready to use. Vending machine operations are usually hasselfree but need regular maintenance and service to keep machine working and full of stock.

Vending Machine

Vending machines are often located at railway stations, bus terminals or at busy community centres to serve eatables or newspapers to common people with or without shelter. After inserting valid metal coin/s, one can get desired product in appropriate quantity.

Benefits of vending machines

- Time saving shopping
- Absence of physical presence
- Space saving shop
- Quick delivery
- Non-store format

Items sold are newspapers, magazines, snacks, beverage (alcoholic and non-alcohlic), cigarette etc.

Following items are sold through Vending Machines Globally

USA 

Adhesive Tape
Batteries
Calculators
Cans of Beer
CDs
Cells
Cheese Items
Cigarettes
Coffee
Erasers
Frogs
Hot Snacks
Live Shrimp
Maps
Milk
Nose Clips
Note Books
Paintings
Perfumes and Deodorants
Poetry
Raw Eggs
Shaving Creams
Shower Caps
Soft Drinks
Temporary Tattoos
T-shirts
Wallet
Watches
Writing Instruments

CANADA 

French Fries
Frogs
Leeches
Live Shrimp
Snacks/Burgers

NETHERLANDS 

Cigarettes
French Fries
Hamburger
Note Books
Pen
Snacks

AUSTRALIA

Beer
Emu Jerky
Gemstones

ENGLAND

Coffee
Comic Books
French Fries
Magazines
News Papers
Snacks

JAPAN

Adult magazines
Batteries
Beer
Beetles
Comic Books
Flower Arrangements
Fried food
Hamburgers
Hot Noodles
Liquor
Oxygen
Pajamas
Popcorn
Snacks
Umbrella
Underwear

INDIA

Comic Books
Espresso
Hot Noodles
Magazines
Newspapers
Novels
Weight Measure
Pens

(B) NON-TRADITIONAL RETAILING

1. Electronic Shopping (WWW)

Electronic Retailing which is also known as internet retailing, e-tailing, cyber-retailing, virtual retailing or e-retailing is the sale of goods /services through and electronic media. This electronic media, we all know is Internet (**World Wide Web**). But these days due to revolution in electronic communications, besides internet, several other medias like digital television, web-enabled mobile telephones (WAP), tele-conferencing devices etc are also operational. The main advantage of electronic/internet retailing is that it does not require any direct human interactions. Besides this, internet retailing offers same quality, convenience of access, reliability and lower cost. In short, this form of retailing allows the customers to evaluate and purchase goods and services without going to any physical retail store.

Internet Retailing

Internet retailing today is considered as the fastest growing format of the retail industry. It helps the shoppers to acquire information about quality, quantity, colour, price and sizes without traveling and incurring any cost. Two systems are used under internet retailing:

(1) Passive retail system: This system is non-interactive and involves all forms of one-way communication such as clubs on television, shopping pages or one-way cable system. This system of retailing includes video catalogues or electronic media, which display the products in use or provide other relevant information.

(2) Interactive System: This system is interactive and allows the user a two-way interaction and includes World Wide Web (www) or kiosks for items such as airline or railway ticketing and promotional touch screen booths. Some interactive systems display the goods and services meant for sale and in the case of touch screens, give printouts or allow further enquiries from the database.

Note: *The common feature of both systems is that a credit or a debit card can be used to secure the sale.*

2. Video Kiosks

The video kiosk is a self-supporting, interactive, electronic computer terminal that displays goods and services on a video screen and permits the viewer to make selections. It uses touch screen for consumers. By simply touching the screen, it shows videos clips, presentations, and product details immediately on screen or on an attached projector or plasma screen. In malls, video kiosk forms the centre piece attraction. Some retailers use video kiosks to enhance the customer service level while other use kiosks to take order from customers, complete transactions, and arrange for goods to be delivered at their doorstep. Video kiosks are used at large levels where there is shortage of space and retailer is not able to display entire product range. Kiosks can be attached with retailers' computer networks or against existing databases or websites.

These kiosks can run any type of software and application on the Internet or a desktop computer. Because every business now relies so heavily on computers, all-in-one systems, which enable businesses to communicate with customers, partners and employees, have an application in every industry. Kiosks can be used in any setting, and are especially well suited for installation in public areas such as lobbies, retail stores, warehouses, entertainment venues, trade shows, museums and colleges[5].

Many companies already have the content they need for a kiosk right on their website. Thus, all-in-one systems Kiosks can easily be connected to the Internet to provide controlled access to a website, or the content of a website may be saved on the kiosk's hard drive, which provides similar functionality. Advanced kiosks can even display full-motion video and other bandwidth intensive applications.

Technology integration further allows kiosks to perform a broad range of functions, developing into self service terminals. For instance, kiosks may enable users to enter a public utility (electricity/ water) bill account number in order to pay the payment online (electronically) or collect cash in exchange for merchandise. Customized components such as coin hoppers, bill acceptors, card readers and thermal printers enable kiosks to meet the owner's specialized needs[6].

[5] www.marketingunlimited.com

[6] http:\\en.wikipedia.org

Video Kiosks

A video kiosk commonly known as all-in-one system, is a self-contained unit that combines software and hardware including a touch screen monitor and computer. Accessories such as credit card reader, printer, and Internet connection are used to promote the available goods and services on self service basis.

Some **video kiosks** provide a free of charge, informational public service, while others serve business purpose. Computer keyboards, touch screens, trackballs, and push buttons are all usual input devices for video kiosk.

Sometimes **kiosks** resemble with telephone booths, but also are used while sitting on a chair or bench. Video kiosks are usually placed in high traffic areas such as airports, hotel lobbies, conference centers, insurance offices or near central parks.

Today's kiosks are small in size, sleeker, light weight and technically advanced than past.

Benefits of having video kiosks in a retail firm

- Anytime anywhere information providers
- Cost saving device
- Customer savvy
- Self service device/terminal
- convenient access to products and services

Types of kiosks

In India kiosks are still in nascent stage. But in developed countries like USA, kiosks are being used for several decades. It is estimated that only in USA more than 13 million kiosk terminals are in existence[7]. The major retailers using such kiosks are Wal-Mart, Northwest Airlines, Future Shop, Jet Blue Airways, GTAA, and The Home Depot. Globally these types of kiosks are used to serve varied purposes.

(i) Building Directory & Way finding Kiosk
(ii) Digital Menu Board
(iii) Digital Order Stations
(iv) Financial Services Kiosk
(v) Instant Print Stations
(vi) Internet Kiosk
(vii) Intranet Kiosk
(viii) Kiosk Manufacturing Industry
(ix) Kiosk Reliability
(x) Movie Ticket Kiosk
(xi) Photo Kiosk

A view of Internet Kiosk

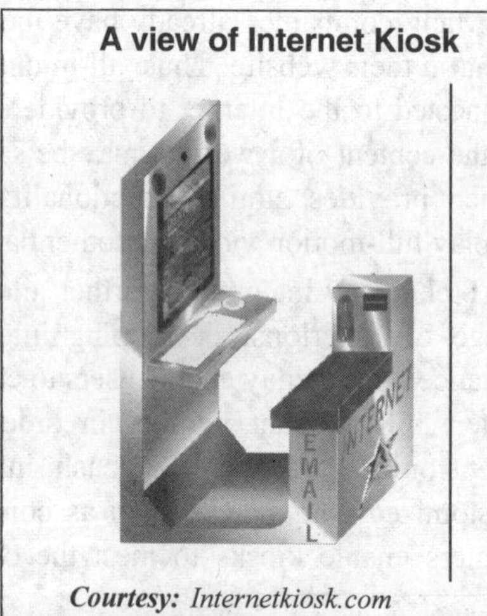

Courtesy: *Internetkiosk.com*

[7] *http://en.wikipedia.org/wiki/Internet_kiosk*

(xii) POS-related "kiosks"

(xiii) Tele kiosk

(xiv) Ticketing Kiosk

(xv) Vending Kiosk

(xvi) Visitor Management and Security Kiosk

3. Airport Retailing

Thanks to consistent double-digit growth in the airport travelers and introduction of low cost carriers, airports today have been renovated from being dull and boring places to cheerful, vigorous and lively destinations. Thanks also go to emergence of airport retailing in India. The 21st century traveler is being attracted in every possible manner. Malls, service stations, parasite stores, duty free shops, consumer durables stores, are all set to change the traditional view of airports.

Being recently explored, Airport retailing offers one of the most promising sectors for retail development. It offers branded luggage, clothing and items of decoration. Food, toys, consumer cells, electronics, souvenirs and wristwatches are other specialized segments. Shoppers' Stop, Future Group and Tata's consumer durable chain, Croma are the few major players in airport retailing.

Figure 2.7

Merchandise Category under Airport Retailing

Entertainment, 1.62%
Car rental, 0.85%
Personal services, 1.91%
Electricals, 2.49%
Food, 1.05%
Personal goods, 17.57%
Duty free, 17.67%
Accessories, 2.42%
CNT, 8.74%
Clothing & Footwear, 12.31%
Catering, 31.89%

Source: *Airport Retailing in UK by Bob Thompson. (www.palgrave-journals.com)*

OTHER EMERGING RETAIL FORMATS

1. Van/Mobile Van Retailing: This is a compromise between door to door selling and store selling. In this type of retail business, retailer keeps one day stock of his merchandise and goes to an area to serve its permanent customers. Sometimes retailers visit some areas which are totally new to them to attract new customers. The kind of products sold in Van retailing can range from everyday household products to different kinds of eatables. The various van goods include soaps, detergents, kitchen appliances, scrubbers, and several other cleaning products. There are some vans which designed to operate at extremely low temperatures. In these types of van customers will find all kinds of in frozen food such as vegetables, meat, dairy products, and ice. In the rural areas this kind of selling of goods still exists though it is not quite popular in metropolitan cities. In some states van retailing may be subject to regulations and entail licensing. State regulations determine the area that van sales can cover and the products that are allowed to be sold[8].

Van retailing is usually found in remote/rural areas and is of two types:

(a) Static retailing: Under this sort of retailing, such vans are parked in public areas where customer traffic is usually high. The items sold under static retailing are snacks and junk food.

(b) Raving retailing is where retailer takes his van to one house to another, selling merchandise to customers at their doorstep.

2. Conference/Party/Event Retailing: In this sort of retailing, retailer invite people from nearby localities and after describing positive aspects of the merchandise, sells it. These types of get together/events are organized by the franchisor (retailer) belonging to a big organization. The products sold under such form of retailing vary from cosmetics from small household items that are of low cost. In order to attract customers, retailer usually distributes sample merchandise or gives some demonstration regarding effective use of his items offered on sale. Event retailing usually takes place on national or regional level events such as Valentine Day, Mother's Day, Father's Day, Diwali, etc. Gold retailing on the day of 'Akshaya Tritiya[9]' in most of the parts of the country is one of such example of event retailing.

Some events are food related like Annual Mango festival at Pragati Maidan, Delhi organized by Delhi Tourism in collaboration with Delhi Government. Further food festivals, special food offers being offered on the occasion of 'Karva Chauth[10] and Navratra[11] in India are none other than event retailing.

---

8 *www.retailsiteshub.com*

9 *Akshaya Tritiya is one of the four most auspicious days of the year for Hindus in India. The day is particularly considered auspicious for buying long term assets like gold and silver, including ornaments made of the same; diamond and other precious stones; and the real estate. With the mass media and marketing, this day has been taken over by marketers to promote sales and bookings for Gold jewellery, houses, and consumer electronics.*

10 *Karwa Chauth is a traditional Hindu festival for married women, and is celebrated in some parts of India. On this occasion, married women fast one whole day without food or water for the long life of their husbands. The ritual signifies extreme love and devotion to the husband, as evidenced by the wife's willingness to suffer for his well being. Usually, falling in the month of October, Karvachauth is celebrated midst harvesting of summer crops.*

11 *Navratra literally means '9 nights'. During these days and nights, prayers are offered to 'Mother Goddess' Hindus believe that the Mother stands for everything that is everywhere in the Universe. These days comes twice in a year and celebrated in different parts of India in different ways.*

3. Distant Retailing: As the very name suggests, under distant retailing, a customer place the order from a remote location by telephone, SMS, internet, pager etc, instead of visiting a store. Retailers who provide such home delivery facility may/may not have physical stores. The leading global retailers who follow such practice are Amazon, Wal-Mart, Arkay Hygiene. The main advantage of such sort of retiling is that any type of item can be supplied by the retailer on demand. The range of items offered depends on the customers' demand, and retailers' resources and the infrastructure of the concerned region.

4. Forecourt Retailing: A new emerging concept in retailing is the establishments of stores in front of large buildings of high traffic areas. This concept caught public attention with oil companies trying to allow private companies to set up convenience stores at their fuel station outlets. The aggressive players in this area are HPCL, IOC, BPCL and Reliance. According to a Business Standard report[12], Vishal Mega Mart has tied up with Hindustan Petroleum Corporation Ltd (HPCL) for opening forecourt retail stores chain, which has been branded as "Vishal Corner Mart" will set up convenience stores at fuel station outlets of HPCL. These marts besides offering convenience goods and services would also provide travel solutions and other facilities as a 'one stop solution'.

Previously, Apollo Pharmacy had tied up and set up 'convenio' stores at Indian Oil Corporation (IOC) petrol pump outlets for supplying groceries and medicines. This experiment was well appreciated by business critics but it did not succeed, perhaps, on account of problems in revenue sharing model. Similarly Kishore Biyani-led Future group had also tied up with IOC to set up fuel pumps in Big Bazaar premises and Big Bazaar stores in IOC premises. However, nothing seems to have emerged so far.

5. Trade Parks: Retailing through trade parks is a recent retail practice and is practiced only in metros and big cities. Under this concept, business complexes are being set up for promotion of retail trade especially the international trade. Some of the examples are India Exposition Mart set up by Handicraft Export Promotion Council in Greater Noida, International Home Deco Park (IHDP) set up by a group of private investors in Noida and World Trade Park coming up in Jaipur. IHDP plans to provide International buyers ready access to approximately sixty world class Indian exporters belonging to Home Furnishings segment. This effort of IHDP would be beneficial to buyers as they would not have to go to remote towns to see the designs and samples of exporters. Exporters apart from getting increased visibility will also get other facilities such as design library, design studio, forwarding services and so on. The parks are built to promote trade and are open to international buyers and buying houses only[13].

---

12 *www.coolavenues.com*

13 *www.coolavenues.com*

Figure 2.8

A View of India Exposition Mart Limited

About Indio Expo Mart

The India Expo Mart is a state of the art exposition center, encompassing over 2.5 million square feet of built up area. It is currently the largest and only one of its kind in India. Located in Greater Noida and easily accessible from the capital, New Delhi, the India Expo Mart aims to be the one-stop shop for Indian cottage industry products. The fairs & exhibitions organised by India Expo Mart is extremely encouraging for various buyers and sellers across the globe. The main objective of the India Expo Centre & Mart is to provide the cottage industry, within India, an infrastructural requirement of international standards for exhibitions, conventions and seminars.

Courtesy: *Company Website and wwwfairwoodindia.com*

SUMMARY

Indian retail industry is under its transformation stage as far as growth and investment trends are concerned. Some of the formats require consumers to visit the physical outlets while others sell their merchandise to customers without any physical visit. At present, out of all store based retail sales mix institutions, hypermarkets and supermarkets are doing well. Apart from these, discount stores and food based super stores are growing fast on the Indian retail landscape. Further, due to cost saving and time saving, non-store based retail formats are also growing very fast. Online retailing is one such recent development where retailers communicate with the customers and offer goods and services for sale through internet. Therefore, it presents business opportunity if availed but a threat if missed.

REVIEW QUESTIONS

True and False Questions

1. Over ninety percent retail outlets in India are independent and hence organized.
2. The independent retailer has no restrictions on who, how or where the business to be set up. He is free to do what he wants and to select a convenient location.
3. The independent store by providing limited but deep merchandise can act as a specialized store to serve a particular consumer segment.

4. A chain retailer or a chain store is a group of two or more outlets carrying the same sort of merchandise assortment, owned and controlled jointly and usually supplied from one or more central warehouses.
5. A Franchise is a contractual agreement between the franchiser and the franchisee that allows the franchisee the right to supply its brand (goods and services) exclusively within a defined area, as per a particular format for a specified period of time.
6. In an area development franchisee system, the franchiser grants development rights of a particular area to the franchisee in turn for a front-end development fee.
7. Under some industries, franchisee agreements are of short duration which requires yearly/continuous renewal upon expiry. If renewal is not made, the whole investment made by the franchisee will go waste.
8. Under leasing agreement, the person who provides the store space to outside party is known as lessor, and the person who takes the shop/store space is known as lessee.
9. A Vertical Marketing System (VMS) is a system in which almost all the members of distribution channel such as manufacturers, wholesalers and retailers work together to satisfy human needs and wants by facilitating the smooth flow of goods and services from manufacturer to ultimate consumer.
10. The reason to setup consumer cooperative is that local retailers are not able to satisfy consumers' needs (whatever the reason may be).
11. Breadth of Assortment refers to the number of distinct goods/services categories that a retailer has purchased and displayed for retail selling in his outlet.
12. Supermarkets usually rely on low inventory turnover and built outside the city or town to provide good parking facilities.
13. In a combination store, luxury merchandise sales usually accounts for 30-40% of total store sales.
14. Discounters typically operate with very low pricing policy by strictly controlling operating costs such as expenses incurred on store layout, cost of land, e-retailing and by offering limited/very few services to their shoppers.
15. A Category Killer or a Power Retailer is basically a small category specialist. Most category killer use on-line selling practice and kills the category of merchandise (*for say Interiors*) for other big retailers of the same line by offering complete assortment in the concerned category.

Answers:

1. False	2. True	3. True	4. True
5. True	6. True	7. True	8. True
9. True	10. True	11. False	12. False
13. False	14. True	15. False	

Multiple Choice Questions

1. According to industry estimates, approximately .... of one million new business created every year, belong to retail industry ?
   (*a*) one fifth (*b*) one tenth
   (*c*) one third (*d*) one fourth
2. Over ninety percent retail firms in India are :
   (*a*) Independent (*b*) Dependent
   (*c*) Huge sized (*d*) Independent and Unorganised
3. India is denominated by :
   (*a*) Independent retailers (*b*) Organised retailers
   (*c*) Grocery retailers (*d*) Chain-store retailers
4. The main feature of independent retailing is :
   (*a*) Big in size (*b*) Ease of entry
   (*c*) Organised (*d*) Most of them are North Indian
5. Independent retailer serves the demand of :
   (*a*) Local area (*b*) Regional area
   (*c*) National area (*d*) International area
6. A distinguish characteristics of chain store system is :
   (*a*) Centrally managed (*b*) Large in numbers
   (*c*) Ease of entry (*d*) Offers deep merchandise
7. A franchise is a contractual agreement between :
   (*a*) French company and Indian company
   (*b*) French company and Multinational company
   (*c*) Franchisee and franchiser
   (*d*) Franchisee and Licensor
8. McDonald's, NIIT, and Koutons are the examples of :
   (*a*) Super markets (*b*) Hyper markets
   (*c*) Chain stores (*d*) Franchising
9. Leased Department store is also known as :
   (*a*) Shop-in-shops (*b*) Franchisee
   (*c*) Organised retail (*d*) Vertical marketing system
10. In a vertical marketing system, almost all the members of distribution channel :
    (*a*) Work together
    (*b*) Work separately
    (*c*) Compete with each other
    (*d*) Are located at one central location
11. Consumer Co-operatives are owned and managed by
    (*a*) Government co-operative societies
    (*b*) Its customers members
    (*c*) Public welfare associations
    (*d*) Trade unions

12. An assortment is the selection of merchandise a retailer carries to :
(*a*) sell in his retail outlet (*b*) purchase from wholesalers
(*c*) keep it in ware houses (*d*) sell when demand is more

13. The main benefit of a supermarket is :
(*a*) Low priced goods (EDLP) (*b*) Convenient shopping hours
(*c*) Enough space for parking (*d*) Self service

14. KFC, Subway and Taco Bell are examples of :
(*a*) Grocery stores (*b*) Optical stores
(*c*) Food stores (*d*) Jewelery stores

15. Speciality stores offer :
(*a*) Discounted merchandise.
(*b*) Unique fashionable goods.
(*c*) Narrow product line with a deep assortment.
(*d*) Apparel merchandise.

16. Wal-Mart, The Kroger company and Home Depot belong to which country :
(*a*) China (*b*) Japan
(*c*) U.K. (*d*) U.S.A.

17. Ware-house club stores usually sell merchandise in :
(*a*) Large quantity but at low prices.
(*b*) Small quantity but at high prices.
(*c*) Fixed quantities at low prices.
(*d*) Proportional quotos

18. The only negative aspect associated with Hypermarket store is :
(*a*) Limited merchandise (*b*) Does not provide self selection facility
(*c*) Limited parking facility (*d*) Far away from the city

19. A parasite store is/has :
(*a*) a huge size outlet.
(*b*) small outlet with its own floor area.
(*c*) its own floor area but not its own customer traffic.
(*d*) neither its own floor area nor its own customer traffic.

20. VPP stands for :
(*a*) Very promising product (*b*) Valuable packed product
(*c*) Valuable priced product (*d*) Value paid on postage

21. Electronic shopping/Electronic retailing are also referred as
(*a*) e-tailing (*b*) Television shopping
(*c*) Catalogue retailing (*d*) Direct selling

22. Asian sky shop is an example of :
(*a*) Electronic shopping (*b*) Catalogue retailing
(*c*) Television shopping (*d*) Vending Machine

23. Under direct selling method, buying and selling
(*a*) takes place at intervals.
(*b*) is done on the spot.
(*c*) takes place through electronic media.
(*d*) takes place through courier/VPP.

24. The main advantage of internet retailing is :
    (*a*) does not require any direct human interactions.
    (*b*) fastest growing format of the retail industry.
    (*c*) Convenient access to product and services.
    (*d*) Self service device/terminal.
25. The 'Akshaya Tritiya' a holy Hindu day, is considered auspicious for buying long term assets such as :
    (*a*) real asset (land, flat, building, property etc.)
    (*b*) Consumer durables.
    (*c*) Gold, Silver, diamond and other precious stones.
    (*d*) Kitchen utensils.

Answers

1. b	2. d	3. a	4. b
5. a	6. a	7. c	8. d
9. a	10. a	11. b	12. a
13. a	14. c	15. c	16. d
17. c	18. d	19. d	20. d
21. a	22. c	23. b	24. a
25. c			

Check your progress

1. What is assortment?
2. What is EDLP?
3. Name few supermarkets?
4. What is 'Catalogue'?
5. What is VPP?
6. What is 'www'?
7. What is Van?
8. Explain SMS?
9. Who is a parasite?
10. What NCR means?
11. What is WAP?
12. What do you mean by format?
13. What is chain?
14. What is VMS?
15. What is service level?

Short Answer Questions

1. Explain the positive and negative aspects of convenience stores?
2. Differentiate between limited line and full line discount stores?
3. Describe the concept of specialty store? Which pricing policy is being followed by them?
4. From a manufacturer's perspective, explain few reasons to have a factory outlet?
5. Do you think traditional departmental stores are loosing their charm?

6. Why membership retailing in India is not so popular?
7. Contrast the strategic mixes of specialty stores, departmental stores and full line discount stores?
8. Explain the pros and cons of electronic shopping?
9. What are the characteristics of direct selling format? Why direct selling retailing is becoming popular in India?
10. Describe the applicability of vending machines in developing countries like India?
11. What are the essentials to become a parasite store?
12. How to become a destination store?
13. Differentiate between direct selling and direct marketing?
14. Explain e-tailing retail format?
15. Why direct selling retailing is becoming popular in India?
16. Describe the applicability of vending machines in developing countries like India?
17. Explain e-tailing retail format?
18. What items are sold under food based retailing format?
19. Briefly explain the significance of signage?
20. Why it is said that franchising is the future of tomorrow's retailing?

Long Answer Questions

1. Do you think that hypermarkets and supermarkets are the future of Indian retailing? Is there enough room for each? Comment with examples?
2. What competitive merits and demerits do hypermarkets have in comparison with supermarkets?
3. What do you understand by non-store based retail mix? Is it present a threat to traditional 'kirana stores' or the other physical retail formats? Describe some emerging retail formats with their types and examples?
4. From a customer's perspective, what are the merits and demerits of the 'www' retailing format? Also explain the future of internet retailing in India?
5. By presenting a retail summary chart, explain various retail formats with regard to variety, assortment, pricing policy, service level, size, SKUs, location and so on?
6. Despite public and private sector initiative, still vending machine concept is not getting popularity as was expected from it, explain why? What suggestions you would like to give to customers and retailers that may enhance the applicability of vending machines in India?
7. Which retailing format you think is best suitable for following parties:
   I. New comers with limited financial resources
   II. Person having limited/no knowledge of retailing business but with adequate funds
   III. Foreign Players entering into India
8. Critically analyze the working of online retailing and TV retailing with its merits and demerits? Out of these two retailing formats which one would you like to recommend to general public?

APPENDIX

Exhibit 2.1: Rich People Love Low Prices, the Poor Need Them

Hypermarkets have caught on the imagination of poor and rich alike. Shoppers are thronging to 25 or so of the country's Hypermarkets. And, there is a scope for 1,000 such markets in 67 retail destinations by 2010.

What makes Hyper markets click?

The convenience of one stop shopping, lower prices, or wider choice of products? May be all, but price appears to be the major driver of increasing footfalls. People may love to shop, but their eyes never stray too far from the price tag. "Rich people love low prices, the poor need them," Unless your prices are the best, especially in the food and groceries (F&G) segment, there's little point. So, how are hypermarket retailers coping with the pressure to offer lower prices and still make money? Here, are a few of the strategies followed by some of them:

Right Product Mix: To overcome lower gross margins of 10 to 12% on Food & Grocery (F&G), retailers are trying to optimize the product mix of F&G and General merchandise. A product mix comprising 40% food and 60% of non-food could enhance gross margins to a respectable 18-19%. While hyper city, is able to achieve a mix of 60 non-food to 40 food, Big Bazaar is able to do even better with 63% of non-food.

More Non-food Display: Higher non-food sales are achieved by allocating higher shelf and display space. Food display space is restricted to around 20%. This works, because shoppers, in any case, are there to shop for food items.

Store Labels: Hypermarkets are also working hard to discourage sales of branded products. They are promoting their own labels, though, it is not easy to promote them beyond a point due to strong customer brand loyalties for a class of goods, such as, FMCG. While Hypercity has achieved store labels sale of around 30%, Trent promoted Star Bazar has been able to touch only 10%.

Increased Volumes: "Suppliers themselves are willing to give away more if the volumes are high enough,"

Bypassing Middlemen: Retailers are also striving hard to keep costs in check by improving sourcing efficiencies. By pruning on the middleman and reaching farm gates, retailers are able to improve margins. Vishal Mega Mart, one of the leading Indian retail stores also stresses on non-involvement of intermediaries as reflected in their business philosophy i.e. "Manufacturing to Retailing".

Source:

1. *Why hypermarts are a hit in India by Shobhana Subramanian, appeared on September 15, 2006 (http://www.rediff.com/money/2006/sep/15spec.htm)*
2. *http://indiaretailbiz.wordpress.com/about, appeared on October 22, 2006*

Exhibit 2.2: Different Formats at Pantaloon Retail India

Product Category	Concept	Status	Formats/Offerings
Food	Brew Bar	Operational	Beers, snacks and set meals
	Cafe Bolloywood	Planned	Eateries
	Chamosa	Operational	Snacks counter in high traffic area
	Food Bazaar	Operational	Supermarket
	Rain	Operational	Food and beverages
	Sports Bar	Operational	Focused on sports lovers
Fashion	aLL	Operational	Fashion apparel for plus-size individuals
	Big Bazaar	Operational	Hypermarket
	Blue Sky	Operational	Fashion accessories
	Central	Operational	Seamless malls
	Fashion Station	Operational	Popular fashion
	Gini & Jony	Operational	Kids' fashion
	Pantaloons	Operational	Department store
Home & Electronics	Collection i Electronics	Operational	Home furnishings
	Bazaar e-zone	Operational Operational	Present within Big Bazaar Consumer electronics
	Furniture Bazaar	Operational	Home furniture
	Got It	Planned	One stop shop for home maintenance
	Home Town	Planned	One stop Destination
Telecom & IT	Gen M	Planned	Hi-tech products Solutions for knowledge,
	M Bazaar	Planned	entertainment and communication
	M Port	Planned	Standalone stores/shop-in-shop
General	Big Bazzar	Operational	Hypermarket
Merchandise	Blue sky	Operational	Fashion Accessories
	Central	Operational	Seamless malls
	Foodwear	Planned	Footwear and accessories
	Bazaar		
	Navarasa	Planned	N.A.
	Pantaloons	Operational	Department store
	Shoe Factory	Operational	Footwear and accessories
Leisure &	Bowling Co.	Operational	Premium family
Operational			entertainment center
	F 123	Operational	For lesiure and entertainment
Wellness &	Health Village	Planned	N.A
Beauty	Star Sitara	Operational women	Beauty salon for men and
	Tulsi	Operational	Pharmacy
	Tumeric	Planned	'Cut-in' formate at Food Bazaar
Books & Music	Depot	Operational	Books and music
e-tailing	online retailing	Operational	futurebazaar.com

Source : *An Insight into the Growth of New Retail Formats in India by Sinha and Kar, Working paper No. 2007-04, Page No. 24 (www.iimahd.ernet.in)*

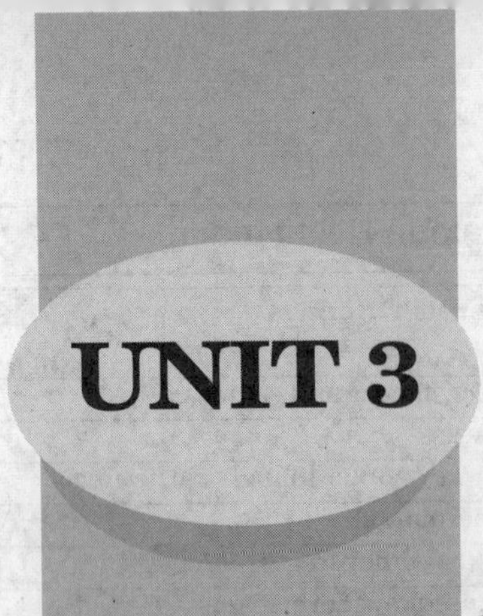

CONSUMER BEHAVIOUR

LEARNING OBJECTIVES

- Understanding the concept of consumer behaviour,
- Examining consumer-buying behaviour,
- Analyzing the factors those have impact on consumer behaviour,
- Knowing different human needs, and
- How a consumer may engage in post purchase behaviour.

"A customer is the most important visitor on our premises; he is not dependent on us. We are dependent on him. He is not an interruption in our work. He is the purpose of it. He is not an outsider in our business. He is part of it. We are not doing him a favor by serving him. He is doing us a favor by giving us an opportunity to do so."

Mahatma Gandhi, Father of Nation

"It's really tough to know a customer just by taking a surface look or a surface descriptor such as male/female or age or ethnic group. To understand your customers' needs today, you really have to understand their lifestyles, opinions and attitudes."

David M. Szymanski
Director, Center for Retailing Studies
(CRS), Texas A&M University.

INTRODUCTION

The reason for setting up a store is the presence of consumers who have some unfulfilled desires. The retailer in order to earn his livelihood, set up the business, sells merchandise, satisfy consumer needs and earn profits. We all are consumers. If we have to survive in this beautiful world, we need to eat something, drink something and wear something. Then several things of daily use like shoes, shelter, vehicles, consumer durables and so on, we require to run our life smoothly. As these things are offered by several retailers, it becomes imperative for one to understand the behaviour of consumers who come to your store. What their needs are? What are their preferences? Why they visit particular store? Why they behave differently in the same level of customer service. Further, studying consumer behaviour is also important for the survival and growth of a retail organization. A retailer who raises such questions and attempt to find answers to them on regular basis, find it easy to face complexities of the changing environment.

Consumer buying decisions consists of the human behaviors that go in making purchase decisions. Successful retailers understand how customers make store choices and purchase decisions. They continuously seek information about the customers changing demands: what goods and services might be useful and how they can be purchased. In addition to identifying the customers' needs and wants, the retailer should know how people take buying decisions. For example, by understanding that a number of different messages compete for our potential customers' attention, we learn that to be effective, advertisements must usually be repeated extensively. We also learn that consumers will sometimes be persuaded more by logical arguments, but at other times will be persuaded more by emotional or symbolic appeals. By understanding the consumer, retailer will be able to make a more informed decision as to which strategy to employ[1]. But this necessitates some familiarity with customer behaviour, which involves the following underlying issues:

(i) Whether to buy or not?
(ii) If yes, what to buy?
(iii) When to buy?
(iv) Where to buy?
(v) How to buy?
(vi) From whom to buy?
(vii) How frequently to buy?
(viii) The changing factors in the society and
(ix) Factors affecting consumer purchases

WHO IS CONSUMER?

A consumer is anyone who engages himself/herself in physical activities of assessing, attaining, using or disposing of goods and services for which he/she pays the money for its usage. If a person buys the product but is consumed by his/her family member then in that case that family member will be the actual 'consumer' and the person who has paid the money will be termed as 'customer'.

From a retailer point of view:

Customer is someone to whom you are selling a product or service.

Consumer is someone who actually buys and consumes the goods and services you provide, although not necessarily a customer (the person who actually does purchasing). Consumers usually refer to general public.

---

[1] *http://www.consumerpsychologist.com*

We take an example to understand the difference between the terms 'customer' and 'consumer'.

A mother buys a Barbie doll for his five year old daughter. Here as the mother has paid the money for the Barbie doll, she will be known as 'customer' but actually the doll is used by her daughter, her daughter will be the 'consumer'.

Another case may be where a mother is buying a DVD player for her family. The mother being the actual buyer is the 'customer' and all her family members (including her) are consumers. That's why it is said that customer can be a consumer but vice versa is not always true.

CONSUMER BEHAVIOR DEFINED

Understanding consumer behavior is the major aspect of retail business. A consumer may describe his requirements and yet may act otherwise. He comes to store to buy a particular thing but ultimately change his mind and buys something else. He may change his mind at any stage of buying process. Therefore, it becomes essential for a retailer to understand customer's buying behavior. Different authors and practitioners have defined consumer-buying behavior variedly.

According to Webster, "Consumer behavior is all psychological, social and physical behavior of potential customers as they become aware of, evaluate, purchase, consume, and tell other people about products and services."

According to Schiffman and Kanuck, the term 'consumer behavior' refers to "the behavior that consumers display in searching for, purchasing, using, evaluating, and disposing of products and services that they expect will satisfy their needs" and the study of consumer behavior is the study of how individuals make decisions to spend their available resources – like time, money, effort – on consumption related items."

The Dictionary of Marketing and Advertising defines consumer behavior as "observable activities chosen to maximize satisfaction through the attainment of economic goods and services as choice of retail outlet, preference for particular brands and so on"

In the words of Professors C.G.Walter and G.W.Paul, it is "the process where individuals decide Whether, What, When, Where, How and from whom to purchase goods and services." The definition can be analyzed in the following ways:

- Consumer behavior is a decision process adopted by the consumer.
- What types of products and services to be bought.
- When the products and services are to be obtained.
- From where the products and services are to be obtained.
- From whom the products and services are to be obtained.

According to Ostrow and Smith's Dictionary of Marketing, the term consumer behavior refers to "the actions of consumers in the market place and the underlying motives for those actions. Marketers expect that they by understanding what causes consumer to buy particular goods and services will make them enable to determine which products are needed in the market place, which are obsolete and how best to present the goods to the consumer."

According to Louden and Della Bitta, Consumer behavior is "the decision process and physical activity individuals engage in when evaluating, acquiring, using, or disposing of goods and services."

CONSUMER BUYING PROCESS

The consumer-buying process begins when a consumer decides to buy a product or service to satisfy his/her unmet demand. The primary objective of studying consumer-buying process is to understand what make consumers to buy or not buy a particular product. In the world of retailing, usually each product has some of its alternate, same product is provided by various brands in various sizes and colors. Two products are identical as far as features and performance is concerned, still consumer response towards one particular product is not good. Sometimes, while store shopping, they are not aware of their deeper motivations and may change their buying decision at any stage.

In a small store where personal attention is possible, retailers provide proper knowledge about the product consumers require. Customers after evaluating the retailer's merchandise offering, prices etc. take decision to buy or not to buy. Eventually customers make a buying decision, use the product and then critically analyze whether it satisfies their needs or not. In some circumstances, customers while visiting to stores like Shoppers' Stop or Big Bazaar, spend enough time and effort to evaluate and finalize the merchandise. In other circumstances, consumers make their buying decisions with little evaluation. Therefore, consumer-buying process plays an important role in evaluating consumer's behavior. It represents a problem solving approach. The retail mechanism is same as is applicable in other processing activities where after supplying some input, followed by processing activity, output is achieved.

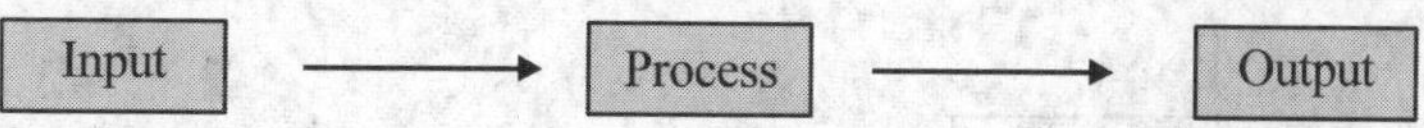

Input: It is a stimulus that encourages a customer to buy a particular product. Two sets of stimulus variables namely the firm's marketing efforts and the consumer's social environment is studied under input stage. Each retailer designs a unique set of marketing efforts to educate, inform and ultimately attract the customers. It includes the retail marketing mix broadly defined as any communication by a retailer that informs, persuades and/or reminds the target market about any aspect of the retail firm. The promotional policy is adopted by retail stores, which intend to sustain themselves by continuous, active and intense promotion. It has one promotional event after another. Typically its appeal is a price appeal that lags emphasis on bargains and sales events. The *social environment* on the other side is not under the direct control of a retailer and therefore, serves as a non-commercial source of consumer information and influences the consumer buying decisions. Under social environment retailing includes reference groups, friends, relatives, colleagues and family members. Undoubtedly, these stimulus variables have impact on consumer preferences and decision-making choices.

The Consumer Buying Process

The consumer-buying process begins with the need recognition where consumers recognize an unsatisfied need and ends at satisfaction (agreement) or dissatisfaction (disagreement). It is composed of several steps and is influenced by a set of factors composed of the consumer's personality, perception, attitude and retailers' promotional efforts. Retailers attempt to influence consumers as they go through the buying process to convince them to buy the retailer's merchandise. For some goods and services that are of daily use, consumer takes no time to decide the item, while in case of luxury goods or expensive items, he thinks several times. Sometimes, he visits several stores, enquires prices and features, collects market report and consults others.

Generally, it has been observed that in the world of retailing, consumer passes through five distinct stages to complete his buying process. These are as presented in figure 3.1.

Figure 3.1

Consumer Buying Process

Need recognition	Step 1: Need recognition
↓ Searching & evaluating for retailers	Step 2: Comparing retailers
↓ Finalizing a retailer	Step 3: Selecting a retailer
↓ Selecting merchandise	Step 4: Evaluation of alternatives
↓ Purchasing merchandise	Step 5: Purchase decision

Step 1: Need Recognition

The buying process begins when people realize they have some unsatisfied needs. An unsatisfied need arises when a customer's desired level of satisfaction differs from his or her current level of satisfaction. He knows from his previous life's experience how well to satisfy these unmet needs like hunger, thirst and shortage of clothing. For example – a fresh management graduate knows that he/she has a need of black color suit with attractive neck tie and shirt whenever he has to face an interview for new job, this would not only make a good impression but will enhance his/her confidence before interview board.

Need recognition in most cases is straightforward when individuals find shortage of something or goods required are of daily use. For instance, there is no wheat/milk in the kitchen. A need may be aroused by an external stimulus such as desire to visit a part of a store while purchasing other usual items.

Types of human needs: Every person has some specific needs. Some requirements are essential to survive and are born with individuals. These fundamental needs are called *psychological needs* and include needs for clothing, food, shelter and emotions. Physiological needs are primary needs or biogenic needs because they are essential to survive and sustain human life.

Psychological needs can be satisfied through shopping and buying merchandise and include learning recent trends, status, social experience, stimulation, power and self-esteem. For example, A 'Parker' pen may not serve the function of writing instrument as compared to 'Luxar/Reynolds', but having 'Parker' pen may satisfy the customer's need to be perceived as a top class executive.

Second type of need, a customer realizes is *functional need* that is directly related to the performance of the goods and services. For example, people who need to style and shine their hair may purchase hair gel. This purchase is because of the reason that the 'hair gel' will assist them in styling hairs.

Recognizing Consumers Need

Spinach, a subsidiary of the Delhi based, Wadhwan owned DHFL, which so far has a cluster of 19 retail stores across Mumbai, as a part of its strategy to garner share from traditional kirana stores, offers customized products to its customers, depending on their socio-economic profile and ethnic domination in a given store locality. Considering consumer behavior, Spinach offers *Khakras* in Gujarati dominated Borivali, while it offers specialty fish in Seven Bangalows area. Taking into account the sensitivities of its customers, it also has exclusive vegetarian outlets in Saibaba Nagar and Ghatkopar. Even the pricing could change according to requirements of a given locality. It has separate range and pricing plan for different Mumabi suburbs.

Source: *www://indiaretailbiz.wordpress.com*

Some products satisfy both functional and psychological needs. For example, the basic reason to buy a BMW car may be to enhance one's self image in the society, but on the other hand, car also satisfies the functional need for conveyance. In metro cities like Delhi and Bangalore, most of the working class has more income than they need to satisfy their functional needs for food, clothing and shelter. As in the urban part of India due to increasing salary packages and disposable income it becomes necessary for retailers that they should give emphasis on store interiors and exteriors, customer service, modern merchandise, ease of payment and provision for on-line retailing.

A distinguishing characteristic of organized retailing in India is that it is largely an urban phenomenon so far (figure 3.2). Organized retail has been more successful in cities, more so in the south and west of India. The reasons for this regional variation range from differences in consumer buying behavior to cost of real estate and taxation laws.

Figure 3.2
Urban vs. Rural Retail Share

	Rural	Urban
Food	64	36
Clothing and footwear	61	39
Misc consumer goods	57	43
Durables	50	50
Consumer services	44	56
Entertainment	33	67

0 25 50 75 100
% respondents

Source : NSSO 5th round; KPMG in India Analysis 2005

Step 2: Search and Evaluation

Under this stage of consumer-buying process, a customer seeks information about potential retailers those can satisfy his needs. Generally a customer shortlists two or three retailers and after evaluating their offerings and prices, finalizes one. This is easy when one alternate is clearly superior to the rest of the options available, Otherwise it becomes difficult for a customer to decide a retailer. The criteria for selecting a particular retailer may include:

(a) Retailer's goodwill and image,

(b) Customer service and

(c) Retailer's offerings with regard to price, payment criteria, delivery method, warranty and so on.

Step 3: Finalizing a Retailer

After evaluating the alternatives, customer ranks various retailers from most suitable to the least suitable and finalizes one from among the list. For some retailers, it is hard to rank and compare with each other because they are performing well and have no reason to reject. When this situation arises, customers compare price, brand options, market standing, proximity to home etc. Retail store staff behavior, store size and traffic flow is an indicator of retailer's quality. Customer finalizes a retailer based on these criterions.

Step 4: Selecting Merchandise

After selecting a retailer, customer visits the retailer's store and evaluates the alternatives available to satisfy his psychological or functional needs. An item with adequate quality and a low price is a must pick over costly and unknown/new brands. However, for a customer, it is not always that simple as it seems and therefore the customer is left with no alternate except to compare the alternatives. The criteria for selecting merchandise are product and service attributes that a shopper considers being valuable. These may include look, price, color, quality, stock in hand, durability, guarantee, warranty and so on. The customer sets his own parameters and ranks each alternate according to its ability to meet the parameters. One thing should be remembered that each customer has its own parameters and selection criteria. For instance, one customer may consider proximity to home as a most important factor, while other gives importance to warranty and assurance.

Step 5: Purchasing Merchandise

After selecting the best alternate, the customer is ready to pay and have the title of ownership. Customers' don't always prefer brand or the item that is continuously advertised. Sometimes retail staff changes the mind of the customer at the last moment by providing expert advice. From a retailer's point of view, this step is always a crucial aspect of the customer-buying process because the customer is mainly concerned with the following issues:

- Attitude of the floor staff,
- Purchase items {cash, short term/long term credit, cash (trade discount etc)}, and
- Convenience in check out

Out Put - *Post Purchase Behavior:* After buying goods or service, customer while using critically analyze the performance to know whether its buying decision was correct or not. If the goods or service matches his expectation after using, the consumer will be satisfied and if not, he will certainly be dissatisfied. Therefore, either customer will continue buying from the store or will look for another store. In short, if product or service-use experience indicates satisfaction and value for money, then repeat buying will occur, otherwise not.

FACTORS AFFECTING THE CONSUMER BUYING PROCESS

The consumer buying decision consists of two parts

(a) the buying process itself, and

(b) the factors affecting the consumer-buying process

Factors that affect a consumer-buying process are compressed in figure 3.3. Among these factors, consumer lifestyle and retailer's purchase terms are more important as consumer is mainly concerned with these factors.

Social factors affecting Consumer-buying decisions	Environmental factors affecting Consumer-buying decisions
• Family size • Reference groups • Culture • Consumer belief & attitude • Taste & preferences • Income level • Gender ratio • Education level • Caste, custom and tradition	• Economic condition of a country • State of inflation • Store location, size & facilities • Government policy with regard to shopping hours, consumer protection etc • Number of working members in home • Emergence of new retail formats & trends • Competition among retailers • Taxation policy

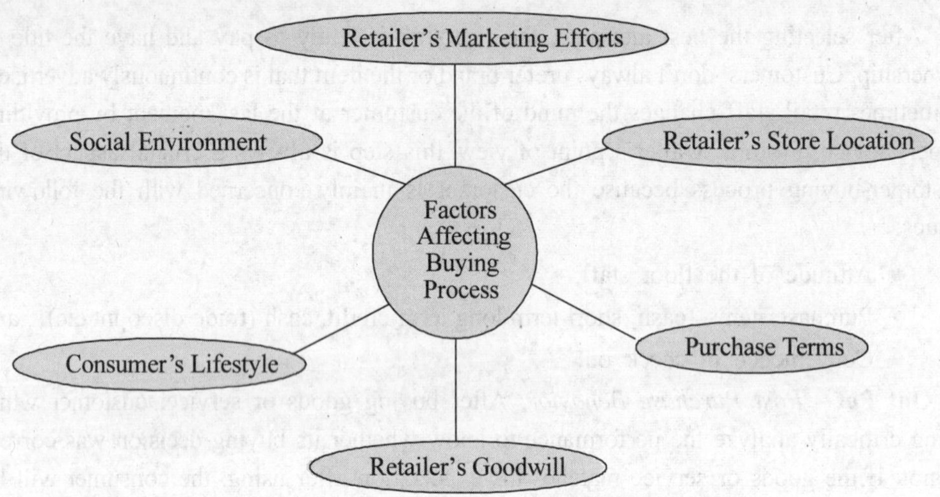

Figure 3.3: Factors Affecting Consumer Buying Process

CONSUMER LIFESTYLE

Lifestyle refers to how people in a particular area live, how they spend their day-to-day routine, how much they spend, what activities they accomplish, what type of relations they have with others and their behavior & thinking about the world in which they live. These styles are the outcomes of both social and psychological factors. Social and psychological behavior is affected by people's demographic background and living conditions in which a child grows and becomes adult. Understanding demographic and psychological behavior is must for retail success. Demographic variables help retailers to identify their target markets, while understanding of psychological behavior provides the great insight into the segment by considering their personality traits, class-consciousness, interests and opinions.

Figure 3.4
Understanding Indian Retail Demographics

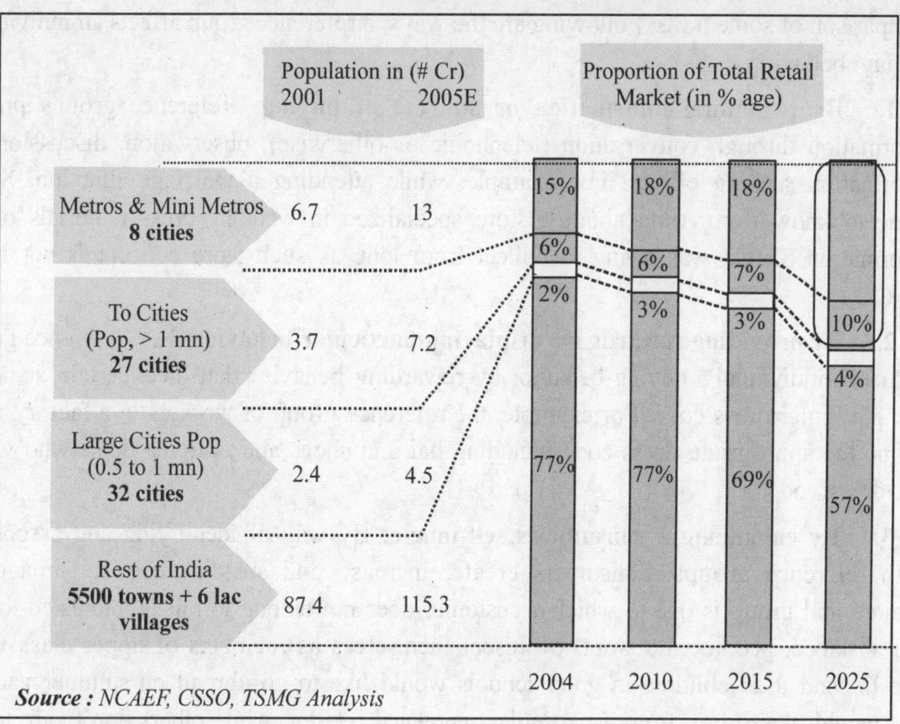

Source : NCAEF, CSSO, TSMG Analysis

What Lifestyle indicates?

1. It is a collective phenomenon and can have influence on others in a particular society.
2. Lifestyle usually reflects consistent behavior pattern of a particular society and is the sum total of one's actions and reactions.
3. It implies a common living habit. For instance, persons visiting abroad in summer vacation are usually from a particular area of the city or country.
4. Any major social change in the society may have its impact on people's lifestyles. For example, as the people become highly educated, more affluent, their lifestyles change drastically upward. They feel the need for a good house, vehicle and education of their children. Even they would prefer leisure, good medical treatment, need for spa and heart centers.

REFERENCE GROUPS

A reference group is composed of one or more people whom a person considers as a basis of comparison for opinions, traditions and feelings. These groups influence people's thinking, behavior and the way they live. It is not always true that a customer will have only one reference group. Sometimes, a customer might have a number of reference groups for comparing various items of use. A reference group may be office (place of work), apartment (place of living), film star; friend circle, celebrity, politician, bus office or family itself.

How reference groups affect buying decisions?

As stated earlier, a reference group is one, which a consumer uses as a basis of comparison of some traits. Following are the ways; a reference group affects an individual's buying behavior:

1. **By providing information or sources of buying:** Reference groups provide information through conversation (telephonic or otherwise), observation, discussion and information seeking efforts. For example, while attending a marriage function, Sheela came to know from Anita about a store specialized in wedding dress materials only – information Sheela was trying to collect from long as such store concept is not in her area.

2. **By providing rewards for displaying particular behavior:** Few reference groups influence individual's buying behavior by rewarding behavior that meet certain standards like particular dress code. For example, the reference group of workers in a factory might define the appropriate dress code including hat and shoes and criticize those who violate the dress code.

3. **By enhancing a consumer's self-image:** By way of identifying and associating with reference groups, consumers create, increase and sustain their self-image. An aspirational group is one to which a customer does not belong to but is interested to join. For instance, people who want to present themselves as members of upper class would like to send their children in good schools would like to go abroad on summer vacation and would like to buy from a particular renowned retailer, while others don't care to buy even from a local store.

SUMMARY

The study of consumer behavior is a rapidly growing discipline under retailing. Understanding consumer behavior has never been an easy subject to study. It is almost unfeasible to predict accurately that how a customer will behave in a given particular situation. Retailers are interested in examining people 'shopping styles, parading, bargaining behavior, to improve their marketing and consumer services.

The consumer behavior study helps a retailer in understanding the issues such as:

- How a consumer is influenced by his personal, social and environmental environment (for instance, value, belief, culture, family size, media);
- How consumer behave while short listing, shopping or making other marketing decisions such as advertisement campaigns, sale offers etc;
- How consumer motivation will result in increased sale and decision to change the products or services they already have selected but not purchased;
- How different types of consumers behave, think, experience, cause, and choose between different substitutes (for instance brands, products); and
- How retailers and marketing agencies can become accustomed and improve their marketing & advertising campaigns to more efficiently reach their customers.

CASE STUDY

WHAT AFFECTS CONSUMER BEHAVIOUR?

Adam Retail was a retail company having 27 stores in the NCR area. The company was carrying grocery, clothing, cosmetics and leather made items. Company was doing well without following any marketing concept. Company basic policy was to cater to loyal customers first. Company executives were of the view that it takes very less to retain the customer but to attract a new one. Therefore, company efforts were primarily concentrated on (a). Their ability to produce and provide, (b). What could be sold by their sales executives, and (c), the items on which company was getting maximum profits. Since its inception in 1983, company followed the same business philosophy. But with the entry of new domestic and international players, company started facing the problem of shrinking profits and decreasing turnover.

To overcome the impact, company thought of recruiting management graduate from India's leading B-School. Mr. Adesh Shrivastava a fresh management graduate (Gold Medalist) later joined the company. After thorough studying the business philosophy of Adam Retail, he was surprised to know that how a company can survive without applying the basic marketing concepts like understanding Consumer behavior, Market Segmentation, Brand Positioning, SWOT analysis and so on. As per his knowledge, he advised the company executives to alter the products and services offered due to change in customers' needs and wants. He also advised the company to stress on socio-cultural and income factors considering rapidly growing earning Indian middle class. Company executives were also convinced with his plan and were impressed by the reasoning he gave behind such policy changes. Further, he modernized the goods and services offered by the company and invested approx 2.75 crore. Company executives were happy and were optimistic about company's future growth over its competitors. But after nine months of such alterations, company did not find any proportionate increase in sales turnover.

This eye opening bitter fact, forced the management to call an emergency meeting of all 27 store managers in the same week. Managing Director (sales), Mr. S. Ramamurti after few rounds of meeting with various store managers, constituted a three member team to oversee the amendments and directed to submit their report within week time. Mean while company decided to continue the Adesh Shrivastava's marketing philosophy.

As decided, on June 21, 2008 enquiry team headed by Mr. R K Agarwal (Senior Regional Manager) submitted its report to the M.D (Sales). Report highlighted, as such there was nothing wrong with the new marketing policy but highlighted the facts that some basic factors related to consumer behavior were ignored.

Questions for Discussion:

1. What should the company do in such situation and why?
2. Where did gold medalist, Mr. Adesh Shrivastava go wrong?
3. As retail expert what others factors, if any, could have been involved? Discuss with suitable examples wherever necessary?

REVIEW QUESTIONS

True and False Questions

1. A consumer is anyone who engages himself/herself in physical activities of assessing, attaining, using or disposing of goods and services for which he/she pays the money for its usage.
2. Consumer is someone who actually buys and consumes the goods and services you provide, although not necessarily a customer (the person who actually does purchasing).
3. The consumer-buying process begins when a consumer decides to sell product or service to satisfy his/her unmet demand.
4. Input is a stimulus that discourages a customer to buy a particular product.
5. In the world of retailing, consumer passes through ten distinct stages to complete his buying process.
6. Psychological needs can be satisfied through shopping and buying merchandise and include learning recent trends, status, social experience, stimulation, power and self-esteem.
7. Under consumer buying process, after selecting a particular retailer, next step is to purchase the merchandise.
8. Lifestyle refers to how people in a particular area live, how they spend their day-to-day routine, how much they spend, what activities they accomplish, what type of relations they have with others and their behavior & thinking about the world in which they live.
9. A reference group is composed of one or more people whom a person considers as a basis of comparison for opinions, traditions and feelings.
10. An aspirational group is one to which a customer does not belong to but is interested to join.
11. It is said that product or service-use experience indicates satisfaction and value for money. If it occurs then repeat buying will occur, otherwise not.
12. The criteria for selecting a particular retailer may include:
    - Retailer's goodwill and image,
    - Customer service
    - Retailer's offerings with regard to price, payment criteria, delivery method, warranty and so on.
13. Retail store staff behavior, store size and traffic flow is an indicator of retailer's quality and performance.

14. A distinguishing characteristic of organized retailing in India is that it is largely a rural phenomenon.
15. The promotional policy is adopted by retail stores, which intend not to sustain themselves by continuous, active and intense promotion.

Answers

1. True	2. True	3. False	4. False
5. False	6. True	7. False	8. True
9. True	10. True	11. True	12. True
13. True	14. False	15. False	

Multiple Choice Questions

1. Consumer is some one who actually :
   (*a*) buys the goods and services.
   (*b*) sells the goods and services.
   (*c*) consumes the goods and services.
   (*d*) decides the goods and services.
2. Input encourages a customer to :
   (*a*) buy a particular product (*b*) change a particular product
   (*c*) sell a product (*d*) Inform a product
3. The consumer buying process begins with the :
   (*a*) need recognition (*b*) Finalising a retailer
   (*c*) Selecting merchandise (*d*) Searching and evaluating for retailers
4. The buyting process begins when people realise :
   (*a*) they have some motivation to purchase.
   (*b*) they have enough resources to purchase.
   (*c*) they have some unsatisfied needs.
   (*d*) they have searched and evaluated a retailer.
5. Psychological needs can :
   (*a*) be satisfied through shopping (*b*) not satisfied
   (*c*) very difficult to satisfy (*d*) be satisfied but in several attempts
6. Functional need is directly related to :
   (*a*) the cost of the goods (*b*) the availability of the goods
   (*c*) the performance of the goods (*d*) comparison of the goods
7. Organised retailing in India is successful in :
   (*a*) remote areas (*b*) urban areas
   (*c*) rural areas (*d*) deserted and hilly areas
8. Lifestyle is the out come of
   (*a*) Social factors (*b*) Psychological
   (*c*) both social and psychological (*d*) None of these
9. A reference group may be :
   (*a*) place of work (*b*) friend circle factors
   (*c*) celebrity (*d*) All of the above

10. What comes under social factors :
    (*a*) Family size (*b*) Reference groups
    (*c*) Culture (*d*) All of the above

Answers

1. c	2. a	3. a	4. c
5. a	6. c	7. b	8. c
9. d	10. d		

Check Your Progress

1. What is lifestyle?
2. What is input?
3. Who is consumer?
4. What is process?
5. Name steps of consumer buying process?
6. List few social factors?
7. What comes under reference group?
8. What is output?
9. What makes psychological needs?
10. What is behavior?

Small Answer Questions

1. Why for a retailer is it essential to understand consumer behavior?
2. Discuss the factors affecting consumer-buying decisions?
3. Differentiate between psychological and functional needs?
4. What all precautions must be taken by a customer while short listing and finalizing a retailer?
5. Why is it important for retailers to know the difference between various human needs?
6. Tell three situations in which you are both the customer and consumer and how it became possible that one man may be the both customer and consumer?
7. List and briefly explain environmental factors affecting consumer buying decisions?
8. What lifestyle indicates?
9. How reference groups affect buying decisions?
10. Being a retailing graduate, what measures you would suggest to a retailer to better understand the varying nature of customers?

Long Answers Questions

1. Explain how a retailer takes his buying decision? What steps are involved and what precautions/measures should be taken by a retailer during each stage of consumer-buying process?
2. Recollect the buying of a consumer electronic item in your family. Illustrate the decision-making process and the factors that have impact on such purchase.
3. Can you describe a procedure under which consumer needs are recognized effectively?

RETAILING STRATEGY

Unit 4 : Store Location

Unit 5 : Retail Marketing Segmentation

Unit 6 : Strategic Planning in Retail

Unit 7 : Financial Strategy

Unit 8 : Inventory Management

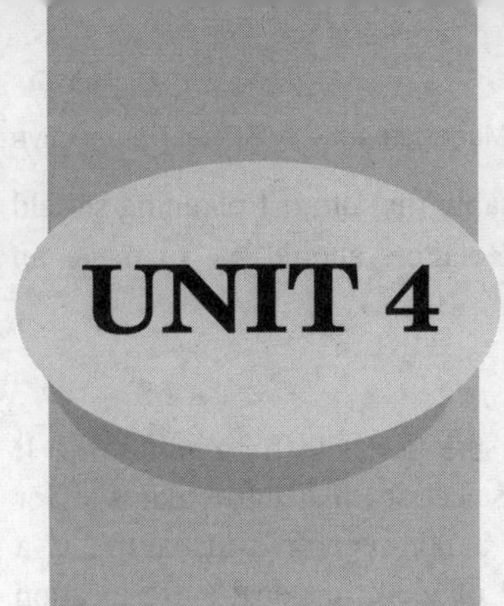

UNIT 4

STORE LOCATION

LEARNING OBJECTIVES

- Understanding an ideal store location
- Identifying factors affecting site location
- Understanding merits and demerits of a particular location
- Examining common errors while selecting store location
- Understanding contemporary issues in store location

"The three most important factors for setting up a retail store are location, location, and location!"

Anonymous

INTRODUCTION

It has rightly been said that there may be good merchandise, good customer service, and good sales promotion, but if the location where retailing has to take place is not proper, retailer will face several day to day selling problems with no solution. Location decision being strategic, long term, involve huge investment and therefore are irreversible in nature. After setting up if it comes to know that the location is not proper for any reason, without closing or suffering losses there is no way out. Therefore while going for store location decisions think again and again not consider only financial aspects but technical, commercial, social, political aspects also. Poor location results in increased distribution cost as well as becomes constant source of poor marketing response, dissatisfaction among the employees, workers, suppliers and the customers.

Therefore, location decisions ultimately decide the future and overall profitability of the organization. Not only in the retailing organizations but ideal location is required for non-retailing organizations too. Buying a good location does not only assure success; but undoubtedly is must for smooth flow and in accomplishment of day to day operations like loading and unloading of goods etc. Therefore, it is advisable that utmost planning should be taken care of. Each individual is a case in itself. Retailers should try to make an attempt for optimum or ideal location.

THE IMPORTANCE OF LOCATION

Every retailer is faced with the problem of deciding the best site for retail store. It deals with the selection of a particular region and the selection of a particular site for setting up a retail outlet. Store location decision being a non-repetitive in nature, is a strategic decision for any retailer. From a retailer point of view, an ideal store location is one where the cost of the merchandise is kept to minimum, with a large market share, the least risk and the maximum social gain. It is the place of maximum net advantage or which gives lowest unit cost of distribution. For achieving this objective, small-scale retailers can make use of location analysis for this purpose.

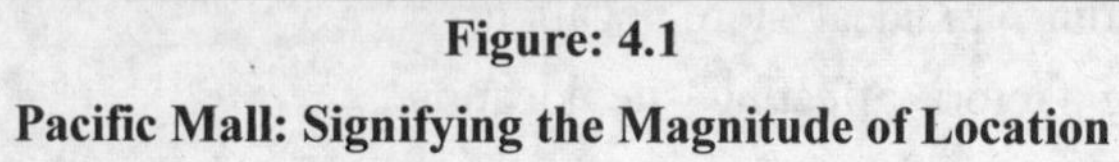

Figure: 4.1

Pacific Mall: Signifying the Magnitude of Location

Pacific Mall, Anand Vihar comes with a major boon and has huge location advantage. Located strategically on a very vital link road at - Plot No.1, Sahibabad Industrial Area, Opposite Anand Vihar ISBT Delhi, it is opposite the Waves Cineplex. This area is one of the fastest developing zones, adjoining to Delhi and getting the best of Delhi and NCR. While the growth of the zone benefits Pacific, the mall's dominating presence shall definitely boost the economy of the entire surrounding area.

***Courtesy:** Company Website*

When Does Location Problem Arise?

The need for searching and selecting a particular location generally arise in these circumstances that also describe the importance of a location.

1. While setting up a new store.
2. In case of expansion of any type (in terms of technology, new product launch, new unit etc) to meet the increased customers' demand.
3. In case of shifting of merchandise market.
4. Due to change in government policies/attitude, where, it becomes compulsory to shift the store from present location to new location; may be outside the city/ town.

5. When a new branch is to be opened in order to tap new market.
6. When due to long stay and near by developments, existing store is not in a position to obtain renewal of lease.
7. In order to overcome the deficiencies of existing store like in case where level of the road goes several feet up and rain water every year causes damage to your store.

TARGET MARKET AND STORE LOCATION

A target is a group of existing or new buyers of a products/service. There exist three types of markets - consumers, industrial and re-seller. But a retailer is concerned about only consumers' market and is usually known as retailer's target market. While identifying a target market, a retailer needs to look at the ability of firm's resources and the future potential of the segment. Further, the kind of investment that would be required and the kind of profits that could be earned are looked into. Store location for constructing a store can be solved in the following four stages.

(a) Home Country Vs Abroad.
(b) Selection of the region.
(c) Selection of the locality or community.
(d) Selection of the exact store

(a) Home Country Vs Abroad

This decision relates to deciding whether the proposed store should be set up in home country or in abroad. Today, in order to avail some low-priced inputs like cheap labour, cheap merchandises, less taxes etc., Indian companies have started venturing into other countries for retailing, marketing, acquisition, and even research and development. There is a long list of Indian retail units abroad yet most of the stores deal with Indian foods, spices, juices and pickles.

Therefore, if management has taken a decision to set up its retail store abroad, very first step is to decide upon a particular country. This is crucial because, due to LPG (liberalization, privatization, and globalization) drive globally, each country across the world is eager to invest foreign capital with unique set of offerings. The following factors should be considered while deciding upon the name of a country. Mainly these are:

- political factors like political policies & political stability
- trade barriers
- synergy
- economies of scale
- regulations
- international competition
- incentives if any

(b) Selection of Region

Generally, each country is divided into various states on the basis of directions (east, north, south and west) or political boundaries. Therefore, after selecting the country, second step is to decide the one such region based on comparative cost advantages available out of the possible regions.

Like India has 28 states and 7 union territories. Where to set up a store is not an easy task. Therefore, it is suggested either to critically analyze the each state or to study the country under its four major divisions, viz. Northern, Southern, Western and Eastern. If the retailer wants to set up for say in Northern Region, then selecting a particular community, viz., Haryana, Punjab, Delhi, Rajasthan, UP, Uttaranchal and Himachal Pradesh, is deciding upon.

The factors influencing such selection are:

- Availability of merchandise
- Proximity to the market
- Infrastructural facilities
- Transport facilities
- Climate conditions
- Government Policy
- Subsidies and sales tax exemptions

(c) Selection of the Locality/Community

After selecting the region, third step in store location is to select a particular locality or community within the selected region. It means to take decisions regarding:

(a) Urban area
(b) Rural area and
(c) Suburban area

The selection of a locality in a particular region is determined by the following factors:

- Labour and wages
- Community facilities
- Community attitudes
- Banking facilities
- Existence of supporting stores
- Local taxes and restrictions
- Water supply
- Personal and emotional factors
- Historical issues and Traffic flow

(d) Selection of the Exact Store

The selection of an exact store in a selected locality is the final step in store location decision. While selecting a particular store, generally a retailer takes decisions regarding following facilities:

This selection is determined by the following factors:

- Availability of funds
- Cost of land development
- Flexibility potential
- Transport facilities
- Local laws/by-laws
- Local taxes, water and fire protection facilities
- Means of communication
- Outlook of local people
- Parking facilities
- Waste disposal provision and
- Property Tax

India Retail Opportunity Unveils

The shop is the most substantive unraveling of intellectual and information exchange for the retail business in the Indian subcontinent. It presents the business of retail in the region to a global audience, with the express aim of facilitating, understanding about and encouraging investment in this massive market place.

At India Retail Forum, it is a congregation of some of the best retail brands, companies and minds from across the globe, from diverse retail-related segments, from retail, real estate, design and architecture, to visual merchandising, retail support, and technology. Indeed, Indian retail has to play a part larger than its definition implies. The industry has a catalyst's role to fulfil in the country's economic destiny, a destiny that is finally finding itself. Economic prosperity also means higher standards of living and higher consumption levels, and only an efficient and organized retail sector can ensure and sustain this growing demands of the evolved consumer. The challenges of the newly found growth are tremendous and, as they say, can make or undo the story. Which is why, The Shop is a market date for all the industry's head honchos, brands, retailers, mall and shopping center developers, real estate firms, architects and designers, and logistics and technology support vendors.

In essence, the shop takes to the world and gets the world to understand and appreciate the fastest-growing consumerist region of modern times.

SELECTION OF LOCALITY

(Urban, Rural, Suburban)

As earlier discussed, under selection of store, broadly a retailer has three options for setting up a store. These are:

(i) Urban area, (ii) Rural area, (iii) Suburban area

The comparative merits and demerits of each area are discussed as follows:

Urban Area

An urban area is a term used to define a geographical area that is highly populated and constitutes a city or town.

Figure 4.2

Trendy Urban Location Advantage

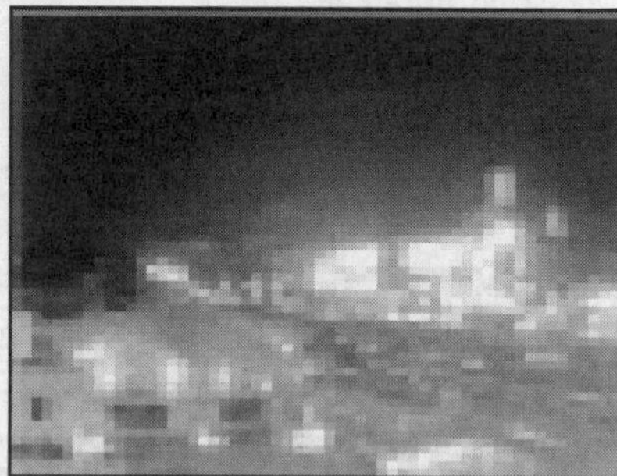

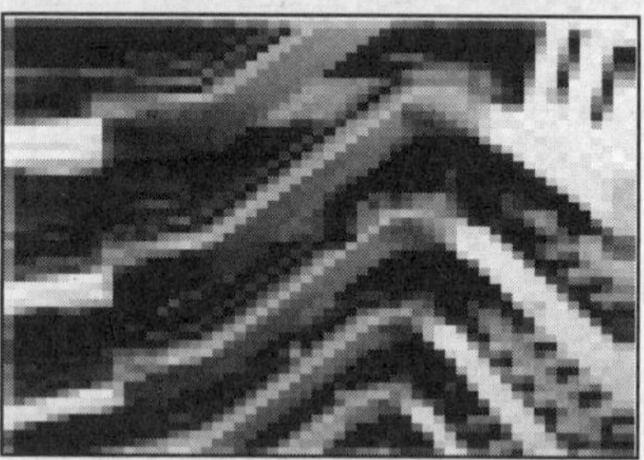

The Great India Place Mall is among the biggest mall of India. Spanning 1,500,000 sq ft, this will be the largest retail development in India. Straddling 1,500,000 sq ft, The Great Indian Place is a retail and entertainment Complex, with multiple theme parks, movie theaters, shops, restaurants, indoor entertainment area, family fashion shops, wedding bazaar, home town, large food court and huge amusement Park. This integrated mix-use destination also convinces with its prime location near Sector 18, right at the entrance of Noida. It takes at least three hours to cover the entire Shopping Mall. The best thing about the Great Indian Place Shopping Mall is the different sections it has – be it the bridal section, men's wear, shoes, cosmetics or food. They all are lined up here to serve you the best.

Courtesy: *Company Website*

Merits of Urban Area

(i) Due to nearness to market (merchandise as well as for selling finished goods), urban location reduces cost of acquisition and distribution to a considerable extent and leads to competitive advantage over competitors.

(ii) All types of transport facilities including rail and road and at times, by water and air.

(iii) Municipal services like water, sewage, fire fighting facilities, public health etc., are available.

(iv) Banking, insurance, courier, postal, internet, ATMs and recreational facilities are easily available and therefore preferred.

(v) Means of advertising and marketing various products are advanced and cost effective.

(vi) Facility of the auxiliary and service units have no problem.

(vii) Sufficient availability of both skilled and unskilled workers and employees.

(viii) Sufficient storage facility like cold storage and godown.

Demerits of Urban Area

(i) The cost of land being high disturbs the whole investment budget.

(ii) Comparative to rural area, local taxes like house tax, water tax, property tax, sanitation tax are high enough.

(iii) Roads are congested and traffic jam, demonstration by political parties, road blockage, '*chakka jam*' are the day to day problems one faces in the city.

(iv) Presence of large number of industries and more job opportunities result in labour turnover rate high.

(v) Ill-constructed and unauthorized constructions make retail area ill-lighted, more congested and ill ventilated which adversely affects workers' health.

(vi) The cost of labour i.e. wage rate is high.

(vii) Restrictions imposed by municipal authorities and district administration put constraint and extra cost due to underground construction, height of the factory, and waste water management.

(viii) Salary and wages are generally high due to high standard of living of urban people therefore this put an extra financial burden on the company.

(ix) More restrictions on constructing multi story building, playing music etc., by district administration.

(x) Today government attitude regarding starting new stores has shifted from urban to rural area due to urbanization. Therefore, government provides financial packages and subsidies to attract stores in rural/sub urban areas.

Rural Area

By definition, rural area is an area outside of cities and towns. Generally no retailer would like to set up a store in rural area but due to problems of urban area and government restrictions towards urban area construction, rural area has become attractive place for new retail stores. Rural area is typically blessed with these merits.

Merits of rural area

(i) Cheaper and sufficient land

(ii) More open space

(iii) Low wages for unskilled workers

(iv) Lesser labour troubles

(v) Less political/municipal interference.

(vi) Less labour turnover

(vii) Fewer problems of air/water/noise pollution

(viii) Few restrictions on constructing multi storey buildings, playing music, lighting etc.

(ix) Less local taxes

(x) Less/no traffic problems, and congested roads which make daily life miserable.

(xi) Government incentives, subsidies, rebates further make rural area an attractive option.

Demerits of rural area

(i) Lack of community facilities like recreation facilities etc.

(ii) Inadequate transport facilities creates day to day problem for workers and employees to reach at such location.

(iii) Shortage of skilled workers.

(iv) Improper supply of electricity, full voltage, water etc.

(v) Absence of training schools, colleges and institutes put extra burden on company to make their own training arrangements.

(vi) Absence of supporting industries and other services.

(vii) Lack of banking and credit facilities.

(viii) Lack of postal, internet, telegraph and other communication activities are not available.

(ix) Inadequate medical facilities like hospitals, nursing homes, path labs and laboratories

(x) Lack of municipal facilities like proper drainage, fire-fighting facilities, pure water supply etc.

(xi) Due to distance from city, it increases cost of procurement as well as distribution cost of retail goods.

(xii) Lack of storing and warehouse facilities.

(xiii) Absence of insurance facilities.

Suburban Area

As the name implies, it is a compromise between the urban & rural area. It is generally located at the outskirts of the city. Suburban area, being located at outer rim of the city, provides comparative advantages of both the locations. For instance, Bawana, Nangloi, Sahibabad, Mangolepuri, Badarpur, Narela are the suburban areas of NCR (National Capital Region Delhi).

Merits of suburban area

(i) Availability of adequate land at affordable price.

(ii) Normally, infrastructural facilities like road, water, electricity, drainage, state transport etc are developed either by government or by retail associations.

(iii) Skilled workers from city and unskilled workers from villages can be acquired easily.

(iv) Store expansion like introducing a new product, adoption of new technology and performing multi-storied operations are easier than in the city.

(v) Availability of ancillary industries, repair and maintenance facilities are available.

(vi) Means of transport are developed as suburban areas are generally connected with cities directly.

(vii) Availability of ready market near suburban area.

(viii) Presence of educational, training and medical facilities in the suburban area itself as well as if desired, can be availed from near by city area due to good connectivity.

(ix) Social security like fire-fighting facilities and police check posts are available.

Demerits of suburban area

Suburban area is generally blessed with all amenities which a retailer requires not only at the time of installation but in performing day to day operations. Due to connectivity with both urban and rural area, whatever is required can be easily obtained from. Therefore, throughout the world, suburban area which sometimes is known as retail area is the foremost choice of each retailer. Perhaps, the only drawback, a suburban area has that over the period of time suburban areas usually get converted into urban areas meaning by congested and overcrowded areas.

In general, urban area is suitable for small scale retailers which are comparatively free from air, noise and water pollution. Rural area offers tremendous advantage to large scale retail manufacturing industries and suburban area is suitable for medium scale retail stores.

SITE ANALYSIS

Site analysis is an integral part in determining the sales potential that generates the major traffic flow for a retail store. With the emergence of various retail formats and product categories, presents a wide choice of locations. Further, the mushrooming of planned shopping centers and malls present an enormous challenge before a retailer. Though a retailer tries his level best to select the site to locate a store, these factors must be considered while selecting a particular site. The major among them are:

1. **Connectivity and ease of traffic flow**: These are the two important issues that a retailer must consider while selecting a site. There may be good merchandising, good customer service, and good interiors but if the man who has to visit cannot reach the store easily, will not be a good preposition. The store sites you have short listed should be well connected through roads, trains and means of public transport. Like Karol Bagh in Delhi is well connected with roads and rail traffic with the neighboring cities.

2. **Parking facility**: Parking today has become the most uncontrollable civic problem for not only metro / big cities but even the small cities and towns are facing the same problem. In a store where tens to hundreds of customers come to shop with their vehicles (two or four wheeler), require space to accommodate their vehicles. In absence of proper and safe parking arrangement, customers hesitate to visit the store, knowing parking today has become the reason for public clashes, stealing and other cases of road rage. There are several ratios that are used to determine the provision for parking lot. For a food store, retailers throughout the globe usually apply the ratio of 3:1, which means 3 sq.ft of parking space for every sq. ft of retail store. One thing may be remembered that no ratio is universal in real life sense but it depends on the product to be sold and the place where your store will be located, i.e. nearby public parking lots.

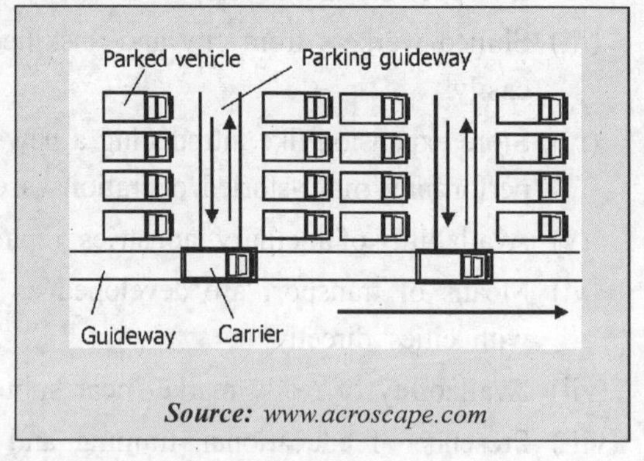

Source: *www.acroscape.com*

3. **Cost effectiveness**: An important factor to be considered before taking the decision on a particular site is the cost consideration. A retailer must remember that so called 'good site' is always a costly affair and retailer should try to go for that because ignorance to such site may be the reason for failure of your store. Retailer may manage the funds to have such site but one thing should not be forgotten that space cost is a combination of mortgage/rent, facilities, lease hold improvements, usual decoration, wear and tear, insurance, security and so on. Therefore, selecting site location only on the basis of cost factor alone may be risky.

4. **Presence of competitors**: While selecting a site, it is beneficial to check the compatibility of the retail store with the other nearby retail stores in that area. It includes

analyzing the type and number of competitors, other industrial parks, shopping complexes, franchisee chains, individual stores and other departmental stores, setting up a new store among established competition means new store will have its market share from the existing ones. Further, under intense competitive area, newcomer must come with unique merchandise, wide merchandise assortment and high level customer service.

Other factors to be considered are:

- Visibility of the store
- Ease of traffic flow
- Local laws and regulations
- Amenities available in that area
- Buy/lease arrangements
- State of infrastructure (water, road and electricity)

TRADING AREA ANALYSIS

A trading area is a contiguous area from which a retailer gets customers for the merchandise he is selling. A trade area may be a town, city, district, state, and country or even beyond the country's boundaries. The trade area may be divided into few layers (zones) depending upon the size and operations of the store, its location, merchandise offered and services offered.

Figure 4.3
Trade Area Analysis

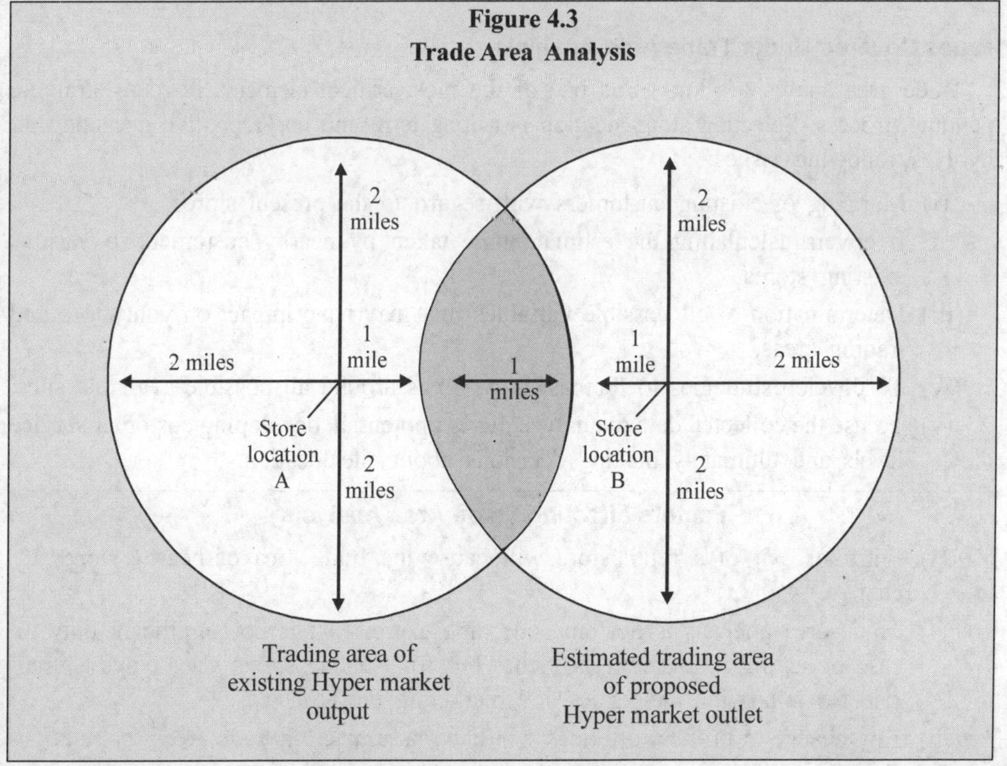

Since most of the retail sales especially in big cities take place at stores, the selection of the store location and analyzing trade area becomes essential. Retailers emphasize on trade area analysis because of the following reasons:

(i) A detailed analysis of trade area provides the retailer a picture about demographic and socio-cultural aspects of consumers. For a new store, the analysis of trade area becomes necessary to understand the prevailing opportunities and threats (if any) that may be a success path for new entrant.

(ii) It helps in identifying the consumer demographics and socio-economic characteristics.

(iii) It helps in assessing in advance the effects of trade area overlapping.

(iv) It helps in highlighting geographic weaknesses. For example, trading area analysis reveals that people from trans-river hesitate to come to city shopping areas due to pick pocketers and thieves in evening. Further, comprehensive study reveals the fact that this is because of improper lighting arrangements and absence of police personnel. Therefore, shopping center could exert political pressure to make the area well lit and crossing safer.

(v) It provides opportunity to understand and review the media coverage patterns.

(vi) It helps in locating better site location by understanding the existing trade areas around the potential locations.

(vii) It helps in understanding customers profile in terms of gender, age, income level, consumption pattern, standard of living, local requirements etc.

Issues Covered Under Trade Area Analysis

Trade area analysis is known as one of the most critical elements in retail strategic planning process. Selecting store location is a long term and non-repetitive decision that involves following issues:

(i) Mapping of existing customers with regard to the present stores.

(ii) It covers calculating the estimate time taken by nearby customers to various existing stores.

(iii) Determination of all possible variables that may have impact on your store and trading areas.

(iv) To develop strategies to forecast trade areas around all possible available sites.

(v) To use the collected data to analyze market potential, developing customer service levels and ultimately making decisions about site location.

Factors affecting Trade Area Analysis

(i) Entry or exit of a retail store will cause the trade area of nearby stores to change.

(ii) Trade area analysis is not only one time exercise. It is not significant only in case of setting up a new retail store but for existing stores also, plays a vital role for improving their sales and marketing performance.

(iii) Any change in product offerings will have its impact on trade areas, population shift, competitors' existence and overall profitability of nearby stores.

The Size and Shape of Trading Areas

Generally, a trading area may be divided into primary, secondary and tertiary zones. ***The primary zone*** is the first layer of any trading area that provides 60-65% of its customers. It is close to the store and includes nearby colonies and residential areas. ***The secondary zone*** comes after primary zone but before the tertiary zone. It is the geographical area that contains around 20% of the total customers of the respective store in terms of customer sales and merchandise demanded.

Figure 4.4
The Layers of Trading Area

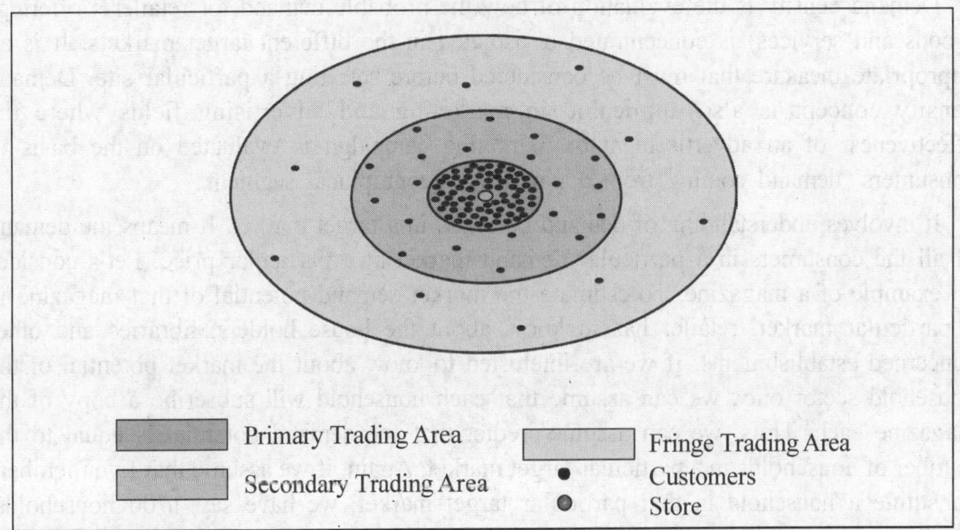

The tertiary zone commonly known as outermost circle contains the remaining 10-15% customers, who occasionally visit the store and shop. These are the customers who travel a long way to reach the store because their nearby stores are not able to fulfill the local demand. Further, there are some forces of attraction that lure the customers from tertiary zone such as wide merchandise assortment, lower pricing policy, payment options and high-level customer service.

Whatever the continent, country may be, each trading area may be studied under three zones:

AREA		CUSTOMERS' DENSITY
(i) Primary trading area	:	50-80% of store's customers
(ii) Secondary trading area	:	15-25% of store's customers
(iii) Tertiary (Fringe) trading area	:	Remaining customers

Factors to be considered while analyzing trade area

1. Total size and density (demand and supply) of the population.
2. Per capita disposable income.

3. Education level.
4. Family system (joint / nuclear).
5. Occupation (job / professional / own business).
6. Standard of living.
7. Age group distribution.
8. Number of residents owning homes.
9. Number of manufactures, suppliers, wholesalers available.
10. Size of competition.

DEMAND DENSITY

Demand density is the evaluation of how the probable demand for retailer's offerings (goods and services) is concentrated or isolated in the different target markets. It is an appropriate measure that must be considered before selecting a particular site. Demand density concept is also applicable in marketing and advertising fields where the effectiveness of an advertisement or marketing campaign is evaluated on the basis of consumers' demand coming from a particular geographical segment.

It involves understanding of demand potential in a target market. It means the demand of all the consumers in a particular demand market at a particular price. Let's consider an example of a magazine. To estimate the market demand potential of that magazine in a particular market, retailer has to know about the house holders, libraries and other concerned establishments. If we are interested to know about the market potential of the household sector only, we can assume that each household will subscribe a copy of the magazine each. Thus, we can assume/predict that the demand potential is equal to the number of households in a particular target market. Again, if we assume that five members constitute a household in that particular target market, we have say 1700 households. Ideally speaking, this is the potential market for a magazine. Further, we know that 25% population is below poverty line and therefore, will not be in a condition to buy a magazine. Besides, almost 35% of Indians fall under the low income group and given the prices of magazine, they too may not be able to purchase it. So, a retailer is left with only 40% of the total population, which is the actual demand potential that requires to be targeted. In the world of retailing, demand density relate to following aspects:

1. Traffic Flow

While selecting an exact site within particular locality, a retailer must analyze the local traffic flow – i.e. searching for most desirable side of a road or street. Sometimes in order to open a store before the competitor makes retailer ignorant about the traffic flow pattern. As with many locations in big cities like Delhi, Mumbai or Chandigarh, if a retailer chooses the wrong side of the road, no customer will prefer to visit that store. Therefore, the way the traffic is increasing in most parts of the country especially in metros, and cities are becoming congested, analyzing traffic flow is most crucial measures of a site location decision. It involves the following:

(1) The direction of traffic flow: e.g. from south to west or east to north or left to right of the road. It also includes one-way/two-way traffic patterns. Other things being same, a site with the highest pedestrian traffic is often most suitable.

(2) Movement of vehicular traffic
(3) Parking facilities
(4) Distance to store
(5) Access from major roads
(6) State of traffic congestion, and
(7) Ease of deliveries.

2. Vehicular Traffic

A retailer before finalizing a site should consider the quantity and characteristics of movements of vehicles including customers' vehicles who will drive in there. The site must have substantial number of vehicles per lane but not too much that create congestion near the store. To know the level of vehicular traffic pattern in the area, where a retailer is interested to buy a site, he may obtain data from regional planning commission including public welfare departments, municipal corporations or city's civil engineer. Further, a retailer should consider the presence of large places of employment like corporate offices, schools, religious places, community centers that are always booked for marriages and religious ceremonies, playgrounds etc. Retailers must analyze carefully that the presence of these places will be a blessing to them or will make shopping experience miserable for the customers.

SUPPLY DENSITY

Retailers always wish to set up their stores in the most attractive and best possible locations. This makes the site location decision even more critical. Selecting inappropriate site can lead to insolvency, huge losses and even closure. The importance of selecting best possible site is a major cost factor because it involves huge capital investments and has effect on transportation and human resources cost. Besides this, site location affects the amount of customer traffic and volume of business. Therefore, while considering other location factors, supply density factor should be considered as it plays a significant role in selection of a particular site or relocating an existing store.

Supply density refers to the measure of how the potential requirements for a particular product are fulfilled by existing retailers irrespective of any size. Retailer is interested to know what gap exists between the market demand and market supply. Higher the gap between demand and market supply (it means supply is less than market demand), higher the chances/opportunities exist for new comers. Measuring supply density is a must exercise for each retailer under going site location decisions.

Drivers of Supply Density

In retailing business, usually five chain drivers are in practice. These are as follows:

1. **Procurement:** This issue is related to the following retailing aspects

(i) What to buy?
(ii) When to buy?
(iii) How to buy?

(iv) Where to buy? And

(v) From whom to buy?

2. **Merchandise Management**: The issues may be related to how much to display and how much to store as reserve stock and where to store the merchandise (in the retail store itself or in the warehouse).

3. **Store location**: A number of issues regarding location such as where to set up a store, where to locate a warehouse facility, how many stories to construct, may have significant bearing on the dynamics of the supply chain, and in turn may affect the overall budget of the retail store.

4. **Transportation**: Under transportation, a retailer is concerned with the following aspects:

How to move a product from one store to another?. For example, in case of centralized retailing, delivery takes from common warehouse to different stores located in different areas at varied distance. Here retailer is always worried about mode of transportation because on one side, he is concerned with economies of scale as desired level of customer satisfaction on the other hand.

5. **Information**: Information is an integrating force that has critical implications for the whole supply chain. For a retailer, information (Data) acts as basis for making various decisions in the supply chain. If information is not understood properly, it can disrupt the whole supply chain and consequences may be fatal for retailer's fate.

Figure 4.5
Supply Density Drivers

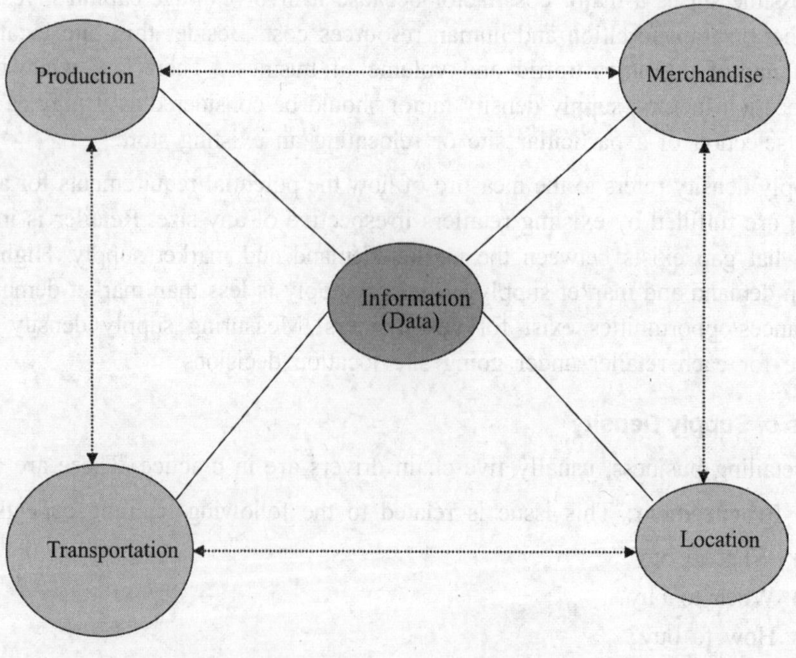

Production

Merchandise

Information (Data)

Transportation

Location

It involves understanding of demand potential in a target market. It means the demand of all the consumers in a particular demand market at a particular price. Let's consider an example of a magazine. To estimate the market demand potential of that magazine in a particular market, retailer has to know about the house holders, libraries and other concerned establishments. If we are interested to know about the market potential of the household sector only, we can assume that each household will subscribe a copy of the magazine each. Thus, we can assume/predict that the demand potential is equal to the number of households in a particular target market. Again, if we assume that five members constitute a household in that particular target market, we have say 1700 households. Ideally speaking, this is the potential market for a magazine. Further, we know that 25% population is below poverty line and therefore, will not be in a condition to buy a magazine. Besides, almost 35% of Indians fall under the low income group and given the prices of magazine, they too may not be able to purchase it. So, a retailer is left with only 40% of the total population, which is the actual demand potential that requires to be targeted.

Market Supply Factors

The market supply of a commodity is the amount of commodity a manufacturer decides to fix up in a market at a particular time and at a given time. The factors affecting market supply are:

1. The price of the commodity: it implies that higher the price of a commodity, higher the supply and less the price of the commodity, less the supply will be.
2. The price of the alternative goods: it refers to changes in the price of a related product due to changes in the supply of a related product (which could be a substitute or complementary).
3. The state of technology used: Better the technology, better the supply and poor the technology, poor the supply.
4. The efficiency of the firm to produce things: it means how many machines, men are efficient to work.
5. The price of factors of production: it means the cost of inputs used to produce a particular commodity. Higher the price of factors of production, less the supply and lesser the price of production, more the supply.

SITE AVAILABILITY

It is the final step in selecting a site location. While deciding upon a particular site, the retailer should make sure that (i) the site is physically available for sale/lease/rent etc. and (ii) the conditions require to secure the site are free from regulatory hassles. The terms and conditions with regard to lease/rental/owning should be studied from all business angles. Supposing retailer decides not to own the property but to secure on the basis of rentals then following issues must be compared and analyzed being a strategic and non-repetitive decision:-

I. For how many years the landlord is agreed upon giving land on lease basis?

1. What will be monthly/quarterly rent?
2. When it will be due?
3. Is there any advance payment? If yes how much? And when to deposit the same?

II. What various taxes will be applicable and when?

The primary objective of site availability exercise is to see that new store is established at an attractive and best possible location. It means selected site is not only preferable from traffic flow point of view but from cost, taxes and their liabilities point of view. In metro cities business incubators have come up that provide space to new retail stores (organized/unorganized) or to retailers who want to start their own trading business. These incubators serve fledgling services by providing vacant space along with management expertise, legal assistance, and clerical assistance on reasonable prices. An incubator renter (retailer) can start his business the same day he enters in, without having electricity, phone, copier, generator, canteen facilities. The objective is to make certain that new business hatch, prosper and leave the incubator.

***Note**: Getting 'best' site is not an easy task for any retailer. All retailers are not fortunate enough to have such 'best' site. The reason is demand and supply differences. The demand for site is increasing from all spheres of businesses but space is limited. Further, the costs to secure a new site may be unaffordable or prohibitive (when it exceeds the retailer's budget).*

Supposing that 'best' site is available, the retailer must decide to purchase or lease. Knowing that purchasing a site and having ownership not only saves several fixed expenses but confers greater freedom, it is always recommended that new retailers must go for lease option because of following reasons:

1. Retailer's financial risk is avoided by substantial investment and by delaying obligations for space until the triumph of store is assured.
2. Leasing avoids hefty cash out flow, which usually each retailer would like to avoid in the beginning of business.

COMMON ERRORS WHILE SELECTING STORE LOCATION

Some of the common errors are:

(i) Personal factors like preferences, emotional attachment, prejudices, liking and disliking of entrepreneurs sometimes result in poor location selection.

(ii) Sometimes, due to political reasons, public stores are set up in backward areas.

(iii) Unwillingness of key executives to move from existing location to a far better new location only because of distance matter.

(iv) Preference to residential or suburban area which already after sometime gets converted into congested and overcrowded area.

(v) Selection without thorough investigation.

RECENT TRENDS IN STORE LOCATION

Gone are the days when a retailer's foremost choice while setting up a store used to be proximity to merchandise market, easy availability of work force and transport facilities etc. These days there is paradigm shift in the store selection choice of a retailer. The old store location deciding factors, reasons have been replaced by modern concepts where traditional factors have no major role to play.

The reason behind this shift is development of infrastructural, transportation, banking, and municipal facilities throughout the country. Further, government's initiatives like subsidies, Export Oriented Units (EOUs), Free Trade Zones (FTZs), Special Economy Zones (SEZs), setting up private colonies, etc, are major deciding factors these days.

The recent trends in the store selection decision in the current years are as follows:

1. Preference to Suburban areas: Today, most of the retailers prefer retail/suburban area for setting up a new store for the following advantages:

(a) No separate permission for conversion for non-agricultural use is required.

(b) Clear title of land is assured.

(c) Speedy clearance issue of construction license, occupancy certificate, etc.

(d) Water and sewage supply is provided and distributed to the units directly by local areas authority without charging additional cost. Alternative arrangements are made whenever necessary.

(e) No shortage of electricity.

(f) Plots are carved out to accommodate small, medium and large scale retail units with various amenities, in a well planned layout and congenial atmosphere and as per the needs of the stores.

(g) Strong institutional network with regard to easy availability of loan.

2. Increased government interference

In order to maintain regional retailing balance and to stop migration of people from rural to urban areas, in search of better jobs and living conditions, government provides several incentive packages to retailers ready to set up stores, industries in rural or remote areas. On the other side, through its persuasive and restrictive measures, does not allow further commercialization in already developed and congested areas.

3. Establishment of commercial estates/areas/parks

Commercial and retail estates have become common features of the global landscape and play a significant role in the production and distribution of goods and services. Retail estates are designed to meet the often compatible demands of different communities within one location.

Figure 4.6
Escalating Attractiveness of Commercial Estates

Ansal Plaza, a part of HUDCO Place built on 35 acres of land, is a shopping complex situated near South Extension, one of the posh markets in New Delhi. The Plaza complex competes with the best ***commercial estates*** in the world in its architectural splendor, aesthetic details and shopping experience. It provides comfort and variety to the customers. One of the finest malls in India today, has made shopping much more enjoyable than before. It offers a climate-controlled environment that removes the fatigue usually associated with shopping. Careful employment of modern technology has created well-lighted, spacious and customer-friendly shopping spaces. Complete with an amphitheater, a shopping complex, twin level parking and best of the brands under one roof, it offers a complete family experience.

Courtesy: *Company Website (www.shipraworld.com)*

A retail estate, in its simplest is an area, located on the outskirts of a city and zoned for a group of retail industries and businesses. While retail parks are usually located close to transport facilities, especially where more than one transport modality coincides: highways, railroads, airports, and navigable rivers. Today, in India, retail estates are the very seat of the breathtakingly-fast commercialization process and greatly affect the location of retail stores.

4. Decentralization of retail stores

In order to avoid concentration of retail stores in a particular area which already has become congested, government through licensing policy has not been allowing new retailing activities. New retailers now can not set up their selling units in some specific congested areas without prior approval. Similarly in case of expansion, existing stores either establish their extended units in less developed areas or in some cases relocate the entire operations in such areas in order to have balanced regional development.

5. Competition between government and private real estate developers

These days what has been observed that like government initiatives, some local organizations, in order to attract retail stores in their areas, offer several incentives like cheap land, rebate in local taxes, cheap merchandise produced in such areas, etc. Consequently, the government objective regarding location of objectives clashes with such offerings made by local real estate developers.

SUMMARY

The selection of a location for a retail store is one of the most crucial strategic decisions a typical retailer makes. Since most of the retail sales in India takes place at stores, utmost care should be taken before taking a site location decision. A good location not only reduces distribution cost to a considerable extent but also attract more customers. No matter what quality merchandise a store offers, customer service or attractive pricing, every retailer has to compete with three success elements: location, location and location.

In this unit you have experienced that the retailer has to make decisions regarding store location, which refers to the selection of a particular place for setting up a retail store/outlet. Before making a decision about a particular location, retailer should go through the detailed locational analysis considering various factors, like financial, political and socio cultural forces. Retailer should understand that store location decision is a long-term strategic decision, which is irreversible and cannot be changed once decided upon. A good location reduces day to day loading, unloading and distribution cost. Consequently extreme care and proper planning is essential to select the most suitable location. And if you follow these tips, you will be able to solve store location problems in an effective way:

In-house Brainstorming

This is a daunting exercise and seems awesome when started, but site location is very practicable for stores of any size and any merchandise. Like a Chinese saying that Journey of thousand miles begin with a single step, site location decision is a very first step towards successful retailing.

The brainstorming exercise should include two issues.

(i) Why store location decision is to be taken?

(ii) What are the preferences-cost of land, merchandise or cost of employees?

Collecting the necessary data

There are a lot of sites in the market but all are not suitable from retail point of view. Some places have good connectivity but are overcrowded. Some places have best infrastructural facilities but are lonely one. Some are customers savvy but are unaffordable.

Therefore, before you start collecting data, you must first apply common sense – you are not going to shortlist- no matter how popular the market is or how better the connectivity it has. These reasons can have cost of the land, socio cultural barriers, over crowded areas, among others. So it is advisable to look at a position map and eliminating the places which you are certain will not be appropriate for long term survival. For this reason, it is better to have a facility comparison chart.

Don't be overestimate or underestimate

During critical examination of facilities chart, don't be overestimate or underestimate. Take view of the members involved. If you decide to relocate, do not compare the facilities of new site to the old site but compare the features of new sites against each other.

Visiting site

It is always recommended that the member of the selection committee should visit several times with different members. The members should consider locational advantages and compare with each other. After comparing, they should shortlist the better place to set up store. Thanks to internet facility, you can get a better view about your probable store location. You can have demographic and economic information related to your short listed sites.

Choose city carefully

Select a city carefully. Within a city there are various good sites for retiling activities. Always crowded places are not recommended for retail stores. If they have the access to customers but can make their shopping experience miserable when it comes to parking problem. Each city has its some peculiar merits and demerits. Compare these and select the best one that meets your financial, technical and cultural expertise long. By doing so, a retailer will be more comfortable while selecting a site for retail store.

REVIEW QUESTIONS

True and False Questions

1. The need for searching and selecting a particular site location generally arise in case of setting up a new retail store or in case of expansion to meet the increased customers demand.
2. A target is a group of existing or new buyers of a products service. There exist three types of markets - consumers, industrial and re-seller.
3. Store location for constructing a store can be solved in the following four stages.
   I. Home Country Vs Abroad.
   II. Selection of the region.
   III. Selection of the locality or community.
   IV. Selection of the exact store
4. The selection of an exact store in a selected locality is the first step in store location decision.
5. Comparative to rural areas, local taxes like house tax, water tax, property tax, sanitation tax are less enough in urban areas.
6. Restrictions imposed by municipal authorities and district administration put constraint and extra cost due to underground construction, height of the factory, and waste water management in rural areas.

7. Rural area is an area outside of cities and towns.
8. Absence of training schools, colleges and institutes put extra burden on company to make their own training arrangements particularly in rural areas.
9. Suburban area is generally blessed with all amenities which a retailer requires not only at the time of installation but in performing day to day operations.
10. Site analysis is an integral part in determining the sales potential that generates the major traffic flow for a retail store.
11. A trading area is a contiguous area from which a retailer gets customers for the merchandise he is purchasing.
12. Selecting store location is a long term and repetitive decision.
13. Generally, a trading area may be divided into primary, secondary and tertiary zones.
14. The primary zone is the first layer of any trading area that provides 05-20% of its customers.
15. The secondary zone comes after primary zone but before the tertiary zone. It is the geographical area that contains around 80% of the total customers of the respective store in terms of customer sales and merchandise demanded.
16. The tertiary zone commonly known as outermost circle contains the remaining 70-80% customers, who occasionally visit the store and shop.
17. Demand density is the evaluation of how the probable demand for retailer's offerings (goods and services) is concentrated or isolated in the different target markets.
18. Demand density concept is also applicable in marketing and advertising fields where the effectiveness of an advertisement or marketing campaign is evaluated on the basis of consumers' demand coming from a particular geographical segment.
19. Supply density refers to the measure of how the potential requirements for a particular product are fulfilled by existing retailers irrespective of any size.
20. The market supply of a commodity is the amount of commodity a manufacturer decides to fix up in a market at a particular time and at a given time.
21. Site availability is the first and foremost step in selecting a site location.
22. Personal factors like preferences, emotional attachment, prejudices, liking and disliking of entrepreneurs sometimes result in poor location selection.
23. In order to avoid concentration of retail stores in a particular area which already has become congested, government through licensing policy allows new retailing activities.
24. These days what has been observed that like government initiatives, some local organization, in order to attract retail stores in their areas, offer several incentives like cheap land, rebate in local taxes, cheap merchandise produced in such areas, etc.
25. A good location not only attracts customers but reduces day to day loading, unloading and distribution cost.

Answers

1. True	2. True	3. True	4. False
5. False	6. False	7. True	8. True

9. True	10. True	11. False	12. False
13. True	14. False	15. False	16. False
17. True	18. True	19. True	20. True
21. False	22. True	23. False	24. True
25. True			

Multiple Choice Questions

1. When does location problem arise ?
   (*a*) While setting up a new store (*b*) In case of expansion
   (*c*) None of the above (*d*) Both of the above
2. The types of markets are :-
   (*a*) consumers, retail and wholesale.
   (*b*) consumers, industrial and reseller.
   (*c*) consumers, industrial and wholesalers.
   (*d*) consumers, import and re-seller.
3. Under store selection, broadly a retailer has following options :
   (*a*) Plain, Hilly and deserted areas.
   (*b*) Urban, rural and remote areas.
   (*c*) Urban, rural and plain
   (*d*) Urban, rural and sub-urban.
4. Sub-urban area is a compromise between :-
   (*a*) Plain and hilly area (*b*) Metro and remote area
   (*c*) Urban and rural. (*d*) Urban and remote area
5. A retail estate is generally located at :
   (*a*) within the commercial city (*b*) outskirts of a city
   (*c*) Hyper markets (*d*) Sub-urban areas
6. Traffic flow analysis includes :
   (*a*) Movement vehicular traffic (*b*) Parking facilities
   (*c*) Distance to store (*d*) All of the above
7. Supply density refers to gap between :-
   (*a*) Import and export (*b*) production and consumption
   (*c*) buying and selling (*d*) demand and supply
8. A typical trading area has how many layer ?
   (*a*) two (*b*) three
   (*c*) five (*d*) seven
9. Primary trading area has how much customers' density ?
   (*a*) 15-25 % of store's customers (*b*) 25-50 % of store's customers
   (*c*) 50-80 % of store's customers (*d*) Remaining customers
10. Cost of land development is considered while :
    (*a*) Selection of locality (*b*) Selection of the exact site
    (*c*) Selection of region (*d*) Selection of country

Answers

1. d	2. b	3. d	4. c
5. b	6. d	7. d	8. b
9. c	10. b		

Check Your Progress

1. What is Ideal location?
2. What is expansion?
3. What is region?
4. What is Economies of Scale?
5. What is synergy?
6. What is traffic flow?
7. What ATM stands for?
8. What NCR means?
9. What do you mean by suburban?
10. What vehicular traffic includes?
11. What is FTZ?
12. What is SEZ?
13. What is skilled work force?
14. What is supply density?
15. What are EOUs?

Small Answers Questions

1. When store location problem arises?
2. What do you mean by semi-urban location?
3. Discuss some benefits of urban location?
4. Tell some demerits of rural location?
5. Write a short note on 'selection of locality'?
6. What are the common errors faced during searching store location?
7. What are the recent trends in store location decisions?
8. How good location problem decreases distribution cost?
9. What do you mean by government infrastructure?
10. Why retailers give first preference to sub-urban areas?
11. Write a short note on decentralization of retail stores?
12. Discuss how competition between government and private real estate developers is increasing?
13. How 'region selection' problem can be solved?
14. Which location you would like to prefer?
15. Why store location decisions are irreversible?

Long Answers Questions

1. What do you mean by store location? How store location problem can be solved in an effective way? Discuss with suitable examples wherever necessary?
2. What do you mean by trading area? How a trading area can be analyzed? What factors must be considered while analyzing a trading area?

APPENDIX

Exhibit 4.1: Store Location Issues Considered by Retailer

Type of Site	• Near or Far • Appropriate/Not-appropriate • How much old the site structure is? • Is it in good condition? • What is the trade area?
Accessibility, Visibility and Traffic	• Can customers and delivery trucks easily get in and out of the parking lot? • How many people walk or drive past the location • Is the area served by public transportation? • Is there adequate parking?
Location Costs	• What's the base rent is? • How much is the average utility bill? • If the location is remote, how much additional marketing will it take for customers to find you? • Who pays for lawn care, building maintenance, utilities and security? • Who pays for the upkeep and repair of the heating/air units? • Will the retailer be responsible for property taxes? Will retailer need to make any repairs, do any painting or remodeling to have the location fit your needs[1]?
Legal Considerations	• Does site meets all legal requirements of state and local administration? • Does site meet all environmental standards and rules? • Are the store displays, external signages meet and as per local laws? • Is the site zoning well-matched with the store?
Special Considerations	• Are there (blue laws) restrictions on Sunday sales? • Are restrooms for staff and customers available? • Does the building have a canopy that provides shelter if raining? • Does the parking lot and building exterior have adequate lighting? • Is there adequate fire and police protection for the area? • Is there sanitation service available? • What is the crime rate in the area? • Will the store require special lighting, fixtures or other hardware installed?

[1] *www.retail.about.com*

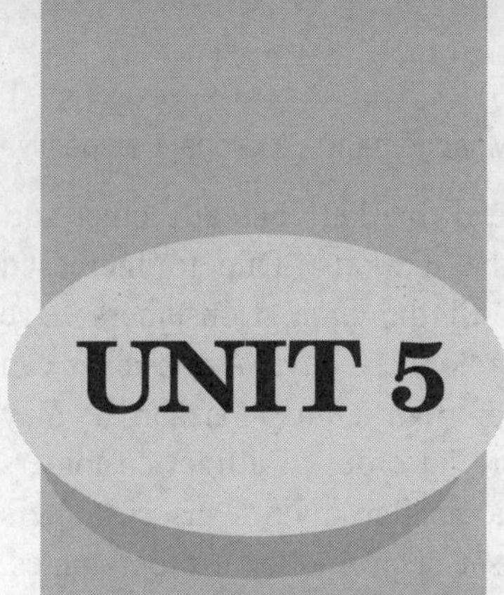

UNIT 5

RETAIL MARKETING SEGMENTATION

LEARNING OBJECTIVES

- Understanding the meaning of market segmentation.
- Discussing the significance of segmenting markets.
- Analyzing the dimensions for segmenting a customer market such as: demographic, behavioral and psychographic.
- Understanding market demand potential and
- Identifying and selecting a target market.

"No business can be all things to all people. Instead, you must reach specific customers and satisfy their particular needs. As an entrepreneur, you must identify those customers and understand as precisely as possible what they want."

Anonymous

"Market segmentation is a natural result of the vast differences among people."

Donald Norman

INTRODUCTION

Retail Marketing deals with identifying and meeting human and social needs. Retail marketing is typically seen as the task of creating promotion and delivering goods and services to retail consumers. The marketer has two options to satisfy the consumers' needs - first he should approach to all customers with identical marketing approach or adopt a differentiated approach for different sets of customers. The first approach in the world of retailing is known as mass marketing, the latter is turned as market segmentation. This chapter is an attempt to discuss the concept of market segmentation and highlights the criteria for market segmentation to gain competitive advantage.

CONCEPT OF MARKET SEGMENTATION

Market segmentation is the process breaking down an entire heterogeneous market into small markets or segments of customers that are identical in terms of some characteristics like needs wants and buying behavior. Retail markets like any other sort of business, may enjoy the benefits of segmenting the markets. Due to increased competition, mass marketing approach is not feasible all the time. Consumers have various retail formats to shop and distance is not an obstacle these days. A consumer can buy any consumer electronic item form a near by shop or from a super bazaar; he may also visit to electronic Gallery to buy the same. Therefore, in order to attract customers and sustain them requires market segmentation where a retailer divides his customers into smaller groups and approaches them with different set of promotional programmes.

In evaluating different market segments, retailer considers two factors: (i) the segment's overall attractiveness (ii) the firm' objectives and overall resources. It helps a retailer to customize the goods & services vis a vis its promotional campaigns according to the needs of narrowly defined customer group.

SIGNIFICANCE OF MARKET SEGMENTATION

Retailers segment the market to identify particular groups of customers in their trading areas so that selling and promotional efforts may be concentrated. The purpose of such exercise is to make the retailer the most attractive destination. Segmenting a market has following advantages shown in figure 5.1.

Figure 5.1
Advantages of Market Segmentation

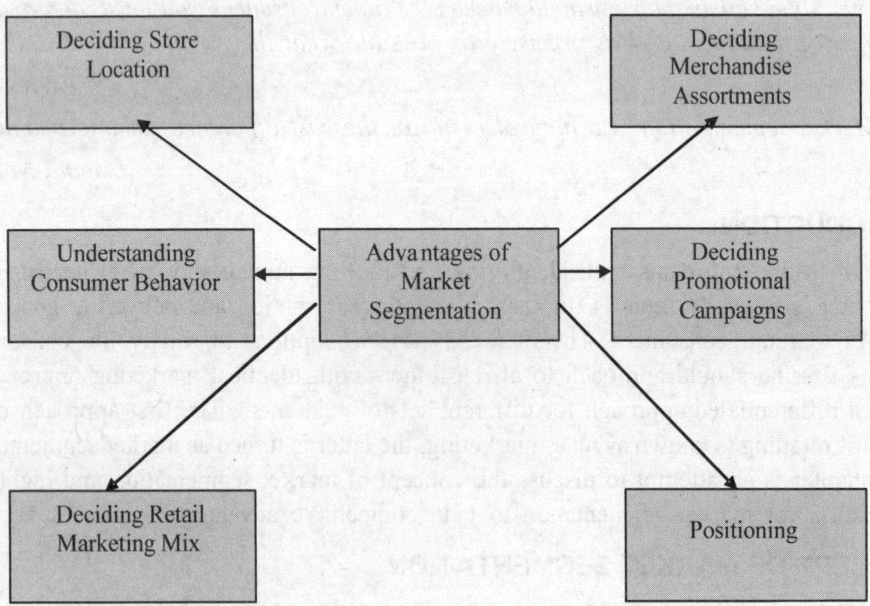

1. Deciding Store Location

Market segmentation helps a retailer in deciding locations for its new outlets in case of expansion. The retail stores may be set up as per the concentration of target population. A location which is attractive and has good traffic flow but serves no target market is of new use to a retailer.

2. Understanding consumer behavior

Market segmentation helps a retailer to understand why consumers behave differently in a same set of marketing and promotional efforts. Once a heterogeneous market is divided into few homogeneous groups, it becomes easy for a retailer to develop an effective marketing & promotional strategy.

3. Deciding retail marketing mix

Marketing segmentation helps a retailers in deciding 7ps (Product, Price, Place, promotion, People, Procedure and presentation) depending upon the target market to serviced.

4. Deciding merchandise assortments

A retailer is always bothered about which item of inventory should be bought and displayed on the store's shelves. Once the market is segmented, retailer can decide which item will go on the shelves. For a merchandise decision to be made successful, a perfect understanding of particular target market is essential.

5. Deciding promotional campaigns

Segmentation helps a retailer in deciding and developing accurate promotional campaigns that hit target at right time and at right place.

6. Positioning

Segmentation helps a retailer in positioning itself in a particular target market. For Instance, Ebony and Shopper's stop have positioned themselves for higher income level while Vishal Mega Mart and Big Bazaar have targeted the Indian middle class.

Strengths of Segmentation (Benefits)

- It helps focus the strategy of the organization.
- Organizations can understand their customers' needs in better way
- Segmentation provides basis for effective resource allocation.

Limitations of the Segmentation (Disadvantages)

- Marketing segmentation can lead to proliferation of products and services.
- Small segments are impractical in long term and may hamper the development of broad-brand equity.
- Targeting multiple segments increases marketing and HR expense.

PHILOSOPHIES OF MARKET SEGMENTATION

Market segmentation is an important element of each marketing strategy. The significance of market segmentation results from the fact that the buyers of a product or service are no homogeneous group. Today, every buyer has individual needs, liking and disliking, resources and behaviours. Since it is virtually impossible to serve for their needs (sometimes similar and sometimes unique), marketers adopt several approaches to segmenting a market. The various approaches as used in retailing area are as under:

Type of Marketing	Features
Mass Marketing	Entire market as one segment
Product variety marketing	Mass marketing with variety products
Target marketing	Serving entire market in different segments
Micro marketing	Serving one segment at a time and at local basis
Customized marketing	Serving to individual customer needs
Personalised marketing	Serving the customer needs

(1) Mass Marketing

A marketing approach where marketers (retailers) decide to ignore market segment differences (if any) and go after the whole market with one offer. Before the onset of marketing era, there was widespread adoption of mass marketing, mass production, distribution and promotion. Therefore, the same product with the same marketing mix used to offer to all the customers assuming that as such there is no significant difference among consumers in terms of their needs and wants. Traditionally mass marketing has focused on radio, television and newspapers to reach broad range of customers. The Coca-Cola Company, Hindustan Motors' Ambassador model, Ranbaxy, Cadbury, Natraj Stationers, Tata Salt, etc. follow this approach. This type of strategy is generally recommended to fruits, pharmaceuticals, bakery items, chocolates, stationery items and so on.

(2) Product Variety Marketing

When marketers realize that one standard product is now no more appreciated by general public, they try to provide same product in different sizes, shapes, colors, qualities and features. For example,

Name of the Product	Product Variety
Maruti	Lx, Lxi, Vx, Vxi, automatic
Colour Television (CTVs)	21", 29", flat TV, with zoom, without zoom, Plasma TV, LCD TV, etc.
Washing Machine	Semi-automatic, fully auto-matic, top loaded, front loaded
Refrigerator	165 litre, 175 litre, 220 litre, 310 litre, 330 Litre, one door, two door, three door, six sense, without coils on back, side-by-side, Top Mount
Reynolds Pen	Ball, Marker, Highlighter, Gel, Fluid, Jetter Range, Retraceable, Liquiflo, Ink Pen
Maruti Omni Van	Omni 5-Seater, Omni 8-Seater, Omni Cargo, Omni Ambulance, Omni Cargo LPG
PGDM	PGDM (General), Marketing, Finance, Retail, Insurance, Banking, Part time, Entrepreneurship, etc.

(3) Target Marketing

A target market or target audience is a group of customers that the business has decided to aim its marketing efforts and ultimately its products and services. Modern marketing concept starts with the definition of target markets. A well defined target marketing resources marketer to take three steps:

(*a*) Market Segmentation.

(*b*) Market Targeting.

(*c*) Market Positioning.

Further, there are several ways to address the wants and needs of a target market. For example, product packaging can be designed in different sizes and colors, or the product itself can be altered to appeal to different personality types or age groups. Manufacturers can also change the durability or warranty of the goods or provide different levels of follow-up service. Other influences, such as, distribution and sales methods, licensing strategies and advertising media also play an important role. Marketing Manager should take all of these factors into account and devise a cohesive marketing program that will appeal to the target customer.

(4) Micro Marketing

Micro-marketing is a term introduced in 1988 by Ross Nelson Kay, as a marketing technique used to describe a form of 'Target' marketing that was more precise and focused than any traditional marketing techniques. Thus with the changing scenario where people are becoming more aware to current issues, income level is increasing, rural demand for products and services is on rise, target market is being changed to micro-marketing. Micro-marketing works when a target market is further bifurcated and the needs of small customer groups are addressed on a local basis. Thus, even after identifying target customer in the target marketing, product is further differentiated and made available at selected places on local basis. Micro-marketing has four levels:

(*a*) Segment Marketing

A market segment consists of a larger market in which the individuals, groups or organizations share similar needs, purchasing power, buying attitude, geographical location or buying habits.

(*b*) Niche Marketing

A niche is a more narrowly identified group whose needs and wants are not served in the way they expect. Niche usually has following characteristics:

(*c*) Local Marketing

As the name suggest, under this form of marketing, marketing efforts are tailored to the needs and wants of local customers. Examples of local marketing are:

(*i*) Different editions of newspapers for different areas covering local news.

(*ii*) Different burgers (Food Stuffs) for different nations like done by McDonalds

(*d*) Individual Marketing

The final level of marketing efforts leads to 'customized' or 'one-to-one marketing'. It is generally practiced by companies whose products are very expensive or unique, such as, gold and diamond jewellery, wooden furniture and so on because these products can be designed to suit the special needs of each customer.

(5) Customized Marketing

Tailoring a particular product to the specific needs of an individual customer is the basic aim of customized marketing. Customized marketing is used by those companies whose products are either unique or do not satisfy the needs of individual customer. Therefore, company's products and services are designed, produced or assembled as per customer order. This practice seems expensive and sometimes infeasible but thanks to technological advancement and use of IT at large level, manufacturing products as per customers' requirement is not a distant dream. This type of marketing is well suited to tailors and drapers, jewelers, furniture makers, boutiques, beauty saloons, etc. Since under customized marketing, company adapts its products and marketing program with such a high degree of specificity, it is considered to be the ultimate form of target marketing.

(6) Personalized Marketing

Customized marketing does its level best to fulfill the requirements of customers on individual attention basis but still the customer might not be willing to retain his loyalty with the retailer because of competition. For instance, a jeweler or furniture maker provides the goods to customers as per their personal order and specifications. Still jeweler or furniture maker find their customers shifting their loyalty to others. Thus personalized marketing is used to change customers' travel behaviour by a combination of persuasion, education and provision of personalized information to either individual customers or a small set of customers.

Marketing through text messages has become the fashion of the day. Given that every other person these days has a cell phone; marketers have come up with innovative ways to reach them. SMS marketing is also effective in the sense that one must click and see the message before being able to delete it. Personalized marketing has also been a great success in interactive media such as internet. A website can track a customer's interests and make suggestions for the future. Many softwares help customers make choices by organizing information and prioritizing it based on the individual's likings. In some cases, the product itself can be customized using a configuration system.

Figure 5.2
Examples of Market Segmentation

SL. NO	PRODUCT'S NAME	CRITERIA FOR SEGMENTATION		
		Criteria 1	Criteria 2	Criteria 3
1.	Television	**Geographic**	**Type**	**Size**
		East North South West	Black & White Colour Screen Flat Plasma LCD	14" 15" 20" 21" 25" 29"
2.	Washing Machine	**Locality**	**Economy**	**Benefits**
		Urban Rural & Suburban	Low Medium Upper Income	Semi Fully Automatic
3.	Refrigerator	**Geographic**	**Size (Capacity)**	**Type**
		East North South West	160 Litre 175 Litre 310 Litre 330 Litre	Top-Mount Side-by-side Mount Bottom Mount French door
4.	Jeans	**Geographic**	**Age/Sex Group**	**Cloth**
		East North South West	Men's Women's Kids	Denim Flat Stretchable Low/High/Medium Waist
5.	Packaged Food	**Geographic**	**Type**	**Pack Size**
		North/East/South/West Plain/Hilly Deserted	Vegetarian Non-Vegetarian	Small Pack Combo Pack Family Pack
6.	Air Conditioner	**Geographic**	**Type**	**Size (Capacity)**
		East North South West	Window Split Packaged Central Air Industrial	1 to 5 Ton

IDENTIFICATION OF TARGET MARKET

A target is a group of existing or new buyers of a product/service. There exist three types of markets - consumers, industrial and re-seller. But a retailer is concerned about only consumers market and is usually known as retailer's target market. While identifying a target market, a retailer needs to look at the ability of firm's resources and the future potential of the segment. Further, the kind of investment that would be required and the kind of profits that could be earned are looked into. After having divided the market into various segments, the retailers now needs to decide on dimensions for segmentation he is going to cater to.

Dimensions for segmentations

The Dimensions that are commonly used for segmenting the market are: demographic, geographic, psychographic and behavioral. These dimensions can be used individually to segment a market or the combination of any two or more at a time. For example, a retailer may use a geographical dimension to locate its trading area, a psychographic dimension to divide buyers into different groups and behavioral dimension to understand their buying practices (consumer behavior). These are discussed as under:

Figure 5.3
Dimensions for Segmentations

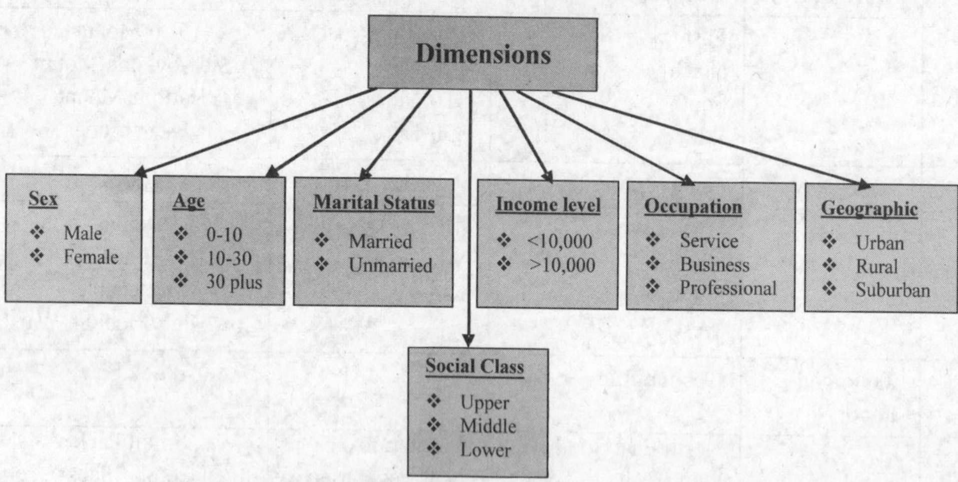

Demographic segmentation involves dividing the market on the basis of statistical differences in personal characteristics, such as age, gender, customs, traditions, belief, income, life stage, occupation, and education level. Clothing manufacturers, for example, segment on the basis of age groups such as teenagers, young adults, and mature adults, college goings, aged. Jewelers use gender to divide markets. Cosmetics and hair care companies may use race as a factor; home builders, life stage; professional periodicals, occupation; and so on. These variables are listed as follows.

- Age
- Gender

- Family size
- Family lifecycle
- Generation: baby-boomers, Generation X, etc.
- Income
- Occupation
- Education
- Ethnicity
- language
- Nationality
- Religion
- Social class

Figure: 5.4
Age & Lifecycle Segmentation

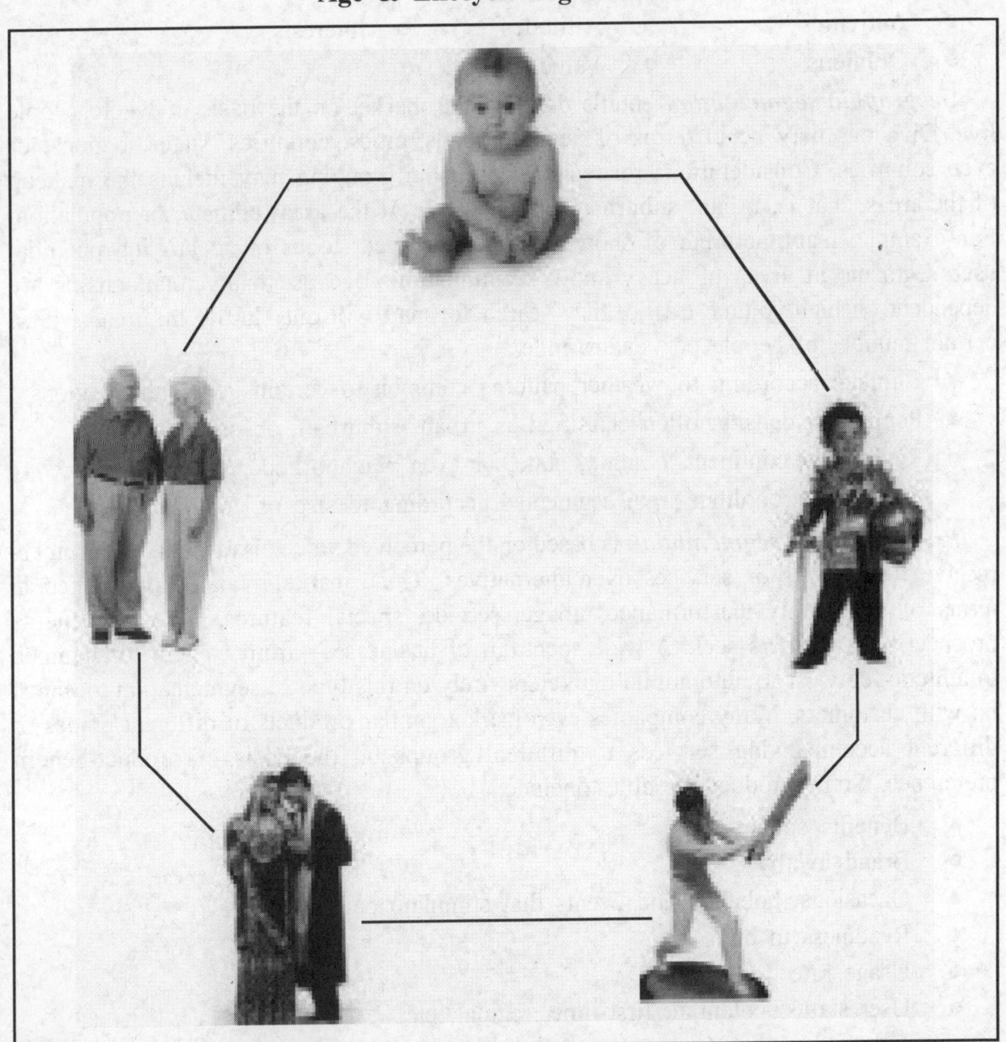

Figure 5.4 describes that as people grow their needs and wants change, some organizations develop specific products aimed at particular age groups for example nappies for babies, toys for children, clothes for teenagers and so on. Such type of gender segmentation is frequently used within the clothing, cosmetics, and magazine industry.

Psychographic segmentation is based on traits, lifestyles, attitudes, and interests of potential customer groups. Companies marketing new products, for instance, seek to identify customer groups that are positively disposed to new ideas. Firms marketing environmentally friendly products would single out segments with environmental concerns. Some financial institutions attempt to segregate and tap into groups with a deep interest in supporting their college, school, favourite sports team, or professional organization through credit cards. Similarly, marketers of low-fat or low-calorie products try to identify and match their products with portions of the market that are health or weight conscious. These psychographic variables include:

- Activities
- Attitudes
- Interests
- Opinions
- Values

Geographic segmentation entails dividing the market on the basis of where people live. Divisions may be in terms of neighborhoods, cities, countries, states, regions, or even countries. Considerations related to geographic grouping may include the makeup of the areas, that is, urban, suburban, or rural; size of the area; climate; or population. For example, manufacturers of snow-removal equipment focus on identifying potential user segments in areas of heavy snow accumulation. Because many retail chains are dependent on high-volume traffic, they search for, and will only locate in, areas with a certain number of people per square mile.

- Climate: according to weather patterns common to certain geographic regions
- Population density: often classified as urban, suburban, or rural
- Region: by continent, country, state, or even neighborhood
- Size of metropolitan area: segmented according to size of population

Product-benefit segmentation is based on the perceived value or advantage consumers receive from goods or services over alternatives. Thus, markets can be partitioned in terms of the quality, performance, image, service, special features, or other benefits prospective consumers seek. A wide spectrum of businesses—from camera to shampoo to athletic footwear to automobile marketers—rely on this type of segmentation to match up with customers. Many companies even market similar products of different grades or different accompanying services to different groups on the basis of product-benefit preference. Some product variables include:

- Benefits sought
- Brand loyalty
- Occasions: holidays and events that stimulate purchases
- Readiness to buy
- Usage rate
- User status: potential, first-time, regular, etc.

Marketing Segmentation strategies used by Titan Wristwatches

Titan entered the Indian market of wristwatches in 1984, at a time when HMT watches were enjoying a monopoly-situation. The venture took birth from the TATA group and today is India's market leader in wristwatches and the sixth-largest watchmaker in the world. The constant innovation and effective market segmentation has been the great boon to the company.

Today the company has a model for every price segment and every market. Initially when the mechanical technology was the norm, Titan went against the tide and built-up its line with Quartz. Styling was not a factor initially with the Indian watch industry but Titan was there to make a difference and gave a fresh breath of life to the age-old rusty style of wristwatches.

Titan is also capturing the rural market very efficiently. Its price range starts from Rs.475-1200 for the basic consumers. It has also appointed Mahendra Singh Dhoni (himself belonging to Ranchi) as the brand ambassador of its Sonata collection to reach out to the rural population. On the other hand, his counter-part Aamir Khan was capturing the minds of the urban segments.

It brought out the Aqua, a trendy collection for the youth. Raga was for the sophisticated Indian woman. This was a significant move as the women were now more liberal in the society and the corporate culture was establishing its roots in India. The needs of women throughout the nation were changing and the brand was aimed to cater these very needs.

- Dash for the kids segment.
- Sonata for the masses and the budget-conscious.
- Fastrack for the cool and funky fetishes of the youth while Insignia, Steel and Nebula were all aimed at the luxury watches segment.

Courtesy: Company Website and www.indiastudychannel.com

Segmentation Variables Considered by Multinationals while Going Global

Geographic	**Economic & Demographic**	**Psychographic**	**Segments**
Country of origin Language Culture	Income Age Life stage Gender Education Social status	Interests, Life goals, Media usage, Cruise brand exposure, Peer status Active, Passive, leisure, engagement, Service expectations, Attitudes towards groups and travel experiences (recency, frequency, amount spent, type and duration)	Explorers Admirals Marines Little Mermalds Escapers Stowaways Adrift

Source: www.cruisemarketwatch.com

MARKET SEGMENTATION PROCESS

Reasons for Market Segmentation

1. To better match the customer needs
2. To enhance store's overall profits
3. To search better opportunities for growth
4. To retain customer base
5. To tap unexplored markets
6. To foray into competitors' markets

Market segmentation is one of most important approaches to understand target groups. In the traditional marketing approach, business houses look at the total market as though all of its parts are same and market accordingly. In the ***market-segmentation approach***, the whole is viewed as being made up of several smaller segments, each different from the other. This approach enables business houses to identify one or more appealing segments to which they can advantageously target their products and marketing efforts. A typical market-segmentation process involves multiple steps (*as shown in figure 5.5*). Possible bases for dividing a total market are different for consumer markets than for industrial markets. The most frequent elements used to separate consumer markets are demographic factors, psychographic characteristics, geographic location, and perceived product benefits.

Although demographic, geographic, and organizational differences enable marketers to narrow their opportunities, they rarely provide enough specific information to make a decision on dividing the market. Psychographic data, operational lines, and, in particular, perceived consumer benefits and preferred business practices are better at pinpointing buyer groupings—but they must be considered against the broader background. Thus, the key is to gather information on and consider all pertinent segmentation bases before making a decision. This task becomes easy if retailers understand the marketing segmentation process and device their strategies accordingly. The market segmentation process is generally regarded as consisting of six stages.

Figure 5.5
Marketing Segmentation Process

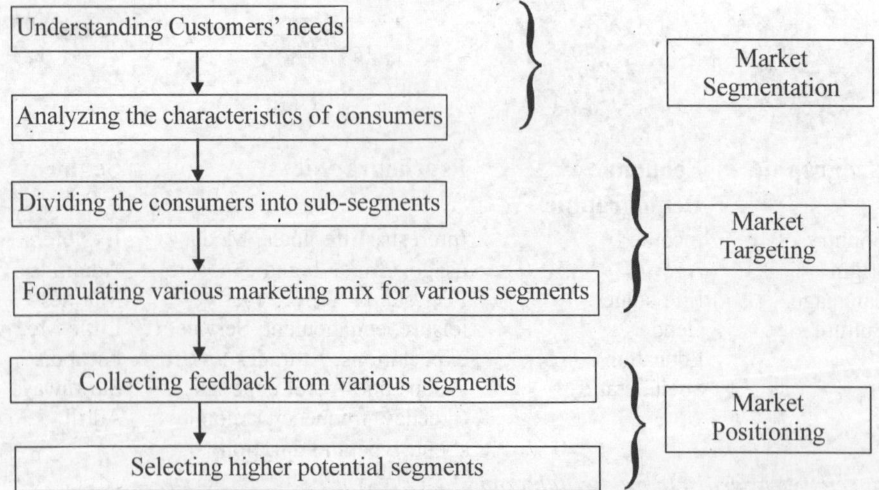

1. Understanding Customers' Needs

Understanding customers' needs and wants is the very first step in a typical market segmentation process. It includes collecting knowledge and data about customers' likings and disliking. it includes answering following questions:

- What customers want?
- When they want?
- Where they want?
- How they want? – In which form? and
- What they want?

The reasons to understand customers' choice is that better you understand your customers, better you'll be able to serve with low/no complaints.

2. Analyzing the Characteristics of Consumers

It means thoroughly understanding the varied characteristics of customers. Usually in the retailing world, customers have four essential characteristics:

I. **Particular Demand**: Most of the customers have some sort of particular demand. They have all kinds of needs including basic survival needs (eg., food, clothing, shelter and health), rational needs (eg., dependability, durability, economy), and emotional needs (eg., love, sex appeal, status, security, acceptance, and power).

II. **Capacity to Buy**: It is imperative for each retailer to know whether they have enough money to buy what you are selling. Being a retailer, remember that just because someone wants to purchase something you are selling does not mean they have enough money to buy it.

III. **Decision Making Power:** The explanation here is to spend your time wisely with customers. Find the customer who has the actual authority to make the choice of buying your product or service.

IV. **Ease of Availability**: Being an astute retailer, make sure that visitors have easy access to your product or service. Accessibility is important. For instance, if you wish to sell baked goods to people in your neighborhood, you must either provide your goods directly to your customers or have a small outlet where they can come to you.

Based on these characteristics, retailer has to answer the following four questions:

a. **What** need does my product or service satisfy?

b. **Who** needs and can afford what I am offering?

c. **Who** has the authority to say "yes" to the product or service I am offering? and

d. **How** accessible is my product or service to my customers?

Your answers to these questions form the base what a retailer need to learn from marketing research efforts. Once retailer knows what he is looking for, he can find more about the specific characteristics of the customers he propose to target by looking at their liking, disliking, ages, heritage, income level, gender, family status, education level and occupations/professions. These factors are nothing but the demographic variables.

The following questions are associated with analyzing the characteristics of consumers and knowledge.

(*a*) Are the customers experienced in dealing with technology?

(*b*) Are the customers' expectations of the end product pragmatic?

(*c*) Are the floor employees trained enough to answer any type of customer queries about the product or service offered?

(*d*) Can the floor staff respond to the customer's requests in a timely manner?

(*e*) Will the floor staff provide proper information about how to use safely and in best manner to customers upon delivery?

3. Dividing the Consumers into Sub-segments

Market segmentation is an important pre-requisite for establishing programme goals and analyzing the determinants of consumers' behaviour. Market segmentation forms an important basis for the success of a marketing campaign, since finding homogenous sub-segments help to devise and implement programme goals and to reach the desired target groups. That is, the markets should be segmented at least to some extent.

In market segmentation process, after analyzing the customers' characteristics, consumer markets are split into ***sub-segments*** that differ from each other in respect to their outlook, values and socio-demographic features (*primarily concerned with income, gender, class, age and education, etc*). A comprehensive and organized segmentation would involve finding out some key characteristics of the markets, in consumer markets, for example, the type of household (single households, couple without children, couple with children, joint families, aged alone households etc.) or geographic differences.

However, in market segmentation it should be kept in mind that each individual has several alternatives and overlapping roles. Initially, people act in double roles as consumers and citizens. As consumers, people look for direct fulfillment of needs and wants without considering sustainability. As citizens their actions are guided by long-term orientation taking environmental matters into consideration. Secondly, people have different roles in their daily lives in work, at home, and in social circles and leisure time activities.

This can be achieved as follows:

Segregate the market into identifiable groups of customers and, taking each group in turn, develop it into a sub-segment by carefully listing what the customers in the group regard as their key features for discriminating between competing offers (*referred to as 'Key Discriminating Features' - KDFs*). When differences are known to occur within a group, capture these differences as separate sub-segments[1].

> **Note:** At this stage of segmenting the groups, it is not advisable to include 'price'. Price is better covered in the next step of the segmentation process.

Recognizing KDFs from the customer's point of view will provide the link to understand the needs and wants that customers want to fulfill. This is because customers seek out specific characteristics not for their own sake but for the particular benefits that they deliver. It is also based on the fact that generally customers don't buy features, they buy the benefits delivered by the features. For this sequence to be successful, however, retailer needs to imagine of features as consisting of both the tangible and intangible components of an offer.

Now retailer should indicate the relative importance of the KDFs to each sub-segment and when significant differences are known to occur within a sub-segment, develop additional sub-segments to accommodate them. An alternative to the above can be to list the customers found in your market (*generally suitable for markets with small customer base*). An additional substitute is to obtain a sample through a market research exercise using a systematic designed sample frame. In many in-company workshops, participants have been surprised at how much they know about their markets when this stage has been conducted rigorously. As best as possible, attribute a size to each sub-segment (volume or value) which reflects how much of the market each sub-segment represents.

TITAN – Successful Segmentation and Targeting

After carrying out an in-depth market study, Titan identified three distinct market segments for its watches. The segments were arrived at using benefit and income level as the bases.

(*a*) The first consisted of the high income / elite consumers who were buying a watch as a fashion accessory not as a mere instrument showing time. They were also willing to buy a watch on impulse. The price tag did not matter to this segment.

(*b*) The next segment consisted of consumers who preferred some fashion in their watches but to them price did matter. While they had the capacity to pay the price required for a good watch, they would not purchase a watch without comparing various offers in the market.

(*c*) The third segment consisted of the lower-income consumers who saw a watch mainly as a time-keeping device and bought mainly on the basis of price.

For the first segment, Titan offered *Aurum* and *Royale* in the gold/ Jewellery watch range. They were stylish dress watches in all gold and precious metals. The prices ranged between Rs.20,000 and Rs. 1 lakh.

For the middle segment, Titan offered the *Exacta* range in stainles steel, aimed at withstanding the rigours of daily life. There were 100 different models in the range. The price range was Rs.500-700. Titan also offered the *RAGA* range for women in this segment.

And, ***for the third segment***, Titan first offered the *TIMEX* watches and later, when the arrangement with Timex was terminated, the *SONATA* range. The price range was Rs. 350 – 500. It was offered in 200 different models. Titan also offered the "*Dash*" range for children.

In-depth segmentation helped Titan launch segment-specific products.

Source: *www.hindustanstudies.com*

4. Formulating various marketing mix for various segments

The next stage of the market segmentation process is to formulate various marketing mix for various segments to fulfill the needs, as well as market conditions of each specific target segment. Although many subject experts limit the market segmentation process to market identification rather on the key elements of the entire process, most companies fail to give due importance to other stages in market segmentation such as product positioning and mix development (Sarabia, 1996).

Once the firm has chosen a market segment it must choose a generic competitive strategy. At this point it is also necessary to review the selected strategy across segments and explore general strategic approaches. In some cases it might become apparent that a counter-segmentation strategy is applicable. In other cases, the development of distinct mixes for each segment uncovers inconsistencies or lack of resources at the corporate level and so it is necessary to revert to the segment evaluation stage.

At this point in the process the company selects those ways in which it will distinguish itself from its competitors. In most cases the differentiation involves multiple elements. In fact, "most successful differentiation strategies involve the total Segmentation - Targeting – Positioning organization, its structure, systems, people, and culture." (Aaker, 1996). One way to differentiate is through brand equity building. A strategy based on brand is likely to be sustainable because it creates competitive barriers. A brand strategy permits the strategist to work with complex concepts and not limit the differentiation strategy to just a few competitive differences. This approach is consistent and reinforces the STP approach. A successful brand strategy builds barriers to protect the selected position by creating associations of the positioning variables with the brand name in the prospect's mind.

Thus ***differentiated marketing*** is used when retailer has to approach multiple marketing mixes. This will involve multiple products, targeted towards multiple segments. *For example*, a clothing brand such as Peter England will have multiple marketing mixes to approach various consumers' segments. This practice is common in the world of retail and is best suitable to fulfill the needs and wants of multiple segments.

Company: Peter England

Marketing Mix 1 -> Utilitarian Guy

Marketing Mix 2 -> Trendy/Casual

Marketing Mix 3 -> Price Shopper

Marketing Mix 4 -> Mainstream

Marketing Mix 5 -> Ethnic

Marketing Mix 6 -> Traditionalist

5. Collecting feedback from various segments

The retailer's main task here is to collect feedback from various sub-segments to know where company should focus its resources, along with their relative importance to each other. Each segment is then assessed against these factors in terms of how well it can met your requirements and by taking the relative importance of these factors into account an attractiveness score is determined. The results are then transposed onto the vertical axis of a portfolio matrix as this is a useful tool for constructing a strategic picture of your market. Measuring the positive impact on the business will help to determine whether the methods used to collect relevant data, evaluate, and implement segmentation:

- Are effective and competitive - in sales/market results/savings and or in process efficiency,
- Are they requiring further improvement?

The criteria to collect feedback involve the following aspects:

Orders	• Average number of orders • Average rupee value; • Number of orders in past 30, 60 and 90 days; • Rupee amount of orders in past 30, 60 and 90 days.
Payment	• Average paid per customer; • Ratio of payments to order; • Payments in past 30, 60 and 90 days; • Proportion of payments on credit card.
Returns	• Average returns per customer; • Ratio of returns per customer; • Returns in past 30, 60 and 90 days.
Activity Status	• Time in days since last communication; • Time in days since last order; • Time in days since last payment.
Customer Lifetime Value*	• Customer retention rates; • Spending rates; • Costs of marketing; and • Discount rates
Response	• Ratio of orders to offers for cross-sell/retention.
Customer Service Inquiries	• Questions; • Change of address; • Billing errors

**CLV analysis is a powerful tool for evaluating marketing strategies and estimating the effect of adopting new programmes. It is a measure of customer profitability over the lifetime of the organization/customer relationship. The value of lifetime revenue potential minus lifetime costs, essentially lifetime profitability, is the foundation for calculating CLV. Customer Lifetime Value may be calculated as the net present value of the profits expected from the average customer during a given number of years.*

6. Selecting Higher Potential Segments

After collecting feedback from various segments, retailer's job is to decide which and how many segments to serve.

Focusing Single Segment

As the name implies, in this case, a retail company selects a single segment. Through concentrated marketing, the firm gains a deep knowledge of the segment's expectations and achieves a competitive market position in that particular segment. In addition, the company enjoys operating economies through specializing its production, distribution, and promotion. In case company is able to become leader in the segment, the firm can earn a high return on its investment. However, concentrated marketing always involves higher than normal risks. A particular market segment can turn sour any time or a competitor may march into the segment. For these reasons, most of the retailing firms prefer to operate in more than one segment.

Focusing Selective Segment

In this case, the company selects a number of segments each independently striking and appropriate, given the firm's objectives and resources. There may be less or no synergy among the segments, but each segment promises to be a moneymaker. Selective segment coverage strategy has the benefit of diversifying the company's risk. Selective specialization is becoming quite popular in FM radio broadcasting. Radio broadcasters that want to appeal both to younger and older listeners can do so by having two different stations in the same market. Similarly most of the car companies, have adopted policies of more than one models to satisfy various income groups.

Focusing Product Specialization

In this case, the company concentrates on producing or acquiring a certain product that it sells to various segments. Product specialization strategy enables a firm in building a strong goodwill in the specific product area. The main shortcoming in adopting such policy is that the product may be replaced by an entirely new technology any time resulting in huge losses to the firm.

Focusing Market Specialization

In this case, the company concentrates on serving varied needs of a particular customer group. The firm gains a strong reputation for specializing in serving the customer group and becomes a channel for all new products that the customer group could feasibly utilize The shortcoming of this policy is that the customer group may have its budgets cut resulting in loosing customers and market share.

Focusing Full market

In this case, as the name implies, the company attempts to serve all customer groups with all the products that they might need. Adopting full market specialization seems to be attractive and lucrative but can be undertaken by only large companies. Large companies can full market in two broad ways: through undifferentiated marketing or differentiated marketing.

Figure 5.6
Various Market segments of Indian Corporate

Single Segment	Merc, BMW
Selective Segment	Kidodent toothpaste (only for kids)
Product Segment	JCB machines, Studds Helmets
Market Segment	Hindustan Unilever
Full coverage Segment	Mother Diary Milk, Pepsi, Coco-Cola, Nokia

UNDERSTANDING TARGET MARKET

After understanding the composition of the target market, retailers then need to know their market in detail. Retailers should study the behavior of consumers in their target markets to develop an effective cost-efficient and cost-effective retail marketing mix. The very first step in developing a marketing mix plan is to develop a customer profile for the market segment or target market. It covers all those information that enable a retailer to know the usage patterns, liking and disliking of his customers. Once the buying patterns are known (regular versus irregular buyers), a retailer can effectively allocate finances to reach its target market in most efficient manner.

Market and retail location

The second step in developing a better understanding of the target market is to take decision about retail location. Retailers consider several issues while assessing the attractiveness of a particular region/location. They would like to know about the people living in that area, and what are their lifestyles? Is the area devcloping or declining? Does it have a favorable working environment? And what is the level of competition in thc retail location? If the retailer believes that he has superior retail format and have unique merchandise to offer, he can choose location of high competition. Further, a retailer would like to know the scope for setting up multiple (more than one) stores in an area or at various locations.

A location having above mentioned characteristics is difficult to find. But a retailer has no option but to select best out of the best. Each location, be it urban, rural or sub-urban, has its own merits and demerits. Before deciding upon any particular retail location, a retailer must consider the proximity to market and workplace besides other financial and marketing issues.

Market Demand Potential

It involves understanding of demand potential in a target market. It means the demand of all the consumers in a particular demand market at a particular price. Let's consider an example of a magazine. To estimate the market demand potential of that magazine in a particular market, retailer has to know about the house holders, libraries and other concerned establishments. If we are interested to know about the market potential of the household sector only, we can assume that each household will subscribe a copy of the magazine each. Thus, we can assume/predict that the demand potential is equal to the number of households in a particular target market. Again, if we assume that five members constitute a household in that particular target market, we have say 1700 households. Ideally speaking, this is the potential market for a magazine. Further, we know that 25% population is below poverty line and therefore, will not be in a condition to buy a magazine. Besides, almost 35% of Indians fall under the low income group and given the prices of magazine, they too may not be able to purchase it. So, a retailer is left with only 40% of the total population, which is the actual demand potential that requires to be targeted.

Target marketing

To predict how large or small a market may be, retail professionals count the potential buyers. For this purpose, retailers usually count loyal customers who do regular purchasing. Certain essentials exist for a useful target market:

1. The buyers' ability to purchase products and services.
2. the willing ness to buy the products and services
3. An eligible number of people in the market to generate profits.

The buyers' ability means that the customers have adequate purchasing power to shop. Most of the customers cannot afford Merc, BMW car because of inadequate discretionary income. The willingness to buy refers to the customer's experience may not to shop at that retail store again. Further, a unsatisfied customer spoils others not to shop from the store. This is the reason why personal touch and efficient customer service is essential for all the retailers. Shoppers who visit first time in the store and have no perceptions about the store are significant from the retailers' target market point of view. And shoppers' who are unwilling and unsatisfied from the retailer's store should not be included in the target market.

Market Supply Factors

The market supply of a commodity is the amount of commodity a manufacturer decides to fix up in a market at a particular time and at a given time. The factors affecting market supply are:

1. The price of the commodity: it implies that higher the price of a commodity, higher the supply and less the price of the commodity, less the supply will be.
2. The price of the alternative goods: it refers to changes in the price of a related product due to changes in the supply of a related product (which could be a substitute or complementary).
3. The state of technology used: Better the technology, better the supply and poor the technology, poor the supply.
4. The efficiency of the firm to produce things: it means how much machines, men are efficient to work.
5. The price of factors of production: it means the cost of inputs used to produce a particular commodity. Higher the price of factors of production, less the supply and lesser the price of production, more the supply.

KEY RETAIL SEGMENTS

Indian retail sector broadly has been studied under following key segments:

FASHION, FITNESS AND PERSONAL CARE

This sector is divided into beauty parlors (both men and women), health centers, spa, gym, and yoga centers. World over, fashion is the largest sector in retail. Lakme, Shahnaz Herbals, VLCC are the key players in this sector. This sector is characterized by large formats, which are fairly price competitive.

With growth in incomes, Indians have been spending enough money on fashion, fitness and personal care products. India has over 1 million retailers, of whom 50 % belong to personal care. As in the case of other retailing sectors, small single outlet retailers also dominate sales of fitness and personal care items. In addition, personal care stores consist of self-diagnostic equipments, natural foods, height increasing products, lotions, body building machines and beauty parlors among other items. However, in recent years, a couple of retail chains specializing in fashion, fitness and personal care products have sprung up. For example, the consumer friendly environment makes the Life Spring chain of personal care stores a perfect example of captive retailing. Besides the regular pharmacy, Life Spring also offers a range of fitness and personal care products like health foods, cholesterol free diet including self-diagnostic items. Another company Glaxo Smith Kline (GSK), the leading Indian Pharmaceutical company has launched fitness retail stores by the name 98.4°. Such developments undoubtedly are unprecedented in India's fitness industry, pointing to the fact that Indian fashion, fitness and personal care is progressing towards a new era of modernization.

Other retailers in this sector are:

(*i*) Apollo Health and Life Style Limited (AHLL)
(*ii*) VLCC
(*iii*) Shahnaz Hussain
(*iv*) Lakme Liver
(*v*) Health and Glow
(*vi*) Avon Beauty
(*vii*) OTC Medicines
(*viii*) Oriflame Stores etc.

HEALTH AND PHARMACEUTICALS

Today due to increase in per capita income, all over the world, people are becoming health conscious and have been spending more on health and pharmaceutical products. Currently, India has over 5 million retailers, of whom 16 % are chemists. Most of the independent retailers in this segment have started providing value added services for the consumers, such as free home delivery, order over phone, prescription records and other reminder services.

In addition, pharmaceutical stores consist of self-diagnostic digital equipment, skin care, blood pressure, sugar control products, and toiletries among other things. Following are the leaders in this segment:

(*i*) Apollo pharmacy
(*ii*) Oriflame Outlets
(*iii*) Life Spring
(*iv*) SRL Ranbaxy
(*v*) Dr. Lal Path Labs
(*vi*) OTC
(*vii*) VLCC
(*viii*) Avon Beauty products
(*ix*) Dr. Batra Homeopathy
(*x*) Subhiksha

Figure 5.7
Major Players in Pharma Retail

Name of the Players	No. of Stores
Apollo Pharmacies	340
Medicine Shoppe	100
Dial for Health	105*
98.4°	15
Pill & Powder	12
Medicine Bazaar	10
Lifespring	7

Source: http://www.expresspharmaonline.com/20060815/market01.shtml
* *Out of the 105, 12 outlets are fully owned*

ENTERTAINMENT RETAILING

Rising middle class income due to economic growth spurred consumer expenditure on leisure and entertainment in India. There are specialized retailers for each category of products in this sector. A few retail chains have emerged particularly in the retailing of amusement parks, music products and movies. This sector is mainly characterized by franchising and retail chain arrangements/tie-ups.

Today most of the high traffic shopping centers have presence of cinema halls, amusement parks, zoo, circus and many other small units for entertaining kids such as water parks, swings, 'bi-scope' etc. The good thing is that these means of entertainment are not only present in metro cities but in small towns too have their presence. This retail segment includes following outlets:

(*i*) theme parks
(*ii*) water parks
(*iii*) cyber cafes
(*iv*) music stores
(*v*) amusement parks
(*vi*) cineplexes
(*vii*) resorts
(*viii*) clubs
(*ix*) zoo
(*x*) Electrical fountain parks etc.

FOOD AND GROCERY

The food and grocery sector is divided in to restaurants, fast food, coffee shops, juice bars, inter continental food courts etc. world over, grocery being the largest sector in retailing. Wal-Mart, Mc Donalds, Ahold and Carrefour are some of the key global players in this sector. Food sales accounted for 77% of total sales, growing to 70.7 lakh crores from 35 lakh crores in 2005. Urbanization, nuclear family concept, double income families, increased disposable incomes and the convenience of one-stop shop with amiable ambience drive growth for organized food retailing in India. The number of food outlets has increased at the rate of 46 per cent from 2005 to 2010. There are large numbers of retailers operating in Indian food retail sector. Some of them are:

(*i*) Subhiksha
(*ii*) Six to Ten
(*iii*) Reliance Fresh
(*iv*) More
(*v*) Vishal Mega Mart(new in grocery segment)
(*vi*) Spencer
(*vii*) MTR (Mavalli Tiffin Room)
(*viii*) Haldiram
(*ix*) Bikaner
(*x*) Mc Donalds
(*xi*) Subways
(*xii*) Pizza Hut
(*xiii*) Nirula
(*xiv*) Sagar Ratna etc.

CATERING RETAILING

This form of retailing is not popular in India. Only in some big cities like Delhi, Hyderabad, Mumbai etc. it comes in picture. Catering retail is the business of providing food and services at desired area. It may include lunch box/Packaged lunch to full service catering with serving staff at dining tables or in the form of self-serve buffet. The food (Breakfast/lunch/Brunch/Dinner) may be prepared at caterer's place and final touching at the place of event or entirely cooked at the place of event. Catering service is usually provided at banquet halls, convention centers, venues for conferences, seminars, official meetings, weddings and orientation programmes of big corporates.

CONSUMER ELECTRONICS

Consumer Electronics Retailing is one of the most amazing developments in the field of retailing since the advent of Direct Response Marketing in the mid of twentieth century in India. Today it is the fast growing segment of the retail industry after food and grocery. The way Indian masses are spending money on luxury and items of standard living, it is the golden opportunity for every businessman who is planning of entering into retail industry.

NEXT, a unit of Next Retail India Ltd is one of the fast emerging leading giant in the Indian organized consumer electronics industry. It is the only consumer electronics retail chain in India that has 385 outlets across 16 states. In order to become a multi brand multi product store, it offers approximately entire range of consumer electronics right from TVs, ACs, Refrigerators, Microwaves, LCDs, Plasma TVs to Small home appliances like juicer, grinder and mixer. It has tie-ups with all leading brands like LG, HCL, Onida, Samsung, Toshiba, Videocon, Sansui, Kenstar, Electrolux, Hyundai, Kelvinator and so on. It is determined to create a network of more than 500 retail outlets and a targeted turnover of more than Rs. 1000 crores by 2010.

Other Indian Consumer Electronics Retailers

1. Infiniti Retail Limited
2. Shah's
3. Rhythm Corner
4. Reliance digital
5. Hyundai Electronics India Ltd plans
6. Home Solutions Retail (I) Ltd
7. HCL Infosystems Ltd

Top 10 Global Consumer Electronics Retailers

1. Best Buy
2. Circuit City
3. CompUSA
4. Dell Computer Corp.
5. Office Depot
6. RadioShack
7. Sam's Club
8. Staples
9. Target Stores
10. Wal-Mart (excludes Sam's Club)

SUMMARY

This chapter besides discussing about various key retail segments, talks about the concept of market segmentation. Market segmentation is a process of dividing a heterogeneous market into smaller groups those have some common characteristics. Retailers must understand that due to intense competition, mass marketing approach is not practicable all the time. Consumers have various retail formats to shop and distance is not an obstacle these days. Therefore, in order to attract customers and sustain them requires market segmentation but utmost care should be taken by a retailer before segmenting a target market. Retailer should know the nature and size of target market besides understanding the nature of competition and own resources.

REVIEW QUESTIONS

True and false Questions

1. Market segmentation involves dividing up the potential market for a product into groups of people who have similar needs, and then addressing these needs in a focused way.
2. Retail marketing is typically seen as the task of creating promotion and delivering goods and services to wholesale consumers.
3. Market segmentation is the process of breaking down an entire heterogeneous market into small markets or segments of customers that are identical in terms of some characteristics like needs, wants and buying behavior.
4. Retailers segment the market to identify particular groups of customers in their trading areas so that selling and promotional efforts may be concentrated.
5. Market segmentation helps a retailer in deciding locations for its new outlets in case of expansion.
6. A target is a group of existing or new buyers of a product service.
7. The Dimensions that are commonly used for segmenting the market are: demographic, geographic, psychographic and non-behavioral.
8. In the traditional marketing approach, business houses look at the total market as though all of its parts are same and market accordingly.
9. Demographic segmentation involves dividing the market on the basis of statistical differences in personal characteristics.
10. Psychographic segmentation is based on traits, lifestyles, attitudes, and interests of potential customer groups.
11. Geographic segmentation entails dividing the market on the basis of where people travel for entertainment and leisure.
12. Product-benefit segmentation is based on the perceived value or disadvantage consumers expect from goods or services over alternatives.
13. Understanding customers' needs and wants is the last and vital step in a typical market segmentation process.

14. Differentiated marketing is used when retailer has to approach single product segment.
15. CLV analysis is a powerful tool for evaluating marketing strategies and estimating the effect of applying old programmes.

Answers

1. True	2. False	3. True	4. True
5. True	6. True	7. False	8. True
9. True	10. True	11. false	12. False
13. False	14. False	15. False	

Multiple Choice Questions

1. Retail marketing deals with :
   (*a*) Marketing goods to customers.
   (*b*) Marketing goods to general public.
   (*c*) Identifying and meeting human and social needs.
   (*d*) Producing goods as per customers' wants.
2. Market segmentation means :
   (*a*) Dividing bulk purchases into smaller lots.
   (*b*) Dividing marketing efforts at regional and state levels.
   (*c*) Dividing marketing budget to various medias.
   (*d*) Breaking heterogenous market into small markets.
3. Marketing segmentation helps in :
   (*a*) Deciding store location (*b*) Understanding consumer behaviour
   (*c*) Deciding retail marketing mix (*d*) All of the above
4. A target is a group of :
   (*a*) prospective retailers (*b*) prospective wholesalers
   (*c*) existing or new buyers (*d*) existing and old buyers
5. The primary reason for market segmentation is :
   (*a*) To better match the customer needs.
   (*b*) To enhance store's overall profits.
   (*c*) To search better opportunities for growth.
   (*d*) All of the above.
6. Demographic segmentation includes following variables :-
   (*a*) Age, Gender, Family size, Income and occupation.
   (*b*) Education, Language, Religion, Social class and Ethnicity.
   (*c*) None of the above.
   (*d*) Both of the above.

7. Psychographic variables include :
   (*a*) Activities, Attitudes and Interest.
   (*b*) Opinions and values.
   (*c*) None of the above.
   (*d*) Both of the above.
8. Geographic variables are :-
   (*a*) Climate, population, Region and size.
   (*b*) Accessibility, Durable and Identifiable.
   (*c*) None of the above.
   (*d*) Both of the above.
9. Essentials of market segments are :
   (*a*) Accessible and durable (*b*) Identifiable and stable
   (*c*) Substantial and uniqueness (*d*) All of the above
10. Market segmentation process begins with :-
    (*a*) Understanding customers' needs.
    (*b*) Analysing the characteristics of consumers.
    (*c*) Dividing the consumers into subsegments.
    (*d*) Formulating various marketing mix for various segments.
11. KDF stands for :
    (*a*) Key Demographic features (*b*) Knitting Demographic flaws.
    (*c*) Key discriminating features (*d*) Koutons Demand forces.
12. Sonata and Timex are the product of
    (*a*) Titan (*b*) H.M.T watches
    (*c*) Orpat (*d*) Rado
13. Peter England is a :
    (*a*) Textile brand (*b*) Shoe brand
    (*c*) Electronics brand (*d*) Clothing brand
14. Customer life time value feed back involve following aspects.
    (*a*) Customer retention rates (*b*) Spending rates
    (*c*) Both of the above (*d*) None of the above
15. SRL Religare comes under which segment
    (*a*) Fashion, fitness and personal care.
    (*b*) Health and pharmaceuticals.
    (*c*) Catering retailing.
    (*d*) Entertainment retailing.

Answers

1. c	2. d	3. d	4. c
5. d	6. d	7. d	8. a
9. d	10. a	11. c	12. a
13. d	14. c	15. b	

Check Your Progress

1. What is a target market?
2. What is consumer electronics?
3. What is marketing mix?
4. What is positioning?
5. What do you mean by Location?
6. Explain 'customer need'?
7. Explain the term 'Grocery'?
8. What comes in Pharmaceuticals?
9. What is alternate good?
10. What is catering?

Short-Answer Questions

1. Discuss the objectives of segmenting a market?
2. What is the significance of market segmentation?
3. Explain the procedure to identify a target market?
4. Describe the various dimensions for identifying a target market?
5. Give some tips to understand a target market?
6. What factors can effect market supply; name them?
7. Differentiate between demographic and psychological factors?
8. Describe the criteria for selecting higher potential segments?
9. How consumers' characteristics can be analyzed?
10. Device an effective criteria to collect consumers' feedback?

Long-Answer Questions

1. What are key retail segments in Indian retail industry? What are the Indian and global retailers under these segments?
2. Explain the market segmentation process in detail? What elements are used to separate various consumer markets?
3. By taking an example of any FMCG company of repute, devise and explain the concept of market segmentation and market targeting.

Appendix

Exhibit 1: Marketing Segmentation Strategies used by Cadbury's Milk

Right now Cadbury's new advertisement campaign is doing the rounds over the television. "*Meetha* hai *khana,aaj pehli tareek hai" is the tagline that the chocolate-giant has come out with. It tries* to bring forth the excitement, which lies in the minds of the general public as they wait for the first date of each month on the calendar. The monthly salary stashed in their hands enables them to celebrate and rejoice by spending it on Cadbury's Dairy Milk. Cadbury's Dairy Milk has come out with such memorable ad-campaigns, which settled into the hearts of everyone.

The story starts with "Once upon a time in 1948..." when Cadbury entered the Indian market. It originated from a town in the United Kingdom, Bournville(also the name of its recently launched high-end chocolate) in 1905. As the Cadbury's official web site suggests, its journey in India has been an eventful one. In the early 1990s, it tried to cater to the sweet tooth of the children. Those days they steered the market and took control over the company's major market share. However, the strategy changed by letting out the secret that "everyone has a child inside "and thus everyone craves for the taste of chocolate. Cadbury strategies went through a considerable change. It now catered from children to adults and from chocolate to *mithai*. As the tagline goes "*Khane walon ko kahne ka bahana chahiye*".

The hole-in-one for the company was when it identified sweets to be a very integral part of the Indian culture. It made sure that the festive and jubilant moods of the society that had paved the way for kilos and kilos of *mithai*, now made way for a large number of Cadbury's.

Meetha did to Cadbury's what *thanda* had done for Coco-Cola. Both helped them crawl their ways through into hearts of the rural population of the country, which had an untapped and astounding potential.

The advertisement campaign of Amitabh Bachchan, dressed up as a villager, proudly announcing that his "daughter-figure" won beauty contests for cattle, brought out the laughs and struck a chord with the same segment of people.

Later came the campaigns of "*Pappu paas ho gaya*" acknowledged the market potential for college-going youth. The treats for passing exams were now a Cadbury instead of a mithai.

With Kuch Meetha Ho Jaye, we knew Cadbury's was now a desert craving as well as a popular gift-item for festivals such as Raksha Bandhan and Diwali. Cadbury's also diversified its range of products with Wowie (with Disney characters for kids), Crackle, Fruit and Nut(variations of the Dairy Milk),Bourn vita(health drink)Deserts, Perk(wafer ingredient) and éclairs(toffee segment). Cadbury's today holds 30 per cent markets share in the confectionaries industry and sells around 1 million bars a day.

Courtesy: www.indiastudychannel.com

UNIT 6

STRATEGIC PLANNING IN RETAIL

LEARNING OBJECTIVES

- Understanding the concept of retail strategy and to know the significance of strategic planning process
- Describing the internal and external factors affecting the retail environment and exploring the alternative competitive strategies before retailers
- Explaining how a retail strategy should be implemented in a retail store and how structural organization of a retail business supports the implementation of a retail strategy
- To gain knowledge about the various departments that are found in a centralized multiple retailers
- Identifying integrated retailing approach and the various steps involved in the implementation process

"The result of planning should be effective, efficient, and economical...that is, suitable for the intended purpose, capable of producing the desired results, and involving the least investment of resources."

Clark Crouch

INTRODUCTION

Retailing strategy outlines the mission and vision of a retail organization. It is a systematic plan which provides the retailers overall framework for dealing with its competitors, technological and international movements. Strategic management actually is of recent origin as far as retailing is concerned. In the past, traditional retailers tended to be mainly reactive to changes in the business environment, but with the increasing business complexities, this is no longer valid as competition in all the disciplines of retailing is increasing and changes in consumers taste, liking and disliking, technological environment and other external environmental variables are taking place with lightening speed. Long term strategically and continuous SWOT analysis is required to ensure that growth opportunities are not missed and action is taken at right time to combat with potential threats in the prevailing business environment.

Retailing strategy sets the tone for creating sustainable competitive advantage through the optimization of available resources. To create the winning edge over competitors, it requires on the part of retail organization to develop its particular mission that defines the scope of store's activities, matching those activities to current business environment, building the organization's resources skilled and competitive and allocating the targets to be achieved in particular time and monetary limit. If this initial exercise is implemented properly, it will lay down the strong base for retail store's long survival.

Formulating a retail strategy comes under the planning process. It implies that what a company should do to achieve the store's objectives? What will be the store's modus operandi? How the plans will be executed? How different resources will be arranged in an effective way? The strategic plan finds a balance between the risk associated with the store's underlined goals and the available resources. Implementation of retail strategy, on the other hand is all about ensuring that the chosen strategy should be properly and effectively put into action in order to achieve the store's objectives. A good strategy without effective implementation can hardly be expected to succeed.

THE STRATEGIC RETAIL PLANNING PROCESS

For the purpose of developing retail strategies, retailers are required to follow a step by step procedure or planning process. The planning process discusses/involves the present stage of business, the formulation, list of available strategic options, and the implementation of the selected strategies. Considering the importance of strategic decisions for the future success of the business, a systematic approach is essential. The strategic planning process, which after considering the HR potential and USP of a particular store takes proper shape, is normally divided into following steps:

1. Deciding the store's philosophy, mission and objectives,
2. Situation analysis,
3. Formulation of retail strategy
4. Strategy implementation and control.

1. Deciding the store's philosophy, mission and objectives

The retail strategic planning process starts with the identification of store's mission for its existence and hence the scope of the retail store. The mission of a store entails identifying the goods and services that will be offered to customers. It also deals with the issue that how the resources and capabilities of a store will be used to provide satisfaction to customers and how the store can compete in the target market vis-à-vis its competitors.

Figure 6.1
Corporate 'Mission Statement' Examples

ITC

"To enhance the
wealth generating capability
of the enterprise in a
globalizing environment,
delivering superior
and sustainable
stakeholder value"

IKEA

"to create a better everyday life for the many people by developing good quality, functional and well-designed products at prices so low that the many people can afford them".

Mc Donalds

"to be the world's best quick service restaurant experience. Being the best means providing outstanding quality, service, cleanliness, and value, so that we make every customer in every restaurant smile."

Global Gilete

"We will provide branded products and services of superior quality and value that improve the lives of the world's consumers. As a result, consumers will reward us with leadership sales, profit, and value creation, allowing our people, our shareholders, and the communities in which we live and work to prosper.

IBM

"Operating a safe and secure government"

The McGraw Hill Companies

"We are dedicated to creating a workplace that respects and values people from diverse backgrounds and enables all employees to do their best work. It is an inclusive environment where the unique combination of talents, experiences, and perspectives of each employee makes our business success possible. Respecting the individual means ensuring that the workplace is free of discrimination and harassment. Our commitment to equal employment and diversity is a global one as we serve customers and employ people around the world. We see it as a business imperative that is essential to thriving in a competitive global marketplace."

Courtesy: *Company Websites*

The ***mission*** also involves the way of store's functioning. How a store will work and accomplish its day to day operations? What is the emergency planning? All are answered in the store's ***mission*** statement. For example, Vishal Mega Marts, they have philosophy of customer satisfaction through "manufacturing to retailing". This reflects not only the way it tends to treat its customers, but discusses the secret of its competitive advantage, i.e. the profit saved from absence of intermediaries like agents and brokers, commission saved is distributed to customers by way of low priced items.

Once the organization mission has been determined, its objectives, desired future positions that it wishes to reach, should be identified. Stores' objectives are defined as ends which the store seeks to achieve by its USP (Unique Selling Preposition) and operations.

The store's objectives may be classified into two parts:

(i) External store objectives, and

(ii) Internal Store Objectives.

External store objectives are those that define the impact of store on its environment, e.g., to develop high degree of customer confidence by providing quality goods at lowers prices.

Internal store objectives, on the other hand, are those that define how much is expected to be achieved with the available resources, e.g. to raise the store turnover by 15% in the coming year.

2. Situational Analysis (SWOT Analysis)

The objective of doing store's situation analysis is to determine where the store is at present and to forecast where it will be if formulated strategies are implemented. The difference between current and future position (forecasted) is known as planning or strategic gap. Under organisational analysis, normally stores study their external (environmental) and internal environments.

External Analysis: The purpose of examining the store's external environment is to study the ***opportunities*** and ***threats*** in the retailing environment. The external analysis studies factors that affect the macro-environment of retailing industry and the task environment. Under external analysis, retailer studies these parameters:-

(i) Economic environment of retailing,

(ii) Political environment of retailing,

(iii) Legal environment of retailing,

(iv) Socio-cultural environment of retailing,

(v) Technological environment of retailing, and

(vi) International environment of retailing.

The store's task environment can be influenced directly by retailer's own policies and includes competitors, suppliers and customers.

Internal Analysis: The objective of studying internal environment of its own store is to identify the store's ***strengths*** and ***weaknesses***. The store will try to increase its capabilities, and overcome the weaknesses that deter the business profit. While doing the internal analysis, store examines the quality and quantity of its available resources and critically analyzes how effective these resources are used. These resources for the purpose of examining are normally grouped into human resources, financial resources, physical resources (assets) and intangible resources (goodwill, image etc).

The types of questions that are enquired under different resources are:

Human resource

- Is present strength of employees at various levels is sufficient for future action?
- Are the employees trained and capable to perform the tasks assigned to them?
- Are the employees loyal to store?
- Are the employees punctual and regular?
- Are the employees skilled in their assigned tasks?

Financial resource

- What is the total cash flow from store's present activities?
- What is the ability of retail store to collect money at the time of requirement/ emergency?
- How much effective and stable financial policies are?
- What is the ratio between fixed and current assets?
- What are the contingency plans in case of negative cash flow?

Physical resources

- What is the contribution of fixed assets?
- What is the position of abandoned/unused assets?
- How effective and update are the store's information systems?

Intangible resources

- What is the present capability of the company's management?
- How effective is the R & D cell?
- How good is the competitor's intelligence system?
- How effective store's loyalty programmes are?
- What is the capability of retail store manager?
- Are customers loyal towards company's products?

3. Formulation of Retail Strategy

In this stage, after analyzing the store's capabilities in terms of HR, finance, physical and intangible resources, a store manager formulates retail strategy with regard to marketing, retail positioning and retail mix.

Marketing is the way to achieve the set objectives. Therefore, marketing strategy should be devised according to store's primary and secondary objectives. Generally, marketing strategy is developed on the basis of product and/or market segmentation instead of the market as a whole.

Retail Positioning is a plan of store's action for how the retailer will enter the target market and will compete with its main competitors. Retail positioning from a retail store's point of view, is a step by step plan to create and maintain a unique and everlasting image of the store in the consumers' mind. This process reveals the fact that understanding 'what customer wants?' is the success key to retail positioning in the market. Under retail positioning, a retailer conveys the message that its products are totally different and as per customers' requirement. The reason here is that customers are attracted towards items that are new for them with the perception that if it is new, it will have some extra/added features.

Retail positioning is made possible under these circumstances:

(i) By differentiating the store's merchandise from its competitors,

(ii) By offering high level of after sales services at nominal/no cost, and

(iii) By adopting low pricing policies.

Retail Mix is the blend of various retail activities which in total present the whole concept of retailing. The retail marketing and retail positioning strategies are put into effect by this retail mix – the set of controllable elements that a retailer can use to satisfy customers' needs and to influence their buying behavior and compete effectively in the target market. Utmost care is required on the part of retail manager to select the various elements for a perfect retail mix. The main elements a retail store manager has to face are:

- Store's location
- Merchandise assortment
- Pricing policy
- Customer service mechanism
- Visual merchandising
- Personal selling efforts
- Advertising efforts and
- Store's internal and external environments.

4. Strategy Implementation and Control: It is concerned with the designing and management of retail systems to achieve the best possible combination of human, financial, physical and intangible resources of a retail store to achieve the formulated objectives, without timely and effective implementation also requires scheduling and coordination of various retail activities. For example, the coordination between the marketing and sales promotion department is a must for sales promotion to make success.

Further, the spirit of team work is an essential part for the success of strategy implementation. If the retail store's strategies are competitive, marketing efforts are as per demand but the sales promotion employees are not taking it seriously or are ineffective, result will not be up to the mark. The implementation of new retailing strategies sometimes require changes in the way of functioning and duties that can lead to resistance from employees. Therefore, stores should take positive steps to reduce this resistance to change and to convince the employees that it in a long term will be beneficial for both the store and employees.

Strategy control on the other hand, deals in three basic concepts:

(i) Inspection,

(ii) Detection, and

(iii) Correction.

It means after implementing the retail strategies, retailer should assess how effectively strategies are being implemented, how far the strategic objectives are being achieved and what has been left to be achieved in the store's objectives list. Therefore, retailers inspect the implemented strategies from time to time and detect the fault (if any) in the implementation of various retail elements. If any deficiency is found during inspection process, that has to be corrected with immediate effect without any further loss to store.

ALTERNATE MECHANISM

Given that the objectives are well articulated, resources are well managed but when it comes to implementation part, due to sudden change in internal or external environment, old concepts/formulated policies are invalid. Now, what a retail manager should do? This is not a common phenomenon but can happen with any retailer. It has rightly been said that 'think for the positive but be prepared for the worst.' Considering retailers who are sensitive to environmental changes, they always prepare a set of alternative strategies in case due to change in technology or change in customers' preferences present schemes are no more effective.

OPPORTUNITIES IN RETAIL SALES

The Indian government in 2005 decided to allow foreign direct investment (FDI) to 51% in case of single brand. This decision has opened a large number of opportunities in Indian organized retail sector. In fact, 350 new malls, 375 departmental stores and 1500 supermarkets are being built which shows the future of Indian retail industry. Further these statistics will grow after the desire shown by world's renowned retail players like Metro AG, Carrefour SA, and Wal-Mart for investing money in India. The opportunities in retailing are divided under two groups:

(i) Management opportunities, and

(ii) Entrepreneurial opportunities

1. **Management opportunities**: Indian retail industry is exploding. In next 8-10 years, industry will witness a change that we cannot imagine right now. With the entry of national and international business tycoons in Indian retail industry, business environment is becoming complex year after year. This wants huge investment, customization and training. Moreover, it is the right time to reap benefits from such global opportunity. Due to increasing complexities, retailers have started hiring people with requisite skills and caliber through placement agencies and campus interviews.

The retailers in India are employing work force under following disciplines of management:

(a) Marketing
(b) Finance and accounts
(c) Advertising and sales promotion
(d) Human resource management
(e) Supply chain management
(f) Information and communication technology (ICT)

Retailing employs entry level (floor staff) to senior managers. Retail managers /store managers are usually given considerable responsibility early in their careers. It is also financially rewarding. With a fixed salary, most of the employees get commission based incentives. A person can start his/her career at the level of management trainee and can go up to manager level. If these employees perform well, within three to five years, they can get twice/thrice of their present emoluments.

2. **Entrepreneurial Opportunities**: These have also increased for those who wish to start their own business. A person can own his business by opening a retail store or just having a 'franchisee' of a popular brand, which has element of both entrepreneurship and managerial assistance. In India, we still have over 12 million retail outlets that are sole proprietorships; many of today's retail giants began as independents like Spencer, Pantaloons, McDonalds, even Wal-Mart and Sears illustrate the entrepreneurial success.

THREATS IN RETAIL SALES

Indian retail industry is facing many threats that are the obstacles in its growing to the full potential. The behavioral pattern of Indian consumers has undergone a drastic change, with the growth of the post-liberalization maturing population; they have the attitude and the desire to spend. Today Indian youth want to shop, eat, enjoy and get entertained under one roof. Their choices are changing frequently. All these have leaded the retailing industry to serve better in fewer prices.

The biggest challenge faced by Indian retail industry is that excluding metros, people still prefer to shop from the traditional '*kirana*' stores, who even change comparatively to a retail store. All the marketing efforts, sales promotion programs have no effect on them. Even advertising has no response from them.

Secondly, even after post-liberalization efforts, India continues to suffer from a multiplicity of government approvals, both at the central and state levels. Bureaucracy, red tapism and corruption in the system further make the entry in Indian retail industry very difficult. Therefore, a single window clearing system and less paper work is an urgent necessity.

There is also a need for developing quality standards in all the segments of retail industry, especially in unbranded food and cloth products. Real estate and lack of human resources also present a big challenge before Indian retail industry. Mall rentals are on unprecedented high than ever before, they have doubled in past few years. Rentals on the ground floor only stand over Rs 750 per sq.ft, while on the upper floors it is Rs 650 per sq. ft in cities like Jaipur, Noida, Delhi etc. This will ultimately affect the customer service offered by the retailer in case they shell out more for retail space.

Trained and educated human resources in retailing are also a great challenge faced by Indian retail industry. A majority of the retail surveys revealed that there are significant competency gaps in India. Supply chain and customer relations followed by merchandising, facilities management and vendor development are areas which have significant gaps that need to be addressed. An area like branding and marketing is considered slightly better since expertise from other industries like consumer products and telecom can be leveraged easily in retail branding as well. Though in the last 2-3 years, some universities and management institutes have started offering degree and diploma programs in retailing but still the output is not as per the industry demand. Retail industry has following two complaints:

(i) Demand for HR is more as compared to the current intake by the Indian Universities and B-schools,

(ii) Curriculum is not updated that hinder their growth.

Figure 6.2

Significant Competency Gaps in Available Human Resources

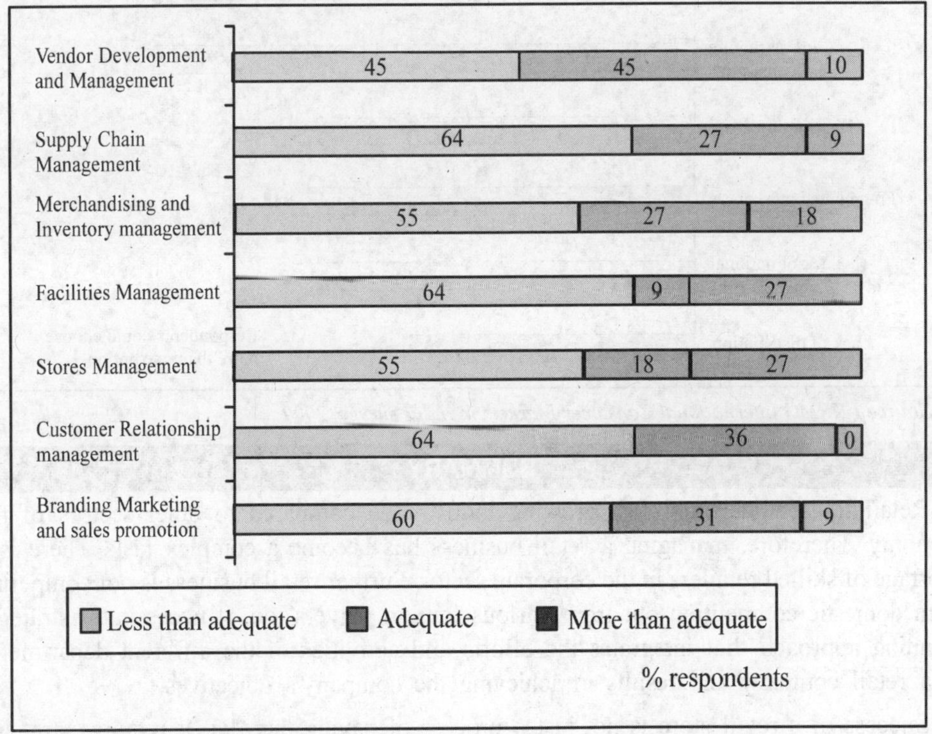

Source : *KPMG in India Retail Survey 2009*

Competition is next such area that presents threat to traditional *'kirana'* stores vis-a-vis new entrants due to presence of Indian and foreign giants in plenty. This too brings down the turnover and ultimate profit of the existing retail players. All these collectively represent as threats before Indian retail industry.

In short, Indian retail industry besides opportunities to Indian and foreign players, presents threats to existing and new comer retailers. If the sector has to grow and prosper, it will have to overcome the challenges posed in front of it. Government regulatory support can do wonder if a committee of experts look into the matter seriously.

According to KPMG, the key challenges (figure 6.3) before Indian retailers for tapping this potential are the fragmentation of the market, given the geographic spread, and infrastructure issues like lack of distribution and logistics. Which are basically:

- Distribution cost,
- Large geographical area
- Infrastructure constraints
- Fragmented market
- Lack of national distribution networks
- Lack of distribution hubs

Figure 6.3

Key Challenges in the Indian Retail Market

Source : *KPMG International Consumer Markets in India Survey, 2009*

SUMMARY

Retailing is a vast and fast growing industry as compared to other sectors of the economy. Therefore, managing a retail business has become a complex task. There is a shortage of skilled retailers in the corporate sector. Further retail business is not competing from domestic competition but from various foreign players too. It necessitates strategic planning approach that integrates the efforts and activities of the different departments of a retail company and results in achieving the company's objectives.

Success of a retail store is not just a process of having the 4Ps. It requires strategic planning. Strategic planning or strategy formulation consists of a set of decisions which leads to the development of an effective strategy. It presupposes situation analysis by way of evaluating internal capabilities. The critical examination of strengths, weaknesses, opportunities and threats (**SWOT**) provides the necessary informational backdrop to the retail planner. The next step is to formulate the retail strategy after considering various alternates, their merits and demerits, so that most suitable alternative should be chosen while formulating a particular retail strategy.

Case Study
Mall Rentals: The Big Price Mania

Since the industrial policy, 1991 retail in India has evolved to support the unique needs of our country, giving its size and complexity. Today, retailing in India has emerged as largest industry, accounting for over 10.5 percent of Indian GDP and around nine percent of the employment. The whole phenomenon of shopping has emerged in terms of format and consumer buying behaviour. A recent study by ASSOCHAM estimates the size of the Indian retail market at Rs. 6 million crores. This sector due to tremendous growth opportunities and good returns has attracted real estate developers resulting in an unprecedented jump in rentals at specialty malls.

Rentals on the ground floor today stand at Rs 750 per sq ft when the going rate in general malls is between Rs 250-450 per sq ft. This is almost 200% higher rental in malls like the Gold Souk, making them the most expensive in the country. An average 1,200 sq ft shop in Gold Souk today commands a rental of Rs 22,000 per day, or Rs 6,60,000 a month. Add to this the maintenance charge of Rs 20 per sq ft and the salaries of the staff and the tenant ends up spending between Rs 1.25-1.50 lakh per month as running expenses.

While the rate on the upper floors in such malls is Rs 450 per sq ft (as compared to the prevailing Rs 100-150 per sq ft in the general category malls), in cities like Jalandhar, Jaipur and Kochi, they command Rs 200 per sq ft on the ground floor. Consider this with the Rs 55 per sq ft rental (for the ground floor) that Gold Souk started its operations in 2003.

Most specialty malls coming up in the country do not exceed the Rs 300 per sq ft figure, that too when they are up and about. However, since most of them like Omaxe's Wedding Mall in Gurgaon, the furniture mall by Crown Plaza in Faridabad, an auto mall and a women's mall in North Delhi etc are under construction, property experts say they do not command more than Rs 45-80 per sq ft at this stage. "It is only when they become fully functional that the rates start shooting up and can reach a maximum of Rs 300 per sq ft," says Rajiv Agnihotri, senior business analyst, propertiesindia.com.

However, the big question is that with these kinds of expenses, how are the tenants able to sustain themselves. The answer lies in the product that they deal in - jewellery. "The profit margins are so high that they are able to sustain themselves as well as agree to pay such high rents," says Ashish Gupta, VC and JMD, Aerens Gold Souk Group. The conversion rate in specialty malls is 80% as compared to the 8-10% in general category malls. For instance, it is estimated that the big and branded jewellery outlets in Gold Souk earn a whopping Rs 30-50 lakh per. Figure 1 gives the idea about mall economics i.e approximately how much budget it takes month to construct a mall – undoubtedly a costly affair.

Figure#1

Mall Economics: What it costs to build a mall

Land: Rs 600 to Rs 1,000 per sq. ft.
Mall size: 400,000 sq. ft. (4 floors of 1 lakh sq. ft. each)
Construction cost (bare shell): Rs 800 per sq. ft.
Interior fit-out (including AC) cost: Rs 1,500 to Rs 3,500 per sq. ft.
Equipment Cost:
6 Escalators: Rs 15 lakh
4 Elevators: Rs 10 lakh
2 Air-conditioning plants: Rs 1 crore
2 Gensets: Rs 1 crore
Approval fees/Misc. expenses: Rs 150-200 per sq. ft.
Marketing cost: Rs 150/200 per sq. ft.

Land price escalations to the extent of five to ten times since 2005 in most Tier I and Tier II cities have become the biggest challenge to mall developers—the end product becomes expensive, the higher rentals hurt bottom lines. But all's not lost for developers, many of which are looking at solutions to get around this problem. The Sunday Express spoke to developers and brokers on how they're coping with this unexpected and unrelenting rise in the price of the most precious commodity in the business and found six strategies to land management[1]. Figure 2 & 3 gives you the idea about prevalent mall rentals in the country.

Figure #2
An Overview of Mall Rentals

Section	Average Rentals
Metros	Rs. 150-400 Sq. Ft
Tier I Cities	Rs. 80-100 Sq. Ft
Tier II Cities	Rs. 60-80 Sq. Ft

Source: *www.imagesretail.com*

Figure #3
Average Rentals by the Mall

Mall	Location	Average Rentals in Rs. Per sq, ft. approximately
Unitech	Noida	Rs. 400-600 per sq. ft
DT City Centre	Gurgaon	Rs. 250 per sq. ft
Metropolitan	Gurgaon	Rs. 300-350 per sq. ft
Shipra Mall	Ghaziabad	Rs. 175-200 per sq. ft
Ambi Mall	Gurgaon	Rs. 250-300 per sq. ft
Select Citywalk	Saket	Rs. 350-400 per sq. ft
Viva College	Jalandhar	Rs. 125-400 per sq. ft
Centre Mall	Chandigarh	Rs. 200-225 per sq. ft
Silicon Square	Zirakpur	Rs. 130-150 per sq. ft

Source: *Balaji Properties, Noida / www.imagesretail.com*

How to keep the mall rentals below?

1. Adoption of Retailer centric philosophy

According to this approach, builders should provide or construct the malls considering the retailers' budget, choices and preference. They should not buy any land which is inexpensive and can hamper the retailers' profitability. Further they should know which retailer enjoys how much margin." Jewellers, for example, usually make a higher margin than shoes or garments retailers. Therefore, builders should decide the rentals accordingly.

2. Need for joint Ventures/Tie-ups with landlord

In order to maintain and keep the land cost reasonable, now mall developers are forming joint ventures with land owners at large scale. The benefit of such tie-ups is that the landlord offers the land at a price which is genuine and comparatively less as per market rate so that mall should be rented to retailers easily without causing them high preliminary expenditures.

3. Shifting to Tier II cities/towns

Overpriced land prices in big cities have led many developers to move to Tier II and Tier III cities/towns. Such shift normally has two benefits which most of the developers admit. These are: first the land is affordable, and second these Tier II cities have a lot of growth potential as the per capita income is increasing year after year.

4. Moving towards sub urban areas

In the last few years it has been observed that sub urban area is becoming the first choice of land developers. Be it Narela (a sub urban area of Sonipat, Haryana), Ghaziabad or NOIDA are becoming hub for mall culture. But it requires utmost care with regard to selection of locality where transport and other basic infrastructural facilities should be developed.

5. Positioning right

It means as per locality and cost of land, developers should offer products that enjoy high margins. For instance, in Greater Kailash, Vasant Vihar, Saket of Delhi, where land is very costly, should be suitable for luxury or jewellery items where the profit is much. Only such retailers will be able to afford the high rentals of these locations. On the other hand, in case of developing a mall at a marginal location, value-for-money kind of goods are more suitable to sell.

6. Location, location, location

There is no doubt that the right location and right catchments does wonders in the world of retailing. For example, the average number of visitors/shoppers at Great India Place (NOIDA) is over 60,000 per day. Because of its superb location, footfalls remain

[1] ***Source :*** *www.indianexpress.com*

consistent throughout the week, otherwise in most of the malls, footfalls is ususlly more on weekends or during festival days.

How to beat high land cost for malls

- Always avoid land that is costly and make certain that rent to revenue ratio is not very high.
- Always divide the long-term profitability of the mall with other investors or developers
- Shift to the outskirts or to smaller cities instead of develoing malls in busy and congested areas
- Twist costly areas into high-end premium malls and affordable areas into value-for-money malls

Concluding Remarks

In the world of business, normally it says that any healthy sales graph has a leveling off. When the time will come to level off but it is sure that recession comes after every boom. In the real estate sector where the land prices and mall rentals are too high, it seems that this sharp increase in rentals will come down in the years to come. It will not be the fashion of the day as demand will rationalize. Even according to market experts, the initial mall ecstasy that had pushed countrywide mall rentals to idealistically high levels seems to have come down with markets such as Gurgaon, Noida, Kundli, Ghaziabad etc. witnessing a price correction. Even in the last quarter of 2007, it was found that many parts of the National Capital Region, Hyderabad and Mumbai see rental stabilization. Even a study conducted by property consultants Chesterton Meghraj, the shopping mall rentals for primary tenants would continue to decline in coming days though the contribution of smaller retailers to mall rentals is relatively higher than the anchors' collective contribution. Therefore, we hope that the mall rentals for primary tenants like retail outfits (anchors) will decline in the country and they will be invited to take positions in malls at affordable rates.

Questions for Discussion:

1. The retail boom in the country has resulted in an unprecedented jump in rentals at specialty malls. Rentals on the ground floor today stand at Rs 650 per sq ft when the going rate in general malls is between Rs 150-350 per sq ft. This is almost 200% higher rental in malls. Discuss few reasons for making the malls the most expensive in the country?
2. According to Financial Daily (a leading newspaper), the initial mall euphoria that had pushed nationwide mall rentals to unrealistically high levels seems to have died down with markets such as Gurgaon now witnessing a price correction, even as parts of the National Capital Region and Mumbai see rental stabilization. Comment?

3. In the real estate sector the steep increase in rentals seems to have negative effect on the retailers' profitability. Considering, the position will continue in the next few years to come, how the tenants will be able to sustain themselves?

REVIEW QUESTIONS

True and False Questions

1. Retailing strategy outlines the mission and vision of a wholesale organization.
2. Retailing strategy sets the tone for creating sustainable competitive advantage through the misuse of available resources.
3. The mission of a retail store entails identifying the goods and services that will be offered to industrial customers only.
4. External store objectives are those that define the impact of store on its environment, e.g., to develop high degree of customer confidence by providing quality goods at lowers prices.
5. Internal store objectives are those that define how much is expected to be achieved with the available resources, e.g. to raise the store turnover by 15% in the coming year.
6. The objective of doing store's situation analysis is to determine where the store is at present and to forecast where it will be if formulated strategies are implemented.
7. The purpose of examining the store's external environment is to study the strengths ands weaknesses in the retailing environment.
8. Retail Positioning is a plan of store's action for how the retailer will enter the target market and will compete with its main competitors.
9. Strategy Implementation and Control is concerned with the designing and management of retail systems to achieve the best possible combination of human, financial, physical and intangible resources of a retail store.
10. According to KPMG, the key challenges before Indian retailers for tapping unexplored potential are the fragmentation of the market, given the geographic spread, and infrastructure issues like lack of distribution and logistics.
11. Strategy planning or strategy formulation consists of a set of decisions which leads to the failure of an effective strategy.
12. The biggest strength faced by organized retail industry is that excluding metros, people still prefer to shop from the traditional '*kirana*' stores, who even change comparatively to a retail store.
13. The difference between current and future position (forecasted) is known as implementation gap.

14. The external analysis studies factors that affect the micro-environment of retail industry and the task environment.
15. The strategic planning process is normally divided into following steps:
    I. Deciding the store's philosophy, mission and objectives,
    II. Situation analysis,
    III. Formulation of retail strategy
    IV. Strategy implementation and control.

Answers

1. False	2. False	3. False	4. True
5. True	6. True	7. False	8. True
9. True	10. True	11. False	12. False
13. False	14. False	15. False	

Multiple Choice Questions

1. Retailing strategy outlines the _________ of a retail organisation.
   (*a*) Mission and vision (*b*) Past and present
   (*c*) Present and future (*d*) Profit and loss
2. SWOT analysis stands for
   (*a*) Side, wide, old and tide.
   (*b*) South, west, offer and threat.
   (*c*) Strength, weakness, outcome and threat.
   (*d*) Strength, weakness, opportunity and threat.
3. The store's objectives may be classified into :
   (*a*) Primary and secondary (*b*) Internal and external
   (*c*) Ins and outs (*d*) Inferior and superior
4. Strategic gap is the difference between :-
   (*a*) Store's current and future positions.
   (*b*) Store's profit and loss.
   (*c*) Store's achievable and non achievable objective.
   (*d*) Company's own standing vs competitiors standing.
5. Internal analysis is used to study :
   (*a*) opportunity and threat (*b*) profit and loss
   (*c*) strength and weakness (*d*) employees and resources
6. Marketing is the way to achieve ?
   (*a*) Sales targets (*b*) Segment the market
   (*c*) Competing efficiently (*d*) Set objectives

7. Marketing strategy should be devised according to
   (*a*) Competitors (Market trends) (*b*) resources available
   (*c*) Capacity of marketing team (*d*) Primary and secondary objectives
8. Retail positioning is to create and maintain :
   (*a*) Profits (*b*) Unique image
   (*c*) Goodwill (*d*) Customers
9. Success of strategy implementation depends on :-
   (*a*) retail mix (*b*) team work
   (*c*) personal selling efforts (*d*) store's internal and external environment
10. ICT means :
    (*a*) Information and communication technology
    (*b*) Income, cost and trade
    (*c*) Income, cost and transport
    (*d*) Internet and communication technology
11. Multiplicity of government approvals poses _______before a business firms :-
    (*a*) opportunity (*b*) strength
    (*c*) hurdle (*d*) no impact
12. The quality standards in Indian retail industry as compared to peers are :-
    (*a*) high (*b*) at par
    (*c*) substandard (*d*) unique
13. What poses threat before a retail industry as a whole ?
    (*a*) Shortage of trained and educated H.R.
    (*b*) Quality standards problem
    (*c*) Supply chain inefficiencies
    (*d*) All of the above
14. What are the opportunities before Indian retail sector :
    (*a*) Entrepreneurial opportunities (*b*) Managerial opportunities
    (*c*) None of the above (*d*) Both of the above
15. According KPMG, the key challenge before Indian retailers is :-
    (*a*) High Distribution cost (*b*) Infrastructure constraints
    (*c*) Fragmented Market (*d*) All of the above
16. India has approximately ______ retailers.
    (*a*) 8 million (*b*) 10 million
    (*c*) 12 million (*d*) 14 million
17. Wal-Mart is a :
    (*a*) Indian retailer (*b*) U.S. based retailer
    (*c*) U.K. based retailer (*d*) China based retailer

18. External Analysis deals with :
    (*a*) Economic environment of retailing.
    (*b*) Political environment of retailing.
    (*c*) Socio-cultural environment of retailing.
    (*d*) All of the above
19. USP stands for
    (*a*) Unique selling point (*b*) Unique source positioning
    (*c*) Unique selling parameters (*d*) Unique selling preposition
20. Internal Analysis deals with :-
    (*a*) Human resources (*b*) Financial resources
    (*c*) Physical resources (*d*) All of the above

Answers

1. a	2. d	3. a	4. a
5. d	6. d	7. d	8. b
9. b	10. a	11. c	12. c
13. d	14. d	15. d	16. c
17. b	18. d	19. d	20. d

Check Your Progress

1. What is ICT?
2. What is SWOT?
3. What is Mission?
4. What do you mean by objective?
5. What is USP?
6. What is intangible resource?
7. What is retail positioning?
8. What is inspection?
9. What is opportunity?
10. What is threat?

Small Answer Questions

1. What do you mean by retail mix? Discuss the concept of retail positioning?
2. Differentiate between external and internal store objectives?
3. Write a short note on situational analysis?
4. Discuss the importance of SWOT analysis? What are the three aspects of strategic control?
5. Why international operations are required?

6. Briefly explain the advantages of strategic planning?
7. Explain the role of a centralized retailer?
8. Why finance is said to be the 'lifeline' of a retail business?
9. What do you mean by management of employees? Is it right to say that success of a retail store depends on a retailer's policy rather than HR resources?
10. Is always international retailing a business of profit?

Long Answer Questions

1. What do you mean by retail strategy? Explain the process of retail planning with suitable examples wherever necessary?
2. What guidelines you would like to suggest to a new comer retailer to face market threats effectively and avail opportunity in the best possible manner?
3. Do you agree that management of retail store is a complex matter? If yes how? Critically access the role of a centralized retailer in modern era and discuss an integrated approach to retailing?

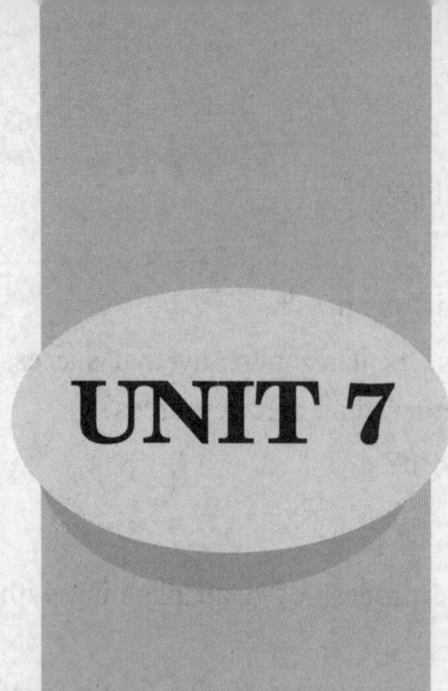

FINANCIAL STRATEGY

LEARNING OBJECTIVES

- Describe the essence of operations management in retailing.
- Discussing the need, utility and structure of profit planning.
- Understanding the financial aspects of operations management.
- Examining the effectiveness of resource allocation.
- Evaluating and describing asset management including key business ratios.

"God gave me my money. I believe the power to make money is a gift from God... to be developed & used to the best of our ability for the good of mankind. Having been endowed with the gift I possess, I believe it is my duty to make money & still more money & to use the money I make for the good of my fellow man according to the dictates of my conscience."

– John D. Rockefeller

INTRODUCTION

Finance is the backbone of any successful business. Be it manufacturing, whole selling or even retailing, without finance no business can survive for long. The retail business that makes consistent profits can survive in the long run and continue to offer products and services to the consumers. A retail firm requires finance to run their business and meet day to day requirements. For the success of a business, there should be continuous movements of funds in and outside the firm. Once a retailer has finalized its organizational structure, it concentrates on operations management. Operations management plays a vital role in a company growth and profitability. This chapter covers the financial aspects of a retail business (operations Management) with emphasis on budgeting, forecasting, profit planning, leverage management, asset management, and optimum resource allocation.

RETAIL CASH FLOW MANAGEMENT

Retail cash flow management is the procedure of monitoring, analyzing, and adjusting the cash flow that comes through selling merchandise. For retail business, the most important part of cash flow management is to avoid extensive cash shortages due to increased gap between cash inflows and outflows. The larger the gap, the more the chances the store will be out of competition. Therefore, effective cash flow management is imperative in planning and in the competent functioning of all aspects of retail operations.

Making money and increasing cash base is not the only part of efficient cash flow management. When a retail store is not able to maintain the optimum balance between cash inflows (the money received through selling the merchandise) and cash outflows (the money paid to vendors and for store expenses), it may not be able to pay the salary to its employees and suppliers' bills. Consequently, the retail organization may be profitable one as per financial statements but in actual it is unable to pay the bills on time. Further, in case of credit facility, if customers do not pay their due bills or pay very gradually in installments, the retail organization may still find unable to pay the employees' salary. Therefore, organization should manage its funds effectively otherwise shortage of cash will result in increased costs, such as late fines if electric, water bills are not paid to government. Further, if loans are not paid to bank or other private lenders, again the organization should be ready to pay hefty penalties.

Effective cash flow management can eliminate these unnecessary costs and make the store financially sound enough to pay their all minor and major bills well in time and create competitive advantage and create the opportunity for more favorable payment terms on some types of purchases. Finally, organizations those know the benefits of effective cash flow management, improve the manner in which they receive the cash through merchandise selling and make proper provisions to make their timely payments.

ISSUES INVOLVED IN EFFECTIVE CASH FLOW MANAGEMENT

From the above discussion it is very much clear that the retail organizations would not be able to continue their day to day operations if they can not pay their monthly bills before the due date. Therefore, the retailers should make proper arrangements to perform a regular cash flow analysis. Use of timely cash flow forecasting can make it easy for retailer to take the necessary steps before the problem of cash inflow and outflow get worsens. Retailer can take the expertise of financial professional. These days retail organizations are also using various accounting software programs that have built-in reporting features and make it easy for the retailer to analyze the cash flow whenever and wherever required by only a mouse click button. Following issues must be considered for managing cash flow effectively and prudently.

1. Developing and using payment strategies that will maintain sufficient cash flow throughout the year. One of such most useful strategies for retail organization is to lessen the cash flow conversion period so that cash should come in business faster.

2. Offering cash discount policy to customers will make them clear their payments in cash. Further, customers who pay their invoices early should be given some early payment discount for say 2.5 percent, will motivate others to pay their bills on time.
3. The retail organizations that are in service sectors like wall paints, repair and maintenance, and software development can ask their customers for paying certain part of the total payment before the service actually starts.
4. Accounting software can help you know the past due defaulters but it depends on the part of organization that how much active and serious it is about such collections. Organizations should do proper arrangement to have an apparent method for pursuing such pending collections. Now organization can adopt reminder method in which series of letters are sent to tell the customers about their unpaid bills pending in their account. Some of the stores when find it difficult to collect the payment, give such cases to recovery/collection agencies.
5. By having a vigilant eye on organizational cash flow, retailers can make arrangements to eliminate it. One of the most effective ways that most of the retail organizations adopt is the continuous monitoring of store's cash flows and its comparative analysis at every fortnight/month so that retail business can bring in money faster.
6. The variety of income a retail organization receives, ultimately decides the cash flow management strategy an organization should consider.

WHO IS RESPONSIBLE FOR EFFECTIVE CASH FLOW MANAGEMENT?

Each retailer has funds to manage and liabilities to control. But question arises being responsible for store's day to day operations, is he the only person who should be made accountable for cash flow management. When this is the duty of finance department, why finance personnel should not be made accountable if the gap between cash inflows and cash outflows is continuously unpleasant. Actually retail business like other businesses, depends on team efforts. Therefore, ideally, all employees, management, and supervisors including finance personnel of finance department should develop 'cash flow awareness.'

Every employee, be it at floor level staff or at supervisory level can improve organizational cash flow by understanding the pertinent issues. For example, floor staff should always suggest the best selling merchandise to be purchased by the organization. Bill section staff can motivate the customers for cash payment. Customer care staff can play its vital role in building store image. When retail store staff lacks clear cash flow understanding and related guidelines or do not follow policies laid down, will result in negative cash flow.

Besides this, managerial staff and board members should understand their respective roles in effective cash flow management. Experience has shown that floor staff and management at every stage can be more committed in tackling adverse cash flow situation if cash flow issues are frequently attended during organizational meetings. Creating an environment for spreading awareness, queries, and follow up can make certain that each employee is working toward the common objective of store's cash flow enhancement. The employees those are directly involved in financial planning, fund raising activities and implementation of cash flows should devote more time. If the above said suggestions are duly acknowledged and the employees concerned give it same level of preferences, organizations would find a remarkable improvement in their fiscal health.

HANDY TIPS FOR MANAGING CASH FLOWS EFFECTIVELY

Retailers have always a big question before them i.e. how they should manage cash flows effectively. Undoubtedly cash management has been a complex matter for retailers always but can be made easier if we follow these handy tips:

1. Try to get the pending money from customers as soon as possible and pay the store's bills at the last possible moment to use it effectively.
2. Concentrate store's inflows and outflows to a single bank account.
3. To speed up customers' orders and deliveries, prompt them to place orders before they come over phone or mail.
4. Send all your invoices, bills the same day merchandise are delivered, not next day or next week.
5. Mention clearly the last date of payment on invoice and also the penalty for late payment.
6. If your store accepts payment through bank checks or cross drafts, make provision for depositing them same day because you in some cases will loose interest.
7. Instruct your cashiers not to deposit checks in a bank's automated teller machines (ATMs) as you have no evidence of depositing these checks.
8. Make certain the financial soundness of a new customer before offering him any credit facility.
9. While offering credit service to a new customer, ask him for three business references and do not neglect to call them.
10. Do not offer too generous discount schemes, such as ten percent discount on cash payment. A better rate in Indian retailing is between two to five percent.
11. Do not hesitate to charge late fee to customers who do not pay on time and charge back customers who enjoy discounts even after the discount period.
12. Instead of giving advances to store's employees, better you should ask them to use their personal credit cards. (if any)
13. If your retail store deals in more than one particular product, identify which product accounts for seventy five percent of your total sales. Then reduce the orders of other products that have poor sales in your retail store.

Last but not the least; ask your bank to send you a monthly or fortnightly bank analysis report that contains both the ledger and available balance of cash.

BUDGET AND BUDGETARY CONTROL

Modern retailing is full of competition, uncertainty and exposed to different types of risks. The complexity of retailing business has led to the development of various managerial tools, techniques and procedures useful for retailers in managing their business successfully. Budgeting is the most popular financial device to control the various activities of retailing business. The budgeting outlines a retailer's planned expenditures for a certain period of time. The budgetary control has now become an essential tool of the management for controlling various costs and increasing profit base.

Retail Budget: A retail budget is a financial plan or blue print of overall financial transactions that shows how the resources will be acquired and used over a period of time.

Budgetary Control: It is the use of budgets as a means of controlling financial activities.

Budgeting: Budgeting refers to the management's action of formulating budgets to facilitate various departments to operate efficiently and economically.

In short, a plan showing how resources will be required and used over a specified time interval is called Budget. The act of preparing a budget is called budgeting and the use of budgets as a means of regulating financial operations is Budgetary Control. Budgetary control starts with the budgeting and ends with control.

Types of Budgets: In retailing business normally budgets are prepared on two bases:

1. On the basis of expenditure: It can further be divided into two heads:
   (i) Capital expenditure budget
   (ii) Operating budget
2. On the basis of activity:
   (i) Fixed budget, and
   (ii) Flexible budget

FORECAST AND BUDGET

In the world of retailing, forecast is mainly concerned with probable events on the other hand budget is concerned with planned events.

- Forecast may be done for longer time but budget is always prepared for shorter periods.
- Forecast is usually a tentative estimate and can be revised as per management requirements and the need of the time while budget remains unchanged for the budget period.
- Forecast is usually applied where there is no control over the events such as forecast of FDI in retailing in the years to come while a budget is endeavor to control the events.
- In short, forecast is the foundation on which a budget is built.

INCOME STATEMENT

A profit and loss account or a Income Statement is the statement of the profit earned or loss incurred during an accounting year, usually a month, a quarter, or a year. This represents a summary of a retailer's revenues and expenses over a particular period of time. Such as April1, 2010 to March 31, 2011 versus April 1, 2011 to March 31, 2012, in order to analyze the profitability. Continuous exercise of preparing income statements can help a retailer in knowing how a firm is performing towards the achievement of company's goals and objectives. Under income statement, income (profit) represents the amount by which retailer's revenues during an accounting year exceeds the expenses incurred during that year. The word profit is used with the several qualifying objectives like gross profit, profit after tax (PAT), profit before tax (PBT) and net profit.

A profit or loss account or an income statement has the following components:

Net Sales

The term Net sales refer to the total revenues received by a retailer after deducting consumer refunds, discounts and all markdowns during a particular period of time, normally one year.

Cost of Goods Sold

This is the amount paid by a retailer to acquire the merchandise sold during a financial year. It is calculated by purchase prices plus freight charges (if any) less all commissions and discounts like (trade discount, cash discount, etc)

Gross Margin

This is also known as Gross profit and gives the retailer a measure of how much profit it is making on merchandise sales without considering operating expenses.

Gross Margins = Net sales - Cost of goods sold

In other words, it consists of operating expenses plus net profit.

Operating Expenses

These are incurred on running a retail business in the normal course of business.

Operating Expenses		
1	Administrative Expenses	Employees salaries + Operations of buying departments + miscellaneous expenses
2	General Expenses	Store rent + electricity bill + water bill + house tax etc
3	Selling Expenses	Sales staff salaries + bonus + commissions

Net Profit: It is the measure of a retail firm. It is expressed either before or after taxes. Generally the firm's overall performance reflects when it is calculated after taxes.

Net Profit = Gross Margin — Expenses

Specimen of an Income statement			
		(in rupees)	
Net Sales	-	22,20,000	
Cost of goods sold	-	11,70,000	
			10,50,000
Operating Expenses:			
Salaries	-	6,24,500	
Advertising	-	22,000	
Insurance	-	13,300	
Repair & Maintenance	-	1,700	
Rent	-	49,000	
Courier & postage	-	1,000	
Misc.	-	4,500	
Total	-	7,16,000	
Other Expenses	-	24,000	
Total Costs	-		7,40,000
Net Profit Before Taxes	-		3,10,000

ASSET MANAGEMENT

Each retailer has assets to manage and liabilities to control. It is the retailer' ability and efficiency how effectively he manages the inputs and outputs. The proper way to find out the financial soundness of a going business at certain moment is to prepare balance sheet. Balance sheet is a statement that reports the values owned by the retail firm and the claims of the creditors and owners against these properties. The period of time is an accounting period/year – The Balance comprises of firm's assets, liabilities and capital at a given date of time. It is static in nature because it tells about the financial position (financial soundness) of a retailing firm as on a certain date. Thus, the Balance sheet of a firm prepared on 31st March reveals the firm's financial position on this specific date.

In an organization, balance sheet is known by different titles (names). These are:

- Statement of assets and liabilities
- Statement of resources and liabilities
- Statement of financial position
- Statement of financial soundness
- Statement of assets, liabilities and owners fund etc
- Balance sheet/ General balance sheet
- Statement of stocks/position

However, in India the most widely used title is "Balance sheet". A balance sheet is supposed to be prepared considering the following basic principles of accounting. Each retailer is expected to know all these principles listed below:

(a) Business entity concept
(b) Monetary unit concept
(c) Going concern concept
(d) Conservatism concept
(e) Cost concept
(f) Accounting equation concept

The retail organization is regarded as a business entity separate from its shareholders. The financial position of a retail organization is shown in a balance sheet in financial terms (rupees). The business organization (retail firm) is considered as going concern, i.e. it has continuous existence till such time as it is legally elucidated. The conservatism concept of business means the philosophy of a business to "anticipate no profit but make provision for all losses". The cost concept implies that financial values of all the assets should be recorded on their market price. According to accounting equation concept, each financial transaction has dual effects, and therefore, a balance sheet indicates the value of all the assets on one side and the liabilities on the other side.

Basic Divisions of Balance Sheet

	Assets		Liabilities
1.	Current assets	1.	Current liabilities
2.	Fixed assets	2.	Non-current liabilities
3.	Intangible assets	3.	Net worth
4.	Other assets		
5.	Deferred expenditure		

These are explained below:

A. Assets: It is an item valuable to run a retail business. The value of an asset may be defined in terms of its capacity to be instrumental in selling of goods and services.

1. Current Assets

These are the assets acquired through cash and easily convertible into cash during the normal course of retail business. These are as follows:

(a) Cash in hand and cash at bank
(b) Inventory on hand
(c) Bills receivable
(d) Government or other marketable securities held by a retailer
(e) Advance payments by a retailing firm.

2. Fixed Assets

These are the items a retailer owns/acquires for the purpose of running a retail firm smoothly. These assets are not for selling purpose to earn profit and are used over a considerable period of time. These are as follows:

(a) Land
(b) Building (retail store, warehouse and so on)
(c) Retail store fixtures and furniture
(d) Conveyance means (trucks, vans, delivery scooters/cars, etc)
(e) Equipments such as cash registers, leasehold improvements.

3. Intangible Assets

Contrary to tangible assets like land, furniture and fixtures, intangible items cannot be seen, touch or realized but are important for any retail business. Intangible assets include the retailer's rights and include the following:

(a) Patents and Trademarks,
(b) Goodwill, and
(c) Copyright, composition/formula, licence etc

4. Other Assets

These are the assets, which cannot be included in any of the above-mentioned categories and therefore are termed as other assets. These assets by nature are tangible but are not used in the normal course of business, like:

(a) Non-trade debtors
(b) Investments excluding marketable securities
(c) Fund earmarked for assets.

5. Deferred Expenditures

As the very name implies, these expenditures are not of recurring nature and do not arise from the present operations. The benefit of such expenditures is that they provide income or benefit in the coming years also. These are paid in advance and written off gradually over few years of business operations, treating each year's share in such expenditure as a charge on operational profit for that year. These include preliminary expenses, advertising expenditure etc.

B. Liabilities: These usually are the financial obligations of a retailer incurse in operating business.

1. Current Liabilities: Current liabilities of a retailer include such obligations or charges that are payable either on demand or in the coming year. All short-term obligations generally due and payable within one year are termed as current liabilities. These include:

(a) Taxes
(b) Short-term loans
(c) Accounts payable
(d) Bank overdraft
(e) Unclaimed dividends
(f) Short-term public deposits
(g) Outstanding or accruals

2. Non-current Liabilities

These are generally the debts of a retailer and are paid over a longer period of time, as after one year. These liabilities are also popularly known as long-term liabilities. These include:

(a) Loan or mortgage

(b) Loans from banks and/or financial institutions

(c) Bonds or debentures

3. Net Worth: Net worth is the excess of the firm's assets over its liabilities. It shows the financial interests of a retailer and is also known as retailer's equity. Sometimes, net worth is also called by the names of net assets, retailer's equity, shareholders' fund, net employed capital etc.

ASSET TURNOVER RATIO

Asset turnover ratio is a retailer's performance measure with regard to its net sales and total assets. The ratio measures the overall performance and activity of a retail organization. It is computed as under:

Asset Turnover = Net Sales/Total Assets

Asset turnover ratio is also known as activity ratios because it highlights the ability of management to convert or turnover the assets of retailing firms into sales. This makes enable a retailer to study the level of sales and the investment in various assets accounts. A sharp rise in this ratio may indicate that the company is expanding too quickly. Conversely any declinc in the ratio indicates a decline in the retailer's efficiency or decline in retailer's products demand.

FINANCIAL LEVERAGE

Leverage indicates how cffectively a retail company uses its borrowed funds to increase the retailer's return on equity. It measures the contribution of financing by retailer's creditors. Financial leverage is a performance measure based on relationship between a retailer's total assets and net worth. High financial leverage indicates that the retailer has substantial debt while a ratio of 1 indicates no use of debt by retailer i.e. assets are equal to net worth. This ratio is expressed as under:

Financial leverage = Total assets/Net worth

***Note**: In case of increasing or high financial leverage, retailer needs to either increase short term store sales by any efforts or to decrease expenditures so that the saving should be used to make large interest payments.*

High financial leverage can lead a retailing firm towards bankruptcy because of non or delay in payments of outstanding debts. On the other hand, low financial leverage ratio increases the retailer's ability to spend money on expansion plans or repair or maintenance. In nutshell, low leverage ratio means retailer's equity is more as compared to debt or marked securities (debt/loan).

RETAILER'S STRATEGIC PROFIT MODEL

The strategic profit model in actual is nothing but a numerical relationship among retailer's net profit margin, asset turnover and financial leverage. It indicates the retailer's return on net worth. A retailer applies strategic profit model in planning or controlling assets. This model numerically expressed as under:

Return on net worth = Net Profit × Asset Turnover × Financial Leverage

$$= \frac{\text{Net Profit}}{\text{Net sales}} \times \frac{\text{Net sales}}{\text{Total Assets}} \times \frac{\text{Total Assets}}{\text{Net worth}}$$

$$= \frac{\text{Net Profit}}{\text{Net Worth}}$$

***Note**: According to retailer's strategic profit model, a retail firm can raise its return on net worth by raising the net profit margin, asset turnover or financial leverage. The reason behind such increase is that these measures ultimately constitute the return on net worth.*

OTHER KEY FINANCIAL RATIOS:

1. Quick Ratio

Quick ratio provides the retailer's ability to meet its day to day business obligations. It signifies a short term (Usually less than one year) liquidity of a retail firm and is computed by current assets minus stock and dividend divided by current liabilities. The philosophy behind deducting stock from current assets is that the stock may not be reduced immediately. This ratio is expressed as under:

Quick ratio = Current Assets – (Stock) / Current liabilities

Note: A quick ratio of 1:1 is usually considered ideal and satisfactory. A quick ratio greater than 1:1 implies that the firm is liquid and has quick ability to pay its short term obligations.

2. Current Ratio

Current ratio indicates the retailer's financial condition (ability) to meet normal operating obligations. It is calculated by dividing current assets by current liabilities. A high current ratio indicates the retailer's financial soundness and the ability to meet its current obligations. A ratio of 2:1 or 2 is a good measure of a retailer's current position. The ratio is expressed as under:

$$\text{Current Ratio} = \frac{\text{Current Assets}}{\text{Current Liabilities}}$$

The current assets of a retailing firm, as already discussed are those assets which in the normal course of action are easily convertible into cash within a short period of time say less than one year like cash and bank balances, work in progress, stock etc. The current liabilities on the other hand are to be paid in one year of time like bank credit, bills payable and outstanding expenses.

3. Accounts Payable to Net Sales

This ratio is used to know the retailer's ability to pay to its suppliers for the volume transacted. This is computed by accounts payable divided by Net Sales. Then this figure is usually compared to industry average to know how much a retailer is financially dependent on suppliers.

4. Gross Profit Margin

This ratio is used to measure the relationship between retailer's profit and sales volume. This is commonly known as gross margin. It is computed by dividing gross profit by sales.

$$\text{Gross profit margin} = \frac{\text{Gross profits}}{\text{Sales}} \times 100$$

The gross margin represents the limit beyond which any fall in sales prices are outside the retailer's tolerance limit.

5. Collection Period

Collection period denotes the amounts retained/owed by customers in case of credit sales. It is computed by accounts receivable divided by net sales and then multiplied it by 365. High collection period means retailing firm has more credit sales.

SETTING PERFORMANCE OBJECTIVE

As it is evident that today field of retailing is a lucrative and first options for an entrepreneur or a business tycoon. Therefore, each successful businessman is looking for retail business. Be it Reliance Fresh of Reliance Industries or 'More' of Aditya Birla Group or Walmart Bharti Joint venture, all present stiff competition in the retail industry. Due to erratic sales, increasing competition, rising human costs, and other resources, retailers are giving stress on improving store's productivity. Productivity refers to the retail store's output relative to its inputs. In simple terms productivity refers to the goods and services sold with the resources used. Productivity in the field of retailing is calculated as:

$$\text{Productivity} = \frac{\text{Quantity of goods and services produced}}{\text{Amount of resources used}}$$

It is very clear from above equation that in productivity there are two variables – the amount of sale and the amount of resources used. Productivity varies with the amount of sale relative to the amount of resources used. Productivity can be improved in these following ways.

I. Increase in sales with usage of same marketing and human resources.

II. Reducing the amount of resources (Human, Marketing etc.) without hampering the sale or even sometime increasing it.

III. Allowing the amount of resources used to increase as long as sales increases more.

IV. Allowing production to reduce as long as the amount of resources used decreases more.

It depends on the retailer which method it will apply to improve productivity but main thing, productivity needs to be improved as increased productivity contributes to the competitive advantage of a retail firm.

Some applied practices :

- Some food stores have been offering 'take away' or 'only packaging' services in their stores resulting in space productivity.
- Conversion of manual operations to automatic brings human productivity.
- Some stores like 'Tuesday Morning' in US operates only in 225 days in a year to save operating and administrative costs.

Productivity

Merits

- Company can pay higher remuneration to its employees
- Higher output from same/less inputs
- Selling cost per unit (SCPU) can be reduced
- Benefits whole economy
- Shareholders are better pay off

Note

Improving productivity always does not mean adding/increasing inputs but using the resources in a better way. Improving productivity doesn't mean store employees should work more or sit late hours but work smart.

SUMMARY

Managing finance effectively and prudently has always been a crucial issue for retailers world wide. Financial aspects of a retail firm can only be managed effectively if firm has proper accounting system in place. Besides having proper records of profit and loss, it covers the way how finance will be raised, managed. Financial aspects, start from forecasting, profit management and lead to increased productivity. For the long term survival and to get a competitive edge over competitors, a retailer has to maintain proper records of cash inflows and outflows. How assets are being managed, what is the status of current ratio and return on net worth should be continuously monitored. In nutshell, don't enter into a business that you don't know how to manage and run.

CASE STUDY # LEADERSHIP REDEFINED

Two years down the line, the dream is a pleasant reality. But there are many who believe that if the dream run has to indeed be along term success story, then there are several issues that the textile-magnate-turned-aviation entrepreneur will have to address urgently. For one, there is virtually no management structure in place. "If Paramount has to be a long term player it needs to have a clear team in place that oversees not just the day-to-day operations, but strategies on the long term vision. The vision of the founder sometimes simply is not enough".

Perhaps that is reason why Thaigarajan is slowly putting people in place. He recently hired two experts to look at key areas – operations and maintenance – of the company's business. He is also looking at hiring others although those who have known him well and interacted with him believe that it is unlikely that there will ever be ***"a hands-off approach"*** as far as Thiagarajan is concerned. Their logic is simple: he is passionate about the airline business and loves to dabble in every aspect of it. Interestingly, of the 36 pilots on board Paramount, 23 are foreign (primarily Thai, the Director –Operations is also one). And, his cabin crew has a pan-Indian flavor right form the plains of Punjab to the distant drums of the North East.

Considering the Paramount announcement to move to the west in 2008 and then slowly, pan out across the rest of the country, it makes sense to get his team in place. Not just that, Thiagarajan states that in daring to dream bigger to make Paramount Airways a truly national airline in four years, he will continue to constantly upgrade his product. So for starters, his jets will continue with the ***'no middle seats'*** concept, the cuisine will continue to be eclectic and varied (Thaigarajan prefers the word gourmet). But he is adding a huge dose of in-flight entertainment with personalized TVs, telecasting current programmes and a mobile link from a sky. All this will cost a lot of money and will the passengers pay? Thiagarajan thinks they will, considering his fares even today are more than the so-called full carriers Jet and Kingfisher charge on similar routes (Thaigarajan says his prices are about 10-15% higher). And to make sure that he was able to fill the aircraft, the airline apparently signed bulk deal with scores of companies. The Paramount chief claims that closer to 90% of his passengers belong to this segment and this is not a ***"price sensitive, but price inelastic band"***. Nonetheless, it won't be a cakewalk as his fleet grows and the market expands. Most recently, the Southern head of Jet Airways stated the 40% of Jet's business was generated in the South and it was growing. Soon Silk Air of Singapore will be flying direct to Coimbatore from the city-state in South-East Asia besides increasing the frequency of SIA to Southern cities of India. Malaysia is planning to increase its frequency to Southern cities.

Perhaps, he sees an opportunity in all these threats. For instance, his Brazil-made all-Embraer can fly non-stop for four hours and can reach Singapore and

KL from his Southern stations. Perhaps, once he completes five years in the flying business or if the government reduces it to three years, he will be ready to fly out.

As on date Paramount has five leased Embraers of which two are E-170 type with 70 seats all business class and three E-175 aircraft with 75 seats comprising 11 first class and 64 business class. The airline prides itself for not offering a Middle Seat to anyone as it does not have one in its aircraft nor is planning to have one in any of its 40 Embraer aircraft it is planning to acquire over the next four to five years at a MoU declared value of US $ 2 billion. The deliveries of these 40 aircrafts will be between mid 2008 and 2011. US $ 2 billion in Indian rupees before it appreciated in early 2007 was equivalent to Rs 8800 crores. Today, it is Rs 7900 crores. So, even before he begins to buy, Thaigarajan is lucky that his same rupee earnings will fetch him more dollars. So, where is the money coming from? From the promoter and debt.

As the fleet strength grows over the next four years, Paramount will add 280 Indian and 120 expat pilots adding up to 400 pilots. There has been no pilot attrition from his airline. Though one may say nobody flies Embraers in India other than Paramount, so where would they go, the fact is that they seem happy with the company and have not left for better pastures overseas. Thiagarajan is proud of this: "Our attrition rate is zero," he claims in a matter-of-fact tone.

Another favorite phrase of the Paramount MD is *"boutique brand"*. So what do you mean by that? Clearly what Thiagarajan means that is being different and classy, the fares are higher, the planes – the only ones of its kind in the country – and the food..... well "gourmet".

"We have marketed some of our city pair flights such a way that businessmen can have their breakfast on board, then attending meetings and return by afternoon to have lunch on board or if they wish dinner, depending upon when they choose to end their business meetings," he says.

The Paramount argument for managing all this is the huge focus on costs. Fuel costs are only 20% of its total operational cost as against 30-35% for other airlines including big dads. Moreover, as his jets are configured to carry less than 80 passengers he also enjoys all the concessions that are available to regional carriers including the crucial exemption from the payment of landing charges.

There is also a bit of tough negotiation and bargaining. Just two weeks back, Thiagarajan was in Kerala to meet with the top brass of the State government. He told the CM that Paramount was ready and keen to connect the three important international airport cities of Kochi, Thiruvananthapuram and Kozhikode provided the Kerala government assure him that 30-40% seats per flight would be booked by the state government for its official travel between the three cities.

Knowing Thiagarajan, one can, perhaps, speculate that he must be having in the back of his mind complete parking arrangement so that he may use his Embraers to tap the Gulf-rich business from Kerala once the Ministry of Civil Aviation takes a final call on who all can fly overseas.

But there are some areas of his business that Thiagarajan is unwilling to talk about. "I do not want to speculate," he said plainly. But those in the know state that financial institutions have been talking to him among who are some who hold nearly 62% in Delhi-based SpiceJet. Asked if his intention was to only take over the parking bays and slots, will it not be too high a price to be pais as realized by Naresh Goyal of Jet for taking over Sahara, Thaigarajan grins and then slowly answers: "This is no reference to SpiceJet. I am not taking any names. But the answer is obviously not. It will be based on

Valuationa and association." Clearly, he does not want to talk any further on the issue, though his appetite for a bigger share of the pie is evident. Similarly, he is non-committal when it comes to a little more insight on his plans to acquire both narrow and wide body aircraft made by Boeing and Airbus. He says blandly, "We are looking at it." He has actually been talking to both and tossing the options.

In essence that really sums up the man and his mission. Keep the powder dry, keep tossing the options and keep pegging away. If you have a good business plan, you will walk away the winner!

Paramount's Fleet Plans

Thiagarajan is looking at the bigger Embraer jets for the simple reason that like the Airbus family there is a huge amount of commonality in the cockpit and the engineering. So, it is easy for the engineers and the pilots to migrate back and forth. At the moment, While two are owned, three are on lease. One more aircraft – Embraer 175 – will join the fleet by end October/early November. Paramount is looking at the total of nine aircraft to service the Southern market. All the five aircrafts are parked at Chennai at the moment and the airline has permission for three more. Beyond eight, they are looking at Hyderabad and Bangalore as possible options. The airline has committed for 20 more Embraer 175s to join the fleet, although they have 40 aircraft on order. Some of the balance could be bigger aircraft from the same company. "Embraer has bigger aircraft and the fleet commonality is an advantage. We will automatically evolve. By 2011, our fleet strength will be close to 40 aircraft. Our aircraft will start arriving from the middle of 2008," said Thaigarajan.

Source: *Cruising Heights, October'07*

Questions for Discussion:

Q1 In two years, Paramount Airways has quietly built a steady reputation as a quality business class carrier out of Chennai. Is it a flash in the pan or is M Thaiagarajan a marathon man. Comment?

Q2 Outline the potential cost savings associated with Paramount and other airlines?

Q3 Comment on the pros and cons of Murugesan Thigarajan's leadership, administration and future plans?

Q4 What factors could account for any airline retailer's requiring to re-engineer its operations?

REVIEW QUESTIONS

True and False Questions

1. Retail cash flow management is the procedure of monitoring, analyzing, and adjusting the cash flow that comes through selling merchandise.
2. A retail budget is a financial plan or blue print of overall financial transactions that shows how the resources will be acquired and used over a period of time.
3. Budgetary Control is the use of budgets as a means of controlling financial activities.
4. Budgeting refers to the management's action of formulating budgets to facilitate various departments to operate efficiently and economically.
5. On the basis of expenditure, budget can be divided in to:
   (i) Fixed budget, and
   (ii) Flexible budget
6. On the basis of activity, budget can be classified as:
   (i) Capital expenditure budget, and
   (ii) Operating budget
7. Forecast is usually a tentative estimate and can not be revised as per management requirements and the need of the time while budget remains unchanged for the budget period.
8. A profit and loss account or an Income Statement is the statement of the profit earned or loss incurred during minimum five accounting years.
9. Net Sales refer to the total revenues received by a retailer after deducting consumer refunds, discounts and all markdowns during a particular period of time, normally one decade.
10. Cost of Goods Sold is the amount paid by a retailer to acquire the merchandise sold during a financial year. It is calculated by purchase prices minus freight charges (if any) plus all commissions and discounts like (trade discount, cash discount, etc).
11. Gross Margin is also known as Gross profit and gives the retailer a measure of how much profit it is making on merchandise sales without considering operating expenses.
12. Current assets are the assets acquired through cash and easily convertible into cash during the normal course of retail business.
13. Current liabilities of a retailer include such obligations or charges that are payable either on demand or in the previous year.
14. Net worth is the excess of the firm's assets over its liabilities that shows the financial interests of a retailer and is also known as retailer's equity.

15. Leverage indicates how effectively a retail company uses its borrowed funds to increase the retailer's return on equity.
16. High financial leverage can lead a retailing firm towards bankruptcy because of no payment or delay in payments of outstanding debts.
17. The strategic profit model in actual is nothing but a numerical relationship among retailer's net profit margin, asset turnover and financial leverage.
18. Quick ratio provides the retailer's ability to meets its day to day business obligations and signifies a long term liquidity of a retail firm and is computed by fixed assets minus stock and dividend divided by fixed liabilities.
19. A quick ratio of 10:1 is usually considered ideal and satisfactory.
20. Collection period denotes the amounts retained/owed by customers in case of credit sales.

Answers

1. True	2. True	3. True	4. True
5. False	6. False	7. False	8. False
9. False	10. False	11. True	12. False
13. False	14. True	15. True	16. True
17. True	18. False	19. False	20. True

Multiple Choice Questions

1. Improving organisational cash flow is the responsibility of :-
   (*a*) store manager (*b*) finance personcl
   (*c*) floor level staff (*d*) all of the above
2. ATM stands for :
   (*a*) All time money (*b*) Automatic Tele machine
   (*c*) Automatic teller machine (*d*) Automatic Trap machine
3. Retail Budget is a financial plan of :-
   (*a*) Overall financial transactions (*b*) Cash in flows
   (*c*) Cash out flows (*d*) None of the above
4. The task of using budgets as a means of controlling financial activities is known as :-
   (*a*) Budgeting (*b*) Budgetory control
   (*c*) Income statement (*d*) Asset Management
5. A Budget is concerned with :-
   (*a*) Probable events (*b*) Planned events
   (*c*) None of the above (*d*) Both of the above

6. Forecast is mainly concerned with :-
   (*a*) Probable Event (*b*) Planned Event
   (*c*) Both of the above (*d*) None of the above
7. Budget is usually prepared for :-
   (*a*) Short period (*b*) Long period
   (*c*) Medium period (*d*) Knowing past accounting mistakes
8. Income statement is also known as ;-
   (*a*) Balance sheet (*b*) Trial Balance
   (*c*) Profit & Loss Account (*d*) All of the above
9. The formulae to calculate gross margin is :-
   (*a*) Net sales + Cost of goods sold.
   (*b*) Net sales – Cost of goods sold.
   (*c*) Gross Margin – Expenses.
   (*d*) Gross Margin + Expenses.
10. Net profit is expressed as :-
    (*a*) Net sales – Cost of goods sold.
    (*b*) Net sales + Cost of goods sold.
    (*c*) Gross Margin – Expenses.
    (*d*) Gross Margin + Expenses.
11. On the basis of expenditure, budgets are divided as :
    (*a*) Capital expenditure budget and operating budget.
    (*b*) Fixed and Flexible Budget.
    (*c*) Short term and long Budget.
12. Balance sheet is also known as :
    (*a*) Statement of assets and liabilities.
    (*b*) Statement of financial position.
    (*c*) Statement of resources and liabilities.
    (*d*) All of the above.
13. Basic divisions of Balance sheet are :
    (*a*) Assets and liabilities (*b*) Profit and loss
    (*c*) Inflows and outflows (*d*) None of the above
14. The example of current assets is :
    (*a*) Cash in hand and cash at Bank.
    (*b*) Inventory in hand.
    (*c*) Bills Receivables.
    (*d*) All of the above.
15. The example of fixed assets is :
    (*a*) Land (*b*) Building
    (*c*) Fixtures and furnitures (*d*) All of the above

16. Which of the followings belong to Intangible asset.
    (*a*) Patents and Trade marks.
    (*b*) Good will.
    (*c*) Copy right, Composition formula, licence etc.
    (*d*) All of the above.
17. Find out the current liability of a retailer :
    (*a*) Taxes (*b*) Accounts payable
    (*c*) Bank Overdraft (*d*) All of the above
18. The example of Non-current liability is :
    (*a*) Loan on Mortgage (*b*) Loans from banks financial Institutions
    (*c*) Bonds or debentures (*d*) All of the above
19. Asset Turnover ratio is :-
    (*a*) Net sales/Total Assets (*b*) Gross sales/Total Assets
    (*c*) Total Assets/Gross Assets (*d*) Total Assets/Net worth
20. Quick ratio is calculated by :-
    (*a*) Current Assets-Stock/current liabilities.
    (*b*) Fixed Assets/Fixed liabilities.
    (*c*) Current Assets/Current liabilities.
    (*d*) None of the above.
21. Gross Profit margin is computed by :-
    (*a*) Net profit/Net sales (*b*) Gross profit/Gross sales
    (*c*) Gross margin/Total Assets (*d*) Current Assets/Current liabilities
22. High collection period means
    (*a*) more credit sales (*b*) less credit sales
    (*c*) more cash sales (*d*) less cash sales
23. Current ratio to computed by :-
    (*a*) Current Assets/Current liabilities.
    (*b*) Fixed Assets/Fixed liabilities.
    (*c*) Current Assets – Current liabilities.
    (*d*) Current Assets + Current liabilities.
24. As compared to budget, forecast is done for :-
    (*a*) Longer term (*b*) Short term
    (*c*) One year (*d*) Present period
25. Deferred expenditures are always paid in :-
    (*a*) Advance (*b*) Cash
    (*c*) As and when due (*d*) No need to pay

Answers

1. d	2. c	3. a	4. a
5. b	6. a	7. a	8. c
9. a	10. a	11. a	12. d
13. a	14. d	15. d	16. d
17. d	18. d	19. a	20. a
21. a	22. a	23. a	24. a
25. a			

Short-Answer Questions

1. Discuss the objectives of preparing a retail budget?
2. Describe few advantages of preparing income statement?
3. How do current liabilities differ from current assets?
4. Explain the significance of financial leverage being a retailer's performance measure?
5. Is excess inventory always bad?
6. How a lifestyle retailer improves its financial leverage?
7. Improving productivity doesn't mean working harder but working smarter? Explain?
8. Give a specimen of profit and loss account showing some imaginary figures?
9. How return on net worth is calculated?
10. Explain Retailer's Strategic Profit Model?

Long Answer Questions

1. Explain the relevance of preparing balance sheet for a retail organization?
2. Distinguish among these following terms: Fixed assets, current assets and liabilities with suitable examples?
3. What are deferred expenditures?
4. Explain the concept of productivity? What are the myths associated with productivity? How these retailers improve productivity?
   a. Food Courts
   b. Shoe Stores
   c. Retail Bankers and
   d. Jewellery Stores
5. An apparel retailer is doing business with past seven years. For last year it had net assets of Rs 9,50,000, and a net worth of Rs. 3,25,000, total assets of Rs. 7,50,000, and a net worth of Rs. 3,50,000.

Calculate the followings:

I. Net profit margin, asset turnover and return on assets
II. Financial leverage and return on net worth
III. How do you evaluate the performance of this retailer?

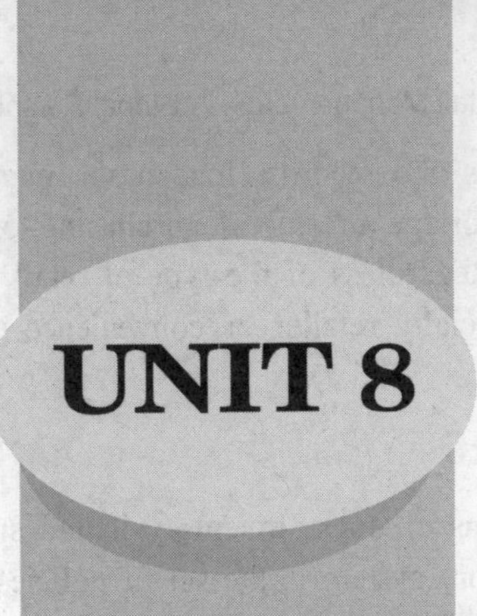

INVENTORY MANAGEMENT

LEARNING OBJECTIVES

- Explaining the need for managing inventory
- Understanding the reasons of poor inventory control
- Discussing various techniques of inventory management
- Identifying different costs involved in managing inventory
- How can an inventory be managed by retailers?
- Understanding the functions of inventory in a retail store
- What measures can be used to avoid shortage?

"Inventory management is primarily about specifying the size and placement of stocked goods. Inventory management is required at different locations within a facility or within multiple locations of a supply network to protect the regular and planned course of production against the random disturbance of running out of materials or goods. The scope of inventory management also concerns the fine lines between replenishment lead time, carrying costs of inventory, asset management, inventory forecasting, inventory valuation, inventory visibility, future inventory price forecasting, physical inventory, available physical space for inventory, quality management, replenishment, returns and defective goods and demand forecasting".

***Courtesy:** www.inventorymanagement.com*

INTRODUCTION

The efficiency of a retail store is based on the retailer's ability to provide the right goods to the consumer, in the right quality, in the right quantity, at the right place and in right time. The entire process of retailing depends on the efficient inventory management. Inventory management is one area that differentiates successful and unsuccessful retail stores. Inventory control is not just a materials management or warehouse department issue. The purchasing, receiving, engineering, displaying, and accounting departments all contribute to the accuracy of the inventory methods and records. Inaccurate inventory management will contribute to dispatch delays, shortage in stores, purchasing of the wrong inventory and stocking too much inventory. Regardless of the type of retail store (department store, super market, hyper market, specialty retailer or convenience store, etc.), deficient areas all seem to remain the same.

MEANING AND DEFINITION OF INVENTORY

Inventory represents a detailed list of all the items in stock. Inventory includes: raw materials, finished products and supplies. An inventory system is the set of policies and controls that monitors levels of inventory and determines what levels should be maintained, when stock should be replenished, and how large orders should be.

The purposes of inventories are:

1. To know how many units to order
2. To allow flexibility in retail scheduling
3. To maintain independence of operations
4. To meet variation in product demand
5. To provide a safeguard for variation in goods delivery time
6. To take advantage of economic purchase order size
7. When to order/inform to senior retail executives that goods in stock will complete soon.

INVENTORY DEFINED

Inventory is the stock of any item or resource (may be food retiling, luxury retailing, grocery/apparel retailing) displayed in a retail store. It is a physical stock of goods/items that a retailer keeps in store (including reserve) for selling to customers when they come to shop. Inventory can be a liability as well as an asset. For instance, large inventory in stores requires larger warehouses and unnecessary increases maintenance and supervision cost which many times is the first indication of wrong decisions in the inventory planning and scheduling.

Some experts of the retail industry define inventory as the blocked working capital of a retail store in the form of goods. As this is the blocked working capital of retail stores, ideally it should be as per store's requirements. But retailers have common practice of maintaining inventory. Sometimes, this inventory is maintained to take care of fluctuations in demand and lead time and in some cases it is maintained to take care of increasing price tendency of commodities or rebate in bulk buying. Inventory is considered a current asset, and shown on the balance sheet, generally at cost.

Another definition of inventory is that it can be used to refer aggregate of those items which are either held for sale in the normal course of business, or are in the process of production for sale (i.e. displayed items).

WHY INVENTORY MANAGEMENT?

The main objectives of managing inventory in a retail organization are:

1. **To Achieve cost-efficient operations:** Inventories allow a retail store to sell the variety goods in normal course of business. Secondly, it maintains a safe level of items throughout the year even when there is seasonal demand for the retail's output. Thirdly, having large stock of items in stores enable the stores to spread some fixed costs like transportation, electricity, maintenance & supervision cost over a larger number of items, thereby decreasing the selling cost per unit. Finally, suppliers often offer extra discount for bulk purchases. To take advantage of extra discount, normally stores go for bulk buying. In this way the selling price per unit comes down resulting in enabling the store to adopt low pricing policy.
2. **To Minimize inventory investment:** When a retailer is able to maintain its inventory to the lower amounts, can use this saved money in other productive areas where comparatively return is very high. In order to know how well a retail store/outlet is managing its inventory, inventory turnover ratio can be used. Inventory turnover is a ratio of the total cost of goods sold in a year to the average inventory level in rupees. The benefit of using this ratio is to know how quickly the retail store is getting its inventories and how quickly customers get the order placed to the stores.
3. **Measuring the gaps in customer service:** Customer service has become a necessary part of retail trade. Customer service is largely a function of perception, customer expectations, and the level of service quality provided. If the customer expects a desired level of customer service (be it after sales or otherwise), and the service provided by a retailer fails to match the customer's expectations, service provided by retailer would be termed as ineffective/poor service. Now question arises how the gap between customer services can be measured. The simplest way to measure the gap between customer services if any is to critically analyze following issues:

- Total number of orders that are received in a particular period (In percentage)
- The number of orders received and delivered at home at or before time
- The time gap between orders received and delayed due to shortage
- The total value of the dispatched orders delivered on time

REASONS FOR HOLDING INVENTORY

Inventory management is a function of central importance in retail stores. Improving product-availability and reducing overall working capital investments, without jeopardizing the store performance is a tightrope that most inventory managers have to stroll and consequently it has to support the objectives of the retail stores as a whole and these are:

1. Ensuring continuity of selling activities by proper and timely supply of goods
2. Hedge against price increases

3. Meet unexpected/ variations in customers demand
4. Reducing inventory holding cost by using appropriate inventory management technique
5. Safeguard against price changes and inflation
6. Smooth-out variations in operation performances
7. Take advantage of quantity/price discounts
8. Transportation saving

CAUSES OF POOR INVENTORY CONTROL

There are certain factors, which lead to poor inventory control in retail stores. These are as follows:

1. Bulk buying due to avail discount or to cut down buying cost can lead to huge inventory storage
2. Over buying inventory due to wrong forecasting
3. When inventory acquisition is more as compare to consumption/sale
4. Over stocking due to some reasons sometimes result in poor customer service
5. Cancellation of delivery orders and unreliable and irregular supplies may lead to bulk inventory storage

STOCK TURN OVER

The stock turn over rate, commonly known as the inventory turnover ratio is one of the most important ratio in the line of retailing that not only shows the health of a sound business but presents a view how a business is operating efficiently.

The inventory of a retail store represents the largest expense to its total expenditure cost. The sale of items from this inventory causes profit to a retailer. Therefore, the money invested in merchandise is of utmost importance to a retailer to have a profitable situation.

Meaning and Definition of Stock Turnover Rate:

The stock turnover ratio is calculated by annual sales divided by average inventory at retail value and is represented as:

$$\text{Stock Turnover} = \frac{\text{Annual Sales}}{\text{Average Inventory at Retail Outlet}}$$

The low stock turnover ratio of a retail business implies that the retailer is carrying high inventory level and high stock turnover ratio presents the retailer's ability to sell quickly. If a retailer at any point of time compares his inventory turnover with his competitor, he must ensure that the formula used by the competitor is same as used by the retailer himself. Any deviation in the formula can lead to different inventory-profit picture.

For example:

	Retailer 'X'	Retailer 'Y'
Annual Sales	Rs 15 lacs	Rs 15 lacs
Average Retail Inventory	Rs 7.5 lacs	Rs 5 lacs
Stock Turnover ratio	2.0	3.0

Importance of Stock Turnover

- It measures the soundness of retailer's inventory methods.
- It also indicates poor inventory planning and lack of controlling techniques.
- By improving stock turnover, a retailer can easily increase his profitability by carrying fewer inventories.
- Stock turnover presents meaningful comparison and informs the retailer about latest trends.

Ways to improve stock turnover

The stock turnover ratio that measures the effectiveness of retailer's merchandise planning and control can be improved in following ways:

1. By increasing retail sales without increasing any expenditure on inventory sales.
2. By decreasing stocks/inventory without disturbing the current sales.
3. By increasing retail sales at one side and decreasing inventory stock on the other side.
4. One way to improve stock turnover is to use less space for retail activity. A low level of inventory takes less space area to display merchandise, resulting in higher sales in a smaller and less expensive retail store.
5. By way of displaying fresh arrivals and new comings, a retailer receives good and quick response and customers prefer to shop more often.
6. By keeping selling price lower, a retailer can turn his inventory into cash quickly resulting in higher stock turns and enhance profitability.

Which approach should be used and would be suitable in the long run depends on the circumstances and vary from retailer to retailer type. One thing can be said undoubtedly that the best way to increase stock turnover ratio over a period of time is to increase the sale without increasing expenditure on inventory held. This can be done using following ways:

(i) By frequent buying but in small volumes.
(ii) By decreasing number of merchandise assortments.
(iii) Replacing slow moving merchandise with fast moving merchandise.
(iv) Don't buy before selling season.

METHODS OF INVENTORY CONTROL

Devising an efficient system of counting and maintaining a stock of inventory items has long been a difficult task for many retail managers. It is said that excess of high inventory isn't a good sign because there is a cost associated with storing the extra inventory. Similarly on the other side it is believed that shortage of inventory is the root cause of all retail disputes. What should be done? Answer is to find out a balance of inventory which is neither excessive nor inadequate.

Selective Inventory Management (SIM)

Therefore, to ensure optimum level of inventory, several classifications are employed to render selective treatment to different types of retail goods/items each classification emphasize on a particular aspect. The right choice of a method depends upon several factors like price of the item, criticality, consumption, lead time, procurement difficulties, etc. Such application of varying levels of control to the total inventory enables retail managers to concentrate on significant matters only. For example, ABC analysis lays emphasis on usage value (consumption of the items in terms of price), VED analysis considers criticality; FSN analysis is based on demand for the items and their stock moving pattern; and HML analysis employs price criterion. Such classification helps the retail managers in controlling the inventory more systematically and scientifically. These are discussed as follows:

1. Economic Order Quantity(EOQ) Model

The primary function of inventory management is to determine

(a) When to order? and

(b) How much to order?

When to order?

This problem of inventory control deals with the issue of point of time when the order for fresh inventory is given. The problem of 'When to Order' is solved by fixing the appropriate re-order levels of each type of inventory. It is determined by compromising the cost of maintaining these stocks and the disservice to the customer if his orders are not delivered in time.

Re-order level

'When to order' is an important query which requires suitable answer.

Buying and issuing the inventories are the foremost tasks of all types of organizations. When the inventories fall below a particular level as decided in advance, they are refilled with fresh procurement. But what should be the quantity for fresh stock is always an alarming question requires suitable answer. In short, the re-order level is that level of inventory at which the order for additional stock should be placed.

Re-order level = Average usage × Lead time

i.e., $R = A_u L$

Re-order point example:

Demand = 10000 units/year

Store open = 320 days/year

Average usage (A_u) = 10000/320=33.33 units/day

Lead time (L) = 10 days

$R = A_u L = (33.33)(10) = 333.33$ units

Note:

This calculation exercise is the responsibility of retail managers but it is the retail staff that informs the retail managers that items in the store is about to finish, which items are in demand in a particular period. Which item should be purchased/acquired on preference basis? Because retail staff is in direct touch with the customers, therefore, is better able to read the customer's buying nerve. Further, retail staff at junior level, one day can/will be promoted at senior level where this calculation takes place. Therefore, concept clarity is must exercise at entry level too.

How much to order?

After solving the problem of 'when to order', next immediate issue is 'how much to order'. Considering over-buying can lead to unproductive use of working capital and under buying leads to unwanted emergency orders and ultimately increases the workload of purchase department, issue of '*how much to order*' is of vital significance. Hence a balance is achieved by selecting the right quantity for each order. This quantity in short is known as Economic Order Quantity (EOQ).

EOQ is an important technique of inventory management. The EOQ refers to the optimal order size that will result in the lowest total of order and carrying costs for an item of inventory given its expected usage, carrying costs and ordering cost. By calculating an economic order quantity, the firm attempts to determine the order size that will minimize the total inventory costs.

Inventory Costs

1. **Ordering costs**: The cost of placing an order and obtaining the supplies is known as ordering cost. It includes costs related to the clerical work of preparing, calling, issuing, transportation, following and receiving orders, the physical handling of goods, inspections and machine set-up costs. This cost does not depend or vary on the number ordered.
2. **Holding (or carrying) costs**: The costs which are required to be incurred on account of inventory storage, handling, insurance etc. from the date of receipt to the date of disposal. It includes store related expenses like salaries of store keepers, electricity expenses, handling, insurance, pilferage, breakage, obsolescence, depreciation, taxes, and the opportunity cost of capital.

The relationship between ordering cost and carrying cost can be understood as follows:

Quantity and size of order	Ordering Cost	Carrying cost
(A) Few Orders of large size	Less	More
(B) More Orders of small size	More	Less

EOQ is simple to understand and use but it has several restrictive assumptions which are also disadvantages in practice. Even with these weaknesses, EOQ is a good place to start to understand inventory systems. EOQ assumes:

1. Demand rate is constant, uniform, recurring, and known.
2. Lead time is constant and known in advance.
3. Price per unit of product is constant; no discounts are given for large orders.
4. Inventory holding cost is based on average inventory.
5. Ordering or setup costs are constant.
6. All demands will be satisfied; no stock outs are allowed.

The EOQ is calculated as follows:

$$\textbf{EOQ} = \sqrt{2 \times D \times C_o / P \times C_c}$$

Where :

D = Annual Demand

C_o = Ordering cost per order

P = Unit price of an item

C_c = Percentage of annual carrying cost to the unit

A BASIC EOQ EXAMPLE

A grocery store sells 10 cases of coffee each week. Each case costs Rs. 80. The cost of placing an order is Rs.10. Holding or carrying cost is estimated to be 30% of the inventory value per year.

So the variables are defined as:

D = 520 cases/year (10 cases/week × 52 weeks/year)

C_o = Rs. 10 per order

C_c = 30% (or 0.30)

P = Rs 80 per case

$$Q = \sqrt{2 \times D \times C_o / P \times C_c}$$

$$Q = \sqrt{2 \times 520 \times 10 / 80 \times 0.3}$$

$$= 20.8 = 21 \text{ cases per order.}$$

How often is the coffee ordered?

520/21 = 25 orders per year. Or every 15 days (365/25= 15)

2. ABC Analysis

ABC analysis is a basic inventory management technique that has been used in business management for a long time. This technique is also popularly known as "Always Better

Control" which is used to exercise control over inventories. Under this method various items of inventory are divided into some groups. These groups are often marked A, B, and C - hence the name.

ABC-analysis is a method originating from material requirements planning, it allows to classify materials by their portion of the overall value of materials. The basic idea underlying ABC analysis is that every item of inventory is not equally important from the view point of control. Certain items are large in numbers but are not of high values, while certain items are very few in numbers but are costly ones. Therefore, items that are perceived as having highest priority is assigned an A, those are of average importance are labeled as B and relatively unimportant items with lowest priority are labeled C.

ABC analysis underlines a very important principle "Vital Few: Trivial Many". ABC analysis, therefore, on the basis of cost and its consumption, tends to segregate items into three categories as mentioned above. Each category should be handled in a different way, with more attention being devoted to category A, less to B, and least to C.

Under ABC analysis, generally for the purpose of controlling inventory, items are classified as follows:

Category	Label	Quantity (%)	Cost (%)
A	Outstanding important	15	70
B	Average importance	30	25
C	Relatively unimportant	55	5

The purpose of classifying inventory in to A, B and C category is to identify where to expend money on inventory and where should be saved. Where care should be taken more and where inventory doesn't demand extra care. During application of this concept, following points should be always considered by a retailer. These are:

1. Category 'A' items are subject to strict inventory control. Therefore, continuous cooperation and interaction is must so that the time spent on placing the order and receiving the inventory should be minimum to the extent possible.
2. For category 'B' items moderate control should be used. As category 'B' items are subject to an intermediate inventory control.
3. Due to low usage value and low costs 'C' items should be procured infrequently and in sufficient quantities. Therefore, strict control is not recommended. Such items are normally kept in an open area inside the store, from where customers can take them according to their requirement. But a periodic monitoring mechanism is established for such items, and quantities almost double the EOQ are ordered at one time.

Category	Degree of Control	Types of Records	Frequency of Review	Size of Safety Stock
A	Tight	Exact & Complete	Continuous	Small
B	Moderate	Good	Frequent	Moderate
C	Loose	Simple	Occasional	large

ABC analysis is frequently combined with 'Pareto' analysis. The 'Pareto' principle is also used in logistics and procurement for the purpose of optimizing stock of goods, as well as costs of keeping and replenishing that stock.

Assumptions of ABC Analysis

1. Demand is known with certainty
2. Demand is relatively constant over time
3. No shortages are allowed
4. Lead time for the receipt of orders is constant
5. The order quantity is received at once

To understand the concept of analysis, we take an imaginary example:

For instance, Indian Star Company has seven different items in its inventory stock. The average number of each of these items held, along with their unit costs, is listed below in table: The Company has decided to introduce an ABC inventory technique from this financial year. Being a expert of the subject you are supposed to suggest the proper breakdown of the items into A, B & C categories.

Item Number	Average Units in Stock	Average Cost per unit
1	10000	30.40
2	5000	51.20
3	16000	5.50
4	14000	5.14
5	30000	1.70
6	15000	1.50
7	10000	0.65

Solution:

Applying ABC Analysis:-

Item (1)	Units (2)	% of Total (3)		Unit Cost (4)	Total Cost (5)	% of Total (6)	
1.	10000	10		30.40	3,04,000	38	
2.	5000	5	15	51.20	2,56,000	32	70
3.	16000	16		5.50	88,000	11	
4.	14000	14	30	5.14	71,960	09	20
5.	30000	30		1.70	51,000	6.38	
6.	15000	15		1.50	22,500	2.88	
7.	10000	10	55	0.65	6500	0.82	10

Explanation

From the above solution one may find how the ABC system works. As per the definition, all the items are classified into three groups. 'A' category inventory constitutes the first 70% of total inventory and hence deserves strict control. The next is 'B' category where moderate control is imposed. The last one is the 'C' category and as per the method, requires least attention and managerial devotion.

Pareto analysis

Pareto principle of inventory was developed by Vilfredo Pareto, an Italian economist who studied the patterns of the concentration of wealth and population in his native country. When he compared the total annual income of Italy to the number of individuals holding the bulk of the wealth, he found that a great majority of the income and the wealth was concentrated in the hands of a relatively few individuals or, conversely, that the majority of the people possessed only a minority of the wealth. In fact, Pareto found that ninety per cent of the income went to only ten per cent of the people. From these observations he formulated a mathematical expression and a generalized principle which states, "... that the significant items in any given group normally constitute a relatively small portion of the total items in the group (often called the 'vital few'). Thus, a majority of the items in the total will, even in the aggregate, be of relatively minor significance (the 'trivial many')".

For many years Pareto's principle was viewed as an interesting academic curiosity, and its practical value was unrecognized until late in the 1930s when it was brought to the attention of people by H. Ford Dickey, who for the first time applied Pareto's law to inventory and observed that when inventory items were plotted on a cumulative percentage graph in order of descending value, Pareto's principle seemed to emerge; that is, a small number of the inventory items comprised a very large percentage of the total inventory value. For example, twenty percent of the inventory items comprise eighty percent of the inventory value.

Today, "Pareto's principle of inventory", often referred to as the "ABC principle", is recognized as an important management tool which affects and influences management control systems of every kind. ABC analysis is used in many areas including inventory control, capacity planning, quality control and production planning and control. Both contribution and sales income have been used as measures of an item's importance to an organization. It is not unusual to find that some products which generate high sales income actually make very low contributions or even losses. Similarly, some products may produce most contribution but their sales income is low. Therefore, both contribution and sales income should be considered.

The following procedure is used in conducting ABC analysis:

1. Obtain the list of the items and estimate their annual consumption (in units).
2. Determine the unit price of each item of inventory.
3. Calculate annual consumption by multiplying items' annual consumption with its unit price.
4. Put together items in the descending order of their annual consumption starting with the maximum annual usage down to the minimum usage.
5. Compute the cumulative percentage for the annual usages and cumulative annual issue.

Advantages of ABC Analysis

Inventory reduction has been a constant goal for all manufacturing concerns. Using the "ABC" concept to analyze and control inventory investment and turns is the simplest and most efficient method. The ABC analysis helps the materials managers that fewer rupees should be tied up in inventory, the more money available for capital investment and expansion. The "ABC" concept also allows a manager to devote resources where it will have the biggest positive impact.

The ultimate goal of ABC analysis is to closely supervise the items according to their share in the inventory investment. This helps to reduce time and minimize efforts towards managing those items which though are not properly taken care of, do not show noticeable effect on inventory performance.

Limitations of ABC Analysis

In ABC analysis, items are divided into various categories for selective management control. These grades are decided on the basis of material price, its usage, availability, size and weight. Further, depending on the type of unit and situation, such classification is made.

ABC analysis despite powerful inventory approach does not guarantee cent percent success. For its successful implementation, the results of ABC analysis have to be reviewed on continuous basis. Some times as advised by ABC analysis, negligence in controlling 'C' type item can be a costly affair during shortage of the same. Like it is common experience that 'sugar & oil' during Diwali will become the high value item.

3. VED Analysis

Just like ABC Analysis for classification of inventories, there is an inventory management technique called VED. In VED analysis inventory items are classified depending upon their criticality in terms of their effect on production function. The degree of criticality states that whether the item of inventory is **vital**, or **essential** or ***desirable*** for the retail store. This classification of dividing inventory is known as **VED** analysis, where **V** stands for *vital*, **E** stands for *essential* and **D** stands for *desirable* items.

Objective

The VED analysis is applied to determine the criticality of an item for displaying in a retail store and its immediate effect on overall buying and other services. It is specially used for material management. Under this analysis, for 'V' items, a large stock of inventory is usually maintained, while for 'D' type items, minimum stock is sufficient.

4. FSN Analysis

This classification works like this:

F = Fast Moving

S = Slow Moving

N = Non-moving

FSN analysis is based on the assumption that all items of inventory are not required all the time in stores. Some items are required on regular basis and some once in a while. Therefore, Fast moving items must be kept nearer to the point of issue and similarly Non-moving items can be kept in a remote place as they are required occasionally.

Therefore for the purpose of controlling items under FSN analysis, **'F'** type items need to be reviewed on regular basis while **'S'** type items may be examined further and their disposal can be considered.

To conduct FSN analysis, the date of receipt or the last date of issue, whichever is later, is considered to determine the number of months, which have lapsed since the last transaction.

5. HML Analysis

This classification works like this:

H = High Cost Items

M = Medium Cost Items

L = Low Cost Items

Likewise ABC analysis, items are classified on the basis of cost of the items. The point of difference between these two techniques is that under HML analysis, for the purpose of classifying inventories into various categories, only cost of the items is considered while their annual consumption value is totally ignored.

Conducting HML analysis

Prepare the list of all the items of inventory in the descending order of their unit value and then to employ price criterion by management for three categories. For Example, in case of luxury retailing, the management may decide all items as follows:

Sl. No	Unit Price	Category
1	2000 and above	H
2	Rs.1000 - Rs. 2000	M
3	less than Rs. 1000	L

INVENTORY COSTS

Five types of costs need to be considered when analyzing inventory decisions:

1. **Holding (or carrying) costs**: storage facilities, handling, insurance, pilferage, breakage, obsolescence, depreciation, taxes, and the opportunity cost of capital.
2. **Setup (or production change) costs**: line conversion, equipment change-over, report preparation, etc.
3. **Ordering costs**: typing, calling, transportation, receiving, etc. This cost does not depend or vary on the number ordered.
4. **Shortage costs (stock out costs):** temporary or permanent loss of sales/future business when demands cannot be met.
5. **Cost of the item**: printed price of an item mentioned over packing wrapper.

MATERIAL HANDLING

Material handling is an integral part of all retail stores and accounts for 10-20% of the total cost of the selling price. It is the way by which the goods of greater efficiency can be attained not only in stores but wherever materials are moved. It is method for moving material. Material can be moved either manually or with the help of slings, or other handling instruments. Material can also be moved by people using machines such as forklift trucks, and other lifting fixtures (mechanical lifting). It does not directly add value to the product but adds to the final cost.

Thus material handling function includes all types of movements within the retail stores. These materials are of various types, shapes and size. At each stage of selling materials are loaded and unloaded are travel widely inside the store. Each handling task poses unique demands on the floor staff. However, workplaces can help store staff to perform these tasks safely and easily by implementing and upholding proper policies and procedures for minimum and automatic materials handling resulting in reduction in handling costs.

Manual material handling operations are carried out in most retail stores because the goods comparatively belong to FMCG sector and these are light in weight. But in case of electronics furniture/luxury retailing, manual lifting can spoil the goods/items meant for sale. As when these items collide with each other, they can create hazards that result in injuries. A load may be hazardous because of:

- absent or inappropriate handles
- ill-shape (making it awkward to handle)
- imbalance (i.e., changing centre of gravity)
- improper temperature
- size (very small/big)
- slippery or damaged surfaces and
- weight

The material handling job sometimes may be dangerous when it involves:

- ➢ lifting or lowering
  - – for extended periods of time
  - – immediately after prolonged flexion
  - – quickly/repetitively
  - – shortly after a period of rest
  - – while seated or kneeling
- ➢ Manual Materials Handling
- ➢ moving the load over large distances
- ➢ accuracy and utmost care required because of
  - – fragile loads, or
  - – specific unloading locations

- ➢ materials positioned too low or too high
- ➢ hazardous arrangements or postures
- ➢ multiple handling requirements (e.g., lifting, carrying, unloading)

Environmental factors that affect material handling are:

- ➢ noise pollution
- ➢ physical conditions
- ➢ poor provision for lighting (Artificial and/or Natural)
- ➢ relative humidity (beyond a 35-50% range)
- ➢ temperature (beyond a 19-26°C range)
- ➢ time restrictions (e.g., machine–paced work or deadline pressures)
  - – obstacles
  - – floor surfaces (e.g., greasy, bumpy or damaged)

Worker characteristics that affect the handling of loads include:

- ➢ general health
  - – height
  - – interest
  - – motivation
- ➢ physical factors
- ➢ pre-existing musculoskeletal problems
- ➢ psychological factors
  - – reach
  - – strength
  - – stress
  - – weight

Symptoms of Poor Material Handling

Different stores have devised different material handling procedures to handle the material in their stores. Sometimes in case of big consignments, cranes are being used at ports. Trucks are normally the means of carrying material from one store to another or from godowns to various chain stores. The purpose of material handling in stores is to prevent any damage to store's assets or to store's employees. If at one place in a store, items are scattered here and there without any reason, is a reason of poor material handling. If in stores at any counter, point of sale, or at supply and dispatch points, there remains a long queue then it conveys the message that retail manager is not efficient in material handling task. As it is a case of poor material handling.

Some indicators for poor material handling are:

- – Damaged floor
- – Delivery of wrong type of materials at different racks/cabins
- – Difference in store records in terms of quantity

- Frequent incidents of accidents, wastage, scrap and rejection of finished goods due to handling fault
- Ideal labor
- Increase in loading and unloading time resulting in long queues at supply and dispatch centers
- Increase in material mix-up rate
- Increasing problem of right materials at wrong place
- Jamming at different areas in store like inward inventory point, quality areas, display areas, receipt and issue areas
- Poor house keeping
- Skilled labor performing work of unskilled workers
- Unable to meet delivery commitments

Purpose of Material Handling (Why Material Handling?)

Material handling function is considered as one of the most significant activities of the retail stores and efficient material handling is must to perform day to day manufacturing operations. According to estimates, one fifth of the total production time is consumed in actual production while remaining fourth fifth of the production time is spent on material handling activities like taking materials from one place to another. Therefore, the primary objective of each production manager is to reduce time in material handling activities so that more concentration should be given to production and after sales activities.

The following may be considered as secondary objectives:

(i) Minimization of fatigues and hard work
(ii) Minimizing material handling cost
(iii) Optimum utilization of material handling equipment
(iv) Prevention of accidents and errors during material handling
(v) Prevention of damages to materials
(vi) Proper housekeeping
(vii) To improve overall productivity without increasing production budget
(viii) To increase storage capacity by proper utilization of space area
(ix) To provide safe environment for movements of materials
(x) To reduce investment in work in progress

Doctrine (Principles) of Material Handling

There is no best criterion to perform material handling activities successfully. But if material handling is planned and well integrated with production activities, it results in maximum overall operating efficiency.

1. Planning Principle

Efficient material handling is the result of efficient planning. Planning not only involves the strategic objectives of the organization but also the existing methods and problems, physical and economic constraints, and future requirements and goals. Therefore, retailers should plan a detailed layout which includes retail's basic requirements, various alternates, and the emergency plans for all possible activities related to material handling and storage. It also includes following supportive principles such as:

- Preparation and selection of best operational sequence and layout with regard to shelves, racks, and cabins which includes the store's possible operations and has potential of arranging material in an effective way. (Layout Principle)
- To effectively utilized the available space in the best possible manner. (Space Utilization Principle)
- To minimize unpleasant effects on the environment while selecting any material handling devise or equipment. (Ecology Principle)
- Delegate planning responsibility of material handling to a separate department/ person. (Delegation of Responsibility Principle)

2. Operating Principles

A material handling is the system developed and accepted for controlling the investments in inventory. The investment in material handling is normally soaring in most of the retail stores. Material handling is a broad concept which includes merchandise buying, retail positioning, selling and distribution. With proper planning and control, the material handling complications can be drastically solved. This requires a system approach and it should include the followings:

- Arrange and move the materials in unit loads rather than on individual basis. (Unit load handling principle)
- Shifting materials from one place to another with in the store while considering limitations related to material safety, floor damage and loss. (Gravity principle)
- Re-handling and backtracking movements should be avoided. Therefore, need is to prepare an operational plan and positioning blueprint for the entire feasible solutions. It will help in selection of alternate arrangements that best integrate resources and capabilities. (Flow of Materials principles)

3. Equipment Principle

Material handling equipment is used for the movement and storage of material within a store. There are several types of equipment available, whose suitability depends on several factors like nature of job, load capacity, ease of operation, speed of operation, space available etc. equipment principle can basically be described as:

- Select appropriate material handling equipment to ensure safe working conditions. (Safety principle)
- Opting those techniques and equipment which are able to perform a number of operations and tasks at a time without disturbing other arrangements. (Flexibility Principle)

- To standardize material handling techniques and equipment in the store whenever and wherever deemed fit. (Standardization Principle)
- To mechanize the material handling methods whenever it is feasible and to increase store's economy and efficiency. (Mechanization Principle)
- Be ready with a preventive maintenance plan and pending repairs for all material handling equipments. Purpose is that prevention is always better then cure. (Maintenance Principle)
- Make handling simple that should eliminate wastes, accidents, errors and omissions by separating or combining some homogeneous activities. (Simplification Principle)
- Organize a long term and cost effective for replacing obsolete and abandoned techniques and methods. This will result in increase efficiency and increased productivity. (Obsolescence Principle)

4. Costing Principle

This principle implies that a store should always compare the cost justification of selected/short listed equipments by its economic life and effectiveness when measured in terms of rupee per unit handled.

- Selection of equipment for total lowest cost. (Economic Principle)
- Amortize the equipment/machinery within a reasonable period of time. (Amortization Principle)
- Calculate your handling cost in advance (Handling Cost Appraisal)

Merchandising optimization

Merchandise optimization is a key activity in the management of any retail store. It not only drives the business strategy of the retailer but also has immense cost and profit implications. Be it small/independent retailer or a franchisee of a chain store, all face a common problem that how right merchandise mix should be provided at each store location so that with satisfying customers, overall productivity should increase. Under the pressure of showing good turnover and profits year after year, retailers find it difficult to provide proper merchandise mix that one side satisfy the customers and on the other side, results in higher level of productivity. Therefore, they have left with no option except to use merchandise optimization technique.

The merchandising optimization is a process under which data related to loyal customers, merchandise and target market is maintained in order to produce merchandise assortment. This is done by merchandise mix which is a blend of marketing intelligence statistics, output from competitors' survey and socio cultural environmental analysis of

Merchandising Philosophy

It sets the guiding principles for all the merchandise decisions that a retailer makes. The advantages of such a philosophy are:

- To have smooth chain of commands
- The buyer's expertise is used in selling
- Enables a retailer to reach its goals.

the near by population. Studies have shown that proper merchandise mix not only results in increased turnover but excellent customer service. Only need is to consider that how your store can create customer interest and differential advantage by the merchandise it is offering? Besides this stores' pattern of breadth, depth, and policies should change over the time as the needs and wants of the customers is tend to change and these changes lead to change in merchandise mix which ultimately have direct impact on the marketing and sales promotion mix.

Points to consider for devising a strategic merchandise assortment plan.

- How a retail manager can implement merchandise assortment plan without disturbing the remaining retail supply chain?
- How a store is intend to use tools such as stock-turnover and stock-sales ratios to support its assortment planning?
- How does the 80/20 principle apply in his retail store?
- How much depth a store can carry?
- How much width a store can carry?
- How much/ consistent a store is towards merchandise assortment?
- What plans a retailer has to maximize the return on inventory investment?
- Which product lines does your store intend to carry?

LATEST DEVELOPMENTS IN INVENTORY MANAGEMENT

Traditional inventory management practices are being made superseded by increasing global supply chains and contract manufacturing, more dynamic product lifecycles, and multi-channel distribution. Therefore, new and new inventions in inventory management are taking place in the field of inventory management. For instancc, in recent years, two approaches have had a major impact on inventory management: Material Requirements Planning (MRP) and Just-In-Time (a Japanese technique). These new techniques are mostly applied by manufacturing organizations but retail stores also find it convenient and cost effective. This is true because these techniques result in tremendous cost cutting and a lot of space saving which can be used for displaying more items.

Material requirement planning is basically a computer-based information system designed to handle ordering and scheduling of dependent-demand inventories (such as raw materials, component parts, and sub-assemblies that will be used in the production of a finished product). MRP is designed to answer three questions: what is needed, how much is needed, and when is it needed. MRP systems are practical for small and medium sized retail stores and are used for planning the future requirements of a retail store.

Just in time retailing is a systems approach to developing and operating a retail store. Just in time has become synonymous with excellence in retailing. Sometimes called lean retailing, it is used in a wide variety of retail stores such as grocery, food & vegetables, electronic goods retailing, luxury retailing, etc. The main philosophy behind the JIT is the elimination of waste to the possible extent. In the end of last decade, when this concept was applying in retailing industries, retailers even had no idea that it will result in cost and space saving. But when the result came in picture, not only the big stores but small stores also started using this technique. It requires that items of sale and display are made available only in the amount required and at the selling hours. To retailers, it makes the compulsion to buy only those items for which there is a demand and in the quantity which could be sold easily. In short, just in time is a philosophy of buying those things which the customers want and providing when the customers want.

The success of JIT depends on these factors:

- Close contact with suppliers
- Continuous interaction with suppliers
- Non-dependency on one supplier
- Retail store layout revision – if it is the demand of implementing JIT
- Set-up time reduction - time taken to arrange merchandise in the store

SUMMARY

Inventory is the stock of any item or merchandise in-stock and on hand. It may be any grocery item or any food/apparel item. An inventory system is the set of policies and controls that monitors levels of inventory and determines what levels should be maintained, when stock should be replenished, and how large orders should be placed. Ideally speaking, inventory is the stock of idle merchandise in a store for present and future sales. In retail stores depending upon the nature, inventory can be of various types. For example in vegetables and fruits store, inventory is not purchased in bulk. While in luxury retailing, due to price rise, inventory is purchased in bulk if it has no expiry or long usage life like gold, diamond and platinum. These reserves represent a major portion of the store's total investment and therefore, should be managed effectively.

The inventory of an 'A' type of goods is always to be maintained in an organization. The control technique which is applied in the case of one particular item and is found successful may not be successful/effective in case of other type of inventory. Therefore, store classifies items into categories A, B, and C based on relevant criterion. The main objective of such classification is to ensure that the inventory level is neither too high nor too low, i.e., inventory should be just optimum so that the total cost is minimum. The *economic order quantity* (EOQ) model helps in finding this optimum level of inventory. The optimum level of inventory calculated by EOQ model and any discount option being offered by the supplier are compared, and the best possible alternate is chosen on the basis of total lowest cost. Therefore, retailer must design their inventory management technique after considering market demand and the store's strategic plan. With the changes in demand, taste, preferences and competitors' retailing practices, retailers should change their inventory management accordingly but the basic principles should remain same throughout the retail life cycle.

The basic building blocks for the inventory management system and inventory control activities are:

– Demand Forecasting
– Sales and Operations Planning
– Production Planning
– Material Requirements Planning
– Inventory Reduction

Effective inventory control helps to strike an optimal balance between these opposing costs and involves determination of economic lot sizes and fixation of operating levels for different types of inventories to ensure availability of required items at minimum total cost to the company all the times.

REVIEW QUESTIONS

True and False Questions

1. Inventory management is primarily about specifying the size and placement of stocked goods.
2. Inventory includes: raw materials, finished products and supplies.
3. Customer service is largely a function of perception, customer expectations, and the level of service quality provided.
4. The primary reason to hold inventory is to ensure continuity of selling activities by proper and timely supply of goods.
5. The stock turn over rate is one of the most important ratios in the line of retailing that not only shows the health of a sound business but presents a view how a business is operating efficiently.
6. The stock turnover ratio is calculated by annual sales multiplied by average inventory at retail value.
7. The problem of '*When to Order*' is solved by fixing the appropriate re-order levels of each type of inventory.
8. Material handling is a method for stocking material.
9. The EOQ refers to the optimal order size that will result in the highest total cost.
10. The ultimate goal of ABC analysis is to closely supervise the items according to their share in the inventory investment.
11. Efficient material handling is the result of efficient planning.
12. In VED analysis inventory items are classified depending upon their criticality in terms of their effect on production function.
13. FSN analysis is based on the assumption that all items of inventory are required all the time in stores.
14. Material handling is an integral part of all retail stores and accounts for 50-70% of the total cost of the selling price.
15. Merchandising philosophy sets the guiding principles for all the merchandise decisions that a retailer makes.
16. Under doctrine of material handling, there is always a best criterion to perform material handling activities successfully.
17. Merchandise optimization is a key activity in the management of any retail store. It not only drives the business strategy of the retailer but also has no immense cost and profit implications.
18. Just in time retailing is a system approach to develope and operate a retail store.

19. Material requirement planning is basically a computer-based information system designed to handle ordering and scheduling of independent-demand inventories.
20. Damaged floor and delivery of wrong type of materials at different racks are the positive symptoms of efficient material handling.

Answers

1. True	2. True	3. True	4. True
5. True	6. False	7. True	8. False
9. False	10. True	11. True	12. True
13. False	14. False	15. True	16. False
17. False	18. True	19. True	20. False

Multiple Choice Questions

1. The main objective of managing inventory in a retail organisation is :-
   (*a*) To achieve cost-efficient operations.
   (*b*) To minimise inventory investments.
   (*c*) Measuring the gap in customer service.
   (*d*) All of the above
2. The primary reason for holding inventory is :-
   (*a*) Hedge against price increase (*b*) Ensuring continuity of selling activities
   (*c*) Transportation saving (*d*) Meeting unexpected demand
3. The reason for poor inventory control is :-
   (*a*) Bulk buying to avail special discount.
   (*b*) Over buying due to wrong forecasting.
   (*c*) Cancellation of delivery orders.
   (*d*) All of the above.
4. Importance of stock turnover :-
   (*a*) It measures the soundness of retailer's inventory methods.
   (*b*) It indicates poor inventory planning.
   (*c*) It presents meaningful comparison and informs the retailer about latest trends.
   (*d*) All of the above.
5. Stock turnover can be improved by :-
   (*a*) By frequent buying in small volumes.
   (*b*) By decreasing number of merchandise assortments.
   (*c*) Replacing slow moving merchandise with fast moving merchandise.
   (*d*) All of the above.
6. SIM stands for :-
   (*a*) Standard Inventory Management
   (*b*) Standard Inventory Mechanism.
   (*c*) Selective Inventory Management.
   (*d*) Selective Inventory Mechanism.

7. FSN stands for.
   (*a*) Fewer, smaller and Non-moving.
   (*b*) Fast, slow and Non-moving.
   (*c*) Far, situated, Non-moving.
   (*d*) Fewer, standard and Non-moving.
8. EOQ means :
   (*a*) Economic order quantum (*b*) Economical order quality
   (*c*) Economic order quantity (*d*) Economic operations quantity
9. The cost of placing an order and obtaining the supplies is known as :
   (*a*) Ordering cost (*b*) Holding cost
   (*c*) Variable cost (*d*) Fixed cost
10. The cost incurred on account of inventory storage is known is :-
   (*a*) Ordering cost (*b*) Holding cost
   (*c*) Temporary cost (*d*) Permanent cost
11. Category 'A' items under ABC control are subject to :-
   (*a*) Moderate control (*b*) Less control
   (*c*) Strict control (*d*) None of the above
12. What kind of control should be applied to 'C' type items :-
   (*a*) Tight (*b*) Moderate
   (*c*) Loose (*d*) Neutral
13. What should be the size of safety stock for 'B' type items
   (*a*) Small (*b*) Moderate
   (*c*) Large (*d*) None
14. The main assumption of ABC Analysis is :-
   (*a*) Demand is known with certainty.
   (*b*) Demand is relatively constant over time.
   (*c*) No shortages are allowed.
   (*d*) All of the above.
15. Pareto Analysis is an extension of :
   (*a*) FSN Analysis (*b*) HML Analysis
   (*c*) ABC Analysis (*d*) EOQ Analysis
16. VED Analysis stands for :
   (*a*) Vital, Essential and desirable.
   (*b*) Vital, Elementary and desirable.
   (*c*) Valuable, Essential and desirable.
   (*d*) Valuable, Elementary and desirable.
17. HML classification works as :
   (*a*) High, Moderate, Low (*b*) High, Medium, Low
   (*c*) High Moderate Level (*d*) High Medium Level

18. Material handling cost accounts for roughly ______ % of the total cost ?
    (*a*) 5-10 % (*b*) 10-20 %
    (*c*) 15-25 % (*d*) 20-40 %
19. The material handling job may be dangerous because of :
    (*a*) Lifting or lowering (*b*) Manual Material handling
    (*c*) Wrong postures (*d*) All of the above
20. Indicators for poor material handling are :-
    (*a*) Damaged floor (*b*) Ideal labour
    (*c*) Poor house keeping (*d*) All of the above
21. The purpose of material handling is :
    (*a*) Minimisation of fatigues and hardwork.
    (*b*) Minimising material handling work.
    (*c*) Proper house keeping.
    (*d*) All of the above
22. Just-in time is an :
    (*a*) Indian technique (*b*) American technique
    (*c*) Japanese technique (*d*) Russian technique
23. MRP technique stands for :
    (*a*) Materials Resource Planning (*b*) Minerals Resource Planning
    (*c*) Materials Recourse Planning (*d*) Materials Requirements planning
24. Selection of equipment for total lowest cost belongs to :-
    (*a*) Handling cost Appraisal (*b*) Amortisation principle
    (*c*) Simplification principle (*d*) Economic principle
25. Material handling equipment is used for :
    (*a*) Movement of material (*b*) Storage of material
    (*c*) Both of the above (*d*) None of the above

Answers

1. d	2. b	3. d	4. d
5. d	6. c	7. b	8. c
9. a	10. b	11. c	12. c
13. b	14. d	15. c	16. c
17. b	18. b	19. d	20. d
21. d	22. c	23. d	24. d
25. c			

Check Your Progress

1. What is inventory?
2. Who developed the Pareto Analysis?
3. What do you mean by ordering cost?
4. What is stock turn over?
5. What is time gap?
6. What is SIM?

7. What is EOQ?
8. What is safety stock
9. What does VED means?
10. Spell out FSN?
11. What is material handling?
12. What is fatigue?
13. What is MRP?
14. What do you mean by carrying cost?
15. What HML analysis implies?

Small Answer Questions

1. Briefly explain the concept of inventory management?
2. What are the objectives of holding inventory?
3. Why stores maintain the inventory knowing that it requires space and unnecessary supervision?
4. How ABC is different from VED Analysis?
5. Why inventory is necessary in a store?
6. What are various inventory costs?
7. What is the significance of equipment principle?
8. What merchandising optimization concept entails?
9. Discuss the main reasons for poor inventory management?
10. Explain the concept of 'optimum level of inventory'?
11. Discuss the importance of 're-order level'?
12. Discuss some causes of poor inventory control?
13. What is 're-order level'?
14. List various features of Just in Time technique?
15. Why is the ABC classification of items done?

Long Answer Questions

1. Explain the kind of problems faced when very high or very low inventory is maintained for items?
2. What do you understand by inventory management? Briefly explain the various techniques used for managing inventory in modern retail stores?
3. Being a retail graduate, what guidelines you would suggest to existing and new retail entrants for effective inventory planning? What measures a retailer should take to manage its inventory especially in following cases:
   (*i*) At the time of delivery
   (*ii*) After Inspection
4. Material handling is an integral part of all retail stores and accounts for 10-20% of the total cost of the selling price. It is the way by which the goods of greater efficiency can be attained not only in stores but wherever materials are moved. Are you convinced with this statement? What is the logic of calling material handling as an integral part?

Appendix

Exhibit 8.1: Inventory Management - New Concept Catching up Fast in India

'Inventory' to many small business owners is one of the more visible and tangible aspects of doing business. Raw material, goods in process and finished goods all represent various forms of inventory. Each type represents money tied up until the inventory leaves the company as purchased products.

Likewise, merchandise stocks in a retail store contribute to profits only when their sale puts money into the cash register. In a literal sense, inventory refers to stocks of anything necessary to do business. These stocks represent a large portion of the business investment and must be well managed in order to maximize profits. In fact, many small businesses cannot absorb the types of losses arising from poor inventory management. Unless inventories are controlled, they are unreliable, inefficient and costly.

Successful inventory management involves balancing the costs of inventory with the benefits of inventory. Many small business owners fail to appreciate fully the true costs of carrying inventory, which include not only direct costs of storage, insurance and taxes, but also the cost of money tied up in inventory. This fine line between keeping too much inventory and not enough is not the manager's only concern.

Others include:

- Maintaining a wide assortment of stock — but not spreading the rapidly moving ones too thin;
- Increasing inventory turnover — but not sacrificing the service level;
- Keeping stock low — but not sacrificing service or performance.
- Obtaining lower prices by making volume purchases — but not ending up with slow-moving inventory; and
- Having an adequate inventory on hand — but not getting caught with obsolete items.

The degree of success in addressing these concerns is easier to gauge for some than for others. *For example,* computing the inventory turnover ratio is a simple measure of managerial performance. This value gives a rough guideline by which managers can set goals and evaluate performance, but it must be realized that the turnover rate varies with the function of inventory, the type of business and how the ratio is calculated (whether on sales or cost of goods sold). Average inventory turnover ratios for individual industries can be obtained from trade associations.

Managing Inventory Effectively (Golden Tips)

At time of delivery:

- After carrier/inspector prepares damage report, carefully read before signing.

- After delivery, immediately open all cartons and inspect for merchandise damage. When damage is discovered
- Call carrier to report damage and request inspection.
- Carefully examine each carton for visible damage — If damage is visible, note it on the delivery receipt and have the driver sign your copy.
- Carrier inspection of damaged items
- Confirm call in writing—This is not mandatory but it is one way to protect yourself.
- Have all damaged items in the receiving area — Make certain the damaged items have not moved from the receiving area prior to inspection by carrier.
- Retain damaged items — All damaged materials must be held at the point received.
- Verify count — Make sure you are receiving as many cartons as are listed on the delivery receipt.

After inspection:

- Keep damaged materials — Damaged materials should not be used or disposed of without permission by the carrier.
- Do not return damaged items without written authorization from shipper/supplier.

Courtesy: www.inventorymanagement.com

Controlling Your Inventory

To maintain an in-stock position of wanted items and to dispose of unwanted items, it is necessary to establish adequate controls over inventory on order and inventory in stock. There are several proven methods for inventory control. They are listed below, from simplest to most complex.

- Visual control enables the manager to examine the inventory visually to determine if additional inventory is required. In very small businesses where this method is used, records may not be needed at all or only for slow moving or expensive items.
- Tickler control enables the manager to physically count a small portion of the inventory each day so that each segment of the inventory is counted every so many days on a regular basis.
- Click sheet control enables the manager to record the item as it is used on a sheet of paper. Such information is then used for reorder purposes.
- Stub control (used by retailers) enables the manager to retain a portion of the price ticket when the item is sold. The manager can then use the stub to record the item that was sold.

As a business grows, it may find a need for a more sophisticated and technical form of inventory control. Today, the use of computer systems to control inventory is far more feasible for small business than ever before, both through the widespread existence of computer service organizations and the decreasing cost of small-sized computers. Often the justification for such a computer-based system is enhanced by the fact that company accounting and billing procedures can also be handled on the computer. Point-of-sale terminals relay information on each item used or sold. The manager receives information printouts at regular intervals for review and action. Off-line point-of-sale terminals relay information directly to the supplier's computer who uses the information to ship additional items automatically to the buyer/inventory manager. The final method for inventory control is done by an outside agency. A manufacturer's representative visits the large retailer on a scheduled basis, takes the stock count and writes the reorder. Unwanted merchandise is removed from stock and returned to the manufacturer through a predetermined, authorized procedure.

A principal goal for many of the methods described above is to determine the minimum possible annual cost of ordering and stocking each item. Two major control values are used:

- the order quantity, that is, the size and the frequency of orders; and
- the reorder point, that is, the minimum stock level at which additional quantities are ordered.

The Economic Order Quantity (EOQ) formula is one widely used method of computing the minimum annual cost for ordering and stocking each item. The EOQ computation takes into account the cost of placing an order, the annual sales rate, the unit cost, and the cost of carrying inventory.

Developments in Inventory Management

In recent years, two approaches have had a major impact on inventory management:

- Material Requirements Planning (MRP) and
- Just-In-Time (JIT and Kanban).

Their application is primarily within manufacturing but suppliers might find new requirements placed on them and sometimes buyers of manufactured items will experience a difference in delivery. A material requirement planning is basically an information system in which sales are converted directly into loads on the facility by sub-unit and time period. Materials are scheduled more closely, thereby reducing inventories, and delivery times become shorter and more predictable.

Its primary use is with products composed of many components. MRP systems are practical for smaller firms. The computer system is only one part of the total project which is usually long-term, taking one to three years to develop.

Just-in-time inventory management is an approach which works to eliminate inventories rather than optimize them. The inventory of raw materials and work-in-process falls to that needed in a single day. This is accomplished by reducing set-up times and lead times so that small lots may be ordered. Suppliers may have to make several deliveries a day or move close to the user plants to support this plan.

Source : *www.inventorymanagement.com.*

MANAGING MERCHANDISE

Unit 9 : Planning Merchandise Assortments

Unit 10 : Merchandise Buying Systems

Unit 11 : Managing A Retail Brand

Unit 12 : Presenting Merchandise

Unit 13 : Merchandise Pricing

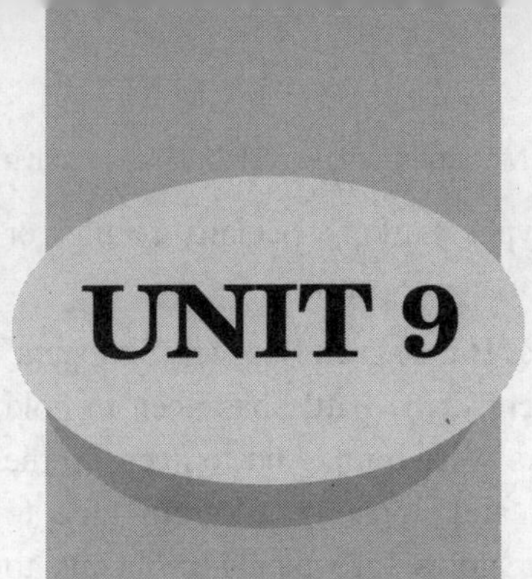

PLANNING MERCHANSIDE ASSORTMENTS

LEARNING OBJECTIVES

- Understanding how a buying process is organized and the dimensions a retailer consider while planning merchandise assortment plan
- Understanding how retailers plan their assortments
- Explaining the role and significance of category management for a sound merchandising philosophy
- Explaining how financial objectives are set for the merchandise plan and knowing the viability of GMROI in an retail organization
- Explaining the assortment planning process and measuring trade offs between variety, assortment and product availability
- Describing how merchandise optimization drives the business strategy and how do retailers determine product mix

"Junk is the ultimate merchandise. The junk merchant does not sell his product to the consumer, he sells the consumer to the product. He does not improve and simplify his merchandise, he degrades and simplifies the client."

William S. Burroughs quotes

INTRODUCTION

The efficiency of a retail store is based on the retailer's ability to provide the right goods to the consumer, in the right quality, in the right quantity, at the right place and in right time. The entire process of retailing depends on the efficient merchandise management. **Planning merchandise assortments** is one area that differentiates successful and unsuccessful retail stores. It is not just a materials management or warehouse department issue. The purchasing, receiving, engineering, displaying, and accounting departments all contribute to the accuracy of the merchandise assortment methods and records. Inaccurate assortments will contribute to dispatch delays, shortage in stores, purchasing of the wrong inventory and stocking too much inventory. Regardless of the type of retail store (Department store, super market, hyper market, specialty retailer or convenience store, etc.), deficient areas all seem to remain the same.

In the retail industry, with the dawn of large players like Big Bazaar, Spencer, Shoppers' Stop, Reliance Fresh, Big Apple, and Globus more recently, the battle has been to hold customer base. Thus loyalty programs for store members were born. And to keep up the enticement, new value additions are constantly sought and implemented from time to time. The result is that our traditional Indian '*kirana* stores' are facing problems to survive their entities. Their resources are limited and can not use these costly sales promotion techniques. In the race of moving ahead and increase their client base, stores are offering wide **merchandise assortments** and lucrative offers to the customers. This chapter discusses the concept of merchandise assortment plan and the essence of product mix. It also talk about the retail buying format and the buying organization process and set the tone for setting financial objectives for the merchandise plan.

PLANNING MERCHANDISE ASSORTMENTS

Planning retail merchandising is a technique of developing, securing, pricing, supporting and communicating the retailer's offerings. This task is done by a retailer who ensures that right product should reach to the customers at right time, right place and at right price. Therefore, a retailer most of the times devote to understand consumers' needs and selling merchandise accordingly. Therefore, what to sell and how much to purchase is an important task for every retailer. Retailer (small or big) has variety of items to buy and each time of merchandise further is available in varied brands. Retailers further are required to choose few suppliers (vendors) out of many. Consequently, if the buying process is not organized systematically, planning merchandise exercise will become chaotic.

Merchandising Philosophy

It sets the guiding principles for all the merchandise decisions that a retailer makes. The advantages of such a philosophy are:

– To have smooth chain of commands
– The buyer's expertise is used in selling
– Enables a retailer to reach its goals.

Planning merchandise assortment is a significant part of a retailer's financial success. To begin with, a retailer first decides the firm's financial objectives. Once the financial objectives are framed, the retailer begins the task of selecting 'what to buy' which is the biggest challenge a retailer faces in his day-to-day life. Any wrong decision in the purchase of merchandise will lead to heavy financial loss to the firm. Ideally, it looks very simple, that if it is kids wear store, a retailer should buy kids' clothes of various sizes and if it is a fashion store, a retailer should buy fashion items or accessories. Practically, it does not work. One thing always should be kept in mind that purchase budget is usually fixed and limited for a particular period of time and even the space allocated to particular merchandise is limited. For instance, in case of kids wear, a retailer will encounter following issues:

- Should I select small variety (for example jeans, capri, and t-shirts) with large assortment of colors and styles?
- Should large variety be selected with small product range?
- How much back up for each category, size number, colour should be kept in store to avoid 'run-out' situation in case of demand?

If a retailer decides to have good back up, it will avoid **'run-out'** situation of a particular item, but large amount of fund will be blocked unnecessarily, resulting in shortage of funds on necessary items. Thus, the problem of buying, managing and having back up is not an easy task, as it seems in a first glance. In actual, this task of managing variety assortment and storing (back up stock) is known as **'assortment planning'** and the culmination of planning the financial and merchandising objectives for a particular merchandise category is called **'assortment plan'**.

Merchandise Assortment

Merchandising: It consists of the activities involved in acquiring particular goods and/or services and making them available at the places, times and prices and in the quantity that enables a retailer to reach its objectives.

Micro Merchandising: A strategy where a retailer adjusts its shelf space allocations to respond to customers and other differences among local markets.

Back up: In order to ensure regular availability of their products and services, some level of inventory is kept aside and is *'not for use'* purpose till the displayed stock is over. The objective of keeping back up/back log merchandise is to meet the regular or seasonal fluctuations in the consumers' demands. Retailers must maintain the equilibrium between displayed and back up stock as too much inventory will lead to financial blockage and too little will hamper the store's sales.

Assortment Plan: An assortment plan is a description of items a retailer would like to have in his store in a particular merchandise category.

ORGANIZING BUYING PROCESS BY CATEGORIES

Category basically is a measuring unit to take merchandise decisions. Before organizing a buying process, retailer must select the quality of its merchandise. Should retailer carry most expensive items to serve upper income level? or It should serve middle class by offering middle-of-the-line merchandising? or Its merchandise should be offered to low Income Group? Or should it serve more than one market segment such as higher and middle income group?

The Category

A category is an assortment of items that a consumer finds as reasonable substitutes for each other. Goods are categorized on the basis of similarities in consumer tastes, preferences, liking and disliking such as Junk food, Bar-be-Que, Razors, burgers, baked confectionary, sweets, etc. The goods are priced, promoted and targeted to same customer base (target market). For instance Vishal Mega Mart, Gokul Mega Mart and few other domestic and global brands have the practice of dividing their apparel on the basis of Gents' Apparel, Ladies' Apparel and Kids Apparel.

Two retailers selling similar merchandise may have different definitions and thus different categories of the same product range. For instance, one retailer divides its 'apparel' under gents, ladies, kids and infants category, while another (for say) may define categories in terms of brands like **Polo figer** be one category and **Rivalry** be the other. *Why it is so?* Because a **'Polo'** customer will buy only **polo figer** not the **Rivalry**. In short, whatever may be the base of defining a **'Category'**, one thing must be remembered that it should suit to customers who ultimately will be affected in terms of time and money spent. Further, supply chain members and suppliers may find it convenient and hassle free.

CATEGORY MANAGEMENT

As the name implies, it is the process of managing retail business that merchandise category outputs rather than the contribution of individual brands or models. Under category management retailer's efforts (promotional, pricing and display) are grouped into categories with the objectives of measuring their financial and marketing performance separately. Consequently, it arranges grouping of products in to strategic business units (**SBU**) in order to better serve the needs and demands of consumers. Most of the emerging retail outlets are managing their merchandise on the same pattern. While on the other side, unorganized Indian retail sector has developed their merchandise items in the categories that serve their customers requirement and are cost effective and time saving for them. Therefore, these categories differ from region to region and outlet to outlet.

CM Defined

According to Institute of Grocery Distribution, "CM is the strategic management of various merchandise groups through trade tie ups and partnerships which aims to maximize turnover and profit by satisfying consumer needs and want."

According to Nielsen (1992), CM is a process of managing product categories as separate business units and customizing them to satisfying consumer needs.

Why Category Management?

1. One foremost reason for the introduction of 'category management' is that all the items of merchandise are not equally important for a retailer from cost revenue generation point of view. Some items are very small but of high value, some items are most popular but of low profit margin. Therefore need was point to categorized the items in to different sub groups.
2. One reason for introduction of 'category management' was the fact that only a definite amount of profit could be obtained from price negotiations and that there was more profit to be made in for the purpose of increasing the total sales.

3. One reason for introduction of 'category management' was that the collaboration with supplier will be helpful in development of categories under three ways:
   (i) Part of the work load like development of categories would be assign to the concerned supplier.
   (ii) Supplier's expertise will be utilized.
   (iii) Supplier will take the venture seriously.

Significance of Category Management

1. Increased sales, goodwill and market share
2. Proper care and devotion to each item of merchandise
3. Increased sales further lead to increased turnover
4. Maximize shelf efficiencies
5. Less inventory shrinkage
6. Recognizes procurement opportunities
7. Enhances customer knowledge level
8. Improves return on investment (ROI)
9. Decreases chances of *out-of-stock* positions
10. Enhances return on money invested in marketing efforts
11. Classifies the performance of brands as doing well, not doing well, problem brands, etc.
12. Purchasing merchandise exercise becomes easy and cost effective.

Essentials / Prerequisite of Category Management

1. Category should be divided and arranged as per consumers' ease not because of retailer's convenience.
2. CM should be based on differentiation and uniqueness.
3. CM should drive multiple item purchases at the same time.
4. It should result in better customers' relations rather than relations with suppliers.
5. Category division should be based on the basis of product response, space, time and profitability.

CATEGORY MANAGEMENT PROCESS

Category management is the process of classifying and managing product categories as strategic business units, rather than simply viewing a retailer's offering as a collection of individual products. The category management approach delivers enhanced business results by focusing on delivering consumer value. It is often a shared process between a retailer and its vendors. This description comes from Category Killers (2005)[1] by Robert Spector:

[1] *www.directionsmag.com*

*For the past couple of years, the term "**category management**" has entered the retail lexicon in virtually every merchandise category. Category management began in the supermarket business, where big retailers of packaged goods learned that they could improve sales and profits if they could more efficiently administer all their different product classifications. The idea was to oversee the store not as an aggregation of products, but rather as an amalgam of categories, with each category unique in how it is priced and how it is expected to perform over time.*

*One vendor is designated as "**category captain**" and charged with helping the retailer define the category; determine its place within the store; evaluate its performance by setting goals; identify the target consumer; divine the best way to merchandise, stock, and display the category; and then influence the implementation of the plan. Becoming a captain is obviously an important position because it offers that supplier an opportunity to sway a retailer's buying decisions.*

Thus the category management process is a repetitive, strategic and long-term business philosophy that promotes cross functional working between companies with the involvement of professionals from very diverse areas such as procurement, finance, supply chain, marketing, store operations, sales and space planning.

Figure 9.1
Category Management Process

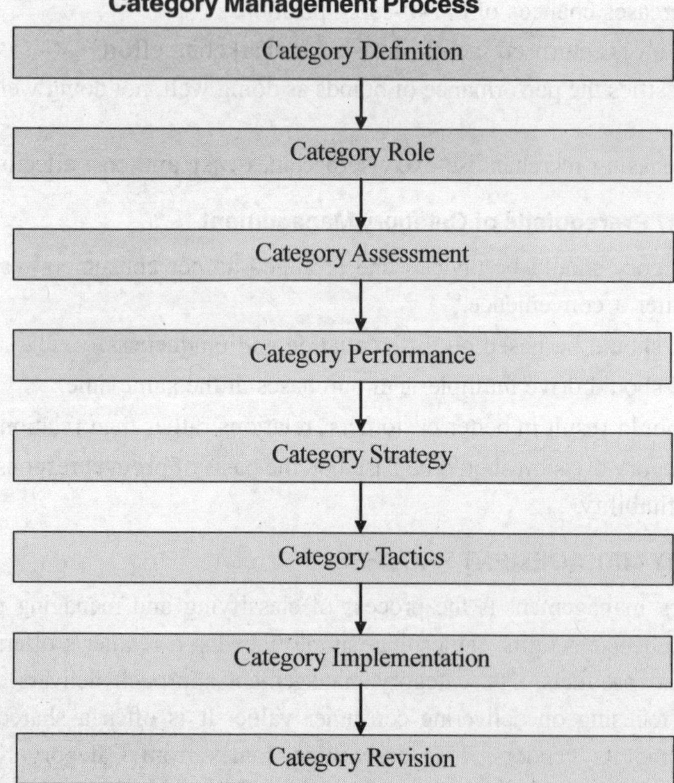

IGD Research (2007) reveals that merely 9% of companies follow this eight step process of category management and is useful for those firms that have developed shorter, streamlined approaches that deliver benefits in a relatively smaller, less resource intensive time horizons. A typical category management process is discussed as follows:

1. Category Definition

Defining a category is the first step in a typical category management process. In this step retailer classifies the store's products into different categories depending on the usage of the product by the consumers and its packaging. What should be the best way to define a particular category is always debatable issues amongst retailers. The category management experts opine that whatever the base it should be, category definition should be based on consumers' buying behaviour not on retailer's buying behaviour. Before beginning with the process of category definition, the retailer and vendor should first understand what exactly makes a category? The supplier know-how about a category and its potential customers becomes vital in developing the correct definition and segmentation of the category. This basically decides the products that fall under a particular category, sub-category and key segmentation. Thus a retailer basically assigns products to the different categories depending upon customers' liking, disliking, quantity size, and packaging. The main objective of defining category is to know what items to include and what items to exclude.

The definition of category varies from situation to situation and one store to another. In one circumstance, category may be narrowly defined or very broadly defined, depending upon several factors. For instance, the category of sandwich may be narrowly defined so as to comprise only vegetarian sandwich, or it may be broadly defined to include all types of varieties such as vegetarian, non-vegetarian, chocolate, fried, baked, grilled, cheese spicy/mutton spicy etc. The point is to be remembered that it is the customer that gives the profit so its perspective should be kept at top priority while defining a particular category. The task further should result into particular product titles with respect to its sizes, color, packaging, sub-categories, variety of products and variety within the product.

2. Category Role

Under this step, retailers usually determine the priority level and then assign a role for the category based on a cross category comparison considering liking and disliking of consumers, and market trends. Basically here retailers develop the base for allocating resources for the entire business. While assessing the role played by a category, retailers should thoroughly consider the nature and size of product category. For instance, some categories may represent luxury brands, whilst others might be denominated by low priced brands. It signifies that if a particular category is denominated by luxury brands, then most of the underlying brands are or will be, lucrative. On the other hand, category largely composed of low priced brands may not provide any opportunity to earn profitable margins for both the retailer and the supplier. Hence, it becomes imperative for a retailer to consider the role played by a category in the store while determining a particular category.

For example, the ice cream product category has been upgraded in UK marked by introducing premium luxury ice-cream, ice cream confectionery, mass scale marketing and sales promotion companies such as Haagen Dazs and the development of premium store brands. Athletic footwear (trainers), toys and beer are examples of other categories that have shifted from value to premium (Vishwanath and Mark, 1999).

The role of SKU within a Category

When a retail product manager is reviewing the choice within a product category, the individual roles that are played by the different brands or product variations will be acknowledged (McGrath, 1997). In a store, some products within a category are '***customers' catchers***', giving high sales and have a large market share. These are the sources of attraction for visitors/customers and their non-availability may result in customer loss. Store brands are clearly concerned with achieving sales targets. Low-priced goods not only attract customers but motivate customers to buy other goods too kept in store. Some stock keeping units (SKUs) create excitement and theatre in stores while other SKUs depict latest fashion and imported goods under same roof. Some SKUs sometimes have been observed for latest fashion and known for first arrivals.

Figure 9.2

The Role Played by a Product Category

Sr. No	Name of the Category	Share in Overall Category (%)	Features/Indicators
1	Retail Brand Builders	10-15%	• Convenience categories • Create attraction for visitors • Latest fashion & design categories • Latest technology product categories • New categories
2	Profit Makers	15-20%	• Fashion categories • FMCG categories • Growing categories • High profit margins • Symbolic categories
3	Cash Flow Contributor	50-60%	• Non-symbolic categories • Proven established categories • Value for money categories
4	Destination	5-7%	• Composed of usually perishable product categories • Consistently deliver superior value • Deep and wide assortment • Mounting or Conventional categories • Usually lead in areas of market share, turnover, service level and customer satisfaction
5	Service Provider	10-15%	• Limited profit margin due to competitive goods • Sluggish or falling categories • Staple product categories • Well established popular brands

Be it profit generator or service provider, all have their own presence and significance for a retail store. Each (SKU) member of the category contributes in the overall turnover and it should be clearly visible. Otherwise astute retailers would like to replace its efforts to another more profitable brand. For instance, will it be feasible to replace one 'non-performing' brand with another more profitable brand. Does a present category enable to create excitement? Considering a category to be a part of growing market, is there any scope for further excitement? Does a particular SKU requires packaging change with regard to quantity packed and offered? Do we offer two or more different pack sizes of a same item like 1 kg, 3 kg, and 5 kg packs? Will the sales be hampered if we offer only two sizes – small and family pack?

While on the other hand, the best practices in category management report suggests a set of four consumer centric categories roles as follows:-

I. Destination Category:

It is used by retailers to position themselves as the most favorite stores of customers through combining the attributes of several categories of stores:

- the size of a mass merchandiser,
- the variety and scope of a department store, and
- the low prices of a discount store.

So that customers should make a special trip to their stores with the specific intention of making a purchase that concentrates on one product category and that combines a huge multivariate selection with low prices. Large discount toy chains, sporting goods chains, and office supply chains are examples of destination categories. Besides this, fresh vegetables and fruits at super bazaars, apparel at departmental stores, fresh bakery produce and food at RPG's Giant Hypermarket are few examples of destination categories. The primary reason for calling them as *destinations* is that people are willing to travel a good distance to shop in these stores.

II. Routine Category (Preferred category)

These are the products and services that customers use in their day to day life on regular basis as a matter of routine or habit. The products placed under routine category include shaving cream, body wash, hair oil, shampoo, toothpastes, soap, and so on. The services under routine category include banking, post office, courier, gyms, spa, health centres etc.

III. Seasonal Category (Occasional category)

These are the products and services which are not purchased on regular basis but occasionally. The products placed under seasonal category include raincoats, umbrellas, sweaters, mangoes, etc. other items such as crackers during Diwali Season, Colours and water balloons before Holi, flying kites before independence day in Delhi and Northern part of India are also examples of seasonal items.

Note: *It has been observed that retailers who only deal in such seasonal items can change their products into destination categories in order to grab the majority of market share.*

IV. Convenience Category

These are the products that a customer always prefers to buy from neighbourhood retail stores. Usually these goods carry a wide range of products but of low prices. The products under convenience category include bread, butter, eggs, routine stationery, and routine medicines and so on. Convenience products can be categorized into staple (milk), impulse (not intended prior to shopping trip).

Category roles are implemented through the appropriate mix of strategies in the category. Certain strategies are implied by role. Figure 9.3 illustrates the type of marketing strategy that is most commonly deployed to implement a category role. These strategies should be considered before other strategies.

Figure 9.3

Strategies Implied by Category Role

Category Role	Implied Marketing Category Strategies
Destination	• Traffic Building • Turf Defending • Transaction Building • Excitement Creating
Routine	• Transaction Building • Profit Generating
Seasonal	• Traffic Building· Excitement Creating • Profit Generating
Convenience	• Transaction Building • Profit Generating • Image Enhancing

Courtesy: *The Partnering Group and Roland Berger and Partner*

3. Category Assessment

Under category assessment step, the retailer conduct an analysis of the category's sub categories, segments with respect to sales, turnover, profits, return on assets by reviewing consumer, market, retailer and supplier information. Category assessment requires a variety of analytical measures designed to determine the strengths, weaknesses, opportunities and threats of a particular category. It provides the retailer an opportunity to identify future prospects in the category.

The retailer's objective to assess categories is to know (a) whether to continue with the present category categorization, (b) Which categories require additional effort to generate profits. (c) What are the areas of highest turnover, profit, and return on asset improvement opportunities, and lastly to know the gaps existed between the chosen category and the present performance level of the category. Besides analytical tools, retailer sometimes assesses the categories with the help of data on the customers, suppliers or competitors.

4. Category Performance

Measuring category performance is the fourth step in the category management process in which the retailer develops bottomline and benchmark to measure the performance of the categories. It involves setting measurable targets in terms of sales, volume, margins, and gross margin return on investment (GMROI).

Establishing category performance measures are essential for measuring performance of a particular category which later on becomes base for further improvement within the category. Category performance measures basically represent the category score card that result in target objectives that are set by the retailer and supplier for the achievement of the implementation of the category business plan.

Sales Volume	Increase in sales (in rupees) Growth over last year The sales per square foot
Profits	Increase in gross profits Growth over last year Growth profits per square foot GMROI Gross margins in percentage Actual margin rcalized
Inventory Turnover	Stock turnover targets achieved in store Stock turnover targets achieved in warehouse
Product Assortment	Number of SKUs carried Number of new products included Number of products withdrawn Major turn arounders
Market Share	Increase in market share Growth over last year Growth changes in percentage
Consumer Served	Number of invoices served Average value of the transaction in monetary terms

5. Category Strategy

Under this stage of category management business process, retailers develop marketing and product supply strategies that determine the category role and performance objectives. The basic purpose behind developing strategies is the retailer's intention to capitalize on category opportunities through creative and optimum utilization of available resources assigned to a category. The sub objectives are:

I. how to horizontally position a store's own brand relative to the incumbent national brand and

II. how to price the store and national brands for retail category profit maximization.

Following seven are the widely applied category management strategies:

(i) Traffic Building

Traffic building strategy is used to draw customers' attention towards store, aisle, and/ or category. This is usually achieved through advertising relatively low priced goods (having enough price difference from the everyday). This strategy typically applies to products that are most price sensitive, have high degree of household penetration, need frequent purchases, frequently promoted, having high sales in the category and generate major portion of sales.

(ii) Turf Protecting

A turf protecting strategy (also known as super traffic building) basically is applied to defend the category sales and market share against a known competitor through competitive based pricing. This policy is only deployed when absolutely essential because it is generally an expensive strategy in terms of profit impact products with large transaction size that are under intense pressure from a defined competitor are considered under turf protection strategy. Turf protection strategy should be applied carefully as and when required because of the essential margin investment. However, proper use of a turf protection strategy can assist the retailer in creating a positive overall price image. Implementing turf protecting strategy requires that if the competitor reduces prices or prices fall in the market, the retailer will follow with price reductions to maintain turf protection strategy.

(iii) Transaction Building

This strategy is issued to increase the sales of a particular category by emphasizing larger sales, multi packs, goods with trade-up options, aggressively pricing and promotion large transactions size terms, and goods that are subject to impulse purchase.

(iv) Profit Generating

This strategy is used to generate profits by focusing on sub-category or parts of the category while keeping prices within competitive ranges. Products generating higher margins usually have a substantial amount of loyalty and which are not like less price sensitive items, with higher than category average gross margins are commonly used in this category. Store's own brands also come under profit generators.

(v) Excitement Generating

This strategy is used to create excitement to a particular category by communicating a sense of dire need (urgency), or opportunity to the prospect. Seasonal items, latest arrivals, special items, limited edition, rapidly growing segments, fashion trends, and high items with a high incidence of impulse purchasing, come under this category.

(vi) Cash Generating

This strategy is used to generate cash flow to ensure the retailer a balanced cash flow across the categories in a store to meet operating cash requirements, larger sales volume products, fast turning products, low inventory turnover goods, and goods with favorable payment terms come under this category.

(vii) Image Enhancing

This strategy is used to enhance retailer's image before customers in one or more of the following aspects:

- Quality
- Variety
- Price
- Service
- Presentation
- Delivery
- Brands Available

Examples with regard to image enhancing are: offering live fishes to customers stocked in fish tanks, exclusive product offerings, combo offers, happy meal menus, meal solution suggestions, wide product assortment, luxury brand assortment, competitive pricing, easy loan options, multiple modes of payment, feel of the product, etc.

6. Category Tactics

Categories tactics are used to determine the optimal category assortment, pricing promotions, and shelf penetration, essential to ensure that strategies put are on right track. Category tactics determine and authenticate the specific actions that are required to implement the category strategies developed earlier.

The areas covered under category tactics vary from retailer to retailer and place to place. But pricing, promotions, assortments and the store's overall presentation are few commonly used areas where tactics are developed.

Therefore, it is expected from a supplier to do proper amount of value addition depending upon the role expected from a category; by assessing this retailers further develop proper strategies. For instance, a SKU may play convenience role for one retailer but a destination role for another. Therefore, while developing the category, category captain (usually supplier) should take an overall view of the category and create a framework suggesting for marketing (traffic building, profit generating, and image enhancing etc.) as well as ensuring product supply. The retailing format (departmental, destination, hypermarkets, etc.) and the product's stage in a product life cycle should be taken into consideration.

7. Category Implementation

This step is used to implement the category business plan through a systematic schedule and list of responsibilities. Implementing category plan as per the objectives laid down, is the path to the success of category management. A typical category plan under implementation stage includes:

I. What specific tasks need to be done?

II. When to do,

III. Where to do, and

IV. Who will do it

Therefore, in a short, implementing category plan on the part of a retailer requires to decide what, where, when a task to accomplish and by whom.

8. Category Revision

This is the final step in a typical category management business plan. Category review enables a retailer and concerned supplier to gauge the performance of a category and identify key areas of opportunity and threats to overcome by adopting alternate plans.

As today category management is an important strategic plan, it becomes imperative for a supplier to revisit the dynamics of the category and the appropriate strategies and tactics. This will enable a supplier to measure performance against the appropriate strategies and tactics. In this regard, one thing should be noted that category business plans are subject to change with regard to change in assumptions laid down. For instance, incase of any specific change in business environment, assumptions made earlier may not hold validate. Therefore, business plan must be modified with respect to change in underlying assumptions without any delay.

Elements of Category Management

Category management aims to maximize sales revenues by satisfying consumer needs and wants through trade partnerships and strategic management of product groups.

The key elements of category management are:

(i) It must provide merchandise as per customers' needs and wants at the cost affordable to them

(ii) Product division should be based on customers buying styles, their needs and demands.

THE CATEGORY CAPTAIN

As retailers and their suppliers work with the same goals of selling merchandise and earning profits, it will be helpful for both of them to share the information (data that may help them to achieve their goals). Therefore, some retailers in order to honor their favorite suppliers assign them the task of developing and managing the entire category. Such supplier is known as '***Category Captain***', who after collecting information about customers; help the retailer in developing his categories. One thing should be noted in this regard that a retailer might have more than one category captains depending upon the number of product categories and supplier expertise in these categories. The category captain is expected to have regular and continuous relations and communication with the retailer, which in turn will be helpful for supplier himself by the way of merchandise sold. Generally, the category captain task is given to that supplier who has maximum turnover in the category although not necessarily but is quite common. The category captain is the first point of contact for advice and information and is normally chosen to lead the strategic direction of the category though others suppliers are also invited to comment and present their ideas.

Essentials of Retailer-Category Captain Relations

1. Unconditional cooperation from both sides.
2. Supplier access to the retailer's database.
3. Reliance on each other.

THE BUYING FORMATS

The retail merchandise plan cannot be properly framed and implemented unless the buying organization and its processes are clearly defined. It includes determining:

1. Who will be responsible for merchandising procurement and related decisions
2. What authority will be given to him?
3. What are the expectations from him?
4. What role and tasks be played by people involved in merchandise decisions to make certain the optimum buying and the relationship of merchandising to overall store operations. It includes buying, selling, selection, price fixing, visual merchandising (display, customer transactions etc). Figure 9.4 below presents the various functions and attributes performed by buying department of a retail organization.

Figure 9.4
Functions and Attributes performed by Buying Department

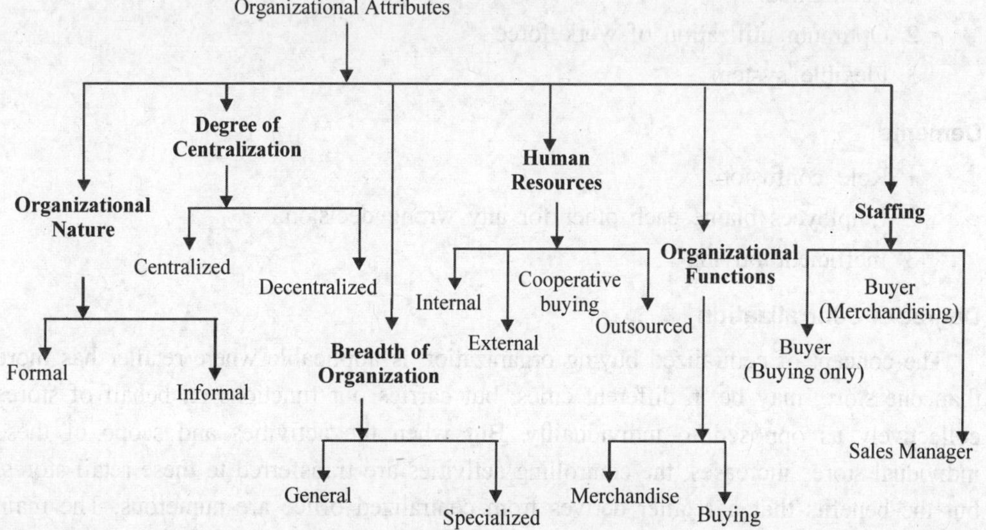

Organizational Nature

Large retail firms generally have formal buying department whose job is to buy the merchandise and making it available to sales floor for selling purpose. This department has full control over buying activities and has separate staff to perform merchandise buying operations, while on the other hand, in case of informal buying organization, merchandise buying is not handled by separate staff but the floor staff along with their usual selling operations, perform buying operations too. It means same floor staff handles merchandise buying and merchandise selling related tasks.

The formal organization generally occurs in large retail firms. No doubt, formal buying is an expensive state of affairs but it has several merits too:

Merits and demerits of 'formal' buying organization

Merits

1 Role clarity
2 Due attention
3 Assistance of dedicated merchandisers
4 Efficient bargaining

Demerits

1. Uneconomical
2. Time consuming task

Merits and demerits of 'informal' buying organization

Merits

1 Economical
2 Optimum utilization of work force
3 Flexible system

Demerits

1 Role confusion
2 Employees blame each other for any wrong decision
3 Inefficient buying

Degree of Centralization

The concept of centralized buying organization is applicable where retailer has more than one store, may be in different cities, but carries out functions on behalf of stores collectively as opposed to individuality. But when the activities and scope of these individual stores increases, the controlling activities are transferred to these retail stores, but the benefits that a retailer derives from centralized office are numerous. The main advantage is the economy of scale and the specialization of activities. Some retail decisions that need to be made for one store is to be made for all stores, hence, a central body of employees becomes responsible for decision making for all outlets. Most of the employees at the head office work in some particular departments dedicated to a particular function of retail management. The central department is commonly known as '**policy-making department**' which carries out the initial planning of the strategic plan. While the independent stores carry out the remaining functions and put policies (as laid by central office) into actions.

On the other hand, in case of decentralized buying organization, purchasing is done at outlet level. It means each store is free to buy the merchandise as and when required under intimation to the regional head. It means if a certain retailer has 15 chains in a city/state, it may allow each outlet to buy its merchandise on its own or separating the branches under geographic territories (like five branches per region) with regional decisions are made by the headquarters' store in each such zone.

Merits and Demerits of 'Centralized' Buying

Merits

1 Benefit of economies of scale
2 Efficient bargaining
3 Integration of efforts and time
4 Nearness to top management
5 Staff assistance

Demerits

1 Time wastage
2 Duplication of work
3 Complexities of overload
4 Lack of flexibility

Merits and Demerits of 'Decentralized' Buying

Merits

1 Enhanced morale of employees at outlet level
2 Quick order processing
3 Degree of flexibility
4 Adherence to local conditions

Demerits

1 Less bargaining power
2 No benefit of economies of scale
3 Less support from staff
4 Some times wrong merchandise buying decisions

Organizational Breadth

Retail store ***organizational breadth*** is a measurement that tracks the store's central business functions affected by a system in practice. Therefore, selection must be made between a general buying organization and a specialized one. As the name implies, in general buying organization merchandise buying exercise is done by one or more persons individually or collectively. For instance, a departmental store owner does the buying for his store on its own. Each type of item is selected and purchased by him or under his control while in the case of specialized buying, merchandise buying is done by separate people committed to separate product categories. For instance, an apparel store has separate buyers for Gents' Clothes, ladies' Clothes and Kids Wears.

Experience has shown that if a retailer is small and deals in limited merchandise, the general buying format is suitable. In case retailer has variety of wide merchandise assortment and within a category, if it has further merchandise depth, specialized buying format is recommended. Each method has its own merits and demerits. Retailer has to select which method will be applicable to his store merchandise.

Human Resources

A retailer has to decide what kind of buying organization will be suitable for him. Will the buying organization be equipped with his internal employees or he should hire employees from outside the organization. Theses employees work on the basis of fixed percentage/commission/sum. According to the capabilities and number of work force, retailers either employ their own employees or seek assistance of outsiders. While some organization, in order to avail the benefits of both the methods, use the mix of two.

Some of the organizations in order to avoid any differences with their employees or outsiders outsource this buying task. It means whole task of merchandise buying is performed buy an outside agency.

Organizational Functions

While planning merchandise assortment, a retailer besides deciding the role of floor staff, outlines the roles of merchandise. Further, the responsibilities and functions of both areas are assigned systematically. It implies if a retailer decides about 'merchandising' view, its merchandising staff does all the acquisition and selling functions including marketing, advertising, pricing, displays, the selection and appointment of employees. On the other hand, if a retailer decides upon a 'buying approach', its merchandise staff oversee the buying of goods, pricing and advertising jobs while store staff supervise assortments, displays, visual merchandising, employees selection and sales promotions. One thing must be noted in this regard that functions must reflect the organizational level of formality, the degree of centralization, and human resources, as enumerated in setting up the buying organization.

Staffing

It is the final organizational decision that deals with the selection of right persons at right job with the right skills, right abilities and right aptitude. In the words of Theo Haiman, "staffing is concerned with the placement, growth and development of all those members of the organization whose function is to get the things done through the efforts of others." Thus floor staff planning, recruitment, training and development, performance appraisal and giving remuneration are the functions of ***staffing***.

Some retail firms hire employees through campus interviews for their entry level positions while for middle and upper level positions; they promote their entry level employees after providing training and relevant exposure. A buyer therefore, must be aware of organizational buying culture and in position to bargain suppliers effectively.

A sales manager, who usually occupies a middle level position in a retail firm, should satisfy the demands and expectations of not only his seniors but those whom he is supervising, analyzing and coordinating. Thus, a retail sales manager has long list of functions such as planner, recruiter, organizer, supervisor, controller, budget manager, communicator and motivator to play and responsibilities to fulfill toward the achievement of the sales objectives of a retail firm.

After understanding the concept of '**category**' and '**category management**', and its significance for a retailer, it becomes important to know where in the buying organization the category fits. Depending upon the nature of products and store size (branches), merchandise-planning group is constructed that works with the buying organization.

THE BUYING ORGANIZATION

After deciding upon the category and the buying format, retailer now has to take decision that wherein the buying organization category will be best placed. The **buying organization** structure varies from organization to organization, country to country and format to format. How many participants will be included in a buying organization scheme depends upon various aspects such as:

- Type of merchandise offered
- Type of retail format
- Areas of business operations
- 'Width' and 'breadth' of merchandise offered

- Management policy
- Level and number of categories
- Competition in the market
- Financial Constraints

For the purpose of understanding, the merchandise classification used by the **National Retail Federation** (NRF) (the world's largest retail trade association), USA has been considered.

About National Retail Federation (NRF)

NRF is the world's biggest retail trade association. It has membership that encompass all sorts of retail formats and distribution channels such as independents, category killer, department, specialty, hyper, super, discount, catalog, cyber, chain restaurants, food stores, drug stores, grocery and consumer electronics stores. It represents more than 1.63 million US based retail companies, approximately 2.5 crore employee work force that belong to more than 100 state, national and international retail associations.

Figure 9.5
Merchandise Classification Scheme
(Levels of Buying Organisation)

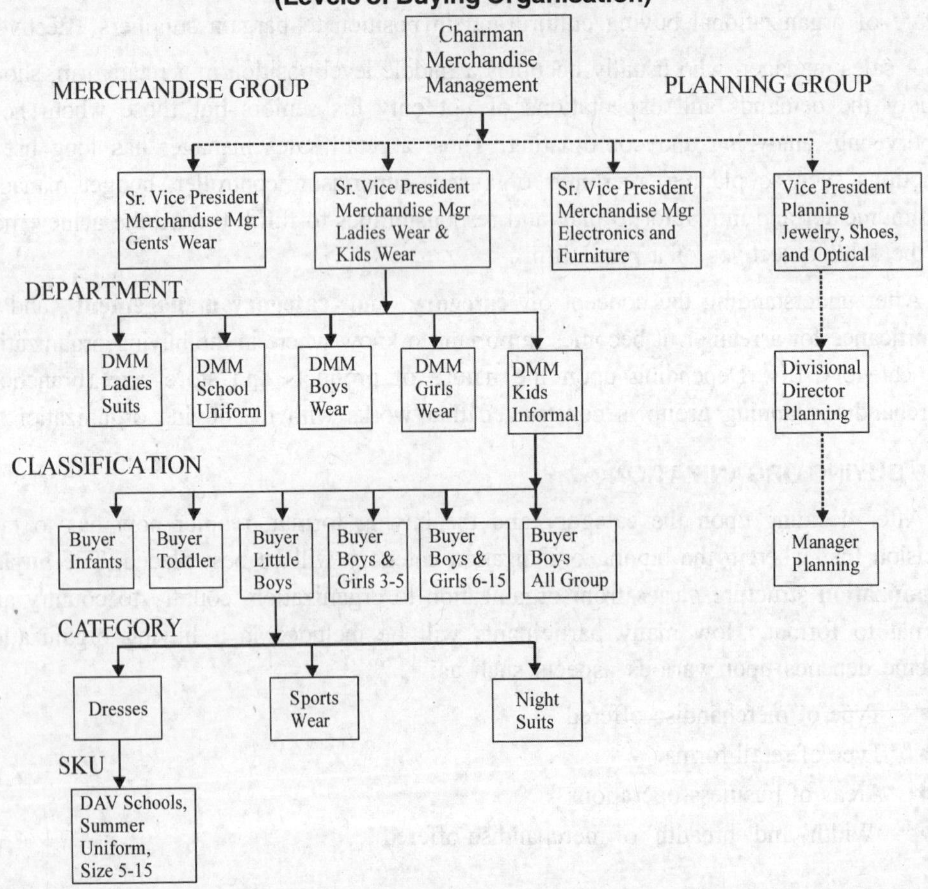

Merchandise Group

Merchandise group is the brain and lifeblood of any merchandising planning group, which is managed/controlled by the senior level officers of the merchandise cell usually by the senior Vice-presidents. These vice-presidents for merchandise are usually known as '**General Merchandise Managers**' (GMMs). These merchandise managers are responsible for the following tasks:

- To lead the team for maximizing the sales and ultimate profits for their respective merchandise areas.
- To determine long-period merchandise strategy for the whole merchandise group from domestic and global perspectives (depending upon the area of operations), considering both economic and competitive pressures.
- Responsible for extending all direct reports and their buyers to achieve organizational goals.
- To search new merchandise categories, fashion, trends and items.
- Responsible for approving all sorts of assortment plans.
- Challenging direct reports to make certain that all financial elements (components) are duly met and exceeded.
- To make certain that on the whole, organizational mission and merchandise strategy is met.

Department

The next step under merchandise organizational chart is the division. These departments are solely run by the **Divisional Merchandise Managers** (DMMs), who are next to vice-presidents. The Division Merchandise Managers provide headship and direction to the merchandise buying staff for preparation of assortment plans that line up with the merchandise strategy and prop up seasonal merchandise plans. Further, DMMs supervise merchandise selection and ensure the success of assortment plan by coordinating with various merchandise strategies. DMMs also play vital role for developing and executing a cost-effective and customer-oriented merchandising strategy, while augmenting the whole department, merchandise group and organizational strategy. As stated above, DMMs directly report to the senior vice presidents/GMMs and escort an organization of buying experts. This link works closely with the merchandise development team, promotional planning team, merchandise placement team and merchant operations team to enhance the overall productivity and shareholders' wealth.

DMMs are entrusted with following responsibilities:

- To anticipate changing market/consumer trends and develop an action plan to respond.
- To oversee market visits.
- To develop relationships with vendors and work with the buyers to strengthen market relationships and product and trend knowledge.
- To study competitors' strengths and weaknesses and action plans.

- To direct assortment selection process and review assortments for balance (major brands, main items, supplement items etc) and adhering to organizational objectives.
- To develop assortment plans while working with the planning organization that support overall strategy of in stock positioning for store's key merchandise categories, classifications, products and vendors.
- To resolve issues related to escalated buyer and associated buyer.
- To compliance with processes, policies, procedures and practices/tools within the group.
- To lineup with the marketing and in store marketing to develop the divisional promotional strategy.
- To review and approve the promotional strategies and plans.
- To overlook and approve line reviews.

Qualifications for Becoming DMMs

Following are the eligible and desirable qualifications to become a DMM:

- MBA (Marketing/Retailing & Merchandise) with 5 to 8 years merchandise related experience, 6 to 8 years experience of merchandise mix buying, planning, and implementing and placement responsibilities or Bachelor (Commerce/Management) degree with 10 years of merchandise related experience.
- Strong communication and analytical skills.
- Dedicated to meet targets.
- Liasoning and negotiation skills.
- Ability to lead teams and getting results through others.
- Ability to build relationships and business tie-ups.
- Ability to interact/communicate with all levels of the executives.
- Capable to analyze financial books and transactions.

Classification

It is the '**third level**' in merchandise organizational chart. Each divisional merchandise manager is responsible for procuring merchandise, deciding prices and markdowns and managing inventories for specific merchandise categories. Each buyer then purchases a particular classification and negotiates with vendors on prices, assortments, quantities, lead time and payment terms. The **merchandise classification** scheme exhibit shows one buyer responsible for infants. In recent years, one buyer may be responsible for several classifications. Further, some retailing firms divide the merchandise buying tasks between a buyer/category manager and a merchandise planner. A merchandise planner is a senior vice president of planning and distribution who work like merchandise managers in the buying organization and are responsible for allocating merchandising and tailoring the assortment in several categories. For instance, a merchandise planner at the Pantaloon India Ltd will alter the basic assortment of sweaters for the different climates in Northern and Southern part of India.

Categories

After classification, next level in a merchandise classification scheme is '**category**'. Each buyer purchases a number of categories. For instance, ladies' suits buyer may buy formal, western, casual and partywear suits. The infant buyer might purchase several categories such as baba suits, baby suits, woolen, cotton, uppers, lowers etc. A category like sportswear may be made up of merchandise from one to several manufacturers.

Stock Keeping Unit (SKU)

A stock keeping unit (SKU) is a unique number (identifier) assigned to an item that describes its features in terms of size, color, style and quantity. Each organization according to its size, level of operations and product categories, develops its own SKU numbers. These numbers are unique and allotted/assigned to a single item. No two items in an outlet will have same **SKU** number and are usually assigned and serialized at an outlet/merchant level. This system allows retailers to track for their merchandise records, for instance, with the help of SKU number system, a retailer will know which item of merchandise is performing well, like whether formal trousers are selling better than casual ones or not.

All retailers following the SKU number system will have different approach to assign the numbers to their merchandise items based on the state or national level data and retrieval strategies.

Stock Keeping Unit

SKU is the smallest and unique unit for managing the inventory stock. Successful retailers have the practice of using SKU for each item of merchandise and for its different variants. It allows retailers to track their merchandise for the following reasons:

- To know the performance of any item.
- To identify various items
- For ordering the supplies
- To know the balance of stock etc.

For Example:

In an apparel store, a SKU number would represent a unique gender/color/style/size combination. For instance, a men' white color shirt with short length and a size of 40 shoulder could be assigned the SKU number 1-03-02-40. Here

'1' represents the gender – male
'03' represents the color - white
'02' represents the length – short
'40' represents the size.

SETTING FINANCIAL OBJECTIVES FOR THE MERCHANDISE PLAN

In retailing, objectives are achieved by plans. These plans are prepared at senior levels and all the other departments tend to achieve them. Further, at the individual level, retailers, planners, divisional managers and other create some low level financial, store item, merchandise assortment and operational plans in order to achieve the organizational overall objectives. In actual, these low level, comprehensive, financial plans describe how the organizational objectives will be achieved. Top management only supervise the overall merchandising strategy and set the merchandising direction for the retail firm by (i) defining the firm's target markets, (ii) establishing performance goals, and (iii) setting various merchandise classification on the basis of market trends.

As discussed earlier, buyers and merchandise planners adopt micro approach towards achievement of overall objectives. They critically analyze their categories in terms of past performance, market trends, market results and consumers' response and try to estimate for their respective categories for the forthcoming quarters.

Be it a small firm, chain store or a supermarket, financial planning process remains the same, the only difference comes that the small retailers have fewer 'levels' in planning and execution process. Small retailers too even begin with their overall financial goals and divide them into categories. The so called resulting merchandise plan is a **financial** buying design for each category that considers the organization's overall financial objectives along with sales forecasts and merchandise flows. It helps the retailer in assessing that how much money is available to spend on a particular merchandise category in each month so that the sales target and other financial objectives are achieved.

Once the merchandise plan is ready, the buyers and planners start developing the assortment plan. The buyers search for vendors to select merchandise, negotiate for prices and preparation of promotional tasks. The planners, on the other hand, breakdowns the overall financial plan into various categories depending upon the number of items and their depth.

General Merchandise Managers (GMMs) while allocating the financial budgets, try to minimize their merchandise budgets, while on the other hand, planners wish to enhance the size of their merchandise budgets. Only way to increase the financial approval in the hands of planners is to increase their sales projections. But here remains a situation that in case planners succeed in getting their increased projections approved, and if the merchandise is not sold, the store's profitability, planners' capability will ultimately be suffered. Further, planner's future predictions will be questioned.

Purpose for setting financial objectives

1. To increase control over inventory and reducing timing involved in acquisition.
2. To increase firm's cash inflow and profitability.
3. To line up between organization's strategy and business operations.
4. To improve the merchandise management as per global standards.
5. To apply best practices leading to improved margins and firm's revenues.

GROSS MARGIN RETURN ON INVENTORY INVESTMENT (GMROI)

Gross margin return on investment or now days known as Gross margin return on inventory investment is used to plan and evaluate the performance of overall retail operations. Since 60-80% of a typical retailer's investment is in inventory, therefore, it becomes essential for a retailer to know how much return he is getting on invested money in inventory. Further, as retailing is becoming competitive and shrinking profits continuously have forced retailers to use some sort of financial tool that should provide a quick feedback to assess how many gross margin rupees are earned on every rupee of inventory investment.

GMROI today has become the widely used measure for any retail execution. It is one of the fastest and easy methods to measure and manage the productivity of a retailer's investment in inventory. A ratio higher than one means, the retail organization is selling the merchandise more than its acquisition cost. GMROI considers both sales velocity of inventory and the overhead in terms of inventory. Following are the essentials to apply GMROI successfully:

1. To understand gross margin.
2. To understand inventory turns
3. Proper access to inventory details with regard to price, acquisition cost, sales volume and inventory turns.

Calculation of GMROI

GMROI indicates the relationship between a retailer's total sales, the gross profit margin retailer earns on that sales and the number of rupees retailer invests in his inventory. Working of GMROI can be understood with the help of this hypothetical example.

A company has five departments. Given are the details of their respective annual sales, annual gross margin and average inventory cost. And out of the five departments, which is more productive?

Table 9.1

Department	Annual Sales	Annual Gross Margin	Average Inventory Cost
A	4,40,500	48%	2,05,400
B	3,18,300	45%	1,04,600
C	2,20,000	40%	57,000
D	2,14,000	47%	78,000
E	1,73,500	43%	38,800

As per the question, Department 'A' has the highest sales, Department 'D' has the highest margin. In order to calculate, which department is more productive, we can calculate the GMROI.

Table 9.2

Department	Annual Sales	Annual Gross margin	Average Cost Inventory Cost	GMROI
A	4,40,500	48%	2,05,400	1.03
B	3,18,300	45%	1,04,600	1.37
C	2,20,000	40%	57,000	1.54
D	2,14,000	47%	78,000	1.28
E	1,73,500	43%	38,800	**1.92**

Form the above table 9.2, it is clear that **Department 'E'** has the highest GMROI, while from table 1, it seems that Department 'E' has the lowest annual sales and margin. Therefore, GMROI is the best way to judge the productivity of a retail store. Annual sales figures and margin alone are not really enough to tell the retailer's actual position. A retailer having various outlets or various departments within a single outlet can calculate GMROI by departments, as mentioned above by categories, seasons, gender, regions or otherwise.

Calculating GMROI

GMROI = (Annual sales) X (Gross margin %) / (Average inventory cost)

Applications of GMROI

The advantage of GMROI is that it is applicable to any store, department or merchandise classifications within a retail store. In case, a retailer's accounting system is fully computerized, a retailer can get GMROI reports automatically on his computer or through a service as a part of monthly accounting reports.

GMROI should not be seen only as *'financial management tool'*, but it can be an effective human resource management tool as well. A retailer can apply GMROI to incentives as a performance appraisal tool for his employees.

Try to involve your staff in improving the firm's **GMROI** by setting targets for achieving a particular gross margin and sales-to-inventory investment for each product category. A retailer should convey these targets, the reasons for setting them and any rewards that the retailer will give to the department that will achieve these targets. Motivate employees to share their suggestions that can improve the firm's productivity in any manner. Encourage them, reward them with appropriate recognition and financial awards.

Let the employees know what actually they are doing/performing and what is expected from them. Provide them latest information about their output and contribution. Further, the sense of healthy competition among various departments can do wonder in terms of improvement in productivity.

In nutshell, **GMROI** is a powerful management tool that involves two significant profitability factors: retailer's gross margin and sales to inventory investment ratio. With the retail space becoming costlier, mall rentals soaring and inventory cost constantly rising; a retailer must get the best possible highest return from every rupee invested in inventory. GMROI will enable a retailer to achieve these goals by keeping a close watch on GMROI.

SOURCING AND SAMPLING

Sourcing is a process of procuring inventory required for selling in the retail stores or it also refers to procuring variety of goods at the best possible prices, in the best quality. Price and the quality are the two main factors that determine the sourcing decision. It has following objectives:

- Reduction in inventory
- Maximizing profits
- Increasing seasonal sales and
- Build customer loyalty

Sourcing criteria and buying operations

The retailers' buying operations are canalized by the policies and philosophy of a retail organization. Further, micro-environmental variables also have deep impact on the business operations of a retail firm. These are:

- The fashion view point of the stores
- Pricing policies
- Promotional criteria
- Nature and structure of retailing mix
- Organizational configuration, and
- Geographical spread

The decisions related to sourcing are usually taken by the regional office and buying operations are delegated to merchandisers (buyers) based on the overall budget, lead time, store's turn over ratios, sales expectations, retail store productivity, profitability and mark-up margin.

In a typical department store, there are usually separate merchandise managers for various product categories and divisional merchandise managers (DMMs) for key group of goods and services for different items. The import choice and the policy proposition are normally handled by the headquarters of the companies, where on the basis of quota availability and other sourcing criteria, open to buy budgets of different product categories are divided among different nations. In few cases, the buying budget is allocated to regional offices and that office will further decide 'from which country to buy' for instance, Singapore office is empowered to decide whether inventory should be purchased from India, Sri Lanka, Nepal, Bangladesh or Pakistan and in how much quantity.

The decision to select one country and giving the order in less or large quantity depends upon the quality standards adopted by the country in question. For example, Liz

Claiborne (New York based Fortune 500 Company) sources from more than sixty countries. The quality standards are centralized and communicated to buying country, who is then responsible for implementing the prescribed quality standards. One thing should be noted in this regard that the retail sourcing decisions depend on the sort of retailer (Chain store, department store, super market, hyper market, catalogue houses etc.) and the type of customer base they serve.

Thus retailers throughout the globe have merchandises and buyers who are generally in charge of the buying operations. The large retailers have their own separate import units and general import divisions and buying cells for (departments) merchandise assortment and development. Some large firms develop in order to create competitive advantage, make their own specialized sourcing sister concerns by providing the right quality, quantity, channel and price mix. For instance, Geoffrey Beene (USA based fashion giant) has its sister concern in New Delhi by the name, 'Triburg'.

About Triburg

Established in 1990s, a leading buying agency in the Indian sub-continent having a staffing strength of 360 people and sources over US$ 200 million worth of merchandise, comprising approximately fourty million garments annually from a vendor base of over 155 factories.

INVENTORY TURN OVER

Inventory turn over ratio, commonly known as Inventory Turnover is one of the most important ratio in the line of retailing that not only shows the health of a sound business but presents a view how a business is operating efficiently.

The inventory of a retail store represents the largest expense to its total expenditure cost. The sale of items from this inventory causes profit to a retailer. Therefore, the money invested in merchandise is of utmost importance to a retailer to have a profitable situation.

Inventory Turnover

Inventory turnover is a ratio of the total cost of goods sold in a year to the average inventory level in rupees. The benefit of using this ratio is to know how quickly the retail store is getting its inventories and how quickly customers get the order placed to the stores.

Meaning and Definition of Inventory Turnover Rate

The Inventory Turnover ratio is calculated by annual sales divided by average inventory at retail value and is represented as:

$$\text{Inventory Turnover} = \frac{\text{Annual Sales}}{\text{Average Inventory at Retail Outlet}}$$

The low inventory turnover ratio of a retail business implies that the retailer is carrying high inventory level and high inventory turnover ratio presents the retailer's ability to sell quickly. If a retailer at any point of time compares his inventory turnover with his competitor, he must ensure that the formula used by the competitor is same as used by the retailer himself. Any deviation in the formula can lead to different inventory-profit picture.

For example:

	Retailer 'X'	Retailer 'Y'
Annual Sales	Rs 15 lacs	Rs 15 lacs
Average Retail Inventory	Rs 7.5 lacs	Rs 5 lacs
Hence Inventory Turnover ratio will be =	2.0	3.0

Importance of Inventory Turnover

- It measures the soundness of retailer's inventory methods.
- It also indicates poor inventory planning and lack of controlling techniques.
- By improving Inventory Turnover, a retailer can easily increase his profitability by carrying fewer inventories.
- Inventory Turnover presents meaningful comparison and informs the retailer about latest trends.

Ways to Improve Inventory Turnover

The Inventory Turnover ratio that measures the effectiveness of retailer's merchandise planning and control can be improved in following ways:

1. By increasing retail sales without increasing any expenditure on inventory sales.
2. By decreasing stocks/inventory without disturbing the current sales.
3. By increasing retail sales at one side and decreasing inventory stock on the other side.
4. One way to improve inventory turnover is to use less space for retail activity. A low level of inventory takes less space area to display merchandise, resulting in higher sales in a smaller and less expensive retail store.
5. By way of displaying fresh arrivals and new comings, a retailer receives good and quick response and customers prefer to shop more often.
6. By keeping selling price lower, a retailer can turn his inventory into cash quickly resulting in higher stock turns and enhance profitability.

Which approach should be used and would be suitable in the long run depends on the circumstances and varies from retailer to retailer type. One thing can be said undoubtedly that the best way to increase Inventory Turnover ratio over a period of time is to increase the sale without increasing expenditure on inventory held. This can be done using following ways:

(i) By frequent buying but in small volumes.
(ii) By decreasing number of merchandise assortments.
(iii) Replacing slow moving merchandise with fast moving merchandise.
(iv) Don't buy before selling season.

Measuring Inventory Turnover

The average inventory is calculated in various ways to determine the retailer's merchandise and performance. To calculate the average inventory, a retailer would first decide how many months should be used? For example, a sportswear retailer calculating inventory for the first half year (two quarters) would use the first six months of end-of-month inventory.

Note: *While calculating Average Inventory, any number of months, up to twelve may be used. It may be for one quarter (three months), half year (six months) or even full year (twelve months).*

Table 9.3

S No.	Month	Inventory's Value (in rupees)
1	EOM January	17,000
2	EOM February	24,000
3	EOM March	29,000
4	EOM April	34,000
5	EOM May	51,000
6	EOM June	55,000

$$\text{Average Inventory} = \frac{\text{Month 1} + \text{Month 2} + \text{Month 3} + \text{Month 4} + \text{Month 5} + \text{Month 6}}{\text{Number of Months}}$$

$$\textbf{Therefore, Average Inventory} = \frac{17{,}000 + 24{,}000 + 29{,}000 + 34{,}000 + 51{,}000 + 55{,}000}{6}$$

Average Inventory = Rs 35,000/-

This is the simplest and widely used method of calculating average inventory. But this method is feasible when the end-of-month (EOM) inventory figures do not vary in any considerable way from usual weekdays. For instance, in North India, June' end-of-month inventory is significantly higher than the other months since it is the hottest month of the year and malls are full with summer collections of men, women and kids' wear.

Merits of high inventory turnover

Inventory turnover is a measure of how many times a retail store sells its average investment locked up in inventory during a particular period of time (usually one year). The higher the merchandise turnover, higher will be the revenue generation. Retailers usually want quick inventory turnover but not too quick as both the quick and slow inventory turnovers has its own merits and demerits that include:

1. **Augmented sales**: A quick inventory turnover results in increased sales volume and hence increased store's profitability. A quick inventory turnover means store has quick response from its customers. Therefore, a store will have fresh stock of merchandise that sells faster than old one. Customers would like to visit a store that keeps fresh merchandise. In short, quick inventory turnover leads to increased store sales as customers get new arrivals frequently.

2. **Improved employees' morale**: Quick inventory turnover increases the morale of the store employees. Store employees are more confident and pleased to sell fresh merchandise to customers. They would like to work with such store where the assortment of sizes is not only complete but up to date, trendy and as per seasonal demand. It takes less time on the part of the store employees to sell fresh merchandise rather than shopworn. When store's employees morale is high, they work sincerely, they think of organization, they remain busy and become the success reason. Further, improved morale leads to:
   (i) Increased client base
   (ii) Improves the image of the store
   (iii) Helps retailers create differentiation and value through their experiences
   (iv) Visitors become customers and customers become loyal to the store
   (v) It is a source of mouth advertisement
   (vi) Strengthens competitive advantage
   (vii) Improves financial performance

> **Morale** is self esteem in action and is the greatest single factor for the success of retail store, as high employees' morale equates to high productivity.

3. **Reduces changes of going obsolete and markdowns**: Today most of us live not according to the reason but according to the fashion and the life of fashion and related merchandise start falling as soon as it comes in market. Quick inventory turnover leads to quick sales, meaning store has less chances of having same inventory for long time. As a result, store will not face financial losses on account of old, not sold, obsolete and outdated merchandise. Therefore, store's markdowns will be reasonable and gross margins on the other hand, go up.
4. **Allows full advantage of economies of bulk purchases and logistics**: Quick inventory turnover enables a retailer to take full advantage of economies of bulk purchases and transportation as money blocked in inventory becomes liquid cash quickly. Therefore, a retailer would like to purchase in bulk resulting in good bargains over trade and/or cash discounts. Further, bulk purchase leads to reduced transportation cost.
5. **Fewer blockages of funds**: When inventory turnover is high, it besides keeping the investment in the inventories as low as feasible ensures availability of reordered inventory by providing adequate protection against uncertainties of availability of funds. As money blocked in inventory is freed quickly, a retailer would have 'ready cash' for fresh purchase and can invest in other emerging areas where return is comparatively more.
6. **Reduction in store's operating expenses**: Quick inventory turnover means less number of staff is required to monitor and administer day-to-day selling activities by controlling store's operating expenses such as salary of employees, supervision charges etc. The reason behind reduced charges is that lower inventory takes lower carrying costs, which is variable cost that increases with the increase in the inventory losses.

7. **Increased asset turnover**: Inventory being a part of current asset increases with the increase in sales or reduction in assets. Therefore, quick inventory turnover leads to enhanced sales from the same level of assets and positively affects the return on assets, which is the key performance measure of a retailer's efficiency.

Demerits of high inventory turnover

High inventory turnover always not leads to merits but has several negative impacts also. A high inventory turnover can be dangerous for a firm if sales decreases or operating expenses increase. Following are the demerits of having high inventory turnover:

1. **Decreased store's sales**: In order to increase inventory turnover, some retailers limit or reduce their total number of categories offered. This results in limited variety with regard to color and sizes. When customers come to such store and do not find the item/size/colour, they are looking for, will be disappointed and if this situation continues, they may stop visiting the stores and influence their friends, known and relatives to visit that particular store. One can imagine the consequences knowing how words of mouth travel with lightening speed.
2. **Augmented operating costs**: High inventory turnover causes frequent orders for inventory and retailer's efforts for meeting vendors, placing orders, negotiations, receiving and stocking merchandise. A retailer spends almost same time, same energy, same traveling / communication expense for both small and big orders. Therefore, high turnover, if not managed properly, leads to increased operating expenses.
3. **Loss of economies of scale**: A retailer can increase inventory turnover by frequent merchandise orders in small quantities, which reduces average inventory without reducing sales. But on the same side, a retailer would not avail the benefits of bulk buying, trade/cash discounts and logistics savings. Therefore, it raises the question how to get benefits of economies of scale without increasing the carrying cost. The answer is that the retailer should buy a long period supply (say six months or one year) at a trading discount that not only covers (offsets) the increased cost of carrying inventory but still provide some monetary benefits to the store.

SALES FORECASTING

The success of a retail store largely depends on how accurately the sales forecasts has been done because the retail supply chain as well as the value chain management depends on the demand patterns for the category as well as for the demand in the market. A retailer is always interested to know the demands for the categories he is offerings so that merchandise procurement can be channelized as per the market demand and budget available/issued for purchase. Sales forecasting helps a retailer to estimate its expected future revenues for sales made in a particular period of time. These forecasts may be at departmental level, company level and for individual merchandise classifications.

As **sales forecasting** has always been a critical step for retailers. With the advancement of information technology and technological advancement, large retailers have started using statistical techniques (like Index numbers, time series and multiple regression analysis) or software packages for the purpose of sales forecasting.

Which forecasting technique or which software package should be implied, depends upon the store's size, employees' skills, availability of funds and retailer's own experience.

Figure 9.6
Widely Used Forecasting Approaches

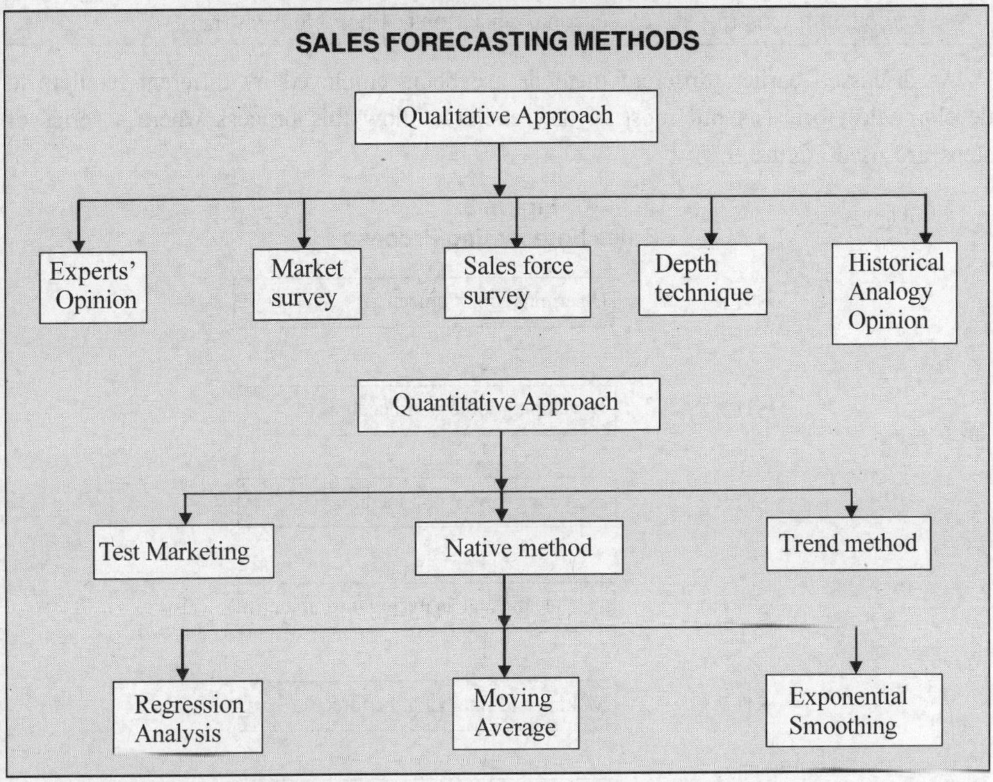

SALES FORECASTING METHODS

Qualitative Approach

Experts' Opinion
Market survey
Sales force survey
Depth technique
Historical Analogy Opinion

Quantitative Approach

Test Marketing
Native method
Trend method

Regression Analysis
Moving Average
Exponential Smoothing

The Sales forecasting process

The sales forecasting process is defined as the series of actions taken by a retailer to estimate the future revenues for a particular time period by considering the past information and current forecasting objectives into account. Sales forecasting for merchandise classifications within the departments usually depends on more qualitative techniques, even for large stores. The easiest way of forecasting sales for narrower categories is to first forecast store's sales on a firm wide basis and by department and then to breakdown these projections into various merchandise classifications. Different firms apply different methods of forecasting, but whatever method is chosen it must carefully predict and take into account external and internal factors. List of commonly considered and most widely encountered factors are as follows:

Internal Factors

- Credit policies
- Working hours
- New store open policy
- Promotion policy
- Additions and deletion of merchandise category
- Remodeling existing stores seasonal variations

External Factors

- Socio-cultural changes
- Competitors' moves
- Economic policies
- Political system
- Technological advancements
- Climate conditions
- New entries

As discussed earlier, different methods are being employed by different retailers to develop sales forecasts but most of the retailers follow this process where a series of steps are used (figure 9.7):

Figure 9.7
Sales Forecasting Process

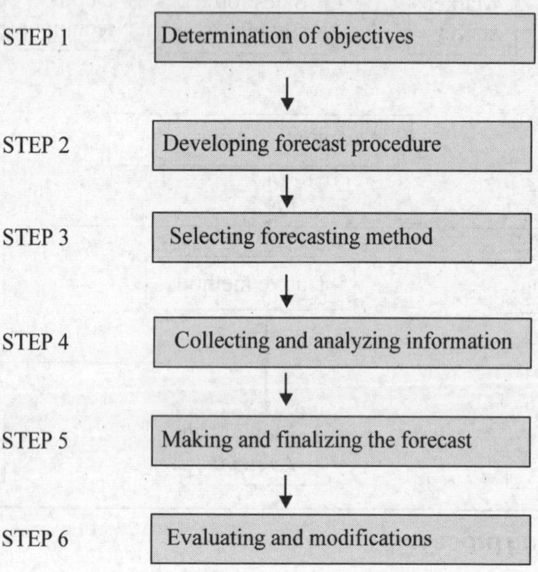

Figure: 9.8

Value-added Aspects of Sales Forecasting

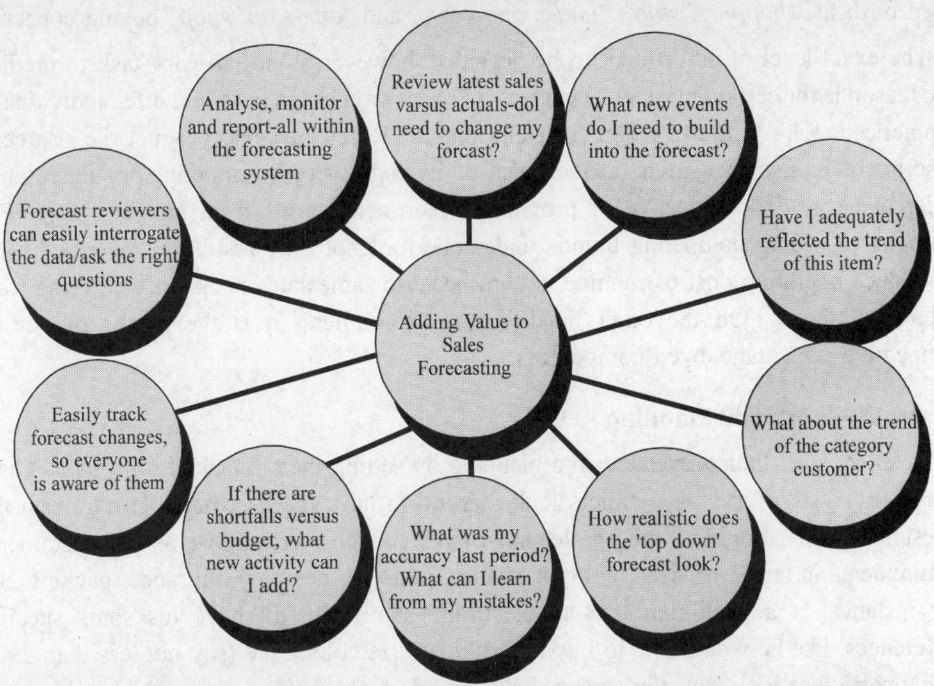

Source: *www.dataperceptions.co*

About Data Perceptions: Data perceptions is a private, self-funded UK software based company based in Hyde Heath, Amersham, about 20 miles from the centre of London, England specialized in the development of Sales Forecasting, Planning and Budgeting software for Microsoft.

THE ASSORTMENT PLANNING PROCESS

Retailers plan for the types of goods and service they wish to sell to the customers. This necessitates thinking about the size of the retail business and the consumers' requirements. Most of the time, consumers demand an assortment of goods and services and not just a single product. For example, you can see the buying style and selection of merchandise picked up by a housewife in her shopping basket in the beginning of the month - she has variety goods, various sizes, various items, and various colors. But one thing should be remembered that a manufacturer produces one or few items only, it is the retailer who collects the merchandise from various manufacturers, vendors and make them available to the customers. To make the concept clear, we take example of our day-to-day life, when we buy a motorbike, we also tend to purchase its accessories like biddings, helmet to wear, side lock, helmet lock, side box, handle guards, mudguard covers etc. Similar is the case with sportswear and grocery shopping. Assortment planning is the process of making available at one point of purchase, products that are inter-related and therefore, bought together. There is a long list of products, which the consumers usually buy in assortments. The reason behind is that these products are somehow inter-related to each other and all are required. Therefore, a customer would like to purchase all of these items at a time rather than visiting several stores for several items. It has given birth to *'shoppers' stop'*, *'under one roof'*, and *'one-stop' shop'* buying concepts.

The exact level of assortment to be provided, however, is not an easy task to predict. The reason is for certain product categories, while assortment is possible, often individually is practiced. Like '**Chhabra 555**' in Delhi and NCR sell just one product, i.e. 'sarees'. Assortment is also measured on the basis of having various competing/popular brands under one roof. The objective of providing assortment varies from store to store. For example, providing competing brands under one roof not only results in increased sales but reduce operating cost of running a store because same sales people are carrying total selling operations. On the other hand, for some retailers, it is the means of getting competitive advantage over competitors.

Strategic Assortment Planning

Retailers start their merchandising planning by setting their financial objectives. Once financial objectives are set, retailers look forward to have the best possible return on the investment made. For this, the retailer must have enough merchandise as per customers' requirements in terms of sizes, colours, shades, patterns, designs, fragrance, packing etc. For instance, if a customer goes to electronic store, he will have his some specific preferences, like he would like to buy a particular size colour TV (say not less than 29"), with a particular look (say flat screen) with specific features (say zoom, child lock, clock, on/off timer etc) and having a particular sound output (say 300-500 W) and digital noise reduction (like Samsung Ultra Slim Fit TV). Therefore, for a retailer of electronics, it becomes essential to have those features and models which customer seeks. Further, it alarms a retailer to have a strategic assortment planning process, which is based on consumers' survey as well as retailer's own predictions about variety. A strategic assortment planning process usually has these four steps shown as under (Figure 9.9):

Figure 9.9

Strategic Assortment Planning Process

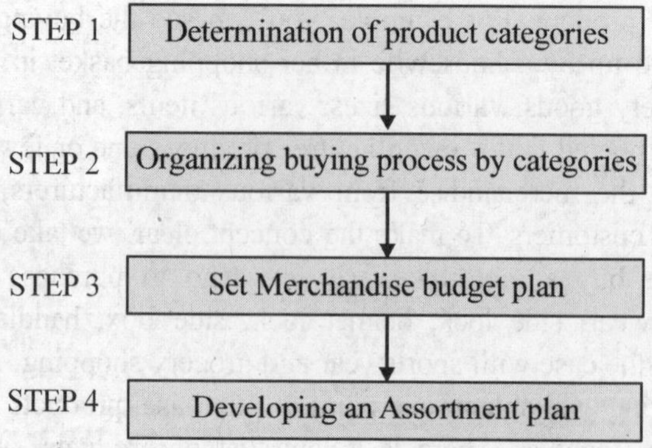

Assortment planning decisions are constrained by the financial budget assigned to invest in inventory and the amount of selling and display space available in the store. Depending upon the financial objectives framed by the top management, decisions regarding variety, assortment and product availability are made as under:

1. **Variety**: offering the right type of item or merchandise in your store is not enough; they also need to turn up in right quantity, quality and in various specifications with regard to colour, size and makeup. **Variety** is measured in terms of width and breadth. Stores offering large variety under one roof are said to have good breadth. For example, 'Subhiksha Mobile' carries latest models of leading cell phones and 'Pentaloon India Ltd' carries seasonal clothes such as sweaters, jackets, coats, trousers etc and other regular categories for all age groups under men's, ladies and kids wear.

Variety

Retailers should provide the customers with the required products not only at appropriate prices but also with an adequate product range or ***variety***, that is, number of different types or classes of products. Further, each product should be made available in enough ***depth*** or ***assortment*** of different styles, colors, sizes and brands.

2. **Assortment**: An assortment basically is the selection of the merchandise a retailer carries to sell to the customers to earn profit. It includes both the breadth of product categories and the depth (variety) within each category.

   Width of assortment: It refers to the number of distinct goods/service categories with which a retailer is involved.

   Breadth of assortment: It refers to the variety within a particular goods/service category.

3. **Product Availability**: Product availability commonly known as level of support or retailer's service level is the total percentage of demand for a particular SKU that is fulfilled during a particular period of time. This time may be one hour, one day or one week. For instance, 150 people visit Gokul Megamart (a retail store chain) to buy 40 size formal shirts but store sells only 120 shirts before the stock runs out of stock. Therefore, in this case the product availability will be

$$= \frac{120 \times 100}{150} = 80\%$$

Availability

Product availability is becoming imperative subject for today's customers that seek convenient shopping under one roof. In the absence of products that they seek, they will switch over to their substitutes or may try different brand. Retailers on the basis of their experience and expertise draw a trade-off between merchandise variety, assortment and product availability. This in general term is called 'assortment planning'.

Assortment planning for service providers

Unlike products, services are perishable in nature and service retailers cannot store as merchandise retailers. Consider Healthcare industry where both big and small hospitals exist. Big Hospitals like AIIMS (Public hospital) and Apollo (private hospital) offer a large variety (assortment) of medical services. From nursing to critical care facilities like microsurgery, plastic surgery, cancer treatments, stitch less cataract surgery (PHACO), nephrology, neurosurgery etc are available under one roof. On the other hand, small (private/public) hospital provide limited medical solutions like RG Stone Hospital, Dhramshila Cancer Hospital & Research Institute, Rajiv Gandhi Cancer Hospital & Research Institute, Indian Cancer Society, Rajan Babu Tuberculosis Hospital etc.

TRADE-OFF BETWEEN VARIETY, ASSORTMENT AND PRODUCT AVAILABILITY

Beggars are not choosers. When options are thought either collectively or individually, to accept one thing or reject another or limiting one thing in order to get more or something else, the phenomenon is called **trade-off**. For instance, when one is allotting his limited funds, the trade-off implies lessening expenditure for some purposes (sacrificing) in order to spend/fulfill for some other urgent need. Evaluating **trade-offs** involves making comparison of costs with benefits of each of the present alternatives. From consumers' point of view, trade-off usually involves whether to buy something more or something less of a good or service considering their purchasing power (limited).

From producers' point of view, trade-off usually involves whether to produce something more or something less of a particular category. Further, another **trade-offs** that producers face in order to maximize their efforts are:

(i) Whether to hire more workers or lay a few off

(ii) Whether to produce automatic or manually

(iii) Whether to purchase new machines or sell-off old machines and so on.

Trade-off

From a layman's point of view, trade-off is a compromise between having one thing or missing other or exchanging something in place of another to get maximum satisfaction under given circumstances.

From a retailer's point of view, as the available space is limited and the cost of the floor space is very high, maximization of profits is possible with proper space allocation within various product categories and across the entire store.

A detailed analysis of **trade-off** helps a retailer to solve issues like what sort of merchandise should be purchased and in what quantity, especially in case of multi-store retail chains. The trade-offs between variety, assortment and availability of product are of strategic significance to each retailer irrespective of size and format. Among all, 'variety' is more significant to satisfy the customers. For instance, what sort of store will it be should a retailer purchase merchandise from many suppliers, manufacturers or from limited? is decided by the retailer's merchandise assortment plan Top management is not bothered about the issue (single/multiple suppliers), it decides about assortment or availability of product. Further, the top management decides whether to delete one category or even a particular department from the store.

Factors affecting **trade-offs** between variety, assortment and product availability basically depend upon the retailer's marketing strategy. If marketing strategy does not run parallel to retailer's variety, assortment and product availability, customers' expectations cannot be fulfilled. And if the above-mentioned three elements do not meet the customers' expectations, a retailer will loose the market share. The factors affecting a retailer's trade-offs are:

(i) The nature and size of retailer's target market.
(ii) The retailer's offerings (goods and services).
(iii) The criteria upon which the retailers will have the competitive advantage.

MERCHANDISING OPTIMIZATION

Merchandise optimization is a key activity in the management of any retail store. It not only drives the business strategy of the retailer but also has immense cost and profit implications. Be it small/independent retailer or a franchisee of a chain store, all face a common problem that how right merchandise mix should be provided at each store location so that with satisfying customers, overall productivity should increase. Under the pressure of showing good turnover and profits year after year, retailers find it difficult to provide proper merchandise mix that one side satisfy the customers and on the other side, results in higher level of productivity. Therefore, they have left with no option except to use merchandise optimization technique.

The merchandising optimization is a process under which data related to loyal customers, merchandise and target market is maintained in order to produce merchandise assortment. This is done by merchandise mix which is a blend of marketing intelligence statistics, output from competitors' survey and socio-cultural environmental analysis of the near by population. Studies have shown that proper merchandise mix not only results in increased turnover but excellent customer service. Only need is to consider that how your store can create customer interest and differential advantage by the merchandise it is offering? Besides this, stores' pattern of breadth, depth, and policies should change over the time as the needs and wants of the customers is tend to change and these changes lead to change in merchandise mix which ultimately have direct impact on the marketing and sales promotion mix.

Points to consider for devising a strategic merchandise assortment plan.

- How a retail manager can implement merchandise assortment plan without disturbing the remaining retail supply chain?
- How a store is intend to use tools such as stock-turnover and stock-sales ratios to support its assortment planning?
- How does the 80/20 principle apply in his retail store?
- How much depth a store can carry?
- How much width a store can carry?

- How much/ consistent a store is towards merchandise assortment?
- What plans a retailer should have to maximize the return on inventory investment?
- Which product lines does your store intend to carry?

ASSORTMENT PLAN

Retailer after deciding about the financial objectives and determining the significance of having variety, assortment and product availability decides about the merchandise to be purchased, displayed and sold. An **assortment plan** is the selection of merchandise a retailer carries to sell in his retail outlet. Assortment includes both the breadth of product categories and the variety within each category. The assortment plan for fashion merchandise usually does not identify specific stock keeping units (SKUs) since these items change frequently and become obsolete very soon even within the same season. The fashion oriented categories usually have fewer details about past history and details of the assortment plan because the retailer would like to have flexibility to adjust the items as per the season demand which cannot be predicted in advance.

Studying an established sales history for specific SKU is the beginning point for developing an assortment plan. A retailer (merchandise planner) besides studying assortment plans for the past seasons; also critically analyze the sales records, GMROI, and turnover forecast too to develop the merchandise plan for the current period. Once the preliminary assortment plan is ready adjustments are then made in order to satisfy the current consumers demand and for the purpose of moving with the fashion trends. For instance, an apparel retailer (merchandise planner) expects that the *low waist jeans* under ladies jeans category will be in demand in the coming season; he will concentrate more on the *low waist jeans* instead of normal size jeans. Therefore, cutting the expenses on normal jeans will be utilized for additional purchase of *low waist jeans.*

Figure: 9.10
A Retailer's Assortment Plan: Raye's Mill

Courtesy: *Company Website*

Preparing an assortment plan is not an easy task. In case of small store, this task can be done at retailer level only but in case of multi store or hyper market; the process becomes tricky and time consuming due to the availability of various sizes, colours, patterns, designs, compositions and price levels. A good assortment plan requires exact forecast about sales, GMROI, and inventory turnover along with retailer's calculations and experience.

SUMMARY

On of the most strategic aspects of the retail business is to decide what kind of merchandise should be purchased and displayed for selling purpose. **Planning merchandise assortment** is a method that helps a retailer to select right merchandise in the right quantity, of right quality at the right place and time, while meeting the retail firm's financial objectives. This exercise also enables a retailer to analyze, plan, procure, handle and control the merchandise investments.

Inventory turnover is a ratio of the total cost of goods sold in a year to the average inventory level in rupees. The benefit of using this ratio is to know how quickly the retail store is getting its inventories and how quickly customers get the order placed to the stores. It measures the soundness of retailer's inventory methods and indicates retailer's ability to understand and implement various strategic techniques like sales forecasting, assortment planning and various trade offs. By improving inventory turnover, a retailer can easily increase his profitability by carrying fewer inventories.

Assortment plan is one of the most valuable and effective endorsement strategies adopted by retailers It refers to variety strategies that are designed to act as a direct inducement, a value addition, or meet customers' latest demands. It is the selection of merchandise a retailer carries to sell in his retail outlet. Assortment includes both the breadth of product categories and the variety within each category. It provides extensive tactical measures to retailers to manage internal or external impediments to sales or profits. A good quality assortment plan requires correct forecast about sales, GMROI, and inventory turnover along with retailer's calculations and experience.

REVIEW QUESTIONS

True and False Questions

1. Planning merchandise assortments is one area that differentiates successful and unsuccessful retail stores.
2. Planning retail merchandising is a technique of developing, securing, pricing, supporting and communicating the retailer's offerings.
3. Merchandising Philosophy sets the guiding principles for all the merchandise decisions that a customer makes.
4. Merchandising consists of the activities involved in acquiring particular goods and/or services and making them available at the places, times and prices and in the quantity that enables a retailer to reach its objectives.

5. Micro Merchandising is a strategy where a retailer adjusts its shell space allocations to respond to customers and other differences among local markets.
6. The objective of keeping back up/back log merchandise is to meet the regular or seasonal fluctuations in the competitors' demands.
7. Assortment Plan is a description of items a retailer would like to have in his store in a particular merchandise category.
8. Category Management is the process of managing wholesale business.
9. One reason for introduction of 'category management' was that the collaboration with supplier will be helpful in development of categories.
10. One of the preconditions of Category Management is that it should be divided and arranged as per retailer' ease not because of customer's convenience.
11. Category management is the process of classifying and managing product categories as strategic business units.
12. It is said that definition of category remains same from situation to situation and one store to another irrespective of location.
13. Under category assessment step, the retailer conduct an analysis of the category's sub categories, segments with respect to sales, turnover, profits and return on assets.
14. Under category strategy step, retailers develop marketing and product supply strategies that determine the category role and performance objectives.
15. Traffic building strategy is used to divert customers' attention towards store, aisle, and/or category.
16. A turf protecting strategy is applied to defend the category sales and market share against an unknown competitor through competitive based pricing.
17. Transaction Building strategy is issued to increase the sales of a particular category by emphasizing larger sales, multi packs and goods with trade-up options.
18. Profit generating strategy is used to generate profits by focusing on sub-category or parts of the category by increasing prices to beat competitors.
19. Excitement generating strategy is used to create excitement to a particular category by communicating a sense of dire need (urgency), or opportunity to the prospect.
20. Cash generating strategy is used to generate credit sales.
21. Categories tactics are used to determine the optimal category assortment, pricing promotions, and shelf penetration.
22. Category Implementation is used to implement the category business plan through a systematic schedule and list of responsibilities.
23. Category revision is the first and essential step in a typical category management business plan.

24. The concept of centralized buying organization is applicable where retailer has only one huge store may be in different cities, but carries out functions on behalf of stores collectively as opposed to individuality.
25. Organizational Breadth is a measurement that tracks the store's central business functions affected by a system in practice.
26. Staffing is the final organizational decision that deals with the selection of right persons at right job with the right skills, right abilities and right aptitude.
27. The buying organization structure remains constant from organization to organization, country to country and format to format.
28. Merchandise group is the brain and lifeblood of any merchandising planning group, which is managed/controlled by the junior level officers of the merchandise cell usually by the floor staff.
29. A stock keeping unit (SKU) is a unique number (identifier) assigned to an item that describes its features in terms of size, color, style and quantity.
30. Gross margin return on investment (GMROI) is used to plan and evaluate the performance of overall retail operations and accounts for 5-10% of a typical retailer's investment in inventory.

Answers

1. True	2. True	3. False	4. True
5. True	6. False	7. True	8. False
9. True	10. False	11. True	12. False
13. True	14. True	15. False	16. False
17. True	18. False	19. True	20. False
21. True	22. True	23. False	24. False
25. True	26. True	27. False	28. False
29. True	30. False		

Multiple Choice Questions

1. Back up inventory is :
   (*a*) not for use (*b*) not for display
   (*c*) not for sale (*d*) All of the above
2. SBU stands for :-
   (*a*) Store buying units (*b*) Stock buffer unit
   (*c*) Stock before utilisation (*d*) Strategic business unit
3. Category Management improves
   (*a*) Return or Investment (ROT) (*b*) Sales & goodwill
   (*c*) Procurement opportunities (*d*) All of the above.

4. Category management should be based on:
(*a*) differentiation (*b*) uniqueness
(*c*) customers choice (*d*) All of the above.
5. Routine category products are used on:
(*a*) day to day basis (*b*) on rare occasions
(*c*) None of the above (*d*) Both of the above
6. GMROI implies:
(*a*) Gross Margin revenues of Investment
(*b*) Gross Margin return on investment
(*c*) Gross market return on investment
(*d*) Gross market revenues on investment
7. Traffic building strategy is used to
(*a*) divert customers (*b*) draw customers
(*c*) Both of the above (*d*) None of the above
8. Turf protecting strategy is also known as:
(*a*) Super traffic building (*b*) Transaction building
(*c*) Profit Generating (*d*) Cash Generating
9. Excitement Generating strategy is used for creating excitement to:
(*a*) a particular category (*b*) a particular store outlet
(*c*) a particular item (*d*) None of the above
10. Image enhancing concentrates on:
(*a*) Quality and price (*b*) Variety and Service
(*c*) Both of the above (*d*) None of the above
11. Category revision is the .... step of a typical category management process:
(*a*) first and foremost (*b*) cast
(*c*) second last (*d*) unnecessary
12. Large retail firms generally have:
(*a*) formal buying department (*b*) Informal department
(*c*) None of the above (*d*) Both of the above
13. The main merit of formal buying organisation is:
(*a*) Role clarity (*b*) economical
(*c*) Time saving (*d*) All of the above

14. The main merit of informal buying organisation is:
    (*a*) Economical
    (*b*) Flexible system
    (*c*) Optimum utilisation of work force
    (*d*) All of the above.
15. The basic function of staffing is:
    (*a*) recruitment (*b*) training and development
    (*c*) Performance appraisal (*d*) All of the above
16. A sales manager typically occupies a:
    (*a*) Low level position (*b*) Middle level position
    (*c*) Top level position (*d*) None of the above
17. GMM implies:
    (*a*) General Marketing Manager (*b*) General Merchandise Manager
    (*c*) General Management Map (*d*) General Merchandise Market
18. DMM belongs to:
    (*a*) Deputy Marketing Manager (*b*) Divisional Merchandise Manager
    (*c*) Direct Marketing Mechanism (*d*) Divisional Marketing Map
19. Sourcing is a process of:
    (*a*) Procuring Inventory (*b*) Stocking Inventory
    (*c*) Issuing Inventory (*d*) Accounting Inventory
20. GMROI is calculated as:
    (*a*) Annual Sales × Gross Margin/Average Inventory cost
    (*b*) Gross Sales × Gross Margin/Average Inventory cost
    (*c*) Net Sales × Net Margin/Average Inventory cost
    (*d*) Net Sales × Gross Margin/Average Inventory cost

Answers

1. d	2. d	3. d	4. d
5. d	6. b	7. b	8. a
9. a	10. c	11. b	12. a
13. a	14. d	15. d	16. b
17. b	18. b	19. a	20. a

Check Your Progress

1. What is SKU?
2. What is ROI?
3. What does category mean?

4. What does SBU mean?
5. What is CM?
6. What is ROI?
7. Who is category captain?
8. What makes a destination?
9. What causes image?
10. What is the principle of staffing?
11. Who is GMM?
12. Who is DMM?
13. What is GMROI?
14. What is the formula for inventory turnover?
15. What is EOM?
16. What is Trade off?
17. What makes a variety?
18. How many steps a sales forecasting process has?
19. What makes breadth of assortment?
20. What is merchandising philosophy?

Short Answer Questions

1. What do you mean by Category Management?
2. Why Category Management is required in retailing?
3. Consider you are a food retailer. How would you like to categorize your merchandise?
4. What would you suggest to a retailer who wants to prepare an assortment plan for its merchandise?
5. Considering an example of your choice explain how buying processes are organized by Categories?
6. Explain the role of merchandise group in a retail firm?
7. What are the responsibilities of DMMs?
8. Take an example of our choice and explain the example working of SKU?
9. Explain the significance of Inventory Turnover Ratio for a retailer?
10. How a retailer can improve his inventory turnover ratio?
11. Describe the assortment planning process for service providers?
12. Briefly illustrate the demerits of high inventory turnover
13. Differentiate between internal and external sources of information?
14. What do you mean by sales forecasting?
15. Explain the formula for calculating average inventory?

Long Answer Questions

1. Critically analyze the role of the 'buying organization' in a retailing organization with the help of standard merchandise classification scheme and organizational chart?
2. The success of a retail store largely depends on how accurately the sales forecasts have been done. Explain this statement and also discuss various techniques used to perform the sales forecast?
3. How a retailer can do trade-offs between variety, assortment and product availability? Explain with suitable examples wherever necessary?
4. Discuss an assortment Plan with its significance to retailer? Also describe what factors must be considered by a retailer or merchandise buyer while preparing plan for staple and fashion merchandise?
5. Being a retail graduate what you would suggest to a person who is facing the problem of categorizing its products and services? How can a retailer adapt the category management process for his new business?

Appendix

Exhibit 9.1: Implementing Category Management

Implementing Category Management process for your business has always been difficult and unanswerable task for retailers. This resource guide will help you to understand the basics of category management, its key elements and how to progress.

Category management is an effective way to utilize market data to help increase sales. Its format provides a consistent merchandising guide and allows management to easily update figures in relation to buying trends. Moreover, it is the modern language of most retailers, and buyers will often expect suppliers to implement category management for the sectors they are trading in.

BENEFITS

Implementing the principles of category management can provide a number of business benefits, including:

- Providing a model for valuable market and consumer information.
- Developing competitive advantage via information and understanding.
- An opportunity of building your relationship with the retail account.
- Building sales.

WHAT IS CATEGORY MANAGEMENT?

Category management is a distributor/supplier process of managing categories as strategic business units, producing enhanced business results by focusing on delivery to the consumer. It has grown in importance since point-of-sale scanning allowed for accurate assessment of product movement.

KEY ELEMENTS

1. It is an organisational design for distributors where buying and merchandising functions are integrated through category management teams responsible for developing category business plans, both internally and with suppliers. These category-based plans are aimed at improving the overall performance of the category.
2. The main aim is to produce an interactive and collaborative business process in which distributors and suppliers work as partners to create and manage consumer-focused category plans.
3. Retailers and suppliers have to focus on the category as a whole rather than concentrating on just one particular line. Supermarkets often have categories for a number of products that are grouped together, e.g. soup or fresh produce.
4. The consumer also benefits from category management. It leads to an improved range, reduced out-of-stocks and shopping will be made easier by the collaboration of retailers and suppliers to improve the effectiveness and efficiency of demand/supply management.

Using the soup category example, the category leader (e.g. Heinz) would advice the retail buyer on which products of all brands should be stocked in a bid to maximise total sales and to grow the category as a whole. This would involve recommending a mix of traditional and more exotic lines – from budget soups to premium lines.. Analysis of buying and consumer patterns would drive the recommended range and what number of facings each product line should have at the fixture.

GETTING STARTED

For the category leader the benefits are enormous – they have the opportunity to control, influence and direct the category. It can be more difficult for a minor player unless they are able to demonstrate how the category as a whole can benefit from their move to a greater position of influence. In such circumstances clarifying the opportunity in strategic terms is the key to success.

To implement category management it is essential to have a consistent strategy and a standardized business process. The process consists of six steps:

1. **Category definition:** decide what category your product fits into.
2. **Assessment:** identify sales, profit and return required.
3. **Strategy:** develop demand and supply chain strategies for the category.
4. **Tactics:** determine the assortment, pricing, shelving and promotions required to achieve the plan targets.
5. **Plan implementation:** implement the category business plan and strategies through the store.
6. **Category review:** monitor category performance versus plans on an on-going basis, e.g. how has your product, your sales and, ultimately, your bottomline improved?

Category management should be viewed as a demand/supply chain process with a manufacturer/ retailer interface. For the manufacturer there are product management functions, which should be organised into category. Similarly, for the retailer there are customer management functions that need to be aligned to the category management functions for maximum impact.

DEVELOPING YOUR STRATEGY

The strategy is the link between a company's overall mission and the role of category management. Retailers and suppliers must answer a number of questions before starting the category management business process. They are:

- What is the company's overall mission?
- What is the basis of competitive positioning?
- What are the key corporate goals?
- Who are the target consumers?
- What are the key strategies relating to price, assortment, promotion, customer service and product supply?

- What is the present relationship between the retailer and the supplier?

The answers to these questions provide key strategic directions and a framework to build upon.

FOCUSSING ON THE CONSUMER

Category management requires the target consumer to be the basis for the competitive strategy. It is essential to understand the target consumer and consumer behaviour that affects retail strategy and consumer purchases. Three questions managers should ask themselves are:

- How do consumers choose stores for shopping?
- How do consumers choose products?
- How do in-store category tactics affect consumer choice?

It is important that space allocation, shelf presentation, assortment, pricing and promotion are dealt with carefully to get the right message across to the consumer. Market research can help with this, but there are also four key points that should be kept in mind when choosing a retail outlet. They are:

- Location of the store.
- Product/brand variety.
- Price.

Shopping environment – fast checkout, friendly staff and the atmosphere within the store. Retailers can influence the consumer through merchandising tactics as part of their category management plan. These include:

- Space allocated to a category and to a brand within a category and the location of the brand, i.e. top shelf versus bottom shelf.
- The assortment offered – items added to or dropped from the category.
- The pricing decision – high/low or everyday pricing.
- The promotion decision – features, in-store displays, sampling.

MANAGING THE RELATIONSHIP

Collaborative relationships between trading partners are not always easy to achieve by the category management business process. Both retailers and suppliers need to develop databases that integrate their internal data with external market/competitive data.

To assist in avoiding problems, category management teams should ensure that:

- Both parties are allowed to put across their perspective
- The category has a co-ordinated internal programme
- The category has a co-ordinated external programme
- It has the appropriate level of resource allocation

A substantial amount of work has to be carried out in terms of research and putting strategies in place to be able to implement category management and, subsequently, improve on business processes. To be successful, suppliers and retailers have to adopt a new way of working together.

HOW TO SUM UP?

1. Develop your strategy and the role of category management in its achievement.
2. Develop your approach to the retailer i.e. why they would benefit from a joint category management approach.
3. Formally begin the process with a start-up meeting involving the team (which will include representation from your business and the retail account).
4. Follow the six-step process described in Getting Started.
5. Remember that category management is not a single initiative; it is an on-going process. Ensure regular reviews and category development. Building this relationship will build competitive advantage.

Courtesy: *www.scotlandfoodanddrink.org*

About Scotland Food & Drink

Scotland Food & Drink was launched as a private limited company in the summer of 2007 with the aim of bringing everyone involved in food and drink together to work towards a common and shared agenda that will deliver greater success in global markets. The scope covers all aspects of food and drink: the drinks industry – both alcoholic and non-alcoholic, and from small farmers to large corporations. Their vision is to make Scotland internationally known as 'The Land of Food and Drink' and their mission is to place Scotland amongst the top 3 of the world's producers of premium food & drink products.

Exhibit 9.2: The Future of Category Management?

After some initial hiccups, it certainly looks like Category Management is not only here to stay, it is going to increasingly become a way of doing business, and those suppliers who cannot do it well, do so at their peril. Okay, now it's time for me to gaze up into the stars, dust off the crystal ball, get the tarot cards out, and make some predictions about Category Management over the next few years.

1. **The spread of Category Management into more diverse retailing sectors**. Initially, Category Management was a grocery or "Mass Merch" concept; however it has now spread into other retailing sectors such as DIY, Pharmacy and Cash & Carry. And in recent times, Borders Bookshop has implemented Category Management as a process within its bookstores. Expect this trend to continue.
2. **The data explosion**. The amount of data has been "exploding" now for 20 years, however it still shows no sign of abating, and Category Management is becoming highly "information technology" and mathematics oriented. That, coupled with the fact that there is still a large "social science" element to Category Management (for example in understanding the psychology of Shopper Behaviour) and you get a very rich and diverse job function indeed!
3. **Streamlined Processes**. The formal 8 step process may well be comprehensive, but is often too labourious, time consuming and not rapid enough in many fast-moving markets. Companies are increasingly looking for faster, more flexible, streamlined processes which deliver results in shorter timescales.
4. **Aisle Management**. Just as products and brands make up categories, so do different categories make up aisles. And as many retail buyers are not in charge of just one category but in charge of a whole aisle, so all the issues around products in categories can be upscales to the same issues of categories within aisles. There may well be good openings for suppliers who can take on the role of "aisle captain" - if they can handle the workload!
5. **Relationship with other disciplines**, eg Supply Chain. The Walmart Retail Link database is already very heavily logistically-focussed, and - given the strong requirement to have the right product at the right place at the right time - who can blame them ? Some of the lines between "day to day category management" and "day to day supply chain management" are already a little blurry with Walmart suppliers and this looks set to be the trend. This paragraph is taking us in the direction of another already-established process and set of buzzwords - Efficient Consumer Response - or "ECR". Let's save the detail of that for another day.

6. The increasing use of **Field Marketing** activity. The explosion of media channels such as satellite channels means that it is becoming increasing difficult to target an advertising message through traditional above the line means. Couple with that the increasing demands of the retailer to have sales and marketing investment not diluted across consumers in general, but spent on *their* consumers and shoppers. Within this, though, expect to see a few counter-trends such as some retailers moving to "clean aisle" policies, or an increasing insistence that suppliers display material must be tailored to *their* corporate feel.
7. **Micro-marketing**. The ability to analyse store sell-out data by barcode and by individual store means that the traditional concept of "one range fits all" may have to make way for a more flexible approach. Already, Walmart in the USA has the concept of "Store of the Community" where individual store ranges are tailored to the demographics of the local population. For example, stores in areas of large Hispanic communities have product ranges more biassed to their tastes. As stores become increasingly keen to use their information technology to squeeze ever more juice out of Category Management, expect to see some more of this.
8. **Development of Category Management across the world**. At the moment, Category Management is carried out predominantly in North America, Canada, (Mexico if you deal with Walmart), Australia, the UK and Western Europe. As other countries develop, their expertise and expectations of Category Management will grow too, fuelled by the growth of International Retailers such as Tesco, Walmart, Carrefour, Auchan and Metro expanding into new countries and immediately injecting their expertise into them.

Source: *www.catmanplus*

MERCHANDISE BUYING SYSTEMS

LEARNING OBJECTIVES

- Understanding the role of merchandise buying under implementation of merchandise plan.
- Describing merchandise buying and handling process.
- Explaining the role of retailer (buyer) under various stages of merchandise buying and handling process.
- Explaining the ethical and legal issues related to merchandise buying.
- Understanding how a buyer (retailer) can guard himself against uncertainties associated with buying process.

"Good merchandise, even hidden, soon finds buyers."

Titus Maccius Plautu

"The best of merchandise will go back to the shelf unless handled by a conscientious, tactful salesman."

James Cash Penney

INTRODUCTION

If store is a body then merchandise is a life blood flowing in it. Store will ensure that there should be proper supply of blood (merchandise) as and when required. As consumers' perception, lifestyle and income (*especially the middle class's income*) is growing continuously, their demand for latest and nearby luxury goods is increasing. Therefore, providing them the right mix of merchandise has become a challenge for retailers.

Retailers should have thorough knowledge of the merchandise buying systems. Not only the merchandise past history but customers' feedback, suggestion, complaints and assistance of category manager should be sought. The sources of buying merchandise can be spread across the globe. The retailer in consultation with category manager should evaluate these sources in order to get proper merchandise that not only satisfies the retailer's needs but also as per consumers' requirements.

MERCHANDISE BUYING SYSTEMS

Retailers throughout the globe usually employ two types of buying systems:

(i) Staple merchandise buying system

(ii) Fashion merchandise buying system

Sales forecasting, which is essential for all types of products, is straightforward in case of staple merchandise buying system but more complex for those with fashion and seasonal merchandise. Efficient buying systems ensure the balance between sales, stock levels, quantity ordered and account for influences on availability of merchandise.

There are several steps in the buying process, which when followed systematically ensure retail success. Buying systems significantly influence these factors:

Sales Volume: Providing right merchandise in right quality in the right price and at right place.

Gross margins: Buying systems influence not only the price (cost) of merchandise but also the pricing policy and the extent of the markup.

Markdowns: Buying systems influence the markdowns as they regulate the quantity, lead time, price and the type of merchandise ordered.

Stock Levels: Buying systems have impact on the balance of inventory (inventory in stock). Further, buying system balances the inventory levels to achieve high sales targets with low level of inventory. Following are the steps in a typical buying process:

Figure 10.1
Steps in a Typical Buying Process

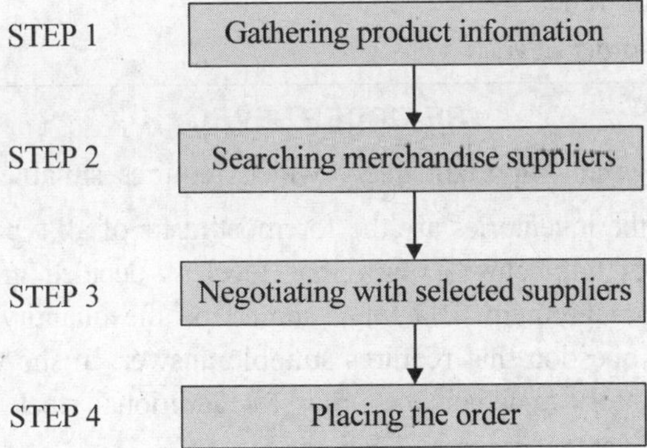

BUYING SYSTEM FOR STAPLE MERCHANDISE

Staple merchandise consists of the items that are regularly purchased, displayed and sold by the retailers. For a grocery store, staple merchandise will be bread, butter, milk, salt, eggs, tissues and so on. Similarly, most of the merchandise at sports store and home improvement centers are **staple**. For a departmental store, staple merchandise is camera rolls, stapler pins, pens, notebooks, briefcase, gift items and house wares.

The reason behind forecasting demand for staple merchandise easily is that these are the items of daily/regular use and are not influenced by season and other factors. A retailer can easily predict the quantity required for these items. Usually for this purpose, retailers prepare a 'basic stock list' that clearly outlines the inventory levels, size, colour, style, packaging, fragrance and so on for various staple items.

Following are the features of a staple buying system:

(i) Easy and straightforward method
(ii) Can predict demand easily
(iii) Provides accurate forecasts comparatively
(iv) Easy to administer
(v) Necessary adjustments can be made to ensure availability of stock
(vi) Monitors and measures present sales for the items at the SKU level
(vii) Guides the ordering sequence for re-stocking of merchandise

Maintaining backup stock in staple merchandise system

Backup stock, commonly known as a 'safety stock' or 'buffer stock' or 'not for general use' is the stock that is kept for unwarranted orders for the purpose to avoid 'out of stock' situation. The size of the backup stock depends upon following factors:

- Size of the product availability, a retailer wish to have
- Time taken to acquire merchandise
- Suppliers' quickness and product availability
- Fluctuations in consumer demand – higher the fluctuation, more the backup will be
- Availability of funds
- Retailer's re-order level

RE-ORDER LEVEL

'When to order' is an important query which requires suitable answer.

Buying and issuing the inventories are the foremost tasks of all types of organizations. When the inventories fall below a particular level as decided in advance, they are refilled with fresh procurement. But what should be the quantity for fresh stock is always an alarming question that requires suitable answer. In short, the re-order level is that level of inventory at which the order for additional stock should be placed.

Re-order level = Average usage × Lead time

i.e., R = Au L

Re-order point example:

Demand = 10000 units/year
Store open = 320 days/year
Average usage (Au) = 10000/320=33.33 units/day
Lead time (L) = 10 days

Note:

This calculation exercise is the responsibility of retail managers but it is the retail staff that informs the retail managers that items in the store is about to finish & which items is in demand in a particular period. Which item should be purchased/acquired on preference basis? Because retail staff is in direct touch with the customers, therefore, is better able to read the customer's buying nerve. Further, retail staff at junior level, one day can/will be promoted at senior level where this calculation takes place. Therefore, concept clarity is a must exercise at entry level too.

BUYING SYSTEMS FOR FASHION MERCHANDISE

Fashion merchandise consists of the items those usually have unpredictable demand and limited sales record. Demand forecasting as discussed earlier, in the absence of any sales history for specific fashion store keeping unit (SKU) becomes difficult. The reason behind this is that these items have cyclical sales and become outdated very easily with the changes in customers' taste and preferences, liking and disliking. Therefore, for few seasons, the demand for such merchandise is high, become outdated for a while and then again becomes fashion of the day. For instance, 'Yoga and meditation' that was part and parcel of Indians' lives before seventies, was replaced by gym, spa and health centers, has again entered in Indians' lives and becoming popular among youths too.

Following are the features of Fashion merchandise

- Unpredictable and unstable demand
- No/limited sales history (record)
- Relatively difficult to forecast sales

Seasonal Merchandise

It consists of items those change season to season but relatively have good demand over non-consecutive time periods. Items such as room coolers, desert coolers, air conditioners, sweaters, umbrellas have excellent demand during one season annually. Since most of the sales of such items take place at the same time every year, it becomes easy to forecast the demand. Further, previous years' sales record may be helpful to predict demand and therefore, sales revenue.

MERCHANDISE BUDGET PLAN (MBP)

A merchandise budget plan, as the very name implies, is a forecast of particular merchandise related activities designed for a particular period of time, say, one year or six months. Under this plan, rather than physical control of items, stress is given towards their financial planning. **Merchandise Budget Plans** usually are made for one season and then broken down into shorter periods like monthly & weekly plans. In an effective merchandise Budget Plan, a retailer forecasts and plans about five fundamental variables, namely, sales level, stock levels, purchases, reductions (markdowns) and gross margin.

The primary objective of having a merchandise budget plan is that a retailer would like to have a proper balance between (a) what will be paid to suppliers for purchase of merchandise and making it available to customers; and (b) the cash inflow that will come in the business from sales to customers. Though in practice, there are several accounting practices that allow some flexibility (for example extended credit terms or easy payment options), this balance is vital to maintain the firm's liquidity. For the effective accomplishment, the firm's internal records, past years experience must be carefully considered instead of relying on historical data alone that will lead to repeating previous mistakes, including previous missed opportunities.

Components of Merchandise Budget Plan

The various components of a merchandise budget plans are as follows: . .

(1) Planned Sales and Stock levels

Planning sales and stock levels is the first step in preparation of a sales forecast for a particular period (say one season) and for each month in that particular season for which a retailer wish to prepare a budget plan. After this, retailer should determine the beginning of month (B.O.M.) inventory in order to specify the desired rate of stock turn for each month of the season under study.

For example, a retailer's stock sales ratio for the month of February is six and predicted sales during February is Rs.80,000, then the planned BOM stock would be Rs.4,80,000.

***Note**: For the purpose of making budgeting effective, it is always suggested to calculate End-of-Month (E.O.M. stock), which is same as B.O.M. stock for the following month. Thus in this case, retailer's EOM stock for January will be same (Rs.4,80,000) to February's BOM stock.*

(2) Planning for Reductions

Planning for reductions is the third step in a merchandising budget plan which involves deciding about markdowns, employee discounts and shortages. Reducing prices is critical because the degree of reduction will have exactly the same effect on the value of stock as an equal amount of sales for that period. **Markdown** is used to push retail sales that offer particular merchandise at a price less than the merchandise marked price (normal price). Shortages result from pilferage (in retailing it is known as shop lifting), accounting frauds, vendor theft and employee theft. Employee discount is also provided by some retail firms in order to build public image and employees' welfare by extra rebate and inviting them to buy merchandise before offering to general public by the way of sales.

(3) Planning For Purchases

After planning sales and stock levels, opening stock (BOM), closing stock (EOM) and reductions, next step under merchandise budget plan is to plan for purchases in Rupees. It is calculated as under:

Purchase Planning = Planned Sales + Planned Reductions + EOM - BOM

Suppose for example, the planned E.O.M. stock for February was Rs 5, 60,000 and that reductions for February were estimated to be Rs 10,000. Therefore, planned purchase will be calculated as under:

Planned Sales (Feb 1 – Feb 28)	=	Rs. 80,000
Planned Reductions	=	Rs. 10,000
Planned EOM stock (Feb 28)	=	Rs.5,60,000
Total:		Rs.6,50,000
Less: Planned BOM stock (Feb 1)	=	Rs.4,80,000
Therefore, planned purchases	=	Rs.1,70,000

The planned purchases figure usually is based on retail prices rather than at cost. In order to determine the financial resources required to procure merchandise, it becomes imperative on the part of retailer that he should determine planned purchases at cost. The underlying gap between planned purchases at cost and at retail denotes the initial mark up goal for the merchandise under consideration. This objective is achieved by calculating by the amount of operating expenses required to attain the estimated sales volume, the profit expectations, and adding it with the reduction figure. Therefore,

$$\text{Initial Mark Up Goal} = \frac{(\text{Expenses} + \text{Profit} + \text{Reductions})}{(\text{Net Sales} + \text{Reductions})}$$

Sometimes, term **Open-to-Buy** is used synonymously with planned purchases where forecasts concur with actual results.

(4) Planning For Gross Margin And Operating Profit

The gross margin usually is the initial mark up attuned for price variations, reductions, shrinkage and other stock shortages. The gap between gross margin and expenses needed to create sales will either contribute to profit or a net profit (i.e. profit before taxes), depending on retailer's accounting practice and the thinness of merchandise budgeting.

Evaluation of Merchandise Budget Plan

As discussed earlier, merchandise budget plan is used by retailers to determine how much money to allocate in each month on a particular merchandise category, considering the firm's sales forecast, inventory turnover and profit margins. After developing a merchandise budget plan, retailer purchases the inventory for the upcoming season in advance and when season comes, retailer sells the merchandise. After the selling season, the retailer should determine how actually the category has performed against the plan forecasted. If the actual turnover and GMROI are greater than the forecasted, then the performance is better than retail's expectations and vice versa.

Evaluating the **merchandise budget plan** aims to balance the money outflows (for supplies) and inflows (received from customers by selling merchandise) for the next financial year or upcoming season. Is there any need to pre-order for some stock or the budget provided was sufficient to meet customers' demand, may be determined through evaluation only. Following issues must be answered to evaluate the retailers' performance:

- Why the performance is better/fall short of expectations?
- Is there any major discrepancy between the forecasted and actual plan? Was such deviation under the retail's control and knowledge?
- Whether retailer responded quickly to marked demand by announcing a sale or by additional purchases?
- What was the reason for deviation? Was it a part of retailer's external or internal environment?

OPEN-TO-BUY SYSTEM

It is a system of monitoring merchandise flow in order to determine how much money was spent on merchandise and how much is balanced to spend. It helps the retailer to ensure that enough budget is available to buy the merchandise as and when required. This system of evaluating merchandise performance begins after the merchandise is bought using the merchandise budget plan.

In open to buy system, a retailer (buyer) must have vigilant eye on the payments made either through checks or cash and when it is to be made. Otherwise, the retailer's account should show different balance than what the retailer actually has. Consequently, the retailer may purchase too much or too less. Merchandise may be available when it it not required and would fall short of requirement when actually the requirement is resulting in declined profits and low inventory turnover. Therefore, even if the retailer's merchandise budget running parallel to the plan may fail in case merchandise and payment /receipt record, are not maintained properly.

For the better understanding of the concept and a merchandise budget plan to be successful, the retailer's attempts to purchase merchandise in volume and with delivery dates; his actual EOM stock should match with the projected EOM stock. For instance, at the end of February month (in case of North India), which is the end of winter season, the retailer must clear out sweater (ladies, gents and kids) so to make space for summer collections. Thus, the retailer's projected EOM stock will match actual EOM stock to both equal zero.

Calculating open-to-buy for past period

Calculating open-to-buy for past periods is an easy task since the months/periods are over. There is no point of buying merchandise or declaring any reductions. Therefore, the actual EOM stock will be equal to projected EOM stock.

Therefore, projected EOM stock = Actual EOM stock

So Open to Buy = Zero

Calculating open to buy for the Current Period

Consider there is a BOM stock of Rs.5,40,000 in the current month, say, February, but there is no EOM stock because the month has not come to end. Therefore, while calculating the open-to-buy for the current month, the projected EOM stock plan will play its role.

For example: Consider a retailer of apparel is checking his open-to-buy for February on the 10th of the month. His actual EOM stock is Rs.4,20,000 for January. This became his actual BOM stock for February. Further additions and reductions are as follows:

Monthly addition Rs.2,80,000 in mens' jeans, received and Rs.70,000 of jeans still on order. The sale plan for February is Rs.1,60,000. Additional reductions (shrinkage, markdowns, employee discounts) are planned at Rs.45,000. The retailer's planned EOM for March is Rs.2,90,000.

Calculate the retailer's open-to-buy?

Solution

The formula for projected EOM stock plan is:

Actual stock +	Monthly Additions	on order (merchandise ordered but not received for the rest of month)	–	Planned Monthly Sales	–	Monthly Reduction Plan	–	Projected February EOM

= Rs.4,20,000 + Rs.2,80,000 + Rs.70,000 – Rs.1,60,000 – Rs.45,000 – Rs.2,90,000
= Rs.2,75,000

Therefore, open-to-Buy for March is:

OTB = Planned EOM – Projected EOM
= Rs.2,90,000 – Rs.2,75,000
= Rs.15,000/-

It implies that the retailer in question should consider Rs.15,000 for placing order for additional stock to meet the projected EOM.

Implications of Open-To-Buy

In case the open-to-buy of a retailer comes to negative (say Rs.45,000) it would mean that the retailer has spent Rs.45,000 extra as compared to the store's projected sales. Therefore, following are the options to avoid such situation:

(i) In case the retailer's actual sales is performing less as compared to planned, the retailer should cancel the merchandise on order if the vendor agrees and loss is negligible; or

(ii) The buyer (retailer) should go for special sales/offers to boost up the sales to utilize the additional stock of inventory and balance it with the projected plan.

ALLOCATION OF MERCHANDISE TO STORES

After selecting the buying system and evaluating the sample merchandise, retailer negotiates the purchases and its terms and delivers the purchase order. Then next step is to receive and stock the merchandise. It means, a firm will physically receive and handle the items after paying for invoices. Once the merchandise is purchased either staple or fashion, it is allocated to stores by the merchandise planner. For this purpose, retailers use, past historical data, in consultation with current demand and supply situations. For instance, if a retailer is not able to meet consumers' demand because of less/no supplies from vendors or sales are slow as compared to forecasted (whatever the reason may be) figures, the retailer has no option to adjust the forecasted data downward.

Table 10.1 Illustrates a traditional merchandise allocation method for allocating an additional stock of Rs.5,00,000 among 20 stores to gents' formal, Rs.450 black colour trousers:

Table 10.1

Store's type 1	No.of Stores 2	Total Sales per Store (in %) 3	Sales per Store (Total sales x Col.3) 4	Sales per Store type (Col.2xCol.4) 5	Unit Sales per Store (Col.4/Rs.450) 6
A	5	10.0	Rs. 50,000	Rs. 2,50,000	111
B	7	4,9	Rs. 24,000	Rs. 1,70,000	54
C	8	2,0	Rs. 10,000	Rs. 80,000	22

Total Sales = Rs. 5,00,000 and Unit Price = Rs. 450

Allocation of merchandise differs from store to store and chain to chain. Chain stores usually divide/rank their stores as A, B or C stores based on their sales performance record (i.e. column 1). In the above mentioned example, the chain has five 'A' type stores, seven 'B' stores and eight 'C' stores, each of which, is expected to sell 10 percent, 4.9 percent and 2.0 percent (column 3) of the total sales equaling Rs.50,000, Rs.24,500 and Rs.10,000 (column 4) per store respectively. The total sales (column 3) per store (in percentage) are based on past historical sales record.

ANALYZING MERCHANDISING PERFORMANCE

Whatever source is chosen, retailer must decide a procedure to analyze the merchandise performance with regard to addition or deletion of SKUs, vendors and departments as an ongoing process. These decisions become necessary because in case of fashion merchandise, consumers' preferences, tastes, liking and disliking change rapidly. Therefore, it becomes necessary for a merchandise buyer to add/delete merchandise, search for new vendors or add/delete/club some categories. Further, poor performance of merchandise, in terms of quality and after use dissatisfaction, force a merchandise buyer to change the vendor in question to avoid further complaints and reduced profits. Three methods are commonly employed to analyze the performance of merchandise. These are:

(1) ABC Analysis

The ABC analysis sometimes known as **Always Better Control** is an inventory classification process where total inventory is classified into three categories:

A - Outstandingly important;

B - Of average importance and

C - Relatively unimportant as a basis for a control scheme.

Each firm whether small or big has to maintain several types of inventories. Some are small in size but are costly ones, some large in size but have less cost. It is never advisable to keep the same degree of control on all the items. The firm should pay maximum attention to those items which are costly and less attention to those which are cheaper. Therefore, firm should be selective in its approach to control investment in various types of inventories. This logical approach is known as ABC analysis and tends to measure the importance of each item of inventories in terms of its value.

Strategy to be followed:

In case of '**A**' items keen attention is paid to work out the requirement, safety stocks, order scheduling, and prompt receipt and inspection. '**A**' and '**B**' items should be frequently reviewed and close watch is kept on their consumption pattern, stock balance and refill orders. For inexpensive '**C**' items control is comparatively stress free.

(2) Sell Through Analysis

This method describes the comparison between the actual and forecasted sales volume to determine whether early markdowns should be applied or fresh order for additional merchandise should be given to satisfy current demand.

There is no universal rule to indicate when a markdown should be introduced or additional stock of merchandise be ordered. It simply depends on the experience with the merchandise, a buyer has in the past year.

Table 10.2

Sell Through Analysis for ladies Jeans

Particulars			Week 1 (Actual to Plan)			Week 2 (Actual to Plan)		
Stock No.	Size	Particular Plan	Plan	Actual	Variation (%)	Plan	Actual	Variation (%)
IDM-2101	32"	Low waist black	30	40	33.33	20	15	-25
IDM-2102	32"	Normal black	40	50	25	30	25	-16.67
IDM-2103	34"	Medium waist white	50	30	-40	40	30	-25
IDM-2104	36"	Normal waist white	30	25	-16.67	10	25	150
IDM-2105	34"	Stretchable blue	20	15	-25	20	15	-25
IDM-2106	30"	Denim Normal Grey	40	50	-25	35	38	8.57
IDM-2107	28"	Denim Low Grey	20	30	50	25	29	16
IDM-2108	32"	Low Normal Grey	40	25	-37.5	35	28	-20

Table 10.2 shows a sell through analysis for ladies jeans for the first two weeks of a particular season. Since the ladies jeans belong to fashion merchandise, demand is not easy to predict, but necessary amendments may be made to the merchandise plan any day after two weeks. The variation between actual and forecasted sales guides the retailer about possible changes with regard to addition/deletion of SKUs, vendors and departments. Further, the significance of sell through analysis is employed in evaluating the performance of fashion merchandise and new arrivals. After carefully analyzing the performance of the various items in ladies jeans category, retailer can plan for whether to buy fresh stock of merchandise (in case of good customers' response) or go for markdowns (in case the items have no good response from customers).

(3) Multi-Attribute Method

This method is used to analyze the various alternatives available with regard to vendors and select one that best satisfies store needs. This method is based on the concept that customers look a retailer or a product as a collection of features and attributes. The model is framed to forecast customers' evaluation/judgement of a product or retailer based on:

(i) Products performance on customers' parameter, and

(ii) The significance of those parameters to the customer.

Retailers/buyers use this method to evaluate the performance of merchandise and vendors. In order to understand the concept, we consider a hypothetical example as shown in Figure 10.2 for a vendor of kids' school uniforms. A retailer/buyer can evaluate vendors as under:

Figure 10.2

Multi-attribute Method: Evaluating Vendor

Performance Evaluation of Individual brand across issues				
Criteria Aspects	**Criteria Weight(I)**	**Brand A(Pa)**	**Brand B (Po)**	**Brand C(Pc)**
1	**2**	**3**	**4**	**5**
Vendor Goodwill	8	5	8	9
Service Offered	5	8	9	5
Meets Delivery Commitments	7	6	5	6
Merchandise Quality	6	5	6	5
Payment Criteria	5	5	5	8
Past Record	5	4	4	7
Country of Origin	4	6	4	6
Promotional help	3	5	6	5
		266	290	308

Σ = sum of the equation.

I_j = criteria weight assigned to the i/th dimension.

P_{ij} = performance evaluation for j/th brand alternative on the i/th issue.

1 = not important.

10 = very important.

Step 1

Decide a list of issues that make the criteria to accept or reject a vendor. Column 1 illustrates nine issues that are considered for the purpose of evaluating vendor's performance. The criteria list should not be either too comprehensive or too small as comprehensive list may consider some less/not important issues that may become difficult to use and small list on the other hand may ignore some vital issues. Therefore, the list should be balanced from number of issues (total) point of view as well as from issues appeal point of view. '*Issues appeal*' here stands for dimension of vendor's performance that gets an attention. It simply means any issue should not get much attention unnecessarily. For instance, if there are four issues dealing with regard to different aspects of merchandise quality and one aspect of payment criteria, then merchandise quality will have undue (extra) weightage in the vendor's overall performance evaluation task.

Step 2

After deciding about the criteria, next step is to assign weightage to each aspect (criteria) in the scale of 1 to 10 (column 2), where 1 represents 'not important aspect' and 2 represents 'very important aspect'. This criteria weights for each aspect must be decided by retailer/buyer in consultation with the merchandise manager/merchandise incharge. One point must be remembered in this regard that different weightage should be given to different aspects. All aspects cannot have some importance over each other. For instance, merchandise buyer and merchandise manager are of the view that Vendor's goodwill must receive 9 points being a very important aspect, payment criteria should receive 5 points being a reasonably important and promotional help should get 3 points being a less important aspect.

Step 3

After allocating the respective weightage to each aspect, now buyer will assign ranking to each brand in question in consultation with the merchandise managers.

Step 4

Under this stage, in order to calculate the overall performance of the Vendors, we multiply column 2 with respective ratings of Brand 'A', 'B' and 'C'. For instance, in case of Brand 'A', we multiply Vendor's goodwill (8) with Brand 'A' performance rating for Vendor's goodwill aspect i.e. 5, totaling 40 for Brand 'A'; similarly, service offered (5) with Brand 'A' ranking (8), totaling 40 and so on. Then, we sum up for 'Brand 'A' that comes to 40 + 40 + 42 + 30 + 25 + 20 + 24 + 30 + 15 = 266; similarly, for Brand 'B' 290 and Brand 'C' 308.

Step 5

Lastly we compare the overall ratings of various Brands, in question, and give preference to the highest overall rating, like in this question, Brand 'C' has the highest overall rating (308), so 'C' is the most preferable Vendor ahead of 'A' and 'B'.

GLOBAL SOURCING DECISIONS

Global sourcing is a procurement strategy that aims to take advantage of global efficiencies for the delivery of goods and services. For MNCs, it has become a strategic sourcing in today's competitive setting. Some popular examples of globally sourced goods and services are: labor-intensive goods produced in China at low production cost, BPOs staffed with low cost English proficient people in India, and IT (software and hardware) tasks performed by Indian and Eastern European low cost programmers. These examples particularly relate to low cost country specific sourcing but the scope and definition of global sourcing is not limited to low cost nations.

In reality, global sourcing is a centralized procurement strategy of a multinational company, wherein a central procurement department seeks the economies of scale through corporate wide standardization and benchmarking. In short, global sourcing is a 'strategic business philosophy' that coordinates the world's most cost effective production and operation inputs such as men, materials, machines, technology, suppliers, engineering and other required facilities. The global sourcing philosophy has following advantages:

- Low cost manufacturing
- Tapping skills and resources that are not available in the home nation
- Seeking the benefit of alternate suppliers
- Utilizing an efficient supply chain management systems
- Learning global business skills
- Meeting competition prudently and efficiently

Disadvantages of global sourcing philosophy

- No exposure of international culture, traditions and beliefs
- Hidden costs related to different time zones and languages
- Financial and political risks associated with emerging economies
- Risk of losing intellectual properties, patents and copyrights
- Long lead times
- Labor problems and labor related issues
- Unnecessary shutdowns and supply interruptions
- Difficulty in supervision
- Difficulty of monitoring goods and services quality

International Procurement Organizations (IPOs)

Due to the complexities of global sourcing, IPOs are doing wonderful jobs to remove the discrepancies that have crept in the global sourcing system. The IPOs take the responsibility of performing all functions and managing the inputs required for economies of scale. Such IPOs provide great help in country based sourcing efforts and meet the requirements of parent organizations. For instance, in case of low cost manufacturing countries like China, which has a large range of sub-markets for raw materials and finished goods and suppliers that span the whole value chain of goods and services, such IPOs' role proved to be very vital. They provide all relevant and essential up to date on ground information. In the years to come, these IPOs may grow upto giant procurement agencies with whole range of buying and category formats.

SOURCING

Sourcing simply means getting the merchandise a retailer wish to sell at the right price, quantity, quality in a firmly manner. It is associated with branding decisions that involve searching the country and the world so as to find the best quality product at best price. Retailers providing private brands usually face these issues.

Sourcing companies provide agents in other countries who handle all sourcing related arrangements. Some countries are more advanced in producing certain things, while some countries are rich with some sort of raw materials/minerals. Therefore, retailers can save cost, time, and reduce consumer complaints by developing relationships with these country-specific suppliers.

COSTS ASSOCIATED WITH GLOBAL SOURCING

It is said that East or West, home is the best. No one is ready to leave his own country but if somebody does, the reason is domestic compulsion. There are some factors that force a retailer to buy merchandise from abroad. Buying merchandise form abroad is full of complexities. Retailers take sourcing decisions due to cost saving and improved quality, but this exercise is not at all simple. A retailer while taking global sourcing decision must consider following costs that have impact on firm's overall profitability. These are:

1. **Country's Origin**: The country's origin has a lot of impact on the sourcing decisions. Buying a handicam from Japan (a developed nation) and from China, India, Korea (developing nations) makes a difference in cost. Japan, USA are famous for producing latest and high quality goods resulting in high cost, while developing nations due to cheap manpower and other benefits of economies of scale produce the same thing relatively in cost effective manner. Further, some countries are technologically advance and therefore, may provide high quality goods in relatively less cost. Therefore, a retailer must consider following issues:
   (i) Technological advancement
   (ii) R&D difficulties
   (iii) Distribution and logistics network
   (iv) Country's specific richness
   (v) Saving associated with buying from a particular country.
2. **Import Duty**: Import duty (commonly known as **tariff**) is a tax imposed by a government on imported goods. Tariff raises the cost of imported goods. Government imposes such taxes to protect the interest of domestic manufacturers and traders. In absence of import duty, India will be dumped with cheap goods (low cost goods) demolishing the Indian business. Therefore, a retailer before

entering into international sourcing agreements must check the rate of import duty on particular merchandise in question.

3. **Foreign Currency Risk**: In recent days, currency fluctuations have become significant consideration while making global sourcing decisions. Currency risk arises due to change in price of one country with respect to another. For example, you are an Indian retailer and you buy merchandise from USA, as usual there exist time gap between placing the order and paying for the supplies, and now while making the payment in dollars, you have to pay more (because dollar is stronger than rupee in international market) and also there is a possibility that you would realize that no gain from merchandise buying.
4. **Trade Blocks**: Trade blocks like **FTZs** (Free Trade Zones), **SEZs** (Special Economic Zones), **EOUs** (Export Oriented Units) are some designated areas in a country that don't come under country's applicable tariffs. Like Free Trade Zone is an area within a country where no taxes are applicable with regard to storage, inspection, packaging, assembly, fabrication or exhibition. Therefore, a retailer while searching for foreign vendors should consider these trade blocks. Also Indian retailers should develop relations with global vendors belonging to these designated areas.
5. **Merchandise Carrying Cost**: The cost of maintaining inventory in a retailer's warehouse like rent, electricity expense, insurance and employees' expenses is known as merchandise carrying cost. In another words, this is basically the cost of holding merchandise in stock.

Carrying Cost = Average Inventory at Cost **X** Opportunity Cost of Capital

6. **Opportunity Cost of Capital**: It is the rate of return that could be earned by investing in the next best possible option. It is the expected return foregone by using capital for other purpose.
7. **Logistics Expense**: It basically includes transportation cost occurred on merchandise travelling. Higher the distance from vendor, higher will be the transportation expense. For example, buying merchandise from China is significantly lower than the cost from New York to India.

MANAGERIAL ISSUES ASSOCIATED WITH GLOBAL SOURCING

Buying merchandise from overseas may be cheaper than from vendors located locally. Vendors that are in foreign country is where majority of the retailers get their merchandise and make a huge profit globally. Following are the managerial issues associated with global sourcing:

1. **Quality Control**: It will take long time for merchandise from outside the country to reach to your store, keep in mind that shipping/air time while sourcing globally. These problems are more common in countries that are under developed or have no bilateral trade with your nation. Therefore, limited/no trade details regarding a country's vendors are available. It can have following consequences:

(i) What will happen if the merchandise delivery is delayed?
(ii) What will happen if the merchandise is of poor quality?
(iii) What will happen if the merchandise is of superior quality but packaging, transport conditions are substandard?

Consequently, it becomes imperative on the part of retailers to assure the quality of imported goods through insurance, agreement with vendor or otherwise.

2. **Building relationships with vendors**: Building relationships with suppliers overseas is difficult but if made correctly, can do wonder for both sides. Domestic retailers look global sourcing not only for lower costs, but also to improve quality, prompt deliveries and develop innovations to keep them a step ahead of their competitors. Following are the problems related to global sourcing:
   (i) Language barrier
   (ii) Cultural difference
   (iii) Climate/time difference
   (iv) Distance issue

Therefore, considering the complexities of global sourcing, retailers should try to remove these obstacles and work for building longlasting relationships. The key to build solid relationships with overseas suppliers is to maintain trust with suppliers.

MERCHANDISE BUYING AND HANDLING PROCESS

Merchandise buying and holding is a vital part of implementing merchandise plans. This is a step by step process and involves following stages: (i) collecting information, (ii) selecting vendors, (iii) evaluating merchandise, (iv) negotiation with vendors, (v) buying merchandise, (vi) receiving and stocking merchandise, (vii) re-ordering, and (viii) re-evaluating, as mentioned in figure 11.1

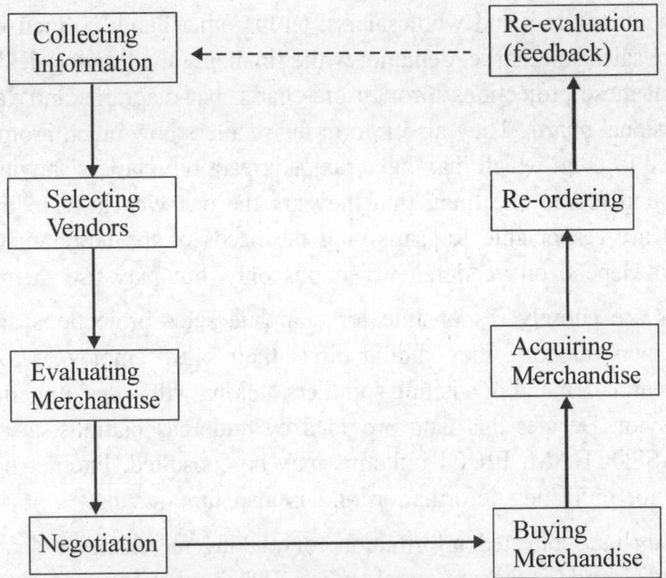

Figure 11.1 Merchandise Buying and Handling Process

These steps are explained in detail below:

1. Collecting Information: This is a very first step of merchandise buying and handling process. Once the firm's overall merchandise plans are defined, exact information about current market needs and potential vendors is required. This is essential as a retailer before buying merchandise would like to know (i) what consumers are looking for, (ii) where the vendors are located and what is their goodwill in the market, and (iii) what their competitors are offering. After understanding these aspects, retailer will be in a position to decide what he wants to buy and from whom.

For collecting information, a retailer/buyer has several possible sources defined as internal and external sources.

Internal Sources

- Employees
- Suggestion boxes
- Complaint boxes
- Want slips
- Feedback record

External Sources

- Dealers
- Vendors
- Competitors
- Sales people
- Internet

It depends on the retailer (buyer) which source he would like to choose. Normally, global retailers rely on both internal and external sources to have the better picture of consumers' requirements. Undoubtedly, the most valuable source is the 'study of consumers'. Global retailers like Wall Mart, Spencer and Noodle Ki Doodle have proper consumer study divisions those continuously monitor the consumers' lifestyles, living habits and their changing demographics in order to study the consumer demand directly.

Vendors (manufacturers and wholesalers), on the other hand, do their own projections about the future sales and market demand, while finalizing the 'buying deal' with retailers. Vendors present these projections through pie-charts, bar-diagrams and various two and/ or three dimensional charts. They also inform the retailers how much promotional support will be provided to them which may have major impact on retailers' buying decision. But retailers must understand one thing that they are the one who have to interact with the customers and are responsible for satisfying the needs of the target market. Therefore, they should not depend on vendors' projections only, but may use them for reference.

As retailers are entirely responsible for complete sales projections and merchandise plans in their own category, they should direct their sales' employees to get a view of customers' potential demand by visiting suppliers, talking with sales' experts and observing consumer behavior. Besides this data provided by trade associations, government bodies projects like ASSOCHAM, FICCI bulletins may be consulted. Internet has also become a vital source for collecting information and is also time saving.

Retailers may use collected information for making merchandise decisions about (i) staple merchandise and (ii) fashion merchandise. The above-mentioned sources are enough to have picture about staple merchandise but for frequently changing fashion merchandise, a mix of internal and external sources may be used.

2. Selecting Vendors: After collecting the information about consumers' demands, the next step is to select sources of merchandise and to interact with them to select the potential vendors. For selecting vendors, the retailers usually have three alternatives:

(i) **Company-owned vendors**: As the very name implies, these vendors are owned by the company themselves. Large retailers have their own manufacturing or wholesale operations. They work only for particular retailers and provide as per their requirements.

(ii) **External, widely used supplier**: This type of supplier is not owned by the retailer but used frequently by him. The retailer is buying merchandise for long and is aware about the quality and services offered by him.

(iii) **External, not used supplier**: This type of retailer has not been used by the retailer as he is either a new entrant or retailer has not purchased anything from him so far. Therefore, what quality he is offering cannot be known in advance.

Retailers may use any one type of supplier as per their requirements, budget and area of operations or they can use a combination of them. Big retailers often deal with all types of suppliers. Therefore, after selecting the supplier category, a retailer should interact with them about the buying terms and conditions. Following points must be considered while selecting the vendors:

(i) Goodwill of the vendor in the market.
(ii) Guarantee and/or warranty offerings.
(iii) Which vendor offers merchandise at the lowest total cost?
(iv) Quality offered by the vendor
(v) Will the vendor provide transport storing and other facilities?
(vi) Is vendor's merchandise line conservative or innovative?
(vii) Is vendor offering credit purchase?
(viii) What promotional support is provided by the vendor?
(ix) Will mark up be sufficient?
(x) Is vendor interested or will be available for long term relations?
(xi) Will vendor fulfill what he has agreed upon?
(xii) Will vendor provide conditional/exclusive selling rights?
(xiii) How quick will orders be delivered?

3. Evaluating Merchandise: After deciding upon the source of merchandise, next step is to evaluate the vendor's merchandise quality. Here, a retailer is encountered with following situations:

(i) Whether the whole lot be examined, or
(ii) Purchasing be made only on vendor's description.

Retailer after interacting with suppliers should **evaluate** merchandise under purchase consideration. Should each unit of merchandise be examined? Or items should be bought only on the basis of description and demonstrations presented by the suppliers. For evaluating merchandise items, retailer has three choices in hand:

1. Inspection
2. Sampling and
3. Description

Which method should be followed depends on the items' features, cost and the frequency of purchase. **Inspection** is a process of examining each item of merchandise thoroughly before the merchandise procurement and also after delivery. Jewelry (diamond, gold, platinum and other precious stones) is one of the examples where retailer inspects all the items of purchase.

Sampling technique is used when retailer is buying items on regular basis in large quantity that is perishable, breakable or costly ones. Therefore, retailer uses **Acceptance Sampling** method. It is "the middle of the road" approach that exercises control over the incoming inventory without going through 100% inspection. It simply means accepting or rejecting the supplier's merchandise assortment. Here decision is taken without going through 100% inspection of the entire lot. It is a compromise between no inspection and 100% inspection. It has two key classifications of acceptance plans: firstly by attributes ("go, no-go") and secondly by variables.

Sampling

Sampling is the process of selecting merchandise (goods and services) from available set of alternatives so that by carefully examining the sample a retailer may understand which product will be more profitable to sell from all points of view. Each observation measures one or more properties such as price, color, weight, packing, demand of an apparent entity specified to distinguish products and services.

Why 100% inspection is not done?

- Time consuming process
- Uneconomical
- 100% inspection means 100% destruction of the products before they are used.
- Handling the products may cause deterioration and is not an easy task.

Description buying is a process of merchandise purchase where a retailer orders the merchandise items after going through supplier's pictorial catalogue mentioning the product features, price, size and other relevant details. For instance, a retailer can order food and clothing items from a catalogue or concerned company website. On receipt of items, they are only counted for matching order size.

4. Negotiation: Once the retailer has evaluated the merchandise quality and other features, he negotiates with the vendor for its price and consequent terms and conditions. Both parties listen to each other carefully and ask questions wherever doubt arises. Terms and conditions are then decided and contract is made involving total amount to be paid by the retailer, delivery date, delivery conditions and other legal aspects. A retailer while negotiating also talk about the conditions for the re-order.

Under Negotiation stage, retailer bargains with the supplier for available discounts and conditions of purchase. A retailer would like to know what will be the additional discount if he goes for bulk buying. What is cash discount? What is trading discount etc? Is there some off-season discount? Once the merchandise is negotiated for its quality, quantity and price, retailer places the order and concludes the buying exercise by paying the amount due. The retailer takes the title of items immediately after the purchase.

5. Buying Merchandise: After negotiating the terms and conditions and agreed upon price, a retailer after placing the size of the order (quantity and quality of each merchandise category), pays the initial money as per the agreement. Big retailers usually place the order and pay the bills online through electronic data interchange (EDI) and quick response (QR) Inventory planning, small retailers due to limited sources, conclude purchase manually. They fill up the order form and deposit it personally or through postage. With the technological advancement and easy access to internet facility, retailers place their orders online. The small retailers who are associated with big vendors also pay their bills and process orders through EDI and QR systems as per policy matters.

6. Acquiring Merchandise: It means after paying for the invoices, retailer should receive the merchandise and stock it properly. While acquiring the merchandise, retailer physically receive the items, counts the supplies, pays the invoices, marks the items, displays the items and stock in godowns/warehouses to avoid any pilferage and damage. In case of centralized buying, goods are received by regional office/central warehouse and then transferred to chain stores as per their requirements and order received from them.

After paying the suppliers' bills, retailer makes provision how and where the items should be received and stocked. Items should directly supplied to store or warehouse, is mentioned at the time of negotiation and merchandise payments. Once the items are received, retailer next step is to make ensure that the items are stocked properly. Sometimes it may take long time to reach from warehouse to store, therefore, when orders are received, they must be checked for its quantity and quality. Invoices must be carefully checked for its description and amount printed to avoid any confusion with supplier later on.

When the merchandise has been procured and stocked, it will be issued to store/s whenever demand pertains. Therefore, retailer should have an eye on merchandise issued and the items left in the stock. Whenever the level of inventory comes close to reorder level, goods are ordered for fresh supplies.

Once a merchandise plan is implemented, it should be re-evaluated at regular interval of time by close monitoring of implementation plan with the objective of satisfying consumers.

In case of central buying, distribution management is the key to store performance. Buyers/concerned staff should take care while shifting merchandise to chain stores or warehouses. Following precautions must be taken under this stage:

(i) Inspect the invoices physically for its accuracy. Once the invoices are signed and paid, vendor will not be responsible for any loss in transit or in case of missing items. Therefore, when orders are received, they must be thoroughly checked for size of order placed and any breakage/pilferage during transit.

(ii) While unloading merchandise, take precautions that their packing should not spoil. Further, keep the items at distance and at proper place as unloading generally causes breakage and mixing of items with one another.

ETHICAL ANG LEGAL ISSUES IN BUYING MERCHANDISE

The retailing sector in India is progressing by leaps and bounds though it has not been given the 'industry' status. Given the hundreds relationships and thousand of transactions between retailers and their vendors, disputes with regard to unethical and illegal situations naturally may arise. Therefore, retailers and vendors need to understand that they can grow with the growth of each other. Retailers on their part should not take any undue advantage of their position with the vendors' supplying terms. Similarly, it is expected from vendors that they should not cheat or betray retailers in any case. Therefore, there is a need of some binding contract for each transaction between vendor and retailer.

Business Ethics

Application of general principles of ethics customary in a society to the areas where business is conducted is known as 'business ethics'. These are concerned with obligations of truth ness, justice and charity that a man assumes when he enters into a business. The significance of ethical code in retail world is of greater importance today because of growing competition, industrialism and the business influence on society. The misuse of socio-economic power by either party may lead to unhealthy atmosphere. Hence, the importance of ethical and legal issues becomes imperative as today most retailers/ vendors websites may emphasize on obligations to promote non-economic social values under various moves such as social responsibility charters, ethics code, extended core values and so on. The following are some ethical issues involved in merchandise buying:

- To honor the binding contract by making commitments.
- To extend fair and human treatment to each other.
- Not to adopt any unfair trade practices such as offering bribes, costly gifts, misuse of market positions by either party.
- Not to manipulate accounts by vendor and hold any part of payment on the part of retailer.
- To observe various business laws and co-operation with the government and trade associations in achieving social objectives.

- Not to corrupt the either's party employees to get any undue advantage or to get any favour from them.

There are certain areas where usually it has been found that dispute arise between vendors and retailers.

1. Dispute over terms and conditions

For buying merchandise, retailer places an order to a vendor specifying quality, quantity, size and other related aspects. Vendor after going through the retailer's desired specifications normally accepts the order by formally informing the retailer; for the vendor to deliver the promised merchandise and on the part of retailer to pay the specified price.

Under such conditions, dispute arises when either party doesn't perform according to the contract. Generally, both vendors and retailers honor the contract because of criticalities of the Indian legal system. Further, no one would like to spoil his image and has no spare time to fight over legal matters in this competitive and busy era. Therefore, in case any differences arise over some terms and conditions, it is settled by mutual consent and negotiations. Consequently, it has been found that in India, parties of contract include 'alternate dispute resolution' under agreement provisions. As per convenience, such provisions may incorporate some clauses like arbitration, mediation or Med-Erb. **'Mediation'** is a process of selecting a neutral third party which helps the parties to solve the dispute by agreeing upon a common solution without going to litigation. The advantage of mediation is that it is less expensive (as compared to litigation expenses) and produces rapid results. **Arbitration** basically is a legal method for solving such disputes without going to court. In India, the arbitration process is based on the UNICITRAL Modcl Law on International Commercial Arbitration which is legally based on English Common Law due to lengthy era of British Colonial influence under the British Raj. Under arbitration, arbitrator listens the arguments of both the parties and makes a decision for which they agree to be bound. **Med-Arb** is a compromise between the mediation and arbitration. Under Med-arb technique, an initial attempt is made to solve the dispute through mediation but later on can become arbitration if no settlement is reached and mediation becomes unsuccessful. In India, such provisions come under The Arbitration and Conciliation Act 1996 that ensures equal status and effect for these settlements like an arbitral award rendered by an arbitral tribunal.

2. Chargebacks

A chargeback occurs when a retailer deducts/stop a part of vendor's money and asks the vendor to remove some charges like transportation expenses etc from the total payment. In the world of retailing, there are two common reasons for chargeback. The first is deducting some part of money from vendor's invoice on account of non-selling of the merchandise in question. The second case arises when vendor does some mistake with regard to wrong size merchandise, wrong color, wrong packaging, late delivery, lost billings, inferior labeling and missing lots. Therefore, retailer for these mistakes deduct the money from their total payments depute the request of vendor to pay full and settle the amount later on after inspecting the matter on the part of vendor.

3. Pricing

Pricing is one of the most crucial reasons for the dispute between vendors and retailers. This is natural that there exist a gap between the order placed by retailer and delivery made by vendor. Sometimes due to increase in prices of some commodities like petrol, diesel, electricity or the raw material used by the vendors/manufacturers, production cost goes unreasonably high therefore, it becomes difficult for vendors to deliver the goods at prices decided earlier. Hence, vendor requests to retailer to co-operate for such price hikes but retailer due to his market position sometimes refuse vendor's request and forced to deliver the goods on old prices.

Vendor in such case will have two options, first either to reduce the quality of merchandise in some way or not to deliver the goods. In both cases, dispute will arise.

COUNTERFEIT MERCHANDISE

Buying and selling counterfeit merchandise goods is as old as currency itself. In includes products exclusively made and sold without the permission of its owner of a copyright, trademark, or a patented invention. Copyrights, trademarks, and patents come under Intellectual Property (IP). **Trademark** is any distinctive sign, word, picture, used by a retail firm to uniquely identify the source of provider. For instance, the 'Maharaja Sign' of Air India, 'M' on McDonalds. A **copyright** on the other hand provides the protection to authors/writers for their literary work. It also relates to artistic creations, musicians, sculptors and others who are related to producing some sort of intellectual work like software developers etc.

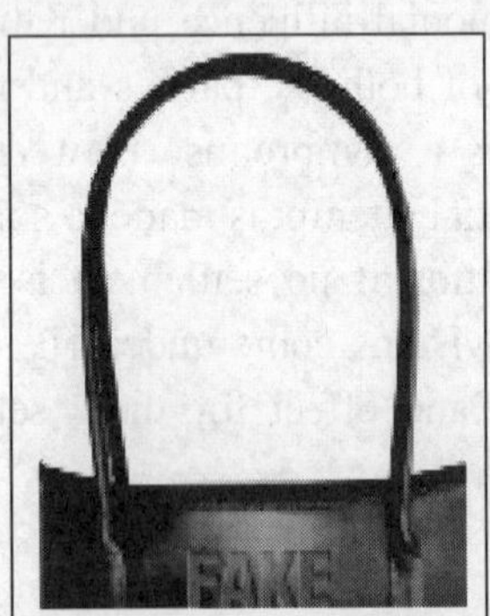

One thing should be noted in this regard that copyright protects the physical expression of the work, not the theme. For instance, in case of copyright music, those sentences, lyrics cannot be used by anyone without the consent of their owners. Similarly, from a copyright book/novel, one cannot take the theme and express it in his different words. Therefore, retailers and vendors can protect themselves from misuse of such intellectual properties in following ways:

1. They should sell/provide the products that are legally 'to be sold' in a country. You might have seen mentioned on some books/goods that "this edition/product is for sale in India, Pakistan, Nepal, Sri Lanka and Bangladesh only". Therefore, avoid such selling.
2. The second way is to protect your company through legal actions. Various laws protect businesses against intellectual property violations such as
   (i) The Patents (Amendment) Act, 2005
   (ii) The Trademark Rules, 2002
   (iii) The Copyright (Amendment) Act, 1999
   (iv) The Design Act, 2000
3. Third, with the initiative of WTO, Indian Government is working for bilateral and multilateral negotiations to combat with counterfeiting.
4. Lastly, global retailers have become serious to protect themselves due to piracy and counterfeiting that is eating their vitals. The International Anti-Counterfeiting Coalition is an Umbrella Union that offers anti-counterfeiting programs to combat piracy and counterfeiting by promoting regulations, rules, laws to protect intellectual property against its misuse in any form whatsoever.

SUMMARY

Any retailer's primary function is to buy merchandise from national and/or international sources and making it available to the customers in a population size at a proper price. Buying and handling merchandise comprises of planning as to what to buy, from where to buy, how much to buy, how to negotiate, how to pay, how to receive, stock and re-order. Merchandise planning, therefore, is the most important aspect of retailing. Issues like negotiation, acquisition and evaluation should be carefully examined besides legal and ethical aspects to avoid complexities of day-to-day business operations.

REVIEW QUESTIONS

True and False Questions

1. Retailers usually have three types of buying systems:
   I. Staple merchandise buying system
   II. Latest merchandise buying system
   III. Obsolete merchandise buying systems
2. Sales forecasting is not essential for all types of products. It is straightforward in case of fashion merchandise buying system but more complex for those with staple and seasonal merchandise.
3. Efficient buying systems ensure the balance between sales, stock levels and quantity ordered and account for influences on shortage of merchandise.
4. Sales Volume means providing right merchandise in right quality in the right price and at right place.

5. Buying systems influence not only the price (cost) of merchandise but also the pricing Buying systems influence the markdowns as they regulate the quantity, lead time, price and the type of merchandise ordered.
6. Buying systems have no impact on the balance of inventory (inventory in stock).
7. There are five steps in a typical retail buying process.
8. Staple merchandise consists of the items that are rarely purchased, displayed and sold by the retailers.
9. The reason behind forecasting demand for staple merchandise is that these are the items of daily/regular use and are influenced by season and other factors.
10. Fashion merchandise consists of the items those usually have predictable demand and unlimited sales record.
11. Predictable and stable demand is the main feature of fashion merchandise.
12. A merchandise budget plan is a forecast of particular merchandise related activities designed for unlimited particular period of time, say one decade or more.
13. The primary objective of having a merchandise Budget plan is that a retailer would like to have a proper balance between (a) what will be paid to suppliers for purchase of merchandise and making it available to customers; and (b) the cash inflow that will come in the business from sales to customers.
14. Planning for reductions is the first step in a merchandising budget plan which involves deciding about markdowns employee discounts and shortages.
15. After planning sales and stock levels, opening stock (BOM), closing stock (EOM) and reductions, next step under merchandise budget plan is to plan for purchases in Rupees.
16. Purchase Planning = Planned Sales + Planned Reductions + BOM - EOM
17. The gross margin usually is the initial mark up adjusted for price variations, reductions, shrinkage and other stock shortages.
18. The gap between gross margin and expenses needed to create sales will either contribute to loss.
19. Evaluating the merchandise budget plan aims to balance the money outflows (for supplies) and inflows (received from customers through selling merchandise) for the next financial year or upcoming season.
20. Open to Buy is a system of monitoring merchandise flow in order to determine how much money was spent on merchandise and how much is balanced to spend.
21. The ABC analysis sometimes known as Always Better Control is an inventory classification process where total inventory is classified into three categories:

    A - Outstandingly important;

    B - Of average importance and

    C - Relatively unimportant as a basis for a control scheme.

22. In case of 'A' items alert attention is paid to work out the requirement, safety stocks, order scheduling, and prompt receipt and inspection.
23. Close watch is kept on the consumption pattern, stock balance and refill orders of 'A' items.
24. For expensive 'C' items control is comparatively stress-free.
25. Buying and handling merchandise comprises of planning as to what to buy, from where to buy, how much to buy, how to negotiate, how to pay, how to receive, stock and re-ordering.

Answers

1. False	2. False	3. False	4. True
5. True	6. False	7. False	8. False
9. False	10. False	11. False	12. False
13. True	14. False	15. True	16. False
17. True	18. False	19. True	20. True
21. True	22. True	23. True	24. False
25. True			

Multiple Choice Questions

1. Staple merchandise belongs to :
   (*a*) Regularly used items (*b*) Rarely used items
   (*c*) Fashion goods (*d*) All of the above.
2. Reorder level implies :
   (*a*) How to order (*b*) When to order
   (*c*) Where to order (*d*) Whom to order
3. Fashion merchandise consists of :
   (*a*) Predictable demand (*b*) Unpredictable
   (*c*) Regularly used items (*d*) Seasonal merchandise
4. MBP stands for :
   (*a*) Merchandise Buying Plan
   (*b*) Merchandise Budget Plan
   (*c*) Merchandise Buying Planogram
   (*d*) Merchandise Before Plan.
5. B.O.M. implies:
   (*a*) Beginning of merchandise (*b*) Beginning of month.
   (*c*) Before open merchandise (*d*) Before order merchandise
6. Safety stock is mainly required in case of:
   (*a*) A type items (*b*) B type items
   (*c*) C type items (*d*) All of the above

7. Sell through Analysis describes the comparison between :
   (*a*) Gross and Net sales volume
   (*b*) Actual and forecasted sales volume.
   (*c*) Gross and Actual sales volume.
   (*d*) Net and forecasted sales volume.
8. Markdown is used to :-
   (*a*) Create shortage of goods (*b*) Restrict retail sales
   (*c*) Push retail sales (*d*) Supervise floor staff
9. For staple merchandise, demand can be predicted :-
   (*a*) Very easily (*b*) Very difficult
   (*c*) Can not be predicted (*d*) None of the above
10. Managing sales history is difficult in case of :-
   (*a*) Seasonal merchandise (*b*) Fashion merchandise
   (*c*) Staple merchandise (*d*) retail merchandise

Answers

1. a	2. b	3. a	4. b
5. b	6. a	7. b	8. c
9. a	10. b		

Check your progress

1. What is ABC analysis?
2. What does BOM mean?
3. What is staple merchandise?
4. Give examples of fashion merchandise?
5. List few seasonal items?
6. What is Gross Margin?
7. What is markdown?
8. What is SKU?
9. How many steps are involved in a typical merchandise buying process?
10. How to calculate reorder level?
11. What is EOM?
12. What is merchandise buying plan?
13. What is open to buy system?
14. What is GMROI?
15. What are stock levels?

Small Answer Questions

1. Briefly explain the concept of sell through analysis?
2. What do you mean by Multi Attribute method?

3. Explain the significance of ABC analysis?
4. How merchandise performance can be analyzed?
5. Illustrate how merchandise is allotted to stores?
6. Describe the implications of Open-to-buy system?
7. How many merchandise systems are in Indian practice?
8. Explain various steps in a typical buying process?
9. How to maintain back up stock in staple merchandise plan?
10. Suggest how 'when to re-order' problem can be solved?
11. How a retailer can evaluate 'the effectiveness of 'open-to-buy' system?
12. How to calculate open-to-buy for past period?
13. Illustrate how 'open-to-buy' for current period can be calculated?
14. What strategies are suggested for handling various merchandise?
15. How a retailer can plan for gross margin and operating profit?

Long Answer Questions

1. Suppose you are a new entrant in this fast growing retail industry, which process what you would like to adopt to buy and handle merchandise? Explain with examples wherever necessary.
2. What do you mean by merchandise budget plan? Explain its various components and also discuss how a retailer can evaluate its merchandise budget plan effectively and prudently?
3. Critically explain the various methods of analyzing merchandise performance with suitable examples wherever necessary?

UNIT 11

MANAGING A RETAIL BRAND

LEARNING OBJECTIVES

- Understanding the scope and essence of creating brands.
- Describing various branding options available to Indian retailers.
- Explaining costs associated with global sourcing.
- Analyzing the role of retailer (buyer) while buying merchandise overseas.
- Understanding managerial issues with regard to global sourcing.

*"A **brand** is the 'personification of a product, service, or even entire company.'*

*Like any person, a **brand** has a physical 'body': in Procter & Gamble's case, the products and/or services it provides. Also, like a person, a brand has a name, a personality, character and a reputation.*

Like a person, you can respect, like and even love a brand. You can think of it as a deep personal friend, or merely an acquaintance. You can view it as dependable or undependable; principled or opportunistic; caring or capricious. Just as you like to be around certain people and not others, so also do you like to be with certain brands and not others.

Also, like a person, a brand must mature and change its product over time. But its character and core beliefs shouldn't change. Neither should its fundamental personality and outlook on life.

*People have character...so do brands. A person's character flows from his/her integrity: the ability to deliver under pressure, the willingness to do what is right rather than what is expedient. You judge a person's character by his/her past performance and the way he/she thinks and acts in both good times, and especially bad. The same are true of **brands**."*

Robert Blanchard, former P&G Executive.

INTRODUCTION

Today be it India, China or USA, retail market is flodded with stores, most retailers have spent a lot of time in searching for new ways to grow their businesses and, at the same time, their brands. It seems impossible to imagine a retailer surviving and expanding consumer base in the years to come without creating a genuinely robust retail brand image. But getting your program off the ground is only the initiative. As the economy shifts and consumers' needs change, retailers must continue to review their brand strategy. Marketers should understand that consumers are finicky creatures, but they can become loyal customers if they are served the way they want. This present an opportunity for retailers to become savvier in the way they present their brand programs to their consumers.

RETAILERS AS BRANDS

The last part of 20th century has seen many fundamental changes in retailing, especially in the grocery and general merchandise industry. On one hand, the rise of promotions and private labels has been seen by many as an indicator of growing retailer power. On the other hand, the mushrooming of discount stores and warehouse clubs has put immense pressure on *kirana* stores and has increased retail competition both within and between retail formats.

Since the major portion of most retailers' earnings comes from selling manufacturer established brands, which many of their competitors also offer, building their own brand & equity is not risk free. Offering own brands, undoubtedly is a good bargain but how many retailers would like to try their luck by doing so. Such offering insulates them from competing retailers, which has the direct impact of increasing revenue and profitability, and the indirect impact of decreasing operational and selling costs as their leverage with brand manufacturers also increases. But if it fails, except having heavy losses, retailers have no other option.

Although retailers while offering own brands, apply all important branding principles, retailer brands are different from product brands that the actual application of those branding principles can vary. Retail brands are typically different in nature than product brands and can rely on rich consumer experiences to impact their equity. Retailers also create their brand images in different ways, e.g., by offering excellent consumer service, unique packaging and delivery service, attractive pricing, wide merchandise assortments and credit policy, etc.

In FMCG and consumer durable industries, the ultimate image and equity of retailer brands also depends on the manufacturer brands they carry and the equity of those brands. Retailers offer manufacturer brands as these are well established and have proved their performance. Therefore, manufacturer brands not only generate consumer interest but loyalty and patronage in a store. Retailers while selling manufacturer brands may offer some of their own brands. Industries like apparel and shoes, offerings own brands by retailers are common practice. In India, Pantaloon, Big Bazaar, Vishal Mega Mart are the main retailers who offer wide range of their own brands with unique brand names. It allows a retailer to differentiate its products from competitors, although often without the support afforded by manufacturers brands.

WHAT IS BRAND?

Brand is an identification mark, symbol, name, design or a combination of all these to uniquely identify a product that differentiate itself from others. The name of a company or its short form like 'coca cola' brand used by the coca cola company doesn't only represents company's face to the external world but also how that name is usually expressed through a logo and now that name and logo collectively be used in company's communications. The components of brand that takes company to heights are brand personality, brand attributes, core value (company's value statement), brand characteristics, brand development strategy (why, what, who and where of brand) and an efficient brand management strategy that keeps pace with the merging opportunities in which the brand will participate. Brands have certain recognizable elements that differentiate a brand from its competitors. These are:

(i) **Brand Name**: Brand name is the verbal part of a branding strategy because of which customers recall and remember a product. Company uses this name in all promotional events and communications.

(ii) **The Logo**: A 'logo' is a recognizable word, graphic element or symbol that represents a company. It is usually in a distinctive way to create uniqueness.

(iii) **The Trademark**: A trademark is any distinctive sign, word, picture used by retail to uniquely identify the source of provider. Usually a ***trademark*** is a legally protected brand mark that gives the producer exclusive rights for its usage such as 'Reliance', 'Big Bazaar', 'Microsoft' etc.

(iv) **Packaging**: Packaging is an extremely important in maintaining brand identification. For instance, the packing of Cadbury chocolates, Pepsi, Nestle products, which represent the company and therefore vital part of product identity.

Essentials of a Good Brand

Brands are all pervasive. Brands explain the way people live in a particular society. The value of a brand comes from its ability to gain an exclusive, positive and prominent position in the minds of customers. Brands are valuable assets to retailers and also are important to customers. Brands not only create wealth for the company but also add value to the consumers' life. There is no defined criterion to select or reject a particular brand. However, research and experience have developed the following features which must be considered while selecting a brand name. These are:

1. It is simple, short and easy to remember, for example, Dabur, Haldiram, Pepsi, Lux, etc.
2. It should suggest something about the product. It may be quality, purpose, action, use, etc. For example, Link locks, Sona Hawai Chappal, Rath Vanaspati, Dabur Oil, Kelvinator Refrigerator, Parle G Biscuits, etc.
3. It should be attractive and unique, for example, Bombay Dying, Chabra 555, Bata, Complan, Surya, Jindal, Nestle, etc.
4. It is stable and unaffected by time. It does not easily change with fashion or style.

5. The brand is consistent.
6. It should provide appropriate value to the customers.
7. It should not be used as a general or common name, for example, Campa, Dalda, Colgate, Maggie, etc.
8. It should be capable of being registered and protected legally under the legislation.
9. It should be properly positioned.
10. It is consistent.
11. The pricing policy is designed as per customers' perception of value.
12. The brand name should not be opposed by any social settings.
13. The brand is easy to publicize and promote.
14. The brand is away from and cut, copy, paste.
15. The brand should not be out of date.

Creating Positive Associations in Customers' Minds

Developing a brand strategy can be one of the most difficult steps in the marketing plan process. It's often the element that causes most businesses the biggest challenge, but it's a vital step in creating the company identity. To create a brand promise that creates such emotional connections, it should be:

1. Grounded in the brand's core values
2. Clearly relevant and engaging to your target market
3. Able to create some sort of positive emotional attachment beyond just being "good"
4. Repeated internally and externally within your organization
5. Adaptable to the business climate
6. Continually reinforced
7. Consistent across advertising and marketing mediums
8. Known and echoed by business

Kinds of Brand Name

The brand name is quite often used interchangeably within brand and comes in many styles. A few include:

(a) Descriptive Name

It includes all those words that describe a product benefit or function. For instance, Nirma washing powder, Godrej locks, Vadilal Ice-cream, Parle-G biscuits, Whole foods, Dabur Chawanprash, Keo Karpin Hair Oil, LG refrigerator, Vim-Bar, Airbus, etc.

(b) Suggestive Name

These types of words basically describe the function of a product, simply stated, the use and application of a particular product. For instance, M-Seal, Quick-fix, Easy-clean.

(c) Arbitrary Name

The name does not suggest neither about the product nor to the producer.

(d) Coined Name

Under the concept of coined name, the importance is given to the producer's identity. For example, Vatika alone is meaningless, unless attached to hair oil. Similarly Vimal to suiting, VIP to briefcase, General to air-conditioners.

(e) Acronym Name

A name made of initials that represent the company or the concept of the product such as IBM, UPS, and ATM.

(f) Foreign Name

Words that are taken from another language like Alpha, Samsung, Volvo.

(g) Founders Name

Using the names of real people who either are founder, or co-founder or whose contribution in the inception of a product or company is significant such as Modicare, Ambuja Cement, Ranbaxy (Ranjeet & Gurbaksh), Chhabra 555, Ford Motors and so on.

(h) Geographical Name

Here brands are named for regions and landmarks like British Airways, Hindustan Petroleum, Fujifilm, Cisco, New York Times, Panipat Refinery, and Barnala Steel.

Elements of Branding

Branding is the art and cornerstone of marketing. Without brands, human beings would be like fish without water. Brands are unique in many ways as they are characterized by enormous amount of complexity, which results from the service attributes of the retailers as well as from the multiplicity of the brand attributes. Considering the presence of more than 12 million kirana stores in the country, neighbourhood kirana store stands to be the strongest retail brands in India. It draws its brand strength from location, accessibility, personal attention philosophy, long trading hours, affordable prices and service. Similarly, in the consumer goods industry especially FMCG and consumer electronic products category, each brand has its position in the customer's mind and delivers high set of values than these of other competing brands. Considering the fundamental nature of the brand management, elements of branding are studied under following four key concepts:

1. Brand identity.
2. Brand image.
3. Brand position.
4. Brand equity.

1. Brand Identity

In retailing world, different brands vary in the power and value they command. Some brands are very popular and have high level of awareness in terms of name recall and recognition while others are entirely unheard by the people. Aaker defines brand identity as "a unique set of brand associations that the brand strategist aspires to create or maintain. These associations represent what the brand stands for and imply a promise to customers from the organization members". Brand identity refers to an insider's concept reflecting brand manager's decisions of what he wants to communicate to its potential customers. However, overtime, a product's brand identity may acquire (evolve), gaining new attributes from consumer perspective but not necessarily from the marketing communications an owner percolates to targeted consumers.

Brand identity needs to focus on authentic qualities – real characteristics of the value and brand promise being provided and sustained by organizational and/or production characteristics. Thus, brand identity refers to an insider's concept reflecting brand manager's decisions of what the brand is all about.

2. Brand Image

Brand identity describes what the brand is all about, what its inherent features are and how it is different from other competing brands while brand image reflects the perceptions of customers about the brand. Brand image is the sum total of impressions created by the brand in the consumer's mind. It is based on the concept that consumers buy not only a product but also the bundle of associations such as wealth, power, sophistication, etc.

Brand image can be reinforced by brand communications such as packaging, customer service, promotion, advertising, word-of-mouth and so on. The image of a brand can lead brand value upwards or downwards. For instance, when the stock broking agent is 'Reliance' or coconut oil is 'parachute', its value moves upwards. This shift is the result of brand name. The name adds visual and verbal dimensions in consumer's mind and acts as intervening variable moving the value upwards. For instance, the name of a product from the house of Tata or Shaktiman adds radical value to the product. Alexander proposed that types of brand associations can be hard and soft and brand images consist of three elements: image of provider, image of product and image of user.

Brand images are usually evoked by asking consumers the first words/images (views come to their mind when a certain brand is mentioned sometimes called "top of mind"). When responses are similar, quick or describe the product/experience in some way, image is said to be strong. In case responses are highly variable, not quick, or refer to non-image attributes such as cost, it indicates weak brand image.

3. Brand Position

A brand is the part of the brand identity and value preposition that is to be actively communicated to the target audience that sets it apart from the competition. A brand manager needs to establish communication objectives and plan the creative execution strategy. The beginning of an execution strategy is the brand positioning statement. The statement basically describes the "place" that a brand should occupy in the minds of target customers. In simple sense, it means how a brand is seen in the market place focuses on what is unique to the brand.

Creating a unique position in the market place involves the careful selection of target market and establishing clear differential advantages in the minds of customers. This is achieved through brand image, brand name, service, design, guarantee, warrantee, packaging, delivery, etc. Here some major factors are discussed that go into defining a brand position:

Brand Attributes

It means what the brand delivers through features, applications and benefits to consumers.

i. Consumer Expectations

Are customers 'expectations' fulfilled from a brand?

ii. Price

It is comparison between your prices and competitors' prices.

iii. Competitive factors

It means what the other brands offer to consumers in terms of features and benefits.

iv. Consumer Perceptions

It is the perceived quality and value of your brand in consumer's minds. It involves:

(i) Does your brand offer what customers want?

(ii) Is it a offer 'value for money'?

(iii) Is it unique in some sense?

4. Brand Equity

Brand equity is one of the popular and widely used concept in marketing that hardly emerged three decades before but is gaining popularity and vital place in marketing strategy. The reason behind the growing popularity of brand equity concept is because of the fact that several marketing researchers have concluded that brands are one of the most valuable assets that a company has.

According to Aaker, "Brands have equity because of their high awareness, many loyal customers, a high reputation for perceived quality, proprietary assets such as access to distribution channels or to patents or the kind of brand associations (such as personality associations).

The brand equity is an intangible asset that depends on associations made by the consumer. There are generally three perspectives from which brand equity can be viewed. These are:

(i) Financial

One of the widely used ways to measure brand equity is to determine the price premium that a brand holds over a generic product. For example, if consumers are willing

to pay Rs.20,000 more for a branded jewellery over the same unbranded brand, this premium provides important information about the value of the brand. However, marketing expenses must be taken into account when using this method to measure brand equity.

(ii) Brand Extensions

A successful brand like Dabur's "Vatika" may be used as a platform to launch new related products. The main benefit of brand extension is to take the benefits of brand awareness and thus reducing the advertising expenditures and risk associated with new launch. Subsequently, appropriate brand extension can enhance the core brand. As compared to financial measures of brand equity, brand extensions are more difficult to quantify.

(iii) Consumer related

A strong brand not only sells itself but increases the consumer's attitude strength toward the product associated with the brand. Attitude strength comes from experience with a product. Reports have shown that actual experience by the customer implies that trial samples are most effective than advertising during introduction stage of building a strong brand. Higher the consumer associations and awareness, higher will be brand loyalty.

Strong brand equity has following underlying benefits:

Increased cash flow by increasing market share and reduced promotional expenses.

(i) Allows for charging premium pricing.

(ii) Facilitates a more predictable income stream.

(iii) Brand equity like an asset can be sold or leased.

(iv) Make the brand easy to remember and develop repeat usage.

Note: *Brand equity is not always positive in value. Some brand acquires a bad reputation that results in negative brand equity.*

Success of a Strong Brand

Customers differentiate brands based on specifications, such as, features, durability, delivery terms and quality. Creating a brand is not a one-day show. It takes years to build a brand. Before becoming a brand, product suffers many ups and downs. A confectioner/ sweet maker took several decades to become 'Handiram', a name one can rely upon. Brand success comes through quality up gradation and differentiation as a continuous process. Brands provide a strong competitive advantage to the retailers owning them and hence they are increasingly becoming important tradable assets.

Following are the inherent benefits of creating a strong brand:

1. A strong brand like magnet attracts customers.
2. A strong brand can command a premium price.
3. Customers take less/no time to purchase them.

4. It creates trust and emotional bond to retailer's product and the company.
5. It is the reason for retailer's good will and image.
6. A strong brand conveys that store is serious and wants to have long lasting relationship with customers not just to sell goods.
7. A strong brand plays vital role in case of mergers, acquisitions and take-overs.
8. A strong brand presents win-win situation for both the customer and retailer.
9. A strong brand strengthens brand awareness and differentiation from the competitors, because it can serve as an anchor for product associations. For instance, 'Spencer', 'Big Bazaar' as a brand stands for value for money and wide range of products under one roof.
10. Strong brands exert halo-effects. The word 'SALE' which no more attracts customers does wonder in case strong brands advertise for small period.

Elements of Branding

The following are elements that should be considered and incorporated into your branding strategy. They will take on a different mix of importance depending on factors such as product life cycles, competitive activity, importance to consumers, loyalty patterns of consumers, commodity/custom perception and others. But within this product environment, these elements will all have to be addressed.

- Existing perceptions of the product category by target market segments.
- Existing structure and infrastructure in this product category.
- Competition for the same dollar from other product categories.
- Product attributes deemed important to target market segments.
- The positions currently occupied by you and your competitors
- Product differentials, real or perceived by target market segments.
- Corporate images of the marketers of products in your category.
- Expectations of buyers about products in your category.
- The programs, activities and policies in support of your brand.
- Relation of a particular brand with other brands from the same company (line extensions, brand adaptations, co-offerings etc.).
- Budget and financial considerations.
- Product expectations for volume, profit, longevity.

The mix of elements and environment make branding a complex and ongoing activity, but it can lead to focused, consistent, powerful and cost-effective marketing performance which in turn can lead to increased market share and profits.

Source Elements of Branding by Martin Jelsema, www.workz.com

Figure 11.1 : Prominent Indian Brands

Figure 13.2 : Prominent International Brands

WHAT IS RETAIL BRANDING?

> **Branding**
>
> Branding is a process by which a manufacturer/producer/retailer develops and communicates brand attributes to persuade customers about product's quality prior to purchase. For a retailer, branding is a must since it enhances goodwill and image among consumers. Building brand value is not an easy task. It takes years to build a brand. Several components like packaging, logo and trademarks play vital role for the success of a brand. This chapter begins with the concept and fundamentals of brand and explains various branding strategies to promote a brand.

A retail brand is basically defined as a niche area earned by a product in the consumer market for which it is demanded and recognized by the consumers. It is something that appeals to a customer to make purchase. According to American Marketing Association's definition of a brand, a retail brand identifies the goods and services of a retailer and differentiates them from those of competitors. A retailer's brand equity is exhibited in consumers responding more favorably to its marketing actions than they do to competing retailers (Keller 2003). The image of the retailer in the minds of consumers is the basis of this brand equity.

It takes years for a product/company to get the status of a brand. For instance, it took several decades to a confectioner to become Haldiram. This is because the retail market is highly consumer driven. For becoming a brand or creating a specific niche area for oneself in the consumer market, the cultural and economic issues play a significant role. The STP (Segmentation, Targeting and Positioning) approach plays very important role. Retailers today assume both brand and inventory management risks that traditionally have been the responsibility of the supplier. The simple reason behind such growing importance is that branding offers customer loyalty which is easy to retain than searching for new customers that demands a lot of initial investments and costs.

When it comes to retail branding, *mom and pop/kirana* stores is a brand in itself. The service level, the flexibility of timings provided by them has no match with all other forms of retailing. However, on the other hand retail giants such as the Aditya Birla Group, Tata Group, Reliance are already a big names in the country, which provide them easy access to venture into a domain that is entirely new to them. Though in India, retail industry is in nascent stage but the largest with an ocean of career opportunities for the Indian youth. And these brands are already popular, well recognized and also offering best deals with bundle of discounts and rebates.

Retail branding is also significant because of tough competition in the industry. With branding that comes an identification and symbol depicts purity, surety and honesty in the form of a punch line or a logo. These punch lines/logos represent the company and what it stands for. For instance, the retail venture of the Reliance Company named Reliance Fresh, hence providing an impression that the customer will always get fresh and selected items by purchasing from here. Similarly 'More' – an Aditya Birla group enterprise gives an impression that it will offer always something more by purchasing from here.

It is impossible for today's retailers to escape the need to regularly sustain the store brand. In a store, the entire retail firm is reflected and the exact nature and feel of a company can be realized. A retail store basically is akin to a container that holds the entire business formula. All the elements of the business formula/equation come together in store. Thus, the business equation/formula should be deliberately shaped from view point of recognition (the 'brand' of the retailing firm) with mutual co-ordination of the elements being important. In short, when branding is applied to retailing the main issue is not of retailers selling brands but branding the retail business itself, like the food chain, grocery store or the luxury store. A supermarket or departmental store, may offer several popular brands, but cannot afford to rest on it. He must attempt to brand himself in different ways, particularly when today's product brands are being launched through their product brand's own outlets. For example, Bata, Liberty, Adidas, Sony, Reebok, VIP, Nike, Action Shoes, Lee and Wrangler offer their exclusive product range through their own outlets.

The objectives that a good brand strives to achieve include:

- Delivers the message clearly.
- Confirms your credibility.
- Connect your target prospects emotionally.
- Motivates the buyer.
- Concretes user loyalty.

PRODUCT BRANDING VS RETAIL BRANDING

Brand is a name, mark, product or anything that provides certain functional benefits in addition to normal products (not always necessary) that some consumers are ready enough to pay a high premium for it. It basically represents a unique set of both tangible and intangible benefits in the mind of the consumers. Brand usually identifies a particular product and differentiates it from its competitors.

In case of product branding, companies build the brand name on the basis of what they want to communicate about what the brand stands for, while on the other hand, retail branding creates a brand preference which goes beyond the product or service in itself. It is through matching the branding with performance.

Product Vs Retail Brands

Product brands make life easier. They make it possible to recognize products, which simplifies the decision making process. Furthermore, product brands make the consumer a part of a group, they create a sense of belonging. But retail brands do even more than that. These brands arc visible platforms for kindred spirits: the physical shop is a container for the entire retail formula and therefore constitutes a large part of the retail brand. The tangible nature of retail makes the familiar slogan 'experiencing the brand' most logical of all, in a physical store.

A big difference between product branding and retail branding is that in a lot of cases most of the products have a mysterious or even pretended presenter, whereas in retail, consumers come in direct contact with the company and/or product. A Nestle Kit Kat bar, for example, is a product made according to a lay down recipe in a factory that is not known to general public. People who work in the factory never come into get in touch with with the consumers because the retail channel lies in between. And those who do sell the 'NKK' to the ultimate consumers (the retailers) do not have very much to do with it by virtue of their function. Therefore it is likely to visualize a brand identity for the product, establish it for a specific target group and then fix it in the minds of consumers. Compare the identities of 'Nestle Kit Kat', 'Munch', 'Milky Bar', Polo and 'Eclairs' : all are very different, yet they are produced by the same manufacturer.

On the other hand, a store like Pizza Hut, for example, because of its direct interaction with the ultimate consumers, must effectively live up to its brand reputation in every aspect, every day. It is not possible for retailers to escape the need to continually sustain the store brand.

In a store, the entire retail organization is exposed and the real nature of a company can be experienced. A retail store in actual is the container that holds the entire recipe. All the elements of the formula (including 4Ps of marketing mix) come together in-store. The formula should be deliberately shaped from the standpoint of identity (the 'brand' of the retail organization) with mutual coordination of the elements being important.

Retail Brand Building

Product brands make ones life easier and comfortable. They make it easy to recognize products, which shortens the decision making process. Furthermore, product brands make the consumer a part of a group; they create a sense of belonging. But retail brands do even more than that. These brands are observable platforms for customers who visit stores. The retail outlet is a container for the entire retail formula and therefore constitutes a large part of the retail brand. The physical nature of retail makes the familiar slogan 'experiencing the brand' most logical of all, in a physical store. Retail brands have gained in popularity in the past few years. Indeed, they have a number of returns above product brands. In the first instance, they are close to the consumer.

The physical retail outlet offers the chance of literally and figuratively communicating with consumers at the moment of purchase (direct marketing). Retailers can show who they are and what they are known for through the store formula. Moreover, in principle, retailers are neutral, because the actual choice of product brand (or store brand, if present) is left to the consumers. Retailers help consumers because they make a smart pre-selection and present their product assortment in a precise manner. Once a consumer knows and believes a retailer and has good experiences and memories about a store, the foundation has been laid for a long-lasting relationship that will ultimately lead to customer loyalty. *Retail branding creates a brand preference, which goes beyond the product or service in itself.*

Courtesy: Idea taken from www.bim.edu/pdf/lead_article Building_Successful_Indian_Retail_Brand

It simply means, when branding is applied to retailing, the point is not of retailers selling brands but branding the retail business itself, like the electronic supermarket chain or the furniture store. A hypermarket or department store, may offer several well-known brands, but in today's competitive world cannot afford to rest on its strategic product assortment and pricing initiatives to bring in the customers[1]. The retailer must attempt to brand himself in a different way, especially when today's product brands are being launched through their product brand's own outlets.

Segments	Examples
Perfumes	Hugo Boss
Shoes	Adidas, Reebok, and Nike,
Jeans	Lee and Wrangler

TYPES OF BRANDS

1. Manufacturer Brands

Generally a retailer's major portion of profits come from sale of manufacturer's brands such as Bata, Vimal, Peter England, Cotton County, Koutons, English Channel, Priknit, Nestle, Samsung etc. These brands are also known as 'National' or 'Global' brands. It has been seen that big retailers have various shops/boutiques within their stores for separate brands, like in case of clothing; a retailer has separate display for Vimal brand, Raymond, Bhilwara, Siyaram, Bombay Dyeing and Donear. Offering a category by national brand rather than in a traditional way (all brands at same place) is always significant and builds the image of a retailer.

Manufacturer brands usually take less promotional efforts as compared to private brands. Manufacturers utilize considerable efforts in terms of money and R & D to create demand for their products. Consequently, on the part of a retailer it takes less time to convince the customers and sell manufacturer goods. Further, customers go to a store and without looking for what is displayed, ask for particular brand by name because they know what they are buying and how the product will perform.

Having manufacturers' brands may build or loose store image, for instance if the manufacturer brand is available in a limited number of stores, customers loyal to the manufacturer brand will automatically become loyal to these limited stores. On the other hand, in case of manufacturer brand is easily available from a number of stores, customers may go to any store as per their convenience and comfort, resulting in decreasing store loyalty, and in this case, retailers will find themselves helpless – how to differentiate from their competitors.

The other problem with offering manufacturer brand is that they can limit a retailer's flexibility towards selling operations such as Koutons and Cantabil (clothes providers) instruct the retailers about how to display the clothes and how and when their merchandise should be advertised.

Lastly, selling manufacturer brands is less profitable option rather than offering private brands, as former one provide very less profit percentage. The reason is that manufacturer would like to meet the promotional expense and retailers' situation for having these brands at any cost. As these brands are easily and widely available, retailers offer significant discount to increase customer traffic on the cost of their profit margins.

2. Licensed Brands

Like manufacturer brands, this category is also becoming popular in newly born organized retail industry. In this category, a well established brand name (known as licensor) enters in a contract with outsider for developing, producing and selling the merchandise under defined set of terms and conditions. This license may be either given to a retailer having large chain stores or to a third party who then sells to the retailers.

In recent years, due to the popularity of outsourcing concept, big and established manufacturer brands are giving license in and/or outside the country under multi-year agreements.

3. Private Label brands

Private Label Brands (commonly known as private or store's own brands) are the brands exclusively developed by a retailer and are sold from that retail store only. For example, Vishal Mega Mart has almost all store brands in each category they are into. Private brands usually are affordable and lead to customers' loyality towards the store as compared to manufacturer brands. Various reasons for the growth of so called store brands are:

(i) These are cheaper to the tune of 20-40% as compared to similar category of manufacturer brands due to own production and absence of intermediaries for selling.

(ii) Due to store's brands, customers don't hesitate to buy as they know there is someone who will listen to them in case of any defect or non-performance.

(iii) As these are stores own creations, replacing the items under warranty or guarantee arrangements, does not make much time as retailer (store) do not has to send these defective items of merchandise to third parties.

(iv) With the emergence of new form of store branding, i.e. the premium brand, offers same quality or in some cases even exceeds that of manufacturer brands while selling it for a low price.

However, retailers need to understand that while creating **private brands** that it is not always feasible and profitable option especially in case where demand for products is limited that can disturb the company's budget on development, manufacturing and packaging the goods. Therefore, private brand programme should have the proper mix of price, quality, features and product differentiation otherwise retailers' gross margin may suffer on account of non-performance of few brands.

The Superbrands List

Aaj Tak,
ACC
Airtel
Anandabazar Patrika
Anchor
Aquaguard
Archies
Ashok Leyland
Barista
Bata
BILT
Blue dart
Bombay Dyeing
Boroline
Bournvita
BSNL
Cadbury Dairy Milk
Canon
Castrol
ColorPlus
Crompton greaves Fans
Crompton Greaves Lighting
Dabur Chyawanprash
Dainik Jagran
DHL
DLF
Euroclean
Everest
Exide
Ezee
Faber
Finolex
Gati
Good Knight
HBO
HDFC
HDFC Mutual Fund
Hero Cycles
Hindware
HSBC
Hutch
IBM
Infomedia Yellow Pages
Jaquar
Jockey
Kajaria
Kamasutra
Kerela Tourism
Kitchens of India
Kitply
Kohinoor
Kurlon
LG Air Conditioners
LG Home Appliances
LG Televisions
LIC
Louis Philippe
Luxor
Malayala Manorama
Milton
Monte Carlo
Moser Baer
NDTV
Nirma
Oriental Insurance
Park Avenue
Parryware
Pepsi
Pillsbury
Prestige
Radio Mirchi
Raymond
Real Fruit Juice
Reid & Taylor
Saridon
SERVO
Shoppers' Stop
SOTC
Star
State Bank of India
Strepsils
Taj
The Economic Times
The Hindu
The Times of India
Times Music
Van Heusen
Wills Lifestyle
Yonex

Sl. No	Segment	Name of the Brands
1.	Fashion	Pantaloons, Central Big Bazaar and Fashion Station
2.	Food	Food Bazaar
3.	General Merchandise	Central Malls and Big Bazaar
4.	Specialty Retailing	All , Blue Sky
5.	Home	Home Town, E-Zone, Furniture Bazaar, Electronics Bazaar, Collection I and Mela
6.	Books and Stores	Depot
7.	Communications	M- Zone and Converge M
8.	Wellness	Star and Sitara
9.	E-Tailing	Futurebazaar.Com
10.	Footwear	Show Factory
11.	Leisure and Entertainment	Bowling Co, Rain, Bollywood Café, Chamosa, Fuel, Sports Bar, Food Stop and Your Kitchen

Table 13.1: Segment and Retail Brand Built By Pantaloon

Pricing strategies for Private Label Brands in India

Usually, it has been observed that three pricing strategies are available to Indian retailers:

(1) Copy Cat Pricing

This pricing policy is one of the widely used and most popular pricing strategies. Under this pricing strategy, retailer prices his brand lower than the existing brands. In order to afford low prices, he does not invest much on advertising the brand at mass level.

(2) Parallel Pricing

As the very name implies, under this method, retailer prices private brands equal to the existing brands. The retailer intention for fixing same price level is that they don't want their brands to be perceived of lower quality than the competitive brands. The retailer opines that the brand equity of the retail store will rub off on the private brands.

(3) Premium Pricing

Under this pricing option, retailer prices the brand at a higher price than the competing brands. This is adopted because to create psychological effect that high prices means high (good) quality goods. Private labels like pantaloon, shopper's stop, bony and lifestyles have adopted such pricing option to attach a snab value with their private labels. Further, charging high prices, private brands promote themselves as up-market brands and to maintain this positioning they priced their in-house brands at a premium.

BRANDING STRATEGIES

Since 2000 onwards, India has seen a drastic upspring in retail sector, especially in grocery and general merchandise areas. On one side, the growth of private brands and promotions represent the growing powers of retailers while on the other side, the growth of category killers and discounters has put enormous pressure on traditional '***kirana***' stores. Consequently, branding choices have been taking new shapes and sizes. Today, retailers (buyers) have various branding alternatives on hand. They can buy either well established manufacturer's brands or can themselves create their own '***private***' brands. The retailers can also adopt the middle path by selling both the brands under one roof to satisfy that segment of customers who prefer only established name and private brands to others who want quality and performance despite of brand name.

(1) Integrated Branding

As the name implies, in this branding strategy, retailer is indirect link with the producer/manufacturer. He is supposed to have not only the complete knowledge about the product but the possible developments in the product in the future. The retailer is involved in process beginning from idea generation to branding the product. Simply stated, manufacturer produces the products, alter the specifications, modify the features, pricing and quality as and when laid by retailer concerned. For this purpose, he practices experience based marketing and leverages the advantage of being in direct contact with the customers. The retailer makes the decision regarding kind of product to be produced. These ideas are then formulated into particular specifications, designs which are then discussed and informed to manufacturer's agent. This agent is a turnkey agent who manages all the necessary things, beginning from locating the manufacturers/producers and manages all other necessary inputs needed. Basically agent's job is primarily to give shape to the ideas generated by the retailer into a product and deliver it to the retailer.

(2) Contract Branding

Under this form of branding, the retailer has no role to play in product development. Here retailer simply out sources goods from external suppliers and has no direct link with the manufacturer. The participation of the retailer is restricted to share the specifications regarding quantity, quality, brand and price. Unlike integrated, here supplier is responsible for product alternations in the future and supposed to have entire know-how of the product and has an established link with the producer. The retailer simply takes advantage of supplier's experience, network and credibility.

(3) Independent Branding

In this form of branding strategy, retailer procures goods from the supplier in bulk and at the lowest possible cost. After buying goods, he becomes the brand owner and total branding investment will be his own. The retailer being the owner of the brand rests entire responsibility for its performance and success. These brands usually are called private brands and are treated differently to other brands. Shopper's stop, Westside, pantaloon, Reliance retail has developed several private brands. Some of these brands in few categories are more popular and demandable as compared to well established brands in the same category.

Retail branding is a philosophy and a distinct approach to manage companies and in its actual form, includes much about changing consumer behavior by persuading him/her to purchase a product by creating willingness. Retail branding is different from just branding because in this case, the retail outlet has to match the branding with product's overall performance in the market. A brånding is said to be retail branding if it delivers both tangible and intangible benefits all in one and at once. Product brands make consumers like easier and make it possible to recognize products, which support in decision making process. In addition to it, product brands make the consumer a part of a group and create a sense of belonging. Retail brands, on the other hand, perform more than that. They present a number of benefits above product brands like they are close to the consumer.

Checklist to test feasibility of Independent Brands

For	Key drivers for successful independent labeling
Retailer	• High sales volume and proven sales record • Large and loyal customer base to leverage upon. • Change of mindset required from monthly ROI to long turn returns. • Special and extensive training to sales staff to promote brand when customer is under decision making process.
Product	• Good relations between retailer and vendors (supplier). • Non-dependability on single vendor. • Comparable quality goods to stock and offer. • Appropriate pricing strategy.Variety of goods and variety within the goods.
Customer	• Should believe and praise the retail share in terms of goods provided, its quality and services offered. • Should be interested to compare with different brands in the product category. • Should have a good post-purchase view of the brand to become a regular customer.

(4) Co-branding

The term 'retail co-branding' is relatively new to the retail world and is used when two companies/products/brands form an alliance to work together, creating marketing synergy. If applied properly, it has the potential to achieve 'best of all world's synergy

that capitalizes on the unique strengths of each contributing brand. A typical co-branding agreement involves two or more companies acting in cooperation to associate any of various logos, designs, colour schemes or brand identifiers to a specific product that is contractually designated for this purpose. The main objective for co-branding is to combine the strength of two brands for following purposes:

(i) To create financial benefits.
(ii) To create operational advantage.
(iii) To provide customers with great value.
(iv) To strengthen an operation's competitive position.
(v) To increase market penetration.
(vi) To adapt to the change markets.
(vii) Making the product more resistant to copying by private label manufacturers.

Key Considerations for co-branding arrangement

The key considerations for a co-branded alliance basically depend upon the economic output which both partners seek to achieve through such arrangement. When ever two or more brands think for co-branding, they must ensure that there is a strategic fit, especially in the consumer's mind. Needless to say that partner should have positive attitude towards the arrangement and have trust in each other. Successful co-branding occurs when both brands add value to a partnership. The value-added potential should be assessed by examining following issues discussed as under:

(i) Whether or not to enter the co-branded venture?
(ii) How to select the best appropriate partner brand?
(iii) When and for how much time the arrangement to continue?
(iv) How to allocate profits between the co-branded brands?
(v) How to split the initial marketing investment?

Examples of Co-branding

1. A successful example of co-branding is the marketing of Indian Premier league (IPL) with youtube (Worlds most Popular video sharing website).
2. HSBC has co-branded credit cards with Spencer's and Westside's Retail.
3. HDFC and Idea have launched various co-branded credit cards.
4. Taco Bell has marketing arrangement with Pizza Hut.

5. Delhi Metro and City Bank have launched co-branded debit and credit cards?
6. Similarly Big Bazaar and ICICI Bank have co-branded credit cards with the names of 'silver', 'gold', and 'shakti' specially targeted to housewives.
7. Another popular example from FMCG industry is the co-branded arrangement between 'Rin' and 'Surf Excel' (both brands owned by Procter & Gamble).
8. Other examples include the marketing of Gillette M3 Power shaving equipment (which require batteries) (both brands owned by Proctor & Gamble).

SWOT Analysis for Co- Branding in Retail

Strengths	Weaknesses
* Ability to adapt to the change markets * Provide one service in exchange of the other * Benefit by association/tie-up * Building of two in house brands	* Long term association with poor performer or weaker brand * Dropping of standard because of the inability of the poor franchisees.
Opportunities	**Threats**
* Outsource to experts * Introduce a new culture change through a new organization * Learn a new trade * Improve consumer trust * Increase market penetration	* Changing Consumer * New entrants from overseas or different market sectors * Consumer confusion * Safety scares and product recalls

SUMMARY

In retail world, the brand name is a major selling tool and one of the most important components of the total product personality. We are infact, living amongst the brands. Brands are all pervasive. Brands explain the way people live in the society. Brands are valuable to the organization and also are important to customers. Brands create wealth of the company depending upon how much value they add to the customers' life. The study of retailing is incomplete, if we don't pay due attention to branding and its various strategies.

The significance of branding can be judged with the fact that out of top ten strongest brands in the world, most of them (nearly six) are retail brands. With the rapid industrialization, malls mushrooming and presence of western culture everywhere, having good brands is the success reason and most valuable intangible assets for retailers. Consequently, branding has emerged as a top management priority in the last few years. Therefore, it is suggested that retailers should apply branding and brand management strategies simultaneously to differentiate themselves from the rest.

REVIEW QUESTIONS

Multiple Choice Questions

1. Private label brands are developed by :-

   (*a*) retailer (*b*) Manufacturer

   (*c*) Licensor (*d*) Any of the above

2. Tata, Bata, Vimal, Koutons are examples of :-

   (*a*) Manufacturer brands (*b*) Licensed brands

   (*c*) Private label brands (*d*) All of the above

3. Import duty is levied on

   (*a*) export goods (*b*) expensive goods

   (*c*) import goods (*d*) branded goods

4. Co-branding is based on ______ aspect :-

   (*a*) Co-operation (*b*) Synergy

   (*c*) Differentiation (*d*) Uniqueness

5. EOU means

   (*a*) Export oriented Units (*b*) Export outlet Units

   (*c*) Efficiency oriented Units (*d*) Electronic outlet unit

6. FTZ means

   (*a*) Flexible Trade Zone (*b*) Free Trade Zone

   (*c*) Free technological Zones (*d*) Flexible Techno Zone

7. 100 % inspection is not done because it is :

   (*a*) Time consuming process.

   (*b*) Uneconomical.

   (*c*) 100 % inspection means 100% destruction.

   (*d*) All of the above

8. Brand is an :

   (*a*) Identification mark (*b*) Symbol and name

   (*c*) design and logo (*d*) All of the above

9. The main component of a brand is :

   (*a*) brand personality (*b*) Brand characteristics

   (*c*) Core values (*d*) All of the above

10. Customers differenciate brands on the basis of :-

    (*a*) Features (*b*) Durability

    (*c*) Delivery terms (*d*) All of the above

Answers

1. a	2. a	3. c	4. b
5. a	6. b	7. d	8. d
9. d	10. d		

Questions to 'Check your Progress'

1. What is Brand?
2. What is Logo?
3. What is trademark?
4. What is packaging?
5. List few branding strategies?
6. What is store brand?
7. What is trust?
8. What creates differentiation?
9. What is Value?
10. Are successful brands affected by times?

EXERCISES AND QUESTIONS

Short Answer Questions

1. What do you mean by brand building?
2. Explain the significance of branding for a retailer?
3. What is licensed brand?
4. Describe few reasons for the popularity of store brands in recent years?
5. Why retailers prefer manufacturer brands over other alternative brands?
6. Differentiate between licensed and store brands with examples?
7. Explain essential elements of a brand?
8. Describe various advantages of branding to a manufacturer?
9. Illustrate the terms brand, logo, trademark and brand name?
10. Describe the key considerations for co-branding arrangement?

Long Answer Questions

1. Take a retailer of your choice and explain the probable problems faced by him for (i) building brand value and (ii) creating private label brands?
2. Critically explain the concept of retail brand and retail branding? Also explain why and how retailers are treated as brands?
3. Compare various branding strategies and highlight the differences that exist in product and retail branding?

Project-work Assignments

1. Select a neighborhood store and evaluate its various private brands and branding strategies?
2. Device a checklist and suggest some tips to test the feasibility of independent brands?
3. Select a retailer in your city that deals in multi-product categories. Take any product of your choice (*preferably from FMCG industry*) and compare the pros and cons of various types (*manufactured, licensed and private label*) of products available in the store.
4. Critically evaluate the branding strategies of three food retailers in your city.

Appendix

Exhibit 11.1 : Retail Branding In India

Branding and Retail Branding

- Brand is a product that provides functional benefits that some consumers value enough to pay a premium price.
- Brand is a mark that represents a unique set of both tangible and intangible benefits in the mind of the consumer.
- Brand is a name that identifies a particular product and differentiates it from its competitors.

In case of branding, companies build the brand name on the basis of what they want to communicate about what the brand stands for. In case of retail branding the store has to match the branding with performance. Thus retail branding has to deliver both tangible and intangible benefits all in one and all at once.

The development of the "whole branding view"* entails creating the store as brand and enforcing this "retail brand" at every point of contact between the prospect and the store. The very essence of this concept is that branding is not merely a synonym for marketing a product, but it is rather the whole host of activities that define and deliver a purchasing experience.

Retailing and India

Let us look at the following examples of retailing in India

- Foodworld - 190 crore business-Belonging to the RPG group
- Shopper's Stop - 180 crore business- Belonging to the Raheja's
- Crossroads - A brain child of the Piramals
- Vivek's - 150 crore, 40 yr old Chennai chain selling consumer durables
- Pantaloons - 50 crore, into apparel retail business
- Margin Free - a discount chain in Kerala dealing in groceries and also the largest retail chain in India
- Subhiksha - Dealing in groceries, pharmaceuticals and the second largest retail chain in India

The above examples show the importance Retailing and Retail Branding has been gaining importance in India. Now consider the following statistics: -

- Retail is India's largest industry, largest source of employment after agriculture, has the deepest penetration in rural India, and generates more than 10% of India's GDP.
- In India the retail market is large with sales amounting to $180 billion and accounting for 10-11% of the GDP.
- India has largest retail outlet density in the world with close to 10 million outlets today.

All these points together collaborate to prove that Retailing is going to go from strength to strength in the future.

The concept of Power Shift

In the Industrial age 'knowledge economy' was the focus area. Today, the economy is customer driven. Concepts like CRM are becoming very important in the field of management. In such a situation the manufacturers have no way but to be dependent on the retailers to provide them with customer information. The retailers are the only people in the entire value chain that have direct interaction with customers. They maintain databases of customer requirements, complaints, etc. Such databases are priceless for manufacturers and so there is a clear shift of power from the manufacturer to the retailer.

The recent surge in the number of brands available in any product line increases the options for the retailer and simultaneously makes it more important for manufacturers that well established retail outlets stock their products. This is an important factor, which has contributed to the growth of the retail segment in the US. In India too, growth of retail can be assigned to the same reason.

Future of Retail Branding in India

Retailing in India is going through a transformation. Increased consumer demand, improved sourcing options and larger availability of real estate are creating the foundation for a significant growth in the organised retail sector. South India, most notably Chennai and, to a lesser extent, Bangalore and Hyderabad - have emerged as centre of organised retailing.

This trend is going to catch up in the other cities soon. The retail industry is going to see ownership changes, consumer spending patterns dissolving and re-forming and the emergence of real e-commerce profits.

The evolution of the organized retail trend in India should follow the trend depicted by the PLC in Figure 1.

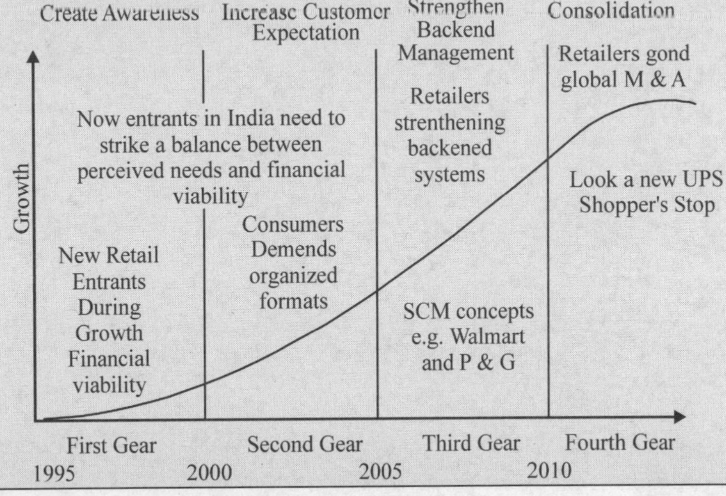

In the US retail branding has reached the third and fourth gear. Retail brands like Walmart have efficiently used IT for the purpose of better supply chain management and outlets like Sears have developed strong USPs. In India the segment is still in the growth phase. Most of the retailers are new entrants. Retailers like Shoppers Stop which have build a strong presence in the urban market based on their USP to stock products of all the big brands will have to think about re-inventing themselves and developing new USPs by the year 2010 since the competition would start catching up by then.

To summarize, the emerging organized retail sector in India offers unparalleled opportunities to entrepreneurs and existing businesses seeking an entry in Retailing. The consumers are open to change, and several USP platforms can be occupied since at present, the "canvas" is more or less blank. The retail branding in India will take sometime and Indian retailers will need to better their customer relations, their value chains if they want to be truly global.

Source: http://www.coolavenues.com

Exhibit 11.2 : Elements of Retail Branding

Key Brands Elements

The most important elements of a brand are:

1. Brand Position

- Who is addressed by company's branded products or services. What the company does and for whom
- The company's unique value and how customers benefit from products and/or services
- Key competitive differentiators, what makes the brand be chosen, be different from its competitors

2. Brand Promise

- The ONE most important thing that the brand promises to deliver to its customers — every time!
- What customers and partners should expect from every interaction, how should they feel as brand's customers

3. Brand Personality

- What the brand is to be known for
- Personality traits that customers, partners, and employees use to describe the company. What comes to the (potential) customer's mind when addressed about the brand

4. Brand Story

- The company's history and how the history adds value and credibility to the brand
- A summary of products/services/solutions

5. Brand Associations

- Physical artifacts: name, logo, colors, taglines, fonts, imagery
- Ideally, it must reflect the all the above statements about the brand and the company

Source: www.brandxpress.net

PRESENTING MERCHANDISE

LEARNING OBJECTIVES

- To understand the purpose and function of retail store display
- To identify the major types of product display
- To recognize the various forms of non-store selling
- To understand the techniques of retail space planning
- To examine benefits and weaknesses of retail store displays
- To explore strategic issues in product displays

"Presenting your goods and services in the most appealing way that will generate a response from potential customers is a much specialized skill."

Anonymous

"Presentation moves customers toward goods;
merchandising moves goods toward people."

Anonymous

INTRODUCTION

Retail is a competitive business and backbone of today's global economy. Retailers in India are the most aggressive in Asia in expanding their businesses, thus creating a huge demand for real estate. Their preferred means of expansion is to increase the number of outlets not only in urban areas but also in suburban and rural area too. Be it Mare store, Reliance Fresh outlets or Big Apple outlets, all are trying their level best to attract the maximum number of visitors. The game is old but rules are new and still developing. Thus relevance emerges from the link between shopping behavior and physical environmental factors. Therefore, in this race of going ahead, only those retail stores get name and fame where the methods adopted for product display are customers friendly and save customers' valuable time spent on walking here and there in search of a particular product.

These characteristics include both interior and exterior elements, as well as layout planning and display. Display in retailing is commonly known as visual merchandising. Display plays a significant role in attracting customers to the store, improve the quality of service experience, create a branding positioning for the outlet, and improve customer retention rates. Effective display attempts to ensure optimum utilization of retail space along with convenience to floor staff and customers.

PRESENTING THE MERCHANDISE

Today's successful retailer is the one making the most profitable use of every square foot of available space in the store. Because space is costly, you need to have a strategy for its use. Strategic floor patterns, location of merchandise, amounts of merchandise and appropriate displays are all key factors to consider.

Layout generally consists of three areas:

(a) The store arrangement,

(b) Classification of particular products, and

(c) The allocation of space (which is undoubtedly the most important area).

For most retailers, the allocation of space to a particular product is usually based on how profitable the product is. To determine how profitable that product is, retailers follow a three-step calculation:

1. Sales per sq. foot = total product sales / total sq. feet of the product
2. Cost of merchandise sold per sq. ft.= cost of product sold / total sq. ft. of product
3. Gross margin per sq. ft = sales per sq. ft. – Cost of mdse. sold per sq. ft.

After determining the gross margin per square foot, we can evaluate which all products are performing well, which aren't doing as well and maybe which you should get rid of them. Give the best selling and the most profitable merchandise in your store the best space. By taking some time to work through these calculations on an ongoing basis, you should be able to produce superior results. Besides this, a lot of factors are required to be considered. These are as follows:

Housekeeping – Somebody has said that 'cleanliness is next to godliness'. A dirty, haphazard store convey the message that the store has lost interest and is not serious about its future and customers. Create a daily and weekly cleaning schedule to take care of all necessary tasks. Dust the shelves, clean the cash counter, vaccum the floor and wash the windows. The cleaner the store is, the more pleasant the shopping experience will be for the customer. Remember this cleanliness drive should be on regular basis. Avoid doing near festivals or special occasion. Because when customers visit whole year then what's the meaning of doing it once in a year.

Create a daily and weekly checklist of every housekeeping duty that must be completed. Assign these duties to various individuals and hold them accountable for getting them done.

- Chase those dust bins away. Vacuum daily.
- Clean the lights.
- Dust the shelves.
- Get rid of the tape on the windows.
- No dust. No grime.
- No smudges. No grease.
- Polish the chrome.
- Remove the clutter behind the cash counter. Tidy up the back room.

Lighting- Lighting attracts maximum attention and highlights items for display. Researches have proved that proper lighting can increase retail sales by up to twenty percent. Start with ensuring that there are no burnt out lights. Use the best bulbs, tubes possible. Cheaper bulbs can cause merchandise to look grey and shabby. Make use of spot lights, preferably halogen to highlight key selling areas. Make the front of your store glow with good light. You need to be noticed and a bright store front is more attractive and appealing.

Music- Music these days is an essential element to a store. Be it food retailing, grocery or luxury retailing, the importance of music can not be ignored. But while playing music in stores, be careful to play the kind of music that reflects both the products you sell and the type of clientele that you hope to attract. Avoid FM radios as commercials can kill the purchasing mood or even advertise a competitor. Purchase a good quality DVD player which will ensure appropriate and continuous music with various options.

Signage - It is the silent salesperson for your business. It costs little but has innumerable benefits. Researches have shown that as much as seventy five percent of all the retail sales are generated at the point of purchase by signage, displays and events within the store. In order to differentiate yourself from the competitar and represent the right image among customers, it would be wise to look into getting your signs professionally done. Following are a few ideas for signs:

- Create a consistent look. Colour, size, type style, and layout should be consistent.
- Make your signs short and sweet. You have only few seconds to tell the customer what you want them to hear.
- It should be clear and understandable.
- Only post positive signs about your policies. If it's negative, either change it or don't post it.
- Use unique feature / benefit / price signs.

Windows – Window in each store is not only desirable but is of utmost importance. Being a retailer, you must think of your windows as an idyllic way to attract new and existing customers. You can use them for: sales promotions, image building, seasonal changes, new arrivals, latest trends and to showcase high demand items. Window displays should be changed frequently so as to avoid becoming stale and easy to ignore. They should be changed at a minimum of once per month.

Shelving and Displays - High margin and profit items get the best space. Research shows that eye level and just slightly below is the best shelves to sell from. While allowing for individual creativity, it is generally agreed that there are effective guidelines for displays:

- Change displays on regular basis.
- Focus on best selling items.
- Focus on impulse items (Items people buy on the spur of the moment).
- Good displays tell a story or have a theme.
- Integrate your advertising into your displays.
- Keep displays simple. Avoid putting in too many items.
- Show complementary / coordinating items together.
- Try portraying your goods in use.
- Use motion if possible to attract attention.
- Use proper lighting and props.

DEMONSTRATING MERCHANDISE

As such, in India no particular type of demonstration layout is adopted for a particular type of retailing. Stores are not of same size. Some stores are very small but some stores on the other side are very huge and some times are not desirable. But one thing is clear that a well-planned retail store layout allows a retailer to maximize the sales for each square foot of the allocated selling space within the store. Appropriate layout makes customers shopping experience memorable and convenient.

Store layouts usually show the size and location of each section, any permanent arrangement, fixture locations and customer traffic patterns. Each floor plan and store layout will depend on the type of products sold, the building location and how much the business can afford to put into the overall store design. The key benefit of store layout planning is that it results in optimum utilization of all available resources. In India, five basic types of layouts are normally in practice. These are:

1. Straight Floor Plan

This type of layout is very common and oldest layout in practice. Its arrangement is not only easy to understand but is less expensive. It is used for any type of retail store. The main benefit of this layout is that it makes use of the walls and fixtures to create small spaces within the retail store. The straight floor plan is one of the most economical store designs so far. The maintenance cost is negligible and even appreciated by floor staff.

Below graphical representation of the straight floor plan is shown for better understanding of the layout.

Figure 12.1

Straight Floor Plan

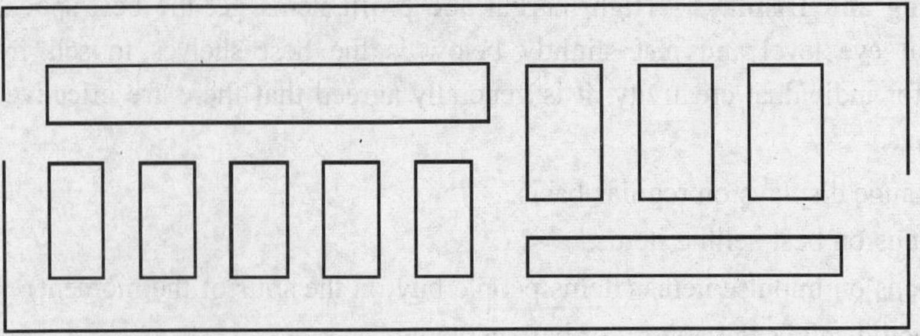

2. Diagonal Floor Plan

After straight floor layout plan, second popular floor plan is the diagonal floor plan. It is an excellent store layout for self-service types of retail stores and offers tremendous visibility for supervisors, cashiers and customers. The diagonal floor plan provides proper movement and traffic flow to the retail store resulting in enhanced sales. The diagonal floor plan looks like in this way.

Figure 12.2

Diagonal Floor Plan

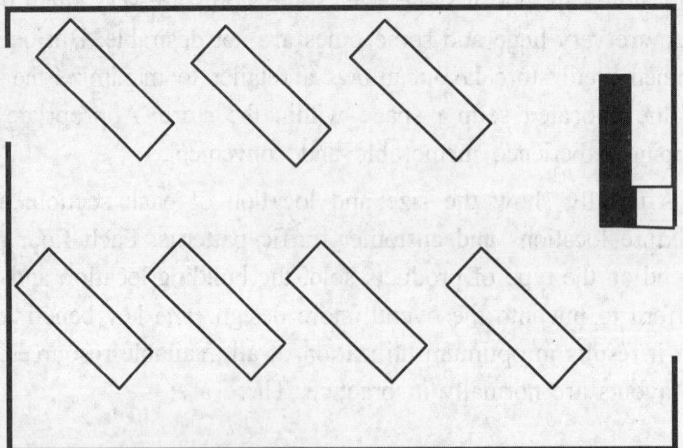

3. Angular Floor Plan

This type of layout is comparatively expensive and hence rarely used. This plan is best suitable for high-end specialty stores where things are costly and not for common use. In angular floor plan the curves and angles of fixtures and walls makes for a more expensive store design. However, the soft angles create better traffic flow throughout the retail store. This type of layout plan can be seen in jewellery/diamond stores.

Figure 12.3

Angular Floor Plan

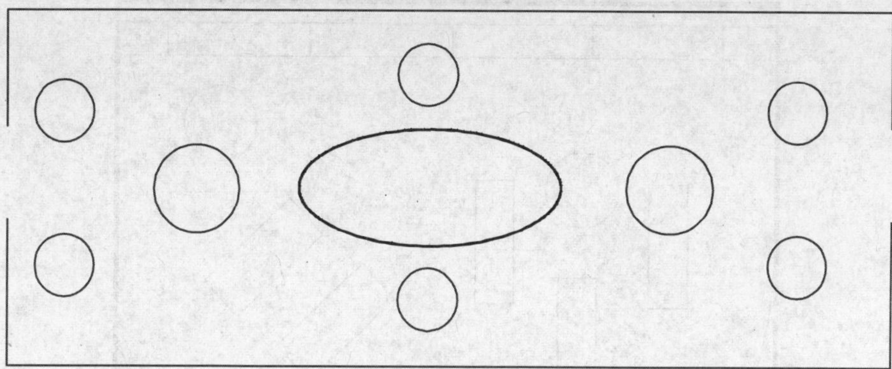

4. Geometric Floor Plan

Geometric floor plan uses racks and fixtures to create an interesting and out-of-the-ordinary type of store design with in a small budget. This plan is recommended for clothing and apparel stores. Due to the proper arrangement of display in this particular layout plan, customers don't find any difficulty while moving around the displayed goods. From economic point of view, it does not involve any extra high cost.

Figure 12.4

Geometric Floor Plan

Source: *www.retail.about.com*

5. Mixed Floor Plan

As the very name implies, this type of plan is the combination of two or more layouts. Some times, a store is engaged in varied retailing. Therefore, a particular type of layout plan is not suitable. Therefore, for convenience sake, stores use the combination of two or more layouts. The mixed floor plan includes the straight, diagonal and angular floor plans to create the most practical store design. The layout moves traffic towards the walls and back of the store.

Figure 12.5

Mixed Floor Plan

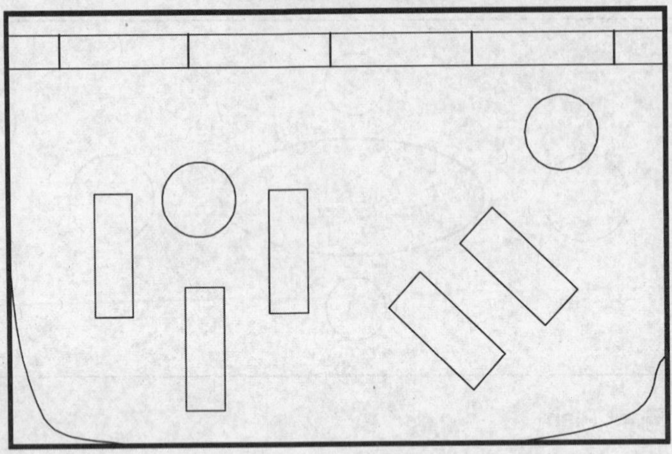

HOW TO CREATE GOOD LOOKING RETAIL STORE DISPLAYS

Driven by changing lifestyles, increased per capita income and favorable demographic patterns, Indian retail is expanding at a speedy pace. The country may have 700 new shopping centres by 2012. Mall space, from a meager forty million square feet in 2007, is expected to touch 100 million square feet by end-2010 and an estimated 200 million square feet by end-2020. Some of the large players in this market are Kishore Biyani's Food Bazaar, Mukesh Ambani's Reliance Fresh, Godrej Agrovet, the Aditya Birla Group's Much More, and the Tata Group (which acquired 70 per cent stake in Innovative Foods from the Amalgam Group) among others. Considering, there is a dire need to spend a lot of money on R&D part to find out what display methods for Indian consumers are best and time saving. Because researches have shown that most of the Indian customers have common complaint that their most of the time in retail store is spent on enquiring and searching the goods they need. Sometimes daily used items are placed behind the seasonal items, some time big packed goods cover the small sized goods of frequent use.

Although every inch size of your store space is precious, it should not be totally used for displaying the goods but some appropriate space should be left for supportive functions like office operations, store, and dispatch cell. Without allotting space to these functions, it becomes difficult to run the store in an effective manner. It is not wrong to allot space to these activities but one thing can be done that effort should be made to allot more and more space to those activities that result into sales. Besides this, whenever store buys any merchandise, it should after proper labeling and other formalities transfer on the proper shelves for the purpose of display. The space for packaging and storing the surplus goods and those goods that has to be delivered at customers' home address should be large enough.

The office area

Select your office area space between the store's back room and the sales floor. Don't take your business operations behind the wall. It is essential that office in retail store should be at that place where clear view of the store is visible from your working desk. Take all necessary purchase or salary record to your office before the customers start coming to your store.

The sales floor

As the very name implies, sales floor is a place where things are displayed and customers come to buy these things. The sales floor is the very important part of retail store as whole future of store depends on the earnings and it is the sales floor which gives earning to the store. In the sales floor, all the items are displayed on various shelves and racks. Therefore, retailer should pay maximum attention to the sales floor and make sure that the arrangements of fixtures, shelves and racks etc. is made according to customers' convenience.

Fixtures normally should be fixed and be arranged at proper gap to avoid any congestion. It is better to visit nearby stores to have the better picture that how fixtures and shelves will look once it is installed. How many racks of which size are required? How many sales counters and showcases will be enough to display all the items? Where lighting is must and where windows will be created?

For the purpose of ease and safety, make sure that all aisles have been allotted proper and enough space for the movement of goods, wheelchairs and safety equipments. The height of the ceiling should accommodate tall stratured persons and sitting arrangement (if any) must be solid enough to used by overweight persons. Don't keep hanging displays over the passage ways. Arrange fixtures and shelves that maximize the store's visibility.

Other considerations

If your store is not a part of any shopping complex or mall where they have separate arrangement of wash rooms, customers can request you to use your wash rooms. Therefore, be prepared and always keep your washrooms clean and hygienic. If your budget allows, have a water cooler in your store that have both cold and hot water outlets with the disposable cups.

In the winter, you can offer tea or coffee to your customers by way of installing instant machine. It can increase the possibility of more sales. Further, don't make much arrangement for sitting in the store. Otherwise it attracts sit arounds. Sit around basically is a class of people who apparently have nothing better to do than sit around and gossip. They are not customers; they do not help your business; and you must discourage them from taking up residence in your shop. Don't let friends or family members hang around either. You are a merchant. You have work to do. Their distractions will only cost you money. Even when you don't have a store full of customers, you need to perform routine upkeep such as dusting, straightening, marking prices, replacing worn signs and creating new displays.

The proper arrangement of fixtures and display is the matter of trial and error. You try your best to provide excellent floor space but when store becomes operational then several small or major mistakes with regard to arrangement become visible that should be rectified immediately to avoid further loss. During installation of fixtures and shelves, it is better to hire some experienced guys that are actively engaged in these installation activities. The layout should be flexible enough to accommodate future requirements and changes if need arises.

Case Let

Malls, Malls and More

A few years ago, asking your friends if they want to go to Noida and hang out would have been a blasphemous. But since the Centrestage Mall came up and better shopping opportunities suddenly emerged in the main market as well, the area around Sector 18 has become the hub of activities, shopping included. The area now has a five star hotel as well: Radisson MBD, Noida. Why just Dilliwallas? For the whole of Noida and Greater Noida and the vast suburbia of East Delhi, Sector 18 Noida and the adjoining Atta Market is GK-II, Sarojini Nagar and CP rolled into one.

Q.1 Why before the arrivals of malls, people used to hesitate about going to Noida?

STRATEGY FOR CREATING ATTRACTIVE RETAIL DISPLAY

Planning designing in hurry can spoil your whole business. Therefore do your homework well. Think what exactly store wants to accomplish. What is your total budget? What percentage is capable enough to spend on retail display? Is display is based on some theme? If yes, where is the theme and whose responsibility is to implement that theme. How this theme will look? It is better to put your theme on a paper and have a feel of that before implementing it. Make proper arrangements for keeping your fixtures, windows and shelves clean and well arranged. It can be done either before or after the opening hours meant for customers. These are some proved strategies that help retailers to create attractive displays that grab customers' interest and curiosity:

1. Keep it simple :

Display is an integral part of the service quality experience for the customer and visitor to the retail store. Physical surroundings, in service settings such as retail shelves, are vital cues to service quality expectations. Therefore, try your level best to keep your displays as simple as possible. The choice of fixtures, shelves, décor, and signage can affect consumer perception about your store. Signs indicate the services offered by the retail store and normally hang above or behind the service counters. This is helpful not only for first time visitors but for regular customers too. Therefore, your planning towards the displayed items should be simple and trouble-free. But in Indian retail stores, it has been observed that most of the retailers have different arrangements for each row or shelf. Remember, in this era of cut throat competition, it is not the customer but the product which gives you profit. Hence, it is the demand of the time that make your display unique but as simple as possible.

2. Make merchandise the focal point :

Not unlike a soft drink commercial in which everyone memorizes the commercial but forgets the product, you do not want your window dressing to outshine your products. A creative or a tiresome one can both have the similar problem of lack of attention. Therefore, make your merchandise the main focal point of your sales floor. Otherwise customers will come and go without buying any item and will put you in dilemma. Being a retail manager and responsible for product display, three points need to be considered:

(i) Where do you want your customers to concentrate?

(ii) Is this a single theme or multiple one?

(iii) Where will the wandered customers concentrate more?

Therefore, put yourself into customers' shoes and look from their eyes. What will be the reaction of a customer when he sees the display? What will be his first action? Possibly a new item may attract him with free gifts placed with it.

3. Be creative while planning product display design

If your probable customers drive rather than walk when they visit to your store, you should understand that there is something wrong with your display method. If steps are not taken to rectify it, it can throw you out of the competition. Therefore, plan and draw customers into the store with innovative, attractive, and compelling displays. Be creative but practical while placing the items for display.

It is better that you should have a rough draft/drawing of display layout to avoid any misunderstanding. When you see from customers' point of view, chances are that you will face no difficulty with your layout. It will give store a design that will be customers' friendly and make them convenient to select a product. Is it horizontal or vertical layout which helps them to shop? Whether the merchandise should be arranged in straight or curved lines, or in a rectangular or circular shape? Whether the layout unites a mixture of elements, or just particular one?

To implement and test this, draw some shapes that suits your product shape. Use models or draw some different shapes as your display space. These shapes can be in the form of circles, rectangles, semi-circles, triangles and bells. It gives a sense of an appealing layout to implement any design. For example, a huge heart shape might represent an arrangement of gift items.

4. Have fun with mannequins (Dummies):

These days, be it any local garments shop or the modern floor of a retail store, use of mannequins is increasing day by day. Mannequins are primarily used in retail stores to display clothing. They are normally found in the front windows of stores in the mall to show off the store's latest fashions and are perfect for saving space while modeling shirts and blouses. The full-size mannequins do take up more room, but they are more versatile in that they can be used to display entire outfits including hats, shirts, pants, and shoes. The main benefits of using mannequins is that shoppers get a good idea what the clothes will look like on a real person when they see them on a display mannequin.

If you are using mannequins in your stores, create interesting poses, and make sure that each one is well lit and easily visible to customers passing by. Use of different mannequins to attract different clientele like boys, girls, bride grooms, and aged is beneficial and always recommended if space allows.

5. Stock up on featured products

This is a fact that items placed in the window at varying heights and depths catch shoppers' attention and make the overall display inviting to their eyes. Therefore, it is recommended retailers should display only those items for drawing customers' attention for which they have enough stock of varied quality and quantity. Don't draw customers in to buy merchandise that you don't have enough of. It can have negative impact rather than increasing sales.

6. Creating balance during display

In a country like India where after several kilometers, a new tradition/custom prevails, the use of 'colour' can be translated as 'caste'. One 'unlucky' color in a particular area can be 'sacred' in another area/locality. Therefore, selection of wrong color can be dangerous not only for stores but can fuel religious clashes resulting in spoiling law and order conditions. Therefore, use of color in any locality is of utmost importance.

Besides this each color has its own impact. Where dark colors look heavier, light color represents light item. This is not as simple as it seems. In order to have balance while displaying the merchandise, light colors items should always be placed over the dark colors items so that top should not reflect heavy items. Arranging dark colors items that look heavy also should not be placed at one place. It looks awkward. If you place light color items at one place then place one or two dark color items that look heavy on its other side to create the balance.

7. Draw attention to products with good lighting :

It has been observed that lighting retail goods not only highlights the displayed goods but makes customers stop and look. Therefore, retailers should make proper provisions for lighting when deciding and allocating budget for visual merchandising. Following points need to be considered:

I. Avoid bright light directly on the mannequin face.

II. Lighting should not be from top to bottom as it will create unnecessary shadow. Better will be when lighting should be arranged somewhat off to the side and to the face of the display.

III. Hide electrical wiring

IV. Light across a display rather than down

V. Lighting arrangement should be changed with the change in display settings.

VI. Whether the window is recessed or under a spotlight, the goal should be to highlight the products within the overall display. If the window design simply features your brand/image, rather than specific products, then balance the lighting throughout.

8. Use backdrops

Backdrops are useful tools to create positive and forceful displays, and to separate the window from the store. Besides attracting the customers' attention, it comparatively has more retention powers in the mind of the visitors. Therefore, sensible use of 'back drops' can be vital for retail earnings and store's image.

AN APPROACH TO RETAIL PLANOGRAM

The planogram is an arrangement of goods that gives an idea how products will be arranged in the retail store. It helps the retailer in knowing that where and how many racks/shelves should be arranged (figure 12.6). Where and at what gap they will be arranged? What item will be placed at which shelf? In short, a planogram is a blue print which gives all major and minor information about the merchandise arrangement. Sometimes, a planogram is also known by following names : POGs, plano-grams, plan-o-grams, and schematics (archaic). The diagram shown below visually communicates how merchandise and props physically fit onto a store fixture or window, to allow for proper visibility and price point options. A planogram is created after taking into account factors like product sales, movement of the products within the product category and the space required for the various products.

Planogram normally list the exact number of square feet used for the various products and the exact number of products to be displayed in a particular area. For a retail company who has number of stores spread over various locations, a planogram is a good way of communicating how displays are to be done. This allows for consistency in display, across locations. When products are presented in the same manner across locations, the customer feels familiar and comfortable at each location. This helps to build brand loyalty and customer trust. If consistency is not maintained and the products displayed are changed month after month then customers will search more and buy less. Some of the chain stores are now using technology/advanced software to create planogram.

Retailers generally receive planogram before the product arrives in a store, and helps the retailer in having an identical look and feel. Manufacturers of the consumer packaged goods provide the new planogram with their new products. The purpose of providing the planogram with the new product is to relate it to existing products. The planogram differs from store to store. For instance, FMCG stores normally use text and box based planograms in order to optimize display area and profit limits. Apparel stores use pictorial or presentation planogram that utilize shelf area optimally.

As the objective of a planogram is to correspond how to arrange the products to increase customer sales, most of the time is used in deciding the layout of a planogram. The attention is devoted to adjust the outer look. Since the objective of a planogram is to communicate how to set the merchandise to increase customer purchases, much research often goes into the layout of a planogram. Attention is given to adjusting the visibility, appearance and presence of products to make them look more desirable, or to ensure sufficient inventory levels on the shelf or display. There are some consulting firms which specialize in retail space layout and planogramming. Some chain stores retailers take help of professionals to create and maintain planograms for their stores.

In short, a plan-o-gram is nothing more than a picture of how various fixtures, shelves and walls will present your merchandise. It is a relatively simple concept, but a very powerful one because it takes into consideration what is known about the psychology of consumer buying habits. Creating a plan-o-gram forces the retailer to carefully evaluate which products go where and how many will be displayed. By forcing yourself to plan the presentation of each department, you will become a more successful and proactive retailer.

Figure 12.6

A Planogram's View

Source: *www.persephone.blueheath.com*

Objectives of Having Planogram

The two main objectives for a retailer to implement planogram in his retail store are the product placement and increased sales. The use of planogram has various benefits such as:

- Allocating selling potential to each square feet of available space
- Excellent product positioning
- Quick and easier merchandise replacement for floor staff
- Rewarding customers with improved visual appeal
- Strict inventory control and lessens obsolete merchandise
- Useful communication tool for floor staff who produce displays

The key to increased store's turnover is the use of proper merchandising positioning and planogram helps in merchandising positioning. Planogram is one of the paramount merchandising tools for presenting products and services to the customer. Therefore, if you are not using planogram in your store, you should start using it. If already a planogram is being used in your retail store, keep on learning how effective you can make your planogram.

The objectives of having a planogram in a store are:

- Communicating how to arrange the merchandise in best possible manner.
- To adjust the visibility, look and presence of products
- To assist communication of retailer's brand distinctiveness.
- To increase retail sales.
- To make accurate selection of products available.
- To make best use of profit per centimeter of shelf space.
- To make certain adequate inventory levels on the store's shelf or in display area.
- To make the products' look more pleasing.
- To provide a reasonable, suitable and inspiring product-customer line.
- To understand the association between space, sales and profit
- To utilize space efficiently whether floor, sheet or virtual

The placement of merchandise that is arriving to the store can be planned out on paper by using a Planogram before the products actually arrive to the store. A planogram is a retailer's drawing (blueprint) which visually communicates how merchandise and props physically fit onto a store fixture or window to allow for proper visibility and price point options. The retailer can plan to mix the new products with current items or initiate entirely new displays. If you have more than one store this is an excellent way to communicate to your staff how you would like displays to be executed.

The intricacy of a planogram may differ by the size of the store, the software used to make the planogram and the requirement of the retailer. Some stores use very simple and some very complex and detailed. According to the size and requirement, planograms can be as straightforward as a photo of a specific division or more detailed with objects, numbered peg holes and colors, presetting exact placement of each item.

VISUAL MERCHANDISING (VM)

Today's successful retailers make the most profitable use of every square foot of space in the store and in the warehouse. Since the space is very expensive, you must take a strategic approach to its use. Floor patterns, location of merchandise, levels of inventory and appropriate displays are all key factors in the proper use of space. Mishandling of space can be as harmful to your success as poor buying or careless hiring. It is very important for every store to create a suitable atmosphere and appealing presentations in order to trigger the consumer's buying decision. In a era where you can find identical merchandise in more than one store, layout and presentation become key differentiating factors.

Visual Merchandising (VM) is the art of creating visual displays and arranging merchandise assortments within a store to improve the layout and presentation and to increase traffic and sales which puts the merchandise in spotlight. VM informs the visitors, creates desire and finally augments the selling process. This is an area where the Indian retail industry, particularly, the unorganized stores lack adequate knowledge and expertise. This inadequacy is best reflected in poor product display and communication during various promotional events. For instance, in clothing stores, mannequins are commonly used as a way to promote products and apparel accessories.

In short, VM coordinates all physical elements in a place of business so that it projects the right image to its customers. Figure 12.7 illustrates how merchandise is visualized within the store area.

Figure 12.7

A Visual aid for Merchandise Arrangement

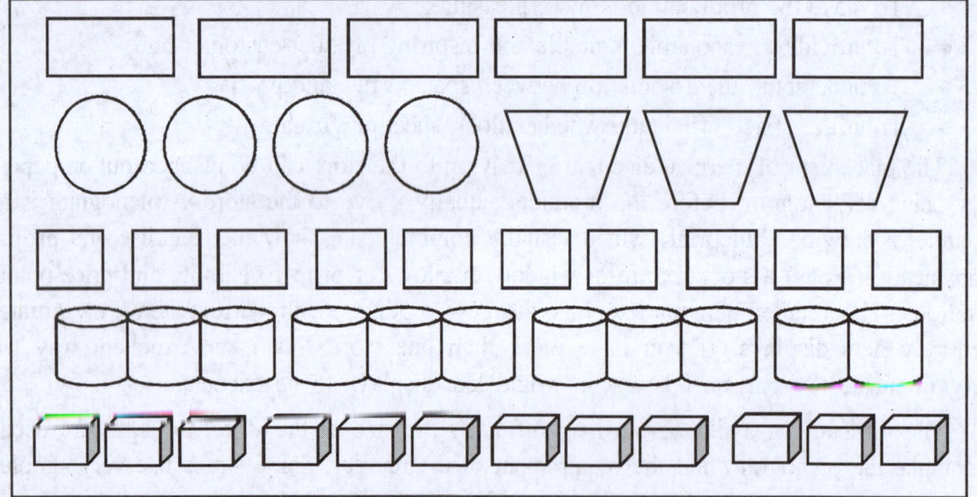

Objectives of Visual Merchandising

- To combine the creative, technical and operational aspects of a product and the store.
- To draw the attention of the customers towards displayed items and to enable them to take purchase decision within shortest possible time, thus augmenting the selling process.

- To educate the potential customers about the product/service in an effective and creative way.
- To establish an innovative medium to present merchandise in three dimensional environment thereby enabling long lasting impact and recall value.
- To establish linkage between fashion, product design and marketing by keeping the product in focal point.

Figure 12.8

Celebrate Life: Maximizing the Store Visual Displays

Courtesy: *Company website.*

Figure 12.9

How Visual Merchandising can Attract Customer Attention (An Inside View of Reliance Fresh Outlet)

Courtesy: *Company Website*

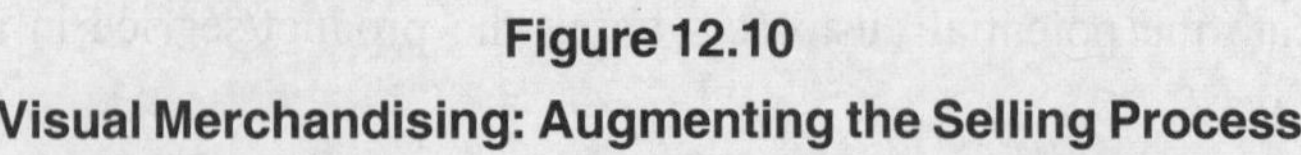

Figure 12.10

Visual Merchandising: Augmenting the Selling Process

(Bata's Super Store Self Selection Shopping Environment)
Courtesy: *Company Website*

Essentials of Successful Visual Merchandising

- **Address the Senses:** Create a sensual experience in your store by paying attention not only to sight, but also to smell, touch and sound. Think of how magical a bakery smells. Doesn't it make you want to buy? Remember how many times you've walked into the movie theater, promising yourself there would be no popcorn this time, only to find yourself elbow' deep in a super-sized bucket? Therefore, pay attention to how your store smells. You can trigger emotional responses in customers that cause them to relax, energize, reminisce, and (hopefully) buy something.
- **Colour:** Use of colour puts life into visual merchandising. It sets the mood to shop the products.
- **Equilibrium:** It implies that symmetry should be maintained during display of various goods. While using colour, objects, lines and shapes consistency should be maintained.
- **Focal Point:** This is the main point of attraction in a store. This point being the central/attractive point attracts the customer and lure to buy these goods. This point has its own charm and importance in a store. Therefore, focal point should be created and presented in an efficient manner.
- **Lighting:** The focus of light should be directed towards focal point to the extent possible. Remember lighting attract maximum attention and highlights items for display.

Figure 12.11
Visual Merchandising Success Factors

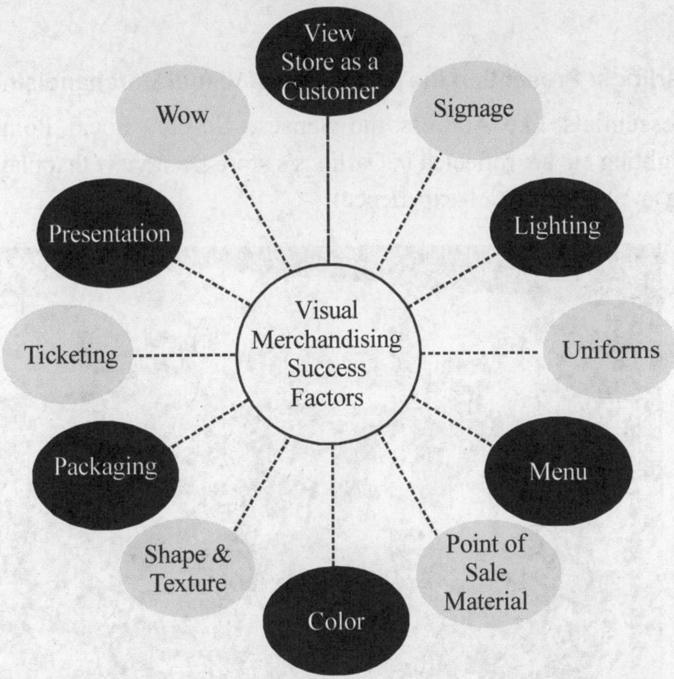

Source: *www.foodconsultants.com*

- **Music:** Music is an essential element in any store. It helps accentuate and build your atmosphere. It can also add texture to the environment. Customers tend to stay longer in environments with appropriate music ... and if they stay longer, they typically buy more. A relaxed and fun work place will also increase the productivity and morale levels of your employees.
- **Store Windows:** Your storefront windows are an ideal opportunity to attract customers' attention and drag them into your store. Windows should be used for these main purposes:
  - ❖ Sales promotions
  - ❖ Image-building
  - ❖ Seasonal changes
  - ❖ New arrivals
  - ❖ High demand items

Successful store windows are changed frequently! In a residential area, potential customers pass by your store at least two or three times a week. Ask yourself "If my windows didn't attract them into the store this week.

What makes me believe they will come next week?"

- **Simplicity:** The Visual merchandising should be simple and easy to understand by the floor staff.

- **Size of displayed objects:** The objects that are large in size should be displayed first in the store's display area.

Figure 12.12
Carlings: Presenting the Essentials of Visual Merchandising

(The VM essentials like Address the Senses, Colour, Focal Point, Simplicity, Equilibrium, Lighting etc are reflected in Carlings's store front view that plays a prominent role in creating a pleasant retail experience)

Courtesy: *http://www.cev-inc.com*

Status of VM IN India

Unlike the western countries, where VM receives highest priority in commercial planning of a product, the Indian industry's understanding and practice of the concept of VM is far behind. With the opening up of industry in 1992 and permission to foreign direct investment in retail sector has fueled the need of western practices towards store designing and layout. Competition is increasing day by day, now retail stores are not competiting with domestic giant stores but countless foreign stores have entered into the line of retailing. Therefore, now retail stores in India have realized the importance of VM. Otherwise most of the retail stores earlier used to consider VM as wasteful expenditure. But with the quantitative restrictions after the year 2004, the retail industry in India, particularly, the textile industry, will have to compete purely on the competitive edge of the products and VM will be a useful tool in projecting the uniqueness of the products and thereby increasing the market access and sales. It is high time that the Indian textile and clothing industry, therefore, understands and adopts the scientific and professional system of VM rather than the traditional practices of display of products and communication which are outdated.

CONCEPT OF SIGNAGE

In the retail industry, signage has become one of the most effective ways to impart the message to the customers. All the store's activities like sales promotion, pricing policy, information about the product, and even the name of the store is conveyed by the use signage. When customer comes to the store, he first sees the signage that tells what items are sold here. It saves customers' precious time. Signages also provide information regarding a store's policy in respect of returned goods, timing to return, prevailing discounts, etc. Most of the independent retailers place such signage boards near their cash counters as most of the customers are habitual of placing orders and respective payment from this point of the retail store. Thus the proper signages provide the right information to the customers about the products. While unprofessional signages confuse the customers about the displayed goods and spoil the store's image.

Definition

Signage is any kind of graphics created to display information to a particular clients, typically way finding information on streets, outside and inside of buildings. It is the "silent salesperson" for the retailer and must reflect your image. Handwritten signs are essentially taboo. Professionalism is everything in your store and the same holds true with your signage. There are four different types of signs:

(1) **Promotional signs**: For off-price events or specials.
(2) **Location signs:** For direction to specific departments.
(3) **Institutional signs:** For store policies, charitable events.
(4) **Informational signs:** For product related features/benefits/prices.

Types of signage:

Today due to the boom in the retail industry and increasing importance of signage, various types of signage are used for the purpose of attracting customers.

1. **Custom made signage** - Signs that are built from scratch to suit a specific requirement presented by a client or a specific project.
2. **MCFT (Modular Curved Frame Technology)** - A contemporary fusion between custom-made signage and modular sign systems. In India these are not so popular.
3. **Modular signage** - A signage system that consists of pre designed elementary units.
4. **Neon signage** – This type of signage is used at busy traffic signal where traffic is slow and two or more roads coincide with each other. This is effective during evening and night time. Here electric lighting is used.

5. **Street signage** – It is a method of signs stamped out of metal with lettering embossed or printed (or both). This method of conveying retail store message is very popular and cost effective. Generally, street signages are used at the time of new product launch or to inform the customers about sale or some promotional offers. The main advantage of using street signage is that it has more retention power as compared to any other type of signage.

Characteristics of Good Retail Signage

1. Quality Production

It has rightly been said that quality speaks itself. Same is applicable in the case of using signage. Selecting a signage requires the retailer to consider the lifespan of the sign. Lesser the lifespan, lesser will be the cost. Whatever the case, you need to understand that your signage should be unique and well written. Be it ink, paint or sticker tape, it should be of good quality and weather proof.

2. Simple Color Scheme

While selecting the color combination for your signage, take utmost care. Remember in India, people are very sensitive about some colors. Some colors represent not only one religion but people respect them, worship them. Therefore, before selecting any color, think its indications and socio-cultural aspects. It is therefore, recommended that you should choose two or three colors at a time and use it all through the store. But ensure that combination of colors should not make the signage difficult to read. If you outline the text with a thin line, it will improve the contrast.

Further, various types of color schemes can be used to communicate the desired image. Some of these schemes are as follows:

- **Complementary schemes:** it is the use of two colors that are directly opposite to each other on the color wheel, for example yellow and blue.
- **Split-Complimentary Schemes:** this involves the use of three colors simultaneously. On central color and remaining two colors on either side of its complement; for instance, red with blue-orange and pink-orange.
- **Double-complementary Schemes:** this combination uses four colors plus their compliments; for instance, yellow with violet and red with green.
- **Triadic Schemes:** this combination is implemented with three colors that are at equal distance from one another.

3. Easy to Read

While making signage, don't make it complex that customers find difficult to read and understand. The language which is used should be understandable to the customers. Further, follow these points:

- Don't give stress on one particular point.
- Signs should not be filled with different objects, colors and jingles.

Sale

- Signages, should not be either too large or too small.
- The font and its size should be selected carefully.
- Signage should be seen clearly by the customers. Therefore, it should be placed at proper distance.
- In case of store window, sign need to be simpler.

You can follow the practice of showing the main theme like '**SALE**' or '**GRAND BONANZA**' or '**LIMITED OFFER**' in your window signage and remaining information in the stores.

LIMITED OFFER

4. Make It Simple

Simple signage always conveys the message quickly and clearly. The place where you have to show the most important message that should be free from any painting or object do avoid any confusion. It will give you more customers will result in decreased complaints and increased sales.

Therefore, keep the signage of your store simple and clear-headed. That should convey the main message. Select that message which actually you want to convey. Instead of saying in paragraph, make your slogan as short as possible. For this put your massage on white paper and then try to reduce it in few words, untill it is of five to seven words and there is no possibility to reduce it further then select and print on the signage. If you think it is not enough, you can use one line message below the main message of five to seven words.

5. Appropriate Placement

Your signage is simple, readable and attractive but if it is not well placed, it will not work. Where the visitors' movement is less and is not a busy area, signage will not catch customers' attention. Therefore, consider the importance of placing a signage. Take care before placing signage anywhere. Place the signage where it attracts more customers. Sometimes what happens that a tree or street light can cover your signage, therefore, this aspect should be considered before giving space to the signage. It should not be at very low or more height. Place it where it will be visible to customers and does not block any essential elements.

Before placing signage, take care that it should not cover any traffic signal or street light and does not block any traffic flow of the city/town. Make sure signs don't block the internal view of your store. Do not forget to check the reflections on the store's window to check that during day time, it should not make your internal signage unnoticed. If you use some lighting, it will not only increase the visibility but will attract the customers. Therefore, while placing the signage, proper arrangement of lighting should be made.

To have the proper benefit of the signage, after placement of signage, you yourself should check whether it is visible or not. What is the reflection position? Lighting is sufficient or not? See from various angles and ensure its readability. Not from retailer but from common man's point of view you should look it and if any change you think can enhance visibility, do not hesitate to do so. Once you have placed, it normally it becomes difficult to alter any change. Therefore, critical analysis is must.

Further, consider the following ideas when designing your next signage campaign:

- Create a consistent look. Colour, size, type, style, and layout should be consistent.
- Make your signs short and sweet. You have three seconds to tell the customer what you want them to know.
- Only post positive signs about your policies. If it's negative, either change it or don't post it.
- Say "Save Rs.100", instead of "10% off". It's usually much more powerful.
- Use feature/benefit/price signs.

Why Digital Signages work

Humans have become masters at ignoring messages from advertisers, merchandisers and public information providers. Our eyes, ears and brains are callused from the continuous proliferation of words and images….. in our mailboxes, on our TV screens, on billboards and the sides of the buses. They are everywhere, and we are experts at blocking them out. Only 1 in 14 TV commercials is watched. Why? Because consumers don't need the advertising information at the time they see it – after all, they can't make the purchase in their homes. Three out of four purchase decisions are made in the retail location. Few of consumers read the labels before buying products. They compare brands and make the decisions on the spot. This is where you must influence their product choices – at the point of decision. Point-of-decision marketing is the rising star of the high-ROI advertising, and you can put it work with digital signage.

Even in its infancy, this powerful medium has already proven its worthiness as a marketing tool. Many businesses have attributed positive, quantifiable revenue gains to digital signage. (A doctor's office improved the customer experience by reducing perceived wait time by 35%! An auto part franchiser increase sales by 8% by digital signage. An international fast food franchise increased sales by 13% by digital signage.) A national movie rental franchise credited digital signage with a 16% increase in rentals. A retailer discovered digital signage could increase brand awareness and revenue by 30% during promotion period.

Unlike static, point-of-purchase marketing, digital signage has the power to compel target audience behavior with motion, color, sound even touch-screen and motion detector technologies. That's right digital signage can react to customers, just as they can react to it. It's interactive, on demand, context specific product information – when the customer is ready to use the information…. at the point of decision.

This incredible medium knows where your customers are, when they are ready to buy. It even has a pretty good idea of what they want. It's infinitely more tunable than most media, allowing you to repeat successes and avoid repeating failures because you control the content. It plays any kind of media – video, sound, graphics or text – from virtually any source.

For retail, restaurant, hospitality and other commercial users, digital signage make it easy to deliver the right selling messages to the right audiences........ at the point of decision which is a crucial moment when they have the inclination and the opportunity to make a purchase. It aids with merchandising, product advertising and brand reinforcement.

From communities, campuses, corporations, places of worship, military bases and other information providers, digital signage gives you control over news, weather, education and safety information. It can work in concert with triggers from smoke, heat and hazmat sensors to alert people and guide them to safety. Neilson Media Research recently confirmed a whopping 38% of digital signage content is watched when it's placed at point-of-decision locations in grocery stores. Fully 62% of consumers demonstrate excellent recall of specific products from digital signage. Purchase decision times are reduced by upto 50%. Well placed displays should yield similar results for information hungry patrons everywhere.

Source: *Images Retail Magazine, June'07*

VISUAL DISPLAY GUIDELINES

In order to get maximum benefit from your display, make it creative and educative. Like a slow moving display, welcoming slogans, sales announcements, welcoming coming season, etc will make a display lively and interesting for the customers. If you have two or more windows in your store, then chances are high to advertise the products at lower total cost and with minimum maintenance.

In India, it has been observed that stores are comparatively small sized and are located in a mall where they lack windows. But retailers should understand that within the store, there may be several points to place the beautiful displays. Only need is to understand the layout sense and making use of the proper place. But one thing should always be kept in mind that windows obviously are good for displaying the items but if it creates obstacle in flow of traffic in the store, it (window) will be of no use to the store. If you think of taking help or guidance of VM professionals, you can take as it is the matter of long term survival.

Focus on best sellers/hot items

1. Focus on impulse items.
2. Good displays tell a story or have a theme.
3. Integrate your advertising into your displays.
4. Keep displays simple. Don't include too many items.
5. Keep signages changing on continuous basis after considering the competitors' move.
6. After completing the display, need is to add proper signage. It is beneficial to have the photo of the display and keeping the daily sales record during the display presentation. It will help you to know what display makes a difference. When you compare the latest record with previous one, you can easily know

whether you should continue to use displays in the time to come or not. Further, if display is successful then record diary will help you to create similar or different displays so that you should not repeat your mistakes again and again.

7. Do not forget that creating an attractive display is an art and requires creativity and some skill like other aspects of retailing. Therefore, do not take display making in an easy way. Keep yourself working to make your display competitive and eye catching as visual merchandising is the key to success.
8. Show complementary/coordinating items together.
9. Take time to plan the display. Consider what you want to accomplish, develop a budget and determine a central theme. You may even want to sketch your display on paper. Gather your visual display tool box, the merchandise and any props. Make sure all materials and location (tables, windows, cabins, and racks) are clean. Choose a slow time of the day or build the display after customer hours.
10. Try portraying your products in use.
11. Unless you're a professional, keep it simple.
12. Use motion to attract attention.
13. Use proper lighting and props.
14. Use well-stocked power walls/displays to show best sellers.

SUMMARY

The recent popularity of the many chain stores, opened by big corporate like Reliance, Godrej, Aditya Birla, and Bharti Communications across India brings an issue that is extremely important in retail industry. The retail store layout is of large concern to its customers. Packed, unsystematic stores are difficult to navigate and customers often wind up leaving irritated and they wind up leaving without making purchases. Stores normally don't consider this aspect but studies have shown that these silent, irritated customers in long run can be harmful for any retail business. When customers are not satisfied with the arrangement and layout of the store, they by nature don't like others to go to the same store. But with the increasing competition in retailing industry, now retailers should understand that store layout and design part is also of utmost importance. Hence, stores should display items in a logical order that simply makes sense. Items are quickly found and they are easily reached. Craft items are placed in the same aisles as other craft items and the other merchandise in the craft aisle relates to crafting, writing, drawing or photography.

Stores need to understand that an organized retail store layout helps potential customers find products quickly and easily and it also helps customers consider purchasing other items related to their target purchases. For example, a customer who is purchasing a executive diary may opt to buy a 'parker pen' if it is displayed in the neighbourhood of the executive diaries resulted in increased sales turnover. Further, it is also important to keep related items in order. Having too much merchandise on display can deter customers who are in a hurry. In this busy and fast moving world, not everyone has time to sort through disorganized merchandise. In short, the retail store layout needs to take the customer's ability to move into consideration. The shopper's comfort is vital. The ability to navigate through attractive displays with ease is directly proportional to the number of times a customer will return.

In nutshell, following are the learning points:

1. Visual Merchandising is first and foremost a strategic activity that requires planning and analysis.
2. Put your best-selling merchandise in your best-selling space.
3. If you want to do one thing with your store, make it professional.
4. Your storefront, including your windows, must tell the right story about who you are as a retailer.
5. Invest in proper signages to take your store to the next level.

REVIEW QUESTIONS

True and False Questions

1. Layout generally consists of three areas:
   (a) The store arrangement,
   (b) Classification of particular products, and
   (c) The allocation of space (which is undoubtedly the most important area).
2. Researches have proved that even proper lighting can not increase retail sales.
3. Music these days is an essential element to a store.
4. Store layouts usually show the size and location of each section, any permanent arrangement, fixture locations and customer traffic patterns.
5. Straight floor plan is very uncommon and new layout in practice. Its arrangement is easy to understand but is very expensive.
6. Diagonal floor plan is an excellent store layout for self-service types of retail stores and offers tremendous visibility for supervisors, cashiers and customers.
7. Angular floor plan is comparatively expensive and hence rarely used layout. This plan is best suitable for low-end specialty stores where things are economical and for common use.
8. Geometric floor plan uses racks and fixtures to create an interesting and out-of-the-ordinary type of store design with in a big budget.
9. Mixed floor plan is the combination of two or more layouts.
10. 'Sit-around' is a class of people who apparently have nothing better to do than sit around and gossip.
11. The planogram is an arrangement of goods that gives an idea how products will be arranged in the retail store and helps the retailer in knowing that where and how many racks/shelves should be arranged.
12. The two main objectives for a retailer to implement planogram in their retail store are the product placement and increased sales.
13. Visual Merchandising is the art of creating visual displays and arranging merchandise assortments within a store to improve the layout and presentation and to increase traffic and sales which puts the merchandise in spotlight.
14. Color, Focal point and equilibrium are not the essentials of visual merchandising.
15. Signage is any kind of graphics created to display information to a particular audience, typically way finding information on streets, outside and inside of buildings.

16. Signage is the "silent salesperson" for the retailer and reflects store's image.
17. There are four different types of signs:
    (a) Promotional signs
    (b) Location signs
    (c) Institutional signs and
    (d) Informational signs
18. MCFT stands for Modular Curved Frame Technology.
19. Neon signage is used at busy traffic signal where traffic is fast and two or more roads coincide with each other.
20. Street signage is a method of signs stamped out of metal with lettering embossed or printed (or both).

Answers

1. True	2. False	3. True	4. True
5. False	6. True	7. True	8. False
9. True	10. True	11. True	12. True
13. True	14. False	15. True	16. True
17. True	18. True	19. False	20. True

Multiple Choice Questions

1. House keeping is related to :
   (*a*) retail cleanliness (*b*) retail accounting
   (*c*) retail sourcing (*d*) retail packaging
2. Which one is the oldest and common layout :
   (*a*) Straight floor plan (*b*) Diagonal floor plan
   (*c*) Angular floor plan (*d*) Mixed floor plan
3. Which floor plan is used for clothing and apparel :
   (*a*) Straight floor plan (*b*) Diagonal floor plan
   (*c*) Geometric floor plan (*d*) Mixed floor plan
4. Which floor plan is comparatively expensive :
   (*a*) Straight floor plan (*b*) Diagonal floor plan
   (*c*) Angular floor plan (*d*) Mixed floor plan
5. Planogram is an arrangement of :
   (*a*) Goods displayed (*b*) Employees arrangement
   (*c*) Colour and Lighting (*d*) Windows and Dummies
6. Visual merchandising is the art of :
   (*a*) Storing goods
   (*b*) Creating visual displays
   (*c*) Arranging merchandise assortments
   (*d*) All of the above
7. Store windows are mainly used for :
   (*a*) displaying new arrivals (*b*) Image building
   (*c*) displaying high demand items (*d*) All of the above

8. For displaying direction to specific departments. Which sign will be used :
   (*a*) Promotional sign (*b*) Location sign
   (*c*) Institutional sign (*d*) Informational sign
9. MCFT is used for :
   (*a*) Materials custom fixed technology.
   (*b*) Modular craft frame technology.
   (*c*) Modular curved frame technology.
   (*d*) Materials curved fixed technology.
10. Neon signage is used at :-
   (*a*) busy traffic signals (*b*) where two or more road coincide with each other.
   (*c*) Both of the above (*d*) None of the above

Answers

1. a	2. a	3. c	4. c
5. a	6. d	7. d	8. b
9. c	10. c		

Check your progress

1. What is house keeping?
2. Name five ways to demonstrate merchandise?
3. What is planogram?
4. What is FMCG?
5. What is focal point?
6. What is signage?
7. List out different signs?
8. What is street signage?
9. What is store layout?
10. What does VM mean?

Small Answer Questions

1. What do you by mean store layout?
2. What are the objectives of using signage?
3. Discuss some guidelines for using displays?
4. What is 'Visual Merchandising'?
5. List various types of store layout with examples?
6. How a attractive store display can be created?
7. What do you mean by retail planogram?
8. Discuss the features of effective retail signage?
9. Explain different elements of an effective visual signage?
10. Why the use of visual merchandising is increasing day by day? Explain the role, objectives and its status in India?

Long Answer Questions

1. Explain the term signage? Discuss its importance in a store and what should be done to create an effective signage?
2. What store layout mean for a store? Explain various types of store layout used in Indian retail industry with its merits and demerits?

UNIT 13

MERCHANDISE PRICING

LEARNING OBJECTIVES

- Understanding the importance of pricing in retailing
- Identifying the effects of pricing on consumer buying decisions
- Understanding various forms of pricing in Indian retailing
- Knowing the factors affecting pricing decisions
- Describing the ways to adjust price markdowns and reductions

"Slowing housing, weak consumer spending and benign underlying inflation give the bank plenty of reasons to leave interest rates right where they are. Fuel prices are up, but thanks to an extremely competitive retail environment and cheap imports, prices for a whole range of items remain weak."

Shane Oliver

INTRODUCTION

Price has always been one of the most important variables in retail buying decision. It is the factor which makes or mars a retail organization. It is also the easiest and quickest element to change. ***Pricing*** helps an organization to achieve its objective. This is particularly significant for new market entrants that need to first establish a brand and they enjoy increasing profits as the brand gets market acceptability. For a customer, price is the main reason to visit a particular store. In this chapter an attempt has been made to know the implications of the pricing decisions which a retailer should consider while deciding the pricing for retail sale.

CONCEPT OF RETAIL MERCHANDISE PRICING

A retailer must price merchandise in a way that besides satisfying the customers, achieves profitability for the firm. Pricing is a crucial exercise due to its direct relationship with a firm's goals and its interaction with other retailing matters. A pricing policy, if not appropriate, send a store out of competition. A pricing strategy must be consistent over a period of time and consider retailer's overall positioning, profits, sales and appropriate rate of return on investment. Lowest price does not necessarily be the best price, but the lowest responsible price is the best right price. The difference between price and cost is profit which can be very high when the sales person wants to exploit an urgent situation.

The Consumer and Retail Pricing

Retailers should understand the importance of pricing because it has direct relation with consumer purchases and perceptions. During pricing decisions, retailers should also under the price elasticity of customers to price changes in terms of the quantities bought.

$$\textbf{Elasticity} = \frac{\dfrac{\text{Quantity 1} - \text{Quantity 2}}{\text{Quantity 1} + \text{Quantity 2}}}{\dfrac{\text{Price 1} - \text{Price 2}}{\text{Price 1} + \text{Price 2}}}$$

If relatively small percentage change in price results in substantial percentage changes in the number of articles purchased, price elasticity will be high. This is the situation where the urgency to purchase is low or substitutes are well available. If large percentage changes in price have small percentage changes in the number of articles purchased, demand is considered to be inelastic. This is the situation where purchase urgency is high and substitutes are not easily available. The formula to compute price elasticity is given below. The price elasticity is calculated by dividing the percentage change in the quality demanded by the percentage change in the price charged. Because in retail market sales usually decline as prices go up, elasticity tends to be on negative side.

Factors Affecting Retail Price Strategy

Following factors have direct or indirect influence on retail pricing. Three are usually basic pricing options before a retailer. Each has its own merits and demerits. These are as follows:

Figure 13.1: Factors Affecting Retail Price

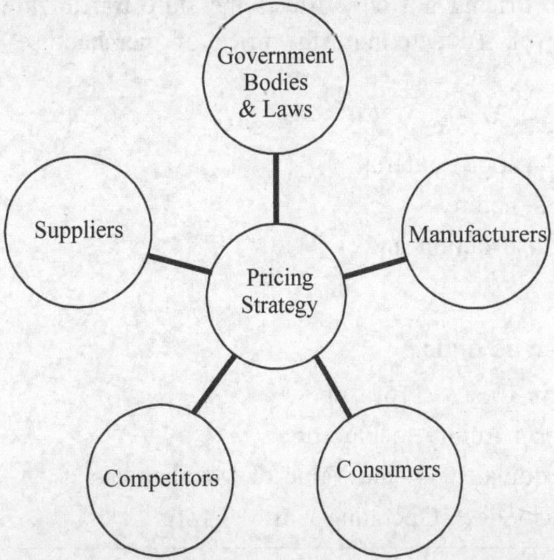

PRICING OPTIONS

(i) Predatory Pricing

It involves large retailers that normally seek to produce competition by selling merchandise at very low prices and create the situation where it becomes difficult for small retailers to stay.

(ii) Prestige pricing

It assumes that customers will not buy merchandise displayed if price fixed are too low. It is based on the price-quality association.

(iii) Price lining

A pricing practice where by retailers sell merchandise at a limited rate/limited range of price points, where each point represents a different level of quality.

SETTING THE RETAIL PRICE

Once price used to be the less important **'P'** of marketing mix & 'Price' was neglected for a long time. But with the complexities of business and increasing competition, the importance of pricing decision is growing because today customers are looking for appropriate **'value'** Value is the relationship between customers' expectation and his paying ability. Retailers, marketers are in business to multiply their invested money. There are several factors that affect the profitability of a retail business but an appropriate pricing policy is a vital decision toward multiplying their invested money. Retailers have various pricing strategies to use in their normal course of business but which one to adopt, depends on costs (operating and running cost etc.) incurred on that products.

Price

Price is an important element of any retail marketing mix. It is expressed as the value of product attributes represented in monetary terms, which a consumer is willing to pay in exchange. Pricing not only affects the store traffic flow but also influences the firm's profit level. To determine the price of merchandise, a retailer considers following factors:

- Pricing objectives
- Demand and supply criteria
- Competition's nature
- Channel of distribution and
- Profitability

Price can be defined as under:

Price = Production Cost + Profit or

Price = Consumer's Ability to Pay, or

Price = Rupee Equivalent of the Value of Merchandise

Price = Cost of Goods + Operating Cost + Profit

Setting the retail price of merchandise is a complicated, but the most important aspects of managerial decision making. If the price is set too low, retailer may not be able to cover its store expenses. If the merchandise is priced too high retailer may price himself out. Therefore, price setting is a complex activity and no formula has been developed so far to set the price correctly.

Retail price setting process includes a series of decisions a retailer makes while determining the price of merchandise. As said earlier, there is no universal way to set the price of merchandise but one thing should be noted in this regard that regardless of the price setting process used, the price of merchandise should meet the cost of obtaining the supplies and expenses to operate the retail firm. Here a five-step process is explained which most of the retailers follow to set the prices for their merchandise. These are as follows:-

Figure 13.2
Retail Pricing Process

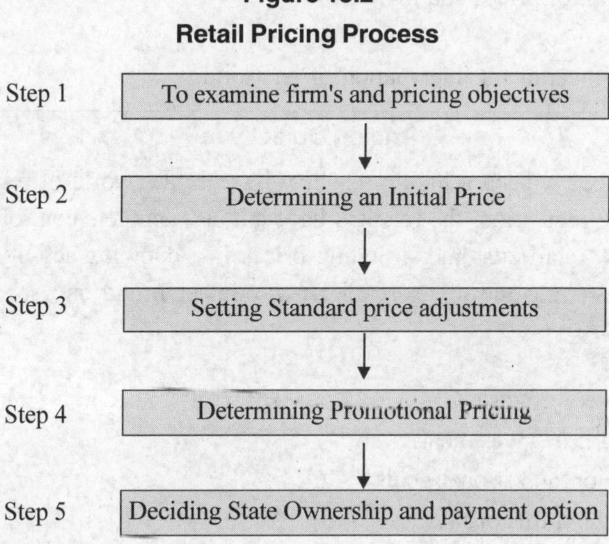

PRICING OBJECTIVES

Pricing objectives are generally considered as part of the general business strategy and give direction to the retail pricing process. While deciding on pricing objectives, a retailer must understand that pricing strategy must reflect the retailer's overall goals that can be stated in terms of profit and sales. Usually, while setting the price, the firm may aim at one or more of the following objectives:

- Achieving pre-determined return on investment (ROI)
- Building company's image, goodwill and brand's name
- Building sustainable competitive advantage
- Creating curiosity and interest about goods and services
- Creating store traffic
- Early recovery of cash

- Having price leadership
- Increasing company' growth
- Increasing market share
- Increasing rupee sales
- Justifying social responsibility of business
- Making the newcomers' entry in the industry difficult
- Matching with competitors' prices
- Maximizing long-term profit volume
- Maximizing short-term profit volume
- Partial Cost Recovery
- Providing ample customer service
- Quality Leadership
- Stabilization of prices and margin
- Survival
- Avoiding government intervention of any kind

Pricing Objectives

Pricing has always been a highly sensitive issue in the world of retailing. With the diminishing price regulation, the retailers have almost complete control over the prices that they offer to retail customers. Setting prices is a complex activity on the part of a retailer, while setting the price, retailer may aim at broad and specific objectives.

Broad Objectives

- Early recovery of cash
- Proper return of investment
- To achieve organizational goals
- To maximize firm's profits
- To maximize the sales volume

Specific Objectives

- To build loyal customer base
- To charge fixed prices
- To clear out reasonable/obsolete becoming merchandise
- To keep the prices stable
- To match with the competitors' prices

PRICING STRATEGIES

Price is a highly sensitive and visible part of a retail marketing mix and has bearing on the retailer's overall profitability. Further, pricing itself is an essential part of marketing mix and has its own place in strategic decision-making process. Out of 4 Ps (Product, Price, Place & Promotion), price is the only element of marketing mix that generates income for the firm, while rest of the elements are parts of the variable cost for the firm. Pricing strategy must consider that it costs to manufacturer to develop a product; it requires expense on distribution and promotion. A lot of pricing strategies are on hand and are practiced throughout the world. The main criterion to adopt a particular strategy is "what objectives' a firm decides to achieve?" A price strategy can be demand, cost and/ or competitive in nature. As charging too high or too low may cause loss to the firm, pricing should take demand, cost and/or competition into account.

1. Demand Oriented Pricing

Under demand oriented pricing, prices are based on what customers expect or may be willing to pay. It determines the range of prices affordable to the target market. Under this method, retailers not only consider their profit structure but also calculate the price-margin effect that any price will have on sales volume.

> **Demand Oriented Pricing**
>
> It focuses on the quantities that the consumer would buy at various prices. It largely depends on the perceived value attached to the product by the consumer. An understanding of the target market and the value proposition that they intend to seek is the base to this form of pricing.

As the very name implies, demand oriented pricing strategy seeks to forecast the quantities (sales volume), customers would purchase at various prices and concentrates on the prices associated with pre-determined sales targets. For example, if customers are highly sensitive to price tags, a price cut can enhance the sales volume so much that profits actually go up. On the other side, if customers are less bothered about 'price', increasing the sales price will directly result into increased profits. In short, demand oriented pricing seeks to estimate the price level that maximizes profits.

To illustrate the working of demand oriented pricing method, we take a hypothetical example of Koutons' summer launch T-shirt for teenagers. Suppose that the fixed cost of designing and developing is Rs 3,50,000 and the variable cost is Rs 10 each.

Table 13.1

Market Region	1 Unit Price	2 Market Demand (in units)	3 Total Revenues (col.1 x col.2)	4 Total Cost of units sold (Rs. 3,50,000 fixed Cost + Rs. 10 variable cost)	5 Total Profit (col.3 – col.4)
1	12	300000	36,00,000	33,50,000	2,50,000
2	15	**225000**	**33,75,000**	**26,00,000**	**7,75,000**
3	18	150000	27,00,000	18,50,000	7,50,000
4	21	75000	15,75,000	11,00,000	4,75,000
5	24	50000	12,00,000	8,50,000	3,50,000

The main advantage of demand oriented pricing strategy is to set the merchandise prices as per customer response towards the product offered. The Gap decides to test the Koutons' T-shirt in five markets at different prices. Figure 13.1 presents the pricing test's results. It is clear from column 5 that a unit price of Rs. 15 is by far the most profitable (Rs.7,75,000).

2. Cost oriented pricing

Under this form of pricing policy, a retailer decides a floor price of the merchandise – a minimum price suitable to the organization to achieve its financial goals. A retailer under this method sets the price to cover production cost, operating costs and a pre-determined percentage for profit. The percentage varies strikingly among industries, among member outlets and even merchandise of the same retail firm. One popular form of such pricing strategy is to **mark up** pricing. In **mark up** pricing, a retailer sets the prices of the merchandise by adding per unit merchandise costs, retail store operating expenses and determined profit. The gap between merchandise price and selling price is the **mark up**. For instance, a retailer purchases a wooden Almirah for Rs 3000/- and sells it for Rs 5000/-, the extra Rs 2000/- is charged to cover its store's operating costs and profit. In this case, the mark up is 80% or 66.67 percent on cost.

The Mark Up Criterion

The retailer's mark up percentage or cost plus percentage depends on following considerations:

- Product's traditional mark up policy
- Competition in the market
- Supplier's guidelines regarding selling price
- Operating expenses of store
- Rented or own retail store
- Inventory turnover
- Level of customers service offered

Calculation of mark up percentage

$$\text{Mark up percentage (at retail)} = \frac{\text{Retail Selling price} - \text{Mechandise cost}}{\text{Retail Selling Price}}$$

$$\text{Mark up percentage (at cost)} = \frac{\text{Retail Selling price} - \text{Mechandise cost}}{\text{Merchandise cost}}$$

Example

A food departmental store desires a minimum 30% mark up at retail outlet. If he feels 100 gm butter cake should sell at Rs 20/-, what maximum price store can afford to pay suppliers?

$$\text{Mark up percentage (at retail)} = \frac{\text{Retail Selling Price} - \text{Mechandise Cost}}{\text{Retail Selling Price}}$$

$$0.30 = \frac{20 - \text{Mechandise cost}}{20}$$

$$\text{Merchandise cost} = 20 - (0.30 \times 20)$$

$$= \text{Rs } 14/-$$

Determination of Initial mark up, Maintained mark up and Gross Margin

With the emergence of various retail formats and enhanced competition, it is not practical for a retailer to sell all the merchandise items at their actual prices. Therefore, retailers compute the initial mark up, maintained mark up and gross margin during their normal course of business.

Initial mark up

It is based on the selling price assigned to the merchandise less the costs of the merchandise sold.

Maintained Markup

It is the amount of profit a retailer plans to maintain on a particular form of merchandise. It is based on the selling price that you intend to wish less the cost incurred on goods sold. As maintained mark ups are concerned to actual prices received, therefore, for a retailer, it is always difficult to estimate in advance.

Initial Markup = Retail selling price initially set for the merchandise – Cost of Goods sold

Where as

Maintained Markup = The actual selling price a retailer want for its merchandise – Cost of Goods sold

The point of difference between initial markup and maintained markup is that initial markup percentage depends on planned retail operating expenses, profit, reductions and net sales while on the other hand, maintained markup represents some additional costs from original retail values caused by discounts, shortages, Inventory theft, markdowns and added markups. The maintained markup percentage can be viewed as

$$\text{Maintained Markup Percentage (at retail)} = \frac{\text{Actual selling price} - \text{Mechandise Cost}}{\text{Actual Selling Price}}$$

Gross Margin:

Gross margin, commonly known as gross profit is an important performance measure in retailing. It indicates the retailer a measure (estimate) of how much profit it is making on merchandise sales without considering the expenses associated with running a store. In other words, gross margin is the difference between Net sales and the Cost of goods sold.

Gross Margin (In Rs.)	=	**Net sales**	–	**Total Cost of goods**

3. Competition Oriented Pricing

As the very name suggest, under this pricing policy, retailers set the prices of merchandise after considering competitors' prices rather than demand or supply considerations. The company following this policy may not react to changes in demand or an increase in cost of merchandise. The retailer can charge higher than the market price, when the location of their stores is attractive and convenient to majority of its customers, offer wide assortments, exceptional customer service, a well established image, long experience and an executive brand. On the other hand, stores with inconvenient location and absence of value-added characteristics can charge less than the market price.

Following are the competition oriented pricing alternatives:-

(i) Competitive pricing below the Market rate

It simply means setting the merchandise prices simply to beat the competitor's price by charging price that is below the prevalent market rate. This policy is advisable only when retailer follows an optimum inventory plan, procure merchandise at right time and at right (minimum best possible) price to gain the benefits of cash payment, trade discount, bulk buying etc.

> **Competition Oriented Pricing**
> Here the prices adopted by competitors play a key role in determining the price of the product. The pricing policies adopted by a retailer can be cost-oriented, demand – oriented or competition oriented.

This policy is followed under following circumstances:-

(i) When retailer has no locational advantage.
(ii) Selling force is not competent and has little product knowledge.
(iii) Customer services offered are average.
(iv) In case of unimpressive layout and visual merchandising and
(v) When retailer has its own manufacturing of some private labels or merchandise.

(ii) Competitive pricing above the market rate

This policy allows a retailer to set the merchandise price above the current market rate. This policy seems to be straight forward and simple but must be applied carefully. This policy is suggested to those retailers who have some competitive advantages like:-

(i) In case of excellent consumer service.
(ii) In case of high level of personal selling, delivery and exchange facilities.

(iii) When retailer has a stock of well known brands that are not available to its competitors in the near by location.

(iv) When retailer has attractive, huge and modern retail infrastructure to offer merchandise that will allow a retailer to charge the merchandise price above market rate.

Retail Pricing Strategies

Generally retailers identify with a specific market type and streamline their efforts in gaining maximum profit. Pricing for certain types of markets mean that market entry is reliant not only on the types of merchandise sold, but the price it sells for. There are three price positions:

1. **Above the market:** It implies that a retailer can safely sell their merchandise at a price or prices higher than their competitors. However, when competitors are located close by, a retailer needs to rely on the perceived quality of their offering to maintain sales.
2. **At the market:** This is the most common policy as the retailer's lowers risk by selling at the same price as surrounding stores. Here the competition is fierce and this may make retailer adopt a different approach. There could be value creation through added benefits like service, or price-cutting like two for one etc. forms a part of this strategy.
3. **Below the market:** This implies that a retailer is prepared to sell merchandise at less than the average price. This is a popular strategy for discount stores and hyper markets formats.

TYPES OF PRICING

Horizontal pricing

This practice involves agreements among manufacturers, wholesalers, retailers to set certain prices. These agreements usually are illegal under Indian sales act.

Vertical Price Fixing

A practice where manufacturers or wholesalers seek to control the retail prices of their merchandise through some sort of agreements.

Price Discrimination

A pricing practice where different prices are charged from different retailers for the same merchandise and same quality.

Minimum Price Laws

These laws prevent retailers from selling certain items for less than their cost plus a fixed percentage to cover overhead.

Unit Pricing

The objective of such legislation is to let the customers compare the prices of product available in many sizes. For instance, Food and Grocery stores must express both the total price of an item and its price per unit of measure.

Item Price Removal

A pricing practice whereby prices are marked only on shelves or signs and not on individual item.

Price Advertising

These are guidelines pertaining to advertising price reductions, advertising prices in relation to competitors' prices.

Manufacturers, Wholesalers and Suppliers – and Retail Pricing

Whatever a business may be, conflict remains between the manufacturers, wholesalers, and Suppliers with regard to pricing decisions. All are interested to have major part in profit and control. Manufacturers always claim that their manufacturing cost per unit (MCPU) is very reasonable; it is the supplier or wholesaler who takes the vitals of the profits. Wholesalers are of the view that they are selling goods costly to retailers as their buying cost is costly. Sometimes wholesalers' view that merchandise is costly retailers are charging too high prices. While retailers control the pricing decisions by threatening wholesalers to stop buying merchandise if their terms and conditions are ignored or dishonored.

It is a normal practice in retailing that retailers sometimes buy manufacturers' brands and place high prices on them so that the sale of local brands should increase and in turn their profits should increase. As local brands normally offer merchandise on very less prices. This practice in retailing is termed as "selling against a brand" and is opposed by manufacturers as it not only harms their image but shrinks their profits. Besides this a retailer also gets supplies from employees, outsiders (advertising agencies), land lords, relatives, and fixture manufacturers. Each of these items has direct or indirect effect on pricing decisions.

PRICE ADJUSTMENTS

After deciding the prices of merchandise, the retailer's next step is to consider whether there is any need to change some prices due to reasons like changing demand patterns, pilferage issues, competition and seasonal shift during normal course of business. Price adjustments include either mark down or additional mark ups.

Mark down

Mark down is a most common technique to push retail sales that offers particular merchandise at a price less than the merchandise' marked price (normal price). The reasons for several types of merchandise include:

- Overstocking / over buying
- Season (climate) change
- Clear out store worn / slow moving merchandise
- Clear out old fashioned / old trend merchandise
- To generate customer traffic

Mark down always does not mean that store is not performing well but this is a part of doing business and to run a retail store efficiently. Sometimes, some retailers initially mark up their merchandise high enough that after reductions and marking downs (whatever the reason may be) the planned maintained mark up is achieved. Thus a retailer's intentions should not be to reduce mark downs. If mark downs are too less, it may mean that the retailer is probably charging the merchandise too low, not purchasing in bulk, or not having interest to purchase particular merchandise.

Types of Mark downs

(i) Temporary Markdowns: This is a policy of reducing the prices of merchandise for a particular time period due to a particular reason. For instance, markdown because of clear out shop worn / substandard merchandise. Once such merchandise is sold, the product will be priced to the normal selling price.

(ii) Permanent Markdowns: In such markdowns, price reduction is made for comparatively longer periods, may be few weeks, few months or more. Unlike the temporary markdown, where price reduction takes place for a particular cause and price eventually will be raised to the original one, the permanent mark down is used to replace the old quality merchandise with the new one. The reasons for permanent markdown are:

(a) Merchandise is of perishable nature and will be of no use after sometime

(b) To replace the old technology goods to new and latest versions

(c) Particular merchandise that a manufacturer / marketer no longer wish to produce / sell.

(iii) Seasonal mark downs: Under such markdowns, prices are reduced to clear out the seasonal retail merchandise, such as 'Ludhiana woolen sales' in the last months of winter season are very common in North Indian states like Haryana, Punjab, Delhi etc.

Additional Markup

Unlike the markdown where the prices are reduced, the additional mark up is intended to increase the retail price above the original mark up due to certain reasons like:

(i) When the demand for merchandise offered is exceptionally high

(ii) Due to monopoly like situation

(iii) When competitors are not able to meet the consumers' demand

(iv) In case private labels are performing well in retail market and have good demand, retailer would like to have quick and fast returns.

Note

In today's world of retailing where brands are easily available and competition is becoming tougher, markdowns are more applied by Indian as well as global retailers rather than additional mark ups.

Besides markdowns and additional markups, a third price adjustment i.e., the ***employee discount*** is becoming popular in retail world. Some retail firms in order to build public image and employees' welfare, offer additional benefits to its employees besides normal salary and perks in the form of discounts on merchandise buying or inviting employees to buy merchandise before offering to general public by the way of sales.

PRICE DISCRIMINATION

It is a pricing policy where a retailer charges different prices from different customers for the same merchandise. Price discrimination is based on the philosophy of 'ability-to-pay' and requires market segmentation. Price discrimination may be studied under few degrees such as first, second and third level price discrimination.

First level price discrimination: This type of price discrimination occurs when retailer charges the price of merchandise according to the customers' ability to pay. Usually for a retailer, it is not easy to identify which customer is able to pay more but when a retailer is able to do so, he would like to increase his profit base. For example, this type of price discrimination practice is usually common for sale of both new and second hand cars. People pay different prices for the cars having same features, model and make. The success of such price discrimination policy depends upon the ability and selling art of the floor employees to convince the customers that they are paying genuine and reasonable price for the merchandise. A customer having less/no bargaining power is welcomed by the retailer.

Second degree price discrimination: It refers to a practice where retail companies charge less prices for bulk buying. A retailer when gets big orders or purchase order for the same items at once in high number, offers the merchandise at a discounted rate. This practice is very common not only in retail business but in wholesaling too. This reduced rate will not be applicable to a customer who places order for a few items. A reduced price (discounted rate) is offered if one buys 5 kg or more instead of 1 kg or two shirts instead of one. It is helpful in clearing out the merchandise and generates quick revenue for a retail firm.

Third degree price discrimination: It refers to a practice where price vary by customer group or by location. One another form of such type of price discrimination is a practice of offering temporary discounts for airfares during particular seasons to cover up the low traffic fleet. In practice, this pricing discrimination takes various forms. For example, 'students' are considered a group and are offered discounts at cinema halls, amusement parks, trade fairs and museums. Some public and private airlines offer discounts to 'senior citizens'. Both students and senior citizens have higher elasticity of demand but less affordability.

SUMMARY

Pricing objectives are the goals that a retail company wishes to achieve through its pricing policy. Pricing is the factor that makes a customer comfortable to a store. Further, the retail market consists of competitors, consumers and suppliers. This means a retailer should have various pricing objectives. For an independent retailer, increasing or decreasing prices can be helpful to increase the store's sales but for brands, such price fluctuations can be harmful even to the cost of out of the market. To develop a pricing policy, retailers should consider the following issues to sustain their customer base.

- Deciding the target market carefully
- Which merchandise to sell?
- Who are our customers?
- What will be the geographical preference to focus on?
- What should be the promotion policy? and
- What makes customers comfortable (Price/Quality)?

REVIEW QUESTIONS

True and False Questions

1. A retailer normally has these three pricing options. These are:
   (a) Predatory Pricing
   (b) Prestige pricing
   (c) Price lining
2. Price is an important element of any retail marketing mix and is expressed as the value of product attributes represented in monetary terms.
3. Setting the retail price of merchandise is a complicated, but the most important aspects of managerial decision making.
4. Retail price setting process includes a series of decisions a retailer makes while determining the price of wholesale merchandise.
5. Price is a highly sensitive and visible part of a retail marketing mix but has no bearing on the retailer's overall profitability.
6. Under demand oriented pricing, prices are based on what customers expect or may be unwilling to pay.
7. Under this form of pricing policy method, a retailer decides a floor price of the merchandise – a maximum price suitable to organization to achieve its financial goals.
8. Initial mark up is based on the selling price assigned to the merchandise adding the costs of the merchandise sold.
9. Maintained Markup is the amount of profit a retailer plans to maintain on a particular sort of merchandise.

10. Maintained Markup Percentage = Actual purchase price - Merchandise Cost/Actual Selling Price.
11. Gross margin is an important performance measure in retailing that indicates the retailer a measure (estimate) of how much profit it is making on merchandise sales without considering the expenses associated with running a store.
12. Under competition oriented pricing retailers set the prices of merchandise after considering competitors' prices rather than demand or cost considerations.
13. 'Competitive pricing above the market rate' allows a retailer to set the merchandise price below the current market rate..
14. Horizontal pricing practice involves agreements among manufacturers, wholesalers, retailers to set certain prices.
15. Vertical price fixing practice where manufacturers or wholesalers seek to control the retail prices of their merchandise through some sort of agreements.
16. Price Discrimination is a pricing practice where different prices are charged from different retailers for the different merchandise and different quality.
17. Minimum Price Laws prevent retailers from selling certain items for less than their cost plus a fixed percentage to cover overhead.
18. The objective of unit pricing is to let the customers compare the prices of product available in many sizes. For instance, Food and Grocery stores must express both the total price of an item and its price per unit of measure.
19. Item Price Removal is a pricing practice where by prices are marked only on shelves or signs and not on individual item.
20. Price advertising is a guideline pertaining to advertising price reductions, advertising prices in relation to competitors' prices.
21. MCPU stands for manufacturing cost per universe.
22. Mark down is a most common technique to push retail sales that offers particular merchandise at a price less than the merchandise' marked price (normal price).
23. Temporary markdown is a policy of increasing the prices of merchandise for a particular time period due to a particular reason.
24. Under seasonal mark downs prices are increased to clear out the seasonal retail merchandise.
25. Price discrimination is a pricing policy where a retailer charges different prices from different customers for the same merchandise.

Answers

1. True	2. True	3. True	4. False
5. False	6. False	7. Ture	8. False
9. False	10. False	11. True	12. True
13. False	14. True	15. True	16. False
17. True	18. True	19. True	20. True
21. False	22. True	23. False	24. False
25. False			

Multiple Choice Questions

1. Predatory pricing belongs to :
   (*a*) Low pricing (*b*) High pricing
   (*c*) Discounted pricing (*d*) Price Lining
2. Value is the relationship between customers :
   (*a*) demand and supply.
   (*b*) buying and selling.
   (*c*) expectations and paying ability.
   (*d*) Inputs and outputs.
3. Price can be defined as :
   (*a*) Production cost + profit.
   (*b*) Consumer's ability to pay.
   (*c*) Cost of goods + operating cost + profit.
   (*d*) All of the above.
4. Out of 4Ps, which one generates income :
   (*a*) Product (*b*) Price
   (*c*) Place (*d*) Promotion
5. Under demand oriented pricing, prices are based on :
   (*a*) What customers expect to pay.
   (*b*) What customers can afford.
   (*c*) What customers may be willing to pay.
   (*d*) All of the above.
6. Gross margin is calculated as :
   (*a*) Gross sales – Cost of production.
   (*b*) Net sales – Cost of production.
   (*c*) Gross sales – Net sales.
   (*d*) Gross sales – Profit.
7. MCPU stands for :
   (*a*) Merchandise cost per unit (*b*) Manufacturing cost per unit
   (*c*) Minimum cost per unit (*d*) Maximum cost per unit
8. Additional mark up is used in case of :
   (*a*) Monopoly like situation (*b*) When demand is exceptionally high
   (*c*) When competitors are weak (*d*) All of the above
9. ROI is used for :-
   (*a*) Rate of Investment (*b*) Retail over Investment
   (*c*) Return on Investment (*d*) Return on income

10. To be successful in retail, pricing policy should be always :-
    (*a*) Lowest (*b*) Highest
    (*c*) Consistent (*d*) None of the above

Answers

1. a	2. c	3. d	4. b
5. d	6. b	7. b	8. d
9. c	10. c		

Answers to check your progress

1. Name three pricing options?
2. What a value demonstrates?
3. What is price?
4. What is ROI?
5. What is early recovery of cash?
6. List out four Ps?
7. What is unit price?
8. What is gross margin?
9. What is price discrimination?
10. What is MCPU?

Short Answer Questions

1. Explain the relationship between consumer and retail pricing?
2. Explain the various types of retail pricing?
3. Describe the various pricing objectives?
4. How manufacturers & wholesalers affect pricing?
5. What are the various pricing options available before today's retailer?
6. List the factors affecting retail pricing strategy with examples wherever necessary?
7. Discuss the formula to calculate price elasticity?
8. Differentiate between demand oriented and cost oriented pricing?
9. Discuss the three levels of price discrimination policy?
10. How a realer adjusts its prices in the normal course of business?

Long Answer Questions

1. What do you mean by the term 'retail pricing'? How elasticity of demand can be calculated? And explain how consumer can affect retail pricing policy?
2. "Setting the retail price of merchandise is a complicated, but the most important aspects of managerial decision making." Explain?

STORE MANAGEMENT

Unit 14 : Retail Store Operations

Unit 15 : Retail Loss Prevention

Unit 16 : Supply Chain Management

Unit 17 : Distribution Management

Unit 18 : HRM in Retail Sales

Unit 19 : Managing Store Employees

RETAIL STORE OPERATIONS

LEARNING OBJECTIVES

- Understanding the store administration and management process
- Describing various tasks performed in the store
- Explaining the concept of store administration & knowing duties and responsibilities of retail staff
- Understanding the features and essentials of a successful retail organization
- Knowing the financial/legal aspects of retail administration

"The person determined to achieve maximum success learns the principle that progress is made one step at a time. A house is built one brick at a time. Football games are won a play at a time. A department store grows bigger one customer at a time. Every big accomplishment is a series of little accomplishments."

David Joseph Schwartz

INTRODUCTION

The success of a retail store depends how efficiently a retail store does its day to day operations. These store operations play very important role in the profitability and long term survival. The rate, at which new and new stores are coming up and are leaving out of the competition, is a serious issue for Indian retail industry. It seems that these retail stores are coming in the market without proper homework. Homework here means that before entering in to a new market, they are not considering the local demand, local tastes and preferences. Even employees are not aware about their key responsibilities. The approach, a store has towards merchandising placement, the visual aspects, the customers, and team work, affects the store's bottom line. The store staff doesn't know how to attend the customers wisely. How to implement new techniques of selling and sales promotion? Even store manger is not effective in training and development part of employees. Money is being spent on training and development of store's employees but still retail staff hesitate to do new experience in their selling behavior. With the increasing competition, they necessitate to be updated when it comes to cost cutting techniques and managing store's day to day activities.

Thus it is the dire need of the time and demand of the retail sector that retail stores should establish a systematic and modern approach towards store and back up operations. This unit provides you the knowledge about store operations, its activities and various warehouse operations which no doubt, when applied efficiently will turn a store into profit making and popular store with in a short span of time. The unit will be also hclpful in identifying in competencies in existing stores' layouts and the tips to remove these basic but not vary important shortcomings related to store operations.

ELEMENTS/COMPONENTS OF RETAIL STORE OPERATIONS

The retail store is a place where customers take a decision to buy a commodity at the spot. The store also knows the customers' mentality and buying behavior. Therefore, store displays all the items under one roof where normally a customer needs not to walk here and there for a particular type of retailing. Customer is the *king* and *queen*. He needs not to ask do you have this soap. Or what the cost of this shampoo bottle is? Everything in the store is displayed with its price tags. Here customer comes and take whatever he/she needs. The concept of self service prevails. But despite self service, managing store operations is not an easy task. It requires a lot of expertise and alertness to manage the day to day activities of the store. In stores everyday retailer has some new experience.

In order to ensure a smooth flow of store activities, it is necessary that management should define the total tasks and the appropriate persons for each task. It has seen that professional stores/chain stores normally prepare an operation manual or blue print which becomes the base for assigning duties and responsibility to various levels of staff.

Be it food and vegetable store or cloth and shoe store, typically, the following five activities are carried in a store. These are:

1. Store Administration and Management of Retail Floor
2. Inventory Management
3. Managing Receipts
4. Customer Service
5. Sales Promotion

The above mentioned activities when put together in a particular manner in which they will perform, are shown in fig.14.1, as illustrated below:

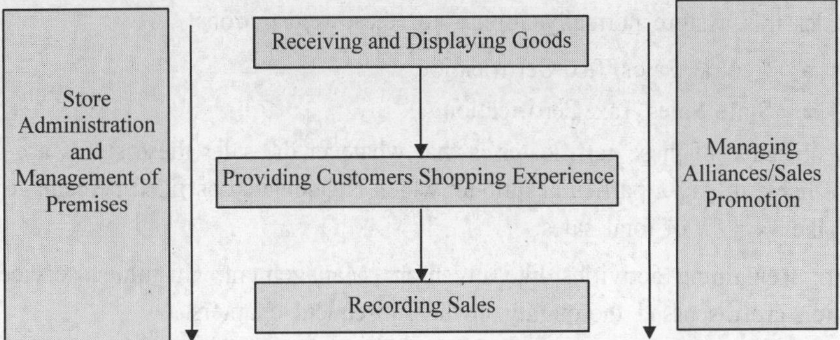

Figure 14.1: Tasks to be Performed at the Store Level

1. STORE ADMINISTRATION AND MANAGEMENT OF RETAIL FLOOR

Store administration deals with various aspects which are necessary to sell the goods to clients without any disruption. It includes cleanliness of the whole store particularly the main floor, maintenance the store façade and the displayed windows, etc. Besides this maintaining the record of each level of employees, using them efficiently and prudently, to keep the records of holidays and the shifts that the staff may be required to work for and the staff's pending leave record.

Administrators make sure that store need to be maintained as per the criteria, rules set by top management. This includes the proper cleaning of the store and arranging/refilling the merchandise before the customers come for shop.

Besides this, administration ensures that all the required permissions, licenses and NOCs (No Objection Certificates) have been properly received on time from all civic authorities. It also includes fulfillment of health and safety norms as required by the law of the land.

Some of these licenses are:

I. **Registration Certificate:** This is needed to run a particular store. This gives an identity to a particular (name) store. The store is then known by that registered name.

II. **Trade License**: The purpose of this license is to apply and take license to sell some day to day eatables like edible oil, sweets, readymade ice creams, candies, chocolates etc.

III. **Dairy License:** As the name implies, this license is required to sell dairy products including cow/buffalo milk.

IV. **License for Weight & Measure:** The purpose of getting this license is to use the weighing machines, weighing balance under weighing and measures rules of a particular state where the store is located.

V. **License for Rationing**: This license allows a store to sell items like food grains, sugar, salt, oils, pulses and dry fruits under retail sale.

VI. **License for Frozen Items:** This license is obtained to sell all types of frozen items such as beef, fish, mutton, bacon, ham, etc.

Besides this a store normally applies for these registrations:

- Central Sales Tax Certification
- State Sales Tax Certification

The objective of these certificates is that whatever the sales these stores are making; they are liable to pay a particular amount which is calculated as fixed percentage to total sales. Like 14.5 % of total sales.

Note: Remaining activities like inventory Management, Customer service, Sales Promotion are discussed thoroughly in the subsequent chapters.

Management of Retail Floor

Opening and closing activities are the primary activities of a store. If a store is not opened, how it can sell the things and if it is not closed, it will be a silly decision. Stores are closed because employees are human being and like machinery they also need some rest. Further, in the night, no one will come to buy except thieves and Stealers. Closing a store enables the store to clean the floor and refill the items that have been sold during the whole day. Therefore, before customers come to a store, the store must not be only opened but refilled with all the items for which customers come to shop.

Closing a retail store not only allows the retail managers to make some changes with regard to price, visual setting and arrangement in displayed items but allows the managers to manage new items and withdrawal of old/expired items in a store. But remember closing a store does not stop the retailer from canceling the orders, but the retailer further cannot modify or make new orders.

Management of retail floor begins by determining (a) what tasks are to be performed? and (b) who will perform these tasks? Following are the set of activities that a retail store has to perform during opening and closing of a retail store.

(a) Pre Store Opening Activities

These activities as clear by the name, take place before the store is opened for the general public. The objective of these activities is that store should be fully operational before the customers come for shopping. It means to prepare a store for its customers. These activities take place before the store's trading hours. Generally under this process, store's shutter or entrance gate remains closed for customers. If a customer comes during this period, he/she is either requested to wait outside or come after sometime when store will be opened. The various activities that take place before opening a store are:

- Cleaning the floor area
- Receiving the inventory
- Maintaining the inventory record
- Arranging the inventory for display
- Checking whether all shelves, racks are refilled properly.
- To check all the electric equipments like bulbs, tubes etc.

- To decide the duty chart (as it varies due to festivals etc)
- To check various weight measuring machines.
- To price the goods kept for display
- To check and refill poly bags, gift wrappers and loose coins at the billing and cash counters.
- Turning off the alarm
- Turning on the power and setting up the computer systems and electronic weighing machines.
- Displaying items that have been locked away overnight.

(b) During Trading Hours Activities

Once this stock is refilled and is prepared for customers' shopping, the store is opened. Shutter up activity and all the concerned staff including floor staff become active and take their positions as assigned before opening the store. The activities that take place during the trading hours are:

- Greeting the customers (welcome).
- To help the customers whenever and wherever is needed.
- Security staff, keeping their luggage, bags and long handy purses and issue a token number.
- Floor cleaning staff, cleans the floor aisles after regular interval
- Retailer supervises the activities of store employees and shoppers by way of anti-theft devices and CCTVs (closed circuit cameras).
- Cashiers keep the record of merchandise sold and accept the payments.
- Floor staff informs the inventory manager regarding status of inventory sold so that shelf should be refilled before the stock ends.

(c) Post Store Close Activities

After the fixed trading hours, store's lights are switched off one by one so that customers in the store should complete their buying and no new customer should be allowed to come. For example, the trading hours of a retail store are 8 am -10 pm, then before half an hour of closing hour, i.e. around 9.30 pm, retailer instruct the security staff to shutter down the store to its half and stop the new customers from coming by saying "*sorry Sir/madam, its closing time, please come tomorrow*". A routine announcement is also made to inside customers that it is store's closing time, so complete your shopping. Once the customers are out of the store, employees after giving their day to day report to their seniors, go out of the store after security check to ensure that store's staff is not carrying any unpaid store item. Then after completing the cash records and depositing the daily cash that comes through sale, cashiers are allowed to leave. The typical store activities that take place after closing the store are as follows:

- Collection of sales and merchandise records from floor staff so that next day shelves can be refilled before the customers come.

- Store manager collects the cash and credit sale record from the cashiers for the purpose of sending sales report to headquarter.
- Inventory store submits the merchandise balance report to the manager.
- Security staff inspects the store's floor staff and reports to staff's manager.
- Janitorial staff makes sure that all the electric, water and other security instruments are properly switched off.
- Supervisory staff ensures that all the windows, display shelves are properly covered and safe from insects, weather, hazardous condition and pilferage.
- Turning on the alarm
- Locking up the display items in an outside the store area.

2. INVENTORY MANAGEMENT

Devising an efficient system of receiving and displaying goods has long been a tough task for most of the retailers. Therefore, deep knowledge of inventory management is essential for retailers who want to maintain a stocking service for quick turnaround to help ensure total customer satisfaction. The "fill rate" of an item on a managed inventory list must be maintained to avoid shortages of frequently used items. Even when utilizing an inventory management system, occasional shortages will still occur[1].

To be successful in complex retailing environment, retailers need to have proper stock of inventory or have reliable suppliers to meet customer demands at a short notice. Either way, retailers must have a realistic, well-organized method for managing inventory in order to satisfy customers and stay in the competition. Sound system of inventory management enables an organization to meet or exceed customers' expectations of goods availability while maximizing net profits or minimizing costs. While managing inventory, retailers must decide on brands, sizes, material, color, style and price points. It involves regular check and adjusting the types of product lines that are added and dropped from the merchandise mix from time to time. Two widely used approaches to monitor and control product assortment and support are:

(a) Inventory turnover: It is the ratio at which a retailer depletes and refills stock over a period of time. A low inventory turnover ratio may position to obsolescence, overstocking, or deficiencies in the marketing line or product line. In some cases, a low rate may be acceptable such as circumstances where higher inventory levels occur in expectation of shortages or rapidly rising prices. A high turnover rate may indicate inadequate inventory levels, which may lead to a loss in retail sales. Inventory turnover is calculated as:

$$\text{Inventory Turnover} = \frac{\text{Sales}}{\text{Inventory}}$$

1 *www. callcentersinindia.com*

(b) Open-to-buy: Maintaining an optimum level of inventory always has been a difficult task. Buying and having too much inventory can slow retailer's cash flow and reduce profit earning with too much markdowns while on the other hand, under buying may lead to shortage and miss sales opportunities by way of loosing customers. Therefore, retailer has left with the option of using an open-to-buy (OTB) plan which ensures that product choice meets targeted consumer needs and requirements.

OTB can be calculated in either units or rupees and is difference between how much inventory is required and how much is actually present including inventory on hand, in transit and any outstanding orders. It is recommended to retailers that in order to take advantage of special buying offers or to add new products, appropriate OTB budget should be kept separate to avail such opportunities. It also allows the retailer to respond quickly to the fast-selling items and quickly restock shelves.

3. MANAGEMENT OF RECEIPTS

Management of receipts involves the policies, procedures and practices retailers follow to receive the payments from their customers. Most of the retailers in India prefer cash payment to avoid any further complexities while some other stores would accept either of these forms of payment like credit cards, debit cards, payment on delivery at home or bank cheques. Some stores also accept payments through co-branded cards. Credit cards are popular and in use in most of the urban parts of India. Due to popularity of credit cards, almost all the stores accept one or the other type of credit card. Major credit cards like ICICI, VISA card etc are accepted everywhere. Therefore, the procedure for accepting payment by way of credit and other cards and thereof collecting payment from the banks needs to be clearly understood by the store staff. The major operational decisions related to management of cash/receipts are as follows:

- Which method of payment should be chosen?
- Who will be responsible for administering credit cards?
- What is the policy for late or non-payment of merchandise?
- What are customer's eligibility requirements to accept a payment through bank cheques and credit cards?
- What are the credit terms and conditions? What interest should be charged? When the interest charge will begin and what will be the minimum monthly payment?

Undoubtedly credit facility offered by stores enhances customers input in the stores if implemented and drafted properly.

4. CUSTOMER SERVICE

Managing a retail store is the toughest task these days. New and new stores are coming up not only in the urban regions but in the suburban regions also. Employees' attrition rate is very alarming. They are leaving the old stores and joining the new ones. Competition is also becoming tougher day by day. Profit margins are shrinking.

Advertisement is no more effective. Customers' preferences, likes, dislikes are changing continuously. Therefore, there is a dire need of experienced and young store managers who should handle daily activities of a retail store in an effective manner and can put loss making stores into profitable entities. Hence, it makes sense to start at the customer interface when considering how a retail business might be managed in order to achieve the store's objectives. Whether a retailer has a practice of applying store or non-store format in his store, the way the customers are attended is a real priority in the management of any kind of retail store.

The retailers who understand the importance of **customer service** and really are customer focused ensure that continuous support should be extended to the team leaders of customer care executives and floor retail staff so that they can concentrate on the task of increasing sales. This support usually comes in the form of a retail store supervisor who organizes the various sales teams to make certain that the present retail staff is matched to the rate of may face. Thus it is expected that retail supervisor should be well experienced and interested in managing store employees. He should be mentally prepared to form the sales team and to take on the extra responsibility of leading the team. But in case of independent or small retailer, the task of supervision may be handled by the store manager itself.

5. SALES PROMOTION

Retailers in recent years have become increasingly inclined toward the use of sales promotion techniques, often at the cost of advertising. Though these promotional efforts are concerned with the store's marketing efforts, ultimately it will have impact on the store's sales. Therefore, retailers must ensure that the place where such promotional events have to take place must be ready for the same. If it requires additional work force, store should not hesitate in hiring such extra staff. If it requires some training to existing employees to get the better result out of promotional program, should be arranged accordingly. To support, an increasing number of retailers are doing tie-ups/partnerships with local dealers offering different merchandise with whom both the dealer and retailer gain win-win situation. Managing promotions, events and alliances all come under store operations and must be managed at store level itself. Further, receiving and displaying merchandise should be handled at store level.

MANAGEMENT OF A RETAIL OUTLET/STORE

Store managers are responsible for enhancing the productivity of the store and the company's investments in its employees. Retailing today is the hot and lucrative area; therefore, most of the entrepreneurs are coming in the world of retailing with foreign expertise and domestic human skills. Due to regular interaction with customers, retailers have the best knowledge of customers' needs and competitors' move. From this point of view, store managers play a vital role in formulating and executing retail strategy. For retail stores to ensure their long turn survival, store operations need to be managed as well as possible. Thus, a decision to change a store format, store's working hours due to seasonal change, or to introduce a new anti-theft device must be carefully examined since these tasks could greatly affect retail performance. Good merchandise does not sell itself. It is the store manager's responsibility to make sure that the merchandise is presented effectively and floor staff offer services that stimulate and help customer buying decisions. Besides this, retail store manager should take a wide range of operational decisions from opening to closing the retail store such as:

- What operating guidelines are used to run the store?
- What are the pre store opening activities?
- What are the operational store activities during the store's trading hours?
- How inventory can be managed effectively?
- What are post store close activities?
- How the safety of the store, its employees and the shoppers can be ensured?
- How to manage the receipts?
- How credit management be made effective?
- How employees' efficiency can be improved?
- Should any part of store activity be outsourced?
- How the use of ICT (Information and Communication Technology) can improve store's efficiency?
- What are the plans to meet any crisis?

The Store Manager

The store manager's role is multifaceted but the main task of a store manager is to meet the sales target as set by the management and is essential for running a store successfully. This target is usually instigated in the form of financial targets, based on store's turnover or profitability ratio. Other targets may be in the form of forming life members, number of clients or the number of dealings. With the increase in the store's size, the responsibilities of the store's manager increase. The bigger the store, the more likely it has increased complexities, in terms of number of increased floor staff, variety of products etc. The diversity in a retail store manager's role depends on the extent to which the central office such as head office or company headquarters' takes on specific tasks, but the under mentioned list gives some areas of responsibility that are common for each type of retail store manager.

Who is Retail Store Manager?

A retail store manager is a person who is responsible for the success or failure of a store. His calculation, forecasting and way of functioning can affect a store in a big way. The designation of a retail store manager holds infinite duties and immense responsibilities. Today there exist various types and various sizes of retail stores. According to the requirement and size of the store, management recruits single or more retail managers to fulfill/accomplish day to day activities performed in a retail store. It is not easy to define the duties and responsibilities of a store manager. It differs from store to store and even some times difference in his portfolio varies from small sized to big size of a same store. In order to understand the duties and responsibilities performed by a retail manager, it is advisable to understand the position and role of a store manger in the retail organization. What in fact these managers do on day to day basis. Once the meaning and position of a retail manager is clear crystal before us, then we will be able to list the duties and responsibilities of a retail store manager in an easy and better way. Let us first understand who actually a retail store manager is?

What Store Manager Means to a Retail Organization?

The retail store manager is a professional/expert in the retailing field and knows the nuts and bolts of a retail stores. He knows what the activities of a retail store are. He supervises the day to day business operations of a particular retail store. He is responsible for managing the daily work of floor staff (junior and senior both). He ensures that customers who come to his store should have a nice shopping experience. He is also responsible for managing the merchandise in the stores. He takes care that at no point of time there should be any shortage of any item in the store. He is responsible for managing the daily complaint register and records related to security staff. Besides this he also makes sure that the store staff at various levels presents team work during the business hours. In short, a retail manager is responsible for success or failure of a retail store.

Duties and Responsibilities of Store Manager

As it has said earlier as such there is not a clear cut duty chart which is expected from a retail manager. Duties and responsibilities vary from store to store. But there are certain duties and responsibilities that are common and a retail manager must perform in all situations. These are as follows:

1. **Management of employees:** Managing employees is the foremost duty of a retail manager. This includes the management of store's employees working at various levels such as sales staff, store staff, cleaning staff and clerical staff.
2. **Maintaining the sales environment:** It involves implementation of store layout plans, displaying merchandise, replenishment/refilling of stock, visual merchandising task and maintaining the sales record effectively.
3. **Cost minimization:** It involves controlling expenses that are essential to run a store. By way of applying cost effective policies, expenses can be reduced resulting in increased profitability. It is possible by elimination of waste, errors and accidents. This task of minimizing cost becomes necessary when store is running on low price policy, like in case of Wall Mart stores where EDLP (every day low prices) policy is being applied.
4. **Recruitment, Training and Development:** The very first duty of any retail store manager is to handle the job of recruiting the right persons at right jobs.

Then train and adjust them according to the store's policies and working environment. If they need any training, they must be provided in or out side the store. These new entrants are those who *make* the store either an achievement or can *mar* the whole business. Therefore, retail manager should ensure that be it cashier, or sales executive or store keeper, they should be hired after considering their minimum qualification and experience in the concerned field. If after recruiting, training and development, still these employees are not performing well after several warnings, they must be fired from the store. In addition to these duties, store manager must ensure that all the employees at different level are honestly doing their duties and are not creating any problem for store or other employees.

If any retail manger, employee or group of employees are lacking in some managerial skill/know how, he/they must be provided with proper training, as trained employees work fast and in more effective way. Also it is the working staff that ultimately put policies/store's objectives into action.

5. **Budgeting and Forecasting:** The store manager is more suitable for predicting the store's future performance, calculating future expenses and accordingly setting budgets. Explaining the set targets and the funds available to departmental heads and collecting their performance at regular interval comes under implementation of retail strategy.
6. **Implementing Marketing plans:** This involves implementation of marketing policies devised in order to pursue store's strategic marketing objectives. For example, to allocate space for sales promotion activities, inspecting effectiveness of sales distribution programs etc.
7. **Team Leadership:** The store manager also has the task of motivating his employees and reducing any resistance to change in working methods that may be required when new strategic directions are set. Retail manager ensures that his all employees should work like a team, leaving any personal grudge.
8. **Maintaining Leave and Salary Record:** Another important job of a retail store manager is to have the proper balance and written record of the money comes in the store by way of selling the goods. He is also responsible for keeping the whole record of all the employees with regard to their working hours, no of days worked by each and every employee. He will take care that each employee is getting the salary according to the number of days and hours served them for the store so that there should not be any partiality with any type of store employee. He will oversee that the provisions related to casual or earned leaves (if any) are applicable to all employees. The necessity of proper and updated records (both sales and purchase) is that it helps in estimating the money which has come in to the store by way of selling goods or providing services to customers and gone out of the store by way of bills and salary payments to employees.

9. **Holding Inventory:** Inventory control is another important activity performed by a retail manager. To ensure regular availability of inventory in the store, retail manager maintains appropriate level of inventory all the time in the store. Since a store's earning is through selling of goods, it becomes the duty of a sales manager to have the full record of incoming and outgoing inventory. So that there should not be any shortage of inventory in the store and side by side there may not excess of a particular good which results in unnecessary blockage of money and also needs storage area. Normally in the small Indian cities, most of the retail managers have practice of keeping the inventory with the nearby godowns to avoid any shortage. The reason is that these cities are not well connected with rail or road networks. But on the other side, retailers in the metros or developed cities avail of just-in-time deliveries with the help of efficient customer response systems, which reduce the practice of having huge inventories in stock all the times. In addition to maintaining appropriate level of inventory, he should make sure that payment has been made for the supplies/ordered goods.

10. **Extending Customer Services:** The retail sales manager being on the senior position is responsible for providing multiple services to immediate customers and the other members of his retail value chain. These services differ from store to store and location to location. Some of the services familiar to all stores are (a) credit facility, (b) free home delivery, (c) after-sale service, and (d) trade discount to bulk buyers or small traders and information and new offers to its regular and loyal customers. For instance, the Titan watch company in India set up its service centers in its own retail chain stores of Titan wrist watches with the name of Time Zone. This has not only thinned the importance of local and unorganized service providers but has also increased the confidence of the retail customers in these chain stores considering after sales service an integral part of watch purchase.

11. **Maintaining Store Harmony:** The retail manager is also responsible for maintaining harmony among different levels of store staff. He ensures that the floor staff is cooperative and has corporate spirit of team work. Store harmony not only includes the good relation between different types of employees but also involves relation between store management and its employees, between public and store, between public and store's employees, store and the government, and also between various stores.

12. **Ensuring Safety of Employees and Inventory:** Since the retail store manager is supposed to be present physically on the store's premise on daily basis, is the suitable individual to ensure the safety of the store including the safety of employees and inventory. He is the appropriate person to inform the corporate office how his store is doing and where and when the changes are needed to introduce in the store. Store manager ensures that all the safety provisions with

regard to requirement of local authorities like municipal corporation, state and central government are duly met. These safety provisions relate to installation of fire fighting systems and provision of emergency exits etc.

In nutshell, a ***retail store manager*** is responsible for day to day activities of the retail store. He undertakes various activities and performs functions that add value to the offerings they make to their potential customers. The retail store manager also serves the manufacturer by performing the function of distributing the goods to the ultimate consumers. For several goods where brand loyalty is not very strong, the retail store manager's recommendation could be very vital in buying decisions of the customers.

Expectations from a Store Manager

Each store has high expectations from its store manager. He is the real representative of management in the store. While recruiting, generally management has following expectations:

(a) Excellent Communication Skills

Communication skill means that the retail manager besides English (the global language), knows the Hindi and the local language (if any). He must have exceptional conversational skills. He should be able to read the body language of customers, what exactly they expect from a store in terms of quality. He should be a person who is ready to work sometimes in the late hours if need arises. He should know how to interact with customers and employees in an effective and pleasing way. He should be aware about the legal and socio cultural aspects of retailing. Considering these essentials, interviewers will be in a good position to select an appropriate retail store manager. Therefore, a lot of homework is required on the part of interviewers and the management while recruiting a retail store manager. Hence, at the time of selection, satisfy yourself about his qualification, know how and his tendency to lead a retail store.

(b) Proper Qualification and Working Experience

It has rightly been said that practice makes a man perfect. It is not the education but experience which speaks and reflects. Therefore, before recruiting a retail store manager, his qualification and proper experience must be duly verified. Although studies have shown that prior working experience is not the right criterion to select a store manger but can not be ignored easily. Yes what type of quality experience a retail store manager has, can be evaluated and examined by proper questioning and cross checks. Selecting a retail store manger that already has some prior working experience in the retail industry decreases the management cost on training and development part. Hence it is strongly recommended that experience must be honored and given priority at the time of recruiting a retail store manager.

(c) Sense of Professionalism

After having examining the experience details in the same field, store management should look for professionalism spirit in a potential retail store manager. It is very difficult to judge in advance how much a store manager is professional. But through rigorous selection technique, it becomes easy to know the deserving candidate. It is also expected that the short listed retail manager must have strong mathematical and quantitative expertise which may assist the employees and the customers. Sense of professionalism helps in managing and carrying out day to day activities of a store in an effective way. A retail store manager should not be either too strict or lenient. He must know where he has to show anger and where he should listen to employees and customers.

(d) Honesty

'Honesty is the best policy' is a legendry aphorism which must be applicable in the case of retail store manager too. If the wholly solely (Retail store manager) is a wrong person how can you expect sincerity from other store employees. If the leader is wrong, it becomes difficult to stay honest for the followers. Followers always do whatever they see is done by their leader. Further, as retail manager has to keep the whole record of the money comes into store and goes out of the store; chances are high that he can commit fraud very easily. Therefore, good remuneration should be offered to the retail store manager which is comparative to the competitors' stores and considers his qualification and past working experience.

An Essential Guide for Retail Store Manager

India is soaring! And nowhere is it more evident than in the retail space. Well, not surprising as it's touted to be one of India's fastest growing sectors. Massive malls, packed multiplexes, hypermarkets, authorized designer wear showrooms, it's all happening here and now. To be shopping now is a delight in itself. What a wide array of products and brands to choose from. There is something for everyone and it seems that everyone is eying for a piece of the action.

But are these retail outfits are successful in luring the customer 100%? Do customers have a good experience shopping at these malls? Do retail outlets ensure maximum brand visibility? These are million dollar questions that need to be answered readily if the retail boom has to be sustained. Selling is not just about the right product in your showroom. It's about displaying them in an appealing fashion – a showroom can make or break a buying decision irrespective of the quality of the product. It's also about creating an identity for the brand quite distinct from the ambience of the rest of the space so that it reaches out to the customers.

To achieve this, retailers need to constantly bring in innovative ideas to make retail space exciting and inline with the brand personality of the brand being displayed. When potential customers step in, showroom needs to create an environment that encourages them to shop. These shop fixtures and fittings should not only draw them to the merchandise but also catalyze a positive choice. It should light up even products that are seemingly not exciting. With customer demand at an all time high, it's imperative that retailers showcase better aesthetics in shopping environment. It's more like a necessity than a choice. Not adhering to such pointers can spell doom for a retailer.

We won't blame you if you thought that this trend is prevalent in the metros only. Hose in the know realize that it's spreading, and spreading rapidly to the 'hinterlands'. Large format stores have been springing up in smaller towns also and **'small towners'** are increasingly savvy and are flocking to other organized retail outlets for want of an enhanced buying experience.

While today's consumers are well-read and exposed to international trends, the retailers themselves face a dearth of knowledge regarding international retail trends and styles. As much as they might want to match (or even surpass) international standards, they simply do not have access to retail fixtures of international quality. This is where Featherlite Steps in.

The Featherlite name is synonymous with international appealing, ergonomically designed modular furniture. For the uninitiated, Featherlite is one of India's largest modular office furniture brands. Headquatered in Bangalore, with state-of-the-art manufacturing facilities spread over 1,75,000 sq. ft, Featherlite operates through a chain of 22 mega showrooms spread across India.

Featherlite presents a distinctive new concept in modular shop fittings and retail showcasing systems. Blending world class aesthetically appealing designs with functionality to match, these shop fittings create an environment that is on par with any retail space in the world. Designed to display a variety of products, these shop fittings/racks come in a variety of shapes and sizes. These can also be customized, taken into consideration the space as well as the product that needs to be displayed.

Aesthetically appealing and highly functional display racks, supermarket racks, heavy-duty racks and product display stands. Featherlite provides solutions that not only spell value for money but also elegance and durability too. Featherlite entered the Indian retail fixtures market when organized retail was not so much top-of-the-mind, approx. 8 years back. Since then Featherlite has come a long way and is unveiling its shop fittings and retail showcasing systems' showroom, the first of its kind in Bangalore and perhaps in India. The neo swanky showroom boasting a 3000 sq. ft sprawl is located on Mysore Road. Here, you get to see an exact view of the retail space that you have in mind as the products are not just displayed as is, but are fitted out to reflect an authentic retail ambience. Retail fixtures are available in both wood and sheet metal. The showroom has retail fixtures for displaying fashion brands, consumer durables, food products et al. all said and done, what is the specialty of the new Featherlite shop fittings showroom? You may ask. What the retailer gets here are a wide range of options and products of international quality. Here, clients can actually test the fixtures before they buy.

With a dedicated, time-tested installation crew at beck and call, Featherlite can install fixtures simultaneously in multiple locations across the country. If you have the ambition to own an international quality retail chain, you now have a 'one-stop shop' for all your retail fixture and shop fitting needs.

Source: *www.featherliteindia.com*

THE ROLE OF CENTRALIZED RETAILER

The concept of centralized retailer is applicable where retailer has more than one store, may be in different cities, but carries out functions on behalf of stores collectively as opposed to individuality. But when the activities and scope of these individual stores increases, the controlling activities are transferred to these retail stores, but the benefits that a retailer derives from centralized office are numerous. The main advantage is the economy of scale and the specialization of activities, some retail decisions that need to be made for one store is to be made for all stores, hence a central body of employees becomes responsible for decision making for all outlets. Most of the employees at the head office work in some particular departments dedicated to a particular function of retail management. The central department is commonly known as 'policy-making department' which carries out the initial planning of the strategic plan. While the independent stores carry out the remaining functions and put policies (as laid by central office) into actions. If we talk about Indian retailers, most of the centralized retail companies have following departments with a team leader:

- Inventory/merchandise management
- Marketing department
- Logistics – a study which is concerned with deliveries (dispatch) to store and from suppliers.
- Personal department – a department concerned with recruiting, hiring, training and development of employees.
- Finance department
- Advertisement department
- Legal and public relation department
- Property department
- Non store operations
- Domestic and international operations.

The detailed explanation of operational responsibilities of each of these departments is as follows:

1. Inventory/ Merchandise Department

This department of a centralized organization is responsible for managing the goods and services for its various chain stores. The department ensures that right quality of goods is purchased at right time that will satisfy ultimate consumers. The merchandise department is usually the largest department in terms of size and operations. This department has highly specialized individuals who are expert in the merchandise management and responsible for investing retailer's large money into those goods which when sold, will give good benefit. If we talk about today's big retailers like Spencer and Tesco & Marks, were also founded by market retailers.

2. Marketing Department

Marketing department has the responsibility of market the goods to the consumers. You can provide a high quality good, offer the goods on low prices but it is the marketing department who does this responsibility of informing the customers. Marketing department informs the customers, attract and lure them so that they should come to retail store. In short, marketing department provides (brings) the customers to the stores. Once the customer has reached a store, now it is up to floor staff/customer care department that how effective they handle the customers. Traditionally marketing department and buying department used to operate separately. But with the introduction of new approaches like category management and other developments in the retailing field forced the two functions together in order to achieve product oriented objectives.

3. Logistics (Distribution) Department

The logistics department provides retail services to the retail stores and deliveries from suppliers to retailers which commonly is known as retail supply chain. Retail supply chain includes means of transportation and storage like warehousing, cold storage, etc. The logistics department in case of centralized retailing deals with both the buying and merchandising and the marketing department to ensure that supply chain operations support the product and marketing strategy of the organization. But in some of retail companies, these both departments are merged. For instance in the case of bread, butter, milk and other fresh produce because here the timely logistics of food stuffs is so essential to the long term survival of the retail store.

4. Personnel Department

Personnel or human factors are must for a retail company, even in the case of e-retailing (at the time of writing/sending supplies). The personnel department (commonly known as HR department) is responsible for recruitment, selection, training and development of store's employees at various levels. HR department ensures that right person should be selected at right position. They must be properly remunerated. Therefore all the activities related to store's employees are managed and planned by HR department. But the success of a retail store depends on the retailer's policy with regard to remuneration, wages and rewards. Unless a retailer is offering a competitive reward package, HR department will not be able to recruit the best caliber staff. Most of the big retail stores operate a system of regional H.R. manager who has the responsibility of recruiting retail staff for its various outlets. But in case retail outlet is very big in size, where hundreds of employees are working then as per requirement HR manager may be dedicated to and based at that outlet.

5. Finance Department

Finance is the life line of any business. Retailing is all about exchange of goods and services for money. The money that comes in to store by way of selling merchandise and goes out by way of salary or supplies payment is controlled by the finance department.

In case of centralized retailing, the regional finance manager (finance head) take care financial dealings of each store. All payments are made from his office and all collection of various stores comes to his office. At the independent stores, cashiers keep record of all financial transactions. As per the guidelines of regional finance head, they can make some payments with in some prescribed limit. But these cashiers are supposed to send weekly, monthly or yearly report of all financial transactions to the regional department.

6. Non-Store Operations

These days most of the retailers have developed new retail channels, and in initial stage this type of non-store operations are managed on a specific project basis, but as it grows then it becomes necessary to integrate with the store's overall organizational structure. For example, in case of food & grocery retail store, free home delivery is originally treated as store's separate entity. But then it is amalgamated with the store's real operations in order to maintain consistency. Other non-store operations are managing customer catalogues and service centres.

7. International Operations

Due to the increased competition in the domestic market, it becomes necessary for the stores to have some international relations with foreign stores so that goods in quality and variety should be made available to the home customers. Further international operations sometimes become essential due to limited opportunities in the domestic market because of high level competition, mature markets and restrictive trade barriers. There is no doubt that international retailing is a business of profit but numerous retailers have failed and were forced to withdraw from international markets. Some of the major reasons for their failure include underestimating cultural differences and lack of supplier and distribution networks. In a centralized retail store, international operations are usually supported by a dedicated team that works in close communication with other sections within the head office.

An Integrated Retailing Approach

Due to the increasing business complexities, the retailers of chain stores require a special sort of approach that not only integrates the efforts of the different departments but provides strategic management approach to its non-store and international operations. The essence of integrated approach is important because it includes the qualitative (non financial issues) as well as quantitative aspects of centralized retailing. For instance, an integrated approach finds the ways in which store's customers evaluate the retailer's strategy such as store's image, customer service, complaint handling effectiveness and number of repeat visits which can not be measured unless thorough customer research is carried out. The way the customers evaluate the store's performance is entirely different from evaluation that share holders may make based on company shares in the stock market. Though the criterion for evaluating the retailer's performance differ from customers to shareholders, but both are valuable measures when it comes to monitoring the effectiveness of a retailer strategy.

Duties and Responsibilities of Retail Floor Staff

In retailing, every day, every shift, every minute being a floor staff, you learn something new about consumer behavior. Every shift is busy and involves many tasks. A typical shift might include any or all of these jobs:

- Bag ice
- Brew coffee
- Check fountain drink quality
- Check in vendors
- Clean and stock beverage areas
- Clean restrooms
- Empty trash
- Greet customers appropriately
- Help customers with their shopping needs
- Restock
- Sweep and wash floor
- Thank customers for shopping at
- Wipe down gas pumps, air conditions, coolers, windows and displays.

OPERATIONS MASTER SCHEDULE (OMS)

Operations master schedule is a plan for retail store which systematically lists all the operating functions to be performed in the store from shutter up to shutter down. This plan / blueprint not only provide the detailed activities to be performed but also explain their characteristics, their timing and those responsible for carrying them out. For example:

- Who will open the store and when?
- What are the pre-store and post-store activities?
- Who is responsible for which job?
- What activities will take place during store's trading hours?

In short, OMS is a detailed document which provides the retailer's information about what to do? Where to do? When to do? And who will do it?

Note: If a retailer is large or in multiple retailing it may use various OMSs. The store then will be having separate blueprints for various operations such as store display, inventory management, credit management, customer care, complaint handling department and store maintenance. Furthermore, whenever a retailer modifies its store format or operating procedures, OMS must be adjusted accordingly to achieve the store's objectives.

STORE MAINTENANCE

Store maintenance includes all the activities involved in managing store's facilities such as management of exterior and interior physical facilities. The exterior facilities include the parking arrangement, the entrances to the store, signs and windows outside the store. While interior facilities include the arrangement for windows, walls, flooring, ceiling, climate control, energy use, fixtures and shelves, displays and signs and sidewalks.

The arrangement and quality of store maintenance affects both the sales generated in the store and the cost of running a retail store. The interior facilities such as cleanliness of floor area affects shoppers perception towards store and exterior facilities such as good parking facilities attract shoppers. Further good store maintenance lengthens the useful life of air conditioning units, floors, electric equipments, shelves and fixtures. Shoppers will not come to a store whose washrooms, stair cases, elevators and floor areas are poorly maintained. Thus, it requires regular cleaning of lights, fixtures, washrooms, elevators, floor areas, dustbins, water coolers and air conditioners, besides replacing burned out lamps and tubes.

Some reputed chain stores even go farther so as to replace all electric bulbs, tubes and lamps after a regular interval to ensure constant color, brightness and light impact throughout the stores.

ENERGY MANAGEMENT

Energy management is all about the management of expenses on lighting, heating and cooling the store area. Due to continuous increase in electricity prices for commercial use throughout the country, energy management is now a major consideration in managing a store for retailers. For retail stores that sell fresh fruits, vegetables and food stuffs, it becomes critical. Therefore, most of the retailers are using energy saving instruments and devices to cut the cost and get competitive advantage. Some of the practices that have been observed and followed by Indian retailers are as follows:

- Instead of using traditional bulbs and tubes, the use of CFL lamps not only reduces the electric consumption drastically but has good lighting effect.
- The photo sensors continuously monitor the light levels in the store and with the increase in daylight, they reduce the artificial lighting in the store resulted in saved electricity and less electric bill.
- The climate sensors like photo sensors control the need for air conditioning in the store.
- Use energy saver elevators that are stopped automatically when they are not in use.
- Use of computerized systems and electronic sensors in washrooms and toilets can reduce water consumption in the store.
- Having centralized computer-controlled systems even let the retailers know whether floor staff has left on lights in closed stores and turn those lights off from their consoles.

STORE SECURITY

Store security relates to the security and safety of store staff and merchandise kept in the store. In India, retail store concept is of recent origin. Retail outlets are only popular and exist in big cities. Yes in some suburban areas some retail outlets have come up but still a big part of the country is uncovered by malls and retail stores. Many consumers and employees especially ladies staff feels uncomfortable in late evening hours in the stores. Fewer people are interested to shop at night in the retail stores. Most of the stores get their major portion of sales during day time shopping. Even studies and surveys have shown that malls are becoming unsafe as far as personal safety is concerned. Parking areas are not properly maintained. Not only the vehicles but the accessories are being stolen in the parking lots especially in the late evening. Some aged people (senior citizens) hesitate or not longer go out in late evening. Therefore, in order to ensure the security of the store, proper arrangements should be made. Some of the provisions made are:

- Appointment of uniformed security guards assures shoppers' safety and presents a warning to potential thieves and merchandise stealers.
- Proper arrangement should be made at entry and exit points of parking lots.
- Without uniformed security guards can be located in and outside the store to locate stealers as they can take a part of stealers.
- Use of TV cameras can be beneficial to catch the thieves and store stealers red handed.
- Cash deposits in banks must be made frequently with fully armed security guards.
- Brighter lighting should be arranged in and outside the store including the parking lots.
- The guards located at various points should have some arrangement of coordination with each other.
- Access to storage areas and ware houses should be restricted.

RETAILING SUCCESS TIPS

Running a retail business is not an easy business amidst increasing competition. The easiness of entry into retail business results in stiff competition and better value for the customers. Therefore, a retail store manager, need to have proper mission and vision before starting his functions. The reason of course is the high costs of real estate and increasing numbers of retail stores in each part of the country. Further, retail sector is the largest employer after agriculture. Employees' attrition rate is alarming and becoming out of control day by day. Therefore, it is the demand of the time that efficient methods and techniques should be devised that should result in to converting retail industry's weaknesses into strengths.

If we talk about the failure rate of retail stores, figures and statistics can put us in astonishing situation. The rate at which new retail stores are coming up near your colonies is approximately not less than the rate at which old stores are closing down their activities. Considering the ample scope of earning the profits, most of the industrialists are starting various retail stores without proper homework. Afterwards, they find difficulties in managing day to day store activities. Therefore, they should understand that running a retail business needs proper planning and strategic implementation than simply having desire.

If we talk about the causes of retail business failure, we will find that the main reason is not to adopt updated methods of retail functioning. It has been observed that retail managers are not responsible for non-implementation of advanced techniques of retailing but it is the employees who resist changing. Employees think that if they apply new techniques/working methods they may not succeed. In this case store management can recruit new and young employees. But they forget instead of standing on a height and think where these routes will go, you at least start your journey sooner or later you'll reach your destination. Same principle applies here; employees should understand that store's existence/survival depends on the employees' potential. If the employees are not ready to work or ready to change, one day the store will be out of race and ultimately out of the market. And then no one will be ready to give them new job because they are not updated to new practices. Hence, good retailers ultimately convince the employees that the 'change' will not change the store's image but will change the employees' efficiency and effectiveness resulting in increased income.

One advice for young and aspiring retailers, remember nothing is impossible in retailing. It you are committed and walking on right track, you'll reach your destination. You can not only beat your competitors but can stop the new entrants to a large extent. Learn some of the nuts and bolts of successfully running your own retail business from experience and studies of various years.

1. **Store's Location:** Where are you located? Selecting a site for your new retail store is very crucial decision. A good location not only attracts the customers but reduces the transportation cost to a possible extent. Store location is the major decision to make your dreams come true. The retail stores can be located where there is a concentration of the target population.

The importance of retail store location becomes important due to these factors:

- Location decisions are irreversible.
- Involves large capital investment
- Affects human resources expenditures, i.e. salaries
- Influence transportation cost

While a retailer can change his merchandise mix, adjust prices, improve communication with customers and offer better services, once a retail store comes into existence, it is difficult to change the location. Therefore, after selecting the location and starting the store if it comes to know that store location is not appropriate, except having losses, there is no alternate. Hence, it is important that before taking a location decision, its managerial, technical and other prospects should be critically examined. Considering factors like population of the locality, purchasing power, nature of competition, rental values, municipal restrictions and value of the property, etc. also play a vital role in selection of good location.

2. Stocking your shelves: 'What to Buy' is a major query that needs to be answered? After selecting the location of a store, constructing the building, installing the racks, shelves and cabins, next big problem before every retail manager is to decide what items should be bought and kept on the shelves. Each product has varied brands and comes in various sizes, even price difference varies sharply. Therefore, selecting goods for store is tedious and time consuming exercise. This should not be taken lightly considering whatever we will display customers will buy. It takes years to build one loyal customer but one second to loose him. In this era, where everyone is busy and normally has shortage of time, retail store managers, must understand and provide the things which customers want not which are likable to them (retailers). Therefore, it is advisable that before buying merchandising for your store, you should visit the near by stores and have a look what type of items they are selling and what brands are placed in these stores. Besides this you can even talk to these retail managers, it seems tricky but you will realize instead of hiding, they will be ready to share their retail experience with you considering you will be in market near to them in the time to come.

3. Keep Yourself Updated but Practical: Don't commit the mistake when it comes to have the knowledge about latest trend. The things that are continuously shown, advertised and talked about in national and international medias will be suitable for your store. So buying these items, stocking on your shelves does not mean that you are up dated, you know and understand the latest trend. Satellite television and fashion magazines are not the final medias to take the decision about your merchandise. You should think will it be sellable in your store? Will customers afford this item? The best way to understand your customers is getting their feedback on continuous basis and direct interaction whenever you get the opportunity. This will enable to understand what customers really want. How much they can afford for a particular item. And instead of relying on televisions and fashion magazines, practical way is to visit the nearest stores and check the latest trend and new arrivals.

4. Right Person at right job: Check all management applicants' references carefully and ask for a resume to send before interviewing them. It will enable you to shortlist deserving candidates. Following points need to be considered while recruiting any retail employee.

- The candidate should be eligible to write and read.
- Preference should be given to experienced candidates.
- Ask about the basic concepts of retailing.
- Interview method should vary from position to position.
- For senior positions, give them some case lets and ask what will be their strategy to combat with the situation.
- Publish the situation requirement in a newspaper, if your budget allows you to do so. Because it will give you long list of applicants.

5. Store Loss prevention. As in the stores, every thing is on customers' display, there are chances of merchandise stealing which is very difficult to stop. You can not watch individuals' actions and body language. It is true that when hundreds of customers at a time visit to a retail store, what they do when they come to store, can not be watched thoroughly. This is not the only point of tension but employees' theft in retail store is also a major reason of retail loss. Your own employees whose duty is to safeguard the store's merchandise is not safe from them. What can you do? You can not stop it but can control to a large extent with the help of cameras (CCTV) and other retail store security devices. If the items are very small in size but costly, can be kept in locked visual cases. Make sure that beforc leaving the store in the evening after working hours, they should be inspected thoroughly by the security staff which is replaced after some interval. It is done in order to avoid any nexus between employees and security staff.

6. Merchandise Positioning: Once the merchandise is purchased and priced, must be positioned in the store at right place. Regular merchandise should be separated from sale items to avoid any confusion. Items should be placed in a way that customers should select them without disarranging the other displayed items. The prices must be clearly visible to the customers. It will help them to take decision whether to pick up the items or move to the next item. Most retail stores classify their merchandise as A, B, or C, based on their sales potential. Each store has its own arrangement of merchandise positioning. One positioning that is effective in one store may not work in all stores. As store's location, size and entry exit position vary from one store to another store. Further, store's signs can lessen the crowd at one place. Similarly, store front signage, can force the customers to stop at a particular point and see the items meant for display.

7. Efficient customer service: Retail industry belongs to service sector. When a customer walks into a particular store, he examines the displayed items, checks the price and quantity offered and compares various brands and products and then decides 'what to buy'. His buying decision is influenced by factors like image of the store, offerings, the ambience, and the level of service offered by the storc. While most of the elements of retail mix like product, price, place and promotion (4Ps) can be copied by the competitors very easily, the experience, a customer gets in the store can be rememberable for long time. This many times becomes the unique and competitive advantage over competitors. The example of excellent customer service provided by McDonald's outlets is not hidden from any body. Really they know how to take care of their customers. They love their customers and behave as they are known to us for a long time. Therefore, always treat your customers delicately and politely. Understand their feelings and emotions. They are the real source of mouth advertisement. Listen to them.

> A distinction is sometimes made between a 'customer' and a 'consumer'. It is to be noted that every shopper is a customer but not every one is a consumer. In another words, the customer is a person who does the buying but does not necessarily consume the product purchased.

Retail Store Effectiveness

Retailers can assess a particular retail outlet's sales effectiveness by examining these four retailing indicators:

1. Number of shoppers passing by on an average day
2. Percentage who enter the store
3. Percentage of those who actually shop
4. Average amount spent per sale

SUMMARY

The store is an important aspect of the retail business. It is the place of a market where customer purchase decisions are made. The perception, image and decision to continue to come to a particular store is formed here. From store's management point of view, to run the day to day activities of a store is a major element of the cost. Having a long term systematic planning and vision are therefore, must for the success of retail store business. For a retail store manager it is not important that he should put his efforts in increasing the sales but he should execute his day to day activities in an effective way. A retail store manager is not known by his name but the contribution they make to uplift the image of their stores among public and the government. The store operation manual is a vital document which gives you the detail what to do in a particular store? How to do it? When to do it? And who will do it? Therefore, precaution should be taken care of while preparing the retail manual. A well prepared operations manual ensures the smooth activities of a retail store and is the starting point of efficient store operations.

The main aspects of store operations include store administration and management of the premises, managing inventory, store layout and designing, managing sales promotions and customer services.

Managing a retail store is a complex activity. Retail store running cost is increasing year after. New and new stores are coming in picture and competition is becoming tough day by day. Profits are shrinking. Therefore, the role of retail manager becomes more crucial under following circumstances. Retail store managers are accountable for successfully running a retail store. Some store managers will run a section, while others are responsible for managing the whole stores. In the changing scenario, besides the routine tasks, you'll be responsible for implementing new techniques through which a store can cut store's expenses and increase profitability. Your enhanced role may be:

1. Analyzing sales records and predicating future sales on continuous basis
2. Ensuring high quality standards for overall quality, customer service and safe trading environment
3. Handling customer complaints as a basis of further growth
4. Having proper check on competitors' movements
5. Making certain that your store meets its sales targets as decided by management with mutual consent.
6. Managing sufficient merchandise levels
7. Organizing sales promotion drives at regular intervals
8. Recruiting, training and developing store staff whenever and wherever required
9. Searching for new ways to increase store's sales and pick up efficiency
10. Continuously managing and motivating staff

CASE STUDY 1

Contacting Customers

Jai Bharat Cinema is located in the cantonment area of Delhi Cantt. It is 20 years old air-conditioned theatre catering to cine goers mostly in Hindi and English movies. It has got a sitting capacity of 500 and as such large audiences are required to run it profitably. This problem does not arise for regular shows as mostly popular hits are screened.

The cantonment area comprises of people from all parts of the country and speaking different languages such as Telegu, Bengali, Punjabi, etc. The theatre has made it a practice to show regional language movies on Saturday evenings. The problem, which they face, is that not always it is profitable venture. As the booking for the regional language movie is made at least one week in advance and as the theatre has a choice, the management was wondering if they could get some kind of feedback from the respective communities about the popularity of the movie and probable large audience before they book it.

Someone suggested to them that they could have opinion poll by telephone interviews so as to reduce the risk of failure.

Q1. Do you think the use of telephonic interview will be a wise decision?

Q2. What are the other goods and services for which telephonic interview technique can be used?

Q3. Suppose it were retail outlet and retailer besides regular goods of daily use, want to sell things used on regional festivals like Onam, Durga Puja etc. Which method do you think would be suitable to collect the views of nearby peoples before entering into a new business line?

CASE STUDY 2

Automobile and Niche Marketing

With the world's leading manufacturer, Toyota, recognizing the power of niche within the automotive sector, the power of this form of marketing is entrenched. The launch of the new Auris, Toyota's money-spinning C-segment hatch, aside form the regular paths of mainstream magazines, prime time television and snappy shopping mall cafes, saw Toyota hit their target market directly with the use of bloggers. Toyota's change tactics comes from Director of Communications, Brian Eades and aims to change the staid image of the Japanese brand. A competition was held to entice regular bloggers to submit entries as to why they should attend the media launch of the stylish hatch, with three winners being selected. In turn, their reviews of the launch produced underground, automotive blogging coverage of the launch and car, targeting the computer-savvy, DINK (double income no kids), and a youthful informed crowd.

Custom publications benefit from the term 'niche' and further add to any company's brand strategy. The Retail Motor Industry Organization (RMI) is responsible for assisting its members with all matters surrounding the motor industry while ensuring members comply with a high level of business practice. With just shy of 8000 members, correspondence can be logistically challenging. For this reason, The RMI decided to start up their custom publication, Automobil. A monthly magazine that has been in existence for more than three decades, Automobil has grown exponentially from near newsletter status to 100 saddle stitched pages providing in-depth coverage on a spread across the automotive industry. Not only does this provide the RMI with the ideal tool to communicate with their members, but it, too, offers a revenue-generating device through its unique niche status. A recent survey completed by Automobil members saw an overwhelming response through fax, email and post. With 98% of members concurring that Automobil provides relevant and informative content and could be referenced for business purposes, the notion of niche is evident.

Considering that 8500 copies are printed each month and read by three or more people with the recipient businesses, Automobil is the ideal mechanism to reach the automotive trade industry. Figures confirmed this with 60% of respondents reporting that they based their business decisions on editorial content in the magazine, while a massive 78% reported that they were influenced by regular advertisers in the magazine. Furthermore, these respondents were not your anticipated grease monkeys. On the contrary, they fell between the LSM groups 8-10 and were in a position of management, ownership or directorship.

All these factors provide an extremely appealing sales pitch to get advertising in Automobil, and its continued growth is testimony to this. However, beyond the income, the brand awareness and communication levels achieved by the RMI to its members through Automobil is priceless. A set percentage of the magazine is decided upon and dedicated to RMI specific news. This provides a template from which topical industry information, special focus features and RMI data can be scribed.

The value added in providing members with a custom publication is insurmountable and can also be seen in industries such as law and accountancy where De Rebus, the law journal has become synonymous with industry-breaking news and foresight. Similarly, the South African Financial Markets journal provides all aspects relevant to those operating businesses within the financial arena. On joining the RMI, the arrival of Automobil in the company's post box is affirmation of membership and provides industry-leading-trends, new products, ideas and international operations structures – the start in the anticipated growth through joining the organization.

A Custom publication transcends the humble newsletter and evolves the base communication device into a profitable brand-aware marketing tool. Generating income through advertising, and maintaining contact with members, the RMI has benefited tremendously from Automobil. Furthermore, their members have gained useful information from the magazine pertaining to their relevant fields, which in turn creates a happier member base and stronger client relations for the RMI. Custom publications are a strong tool available for use in most fields, and the benefits are tremendous.

Question for Discussion:

1. What is Niche marketing?
2. As an automobile retailer, what would you propose to increase sales volume through Niche marketing?
3. Explain the role of RMI?

REVIEW QUESTIONS

True and False Questions

1. The retail store is a place where customers take a decision to buy a commodity at the spot.
2. Typically, the following five activities are carried in a store. These are:
   a. Store Administration and Management of Retail Floor

b. Inventory Management

c. Managing Receipts

d. Customer Service and

e. Sales Promotion

3. Store administration deals with various aspects which are necessary to sell the goods to clients without any disruption.
4. Registration Certificate is required to run a particular store. This gives an identity to a particular (name) store and the store is then known by that registered name.
5. The main objective of applying trade license is to purchase some day to day eatables like edible oil, sweets, readymade ice creams, candies, chocolates etc.
6. 'Dairy license' is required to purchase dairy products including cow/buffalo milk.
7. 'License for weight & measure' is required to use the weighing machines, weighing balance under weighing and measures rules of a particular state where the store is located.
8. 'License for rationing' allows a store to purchase items like food grains, sugar, salt, oils, pulses and dry fruits under retail sale.
9. 'License for frozen items' is required to buy all types of frozen items such as beef, fish, mutton, bacon, ham, etc.
10. Opening and closing activities are the secondary activities of a store.
11. Closing a retail store not only allows the retail managers to make some changes with regard to price, visual setting and arrangement in displayed items but allows the managers to manage new items and withdrawal of old/expired items in a store.
12. Inventory turnover is the ratio at which a retailer depletes and refills stock over a period of time.
13. A retail store manager is not responsible for the success or failure of a store.
14. Management of employee includes the management of store's employees working at various levels such as sales staff, store staff, cleaning staff and clerical staff.
15. Maintaining the sales environment involves implementation of store layout plans, displaying merchandise, replenishment/refilling of stock, visual merchandising task and maintaining the sales record effectively.
16. Cost minimization involves controlling expenses that are essential to run a store. This task of minimizing cost becomes necessary when store is running on high price policy, like in case of Wall Mart stores where EDHP (every day high prices) policy is being applied.
17. Communication skill means that the retail manager besides English (the global language), knows the Hindi and the local language (if any).

18. It has rightly been said that practice makes a man perfect. It is not the education but experience which speaks and reflects.
19. The concept of centralized retailer is applicable where retailer has only one store.
20. The central department is commonly known as '*policy-making department*' which carries out the initial planning of the strategic plan.
21. Marketing department separates the customers to the stores.
22. The logistics department provides retail services to the retail stores and deliveries from suppliers to retailers which commonly known as retail supply chain.
23. Operations master schedule (OMS) is a plan for retail store which systematically lists all the operating functions to be performed in the store from shutter up to shutter down.
24. Store maintenance includes all the activities involved in managing store's facilities such as management of exterior and interior physical facilities.
25. Energy management is all about increasing the expenses on lighting, heating and cooling the store area.
26. Store security relates to the security and safety of store staff and merchandise kept in the store.
27. A good location not only attracts the customers but increases the transportation cost to a possible extent.
28. Is it right to say that every shopper is a customer but not every one is a consumer.
29. Having a long term systematic planning and vision are not essential for the success of retail store business.
30. The store operation manual is a vital document which gives you the detail what to do in a particular store? How to do it? When to do it? and plan who will do it?

Answers

1. True	2. True	3. True	4. True
5. False	6. False	7. True	8. False
9. False	10. False	11. True	12. True
13. False	14. True	15. True	16. False
17. True	18. True	19. False	20. True
21. False	22. True	23. True	24. True
25. False	26. True	27. False	28. True
29. False	30. True		

Multiple Choice Questions

1. Deciding duty chart belongs to :
   (*a*) Pre store opening Activities (*b*) During Trading hours Activities
   (*c*) Post store close Activities (*d*) None of the above
2. Inventory turnover is equal to :
   (*a*) Sales/Profit (*b*) Sales/Inventory
   (*c*) Purchase/Profit (*d*) Purchase/Inventory
3. EDLP stands for :
   (*a*) Every day luxury prices (*b*) Every day low prices
   (*c*) Every day left prices (*d*) Every day low products
4. For Energy management what is recommended in a store :
   (*a*) Power Back up (*b*) CFL Tubes
   (*c*) Windows (*d*) Solar Energy
5. CCTVs are used for:
   (*a*) Energy Management (*b*) Inventory Management
   (*c*) Loss Prevention (*d*) Finance Prevention
6. The store manager is primarily responsible for:
   (*a*) Managing Inventory (*b*) Managing Employees
   (*c*) Cost Minimisation (*d*) All of the above
7. What attracts a customer:
   (*a*) Customer service (*b*) quality of merchandise
   (*c*) Both of the above (*d*) None of the above
8. Senior citizens are:
   (*a*) Old customers (*b*) Loyal customers
   (*c*) Aged People (*d*) Affluent people
9. A typical OMS describes:
   (*a*) Marketing Functions (*b*) Finance Functions
   (*c*) Human Resource Functions (*d*) Operating Functions
10. International relations with foreign stores are :
    (*a*) Mandatory (*b*) Not required
    (*c*) Wastage of money (*d*) Need of the time

Answers

1. a	2. b	3. b	4. b
5. c	6. d	7. c	8. c
9. c	10. d		

Answers to Check Your Progress

1. What is EDLP?
2. What is NOC?
3. Why trade license is required?
4. Why diary license is required?
5. What are trading hours?
6. What is CCTV?
7. What is OTB?
8. What is ICT?
9. What is OMS?
10. What is Energy Management?
11. Why CFL Lamps are becoming popular?
12. Who is consumer?
13. Why shelf is used in retail store?
14. What are 4Ps?
15. What is store maintenance?

Small Answer Questions

1. What do you mean by management of store premises?
2. Discuss few elements of retail store operations?
3. Why store manager should have some prior experience while applying for a new retail job?
4. What do you mean by opening or closing of a store?
5. What expectations management has from a retail store manager?
6. Explain the concept of store administration and management of the store floor?
7. Discuss some operational decisions during opening and closing a store?
8. Discuss pre store opening activities?
9. Briefly describe the activities take place during trading hours?
10. Highlight some of the post store activities? Why OMS is used?
11. What do you mean by store security?
12. What store maintenance includes?
13. Discuss the importance of energy management?
14. Explain the duties of security staff?
15. Write a short note on art of managing a retail store?

Long Answer Questions

1. Discuss the duties and responsibilities of a retail store manager in the today's competitive era?
2. Why it is said that managing a store is a complex activity? Critically analyze the some of the activities that take place during pre opening and post closing the store?
3. Being a retail graduate and after having enough experience in retail store management activities at various levels, now you plan to teach retail store management subject in a management school. During a discussion on effective retail store management, what suggestions and tips you would like to share with your students that result in retail store effectiveness. Also explain few indicators of measuring retail store effectiveness in a competitive arena?

UNIT 15

RETAIL LOSS PREVENTION

LEARNING OBJECTIVES

- Demonstrating the importance of retail loss prevention for a retailer
- Discussing the various forms of retail losses and theft
- Understanding the cost of store theft to a retail organization
- Knowing the ways to combat with retail theft
- Examining the challenges in retail loss investigations

"There is no better than adversity. Every defeat, every heartbreak, every loss, contains its own seed, its own lesson on how to improve your performance the next time."

Malcolm X

"An ounce of prevention is worth a pound of cure."

Henry de Bracton

INTRODUCTION

Retail store loss prevention or assets management is a line of work that is responsible for reducing inventory losses that arise within the stores without the knowledge of the retailer. Retail loss prevention manager ensures the overall security of the store to avoid any inventory shrinkage. Retail losses occur due to stealing (in retailing it is known as shoplifting), accounting frauds, vendor theft and employee theft. Similar to other forms of security, retail loss management professionals must continuously interact with store staff and store customers whenever any retail theft comes into notice with the objective of maximizing profits through reducing merchandise shrinkage. It is always risky for a store to accuse somebody carelessly considering what will happen if the store is on fault. Consequently utmost care and sense of professionalism is required while dealing with retail loss investigation cases.

AN INTRODUCTION TO RETAIL LOSS PREVENTION

Retail loss prevention is the store's initiative to control any kind of retail theft which is the main reason for increasing merchandise losses inside the retail stores. This is a sort of private investigation where loss prevention managers/professionals manage in-store security programs for the purpose of reducing merchandise losses due to shoplifting, employee theft, vendor theft, credit card theft, frauds and accounting mistakes. Retail loss prevention or RLP is a term used to describe all the methods adopted by loss prevention managers to keep merchandise shrinkage to a minimum. The objectives to appoint loss prevention managers are:

(a) To maximize profits by reducing shrinkage,

(b) To make proper provisions to stop store lifting,

(c) To develop a system within the retail store that discourages store's employees to steal any merchandise, and

(d) To analyze the store's records continuously to expose any type of internal fraud and/or accounts discrepancies.

Thus store loss prevention manager is a professional who is responsible for reducing merchandise losses, leading the losses control programs for the retail store and also to ensure the safety of customers, employees and merchandise. The loss prevention manager in case of centralized retail stores, reports directly to the regional loss prevention manager sitting in the head office. The loss prevention manager is entitled to perform following responsibilities:

- To reduce merchandise shrinkage within the retail store.
- To hire, train and supervise the loss prevention team.
- To develop, implement and execute various loss prevention programs from time to time.
- To ensure effective use of CCTV cameras, alarms and others security instruments installed in the store.
- To ensure physical security of facilities to keep a check on retail theft.
- To build co-ordination and proper partnerships with store management to implement LP (loss prevention) programs.
- To ensure that all in and outside retail theft cases are investigated and resolved in accordance with state administration and local laws.
- To have a strong liaison with local law enforcement agencies.

ESSENTIALS/EXPECTATIONS FOR STORE LOSS PREVENTION MANAGER

- He must have some prior retail store loss prevention experience.
- He must have good communication skills, leadership qualities and knows about motivating and training skills.
- He must be willing to work on weekends, holidays, festive seasons and flexible working hours.

- He must be ready to travel whenever required including overnight stay.
- He must have exposure to ICT (Information and Communication Technology).
- He should be expert in the use of retail security devices like CCTVs etc.
- He should have good track record of reducing, investigating and controlling merchandise shrinkage.

TYPES OF RETAIL THEFT

Shoplifting and employee theft are the two common reasons of excessive costs in the newborn Indian retail industry. The employees who are responsible for the safety of store's merchandise have been carrying merchandise with them. This retail theft is not only prevalent in India but European retail stores also claim that shoplifting is the main reason of their excessive costs while employee theft accounts for fifty percent of the loss.

Most of the shoplifters and store's employees when caught red handed rationalize that the store merchandise is expensive and over-priced. The reality is that the retail theft actually damages the store's bottomline and forces the store to increase their unit prices. The retail stores have no provision to combat with retail theft and we as consumers ultimately suffer by paying more due to retail theft. According to a survey conducted by Efficient Customer Response (ECR), in Europe, the top six measures used by retailers to reduce shrinkage are:

- Cash protection equipment: safes' caches
- Electronic article surveillance equipment
- Employee integrity checks
- Intruder alarm systems
- Live closed circuit television (CCTV)
- Mystery shoppers

Retailers in India are increasingly adopting these measures. Globally best-practice Organizations embed loss prevention into every facet of retail operations and this is what Indian organizations should work towards as well. Broadly store thefts are classified under three categories:

(a) Shoplifting
(b) Employee Theft
(c) Card Theft

(A) Shoplifting

Shoplifting is a type of retail crime that occurs when somebody steals the store's merchandise displayed in store for the purpose of selling. Only in USA, shoplifting from retail outlets costs owners an estimated loss of thirteen to fifteen billion US dollars annually. Shoplifting usually occurs when stealers conceal store's merchandise in their purses, pockets, bags or garments. This is not the only list but shoplifting may occur by variety of methods. Anyone can be a shop stealer. It has no relation with age, religion or sex. Reports have shown that most of the shop lifters are young and amateurs. They come in all ages, sexes, shapes and sizes and vary in educational and economical status and in religious backgrounds. Some shoplifters steal the store's goods for excitement, some steal due to unaffordability, some because they have no other source of income, some steal out of necessity and some people steal store merchandise to show their friends and relatives that they are very clever and smart they can befool anyone and anywhere. In India, it has been found that some shoplifters are opportunistic and some even are of unsound mind and do not know its consequences. Some professional shoplifters work in small teams, use force and fear and commit take-and-run retail thefts. The term 'professional' here is used in the sense that these people steal merchandise for their bread and butter and like other professions, they are expert in their stealing jobs.

Cost of stealing to retail store

Shoplifting from retail stores (including employee and vendor stealing) cost Indian retailers crores of rupees per year. Comparative to big brands, independent retail stores are most successful in controlling shoplifting due to their personal interest. Retail loss varies from store to store, brand to brand and type of retail merchandise sold. According to one estimate, retail merchandise loss in India ranges from 0.5% - 2.5% of the gross retail sales. This is also the reason that in the last few months, some of the well known retail store chains have gone out of business due to increasing daily operating costs and their inability to control retail theft losses. The worse part is that the cost of these retail losses is passed on to customers like us.

Shoplifting cases differ by merchandise type but can account for about one-forth of the total merchandise shrinkage. When we count employee and vendor theft, this average estimates more than one-third of the total store loss.

Prevention of Shoplifting

Studies and surveys have shown that in metros where many retail stores have flourished, as many as one in ten customers is a shoplifter. The shoplifters commit an average of twenty five thefts before they are caught red handed. To control retail store theft, retailers in big cities sometimes take extreme measures. Most of the big retailers in India employ plain clothed security staff to observe customers' actions while they shop. Many retail stores use closed circuit TV cameras and other electronic surveillance devices to watch the customers' intention. Some big retail stores use Electronic Article Surveillance (EAS) devices that are attached to the products displayed and cause alarms to blow if not deactivated by retail cashiers or concerned floor staff. Some of the retailers have the practice of displaying costly and small items in glass locked enclosures like diamond watches, imported perfumes, pens, liquor, purses and cigarettes.

In apparel retailing, retailers use long cables or hanger locks that are to be unlocked by the floor staff before any expensive piece of clothing be inspected by the customer.

Most of the first time visitors and aged persons get annoyed when a store security staff or sales executive first count their items before entering and exiting the try room. It obviously is annoying when merchandise you wish to try on has an electronic surveillance device on it and sometimes make difficult to have a proper look of the item. It is very disgusting when a sales executive follow your each move within the store. Therefore, it is important for customers that they should not take it otherwise but be patient with stores that adopt these ways to control store theft, otherwise they will be left with no option but to hike prices. If these tactics make you feel uncomfortable and annoyed, think how the shoplifter will feel. Therefore, shoplifters before targeting a store make certain where anti-theft devices are placed. If they feel insecured, they left the store and go to the next store.

Shoplifters prefer retail stores with less anti-theft devices and places where they have ease of privacy and merchandise accessibility. In nutshell, this is the demand of the day but no doubt in saying that these anti-theft devices make shopping experience dull if applied thoughtlessly and in excess.

The Shoplifter Detention

For a store staff, the task of physically detaining and arresting shoplifters is not free from risks and challenges. As at the time of physical detention, it becomes difficult to catch an aggressive shoplifter. No one can imagine while physical detention how a shoplifter will react and oppose. Sometimes during such detentions, customers and even store employees' lives could be at risk if an aggressive shoplifter tries to throw displayed items in order to escape. Therefore, to avoid such situations, two or more loss prevention employees should work very close to the suspect and while speaking in a calm manner should make shoplifter realize that this is an unfair practice and he/she should return store's merchandise. It is not recommended to chase a shoplifter especially if before escaping he has thrown the stolen item. Further, chasing a shoplifter on a road or in a vehicle has never been a good idea and can be fatal and expensive as compared to the cost of the stolen item. In India, such cases have not come in picture at large but possibility of retail theft cannot be overruled.

Shoplifter Detention Mechanism

To establish a sound shoplifting detention mechanism and to avoid false detention claims, a retailer should follow these three globally accepted steps before detaining someone suspect of shop lifting:

1. Inspection
2. Detection and
3. Collection

Step 1: When a customer enters into your store, make sure that he is not having any item in his bag, purse, pocket and in his hands to avoid any confusion. This is a very important step but most of the retailers miss it. This step usually prevents a normal mistake that occurs when a customer comes to a store not for buying but return counter first. Therefore, you must inspect a customer and watch continuously his move. Floor staff normally misunderstand when they see a customer putting an item in his/her pocket or purse and does not realize that innocent customer brought the item with him/her only for the purpose of comparison.

Step 2: You must detect a shoplifter when he tries to hide, carry away or exchange any merchandise. You must identify him when he wears any item by removing security tag, or hide it in clothes or in bags. Shoplifting sometimes occurs because of conversion, for instance, consuming or eating food before buying. An exception to the detection rule is inside a try room. The point to consider here is how many items go into the try room and how many items are returned out of it.

Step 3: You must have continuous observation of the suspected shoplifter. Sometimes, trained and professional shoplifters leave the concealed item without your observation, if they find themselves being watched. You, after such physical detention may be worried of not finding anything on inspection. The best and sensible practice is that if you loose sight for a minute for any reason, show your presence to the shoplifter and give him/her an opportunity to leave the item (merchandise) and go out of the store immediately. This can be done by mere announcement or by turning up their mobile to alert the shoplifter that he is standing near plain-clothed security guards.

If you follow these three steps mechanism, your store will have no problem in combating shoplifters. Depending upon the type of locality and geographical conditions, store can install various EAS systems and can develop their own security mechanism to beat shop lifters.

Retailers Loose $5.8 Bn. in Shoplifting and Thefts

Despite all the closed-circuit television cameras, electronic article surveillance (EAS) and security personnel, retailers continue to wage a losing battle against shoplifters, says Jack L. Hayes International Inc., a leading loss prevention and inventory shrinkage control consulting firm.

Among 24 major retailers surveyed by the firm, which represented 13,313 stores nationwide (U.S.) with combined 2005 annual sales of more than $519 billion, a staggering $5.8 billion (or 1.6%) was lost to shoplifters and employee theft. But according to the survey, an even more worrisome concern to retailers is the growing threat posed by dishonest employees. In fact, the survey shows that for every 26 employees, one was caught with a hand in the cookie jar in 2005.

The survey also found that the number of employees caught stealing in 2005 rose to 68,994, an increase of 11.4 percent over the previous year. By the same token, $49.9 million were recovered as a result of those apprehensions, an increase of 17.8 percent over 2004. Mark Doyle, president of Jack L. Hayes International, says the $5.8 billion figure was derived by multiplying total sales by 1.6 percent, which is the average shrinkage according to the 2005 National Retail Security Survey conducted by the University of Florida. Doyle says the total theft loss amount may be even higher. "We took 30% (against usual 20%) for paperwork and systems errors. If anything, we were more conservative."

"The dollar losses are staggering," says Doyle, adding that in the end everybody gets hurt because retail theft "drives consumer prices higher." Look for the cat-and-mouse posturing between retail surveillance and shoplifters to get even dicier as the holiday season approaches. "Without looking at hard data, retail thefts tend to increase during all busy shopping seasons," said an expert.

Source: *www. indiaretailbiz.wordpress.com, appeared on October 26, 2006.*

Shoplifting Beating Tips

Beating shoplifting has always been a complex subject but can be made easier if we consider these handy tips:

- **Fix retail fixtures**: Fix your retail fixtures in such a way that floor staff and supervisors should be in a position to look down almost every aisle in the retail store. Use convex mirror to have the view of any unavoidable hiding places behind the fixtures or otherwise as shoplifters require privacy to hide merchandise.
- **Lock up small and expensive items:** It is a well known saying that the smaller and more valuable merchandise are more pleasant to shoplifter. Make practice of displaying such small sized but costly items in a locked showcase. Genuine customers will not object to this as they know the essence of locking, they will request you to show if they want to have a close look before buying.
- **Return with receipts:** Some shoplifters steal the merchandise with the intention to return for a cash refund. This can be tackled easily by producing a cash receipt for all returns. This appears to be an unhealthy sales practice as far as quality customer service is concerned but it is the demand of the day. Follow a policy of same-item-only exchanges without one that makes the real customers to exchange their wrong size or color but not to the stealer.
- **Monitor your try room:** A try room is an ideal place to conceal store's merchandise that is kept for display. If shoplifters took the merchandise into the try room they can have ample privacy and even a good mirror to tell how tactfully he has concealed the merchandise. Make provisions that your try rooms do not have any place or chance to remove security labels and exchange for price tags. As shoplifters normally place several items of clothing on a single hanger and then change a price tags having higher prices with those of lower prices and then pay the bills. Buying an item of one thousand and paying three hundred rupee is also a part of shoplifting and a hard nut to crack on the counter of cashiers where long queue problem always prevails.

- **Use of creative signage:** Signages are not only used for sales promotion but if used differently can stop shoplifting to a great extent. Knowing that shoplifters are not honest people, do not hesitate about bringing the truth a little on your retail signage. For Instance, in your retail store, you can post the classic signage having slogans such as "smile, you are on CCTV" now or "use your camera or not, it does not make any difference, or simply a warning message to shop lifters on electronic displays saying "102 shoplifters caught this year, Are you the next one?"
- **Change directions of Clothing hanger:** It has been found that one of the easiest way the shoplifters can steal a large number of clothing is to pick up the clothing items displayed or kept near the exit gate and run out of the store towards a waiting vehicle before the store's staff become active. Therefore, to avoid such clothing theft, the way is to alternate the directions of every hanger on the display, mainly of those that are close to the store's exit. The advantage of such an arrangement is to make it difficult to quickly grab an entire lot of clothing from a circular rack.

(B) Employee Theft

Employee theft is a term that is commonly used in retailing business when an employee of a retail store conceals merchandise, cash, food, equipments installed, or supplies while on duty. According to Indian law, employee theft is akin to theft as the basis of the crime is same. To commit employee theft, he/she must steal the item and take it outside the store without paying its price. Employee theft, like shoplifting happens by hiding merchandise in lunch boxes, purses, pockets, inner garments and taking it out from the store without paying the cost.

> *"Most shrinkage is due to our store personnel. Employee integrity is an area of concern for us."*
>
> *Founder, department store*

Employee theft actually has various dimensions. It not only happens by concealing of any item but also by stealing cash, fraud, allowing known/others to take merchandise without paying, eating food and by refund, cheque or credit cards fraud. Whatever the method is used, it will be counted as employee theft. Reports have shown that store employees can be more harmful than shoplifters because they are trusted and know the ins and outs of the store security measures.

Impact of Employee Theft

According to the recent National Retail Security Survey Report from the University of Florida, employee theft again indicates the most crucial area as the most significant source of inventory shrinkage[1].

[1] *www.integriview.com*

The report reveals the following facts:

Figure 15.1

Inventory Shrinkage Sources

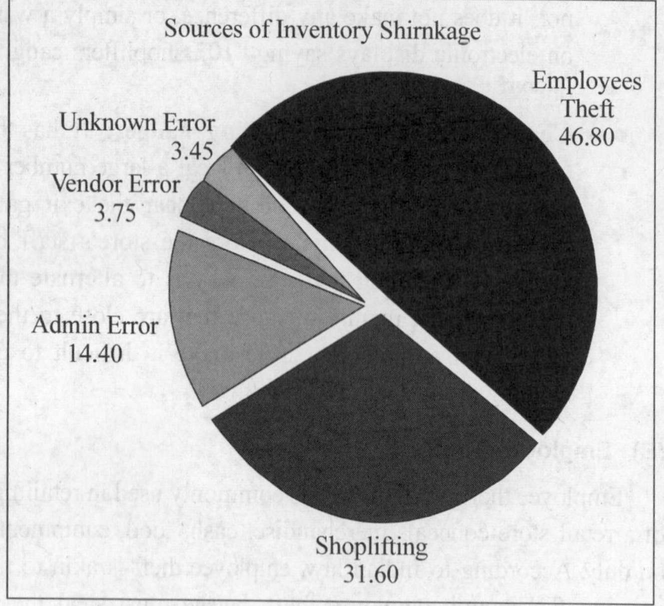

1. Retailers attributed 47% of their inventory shrinkage to employee theft;
2. Total employee theft cost retailers $19 billion annually;
3. 16 out of 24 types of retail chains reported employee theft rates well above the 47% average;
4. No other form of larceny costs US citizens more than employee theft;
5. Losses from employee theft are 30% higher than losses from shoplifting.

Profile of Employee theft

Employee theft has no relation with age, designation, height, color and time the employee has spent with the store. They come in all ages, shapes, sexes, sizes, educational levels, religions and financial status. It is not easy to predict who will steal the merchandise on the basis of their economic and demographic situations. Teenagers are more dishonest or the aged never has been an easy forecast. But a retailer can make his assessment on the basis of his experience in retailing line, employee's conduct, integrity and commitment. Besides this employee's past track record, in terms of his conduct, devotion and commitment are the best measures to judge and provides his future behavior.

Retail store employees have unlimited access to merchandise. They can therefore steal merchandise or cash very easily, as they know the best time to steal and best place to hide. If we study the reasons for employees becoming dishonest, we found that their moral character, loyalty, respect for the employer, wish to be viewed as loyal employee and their future prospects in terms of promotion are the common reasons. Reports support the evidence that unlike European stores, in India, merchandise shrinkage is comparatively less in stores with less attrition rate and less part time employees.

In India, the employee theft comparative to shoplifting is not alarming because employees have the fear of getting caught red handed. Further, the risks of getting fired, being detention and jailed, fined and paying penalties, besides public insult are other barriers to dishonesty.

Employee Loss Prevention

Employee theft has been a continuous challenge for retailers. The retailers wish to prevent but unable to understand how to go ahead. Initially a retailer should design a loss prevention mechanism that eliminates the opportunity for employee theft, desire and encouragement for employee theft. Basically loss prevention mechanism should involve sound procedure for recruitment, training and development and continuous employees' monitoring at all levels. Loss prevention methods that are clearly defined, articulated, and fully applied can reduce the chances, desire and motivation to a great extent.

According to Jack L. Hayes International (a well known USA based loss prevention and inventory shrinkage control consulting firm), "*shoplifting and employee theft are serious crimes which continue to take their toll on retailer's bottom-line profits. These types of losses continue to hurt our economy, costing consumers higher prices at the cash register, and causing a loss of jobs when retailers are forced to close stores or even go out of business*[2]."

Experts' Views

Experts opine that the very first step to curb employee theft is to create a climate atmosphers of honesty & dedication within the organization. Retailers should convey it to its employees and aspirants that fraudulent behavior will not be accepted in any case and implement programs to make certain they are employing candidates who would not be considered high risk for stealing from the company stores or acting aggressively towards customers, store employees or executives. Store employees who are honest tend to follow the rules and rarely steal from their employers.

Merchandise theft by employees is often caught by CCTV cameras (Figure 15.2). The items stolen by retail store employees normally are small sized but expensive ones. The store ware houses, fitting rooms have more chances of employees' theft and can be made tough by using CCTV cameras placed in the areas of high opportunity for employee theft.

Figure 15.2: A View of Various CCTVs Used in Retail Stores

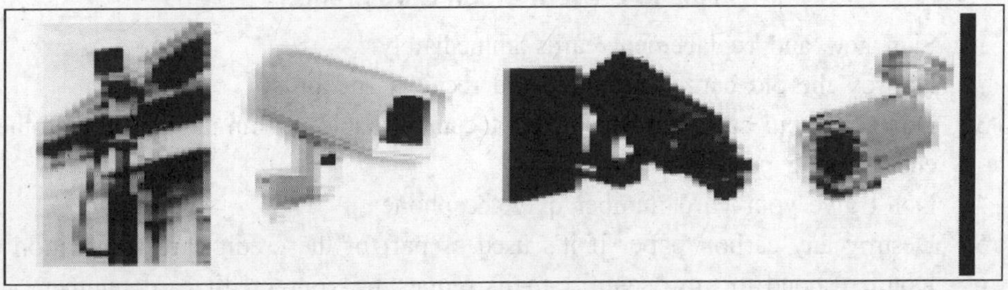

[2] *www.integriview.com*

(C) Credit Card Theft

Credit card theft is becoming popular in big cities where these are used at large scale. Credit card theft is a term that is used to purchase store's items through stolen credit cards directly or through e-retailing. The reasons for increasing credit card theft are many. Sometimes retailers in order to offer quick service relax their procedures for inspecting the authenticity of credit cards. Also purchasing store's merchandise personally/ first hand offers a credit card thief some level of secrecy as compared to e-retailing where he is supposed to mention his billing address.

The inherent problems with credit cards theft lie in lack of employees' training. Employees' sometimes do not enquire the details about credit cards and sometimes even do not verify the signatures. Due to loopholes in the Indian laws, most retailers are not liable for the use of any stolen card. Therefore, in order to maintain their customer base, they even do not verify card holder signature and address.

Online Fraud

Online fraud is costing retailers £580 million a year, which could rocket to £5.1 billion by 2010, according to research by Visa voucher firm 3V in conjunction with IMRG. Almost two-thirds of online retailers have fallen victim to internet fraudsters and it is costing some of them about 5% of their annual turnover.

More than one third said that they have experienced an increase in fraud since the introduction of Chip and PIN on the high street. About 40% of retailers said that the threat of being hit by fraud is becoming a massive concern.

While two-third of retailers are increasing their online security measures, one fifth feel systems introduced in the past three years by payment providers are placing an increased burden on the consumer. More than 60% said customers have difficulty signing up to the likes of Verified by Visa and Mastercard's Secure Code, citing reasons such as the need to remember multiple passwords.

Source: *www.imagesretail.com*

Tips to Prevent Credit Card Fraud

1. Sign new and replacement cards immediately
2. Destroy the old cards and shred old receipts and bills
3. Don't fax your card number. Faxed document could remain in sight at the other end for long periods of time
4. Don't give your card number over the phone
5. Destroy any carbon paper if it's used as part of the credit card transaction
6. Don't respond to any 'scam' e-mails requesting your credit card number
7. Never e-mail your card number to anyone

8. A good option for discouraging theft is to choose a credit card that includes your photo and signature
9. If there are mistakes or unauthorized items on your statement, you have the right to challenge them
10. Don't leave your card lying around your home or office where others can see it, and don't lend it to anyone. If you want someone else to be authorized to use your account, make those arrangements through your card issuer. Only give your credit card number when you are actually making a purchase.
11. If your card is lost, stolen, or you suspect fraudulent use, call the credit card company's 24 hour hotline immediately to block its use

Source: *Mail Today & www.fraud.org*

CHALLENGES IN RETAIL LOSS INVESTIGATION

Many big sized retailers have set up centralized control structure to combat store loss prevention. Typical centralized system consists of few floor level investigators, who are appointed generally on contract basis. Next comes the retail store loss prevention manager who heads the loss prevention department. These managers are commonly ex-employees who have enough experience in the related field. In case of centralized stores, head office prefers to appoint ex- army or ex-police personnel who work as a regional security officer with significant amount of loss prevention experience.

Indian retail industry is facing various problems in the field of loss investigation because firstly there are no proper guidelines from state governments and secondly because of the shortage of eligible staff. Some retailers have renamed their loss prevention department to "Assets protection department". Assets protection department usually hire the services of private security agencies by using more visible means of security, such as well uniformed security guards standing outside the retail stores. Following are the common challenges faced by Indian retail industry:

(a) Lack of experienced personnel
(b) Lack of support from government machinery
(c) Shortage of training to security guards
(d) Wage associated with entry level investigators is insufficient
(e) Even compensation scale at manager level is not sufficient as retailers consider loss prevention department as an expenditure rather than human asset.
(f) Loss prevention staff sees themselves as being pro-active, whereas security agencies are usually reactive in nature.
(g) The use of IT applications in managing retail activities is quite negligible. The level of bar-code usage is also largely due to retailers' initiatives of printing these codes at their warehouses, unlike in developed countries where all the suppliers print bar codes. Most retailers do not have integrated IT systems today. Few national level retailers have few IT systems in the areas of supply chain management, vendor development, merchandising and inventory management.

Figure 15.3
IT Usage in Indian Retailing

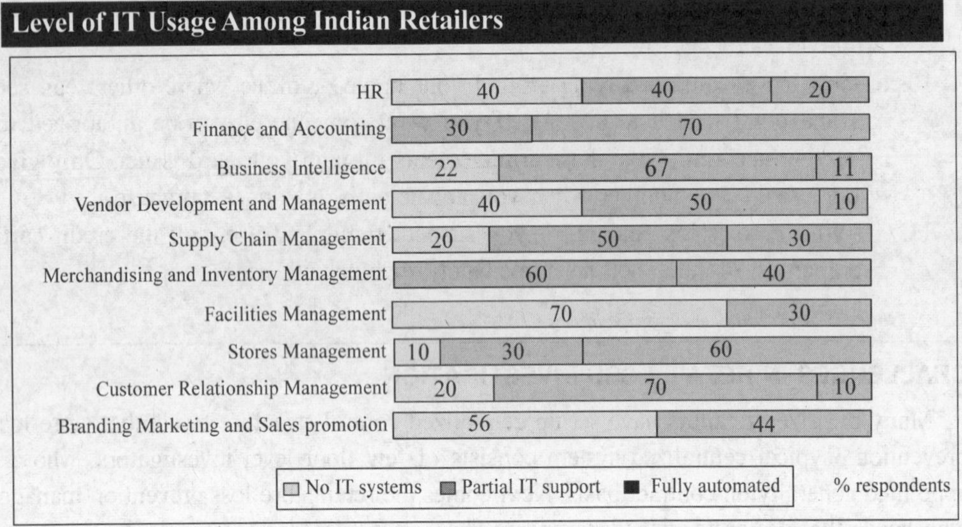

SOURCE : *KPMG in India Retail Survey 2005*

Hence, the shortage of manpower required to investigate and to make shoplifters' detention safely. Further, security guards are under the impression that the potential consequences associated with investigation and detention are not worth for near minimal wage and thus they sometimes knowingly ignore, quit, hesitate to make any detention or, worse yet, they themselves act dishonestly. In short, the objective of bag check by security guards is often questioned.

SUMMARY

The practice of reducing the amount of theft and merchandise shrinkage within a retail store is known as retail loss prevention (RLP). Conducting a retail store merchandise inspection, checking employees' bags before leaving the store, and installing security scanners at various possible locations within the store are examples of controlling retail losses. Shoplifting and employee theft are the two major reasons of increasing costs to Indian retail stores. Shoplifters sometimes can also be store employees and among security staff those have the knowledge of store's ins and outs. Reports have shown that, in the united state of America, out of eleven shoppers, one is a shoplifter. India is also not an exception where due to lack of loss prevention awareness, theft figures are becoming worse year after year.

REVIEW QUESTIONS

True and False Questions

1. Retail store loss prevention or assets management is a line of work that is responsible for increasing inventory losses that arise within the stores without the knowledge of the retailer.
2. Retail loss prevention manager ensures the overall security of the store to avoid any inventory shrinkage.
3. Retail losses don't occur on account of stealing, accounting frauds, vendor theft and employee theft.
4. Store loss prevention manager is a professional who is responsible for increasing merchandise losses, leading the losses control programs for the retail store and also to ensure the safety of customers, employees and merchandise.
5. The loss prevention manager in case of centralized retail stores, does not reports directly to the regional loss prevention manager sitting in the head office.
6. Shoplifting and employee theft are the two common reasons of excessive costs in the newborn Indian retail industry.
7. Shoplifting is a type of retail crime that occurs when somebody steals the store's copyrights and patents displayed in store for the purpose of selling.
8. Electronic Article Surveillance (EAS) device is attached to the products displayed and cause alarms to blow if not deactivated by retail cashiers or concerned floor staff.
9. In apparel retailing, retailers use long cables or hanger locks that are to be unlocked by the floor staff before any expensive piece of clothing be inspected by the customer.
10. Employee theft is a term that is commonly used in retailing business when a customer of a retail store conceals merchandise, cash, food, equipments installed, or supplies while on duty.
11. Credit card theft is a term that is used to purchase store's items through stolen credit cards directly or through e-retailing.
12. The practice of reducing the amount of theft and merchandise shrinkage within a retail store is known as retail loss prevention (RLP).
13. Conducting a retail store merchandise inspection, checking employee bags before leaving the store, and installing security scanners at various possible locations within the store are examples of wasting retail employees' precious time.
14. Retail store employees have limited access to merchandise.
15. A try room is an ideal place to conceal store's merchandise that is kept for display.

Answers

1. False	2. True	3. False	4. True
5. False	6. True	7. False	8. True
9. True	10. False	11. True	12. True
13. False	14. False	15. True	

Multiple Choice Questions

1. Retail store loss prevention is commonly known as :
   (*a*) Asset Management (*b*) Inventory Management
   (*c*) Merchandise Management (*d*) Cash Management
2. Retail Loss can be minimised through:
   (*a*) CCTVs (*b*) Burgers and Alarms
   (*c*) None of the above (*d*) Both of the above
3. Shoplifting occurs when:
   (*a*) Somebody steals the merchandise
   (*b*) Somebody without paying leaves the store
   (*c*) Somebody changes the price tag and pays for low priced goods
   (*d*) All of the above
4. Employee theft term is used for:
   (*a*) Employees only
   (*b*) Customers only
   (*c*) Both employees and customers
   (*d*) None of the above
5. The example of Employee theft involves:
   (*a*) Stealing cash (*b*) Fraud
   (*c*) Eating food without paying (*d*) All of the above
6. The primary reason for retail theft is:
   (*a*) Goods are expensive (*b*) some have no source of income
   (*c*) Excitement (*d*) All of the above
7. Beating shoplifting can be made easier by:
   (*a*) fixing retail fixtures (*b*) Lock up small and expensive items
   (*c*) using warning signage (*d*) All of the above
8. Reports have shown that most of the shop lifters are:
   (*a*) Middle aged (*b*) Young and amateurs
   (*c*) Employees (*d*) Uneducated

9. Shoplifters prefer retail store places where they have:
   (*a*) Ease of privacy (*b*) Costly things displayed
   (*c*) Crowd of people (*d*) Easy exit
10. Retail loss prevention is the primarily responsibility of:
   (*a*) store manager (*b*) floor staff
   (*c*) security people (*d*) All of the above

Answers

1. a	2. d	3. d	4. a
5. d	6. d	7. d	8. b
9. a	10. d		

Answers to Check Your Progress

1. What is shrinkage?
2. What is RLP?
3. What is CCTV?
4. Who is shoplifter?
5. What is ICT?
6. What is ECR?
7. What is EAS?
8. What is try room?
9. List three thefts?
10. What is investigation?
11. What is liaison?
12. Who is employee?
13. What is ATM?
14. What is detection?
15. What is credit card?

Small Answer Questions

1. What are the objectives of retail loss prevention?
2. Explain the responsibilities of loss prevention manager?
3. What are the expectations from a loss prevention manager?
4. What do you mean by shoplifting?
5. How to prevent shoplifting?
6. Explain the shop lifting detection mechanism?
7. Give some tips to combat shoplifting?
8. Explain the meaning of employee theft?

9. What is credit card theft?
10. How try room act as a place for stealing?

Long Answer Questions

1. Explain the term retail loss prevention? What are its types? And explain the challenges faced by retailers in retail loss investigation with suitable examples wherever necessary?
2. Some experts say that installing electronic devices in retail stores only increase the store's operational expense and are of no significant use? Are you satisfied with this statement if no then give examples or narrate circumstances where you've come across with incidents/news where thieves were detected by use of these electronic devices?

Appendix

Exhibit 15.1: Strategies for Managing Dishonest Retail Employees

Discovering a trusted employee has been dishonest can be an employer's worst nightmare. All businesses that employ staff are at risk purely because of the 'people factor'. This article focuses on employee dishonesty in retail settings and provides practical suggestions for prevention and detection, as well as for creating an honest workplace.

The risk in retail

In a retail business, the risk is greater where the following factors apply:

- Employees are young
- Pre-employment screening is hasty and poor
- Access to company's cash and product is high
- There is a high level of trust to open and close stores and handle money
- Day to day supervision is low
- Computer literacy (understanding how to manipulate point of sale systems) is extensive.

In a retail business, internal exposure can well outstrip external theft or shop stealing.

One way of dealing with internal theft is to engage the services of a qualified investigator.

Investigations can range in complexity and scope from staff theft of Rs 100 from the register, to systematic long-term thousand rupee fraud by a member of senior management.

Who are the risk factors?

There is no specific profile for a dishonest employee, but in every workplace at some time there will be employees who fall into one or more of the following categories:

- **'In the right (or wrong) circumstances I will'** – generally not dishonest, however in a significant personal situation, for example unexpected debt, this employee may resort to dishonesty at work.
- **'If I can I will'** – based on the opportunities that present themselves, risk of detection at the time and how loyal the employee feels.
- **'Where there's a will there's a way'** – dedicated to dishonesty in the workplace. This employee has justified to themselves that he or she is entitled to what they take and accepts the risk of detection.
- **'This is what I do – I want more than just my pay from my employment'** – a serial offender. This employee has a history of dishonesty in the workplace, generally uses the same methods and moves on in search of the next employer whose employment practices are not thorough enough to discover this history.

The culture, management and systems of an organisation can often provide an effective filtering system, deterring and de-motivating some of these people, or vice versa.

What is the scope?

Every year loss prevention management companies conduct hundreds of investigations resulting in the following outcomes:

- Dismissal
- Civil restitution
- Criminal charges

So where do these people go?

Generally back into retail service.

How do they do this if they were detected being dishonest in their last job?

They seek out employers who don't analyze their resume too closely, don't conduct pre-employment screening, and don't do thorough reference checks.

What happens if their past is discovered after they have been employed?

If they have not 'failed to disclose', that is: have not been asked to disclose previous dismissals, charges etc, and they have not lied about their previous employment, this new information does not constitute grounds for dismissal.

We see too often an investigation conducted in one business resulting in a suspect being identified/dismissed/charged, and subsequently find that the same person is a suspect/offender in an investigation in another business, often involving the same method of dishonesty. Exacerbating this situation is where the employee actually nominates the previous employer on their resume, and a reference check, that would have exposed the negative history and precluded the hire, is not done.

CASE STUDY – REPEAT OFFENDER

In July 2006, a 23-year-old female, who we will call 'Emily', was employed as an Assistant Store Manager for a national level retail chain.

A day's cash takings were discovered missing at her store and an investigation was initiated.

It was discovered that up to eight staff had access to the missing takings over a period of two days.

These staff was interviewed, and Emily was identified as a 'most likely' suspect based on the instincts of the investigator. However, due to lack of evidence, she remained on-staff until another incident occurred involving Emily's misappropriation of product and breach of staff purchase policy. She was dismissed.

Take two

In February 2007, we conducted an investigation for another national retailer, again involving the theft of a day's cash takings from a Wednesday's trade, with the theft discovered at banking time on Friday. Emily had been the Assistant Manager in this store for a period of six weeks. On the Thursday of that week, she had been involved in a public dispute with another staff member, which resulted in her being 'let go' that day as she was on probation and had demonstrated inappropriate conduct.

The investigation identified that the staff who had access to the takings were limited to the long-time store manager, and Emily.

The manager and other staff were interviewed, and it became apparent that Emily, for a period of a few hours on the Thursday, had retained possession of her safe key after her dismissal.

Motive pointed to Emily as the most likely suspect, but it was critical that the business establish who the offender was, in order to maintain trust in the store manager.

The investigator contacted Emily who participated in an interview where the situation was outlined to her and questions were asked.

She subsequently admitted to taking the cash from the safe in the final hours of Thursday's trade, and spending the majority of the money that she had stolen.

She insisted that this was a split-second decision and was something totally out of character.

She agreed that she owed the total amount to the business and a plan was agreed to for the repayment of the money, including recovery of remaining cash from her home, withdrawal of funds from an ATM, and authority for forfeiture of part of the pay owed to her on dismissal.

At the same time her resume was re-examined and it was discovered that she had omitted listing her previous employer (where the earlier theft and dismissal had occurred) and had listed another retailer as her employer during this period.

The investigator established that the referee nominated was Emily's partner, who at the time was store manager of the retailer listed on her resume. Emily had never worked for the company. This fiction covered that period of employment.

Not surprisingly, when the client learned all of this, he opted to report the matter to police for criminal prosecution.

Reflection

One might imagine Emily to have some sort of readily identifiable criminal element.

The opposite was true. She was presentable; she spoke well, was undertaking tertiary studies, and had a very convincing backup story with suitable responses to cover likely questions about her employment history.

These situations are not unusual.

Strategies for managing dishonest employees

The first step is to accept that the risk is always present and that the strategy focus should be on:

Prevention and early detection

Prevention strategies include:

- Pre-employment screening – knowing who you are hiring so that you don't put someone into your business who has been dishonest in someone else's, and/or has fabricated his or her resume or application to cover past dishonesty.
- Honesty policies – clearly communicating a comprehensive honesty policy, specifically what the business expects from its employees in terms of both dishonest and unacceptable practices, and getting this document acknowledged as a condition of employment before the candidate commences.
- Adequate supervision – ensuring that there is supervision, particularly of critical activities such as cash handling and banking.

Detection strategies include:

- Reporting avenues – encouraging reporting of dishonesty and having a variety of reporting mechanisms available, including an external 'hotline' where there is an opportunity to report anonymously.
- Business indicator analysis – using available data to ensure that 'spikes' or exceptions are flagged and can be promptly investigated.
- Initial action guidelines – management having an understanding of the 'initial action' steps, including investigation process, preservation of evidence, and industrial relations implications.
- Professional investigation – so that the best possible outcomes are achieved in terms of minimal loss and disruption to the business, maximum restitution, and low risk of industrial relations action.
- Gaining and learning – from the incident to take steps to reduce the risk of it occurring again.

Responding to detected dishonesty

When a situation of suspected staff dishonesty is reported, the employer should address the report in a timely manner. The desired outcomes are:

- Investigation to establish facts (versus assumption)
- Evidence to support suspicions/ or;
- Exoneration after investigation.

The outcomes can involve three quite separate areas –

1. The employment relationship
2. Recovery of losses and costs from the offender
3. Criminal charges

The first priority is addressing the employment relationship. Calling the police will not deal with this area of the employer's responsibility and may indicate that the employer has assumed a criminal offence before conducting any investigation.

Initial action

- What is done initially is crucial to the end result
- Maintain confidentiality
- Remain objective
- Seek expert advice
- Write an account of what you know and what has occurred
- Cover – what, where, when, who, why
- Follow the advice of investigators/HR managers/supervisors
- Ensure all information is documented
- Keep original documents secure. The obligations are to:
- Investigate thoroughly and in a timely manner
- Be fair and follow a sound process
- Give the suspected employee the opportunity to answer the allegations
- Be consistent in your response to such situations
- Ensure that where a dismissal is warranted the reasoning is sound and clear

The honest workplace

The concept of an honest workplace means different things to different people.

To guard against and detect dishonesty, businesses must realize the very real possibility of its occurance. Discuss it openly and then implement strategies to deal with it.

Handled well, a discussion about honest workplace expectations will be welcomed by staff who would appreciate the openness and that clarification is given to 'the rules of the game'.

Source: *Strategies for Managing Dishonest Retail Employees by Renata Ringin, www.retailtimes.com visited on November 24, 2008.*

About Author: *Article first published in Security Solutions Magazine July 2007. Renata is the Managing Director and founder of Pro Active Strategies (see www.proactivestrategies.com.au), an International Loss Prevention Consultancy, has spent past 16 years working in Loss Prevention management and is a former Detective with Victoria Police. She has studied Loss Prevention worldwide as part of a Winston Churchill Trust Fellowship and is a former Director of NSW Crime Stoppers.*

SUPPLY CHAIN MANAGEMENT

LEARNING OBJECTIVES

- Understanding the emergence of supply chain management in modern retailing
- Knowing why SCM is getting world wide attention
- Explaining the significance of warehousing
- Analyzing the major drivers of supply chain management
- Examining the components of an effective supply chain

"You'll never have a product or price advantage again.
They can be easily duplicated, but a strong supply chain network can't be copied."

Anonymous

INTRODUCTION

Supply chain management represents the logistics aspect of a value delivery chain. It represents the inter-linkage of a business organization with other organizations, which in turn have their separate integrations. It involves all the members of a retail logistics process, i.e. manufacturers, wholesalers, intermediaries and the retailer.

Retailers are the most important link in the supply chain process as they provide the link between a wholesaler/vendor and the ultimate consumer. Retailers, by their business nature, continuously explore and try to find out what customers' requirements are? And by working with the other members of the supply chain process like wholesalers, manufacturers, transportation companies, importers etc, make certain that customers' requirements are fulfilled when they come to shop. The primary objective of the supply chain management (SCM) is to ensure merchandise in right quality, quantity, price and place by minimizing/eliminating the uncertainties associated with the supply chain process.

THE SUPPLY CHAIN

A supply chain is a network of retailers, distributors, transporters, storage facilities, and suppliers who take part in the production, delivery, and sale of a product that convert and move the goods from raw materials to end users. it describes the processes and organisations involved in converting and conveying the goods from manufactures to consumers. The activities close to the raw material stage are known as ***upstream activities*** and activities between the manufacturer and end consumer are ***downstream activities***. Marketing distribution concerns these downstream activities. A typical supply chain consists of multiple companies which coordinate activities to set themselves apart from the competition.

A supply chain basically has three key parts:

- **Supply:** It focuses on the raw materials supplied to manufacturing, including how, when, and from what location.
- **Manufacturing:** It focuses on converting these raw materials into finished products.
- **Distribution:** It focuses on ensuring that these products reach the consumers through an organized network of distributors, warehouses, and retailers.

Figure 16.1

A Typical Supply Chain

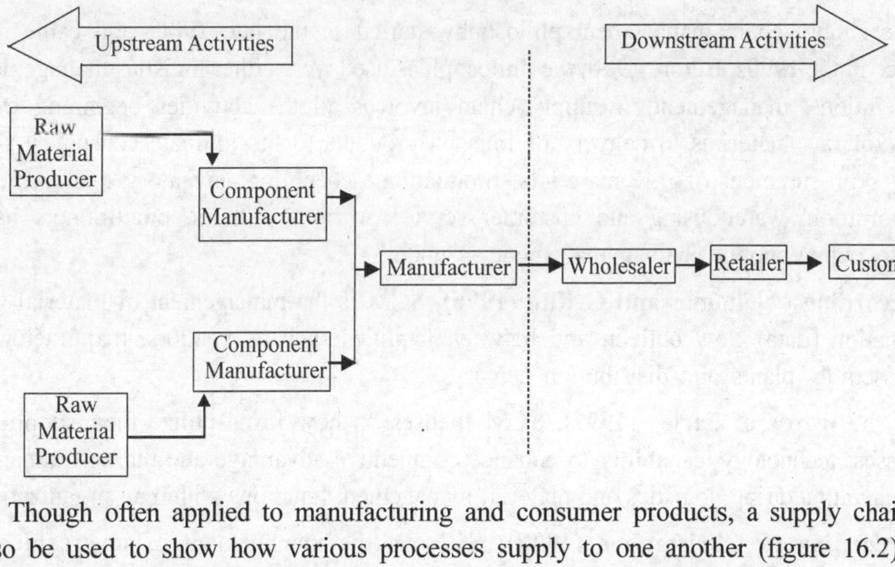

Though often applied to manufacturing and consumer products, a supply chain can also be used to show how various processes supply to one another (figure 16.2). The supply chain definition in this sense can apply to Internet technology, finance, and many other industries[1]. A supply chain strategy defines how the supply chain should operate in order to compete in the market. The strategy evaluates the benefits and costs relating to the operation. While a business strategy focuses on the overall direction a company wishes to pursue, supply chain strategy focuses on the actual operations of the organization and the supply chain that will be used to meet a specific goal.

[1] *www.wisegeek.com*

Figure 16.2
A Network of Supply Chains

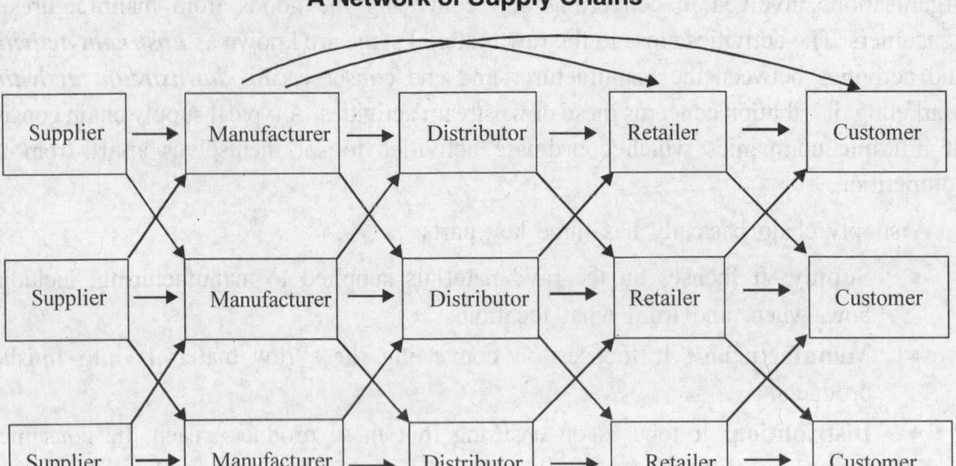

WHAT IS SUPPLY CHAIN MANAGEMENT?

The supply chain management philosophy started in the late 1980, and came into practice in the 1990s. Before 1990, the philosophies used were either logistics management or operations' management. A supply chain involves all the activities beginning from supply of raw materials to delivery of finished products to the ultimate consumer. This involves procurement of raw materials, production, scheduling, inventory management, transportation, warehousing and customer service. Various authors, practitioners have tried to define supply chain management as under:

According to Thomas and Griffin (1996), SCM is the management of material and information (data) flow both in and between facilities such as vendors, manufacturing and assembly plants and distribution centers.

In the words of Farley (1997), SCM focuses on how firms utilize their suppliers' processes, technology, capability to enhance competitive advantage and the co-ordination of the manufacturing, logistics and material management functions within an organization.

According to Christopher (1998), SCM is the management of upstream and downstream relationships with suppliers and customers to deliver superior customer value at lesser cost to the chain as a whole.

According to Hansfield and Nichols Jr (1999), SCM is the integration of activities associated with flow and transformation of goods from raw material stage through to the end user as well as associated information flows through improved supply chain relationships to achieve sustainable competitive advantage.

According to Zheng et al (2000), SCM is the process of optimizing a company's internal practices and improving the interaction with its suppliers and customers.

According to Stock and Lambert (2001), "SCM is the management of eight-key business processes: customer relationship management, customer service management, demand management, order fulfillment, manufacturing flow management, procurement, product development and commercialization and returns".

Mohanty and Dsehmukh (2004) define SCM as a loop:

- It starts with the customer and ends with the customer.
- Through the loop flow all the materials, finished goods, information and all the transactions.
- It requires looking at the business as one continuous, seamless process.
- This process absorbs distinct functions such as forecasting, purchasing, manufacturing and distribution, sales and marketing into a continuous business interaction.

Example of Supply Chain

Consider a customer walks into Spencer Store to purchase beauty soap. The supply chain begins with the customer and his need for beauty soap. The next stage of this supply chain is the Spencer retail store where the customer visits. Spencer stocks its shelves using inventory that may have been supplied from a finished goods warehouse managed by Wal-Mart or received from third party (vendor). The vendor in turn is stocked by the manufacturer [say Hindustan Uni Liver (HUL)]. The HUL manufacturing plant receives raw material from a variety of suppliers who may themselves have been supplied by lower tier suppliers. For example, packaging material may come from Home-foil (an aluminum foil company) while Home-foil receives raw material to manufacture the packaging material from other suppliers. This forms a typical supply chain.

Figure 16.3
Stages of a beauty soap supply chain

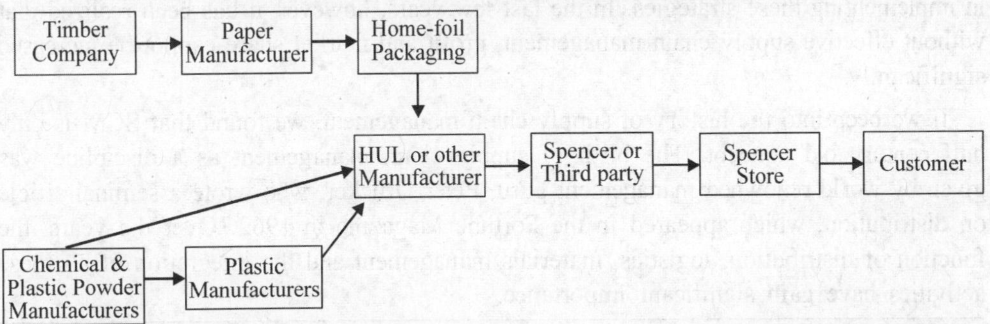

In another example, a customer purchases a wrist watch and traveling bag online from Reliance retail. The supply chain includes, among others, the customer Reliance Website that accepts the customer's order, the Reliance store, and all of Reliance's suppliers and their suppliers. The Reliance Website provides the customer with information regarding pricing, product features, and product availability. After selecting the product, the customer clicks on 'order form' and pays for the product. The customer may later return to the Website to check the status of the order. Thus a typical supply chain may involve a variety of stages discussed as under:

- Customers.
- Retailers.
- Wholesalers/Distributors.
- Manufacturers.
- Component/Raw material supplier.

Benefits of Supply Chains

(1) It bridges the gaps between the suppliers and the customers.

(2) It helps manufacturers in reducing inventories as finished goods are stored nearer to the customers.

(3) It allows firms to conduct operations at an appropriate time and place for the benefits of suppliers and customers.

(4) Effective supply chains results in enhanced customer service as retailers get a choice of goods and also carry less stock.

(5) Supply chains make movements simple, cost-effective and efficient as transport is simpler.

(6) Expertise can be developed in a particular type of operation.

(7) It allows firms to conduct operations at an appropriate time and place for the benefits of suppliers and customers.

EVOLUTION OF SUPPLY CHAIN MANAGEMENT

The main driving force behind the development of SCM over the past 20 years has been the desire to minimize inventory level. In the 1980s companies discovered new manufacturing techniques that allowed them to reduce costs and better compete in different markets. Strategies such as just-in-time, manufacturing, team manufacturing, total quality management, and other became very popular and vast amount of resources were invested in implementing these strategies. In the last few years, however, it has been realized that without effective supply chain management, profit and market share cannot be increased significantly.

If we peep into the history of supply chain management, we found that SCM is only half century old concept. The birth of supply chain management as a discipline was given by world renowned management guru, Peter Drucker, who wrote a seminal article on distribution, which appeared in the Fortune Magazine in 1962. Over the years, the function of distribution, logistics, materials management and the integration of all these activities have gain significant importance.

The Evolution of Supply Chain Management

Early 1960s	:	Physical Distribution Management (PDM).
Late 1970s	:	Logistics and Total Logistics.
Early 1990s	:	Logistics and Business process Re-engineering (BPR).
Late 2010 (Last 20 years)	:	Supply Chain Management (SCM) and its Optimization.

From 1970s to early 1980s

This period of supply chain management was characterized by large scale changes, re-engineering, downsizing driven by cost reduction techniques and widespread attention to the Japanese manufacturing techniques.

In the early 1990s

In the early 1990s industries began to focus on "Core Competencies" and adopted a specialization model. Companies abandoned vertical integration, sold off non-core operations, and outsourced those functions to other companies. Thus companies extended their supply chain operations well beyond company walls and entered into supply chain partnerships with externals (vendors) resulted in vendor managed inventory (VMI) control. Thus managing inventory levels was the sole responsibility of vendors. The retailer was supposed to send the sales and inventory data to the vendor via EDI.

Late 2010 (Last 20 years)

In the last twenty years especially after year 2000. Outsourced technology hosting for supply chain solutions was replaced by on-demand model from approximately 2003-2006 to the software as a service (SaaS) model currently in focus today. Furthermore, the last two decades have seen the introduction of large number of operation and quality management and control issues like JIT (Just-in-time), ZI (Zero Inventory), TQM (Total Quality Management), ECR (Efficient Customer Response), VMI (Vendor Managed Inventory) and CD (Cross docking). All of these techniques now have been integrated within the domain of supply chain management process.

WHY SCM IS REQUIRED?

As a result of the shrinking profits, declining delivery commitments, decreasing product lifecycle, mass outsourcing, increasing customization and most importantly due to LPG (Liberalization, Privatization and Globalization), the need for **SCM** is being felt by all types of retail organizations. Today customer is the '*king*' and '*queen*'. In this era of cut throat competition and mall mushrooming culture, it is not the product but the customer that gives the profit. Therefore, customer has become very much demanding and the focal point of all retail strategies. Here, supply chain management is the answer to the unanswered questions; **SCM** provides opportunities for organizations to meet these challenges by accurate and prompt deliveries. The need for SCM may be understood under following heads:

> *Wal-Mart has been widely recognised as a leader in supply chain management and for passing its savings on to its customers.*

- **Continuous Supply:** SCM as a system approach to manage the whole set of information, materials and services from raw material procurement to delivery of finished goods to the ultimate consumer, ensures the continuity of goods and services by eliminating the possibilities of supply disruptions.

- **Quality Assurance**: In the total quality management (TQM) and six sigma era, the products and services should be virtually defect free. Like in six sigma applications, quality assurance team ensures even less than 10 defective units per million (ppm). Without efficient working of SCM, minimizing/eliminating this defect rate is not feasible.
- **Technological Competitiveness**: In today's rapidly changing business environment, there is need for an integrated approach that should ensure that the firm's supply base provides appropriate technology in timely manner and is carefully controlled while dealing with external parties (suppliers and customers).
- **Cost effectiveness**: For a retailer cost effectiveness implies that SCM function must focus on cost cutting throughout the supply chain process from supplier to the ultimate consumer. SCM ensures and is capable enough to reduce the total cost associated with acquisition, movement, holding and supplying.
- **Time Management**: SCM by monitoring all aspects of supply chain, optimizing retailing processes and eliminating all process waste including wasted steps, duplication of activities (if any) and excess inventory results in timely deliveries in less efforts in same or reduced time horizons.

> *The presence of global retailers in the Indian market will enhance sourcing and exports from india, as retailers develop and leverage relationships with local suppliers.*

Supply Chain Management (SCM)

SCM is the process of effectively managing the flow of materials, information and finished goods from manufacturing and distribution chain to the ultimate consumer. The objective of managing supply chain is to synchronize the needs and desires of customers so that deliveries should meet customers' requirements at lesser cost as a whole. Following are the objectives of SCM:

a. To provide an uninterrupted flow of goods and services.
b. To meet quality criteria.
c. To reduce the inventory investment to the extent possible.
d. To offer high customer service, low inventory management and low unit cost.
e. To ensure quick responsiveness to the customers' changes.
f. To select and maintain competent suppliers.
g. To ensure purchasing at lower total cost throughout the supply chain process.

INNOVATIONS IN SUPPLY CHAIN MANAGEMENT

(1) Vender Managed Inventory (VMI)

Vendor Managed Inventory is the process where the vendor (the manufacturer or supplier) manage the inventory of the retailer. The vendor receives the electronic messages, usually via EDI (Electronic data interchange) from the retailer. These messages inform the vendor various bits of information such as what the 'retailer has sold' and 'what they have currently in inventory'. The vendor reviews this information and decides when it is appropriate to generate a purchase order.

The VMI process is a combination of e-commerce software and people. The e-commerce layer is a mechanism through which companies communicate the data. VMI is not tied to a specific communications protocol. VMI data can be communicated via EDI, XML, FTP or any other reliable communications method. The key feature of e-commerce layer is that the data be timely and accurate. The vendor's computer acquired the data electronically which helps in reducing the lead time and in eliminating the vendor's recording errors. It increases the product availability and lowers inventory investments. Furthermore, vendor representatives in a sore benefit the vendor by ensuring the product is properly displayed and store staff are familiar with the features of the product line.

Benefits to Retailers

(i) Reduced level of inventory at retailer's end.
(ii) Less chances of stock outs.
(iii) Reduced forecasting and purchasing activities.
(iv) Increased sales due to product availability.
(v) Less paper work.
(vi) Increased return on assets (ROI).
(vii) Increased service level to the end customer.
(viii) Reduced fulfillment costs/lead times.
(ix) Shared risk.

Benefits to Supplier

(i) No/less chances of mistakes and errors while preparing purchase orders.
(ii) Encourages supply chain cooperation.
(iii) Timely and accurate data results in better forecasting.
(iv) It reduces purchase order related errors and conflicts.
(v) Reduced fulfillment costs/lead times.
(vi) Smoother demand patterns.
(vii) Increased service level to the end customer.

Limitations/Challenges of VMI

(i) Some vendors continue to stock without leveraging customer – specific data effectively for production planning.
(ii) High expectations from retailers.
(iii) Resistance from sales staff due to concerns of losing control, affecting sales based incentive programmes.
(iv) Lack of trust and skepticism from employees.

Vendor Managed Inventory (VMI)

VMI in its simplest form means that the vendor manages the inventory of the retailer. The retailer sends the sales and inventory data to the vendor via EDI and the supplier creates the purchase orders based on the established inventory levels and fill rates.

The working of VMI process

(1) The purchase order is prepared by vendor and not by retailer.

(2) The vendor sends the delivery notices before sending the goods to the retailer's store.

(3) Soon after this, the vendor sends the invoice to the retailer.

(4) Upon receiving the goods, the retailer does the invoice matching and handles payment through their account payable systems.

EDI documents used in VMI

- Purchase orders.
- Product activity.
- Purchase order acknowledgement.
- Advance delivery notice.
- Invoice.

VMI today is one of the successful business models used by Wal-Mart and many other big retailers. Oil companies in India and abroad use technology to manage the gasoline inventories at the service stations that they supply. Home Depot also uses VMI technology with larger vendors of manufactured goods.

(2) Collaborative Planning, Forecasting and Replenishment (CPFR)

Collaborative Planning, Forecasting and Replenishment or CPFR (a Wal-Mart's initiative) is one of the prominent business model in today's supply chain context. CPFR is a business practice that combines the intelligence and skills of multiple trading partners in the planning and fulfillment of customer demand. It links the best practices of sales and marketing to supply chain planning and execution process with the objective to increase product availability to the customer while reducing inventory, transportation and logistics cost.

Facts about CPFR

(1) The model was developed by VICS in cooperation with leading retailers like Wal-Mart, IBM, SAP and Manugistics.

(2) It is a business practice wherein trading partners use information technology (IT) and a standard set of business procedures.

(3) CPFR basically is based on EDI.

(4) It basically works to solve two challenges faced by retailers and vendors:

(i) Stock out of critical products.

(ii) Unneeded safety stock lying on the shelf gathering dust.

CPFR Model

The economic benefits of CPFR Model are now well recognized and publicized in practice by successful retailers such as Wal-Mart. The model provides a basic framework for the flow of information, goods and services. In the retail industry the participants namely retailer, vendor (manufacturer) and the consumer basically follow following roles respectively.

The Retailer	–	the role of buyer.
The Manufacturer	–	the role of seller, and
The Consumer	–	the role of end customer.

Under CPFR model, centre is represented as the consumer, followed by the middle ring of the retailer, and finally the outside ring being the manufacturer. Each ring of the model represents different functions within the model. The consumer creates demand for good and services while the retailer fulfils these demands by obtaining supplies from the manufacturer.

The CPFR model represents voluntary guidelines aimed at structuring and guiding supply chain partners in setting up their relationship and processes. Some of the main processes are shown in the second ring of the model that has allows in circular pattern. This is displayed with collaboration arrangement. Joint business plan, sales forecasting, order fulfillment etc. as shown below:

Figure 16.4
CPFR Model

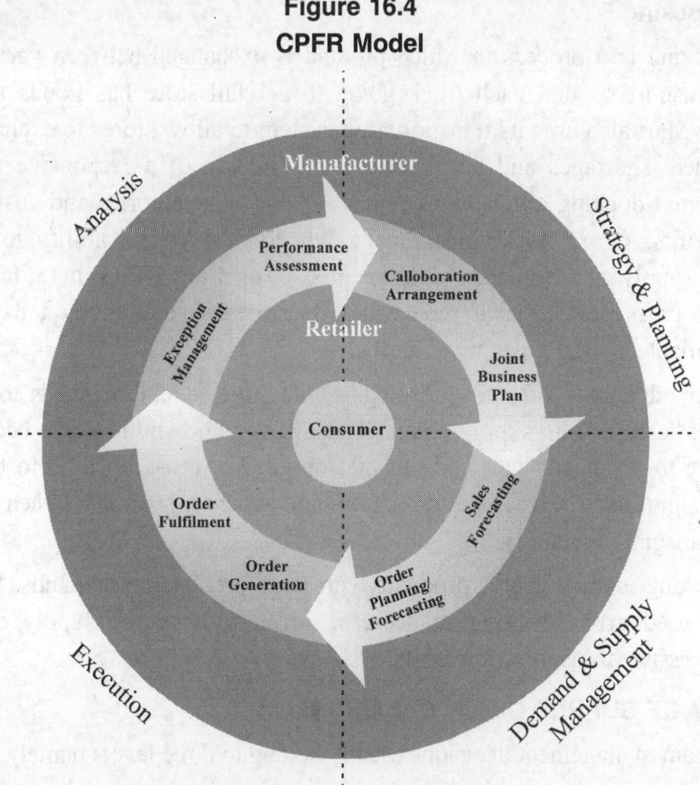

The various steps in a typical CPFR Model are described as under:

Step 1 : Collaboration Arrangement.
Step 2 : Joint Business Plan.
Step 3 : Sales Forecasting.
Step 4 : Order Planning/Forecasting.
Step 5 : Order Generation.
Step 6 : Order fulfillment.
Step 7 : Exception Management.
Step 8 : Performance Assessment.

Crux of CPFR Model

The CPFR process starts with a mutual agreement between all the trading partners for the purpose of sharing information with each other. They also collaborate on planning, with the ultimate goal of delivering goods and services on actual market demand. The trading partners share their forecasts, results and data on line. FPFR system analyses the data and in case the forecasts do not match, it immediately informs planners at both the firms. The trading partners then work together and cooperate to resolve these differences. As a result, a final plan is agreed upon by both describing what is going to be sold and how it will be materialized.

(3) Cross Docking

Cross docking is a process in which product is exchanged between various trucks or means of transport so that each truck going to a retail store has goods from different vendors. Wal-Mart also uses its transportation system to allow stores to exchange products based on where shortages and surpluses occur. The use of a responsive transportation system and cross-docking allows the company to lower inventories and costs resulting in increased profits. Cross docking is thus a key to Wal-Mart's ability to improve the matching of supply and demand while keeping costs low. 7-Eleven (a Japanese based retailer) uses cross docking that replenishes its stores several times a day so that the products available match customers' needs.

The major advantage of cross docking is that little inventory needs to be held and product flows faster in the supply chain. It also saves on handling cost because product does not have to be moved into and out of storage. For cross docking to be successful, it requires a significant degree of coordination and synchronization between various truck managers managing inventory.

Cross docking is suitable for products with large predictable demands. Wal-Mart has successfully used cross docking to decrease inventories in the supply chain without incurring excessive transportation costs.

HIERARCHY OF SUPPLY CHAIN DECISIONS

Supply chain management decisions usually belong to three levels namely, the *strategic*, the *tactical,* or the *operational* level, as shown below in pyramid shape. The decisions taken at higher level in the pyramid will set the guidelines under which lower level decisions are made. On the strategic level, decisions such as location, production, inventory and transportation are taken. Location decisions basically are related to size, number and geographic location of the supply chain entities, such as plants, inventories or distribution centers. Production decisions are related to issues such as which product to produce, where to produce, how many, which supplier to involve, and so on. Inventory decisions are related to management of inventories throughout the supply chain.

Most of the strategic level decisions are inter-related. For example, which transport mode to be used, depends upon the geography of the plants and warehouses. Similarly inventory policies are influenced by choice of suppliers and production locations.

Tactical level decisions basically belong to medium term decisions such as monthly/weekly demand forecasts, production planning, materials requirement planning (MRP), and transport planning. While at operational level, very short term decisions made from day-to-day are taken.

Figure 16.5
Hierarchy of supply chain decisions

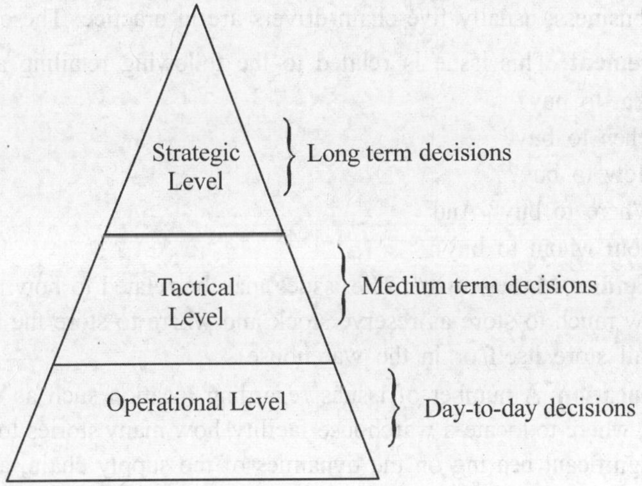

WAREHOUSING

In the world of retailing it is said that customer can come to shop any time and any day. He will not inform you when he will come, what he will buy and how much he will buy? Considering, each retailer has to store each type of inventory in its stock room in some quantity besides the quantity kept for display. Further, it takes time to order and deliveries to come. The storage function helps a retailer to smooth discrepancies between inventory buying, stocking and quantities desired by the customers. Warehousing is an old concept which can be used as an instant tool by modern retailers by satisfying consumer needs promptly due to increasing mall rentals and limited sizes, some goods are kept at or near the store and the rest is located in warehouses in other locations. The retail store might own rented warehouse and also own private warehouse.

Types of warehouses

Usually two types of warehouses are found in the world of retailing:

1 **Storage warehouses:** store goods for medium to long periods of time.

2 **Distribution warehouses:** receive multiple goods from various suppliers and move them out as soon as demand comes from retail outlet.

Warehouse

Warehouse is a part of retail store building where goods are stored for a certain period of time. Sometimes due to limitation of retail space, warehouses can be located at distance from the retail store. These are normally large plain buildings or big hallrooms in a business complex in commercial areas of cities and basements of malls. Warehouses may be automated with no staff working inside. Recent developments in methods of procurement and adoption of Japanese selling techniques like JIT (Just in time) buying, KANBAN etc. traditional warehousing has been loosing its identity since few years.

MAJOR DRIVERS OF SUPPLY CHAIN

In retailing business, usually five chain drivers are in practice. These are as follows:

1. **Procurement:** This issue is related to the following retailing aspects :
   (i) What to buy?
   (ii) When to buy?
   (iii) How to buy?
   (iv) Where to buy? And
   (v) From whom to buy?
2. **Merchandise Management**: The issues may be related to how much to display and how much to store as reserve stock and where to store the merchandise (in the retail store itself or in the warehouse).
3. **Store location**: A number of issues regarding location such as where to set up a store, where to locate a warehouse facility, how many stories to construct, may have significant bearing on the dynamics of the supply chain, and in turn may affect the overall budget of the retail store.
4. **Transportation**: Under transportation, a retailer is concerned with the following aspects:
   How to move a product from one store to another. For example, in case of centralized retailing, delivery takes from common warehouse to different stores located in different areas at varied distance. Here, a retailer is always worried about the mode of transportation because on one hand, he is concerned with economies of scale and desired level of customer satisfaction on the other hand.
5. **Information**: Information is an integrating force that has critical implications for the whole supply chain. For a retailer, information (Data) acts as basis for making various decisions in the supply chain. If information is not understood properly, it can disrupt the whole supply chain and consequences may be fatal for retailer's fate.

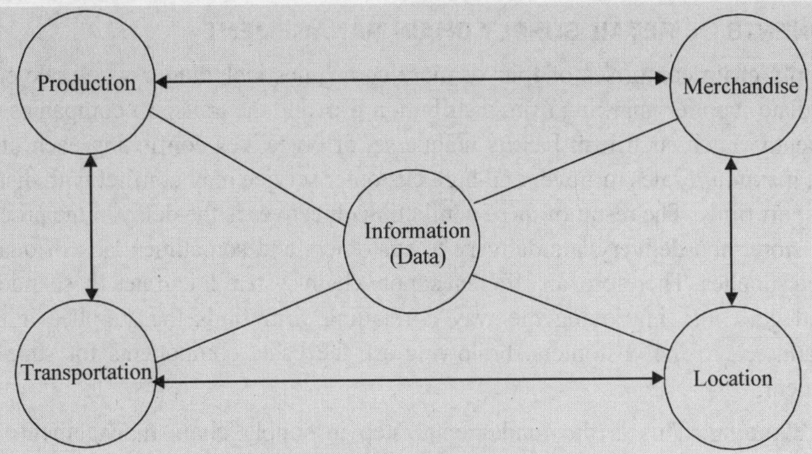

Figure 16.6: Supply Chain Drivers

SCM Skills

SCM professionals/experts working in retailing line of business are required to take a variety of decisions in their day to day store operations. Undoubtedly their decisions can make or mar any retail store. In large retail organizations, there exist a supply chain department consisting of several employees assigned to specialized tasks, and led by a responsible manager or vice president who directs the overall sourcing operations.

The supply chain management professionals' existence is felt in all types of retail stores, including luxury, clothing, healthcare, electronics, good living and even cyber retailing. Procurement and supply management can affect store's profitability and operational success. Therefore, following are the essential to manage supply chain effectively:

1. The logistics skills: It includes functional competencies to have balance between organizational goals and customer services in terms of low cost, regular supply and appropriate quality.
2. The system skills: It includes basic skills to understand the supply chain process under different circumstances as and when arise. Data capturing, decision analysis, e-commerce know how and information routing come under system skills.
3. Analytical skills: It includes the ability to forecast, competitiveness in quantitative decisions and the power to understand the issues quickly.
4. Technical skills: It includes the ability to understand and manage issues related to store process technology, store engineering, merchandise management, job related etc.
5. Commercial skills: It includes the sense to understand economic, price and value issues.
6. Interpersonal skills: It includes the professionals' ability with regard to team building, equity, dedication, commitment, negotiations, social skills, integrity and relationship building.

COMPONENTS OF RETAIL SUPPLY CHAIN MANAGEMENT

A supply chain comprises of four or more companies including a wholesale company, an immediate supplier, marking firm, distribution firm and the transport companies working independently. Each such firm has its unique set of objectives conflicting each other. For example, maximum sales turnover and high customer service may conflict with distribution and transport firms. The result of these conflicting objectives is the delay in the procurement by retail store, non-delivery/late delivery to customers and sometimes lack of quality due to delayed supplies. Therefore, an efficient supply chain system integrates these independent firms and goes into improving the way a retailing firm finds the supplies it needs to display and sell to the customers. Following are the basic components for supply chain management:

1. **Planning**: This is the fundamental step in supply chain management. Retailer needs step by step plan to manage all the resources that not only go towards meeting customer demand for a product or service but key to competitive advantage. Many retailers are under the impression that having a plan is same as having a retail strategy. They must understand that having a plan is not enough to ensure retail success but devising and implementing a set of metrics to monitor the supply chain will ultimately work.
2. **Source**: The retailers must carefully select the suppliers that will deliver them goods and services as and when required without compromising with quality. It includes developing proper policies that ensure proper pricing, delivery and payment mechanism suitable to both parties. More specifically, it's a periodic event that includes the identification and selection of initial commercial agreements with short listed suppliers that either create or reset a relationship.
3. **Procurement**: This is a buying and receiving step. This includes ordering, receiving and displaying merchandise in a retail store. This also includes how much merchandise should be kept for display and in warehouse. This is the most critical phase of supply chain management as it requires measurement of quality levels, following planograms, sales turnover and floor staff productivity.
4. **Sell**: This involves coordination between the customers' orders and retailers' supply to deliver goods and services ordered and setting up billing and invoice system to collect payments and returning balance thereof.
5. **Return/Exchange**: Under this heading, we include the items that flow from customer back to the retailer. This is because of defective supplies or different item provided by retailer unknowingly. It also involves customers' complaints handling issues related to dissatisfaction due to non-performance of the products and delayed supplies.

SUMMARY

Supply Chain Management is the integration of business processes from end user through original suppliers, assembly, manufacturing, logistics and distribution facilities that add value for customers. Retail supply chain management is different from supply management in the sense that retail supply chain management emphasizes only on the retailer -supplier relationship for attaining a sustainable competitive advantage. Retail supply chain management has emerged as the new key to productivity and competitiveness of retail stores. Customers are demanding better product availability and broader assortment than in the 20th centaury. Their demands are changing frequently. Considering, retailers are reacting to rapidly changing retail environment by changing the way they sell and provide the merchandise. Cyber (On-line) retailing is the fashion of the day. Further, some retailers are using distribution outlets for cross docking instead of storing merchandise.

REVIEW QUESTIONS

True and False Questions

1. A supply chain is a network of retailers, distributors, transporters, storage facilities, and suppliers that take part in the production, delivery, and sale of a product that convert and move the goods from customers to manufacturers.
2. The activities close to the raw material stage are known as ***downstream activities***
3. Activities between the manufacturer and end consumer are ***upstream activities***.
4. Marketing distribution concerns with only upstream activities.
5. A supply chain basically has three key parts: supply, manufacturing and distribution.
6. A supply chain strategy defines how the supply chain should operate in order to compete in the market.
7. SCM is the management of upstream and downstream relationships with suppliers and customers to deliver superior customer value at lesser cost to the chain as a whole.
8. Warehouse is a part of retail store building where goods are stored for a certain period of time.
9. A supply chain comprises of four or more companies including a wholesale company, an immediate supplier, marking firm, distribution firm and the transport companies working independently.
10. While planning retailers must understand that having a plan is enough to ensure retail success instead of devising and implementing a set of metrics to monitor the supply chain.
11. Source includes developing proper policies that ensure proper pricing, delivery and payment mechanism suitable to both parties.
12. Procurement is a buying and receiving step which includes ordering, receiving and displaying merchandise in a manufacturing unit.
13. Selling involves coordination between the customers' orders and retailers' supply to deliver goods and services ordered and setting up billing and invoice system to collect payments and returning balance thereof.
14. Return/Exchange includes the items that flow from customer back to the manufacturer.
15. Retail supply chain management is different from supply management in the sense that retail supply chain management emphasizes only on the retailer -supplier relationship for attaining a sustainable competitive advantage.

Answers

1. False	2. False	3. False	4. False
5. False	6. True	7. True	8. True
9. True	10. False	11. True	12. False
13. True	14. True	15. True	

Multiple Choice Questions

1. The activities close to raw material stages are known as :
   (*a*) Downstream activities (*b*) Up stream activities
   (*c*) Cross screen activities (*d*) Horizontal activities
2. Activities between manufacturer and end consumer are known as :
   (*a*) Horizontal (*b*) Vertical
   (*c*) Up stream (*d*) Down stream
3. KANBAN and JIT are .... techniques.
   (*a*) Indian (*b*) American
   (*c*) Russian (*d*) None of the above
4. Procurement is related to :
   (*a*) What to buy (*b*) When to buy
   (*c*) How to buy (*d*) All of the above
5. EDI refers to :
   (*a*) Electronic data Interface. (*b*) Electronic data Interchange.
   (*c*) Efficient data Interchange. (*d*) Employee description input.
6. VMI is a combination of :
   (*a*) e-commerce hardware, and people.
   (*b*) e-commerce software, and people.
   (*c*) Software, hardware and people.
   (*d*) Software, technology and people.
7. CPFR refers to :
   (*a*) Collaborative positioning, Forecast report
   (*b*) Collaborative positioning, financial report
   (*c*) Collaborative planning, forecasting and replenishment.
   (*d*) Collaborative planning, financial and replenishment.
8. Under cross-docking process, merchandise is exchanged between
   (*a*) Various stores (*b*) Various trucks
   (*c*) Various warehouses (*d*) All of the above.
9. Storage ware houses store goods for .... periods of time.
   (*a*) Small to medium (*b*) Medium to long
   (*c*) One day only (*d*) Less than 15 days.
10. The objective of SCM is:
   (*a*) To provide an uninterrupted flow of goods and services.
   (*b*) To reduce the inventory investment to the extent possible.
   (*c*) None of the above.
   (*d*) Both of the above.

Answers

1. (*a*)	2 (*b*)	3. (*d*)	4. (*d*)
5. (*b*)	6. (*a*)	7. (*c*)	8. (*b*)
9. (*b*)	10. (*d*)		

Answers to Check your Progress

1. What is SCM?
2. What does LPG mean?
3. What CAGR stand for?
4. What is ppm?
5. What is JIT?
6. What is procurement?
7. Who is supplier?
8. What is time management?
9. List various warehouses?
10. What is merchandise?
11. What is quality assurance?
12. What is warehouse?
13. What is cyber retail?
14. What is upstream activity?
15. What is downstream activity?

Small Answer Questions

1. Describe the factors affecting a retail supply chain?
2. Differentiate between upstream and downstream activities?
3. Explain why supply chain management is getting worldwide attention?
4. What are the essential to manage supply chain effectively?
5. What challenges do companies face as they try to improve SCM?
6. What is a supply chain?
7. What is logistics?
8. What is supply chain management?
9. What kinds of jobs (and salaries) are available for SCM graduates?
10. What skills students need to build in preparation for a supply chain career?
11. Why is supply chain management important?

Long Answer Questions

1. Critically explain the components of a typical supply chain?
2. What a retailer can do to control the impact of rising transportation costs?
3. Is it right to say that "SCM is the process of effectively managing the flow of materials, information and finished goods from manufacturing and distribution chain to the ultimate consumer" Explain?
4. Is it necessary for successful retailing to have efficient provision for flawless supply chain?

Appendix

Exhibit 16.1: Underdeveloped Supply Chain - Biggest Challenge for Retail

Behind the glitz and glamour of the neighbourhood retail chain that you are fond of nowadays (the local *kiranawalla* is not a priority anymore), remains a very efficient supply chain. The job isn't complete if you happen to have just products stacked up in the shelves. Somebody has to manage the supply chain as well. This is where Supply Chain Management (SCM) comes. But as far as India is concerned, therein lies the risk too.

From movement and storage of raw materials, inventory, and finished goods from points of origin to consumption — the current retail boom in India can only sustain its momentum if supply chain management is given top priority by retail players. An under-developed supply chain cannot help retail stores. It will cause more harm.

"To achieve profitable growth over the longer term in the retail sector, supply chains need to be realigned into efficient, agile and adaptable network that can handle larger volumes, expand reach, balance costs and address the demographic variations while providing scalability," said Pinakiranjan Mishra, Partner, Retail & Consumer Practice, Ernst & Young to *Business Line* in an a e-mail interview.

As the process that looks after first planning, secondly implementing and then finally controlling the operations of the supply chain as efficiently as possible, the importance of SCM is paramount.

Excerpts of the interview

Where does India's back-end supply chain stand today?

The most significant challenge that impedes the development of an efficient and modern retail sector is an underdeveloped supply chain. India today has an underdeveloped unidirectional supply chain that increases inventory build-up and operational inefficiencies for companies.

What about the traditional supply chain?

Traditional supply chain network in India has a host of intermediaries. There are considerable gaps in the transportation and storage network of the country. Third-party logistics providers, a mainstay in any well-developed supply chain, are largely non-existent in India. There is also very little sharing of supply network infrastructure among leading Indian retailers.

Okay. So what is the biggest problem in developing a robust back-end supply chain?

The most significant challenge in developing a smooth supply network is the lack of adequate infrastructure particularly the road infrastructure, reliable power supply, insufficient investments in alternate modes of transport (marine, railways, air transport), a well-connected cold chain and warehousing infrastructure.

Infrastructure; What else?

Lack of technology usage, a fragmented supplier base and a multi-layered tax structure pose significant challenges to the evolution of a streamlined supply network. Local, regional and national regulations pose major hurdles for retailers in obtaining permissions to establish supply chain infrastructure.

Coming back to the infrastructure issue. Is low optimisation of available infrastructure an issue?

Sure it is. For instance in transportation, railways could accelerate freight earnings by 100 per cent. Railways today hardly transport about 22 per cent of cargo whereas they don't suffer from the typical issues of our roadways like congestion and poor maintenance.

Guess, the rest of cargo travels by road. Then, what is the problem?

Two per cent of roads constitute national highways but carry 40 per cent of all cargo. Only 48 per cent of villages are covered by road network. Indian cargo travels 250 to 300 km per day vis-à-vis 600-800 km as per international norms. This severely limits the access of rural producers to the consumer markets.

By connecting specific producing regions like 'food parks' and building storage and handling capacity, railways could double their freight growth from the current 10-11 per cent to about 20 per cent while providing market connectivity to farmers. A study by the US Federal Railroad Administration had revealed that relative fuel efficiency of railways was about 4.5 times that of roadways.

We keep on hearing about third-party logistic providers. Is there a market for them?

Third-party logistic providers (3PLs) have a significant opportunity of growth with the outsourced logistics market in India, estimated at $10.2 billion, expected to grow at a CAGR (compounded growth annual rate) of 15 per cent to 20 per cent during 2007-10, driven by a growing trend towards annual contracts.

Indian companies are increasingly using specialist logistics service providers to reduce costs and focus on their core competence. Growth in industry and trade has created demand for a range of logistics services including transportation, storage, warehousing and inventory management that benefits the productivity and efficiency of the customers' entire supply chains. This offers a huge opportunity for 3PLs.

Tell us more about the scope for organised players?

With 54 per cent share of the retail market and penetration rates of just over 1per cent, F&G (food and grocery) represents the biggest opportunity for organised players.

Owing to land parcels, multiplicity of regulations, large number of intermediaries and inadequate processing infrastructure, the final price for the products increases significantly.

Consumer prices for fruits and vegetables in India are as high as 3.5 times the farm-gate prices. Milk and dairy products are another large-consumption category and offer huge opportunity for the processing industry, with 35 per cent of milk currently produced undergoing some form of processing.

The emergence of 3PLs, backward integration, which is being facilitated, by large retailers and the increasing presence of large international retailers will enhance efficiencies in logistics and warehousing.

But can technology help in all of this? Is there a case to be made out for its low usage?

You are right. The usage of IT in the back-end supply is fairly low in India. The unorganised sector, a considerable portion of the retail industry, is lagging behind in IT usage. This could be one of the key reasons why IT usage percentage remains low in the Indian retail industry.

Even though technology is available to cater this segment, factors such as money, low understanding of benefits etc. deter its usage. Currently, national and multi-format retailers are the most aggressive players in IT spending.

This means we are lagging in the adoption of even basic IT in the case of retail...

No. In fact, Indian retail is quite advanced in basic IT adoption like enterprise resource planning (ERP), network, etc. as compared to foreign retailers. However, implementation has not been managed well due to the lack of sector understanding, both with clients as well as IT consultants. Where we are also lagging is in the realm of advanced IT products and solutions such as replenishment planning, analytics, RFID (radio-frequency-identification), and warehouse management systems.

Given the big budgets for IT, what benefits does it have to offer?

Supply chains have evolved into complex networks keeping pace with the increasing demands of retail business. Technology intervention at every level of the supply chain helps track products and provides data visibility.

Couple of key benefits comprise tracking of inventory and leakage, planning and replenishment of SKUs (stock-keeping units), CRM (customer relationship management) and potential of cross-selling other products, performance management across locations and categories, to name a few.

So, if we have IT and developed infrastructure, will that give us an Intelligent Supply Chain?

An intelligent supply chain network aims to help an enterprise understand and operate its business profitably. Intelligent supply chain utilises past performance to provide a predictive model for future performance. It also identifies deteriorating supplier performance which helps take preventive action.

Significant features of the intelligent supply chain comprise web-enabled global visibility, 'componentised' application architectures, real-time planning/ execution linkage and reporting and analytics.

An efficient and effective supply chain execution would help manage costs, ensure product availability and be highly responsive.

In short, what do retailers need to do?

Going forward, retailers would need to collaborate with suppliers to assist them in building required capabilities and manage the demand supply gap.

Simultaneously, retailers would need to work towards building the execution capabilities by establishing robust supply chain performance management framework and developing ways and means to capture unstructured information and using it for competitive advantage.

The retail industry needs to focus on making IT implementation successful and sustainable. Further, they should concentrate on using retail analytics to understand consumer demand side and planning for fulfillment/supply side.

Last question. Can the Government boost development of supply chains?

The Government needs to actively engage with the retail players to address taxation and infrastructure issues that would facilitate large-scale investments.

The introduction of a uniform goods and services tax (GST) across the country will allow companies to design a lean and effective supply chain infrastructure. The Government should also provide tax holidays for cold chain infrastructure investments and encourage the food processing industry to set up in areas near the source. This will cut down losses to farmers and also generate employment.

Courtesy: *http://www.thehindu.com, visited on July 20, 2008*

Exhibit 16.2: Components of a Supply Chain

SCM in actual is so vast that it becomes difficult to exemplify each and every component of it. The basic function of SCM is to plan, organize, coordinate and control all the supply chain activities.

A supply chain comprises mainly of suppliers, distributors and customers. The supply chain broadly can be classified into three parts: upstream, internal and downstream.

(a) Upstream Supply Chain

This part of the supply chain is mainly concerned with the procurement of raw materials. In includes suppliers that could be manufacturers themselves. As in case of assembled laptop, these suppliers can have their own supply chains e.g. a micro processor may be one of the first items for an assembler but it has its own supply chain, which is even longer than the chain of the assembler. The major activities in this part of the supply chain are purchasing and shipping.

(b) Internal Supply Chain

This part is mainly concerned with transforming the inputs obtained in the upstream supply chain into outputs. It starts from the time raw material comes to an organization and continues till it gets converted into finished goods and is sent for distribution. In this part, major activities are material handling, inventory management, manufacturing and quality control.

(c) Downstream Supply Chain

This part is mainly concerned with the processes involved in delivering the finished products from the internal supply chain to the final customers. In the case of an assembled laptop, downstream activities are packaging, shipping, after sales service, guarantee, warranty, etc. Many wholesalers and distributors are involved in these activities.

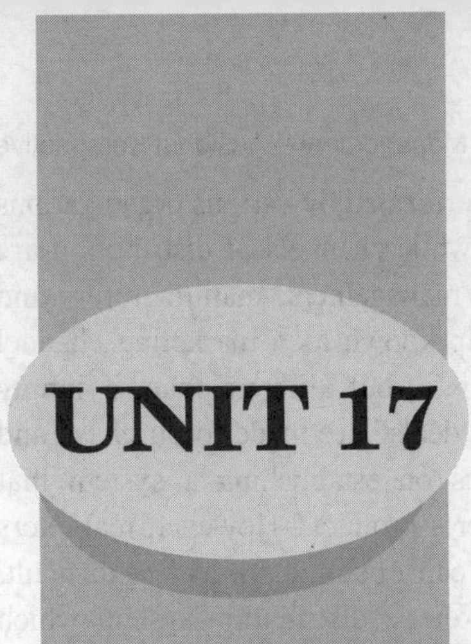

UNIT 17

DISTRIBUTION MANAGEMENT

LEARNING OBJECTIVES

- Understanding various functions performed by distribution channel intermediaries.
- Knowing various types of distribution channels and their respective role in effective distribution management.
- Explaining the issues and components of a retail channel strategy.
- Describing the significance, various types and benefits of warehousing.
- Understanding the concept, importance, systems and approaches of physical distribution.

A distribution system.....is a key external resource. Normally it takes years to build, and it is not easily charged. It ranks in importance with key internal resources such as manufacturing, research, engineering, and field sales personnel and facilities. It represents a significant corporate commitment to large numbers of independent companies whose business is distribution – and to the particular markets they serve. It represents, as well, a commitment to a set of policies and practices that constitute the basic fabric on which is woven an extensive set of long-term relationships.

E. Raymond Corey

INTRODUCTION

In the world of retailing distribution is termed as 'the second half of marketing'. The reason is that the expense incurred and efforts involved in distribution and supplying nearly accounts close to 'fifty' percent of the total marketing budget. Manufacturers only produce the goods and at maximum provide them to wholesalers. These produced goods must be provided in proper quantities, convenient locations and at times when customers want them. Simply stated, distribution is a value added task through which the finished goods are supplied to the place of demand and stored till sold.

The supply chain is the sequence of linked activities performed by various organizations to move goods from the sources to ultimate consumers while channels of distribution are part of the overall supply chain. Besides supply chain management, manufacturers and retailers take part in one more give-and-take relationship known as a marketing channel or distribution channel. A distribution channel is similar to, but different than, a supply chain. The distribution channel plays its role where the "deals" are made to purchase and sell goods and/or services. Distribution decisions focus on establishing a system that allows customers to gain access and purchase a marketer's product. However, marketers may find that getting to the point at which a customer can obtain a product is difficult, time consuming, and costly. The bottom line is a marketer's distribution system which must be both efficient and quick reactive.

DISTRIBUTION CHANNEL

Distribution channel is a means used to transfer merchandise from the manufacturer to the end user through retailer and other necessary intermediaries. An intermediary in the channel is called an agent/middleman. Channels normally vary from two-level channels without intermediaries to five-level channels with three intermediaries. For example, a leather handbag manufacturer who prepares handbags and sells it directly to the customer is in a two-level channel. A poultry farmer sells chicken and eggs to a restaurant supplier, who sells to individual restaurants, who then serve the customer, is in a four-level channel. Agents/intermediaries in the channel of distribution are used to facilitate the delivery of the merchandise as well as to transfer title, payments, and information about the merchandise.

According to Philip Kotler, the channel decisions are among the most important decisions that management faces and will directly affect every other marketing decision. These decisions are set of interdependent organizations (intermediaries) involved in the process of making a product or service available for use or consumption by the consumer or business user.

FUNCTIONS OF A DISTRIBUTION CHANNEL

Distribution channels are well organized arrangements that perform all the necessary tasks to assist exchange transactions. The basic function of a distribution channel is to provide a link between production and consumption and to create time, place and possession utilities which constitute the added value of distribution. Intermediaries (wholesalers, retailers, agents, brokers) are needed because manufacturers lack the necessary financial and human resources to carry out direct marketing. Maruti Suzuki Corporation sells its cars through more than 600 dealer outlets in India and abroad. It will not be feasible for Maruti Suzuki Corporation to buyout its dealer network and sell car throughout the country and abroad. Distribution channels can be exemplified by the number of intermediary levels that separate the manufacturer from the end consumer. The choice of a particular distribution channel is determined by factors related to market size, buyer behaviour and organization's characteristics. A typical distribution channel has to perform various functions as mentioned below.

Figure 17.1

Functions of Distribution Channels

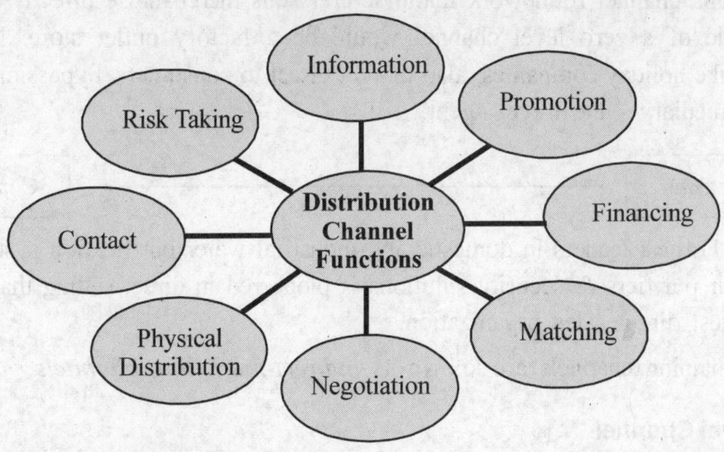

Distribution Channel Functions

Information	It involves collecting and sharing market research and intelligence - important for marketing planning and decisions.
Contact	It involves finding and communicating with prospective buyers
Financing	Financing basically involves acquisition and allocation of funds to cover the costs of the distribution channel in a cost effective manner.
Matching	Matching is to adjust the offer to suit a buyer's needs, including grading, assembling and packaging
Negotiation	Negotiation is to reach at an agreement on quality, price and other terms of the offer.
Physical Distribution	Physical distribution basically is to transport and store the goods in the warehouses.
Promotion	It is to develop and spread communications about offerings.
Risk Taking	It is to assume some inherent commercial risks by operating the channel (e.g. holding stock for precautionary or speculative motives)

All the above mentioned functions should be considered logically in any market. The idea is to know what functions are to be performed, who will perform them and how many levels it requires to make the distribution efforts cost effective, is another important decision to take.

CHANNEL LEVELS

Each layer of distribution intermediaries that performs some work in bringing the product to its final consumer is a ***channel level***.

A Zero Level Channel

A zero level channel, commonly known as direct marketing channel has no intermediary levels. In this channel framework manufacturer sells merchandise directly to customers. An example of a zero level channel would be a factory outlet store. Many service providers like holiday companies, also market direct to consumers, bypassing a traditional retail intermediary - the travel agent.

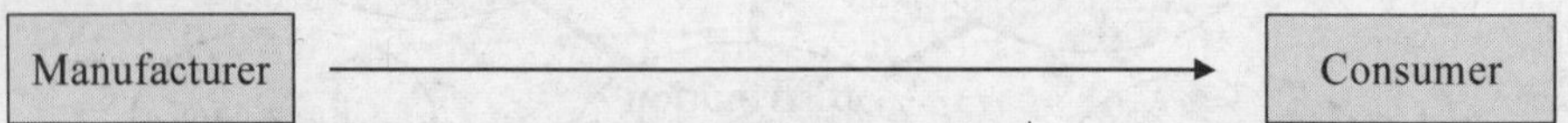

Eureka Forbes, leaders in domestic and industrial water purification systems, vacuum cleaners, air purifiers & security solutions is pioneered in direct selling that makes it an Asia's largest direct sales organization.

The remaining channels are known as ***indirect-marketing channels***.

A One Level Channel

A one level channel contains one selling intermediary. In consumer markets, this is usually a retailer. The consumer electrical goods market in the United Kingdom is typical of this arrangement whereby producers such as Sony, Panasonic, Canon etc. sell their goods directly to large retailers such as Comet, Dixons and Currys which then sell the goods to the final consumers[1].

A Two Level Channel

A two level channel encompasses two intermediary levels - a wholesaler and a retailer. A wholesaler typically buys and stores large quantities of merchandise from various manufacturers and then breaks into the bulk deliveries to supply retailers with smaller quantities. For small retailers with limited financial resources and order quantities, the use of wholesalers make economic sense. This agreement tends to work paramount where the retail channel is jumbled - i.e. not dominated by a small number of large, dominant retailers who have an encouragement to cut out the wholesaler. Distribution of drugs/ pharmaceuticals in the Europe and United Kingdom is typical example of such arrangement.

A Three Level Channel

A third level channel, as the name implies, encompasses three intermediary levels – a wholesaler, a retailer and a jobber. In the poultry industry, products like mutton, chicken, eggs etc. are first sold to wholesalers; he then sells it to jobbers, who sell to small and

[1] *www.tutor.2u.net*

unorganized retailers. One point in this regard, is to be noted that the levels of distribution vary from industry to industry and country to country. In Japan, food distribution system usually may involve as many as five or six levels while rest of the world, rely on two to three levels distribution network.

> **Jobber**
>
> A ***jobber*** is a person or firm that purchases large quantities of goods and services from manufacturers and importers and resells to merchants rather than to the end customers. A type of intermediary in the apparel industry, who buys bulk merchandise from several wholesalers of varied brands throughout the world and then sells it to small retailers, is typical example of jobber's presence in a distribution channel.

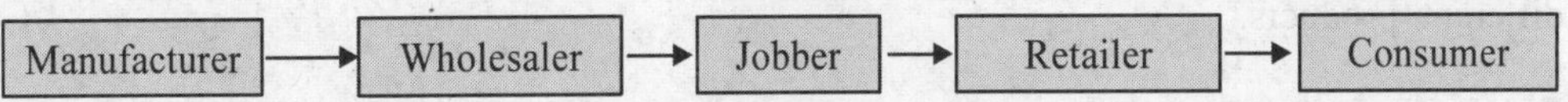

Note: *Because of the negative connotations of the word "jobber," they are now referred to by the more politically-correct term - "Off-price specialists."*

Figure 17.2

The Business Functions/Tasks Performed By Direct and Indirect Sales Channels

Business Function/Task	Direct Employees Direct Sales Force	Indirect Product Ownership	Product Non-ownership
1. Fixed Expenses	Yes	No	No
2. Variable Expenses	No	Yes	Yes
3. Tasks ownership of product	Yes	Yes	No
4. Product bears full sales cost	Yes	No	No
5. Sales cost spread over several product lines	No	Yes	Yes
6. Receives payment for product	Yes	Yes	No
7. Order Acceptance	Yes	Yes	No
8. Commissioned	Yes	No	Yes
9. Discount from manufacturers	No	Yes	No
10. Customers invoicing/billing	Yes	Yes	No
11. Ships to customers	Yes	Yes	No
12. Inventories Product	Yes	Yes	No
13. Determines Prices	Yes	Yes	No
14. Managerial Control	Yes	No	No
15. Has a sales force	Yes	Yes	Yes
16. Control over company image	Yes	No	No
17. Bureaucratic	Yes	No	No
18. Entrepreneurial	No	Yes	Yes
19. Possible Inter-channel Conflict	Yes	Yes	Yes
20. Sells only one product line	Yes	No	No

Source: *Channels of Distribution: The Marketing Executives Complete Guide by Kenneth Rolniki, pp 10.*

PARTICIPANTS IN THE DISTRIBUTION CHANNEL

Manufacturers can only produce the goods but it is the intermediary who supplies these goods to the people who are in need of it. To reach end consumers effectively, businesses need a well knitted network. The network includes manufacturers, retailers, wholesalers, agents and brokers commonly known as channel participants. These participants play a vital role in success and failure of any business. They actually bridge the gap between suppliers and end consumers thus framing the outline for a company in end users mindset. In the world of retail, several types of participants make up a distribution channel. Some of these might overlap each other because of the simple reason that retailers belong to several supply chains, each group focused on making and marketing different products.

Retailers

Retailers are the gate keepers to the market for all other members of the sales distribution process. The distinguishing feature that sets a retailer apart from other members of its distribution channel is that the retailer is the person who ultimately sells the goods to its end consumers.

Wholesalers

Wholesalers are intermediaries or middlemen who buy products from manufacturers and resell them to the retailers. They take the same types of financial risks as retailers, since they purchase the products, keep them in inventory until they are resold to retailers, and may arrange for shipment to those retailers. Wholesalers can gather product from around a country or region, or can buy foreign product lines by becoming importers.

Agents and Brokers

Agents (occasionally called brokers) are also intermediaries who work between suppliers and retailers, but their agreements are different, in that they do not take ownership of the products they sell. They are independent sales representatives who typically work on commission based on sales volume, and they can sell to wholesalers as well as retailers. In B2B arrangements, this means they sell to distributors and end consumers.

Resident Sales Agents

Resident sales agents are good examples in retail. They reside in the country to which they sell products, but the products come from a variety of foreign manufacturers. The resident sales agents represent those manufacturers, who pay the agent on commission. A resident sales agents does not always have merchandise warehoused and ready to sell, but he or she does have product samples for which orders can be placed and is responsible for bringing the items through the importation process[2].

The concept of resident sales agents in recent decade is getting popularity because it is not always practical for retailers to send someone abroad to check manufacturers'

[2] *www.media.wiley.com*

offerings and place the orders. On the other side by appointing resident sales agents in various countries, manufacturers can tap large number of small and big retailers who otherwise are difficult to knock.

Buying offices

Buying offices are also considered a type of commission agent or broker, since they make their money pairing up retailers with product lines from various manufacturers.

WHY DISTRIBUTION CHANNELS ARE REQUIRED?

Considering the fact that increase in number of participants in any distribution channel results in decreased profits and increased product cost, question arises why various participants are required in distribution? Why can't a manufacturer directly sell goods to a retailer, who sells to a consumer? It's a genuine question and must be answered. The fact actually lies with the limitations on the part of both the manufacturers and retailers. In fact most of the retailers are either too small or too large to handle all the essential functions themselves to get their products to end consumers. For instance, a specialty manufacturer who is excellent in making coloured candles may not have the skill to market its products or he may not have the enough financial resources to hire sales people, train them, motivate them and keep record of their sales performance. An agent who works for various small, non-competing firms can easily handle those functions in cost effective manner. It not only reduces a manufacturer's financial resources but precious time too.

The Necessity of Distribution Channels

Most business firms employ third parties or **intermediaries** to bring their products to market and ultimately to end consumers. They try to form a "distribution channel" which can be defined as

"...all the business firms through which goods and services must pass between its point of production and consumption"

Why does a business firm give the job of selling its goods and services to agents/intermediaries? Using intermediaries, simply means giving up some control over how goods and services are sold and who they are sold to.

The simple explanation to this query lies in the efficiency of distribution costs. Agents/intermediaries are expert in selling. They have the skills, contacts, know-how and scale of operations which means that better sales can be attained than if the manufacturer tried running a sales operation itself.

On the other hand, large companies need channel participants because they are also in the business of manufacturing, not marketing. Turning out tens of thousands of cases of soft drinks, for instance, do you think Coke has enough time to take retail orders? Channel members like wholesalers and retailers are useful because they are best at specific aspects of sales in their markets, leaving the manufacturers to do what they do best—which is turn out the best possible product.

Further, a distribution channel breaks the whole buying and selling process and all its allied negotiations into manageable tasks, each performed by companies that specialize in certain skills. Using a resident sales agent, can be profitable because these agents despite knowing the communication barriers are expert in laws and customs of the suppliers' nations and they generally offer their own lines of credit so the retailer won't have to deal with currency exchange or negotiate payment terms with a bank in another country, resulting in win-win situation for all the parties involved.

One more benefit of having distribution channel is its ability to counter with the unforeseen ups and downs of a supply chain. This usually comes from the capability of some channel participants to store surplus goods until they are required, and to store goods in expectation of seasonal sales hikes. Depending on how close their relationships, channel participants may also work together to acquire goods or services in greater quantity at discounts, transferring the savings to customers.

Consumers also find a distribution channel more convenient. It is the contribution of a distribution channel that provides today's customers all the things under one roof they can think of. Supermarket and hypermarkets are the examples of having the need for a distribution chain. Otherwise one can imagine how much more time and money he/she will spend having to buy every item at its source?

PHYSICAL DISTRIBUTION DEFINED

Physical Distribution is the set of activities aiming to provide intermediaries and customers with the right quality goods in right time and at right locations. Sound system of physical distribution does not result in cost cutting but leads to high level of quality service. Cost cutting is achieved through maintaining low inventory level to the extent possible with the use of cheaper forms of transportation and shipping goods in bulk. While high customer service levels can be achieved through quick and reliable delivery systems and having high inventory so that customers would have deep assortment of products without the chance of stock outs. ***Physical distribution*** takes place within numerous wholesaling and retailing distribution channels and includes such important areas as inventory control, customer service, packaging, warehouse, transportation, site selection and so on. In actual, physical distribution is a part of larger process called "distribution", which includes wholesale and retail marketing as well as physical movement of products.

In the recent years, physical distribution has attracted the attention of managers of modern organized retailers because of a number of reasons:

(i) Continuously increasing distribution cost

(ii) A major area for cost cutting and

(iii) Contribution towards sales promotion

These reasons are discussed as under:-

(i) Continuous rising costs: Due to the rising prices of petrol, diesel and other associated reasons like costly automobile vehicles, costly parts and their maintenance, the distribution costs are increasing day by day. Further, the elements of distribution costs such as labor, tools, and storage facilities like warehouses, transportation cost, inventory holding cost etc are becoming costlier year after year. Considering, it has attracted the attention of retail executives to plan and make policies to control rising costs.

(ii) Cost cutting: If distribution is handled properly, it can control the distribution cost to a major extent. Experience has shown that logistics areas, compared to others, always have the possibility to reduce cost. It can be done by effective inventory control, suitable site location, warehouse control, by optimizing the modes of transport and by effective supervision over elements of distribution costs.

(iii) Sales promotion: The main objective of physical distribution is to make the goods available to the customer. If distribution is properly managed, it can result in prompt deliveries, resulting in efficient customer service levels.

Physical Distribution

Physical distribution (PD) is concerned with effective movement of goods and services from the producer/provider to the ultimate consumer. In simple words, PD is concerned with transportation of merchandise, raw materials or by-products from place of manufacturing to place of selling (retail stores). On the other hand, physical distribution management (PDM) is concerned with controlling the movement of merchandise from their source (manufacturing unit) to their destination (retail store).

Retailers believe it a highly complex process, and one of the essential aspects of any business especially the retail one. The reasons to study physical distribution are many, the main among them is the critical cost area that is:

- 50% of total marketing costs,
- 25% of total manufacturing costs,
- 33% of food retailing, and
- 20% of GNP

Elements of Physical distribution system

(i) **Customer service:** It implies 'what type and level of customer service customers' require?'

(ii) **Order processing:** It implies 'how effective the sales ordered be handled?'

(iii) **Inventory control:** It implies 'determining the optimum level of inventory?'

(iv) **Warehousing:** It implies 'how many warehouses should be managed? Where should inventory be placed?'

(v) **Transportation mode:** It implies 'what type of transportation mode should be used without compromising with timely deliveries and transit damage?'

(vi) **Material handling:** It implies "how effectively the merchandise be handled during transportation?'

Criteria for Choice of Physical Distribution Channel

- acceptable product quality
- dependable deliveries
- efficient order processing
- fair price
- sizable inventory

New trends in Physical Distribution

- Changing role of warehouses/distribution centres
- Growth in air and sea transport
- Growth in heavy goods vehicles
- Growth in JIT production
- Growth in light vehicles goods
- Increase in road and decline in rail transport
- Increased road congestion
- Restrictions on driver hours

ELEMENTS OF PHYSICAL DISTRIBUTION

The overall objective of any physical distribution system is to provide right quality of goods to the customers in right time and at right place.

The various elements of a physical distribution system are:

1. Customer service

Customer service is a predefined standard of customer satisfaction, which a retailer plans to provide to its customers. Without defining and setting 'standards of customer service', retailers cannot achieve competitive advantage over their competitors. A customer service standard may be that 95% of the orders are delivered within 5 hours of receipt and 100% are delivered within 24 hours. Retailers maintaining higher service standards bear costs of maintaining higher inventory level or expenditure incurred on fast mode of transportation. The effective distribution systems must keep proper records of costs of meeting various customer service standards (90%, 95% or 100% of orders delivered within 24 hours), and additional customer satisfaction that results from raising standards.

Physical Distribution's Goal

The primary goal of the physical distribution system is to place the right goods in the right place, at the right time, in the right quantity, and with the right support services.

These days, specialized software packages are being used by modern retailers to track the merchandise during its transportation to ensure fastest, cost-effective deliveries on time. Customer service levels may be improved by following steps too:

(a) By ensuring product availability all the time.

(b) By improving order cycle time – it implies reducing the gap between placing the order and its delivery time.

(c) By providing proper training to sales persons and employees engaged in transportation.

(d) By having separate plans for

- quick deliveries in case of urgent orders
- in case of natural/unforeseen problems
- loss in transit etc

2. Order Processing

Order processing, alternatively known as order fulfillment is the handling of customer orders within the distribution center (may be warehouse, retail store itself) involving the keying of customer and order details into the computer system in order to produce the invoices for picking. The basic idea is to deliver the orders as per customers' wants of place and timing. Therefore, action should be taken quickly as an order has been placed and the customer must have fast confirmation of the order's receipt and the exact delivery time. In today's high tech world, computers are used to check the customer's credit rating, stock levels, and delivery promptness so that management can obtain an accurate picture of distribution status. Accuracy plays a vital role in successful order processing, as are procedures that are designed to lessen (shorten) the order processing cycle.

The task of order processing begins with the receipt of an order from a customer through telephone, personal visit or by fax or email.

The basic areas for improving order processing tasks relate to following questions:

(a) What a sales person does when he receives an order?

(b) What happens when such an order is received by the order department directly?

(c) How much it takes to ensure inventory status?

(d) What methods are in practice for checking inventory?

The intelligent retailer would take proper steps to minimise the gaps in above-mentioned situations to fulfill the customer order. Plugging these gaps certainly will result in high customer service levels.

Figure 17.3
Functions of Physical Distribution

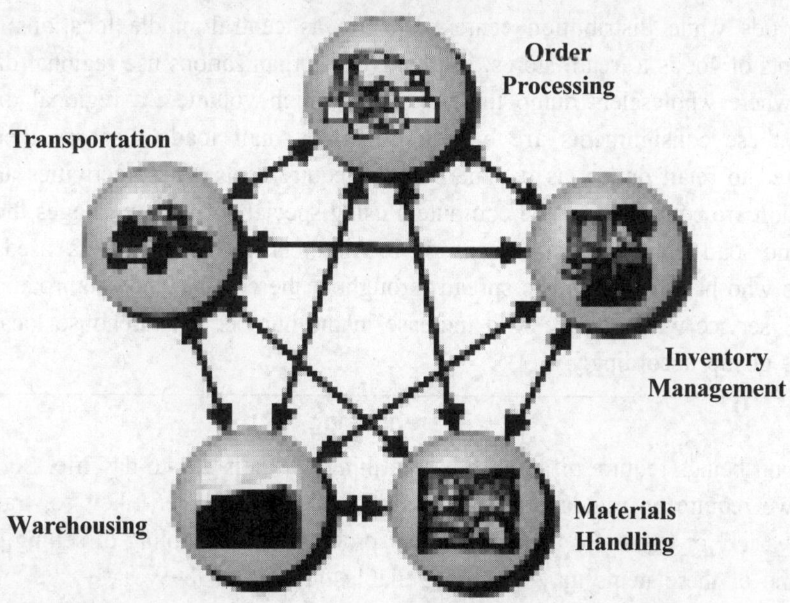

3. Inventory control

Inventory control is a major component of a retail organization's physical distribution system. It includes money invested in inventory, wear and tear and possible obsolescence of the goods with the passage of time. In a retail organization, where finance executives seek inventory minimization, marketing executives advocate large inventories to prevent stock outs. Therefore, retailers should to try minimize optimum level of inventory to meet the customers' demand close to customer service standards of 100%.

The companies offering wide merchandise assortments find it difficult to have all the probable items in large quantities that a customer might order. For them, it is suggested to segregate patterns as:

(a) fast moving items, and

(b) slow moving items.

A high customer service standard is then applied to fast moving items but a much lower standard is used for those moving slowly or have less demand. Inventory control experts have developed a number of methods, which can help retailers control inventory effectively. The widely used method is economic Order Quantity (EOQ) model. Besides this, ABC analysis is also applied throughout the globe. (*discussed in detail in unit 9 – Merchandise Management*)

4. Warehousing

It involves all the activities required in storage of goods between the time these are procured and the time these are transported to the customer upon receipt of order. This function basically involves receiving the merchandise, breaking bulk, storing and loading for delivery to customers as per their details. Storage warehouses usually keep goods for long periods while distribution centers operate as central/middle locations for quick movements of goods to retail stores. Further, retail organizations use regional distribution centers where wholesalers dump the products in high volume. At regional distribution centers, these consignments are broken down to small loads that are then quickly transported to retail outlets as per the outlet's requirements. These activities and related information are controlled by the computers using special software packages those gather goods and load them to their places of requirements. This system is used by large suppliers who have retail outlets spread throughout the country and/or abroad. Levels of customer service will increase with increase in the number of warehouse locations, but cost will go up accordingly.

Warehousing

Human beings require different types of things in their day-to-day life. Some items, which we require on regular basis are usually stored in home. Likewise, traders also need a variety of goods for their day-to-day production, assembling or selling purposes, and some of these items may not be available throughout the year.

To understand this concept, take an example of flourmill. It requires wheat as main raw material for producing flour, but we know that wheat is a seasonal item and is produced during a particular period in the year. Since, flour production takes place throughout the year, it requires the supply of wheat whole year without any interruption. But how is it done? The answer is to store the wheat as per the requirement. Once the flour is produced, it is not certain that it will be sold or distributed at the same time in one go. Therefore, it requires storage of not only the raw wheat but finished products, which involve proper arrangements from the time of their production or procurement to the distribution time or final sale. Simply stated, when the storage of goods (raw material/ semi-finished/ finished goods) is done in a systematic manner and at large scale, it is termed as 'warehousing'. The place where goods are stored or kept is known as 'warehouse' and the person who takes care of warehouse is called 'warehouse-keeper' or 'storekeeper'.

The warehousing function which helps manufacturers to smooth discrepancies between production and consumption cycles that hardly match, helps retailers to meet unforeseen demand. The retailer must decide about the size, number and location of warehouses. Warehousing location means the goods can be delivered to customers as and when desired. Some merchandise is kept at or near the retail stores, and rest is located in warehouses at some distance. Therefore, an optimum strategy must be established that reflects and results in desired level of customer service.

5. Transportation Mode

Transportation is indispensable for physical distribution of goods and services. Transportation mode enables channel members like producers, wholesalers and retailers to make goods and services available at the customers' place of purchase or at his doorstep. From cost point of view, transportation accounts nearly 25-40% of total distribution costs. Quick and timely delivery, security of goods during transit and proper handling results in customer satisfaction. Following aspects signify the increased role of transportation:

(a) To supply goods in proper quality and quantity
(b) To supply goods at right time and at right place
(c) To satisfy customers' demands
(d) Quick and easy availability of goods
(e) Cost considerations

Due to technological developments and variety of transportation modes available, a retail organization can use anyone or a combination of following modes of transport:

- Rail,
- Airway,
- Roadways,
- Water ways, and
- Pipelines

6. Materials Handling

Materials handling implies the movement of goods inside the retail organization, warehouses and retail stores/outlets. In case of chain stores, the raw materials, finished goods etc move from a common warehouse to various store locations. Similarly, in case of multistory or even single-story storage houses, movements of goods take place. Some items or materials may be light weight but few may be heavy, which may requirc proper handling and utmost care. In modern storage facilities, material handling is through equipments meant for moving/transferring goods. These handling equipments also vary with method of loading and modes of transport used like railways, water ways, airways etc. Type of handling equipment used will depend upon the following reasons:

(a) Mode of transport: rail, air, water, road and others.

(b) Nature & size of goods (materials: heavy, light, solid, liquid or gases).

(c) Place of operation: warehouse & selling floor

WHOLESALING

Wholesaling, commonly known as wholesale trade, involves selling goods or services to those who buy goods with the intention to resale or redistribute (but not directly to the ultimate consumers). Wholesaling does not include farmers and manufactures because basically they are engaged in production.

The persons involved in wholesale business are known as wholesalers or distributors. They even differ from retailers in several ways:

(i) The wholesaler deals with the sales to any customer except the ultimate consumer who buys things for his/her own requirement (use), while a retailer has direct interaction with the ultimate consumer.

(ii) Wholesalers are concerned with manufacturing goods at affordable prices – a price which results in minimum variable cost. Therefore, in order to minimize manufacturing cost per unit (MCPU), manufacturers do not pay much attention to location, promotion and atmosphere because they don't have to deal with the ultimate customers, while on the other hand, retailer's success in the business will depend upon these factors only.

(iii) The government rules, regulations, laws and taxes vary from manufacturers to retailers.

(iv) Wholesaling generally is done at large scale. The number of transactions in wholesaling may be less from retail business but are large in volume (monetary terms).

(v) Wholesalers as compared to retailers cover large trading areas targeting several regions at a time.

Some examples of wholesale business are:

(i) A business organization purchases helmets from manufacturers for resale,

(ii) A firm selling fruits to juice shops for selling juices to customers,

(iii) A dress material company makes identity cards and sells it to schools, colleges and institutions for their employees or workers, and/or

(iv) A firm selling sugar packets to confectioners to prepare sweets for customers.

Why retailers don't buy from manufacturers?

Wholesalers are the link between manufacturers and retailers. If retailers buy from the manufacturer directly, they can save commission charged/profit earned by the wholesalers. Then the question arises that is the wholesaler a necessity or a compulsion? Here are the few reasons mentioned, which advocate the essence of wholesalers in any distribution channel:

(i) Limited infrastructure: This is a fact that most of the manufacturers belong to small and medium sized enterprises (SMEs). Undoubtedly, they are specialist and have expertise in manufacturing but do not have as much infrastructure that may meet or sell to all the possible buyers. Wholesalers' presence becomes essential here.

(ii) Skill and efficiency: Wholesalers buy goods and resell them quickly, they are the experts in their areas. Such skills, expertize and efficiency are missing with most of the manufacturers and retailers.

(iii) Economies of scale: Wholesalers, due to specialization in their field keep the prices of goods stable and result in cost reduction due to continuous supply and economies of scale.

(iv) Size of retailers: In developing countries like India, Pakistan, China etc, most of the retailers are small and do not have enough funds and space to buy goods in bulk from the manufacturers. In India only, we have more than 12 million retailers who earn primarily for their own livelihood. Even employment provided by them is negligible because family members help them. Here, retailers are required.

(v) Transaction economy: This is a fact that presence of wholesalers in any business reduces number of business transactions. This is nothing but economies of scale. This is also evident from figure 17.4 shown below:

Figure 17.4
Business Transactions

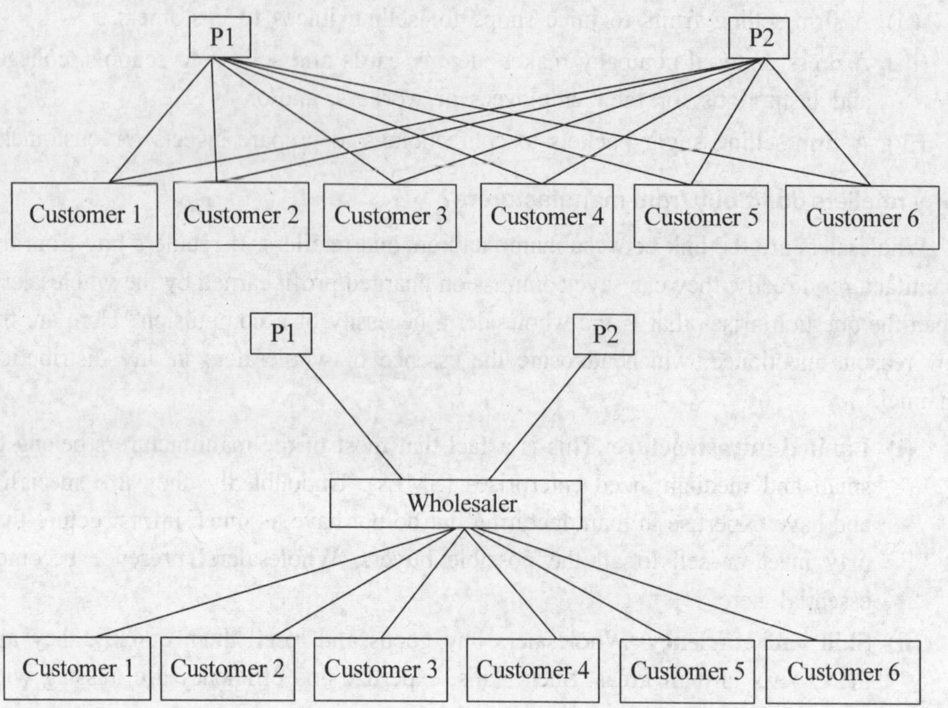

In figure 17.4 without wholesalers and with the presence of two producers (P1 & P2) and six customers (C1 – C6), total number of transactions are 12, but with the presence of wholesalers, the transactions between same numbers of producers (P1 & P2) and six customers (C1 – C6) reduce to 8 only.

Hence, wholesaling becomes necessary for smooth selling operations. In the absence of wholesalers, retailers will have to purchase in bulk to ensure availability of stock throughout the year or as and when required, which will result in their increased expenditure. Further, retailers are so scattered that it is not even feasible for the manufacturers to reach each retailer.

Besides the above-mentioned reasons, wholesalers are being widely used because they perform following functions effectively and prudently:

(i) Sales and promotion: Wholesalers bridge the gap between manufacturers and retailers with their sales force. They facilitate manufacturers to reach large number of scattered small shopkeepers at affordable prices. Wholesalers are good in public relations, they have large number of contacts and therefore, they can reach to retailers and convince then to buy goods. Even retailers trust wholesalers than remote situated manufacturers.

(ii) Credit facility: Wholesalers usually sell goods to retailers on credit basis. In the absence of wholesalers, retailers will have no option to buy on credit basis.

Sometimes, wholesalers finance customers by granting trade credits and finance suppliers by ordering early and paying payments on time.

(iii) Warehousing: Wholesalers usually use warehouses at large numbers. By holding inventories in stock, all the time, retailers at least save inventory related expenditures and risks to suppliers and customers.

(iv) Assortment building: Wholesalers buy in bulk, select items and build assortments for their customers as and when required by them, which involves saving customers' valuable time and efforts.

(v) Quick delivery: Wholesalers as compared to manufacturers are close to retailers. Therefore, they are capable of providing quick deliveries even at short notice.

(vi) Absorption of risk: Wholesalers due to complexities of their business, absorb few risks by taking title and bearing the losses for obsolescence, damage, spoilage, theft and deterioration.

(vii) Source of information: Wholesalers due to their role and market position, guide retailers about competitors' move, products and trade policies. Wholesalers are an easy and reliable source of information for retailers.

(viii) Expert services: Wholesalers due to large exposure, retain retailers, help them by providing training to their employees and marketing & selling staff, guidance for store layout & design, inventory control, planning merchandise assortments and so on.

Ways to Categorize Wholesalers: Classification and Characteristics

Liberalization, privatization and globalization (LPG) throughout the globe have increased the level of services rendered by wholesalers. Now besides leading activities like storage and accounting, wholesalers act as category captain, transporter, financer and risk bearer. Consequently, many varieties of wholesalers have emerged and still under transition stage. There are nearly ten major wholesaler types. Some of these wholesalers also have online presence but still the wholesalers offer and expect from their customers to place orders among phone, fax and couriers. With the wholesale industry, online retailing is just another communication option rather than a significantly separate distribution channel. These are classified as below:

(i) General merchandise wholesalers: This type of wholesalers deal with broad but shallow product lines to market to the small general merchandise retailers such as convenience stores or variety stores dealing with wide range of products mix like pharmaceuticals, cosmetics, foods and hardware. As general merchandise retailers deal with wide product assortments, their expertise about individual products may not be very strong.

(ii) Speciality merchandise wholesalers: These wholesalers offer one or two specialized lines like handicrafts, seafood, woolen items, hand-made items, Persian carpets, wooden furniture etc. In order to focus on specific product lines, most of the speciality merchandise wholesalers direct their marketing and promotional efforts to few selected industries. Since, speciality wholesalers deal with narrow product assortments, they tend to be highly knowledgeable of the markets they cater.

(iii) Contractual wholesalers: As the very name implies, contractual wholesalers provide wholesale services to the limited number of retailers those are involved in the contractual arrangement. Contractual wholeselling basically focus on wholesaler-sponsored channel arrangements where a wholesaler brings together and manages several independent retailers.

(iv) Cash and carry wholesalers: These are limited service merchant wholesalers who usually offer Fast Moving Consumers Goods (FMCG) to small retailers for cash. Food industry is the typical cash and carry operation where buyers visit the wholesaler's facility, select items, pay in cash and handle their own delivery to their place of business. Simply stated, cash and carry wholesalers perform most of the wholeselling functions except the following:

- Transportation (delivery),
- Financing, and
- Promotion of products

The items sold under cash and carry operations are fast moving like grocery, electrical fittings, building materials, cosmetics, beauty products etc.

(v) Industrial wholesalers: Industrial wholesalers commonly known as industrial distributors direct their wholesale operations to the industrial/business customers rather than to the resellers. Further, depending upon the nature and size of distributor, wholesaler offers either broad or narrow product lines.

(vi) Truck wholesalers: These wholesalers mainly sell and deliver a limited line of semi-perishable merchandise such as certain groceries like fish, vegetables, fruits, bread, butter & oils to small retailers, cafeterias, hospitals, airlines, supermarkets, restaurants and hotels. Such wholesalers often have limited geographical locations to deliver, on the spot inspection and acceptance. Truck wholesalers usually offer specialty product lines with many being found in the retail food industry and the industrial retailing.

(vii) Rack jobber: Like truck wholesalers, rack jobber sells merchandise from a truck and is also known as service merchandiser. However, the main difference between a rack jobber and truck wholesaler is that rack jobbers are assigned and manage space within the retailer's store. Rack jobbers usually serve non-food items such as drugs, grocery, magazines, cosmetics and house wares. They send their delivery trucks to stores and delivery people set up display counters, price the goods, keep them fresh, sell and keep the uptodate inventory record. Rack jobbers, sometimes known as service merchandisers, perform purchasing, stocking, financing functions for retailers. They may prefer 'consignment selling' wherein a retailer pays for merchandise after these are sold out.

WAREHOUSING

Warehousing is the overall design and operation of storage facilities. In warehouses, traders store goods until these are drawn by channel members for further movement for sales and delivery. Storing the goods is not the only function of warehouses. Warehouses perform a series of functions such as storage, assembling, dividing, receiving and sorting.

The main objectives of warehousing are:

(i) To minimize the cost of transportation

(ii) To enhance customer satisfaction level

(i) Minimizing costs: As we know that transportation account for fifty percent of overall marketing budget. If most of the time, a customer demands an item and the item has to be transported to the warehouse from the manufacturers' premises, the cost of transportation will be non-bearable, knowing that bulk transportation reduces transportation cost per unit (TCPO).

(ii) Enhancing cost: There is no doubt that in case of warehousing, overhead expenditure can be saved. Warehouses besides ensuring product availability reduce the prices of products resulting in enhanced customer service level.

Functions Performed By Warehouses

Warehouses are must for retailing success. Warehouses usually perform following functions:

(i) Procurement: Procurement is the very first step in warehousing. Under this step, goods are received, unloaded and moved to pre-receipt inspection point and for accounting purpose.

(ii) Sorting: Sorting is a step in which items are received in bulk are sorted out itemwise for its better storage and easy identification. Heavy and big sized items are kept separate.

(iii) Breaking (dividing): Under breaking, items received in bulk are broken down into smaller portions and packed separately to cater the requirements of various retail outlets and customers.

(iv) Storage: After sorting and dividing, items are stored with proper identification and location so as to take them out as and when required. Bin location cards are used for this purpose. Big retailers also use computers and merchandise based software packages to locate, identify and maintain accounting of the items.

(v) Making items available for consignment/shipment: In warehouses, goods are stored for short period, as per the orders from retail outlets or customers, goods are dispatched to the destinations.

(vi) **Material handling**: Material handling is a part of physical distribution system consisting of proper handling equipments used for loading, unloading, lifting and moving goods from one place to another.

(vii) **Display**: In order to promote sales, some warehouses display products.

(viii) **Inventory control**: It includes procuring goods and keeping proper records of the goods. Warehouses are also responsible for inspection, maintenance and accounting of goods to avoid them from theft and unforeseen mishaps. Proper accounting results in avoiding large fluctuations in inventory levels.

(ix) **Processing**: Certain goods are not to be consumed in the form they are produced. It requires processing to make them consumable. For instance, fruits are ripened, timber is seasoned, wheat is crushed, paddy is polished and juices are filtered etc. Some warehouses also perform these activities as per the demand from the owners.

(x) **Grading and branding**: Some warehouses perform the functions of grading and branding of goods on the behalf of the producers, wholesalers or the importer of goods. Besides usual activities, some warehouses provide mixing, blending and packaging assistance for the convenience of handling and sale.

(xi) **Transportation**: In few cases, warehouses provide transportation facility to big depositors. It collects goods from the factories and sends these goods to the place of delivery on the request of the depositors.

Features of Ideal Warehouses

An Ideal warehouse

(i) **Proper location**: For effective movement of goods and cost saving, warehouses should be established at places, which are convenient to both the buyer and the seller. These warehouses should be set up near railway stations, major highways, seaports and airports, where goods can be loaded and unloaded conveniently. It is also recommended to have godowns in open places so that the vehicles can move around easily.

(ii) **Use of Mechanical Appliances**: In the warehouses, mechanical appliances should be used to load and unload the goods. It not only results in safety of men and material but also reduces wastages in handling goods and overall handling costs.

(iii) **Sufficient space**: For an ideal warehouse, adequate space should be covered for maximum storage and to keep the goods in proper order. Each trader (big or small) would want that all of his merchandise should be accommodated in one warehouse so that he need not travel to different places to manage the loading and unloading of his goods.

(iv) **Proximity to the market**: The warehouses should be established at a place where market for raw materials and for selling finished goods is as close as possible. This is the reason that big warehouses are close to commercial places or bus stands.

(v) **Parking Facility**: Parking along road, public places in the urban/suburban areas continue to be a harrowing experience for the traders who visit from outstations. Hence, in warehouses, proper arrangements should be made inside the premises to assist quick loading, unloading and safe parking.

(vi) **Safety Measures**: A warehouse, which basically is used to store eatables or perishable goods like bread, butter, fruits, eggs and vegetables should be equipped with proper cold storage, moisture resistance etc facilities. Further, efforts should be made to secure the warehouse against possibilities of theft and damage from heat, rainwater, insects, pests and fire. The use of fire extinguishers, safety alarms, budgers and round the clock security arrangements should be there to secure warehouses from unforeseen mishappenings.

(vii) **Economical**: The warehouse location, layout, construction and maintenance should be done in such a way that ensures maximum storage of goods at minimum expense.

(viii) **Proper Management**: If warehouses are not managed properly, all the money spent will go waste. Mismanagement may lead to theft, loss, errors and omissions of goods stored by various traders. Hence, a strict control over the warehouse is essential on permanent basis. A permanent officer should be appointed for proper arrangements of incoming and outgoing goods.

Classification of Warehouses

1. **Private Warehouses**: These are owned and managed by the channel suppliers (manufacturers/traders) and resellers and are used exclusively for their own distribution activities.

Examples:

(a) Warehouses constructed by farmers/producers near their fields/places of work.

(b) Warehouses owned and managed by wholesalers and retailers close to their selling centers.

(c) Warehouses constructed by manufacturers near their production units.

(d) Warehouses taken on rent by retail stores.

(e) Retailers may have several regional warehouses to cater the needs of their stores.

(f) Warehouses owned/leased by a wholesaler where it stores and distributes.

Maintaining private warehouses involves fixed as well as variable costs. Examples of fixed costs are basically the investments made in terms of insurance, capital, interests and taxes. The variable costs on the other hand, include maintenance costs and operating costs. Therefore, due to large expenses, private companies prefer to have assistance of public warehouses and will go for private warehouses under following situations:

(i) Wide presence and firm commitment in the region and necessity to have permanent base in an area.

(ii) Considering long term strategic advantage

(iii) Scope of optimum utilization is assured for long periods.

(iv) To build advantage over competitors.

2. Public Warehouses: These warehouses are owned by government[3] and semi government bodies and are made available to private firms to store goods on payment of rent. The public warehouses are usually set up to help small traders who are not in position to have their own warehouses due to financial constraints. Therefore, in order to promote trade and industry, central or state governments come forward to cater such storage needs of traders/retailers. Anyone can avail these facilities to solve its short-term distribution needs. Retailers sometimes due to increased sales even find their private warehouses insufficient if their facilities have reached capacity or if they are making a special, huge purchase of products for some reasons. For example, before festivals or before marriage seasons, retailers may order extra merchandise to avoid 'out of stock' situations. These warehouses are typically regulated by the government bodies. Costs incurred by the private firms for the use of public warehouses are considered as variable. These warehouses are mainly used by manufacturers/producers, exporters and importers.

3. Bonded Storage: These warehouses are owned, managed and controlled by government as well as private agencies. Bonded warehouses are storage facility used to store imported goods for which import duty is still to be paid. The bonded warehouses run by private agencies have to obtain license from the government. In actual, this enables the government bodies to hold control on private firms to pay their taxes on time. Without paying duties, importers cannot take over or open the goods. Globally, it has been seen that these warehouses are found near the ports and are usually owned by dock authorities. Bonded warehouses are subject to two types of taxes: (a) Excise duty[4] and (b) Custom duty[5].

4. Co-operative Warehouses: As the very name implies, these warehouses are owned, managed and controlled by co-operative societies. These societies provide storage facilities on the most economical rates to their members only. The basic purpose to run such warehouses is not to earn profit but to help their members.

---

3 In India, Container Cooperation of India Ltd (CONCOR) is a government of India' enterprise committed to provide cost effective, reliable and responsive logistics solution to its customers. Today, it strives to be the first choice for its customers and offers bondage facility for deferral to duty payment and at the same time, allows for cargo to be stored at an affordable rates. CONCOR offers such facility at Tuglakabad (New Delhi), Ton-diarpet (Chennai), Sanathnagar (Secundrabad), New Mulund (Mumbai), Gwalior etc.

4 Excise duty, sometimes called excise tax, is a type of tax charged on goods produced within the country usually before wholesale stage.

5 Customs is a government body responsible for collecting and safeguarding custom duties and for controlling the flow of goods including eatables, cosmetics, personal effects and hazardous items in and outside the country. This duty is levied on import and/or export of goods.

5. Distribution Centres: This type of storage facility usually has large space, which enables fast movement of large quantities of stores for short period. While, on the other hand, conventional warehouses hold goods for long time, say 2 months or 1 year. These warehouses basically by nature, serve as points in the distribution system at which goods are procured from different suppliers and quickly transferred to various customers. These centers provide computerized control, which make movement of goods quick, fast and reliable. In order to minimize delivery time, these storage facilities are found close to transportation centers. In some cases, distribution centers handle the goods for less than a day period such as in case of fast foods or perishable products. Most of the goods enter in the early morning (dawn time) and is transferred/distributed by the evening time.

Automated Warehouse

With technological advancement and use of computers and internet, some warehouses be of any nature, provide automated capabilities. According to the location, nature and size of warehouse, automation and use of robotics technology may vary from store to store. For instance, in many warehouses, machines are used to handle nearly all physical distribution activities around multistory buildings spreaded in long and wide areas.

Climate-controlled Warehouse

This is a warehouse with different facility. Such warehouses handle storage of goods that require proper temperature or special handling conditions such as freezers for storing frozen items, dirt free facilities for storing highly sensitive technological/computer accessories, produce or flowers for humidity controlled environments for delicate/low weight items.

Need for Warehousing

The warehouse is a place where the supply chain holds or preserves the goods. The need for warehousing arises because of the following reasons:

(i) Seasonal production: We know that certain items are produced during 'particular period of the year, like agricultural goods are harvested during a particular season say summer, winter or monsoon, but the requirement of consumption takes place all over the year. Therefore, it requires proper storage or warehousing for these goods, so that supply should be ensured throughout the year.

(ii) Bulk production: Due to borderless economies and globalization, manufacturing generally takes place throughout the year not only to meet the domestic demands or existing demands but also for the future demands. In order to enjoy the benefits of economies of scale, manufacturers produce goods in bulk because by purchasing large volume of raw materials, the raw manufacturer can reduce the ordering cost as well as carrying cost.

(iii) Non-stop production: Non-stop production commonly known as continuous or regular production of goods requires the adequate supply of raw materials. Considering the uncertainties of future and country specific problems like traffic jams, bad climatic conditions, inadequate infrastructure facilities like bad roads, waterlogging, road blockage etc, it becomes essential to have sufficient supply of raw material in the warehouse to ensure non-stop production.

(iv) **Seasonal/irregular demand**: In our day-to-day life, we use certain items, which are required seasonally, like umbrellas in rainy season, woolen garments in winters. But the production of these items takes place throughout the year because manufacturers cannot close their factories. Therefore, it requires storage facility to store/stock these items to make them available as and when required.

(v) **Ensuring supply near the place of consumption**: This is a fact that agricultural as well as industrial (including FMCG) goods are produced at separate locations but are consumed throughout the nation. Therefore, traders (suppliers, wholesalers or retailers) in order to meet regular and uncertain demands of the customers, stock adequate quantities of raw materials in the warehouses. Further, they have the fear of loosing customers in case of stock out.

(vi) **Price consistency**: As we know that shortage of any thing in the market will lead to increased prices, likewise excess supply of goods in the market results in full prices of the goods. Therefore, in order to maintain consistency in the prices of goods, it requires adequate stock in the warehouses all the time. By doing so, traders can maintain a balance between supply of goods and its prices.

Benefits of Warehousing

Warehousing has many benefits to offer to traders/businessmen, whether it is wholesale or retail, it provides a number of benefits listed as under:

(i) **Safety and preservation**: Manufacturers, importers, wholesalers, exporters, traders and stockiest use warehouses to store their goods (raw materials and finished items) before distribution and sale. Besides, serving the storage purpose, warehousing facilitates preservation facility against water, fire, theft and climatic changes. Due to technological advancements, safety measures and computerization, warehouses minimize spoilage, errors, accidents, omissions, breakage, deterioration in quality etc.

(ii) **Trouble free handling**: Today warehouses are usually large plain buildings in industrial or institutional areas of cities and towns equipped with loading docks to load and unload trucks, from railways, seaports or airports. They also have automatic fork lifts and cranes for moving goods from one place to another within the warehouse area. Some warehouses are completely automated with no workers working inside resulting in minimum wastage and easy handling during loading and unloading goods.

(iii) **Ensuring continuous supply**: Certain commodities like agricultural products are produced during a certain period of year but consumed or required throughout the year. Warehouses ensure adequate supply of such seasonal products throughout the year without any break.

(iv) **Lifeline for small traders**: Due to rising costs of land and financial limitations, small traders cannot afford to have their private warehouses. Public or government warehouses facilitate them to store goods at affordable rates. In absence of warehouses, it will be difficult for small traders to survive in cut-throat competition because 'stock out' situation if persists for long, can disrupt the image and goodwill of the traders especially the small traders who have no/limited marketing budget to spend.

(v) **Assisting in continuous production**: Warehouses facilitate the manufacturers to produce goods throughout the year without much attention of raw material shortage. The manufacturers who usually produce in bulk require raw materials in large quantity. Warehouses assist them to provide agricultural (seasonal) and industrial goods all over the year.

(vi) **Location advantage**: Most of the warehouses are located at a convenient place near railways, highways, seaports and airports that facilitate smooth movements of goods. Further, convenient location reduces the distribution cost to great extent.

(vii) **Employment generation**: Warehouses are usually large plain buildings in industrial areas of cities and towns covering huge storage area. Warehouses located in or near industrial areas are so big that can store goods of large number of businessmen at a time. Further, besides storage, warehouses perform several functions like procurement, sorting, dividing, marketing, preparing for shipment, handling, inventory control, display, order processing, financing, transportation, grading and branding and so on resulting in employment generation in various sections and at various levels. It is the source of bread and butter for several laborers, workers, employees and officers.

(viii) **Financing**: When businessmen store goods in the warehouses upon certain formalities, they get 'deposit receipt', which acts as a proof about the deposit of the goods. Warehouses also issue a document in the name of owner against storage of goods, which is known as warehouse-keeper's warrant. This document can be transferred by simple endorsement and delivery. Businessmen on account of these documents (warrants) may get financial aids/loans from banks, private tenders on financial companies. In some cases, warehouses also provide finance to the businessmen on keeping goods as collateral security.

(ix) **Risk reduction**: Warehouse owners/authorities make certain that the goods stored in their warehouses are well protected, preserved and monitored. In order to keep proper information about good details, to save goods from theft and pilferage, warehouses employ employees and security staff. For perishable items, they provide cold storage facility, to protect warehouse from fire, fire-fighting equipments are used. On requirement, goods stored may be insured against unforeseen mishaps like loss due to fire, theft and natural disasters.

(x) Assisting in selling: Most of the warehouses, as per requirements from depositors' side, provide assistance towards inspection of goods, sorting, branding, packaging, financing and labeling that is essential towards sale of goods. In certain cases, transport arrangements may be availed to depositors for their bulk deposits.

SUMMARY

A distribution is the path followed by product and services to move from manufacturer to end consumer. Manufacturers have the option to sell their manufactured goods either through *direct* or an *indirect* channel of distribution (COD). In case of direct channel, manufacturer hire sales force, train them and sell goods directly to end consumers. In the early fifties, the only way to get an IBM typewriter was to order to IBM offices run and managed exclusively by IBM. As the time passed, technology developed, business expended across the borders, the path between manufacturer and end consumers developed a hundred folds and the concept of indirect distribution became popular. The direct channel of distribution offers a number of benefits to the manufacturers. The main advantage it offers is the control over sales force. The manufacturer's representatives/officials further can guide its sales force where to sell, what to sell, how to sell and how much to charge without any harm to company's image. But a direct channel is not suitable for every manufacturer and is also not recommended to small manufacturer who lack enough financial resources. The reasons why customers buy from indirect channel are:

- Customer service and technical support
- Logistical support and
- Convenience of one stop shopping

REVIEW QUESTIONS

True and False Questions

1. Distribution channel is a means used to transfer merchandise from the manufacturer to the end user through retailer and other necessary intermediaries.
2. An intermediary in the channel is called an agent/middleman.
3. The basic function of a distribution channel is to provide a link between production and consumption and to create time, place and possession utilities which constitute the added value of distribution.
4. A zero level channel has infinite intermediary levels.
5. A one level channel contains one selling intermediary.
6. A two level channel encompasses two intermediary levels - a manufacturer and a retailer.
7. A wholesaler typically buys and stores large quantities of merchandise from various manufacturers and then breaks into the bulk deliveries to supply retailers with smaller quantities.
8. A third level channel, as the name implies, encompasses three intermediary levels – a wholesaler, a retailer and a manufacturer.
9. A ***jobber*** is a person or firm that purchases small quantities of goods and services from manufacturers and importers and resells to merchants rather than to the end customers.

10. Retailers are the gate keepers to the market for all other members of the sales distribution process.
11. The distinguishing feature that sets a retailer apart from other members of its distribution channel is that the retailer is the person who ultimately sells the goods to its end consumers.
12. Wholesalers are intermediaries or middlemen who buy products from manufacturers and resell them to the retailers.
13. Wholesalers can gather product from around a country or region, or can buy foreign product lines by becoming importers.
14. Agents are intermediaries who work between suppliers and retailers, but their agreements are different, in that they do not take ownership of the products they sell.
15. A resident sales agent always have merchandise warehoused and ready to sell, but he or she does have product samples for which orders can be placed and is responsible for bringing the items through the importation process.
16. The concept of resident sales agents in recent decade is getting popularity because it is not always practical for retailers to send someone abroad to check manufacturer's offerings and place the orders.
17. Buying offices are also considered a type of commission agent or broker, since they make their money pairing up retailers with product lines from various manufacturers.
18. Physical distribution takes place within numerous wholesaling and retailing distribution channels and includes such important areas as inventory control, customer service, packaging, warehousing, transportation, site selection and so on.
19. Despite of rising prices of petrol, diesel and other associated reasons like costly automobile vehicles, costly parts and their maintenance, the distribution costs are stable since decades.
20. The main objective of physical distribution is to make the goods available to the customer. If distribution is properly managed, it can result in prompt deliveries, resulting in efficient customer service levels.
21. Physical distribution (PD) is concerned with effective movement of goods and services from the producer/provider to the ultimate consumer.
22. The primary goal of the physical distribution system is to place the right goods in the right place, at the right time, in the right quantity, and with the right support services.
23. Retailers maintaining higher service standards enjoy costs of maintaining lower inventory level or expenditure incurred on fast mode of transportation.
24. Inventory control is a minor component of a retail organization's physical distribution system.
25. Warehousing involves all the activities required in storage of goods between the time they are procured and the time they are transported to the customer upon receipt of order.

26. Warehousing basically involves receiving the merchandise, breaking bulk, storing and loading for delivery to customers as per their details.
27. Storage warehouses usually keep goods for long periods while distribution centers operate as central/middle locations for quick movements of goods to retail stores.
28. Transportation is indispensable for physical distribution of goods and services. Transportation mode enables channel members like producers, wholesalers and retailers to make goods and services available at the customers' place of purchase or at his doorstep.
29. Material handling implies the movement of goods inside the retail organization, warehouses and retail stores/outlets.
30. Wholesaling, commonly known as wholesale trade, involves selling goods or services to those who buy goods with the intention to consume.
31. Wholesalers are concerned with manufacturing goods at an affordable prices – a price which results in minimum variable cost.
32. Wholesalers are the link between manufacturers and customers.
33. General merchandise wholesalers deal with broad but shallow product lines to market to the large general merchandise retailers such as hyper market, super bazaar etc.
34. Specialty merchandise wholesalers offer one or two specialized lines like handicrafts, seafood, woolen items, hand-made items, Persian carpets, wooden furniture etc.
35. Contractual wholesalers provide wholesale services to the limited number of retailers those are involved in the contractual arrangement.
36. Cash and carry wholesalers are limited service merchant wholesalers who usually offer fast moving consumers goods (FMCG) to small retailers for cash.
37. Food industry is the typical cash and carry operation where buyers visit the wholesaler's facility, select items, pay in cash and handle their own delivery to their place of business.
38. Industrial wholesalers direct their wholesale operations to the industrial/business customers rather than to the resellers.
39. Truck wholesalers mainly sell and deliver unlimited line of perishable merchandise such as furniture and consumer electronics.
40. Rack jobbers sell merchandise from a truck and also known as service merchandiser.

Answers

1. True	2. True	3. True	4. False
5. False	6. False	7. True	8. False
9. False	10. True	11. True	12. True
13. True	14. True	15. False	16. True
17. True	18. True	19. False	20. True
21. True	22. True	23. False	24. False
25. True	26. True	27. True	28. True
29. True	30. False	31. True	32. False
33. True	34. True	35. True	36. True
37. True	38. True	39. False	40. True

Multiple Choice Questions

1. In the world of retailing, distribution is termed as:
   (*a*) First half of marketing. (*b*) Second half of marketing
   (*c*) Third half of marketing (*d*) Fourth half of marketing
2. Zero level channel is also known as:
   (*a*) Direct distribution channel (*b*) Indirect distribution channel
   (*c*) Multi distribution channel (*d*) None of the above
3. A jobber buys things in .... and sells in ....
   (*a*) Bulk, small (*b*) Credit, cash
   (*c*) None of the above (*d*) None of the above
4. Agents are occassionally called ....
   (*a*) brokers (*b*) wholesalers
   (*c*) providers (*d*) retailers
5. The criteria for choice of physical distribution channel is :
   (*a*) efficient order processing. (*b*) fair price.
   (*c*) sizable inventory. (*d*) All of the above.
6. From cost point of view, transportation accounts nearly .... percent of total distribution costs.
   (*a*) 5 to 10 percent (*b*) 25 to 40 percent.
   (*c*) nearly more than 50 percent. (*d*) nearly half of product cost.
7. MCPU refers to :
   (*a*) Manufacturing cost per unit (*b*) Materials cost per unit
   (*c*) Middlemen cost per unit. (*d*) Managerial cost
8. Rack jobbers are sometime known as
   (*a*) Industrial wholesalers (*b*) contractual wholesalers
   (*c*) service merchandiser (*d*) speciality merchandise wholesalers
9. Customer service levels may be improved by :
   (*i*) By ensuring product availability all the time
   (*ii*) By improving order cycle time
   (*iii*) By providing training to sales people.
   (*a*) Only (*i*) and (*ii*) (*b*) Only (*i*) and (*iii*)
   (*c*) (*i*), (*ii*) and (*iii*) (*d*) (*ii*) and (*iii*) only
10. Wholesaling .... the gap between manufacturers and retailers.
    (*a*) widened (*b*) bridge
    (*c*) Remove (*d*) None of the above

Answers

1. (b)	2. (a)	3. (a)	4. (a)
5. (d)	6. (b)	7. (a)	8. (c)
9. (d)	10. (b)		

Answer to Check Your Progress

1. Who is intermediary?
2. Who is rack jobber?
3. What is negotiation?
4. What is LPG?
5. What is CSL?

6. What is B2B?
7. What is credit facility?
8. What is B2C?
9. What is COD?
10. What is sorting?
11. What is TCPO?
12. What is ABC?
13. What is MCPU?
14. What is warehouse?
15. What are SMEs?
16. What is credit facility?
17. What is EOQ?
18. What is non-stop production?
19. What are bonded stores?
20. What do you mean by channel?

Small Answer Questions

1. Explain basic functions of distribution channel in a business firm?
2. Explain few channel levels, you've come across?
3. Describe the participants in a typical distribution channel?
4. Why distribution channels are required?
5. Differentiate between retailers and wholesalers?
6. Differentiate between agents and resident agents?
7. Explain some emerging trends in physical distribution?
8. Why inventory control is known as major components of an organization's physical distribution system?
9. Why transportation is said to be an indispensable for physical distribution of goods and services.
10. Briefly explain the need for warehousing?
11. Illustrate the functions performed by warehouses?
12. What are the benefits of warehousing to a retailer?
13. Discuss various ways to categorize wholesalers?
14. Why non-stop production has become the trend with FMCG companies?
15. What do you mean by 'cash and carry' wholesalers?

Long Answer Questions

1. What do you understand by the term 'Physical Distribution'? What are its inherent elements? Explain with the help of proper examples wherever necessary?
2. Despite knowing that use of a distribution channel simply increases merchandising cost, still most of the manufacturers, use intermediaries? Explain?
3. Explain some general merits and demerits of having warehouses by any party, be it retailer, manufacturer or wholesaler?
4. What makes a warehouse an ideal one? Also explain various common types of warehouses used throughout the business community?

UNIT 18

HRM IN RETAIL SALES

LEARNING OBJECTIVES

- Understanding the role of HRM in retail industry
- Describing the procedure, policies and practices involved with HRM in retail
- Knowing the various organizational structures applied in retailing
- Analysing the essence of employment relationship in retail
- Understanding various organizational patterns in retailing.

The only vital value an enterprise has is the experience, skills, innovativeness and insights of its people

Leif Edvinsson

The soft stuff is always harder than the hard stuff

Roger Enrico

I believe in the adage: Hire people smarter than you and get out of their way

Howard Schultze, CEO of coffee chain Starbucks (1994)

Do you want to spend the rest of your life selling sugared water or do you want a chance to change the world?

Steve Jobs of Apple Computer, inviting John Scully, then President of PepsiCo, to join Apple in Fortune, September 14th, 1987

Take our 20 best people away, and I will tell you that Microsoft would become an unimportant company

Bill Gates

If an institution wants to be adaptive, it has to let go of some control and trust that people will work on the right things in the right way

Robert B.

INTRODUCTION

The Human Resource Management (HRM) includes recruitment and selection of appropriate employees at various levels to perform day-to-day operations of a retail organization. The main objective of human resource management is to help an organization to meet its strategic goals by attracting, maintaining and managing them in an effective way. HRM basically is the organizational function that deals with issues related to people such as compensation, hiring, performance management, organization development, safety, wellness, benefits, employee motivation, communication, administration and training.

Retailing being a dynamic and growth-oriented industry does require effective management of human resources to achieve organizational financial objectives. Further, human resource management is particularly significant in retailing because success in retailing depends more on its human resources who have direct interaction with the customers and if the employees whose duty is to convince the shopper and make them buy, are not trained and motivated, results will not be up to the mark. In production/manufacturing organizations where most of the work is performed by machines, robots and electronic devices, much significance is given to its capital resources such as machines, tools and computer devices), while on the other hand in the retail world, almost all the activities (procurement, display and selling) are performed by human beings.

The activities to be performed by employees working in a retail organization are very comprehensive and vary from organization to organization. The retailing activities are dependent on store size, store format, nature and location of organization. Further, market conditions, nature and size of competition, country's economic, cultural and politico-legal environment and the community's attitude also influence retailing activities.

OBJECTIVES OF HRM IN RETAILING

The HRM objectives in a retail organization serve as standards against which performance is evaluated. If objectives are well defined and accepted by employees, these promote harmony among human efforts and invite voluntary co-operation. The pace with which new and new corporate are entering into the retail industry, a retail organization may have to structure and assign tasks, policies and resources in order to meet this fast changing requirements of the target market, management administration and employees. Due to high attrition rate and increased demand for skilled employees, retail organizations have prioritized retention policies and growth of its employees within the organization.

The scope of HRM in retailing is indeed vast and multifaceted. All the activities a retail store employee has to perform from his entry to exit broadly come under the purview of HRM. HRM in retailing is composed of survival-integrated activities such as employees' recruitment, selection, induction, training and development, supervision and compensation.

The main objective of HRM is to ensure that right person should be appointed at right position according to his or her caliber, interest and experience in the relevant field. Broadly, HRM in retailing has four specific objectives to perform. These are as under:

1. Societal Objectives

Retailing is all about selling goods or services or both to consumers for their personal or family use. Retailing is perhaps the only sector where the owner of the business has direct interaction with its customers. Further, retailers in a society are the final businessmen in any distribution channel that links manufacturers to end consumers. Therefore, considering all these factors, socially and ethically, it becomes imperative for a retailer to satisfy the existing and would be needs and wants of the society. The organization, which ignores this aspect, soon may find itself out of competition. Keeping pace with the market trends and continuous changing fashion is another criterion that retail organization should consider as a part of their social organization. In fact, societal objectives are basically responsible for the needs and challenges of society. While performing societal objectives, retailers should try to minimize the negative impact of such demands upon the organization. The inability of the organizations to use their resources for society's benefit in social and ethical ways may lead to restrictions. For instance, having no option, society may limit HR decisions to laws that enforce reservation in hiring retail employees and laws that address discrimination, safety or such areas of societal concern.

2. Personal Objectives

When an employee joins an organization, he does not come alone. He brings with himself experience, attitude, skill, knowledge, personality and he tries his level best to take the organization to zenith. He seeks the organization for realization of his personal growth. If the organization requires employees for fulfillment of organization objectives, it becomes important for an organization to help its employees to grow further and achieve their personal goals. Personal objectives of the employees must be fulfilled if a retailer is serious about long-term survival of its organization. If organizational efforts are only directed towards profit maximization, sooner or later, it will become difficult for the retailing firm to retain or maintain its employees, resulting in decline in turnover and employees' performance.

3. Functional Objectives

Retailing is termed as hard & rigorous business. The store employees stand on their feet from eight to nine hours in a day. The job of sales people in the retail outlet is physically demanding and expressively draining. Functional objectives help an organization to support and enhance the role of its employees within the organization through provision of information, advice, facilities and training. Simply stated, functional objectives attempt to uphold (sustain) the department's contribution at a level suitable to the organization's needs. All the efforts, policies and resources spent on HR will go waste in case HRM in an organization is found to be more or less sophisticated. Therefore, it becomes imperative on the part of HR manager to adjust its HR that should exactly meet its organization's requirements. Further, the department's level of service must be tailored to fit the organization it serves.

4. Organizational Objectives

Organizational objectives identify the job of HRM in bringing about organizational overall effectiveness. It involves HR planning, maintaining good relations with employees, selection, training & development, appraisal and assessment. HRM assists the organization to achieve its primary objectives. It is the department that co-ordinates the activities of rest of the organization to achieve organizational mission. Therefore, an astute retailer will infuse passion for success in its employees. If the store staff is actually on the company's pay roll, rather than outsourced from agencies, there will be greater commitment.

Figure 18.1
Retail HRM Objectives and Functions:

HRM Objectives	Functions
1. Societal Objectives	1. Legal and ethical compliance 2. Satisfying society's needs and wants 3. Harmony among union-management relations
2. Organizational Objectives	1. Human resource planning 2. Employees' relations 3. Recruitment, selection, training of retail employees 4. Performance management 5. Compensation and benefits 6. Managerial relations
3. Functional Objectives	1. Performance management 2. Compensation and benefits 3. Labour relations 4. Managerial relations
4. Personal Objectives	1. Training & development 2. Performance management 3. Compensation and benefits

HUMAN RESOURCE FUNCTIONS IN RETAILING

HRM in people centric industry is concerned with the 'people' dimensions of the organization. In order to achieve the objectives as stated above, HRM must perform certain functions. Generally, it is said that to achieve the organizational objectives, retailers must set up a proper correlation between the objectives and the functions. Usually a particular set of functions helps realize specific objectives. For example, personal objectives are thought to be realized through training & development, performance management and compensation & benefits functions, while on the other hand, organizational objectives are achieved through human resource planning, employees' relations, recruitment, selection, training, compensation and managerial relations functions as discussed in figure 18.2.

One point should be noted in this regard that most of the Asian and African countries are still dominated by local/kirana/unorganized shops. Likewise, in India, we have over 12 million '*kirana*' stores. All the employees of that shop report to him or her. Be it strategic decision or day-to-day operations of the establishment are taken by the proprietor. All issues related to recruitment, selection, promotion, training & development, hiring, firing and so on depend upon the proprietor's sole discretion.

Benefits

Providing benefits is another way to compensate employees other than salary for the work performed. In modern retailing, the significance of 'benefits' has risen to such a point that it has become a major consideration for both the employers and employees. Benefits include the legally required items and those offered at employer's discretion.

Actual need for HRM is felt by big retailers like Big Bazaar, Reliance Mart, Pantaloons, Shopper's Stop, etc. Further, the number of functional areas also varies from company to company according to nature, size and merchandise offering. Following are the common human resource functions, any typical retail organization will be having:

1. Job analysis and job design
2. Recruitment and selection of retail employees
3. Employees' training and development
4. Performance management
5. Compensation and benefits
6. Labor relations
7. Managerial relations

These seven human resource areas and their associated functions share the common objectives of an adequate number of competent employees with the abilities, experience, knowledge and skills required for fulfilling organizational goals. Though a human resource function can be assigned to one of the seven areas of human responsibility, some functions serve a variety of objectives. For example, performance management besides motivating the retail employees leads to employees' development as well as compensation and benefits. Similarly, compensation and benefits function facilitates retention, training and development and also serves to have cordial labor and managerial relations. These human resource functions are expressed as under:

1. Job analysis and job design: Job analysis is the process of describing the operations, duties and responsibilities of the job. In order to recruit retail employees on a scientific and rational basis, it becomes necessary to determine in advance a standard of personnel with which interested candidate can be compared. This standard must establish the minimum acceptable qualities necessary for the accomplishment of tasks by retail employees.

Job Analysis

It is the detailed and systematic study of information relating to the operations and responsibilities of a specific job. Each retail store needs to find out the jobs to be offered to the prospects from time to time. The main objective of this analysis is to describe and define the distinctions among various jobs in the organization and their relationships.

Simple stated, the process through which these qualitative requirements (standards) are determined is known as Job analysis. Various experts have defined Job Analysis as under:

In the words of Edwin B. Flippo, "Job analysis is the process of studying and collecting information relating to the operations and responsibilities of a specific job".

In the words of John A. Shbim, "Job analysis is the methodical compilation and study of work data in order to define and characterize each occupation, in such a manner as to distinguish it from all others".

According to Michael J. Jucius, "Job analysis refers to the process of studying the operations, duties and organizational aspects of jobs in order to derive specifications, or as they are called by some job descriptions".

According to Scott Clothier and Spriegal, "Job analysis is the process of critically evaluating the operations, duties and responsibilities of a specific job".

JOB ANALYSIS PROCESS

The process provides information about what the job involves and what human features are essential to carry out these activities. This information becomes vital to decide what sort of people to recruit and hire. The data derived from job analysis process is beneficial for estimating the value and appropriate compensation for each job. The reason behind this is the belief and practice that compensation generally depends on the job's required skill and education level, safety hazards, degree of responsibility, and so on all these factors that are assessed through job analysis. This ultimately provides the base for determining the relative worth of each job so that each job should be properly classified. Hence, job analysis is a data collection function performed by the HR department that includes the following steps:

Figure: 18.2

Job Analysis Process

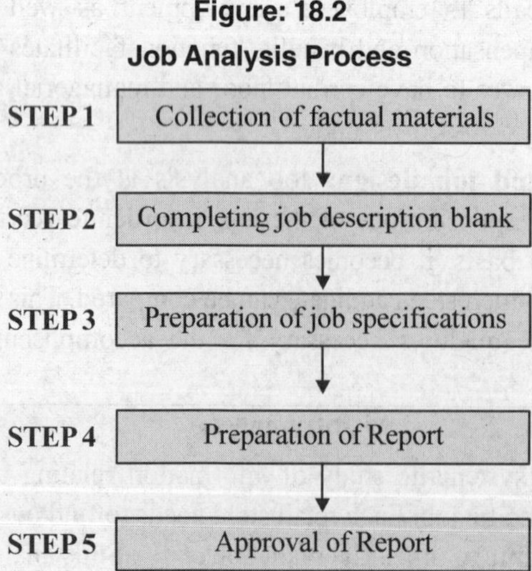

The above mentioned steps are discussed as under:-

(i) Collection of factual materials: The first step of job analysis process includes collecting factual information relating to the job. This task is usually accomplished in four ways:

(a) with the help of structured questionnaire

(b) using narrative descriptions

(c) observations, and

(d) by interviews

Two types of information is collected through above mentioned four techniques:

(a) Belonging to the job environment, i.e. its physical environment such as use of computers, sitting arrangements, comforts, lighting, restrictions etc; its financial obligations (salary, bonus, commission, DA, TA, fringe benefits, incentive schemes etc); its social environment (whether job is individual or in groups, shifts, working hours, team work).

(b) Belonging to employees' qualities: It includes following qualities of employees performing retail tasks:

- **Physical demands**: number of working hours, store job/field job, physical (muscular energy).
- **Intellectual demands**: degree, diploma, working experience, fresher, problem solving ability.
- **Personality demands**: look, height, spoken language, humbleness, ability to listen, working under stress, employees' complaint handling.

(ii) Completing job description blank: After collecting the information, job analysis puts such information in a standard job description form as a comprehensive draft which shows full details of the activities of the retailing job. As per the nature and format of the retail organization, separate forms may be used for various activities in the job and may be compiled later on. In actual, the whole task of job analysis depends upon these forms, which are regularly consulted as reference guide for the future planning tasks.

(iii) Preparation of the job specifications: Job specifications are also prepared on the basis of information collected through data collecting techniques. Job description basically refers to a statement of minimum acceptable qualities of a candidate whose selection should be made.

(iv) Preparation of Report: This report indicates various activities to be performed by the retail staff and expectations from them. It is prepared by the job analyst on the basis of information collected. The report is then submitted to the HR department for its suggestions and amendments.

(v) Approval: The report submitted by the analyst and reviewed by the HR department may now be revised by the top executives for:

- Competitive policies
- Comments of HR department (if any)

- Views of Trade Unions (if applicable)
- Mission and vision of the organization

In some organizations, such drafts are usually approved by the HR manager while in some organizations by the top executive, who has the ultimate responsibility to finalize it.

Note: In actual, it is the prime duty of the retail store manager to prepare the job design since he/she is responsible for conducting day-to-day activities of the store and also the reason for retail success. But it has been seen that in most of the cases, job design is drafted by the HR department may be in consultation with the store manager.

2. Recruitment and selection of retail employees: The success of a retail organization largely depends upon the team of efficient store employees who are chosen out of a number of applicants for the job. Recruitment is a very first step in the employment process, which aim at obtaining and maintaining an efficient store staff (floor employees) as a means of achieving sales targets. Recruiting employees basically involves three major sub-functions:

(i) Recruitment,
(ii) Selection, and
(iii) Placement on the job.

Recruitment defined

According to Edwin Flippo, "Recruitment is the process of searching for prospective employees and stimulating them to apply for the jobs in the organization".

According to Werther and K. Davis, "Recruitment is the process of finding and attracting capable applicants for employment. The process begins when new recruits are sought and ends when their applications are submitted. The result is a pool of applicants from which new employees are selected".

Recruitment

Once a determination of HR recruitment has been made, the recruitment and selection process has to be done very seriously because it is a vital function even for the establishment and development of the business. A faulty recruitment and selection can spoil the company plans and all its future vision to the extent jeopardy.

Factors affecting Recruitment

1. Nature and size of the organization.
2. Employment conditions in the concerned retail format.
3. Compensation and benefits offered by the organization.
4. Rate of growth of the organization.
5. Socio-cultural, legal and economic factors.
6. Level of seasonality of operation and future expansion plans.
7. Company's track record which reflects the organization's ability to locate and keep good performing people.

Theoretically, recruitment is the positive process of employment aiming at searching for the prospective employee and inspiring them to apply for jobs in the organization. In short, it increases the number of applicants and number of posts vacant and thus provides an opportunity to the management to select the suitable person.

Selection defined

Selection is the process by which qualified and suitable store employees are selected and placed on the jobs according to their capabilities and organization's requirements. Thus, it is a tool in the hands of the management to differentiate the suitable and unsuitable applicants by applying various techniques such as group discussions, personal interviews, game tests etc.

According to Thomas stone, "Selection is the process of differentiating between applicants in order to identify those with a greater likelihood of success in the job".

According to Dale Yolder, "Selection is the process in which candidates for employment are divided into two classes, those who are to be offered employment and those who are not".

Selection

Selection means choice, i.e. a choice of an applicant suitable for the job out of several candidates who have offered their services to the organization. In short, it is a tool in the hands of the HR department by which undesirable applicants can be weed out and most suitable could be selected out of shortlisted ones.

Selection procedure employed in large retailing concerns: Selection is a long process beginning with receipt of applicants and ending with the final placement. The selection process varies from organization to organization and also between two different positions. For example, in a retail company, when they are looking for entry level sales personnel, they tend to reply on educational institutions, advertisements and employee recommendations. Moreover, when a retail company is looking for middle-management positions, they are likely to use employment agencies, competitors, advertisements and current employees. The recruitment process can be very costly. It takes a great deal of time to set up an effective recruitment process. Therefore, the company has to carry this job out in a systematic way[1]. For instance, selection procedure for store accountants, store supervisors, store managers will be long drawn and rigorous as compared to those applicants who apply for floor staff position. The various steps in the selection of desirable employee in the organization should be decided by the top management.

Placement

Placement means offering of the job to the finally selected candidates. It is the duty of the HR department or the store manager to dictate the job title and offer a job to the new entrant, who is the most, suited to his/her abilities, skills, degrees and past experience. The following principles should be followed during placement of employees:

[1] HRM – Retail Industry by Mary Anne Winslow, (www. Fibre2fashion.com), Visited Nov 11, 2008.

1. Right person should be placed on right job.
2. 'Job first, man next' should be followed.
3. Job should match applicant's qualifications.
4. Placement should be followed by induction.
5. Different methods for different levels of employees should be followed.
6. Selection procedure should be unbiased and employment-oriented.

Note: *The applicants are screened out at each step of selection process and those who are found suitable and fit for the job, ultimately are selected. At any stage, any unfavorable criteria like unfavorable test scores or physically unfit will simply lead to rejection of employees.*

Following are the commonly used steps involved in the selection of retail employees:

Figure 18.3

Selection Process

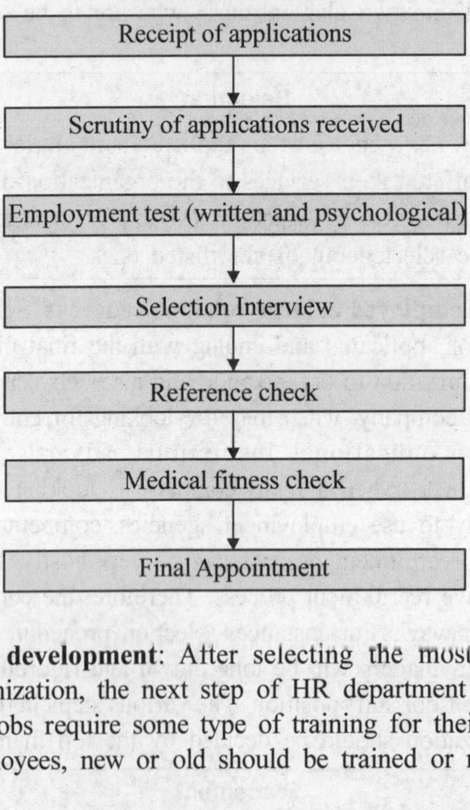

Receipt of applications
↓
Scrutiny of applications received
↓
Employment test (written and psychological)
↓
Selection Interview
↓
Reference check
↓
Medical fitness check
↓
Final Appointment

3. **Training and development**: After selecting the most suitable and eligible candidates in the organization, the next step of HR department is to arrange for their training. All types of jobs require some type of training for their efficient performance and therefore, all employees, new or old should be trained or re-trained from time to time.

Further, the way new and new retail formats are emerging, new developments are taking place throughout the globe, it becomes imperative for any retail organization to systematically plan for the training program aiming at increasing the knowledge, skills, abilities and aptitude of employees to perform the new competitive tasks.

4. **Performance Management**: After selected, training and motivation, the next task, a HR manager has to perform is to evaluate the personality and performance of each

employee by quantitative factors (such as targets achieved). In actual, with the help of performance management, the management through HR department would like to find out how effective it has been hiring and placing employees. Performance management allows retailers gain access to the reliable, timely information that drives better decisions.

The term 'performance management' and 'performance appraisal' are used synonymously by few authors and subject experts. But the retailers throughout the globe believe that performance management is a broader term that may include performance appraisal too. A typical performance management system involves following actions:

(i) To develop job descriptions clearly.
(ii) Selecting right employees at right jobs with right selection process.
(iii) To negotiate requirements and accomplishment based performance standards, outcomes and measures as and when required.
(iv) To provide appropriate training, education and induction.
(v) To facilitate ongoing coaching and feedback.
(vi) To conduct quarterly/half yearly performance development discussions.
(vii) To design appropriate compensation and appraisal system that rewards employees for their outstanding contributions.
(viii) To provide career development opportunities for employees.
(ix) To assist with exit interviews to understand why loyal employees leave the organization.

5. **Compensation and Benefits**: Compensation and benefits represent a substantial part of total cost in most of the organizations. Compensation is not only the concern of the organization but is equally important for the workers and employees to maintain their social image. The main objective of such compensation and benefits are to control the costs, to establish a fair and equitable remuneration to all, to utilize the compensation and benefits device as an incentive for greater employee productivity and to establish a satisfactory public image. Hence, it becomes imperative for the HR department of any retail business to have clear-cut policy guidelines regarding employees' compensation and various benefits. For effective implementation of compensation plans, HR department should be aware about the benefits given to the employees in similar kind of organizations.

Compensation and Benefits

It is extremely important to have a well-designed compensation system. A properly planned and administered compensation and benefits system is one of the most important aspects of modern retailing. Deciding how and what should be paid for employees' contribution is covered under compensation and benefits administration. Commonly this is termed as 'wage and salary administration'. Although, wages include salaries yet there is slight difference in wages and salaries. The compensation given to labor engaged directly in manufacturing activities is called 'wage. Simply stated, wages have direct relation with the production. Salaries, on the other hand, are the remuneration for the quantum of services rendered by the person whose output is difficult to be measured, such as remuneration paid to floor staff, security personnel, VM professionals or supervisory staff. It is paid on time/shift basis, generally on monthly basis.

The attitude of the employees towards his employer will usually be determined by the extent to which he/she is satisfied with the wages he/she is getting, though it is not the only reason for employee satisfaction. Even motivation comes after an employee is satisfied with his/her basic compensation. It is also the best way to satisfy the employee at the lower and middle level of management.

6. **Labor Relations**: In modern days, retailing is carried on a large scale where hundreds of employees work together. The HR manager is basically responsible for the control of labor (workers and employees) through human relation approaches. Employees differ in nature and therefore, it is but natural that due to any communication gap, labor relations may spoil within the organization. Therefore, the HR department should know the proper policies, rules and regulations with regard to labor relations. Harmonial relationships are necessary for both retailers and employees. It not only results in industrial peace but also leads to better and higher sales targets. Most of the retail organizations these days besides having HR department also take the services of legal experts (practitioners) for consultation from time to time. Further, hiring legal experts within the organization has become necessary considering that each state has its different set of rules for managing HR with some standard rules.

7. **Managerial Relations:** The employment relationship, irrespective of nature of organization, usually has two parts: labour relations and managerial relations. The former which covers the price of labour is more obvious. The labour relation is also known as 'market relations'. The managerial relations on the other side are the relationships that define how the process takes place. Labour relations describe the price for a particular shift (a set of number of hours) but managerial relations determine how much work is performed in that time, at what specific task or tasks, who has the right to define the tasks and change a particular mix of tasks and what penalties will be deployed for any failure to meet these obligations (Clegg 1979:1).

Figure: 18.4
The Employment Relationship

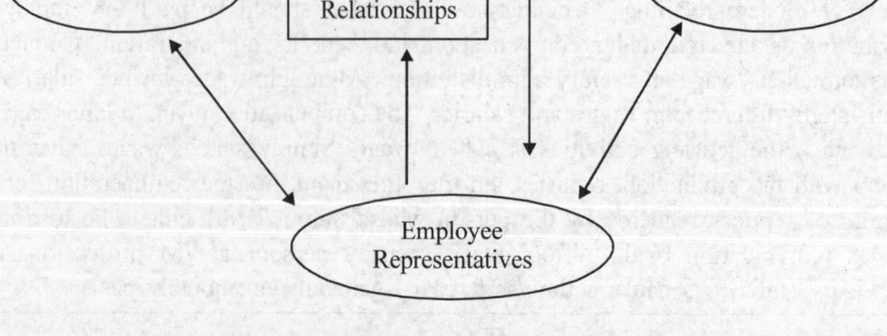

CREATING ORGANIZATION STRUCTURE

The term retail organization refers to the basic format or structure of a retail company designed to fulfill the needs of the customers, organization structures are important as they not only defines the hierarchy levels but also the reporting relationships that help the retailer in performing his day-to-day store operations. Although most of the Indian retailers fall in the category of un-organized small scale units, there are also some big retailers like Reliance Fresh, Big Apple, The Mobile Shop and Six to Ten. These organized retail stores usually characterized by large, professionally managed store formats providing large variety of goods and services at reasonable prices, in an ambience that is conducive for shoppers and provides them a memorable experience. In this unit, an attempt has been made to examine the various types of organization structures that exist in Indian retail industry.

Making a Choice of Proper Forms of Organization

To select a suitable business form for your organization depends on various requirements that are to be met. Some requirements which guide retailers in making such choice are:

(i) Nature of Retailing – food, luxury, grocery, mobile, etc.

(ii) Expected life span of business;

(iii) Requirement of capital and the availability of funds;

(iv) Expected volume of business;

(v) Area of retailing – local, national or international;

(vi) Legal formalities for setting up store and organizing the business;

(vii) Government control and restrictions;

(viii) Rights and responsibilities (including personal liability of the retailer) of the retailers;

(ix) Tax advantage under different types of organizations;

(x) Opportunities and requirements for decision making.

Setting up a Retail Organization

Retail organization enables the store, to assign responsibilities, resources, policies and rewards so that it should satisfy customers demand and the requirements of its target market. Essential factors that must be considered while planning and assessing a retail organization are:

From management's point of view

- Is it possible to get right employee at right job?
- Are HR policies clearly defined?
- Are the levels of organization properly developed?

- Are there proper arrangements for employee's supervision and control?
- Is there any need to motivate employees?
- Is absenteeism an issue of worry?
- Are the employees trained under position rotation system?
- Is the store well flexible to adapt to changes in customers' preference?
- Are the duties of store employees working at different levels clearly defined?
- Are the organization's objectives clearly defined to all employees?

From Employees' point of view:

- Are employees turnover rate is satisfactory?
- Is the remuneration competitive enough?
- Are employees welcomed to participate in decision making process?
- Is the authority-responsibility relation properly balanced?
- Are employees rewarded for showing good performance?
- Is there any partiality with any type of employees?
- What is the promotional policy?
- Are employees promoted at regular interval from within?
- Is job description properly laid down?

From Marketing point of view:

- Is the store strength enough to attend customers and to provide customer service?
- Are the changes in customers' demand, liking and disliking, new innovations properly addressed?
- Are chain stores are well and effectively maintained?
- Is the mechanism to understand the specific needs of branch stores are operational?
- Are employees knowledgeable and properly trained?
- Is the complaint handling department properly maintained?

Process of Organizing a Retail Firm

Retailing today is one of the most competitive industries in India. Some retailers pursue the strategy of providing better customer service, while others try to make shopping more pleasant by investing money in their entertainment. Whatever is the strategy, a retailer adopts is dependent on the performance of his subordinates. The process of organizing is nothing but developing an organizational chart, creating designation and assigning various tasks that will be performed on the behalf of a retailer.

The process of organizing a retail firm basically has five following steps –

Figure 18.5: Process of Organizing a Retail Firm

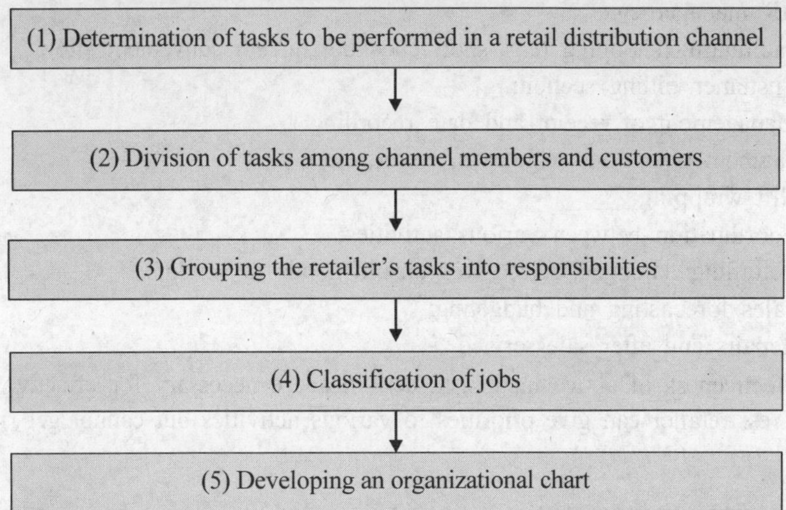

As a policy matter, a retailer cannot survive unless its retail organization satisfies the needs and wants of the customers. In retailing, a retailer can compete with competitors only if the needs of customers are fulfilled. No one will give you credit and acknowledge how well management and employees needs are effectively met. Thus, an organization structure that has adopted policy of central buying in order to cut costs but ignores the specific requirements of its various chain stores would be a fatal decision in the long run. This practice is normally common in newly born retail stores but ultimately retailers will have to understand that individual attention should be given to buying, pricing, wrapping and displaying merchandise considering geographical and cultural differences. There are many ways of organizing to perform these functions and focus on customers, employees and management requirements. The process of setting up a retail organization is divided into five steps. These are discussed as follows:

(1) Tasks to be performed

The general tasks in a retail organization vary from organization to organization and size to size but these are some common retail activities that are usually applicable to all sorts of retail distribution channel:

- Arranging and buying merchandise for the retailer;
- Receiving merchandise and check for its quality;
- Determination of prices i.e., price setting/labeling;
- Marketing the merchandise;
- Inventory management and control including stores;
- Classifying merchandise and window displays;
- Store maintenance;
- Customer research and development cell;

- Customer complaint handling;
- Customer contact (e.g. personal selling, advertising);
- HR management;
- Facilitating shopping (e.g. short checkout queue, convenient site);
- Customer billing section;
- Management of receipt and date recording;
- Payment operations (e.g. cash, credit, etc.);
- Gift wrapping;
- Coordination between various activities;
- Returning damaged, rejected or unsold goods to vendors;
- Sales forecasting and budgeting;
- Repairs and after sale service.

The effectiveness of above mentioned activities are necessary for effective retailing to occur. Yes, retailer can give priorities to various activities but cannot get rid of any one.

(2) Division of tasks among channel members and customers

Although the above mentioned various activities take place in a retail channel but a retailer is not supposed to accomplish all the tasks. Some of these activities are usually performed by the manufacturer, wholesale professional, customer or retailer itself. The below mentioned figure provides the details of activities that are performed by different parties of a retail chain:

Figure: 18.6

Division of Retail Activities

Party	List of Activities
Manufacturer or Wholesaler	Manufacturer/wholesaler functions include: pricing merchandise, inventory control, display layout preparation, research, sales forecasting, checking quality of incoming inventory, etc.
Professional	Professionals can take up these activities: site arrangement, R&D, advertising agency, warehousing, legal matters, credit maintenance, computer service provider, lift maintenance, etc.
Customer	Customer is responsible for: acceptance of delivery, bill payment, self service, selecting merchandise, product replacement (do it yourself).
Retailer	Retailer is normally responsible for buying merchandise and coordination between various activities. *Note:* if store's size is small, then most of the activities a retailer can perform.

This is a list of possible activities that are normally performed in a retail chain. But an activity should be performed only if it is as per the need of the target market. For example, free home delivery; it should not be provided unless required by the majority of the customers. In luxury and cosmetic retailing, customers would like to take their ornaments, cosmetic items with them but in case of grocery, they would be requiring home delivery. Therefore, unless a retailer finds some facility ignorable, he should not provide it.

Once a facility/activity is provided, it should be done with proper competence. For instance, a customer follows up and complaint handling activity may require a dedicated staff that could understand customer's feelings and has soft communication skill. In case of some retail store, this activity can be handled by retailer itself but when the store grows in terms of size and volume of merchandise, it requires separate staff for both personal and telephonic customer care.

(3) Grouping tasks into responsibilities

After considering and finalizing various retail activities necessary to be performed in a store, a retailer groups these activities into job profiles those will be handled by a particular employee/group of employees. To make the retailing successful, various activities must be defined and properly grouped. Figure 18.7 gives you an idea how a retailer does task grouping and assign tasks into jobs.

Figure 18.7
Grouping Tasks into Responsibilities

Activities	Jobs
Arranging and displaying merchandise, customer's reaction, customer views collection, gift wrapping, guide to customers	Floor Staff
Receiving inventory, checking for its quality, keeping record of issue and receipt, inventory storage, returning inventory to vendors, making inventory	Inventory Staff
Management of receipts, ledger maintenance, providing poly bags/packaging materials, bills issuance maintaining data related to credit/card purchasing	Cashier
Inventory repairs, alterations and setting, attending queries, complaints handling, R&D, follow up	Customer Care Staff
Recruitment, training and development, sales forecasting, budgeting, pricing, coordination between various activities	HR staff
Cleaning store, washing floor, repairing shelves, racks and cabins	Janitorial staff

***Note:** In order to avoid the problems of role conflict, a retailer should use the rule of 'specialization'. According to the rule of specialization, each employee should be responsible for definite range of functions as per his expertise and depth of knowledge. Specialization results in role clarity, reduced training costs, greater efficiency and increased output. Rule of specialization further results in right person at right job.*

After grouping the activities, job descriptions should be prepared. A job description, as the name implies, outlines the title of a job, objectives and expectations from a job in terms of duties and responsibilities. The job description further helps the HR department in recruitment, selection, supervision and assigning pay scales to each job title.

(4) Classification of jobs

After grouping tasks into jobs, next step in setting up a retail organization is to classify the jobs under functional, products, geographical, or combination classification system. Under functional classification, jobs are divided in terms of various retail functions, like sales promotion, customer care, inventory management and store operations.

Under products classification, jobs are divided on the basis of nature of goods and services. Thus a retail store recruits different employees for apparels, vegetables and fruits, furniture, electronics, grocery food and so on. Product classification is based on the concept that employees' requirement in terms of experience, age, look, qualification, etc. varies from product to product.

Under Geographical classification, jobs are classified according to spread of the organization in various cities and states. Therefore, job locations are assigned in such a way that employee to the extent possible should work in or nearby home town. As he/ she is aware about the locality, its preferences and buying behaviour. For example, if recruitment is done by head office and two shortlisted selected candidates belong to Garhwal – a hilly area then these two candidates should be offered job to a store which is nearest to Garhwal region.

Under combination classification system, stores use more than one classification. For example if a branch retail store of luxury items like Jewellery, gold, diamond and platinum recruits its own staff for selling goods, but buys employees for each product line from head office and controlled by head office, then it will be a combination of functional, geographical and product formats.

(5) Developing an organizational chart

This is the last step of organizing a retail firm. For the purpose of understanding the concept, various organizational patterns are given as under:

A. Organizational patterns in Retailing – On the ground of functions

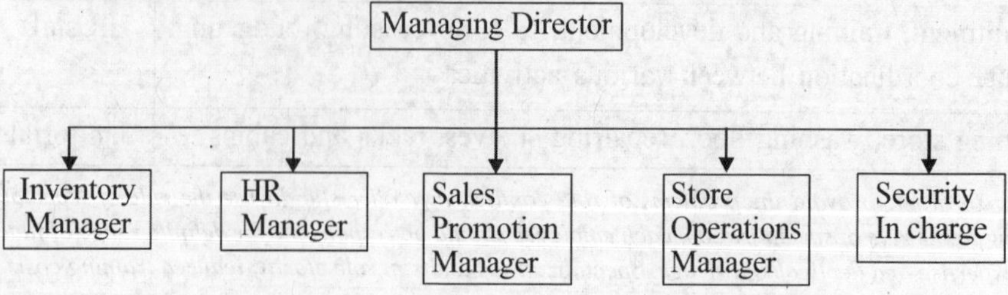

Figure 18.8 : Organization Pattern on the Basis of Functions

B. Organizational patterns in Retailing – On the ground of Merchandise Offered

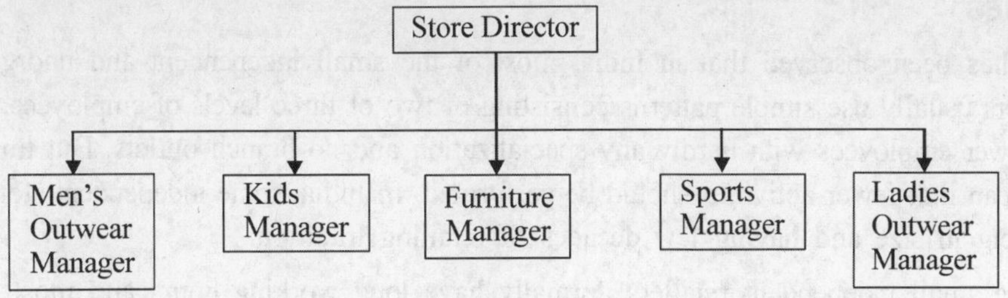

Figure 18.9: Organization Pattern on the basis of Merchandise Offered

C. Organizational patterns in Retailing – On the ground of Geography

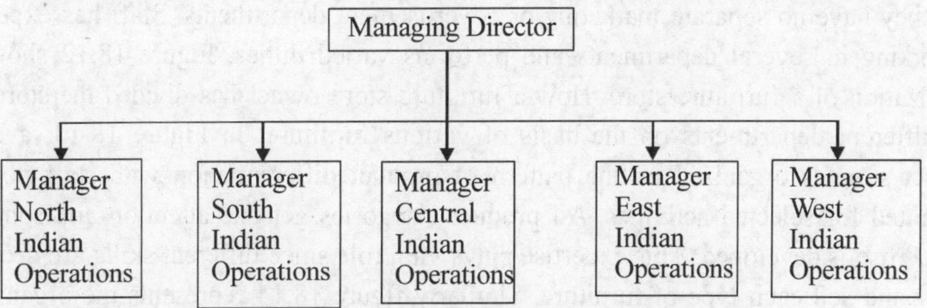

Figure 18.10: Organization Pattern on the basis of Geography

D. Mixed Organizational Pattern

As the very name implies, these types of organizational patterns involve two or more organizational patterns available. Thus, they have the features of various organizational patterns. These are used when the store is expanded in terms of branches, customers and variety of merchandise.

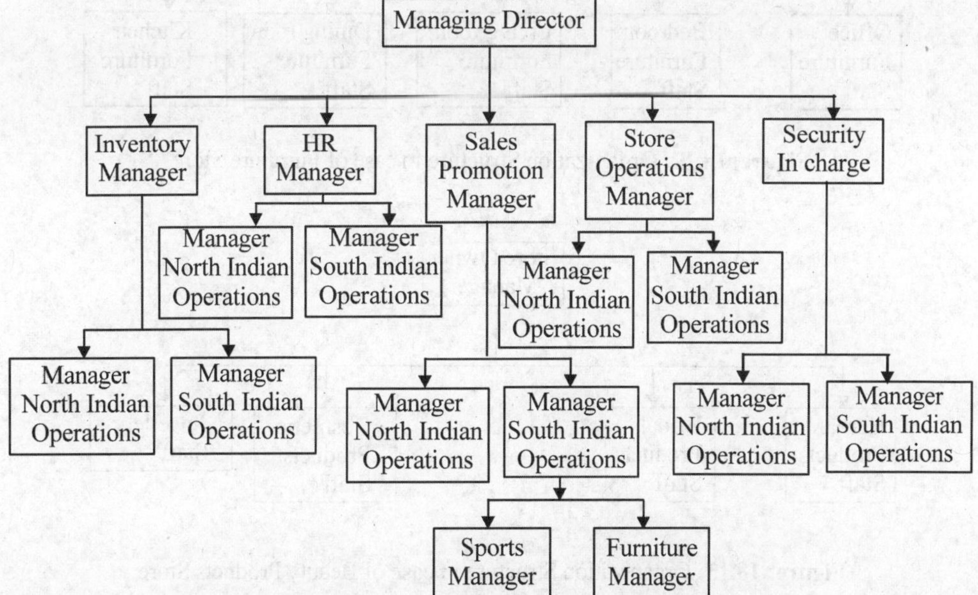

Figure 18.11 Organization Pattern on the basis of Mixed Pattern

ORGANIZATONAL STRUCTURES APPLIED BY SMALL AND INDEPENDENT RETAIL STORES

It has been observed that in India, most of the small independent and unorganized retailers usually use simple patterns consisting of two or three levels of employees. There are fewer employees with hardly any specialization and no branch outlets. But this does not mean that fewer activities should be performed. In India, some independent stores are very big in size and having few decades of retailing tradition.

The small independent retailers normally have long working hours and most of the supervision is done directly by the retail owner. Merchandising staff is involved with buying and selling goods and services, sales promotion, displays and advertisement. As such they have no separate marketing or advertisement departments. Staff has experience of working in several departments and performs varied duties. Figure 18.12 shows the organization of a furniture store. How a furniture store owner has divided the store in to five different departments on the basis of various furniture. In Figure 18.13, a beauty product store is organized on the pattern of product differentiation with staff normally committed for selected activities. All product categories get due attention and some sort of expertise is developed. This expertise plays vital role since different skills are necessary to buy and sell each type of furniture. Similarly figure 18.14 represents the organization structure of a local *kirana* store while Figure 18.15 represents the organization structure of an electronic appliances store.

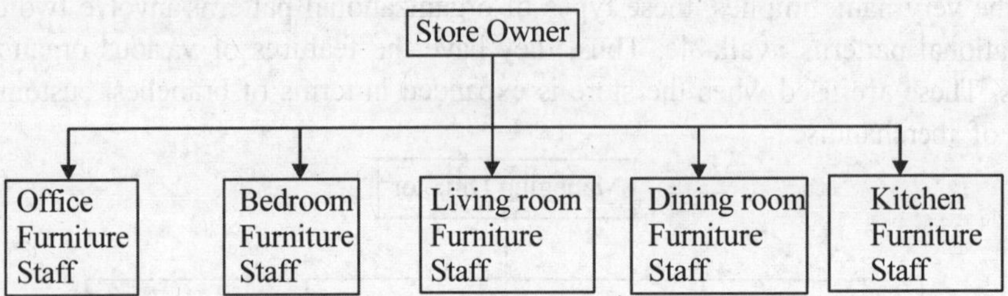

Figure: 18.12: Organization Structure in case of Furniture Store

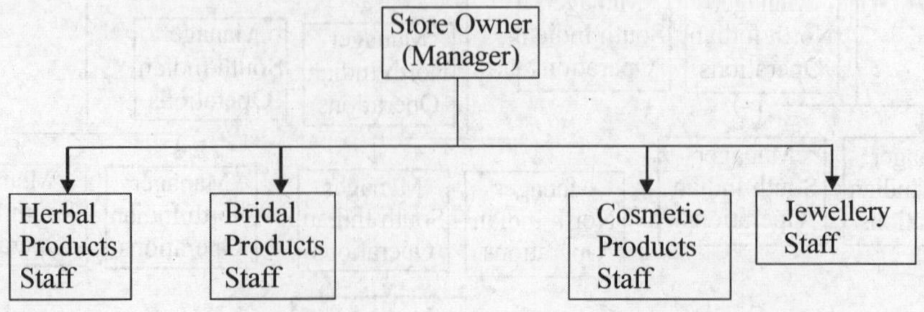

Figure: 18.13: Organization Structure in case of Beauty Products Store

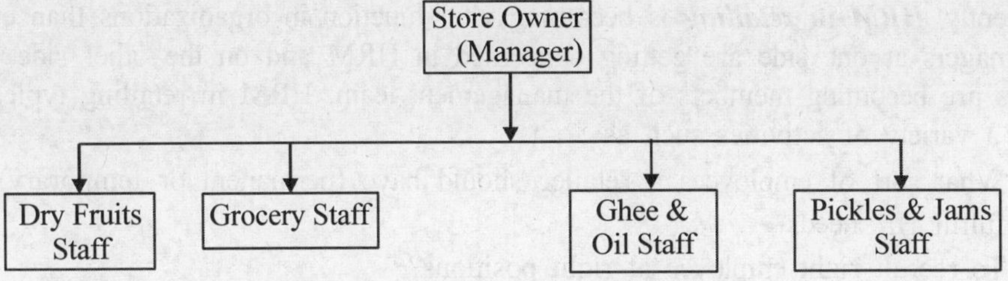

Figure: 18.14 : Organization Structure in case of a *Kirana* Store

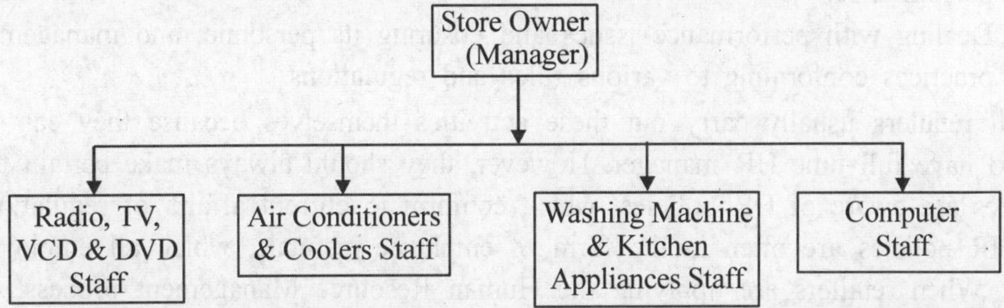

Figure: 18.15: Organization Structure in case of Electronic Appliances Store

SUMMARY

Since the dawn of LPG (Liberalization, Privatization and Globalization), process management, human engineering, ergonomics, and value based management concepts are being talked about in retailing conferences and seminars frequently. Therefore, there has been an increasing realization that human resource like other resources is one a company's key assets. Rctiling being customers centric, calls special attention from retailing industry to fulfill the demands of an increasing number of educated and well informed customers. Considering these necessities, it becomes imperative for retailers to have right people to gain competitive advantage over its competitors.

Human Resource Management provides a 'facilitator' not only to organize, but also to support employees and management effectively in fulfilling their tasks in terms of future company's goals. Employees (Human Resource) are a key resource in any business. This is predominantly correct in retail industry, which entails large number of employees for providing a range of services to its customers. Typically a HR manager in a retail concern performs following functions that increase company's success each day:

- Human Resource planning
- Recruitment and Selection
- Training and Development
- Performance management and
- Compensation

The ***HRM in retail*** has its own particular features: a large number of inexperienced workers, elongated working hours, vastly visible employees with permanent and temporary staff, and dissimilarity in customer demand. These features impose difficulties before retailers in their day to day business operations. Among them high employee turnover, poor performance, absenteeism and opinion differences among employees are common.

Consequently, ***HRM in retailing*** is becoming vital function in organizations than ever. Line managers at one side are getting concerned in HRM and on the other side HR managers are becoming members of the management team. HRM in retailing typically involves a variety of activities such as :

- What sort of employees a retailer should have (permanent or temporary) to fulfill HR needs?
- To recruit right employee at right positions?
- Providing training and development to the best employees to ensure higher performance.
- Dealing with performance issues and ensuring its personnel and management practices conforming to various rules and regulations.

Small retailers usually carry out these activities themselves because they can not afford to have full time HR manager. However, they should always make certain that employees are aware of HR policies, which conform to current affairs of regulations. These HR policies are often in the form of employee manuals, which all employees possess. When retailers are applying the Human Resource Management process, the country specific labour laws, diversity and employee privacy has to be considered.

REVIEW QUESTIONS

True and False Questions

1. The main objective of HRM is to ensure that right person should be appointed at right position.
2. Retailing is perhaps the only sector where the owner of the business has indirect interaction with its customers.
3. Functional objectives help an organization to support and enhance the role of its employees within the organization through provision of information, advice, facilities and training.
4. Organizational objectives identify the job of HRM in bringing about organizational overall effectiveness.
5. Providing benefits is another way to compensate employees other than salary for the work performed.
6. Benefits include the legally required items and those offered at employee's discretion.
7. Job analysis is the process of describing the operations, duties and responsibilities of the job.
8. The process of job analysis provides information about what the job involves and what human features are not essential to carry out these activities.
9. Physical demands include: degree, diploma, working experience, fresher, problem solving ability.
10. Intellectual demands include: number of working hours, store job/field job, physical (muscular energy).

11. Personality demands include: look, height, spoken language, humbleness, ability to listen, working under stress, employees' complaint handling.
12. Recruitment is the process of searching for prospective employees and discouraging them to leave the jobs especially in case of credit crunch.
13. Selection is the process by which unqualified and non-suitable store employees are selected and placed on the jobs according to their capabilities and organization's requirements.
14. Usually all types of jobs require some type of training for their efficient performance and therefore, all employees, new or old should be trained or re-trained from time to time
15. Compensation is not only the concern of the organization but is equally important for the workers and employees to maintain their social image.
16. The employment relationship, irrespective of nature of organization, usually has two parts; labour relations and managerial relations.
17. The labour relation is also known as market relation.
18. Labour relations describe the price for a particular shift (a set of number of hours) but managerial relations determine how much work is performed in that time.
19. The process of organizing is nothing but developing an organizational chart, creating designation and assigning various tasks that will be performed on behalf of a employee.
20. In retailing a retailer can compete with competitors only if the needs of customers are not fulfilled.
21. Manufacturer/wholesaler functions include: pricing merchandise, inventory control, display layout preparation, research and sales forecasting.
22. Professional can take up these activities: site arrangement, R&D, advertising agency, warehousing, legal matters, credit maintenance, computer service provider, lift maintenance, etc.
23. Customer is responsible for: acceptance of delivery, bill payment, self service, selecting merchandise, product replacement.
24. Retailer is normally responsible for buying merchandise and coordination between various activities.
25. Cleaning store, washing floor, repairing shelves, racks and cabins don't come under the responsibility of janitorial staff.
26. Under Geographical classification, jobs are classified according to spread of the organization in various cities and states.
27. The small independent retailers normally have short working hours and most of the supervision is done directly by the retail owner.
28. LPG stands for local, private and groupism.
29. Human resource management provides a 'facilitator' not only to organize, but also to support employees and management.
30. Induction should be followed by placement.

Answers

1. True	2. False	3. True	4. True
5. True	6. True	7. True	8. False
9. False	10. False	11. True	12. False
13. False	14. True	15. True	16. True
17. True	18. True	19. False	20. False
21. True	22. True	23. True	24. True
25. False	26. True	27. False	28. False
29. True	30. False		

Multiple Choice Questions

1. The main function of societal objective is :
   (*a*) Legal and ethical compliance. (*b*) Performance Management
   (*c*) Both of the above (*d*) None of the above
2. The function of personal objective is :
   (*a*) Training and Development. (*b*) Performance Management
   (*c*) None of the above (*d*) Both of the above
3. Recruitment is the process of employment :
   (*a*) Positive (*b*) Negative
   (*c*) Neutral (*d*) Only
4. Selection is the .... process of employment.
   (*a*) Positive (*b*) Negative
   (*c*) Neutral (*d*) Complementary
5. Placement means :
   (*a*) Selecting candidates. (*b*) Rejecting candidates
   (*c*) offering job to the candidate (*d*) training to candidates
6. The appropriate principle for placement is :
   (*a*) Right person at the right job
   (*b*) Job first, man next.
   (*c*) Placement should be followed by induction.
   (*d*) All of the above.
7. The labour relations are also known as :
   (*a*) Managerial relations (*b*) Market relations
   (*c*) Employment relations (*d*) All of the above
8. The duty of floor staff involves
   (*a*) Guide to customers (*b*) Complaint Handling
   (*c*) Budgeting (*d*) All of the above
9. A customer is responsible for :
   (*a*) Acceptance of delivery
   (*b*) Buying merchandise
   (*c*) Checking quality of incoming materials.
   (*d*) Attending queries
10. Recruitment process is affected by :
    (*a*) Nature and size of the organisation
    (*b*) Employment conditions
    (*c*) Compensation and benefits offered.
    (*d*) All of the above

Answers

1. a	2 d	3. a	4. b
5. c	6. d	7. b	8. a
9. a	10. d		

ANSWERS TO 'CHECK YOUR PROGRESS'

1. What is HRM?
2. Define job analysis?
3. What is job design?
4. Who is cashier?
5. What is intellectual demand?
6. What is job description blank?
7. What is placement?
8. Describe Janitorial staff?
9. What is R & D?
10. What 'staff' includes?

EXERCISES AND QUESTIONS

Small Answers Questions

1. Discuss the objectives of HRM in retail sector?
2. Differentiate between selection and placement?
3. How compensation is different from benefits?
4. Explain the role of training and development in HRM?
5. Write a short note on role of performance management?
6. List few factors of recruiting retail employees?
7. Being a retailer what factors would you consider while selecting a business form?
8. Why it is said that smooth labour relation is the backbone of any business especially retailing?
9. How you would like to divide various tasks among channel members and customers in a retail firm?
10. The general tasks in a retail organization vary from organization to organization and size to size but some retail activities are common to all sorts of retail distribution channels. Discuss?

Long Answer Questions

1. Being a Business graduate, discuss a strategy for developing an organization chart for a person who is interested to start a garment (ladies and gents) store? Also illustrate few organizational structure charts as applicable to small and independent retailers in Indian context?
2. Suppose you are recently appointed a HR manager of a newly opened retailing firm? Your MD wanted you to develop a selection procedure for recruiting talented floor staff? Which selection procedure you would develop that not only results in talent acquisition but is time saving and cost effective too?

Appendix

Exhibit 18.1: The Special Human Resource Environment of Retailing

Staffs are a major resource in any business. This is particularly true in retail industry, which has a very large amount of employees and which provides a range of services to its customers. The retail human resource environment has its special features: a large number of inexperienced workers, long hours, highly visible employees, many part-time workers, and variations in customer demand. Those features also create difficulties to retailers.

First of all, a large number of inexperienced workers and part-time staffs in a retail business may lead high employee turnover, poor performance, lateness and absenteeism. This is due to several seasons. One is that inexperienced workers can apply retail positions, such as check out clerks, wrappers, stock clerks and some types of sales personnel, which doesn't require high education, training and skill. The other one is that employees who work in retailing companies likely live near the retailing stores. In addition, part-time staffs are very easy to quit their jobs.

Secondly, long working hours may result in that retailers need two shifts of employees. As the trend of longer store hours (evening and weekend), retailers need to consider employ staff for evening and weekend use.

Thirdly, high visible employees mean that retailers have to monitor employees very closely. As consumers now a days play a very important role in retail industry and employees are highly visible to the consumers, retailers must select and train employees carefully, especially taking care about their manners and appearance.

Finally, variations in customer demand may create difficulty to retailers to predict exactly how many employees are required. Retailers need to have the knowledge about in which season, how many number of employees are required and which period of a day, what number of employees.

Source: *HRM – Retail Industry by Mary Anne Winslow, (www.fibre2fashion.com), Visited Nov 11, 2008.*

Exhibit 18.2: Motivating Your Retail Sales Staff in Slow Times

Keep a Positive Mindset

Retail is a day to day business. Some days you are HOT and some days your are not. Don't buy the down economy. This is not a bad economy - the US will experience a 10 Trillion dollar economy this year alone. There is a lot of money to go around! If you are doing the right things to market your business and staying in touch with your customers on a regular basis they will return after your slow period of summer vacations, back to school, etc.

When you keep your positive mindset it will flow onto your sales staff and motivate them to keep a positive mindset on the sales floor. This will keep your register ringing and your sales UP. When you encourage a positive atmosphere with enthusiasm it is contagious.

Enthusiasm = Positive Emotions

Positive Emotions = Happy Customers

Happy Customers = More Sales and More Profits for You

Offer More Flexible Hours

Ask your staff to let you know in advance of your scheduling what days they will need off. Discuss your willingness to make it work for them. If business is slow offer some bonus paid vacation time to your best salespeople. They will appreciate and surprise benefit will motivate them to become more loyal to your organization and they will return the favour with hard work and more determination to succeed.

Encourage Creativity

When times are slow hold more sales meetings to discuss new promotions, advertising, inventory, customer service and future goals. Always get input from your staff at these meetings and have some fun with a creative brainstorming session that puts every one's ideas to work.

Be Open, Not Intimidating

Let your staff know that your door is always open to support them and listen to their ideas and concerns. Create a family atmosphere where people can feel they trust and support one another through good times and the bad.

Have Fun

All work and no play can make a dull day. Don't take your business too seriously. Lighten up, relax and enjoy some free time when your retail business is not in full swing. If you can't stand being around in during the down times - get out of the store and take a short vacation or attend workshops to build your business. Make sure to plan for a lot of relaxation time to refocus.

Discover new ways to look deeper into your business and focus on what you are thankful for and where you plan to go in the future. Upon your return, share your new discoveries with your sales staff during a fun and relaxed meeting. They will pick up on your motivation and feel more confident about their own future within your organization.

Remember Birthdays and Anniversaries

Recognize and celebrate with your staff often. Host an annual anniversary party for all the sales staff that have been with your retail store from one year or longer. Make them feel special with surprise gifts and a very special evening out on the town, or host an off-site meeting at a restaurant or a picnic in the park for their entire family.

Snoop Days

Take out your entire staff to shop the competition. If you have a large staff you may want to break this up during two or three different days and maybe even rent a large van so that you can all travel together and have some fun during your adventure. Introduce yourself to the competition. Let them know why you are shopping their store and offer to send them to business in areas that you do not focus on in your retail store.

Your competitors can often be your best alliances. It will be a good lesson for your staff to learn and understand this competitive advantage of making friends with the competition. After your tour, take your staff out for lunch or dinner and discuss all the things your competition is doing RIGHT. The areas where they excel are the areas to watch out for. By educating yourself and your sales team to your competitors strengths and weaknesses, you will automatically feel more confident and motivated to move forward and succeed.

***Source**: Motivating Your Retail Sales Staff in Slow Times by Debbie Allen, (retail.about.com)*

About Author: Debbie Allen is one of the world's leading authorities on sales and marketing. She is the author of five books including Confessions of Shameless Self Promoters and Skyrocketing Sales. Debbie has helped thousands of people around the world attract customers like crazy with her innovative, no-cost marketing strategies and secrets to sales success. Her expertise has been featured in Entrepreneur, Selling Power and Sales & Marketing Excellence. Sign up for her free 6-week e-Course Business Success Secrets Revealed and take the online business card quiz to rate you marketing online now at www.DebbieAllen.com.

Exhibit 18.3: Retail Store Organization – Structuring Your Business

The organizational structure of a retail store will vary by the size and type of the business. Most tasks involved with operating a retail business will be the same. However, small or independent retail stores may combine many sectors together under one division, while larger stores create various divisions for each particular function along with many layers of management.

For example, the small specialty shop may have all of its employees under one category called 'Store Operations'. A large department store may have a complete staff consisting of a manager, assistant manager and sales associates for its Sporting Goods department, Home and Garden, Bed and Bath, and each additional department.

In order to define the store's organization, start by specifying all tasks that need to be performed. Then divide those responsibilities among various individuals or channels. Group and classify each task into a job with a title and description. The final step is to develop an organizational chart.

Retailing Structure

The following is a brief outline of some of the divisions in a retail organization.

Owner/CEO or President

Store Operations : Management, Cashier, Sales, Receiving, Loss Prevention
Marketing : Visual Displays, Public Relations, Promotions
Merchandising : Planning, Buying, Inventory Control
Human Relations : Personnel, Training
Finance : Accounting, Credit
Technology : Information Technology

As the store grows and the retail business evolves, the dynamics of the organization's structure will change too. Therefore, it is paramount to redesign the store's organizational chart to support the decision-making, collaboration and leadership capabilities that are essential during and after a growth period.

Source: *Structuring Your Business by Shari Waters, from retail.about.com*

Exhibit 18.4: When and Who Should You Hire?

As your business begins to grow and evolve, you'll be challenged by the decision to expand. If you are doing all of the work yourself, your first thought may be to hire employees. Before you begin the hiring process, take a moment to determine whether or not you really need the help.

Time Management

Are you doing everything you can to make your time as productive as possible in your store? Becoming better organized may eliminate the need for outside help. If you're having trouble managing your time, sign up for a seminar at your local library or college.

Many retail owners try to wear all the hats and then feel they need to hire help. You can reduce some of the workload by outsourcing any part of your business that would be better served by a professional. Book keeping, marketing and information technology are the areas that may be outsourced.

Don't expect to have a lot of free time on your hands right away if you hire a new employee. Your new management role will involve a lot of time in the hiring process, the training of the new worker and the additional payroll paperwork. These new responsibilities will require you to have the organizational aspects under control.

Hiring Is Expensive

Can you afford an employee? Hiring an employee is an investment but for each new hire your retail business makes, valuable resources like time, energy and money are dedicated to the effort. Examine your operating budget. Is there room to pay an extra worker? Keep in mind that you'll need to pay at least the minimum hourly wage and you'll also have payroll taxes and workers compensation to pay.

An extra employee may generate enough new sales to more than compensate the salary of the employee. The additional help could give you a chance to produce more products or serve more customers efficiently. If the added business does not outweigh the minimum salary that you would have to pay, then consider other alternatives to hiring a permanent employee. There are many staffing options available and each has some pros and cons.

Staffing Options

Full-time Employees: A person who works a set number of hours and generally receives benefits like health, dental and life insurance along with a standard salary is considered full-time. Having someone around full-time can provide a peace of mind knowing someone is manning the store even when you can't be there. There are also many labour laws which govern the full-time worker.

Part-time Employees: These workers may offer more flexibility in scheduling and cost less than full-time employees, but you may spend extra time in training more people and if they have jobs elsewhere, worker loyalty may be compromised.

Temporary Employees: Staffing agencies usually charge for the convenience of providing full service, as they handle the payroll administration and fringe benefits. However, temporary help may be useful for the short-term projects such as the busy holiday selling season.

Independent Contractors: Contractors usually provide work on a project-by-project basis where specialized training or certain skills are required. Fees for work performed are paid based on results and negotiated in advance. Be sure to have a written contract in place before hiring independent contractors. Once your business becomes successful, you will obviously need help on a temporary or permanent basis. Good employees can be a business's biggest asset but the legal and accounting concerns that come with hiring can almost make it seem having employees is more trouble than it's worth. Be sure you understand all the responsibilities before recruiting and hiring.

***Source:** Getting help by Shari Waters, from retail.about.com*

Exhibit 18.5: Training and Development in Retail-FMCG Sector

Retail/FMCG Sector is the most booming sector in the Indian economy and is expected to reach US$ 175-200 billion by 2016. With this rapid expansion and coming up of major players in the sector, the need of human resource development has increased. Lack of skilled workers is the major factor that is holding back the retail sector for high growth. The sector is facing the severe shortage of trainers. Also, the current education system is not sufficiently prepared to address the new processes, according to the industry majors.

Training Programs in Retail/FMCG Sector

Some of the training programs that are given in the retail sector are:

- Sales Training
- On-the-Job Training
- Seminars/Workshops
- Customer Relationship Management
- Online Course
- Group Study
- Computer-Based Training
- Self-Directed Training

Training Institutes for Retail Management

Some of the institutes for retail management are:

- Indian Retail School
- Loyola Institute of Business Administration (LIBA)
- S P Jain Centre of Management
- Institute for Integrated Learning in Management (IILM)
- Welingkar Institute of Management, Centre for Retail Studies
- K J Somaiya Institute of Management Studies & Research
- Mudra Institute of Communications
- Amity Business School

Courtesy: *www.traininganddevelopment.naukrihub.com*

UNIT 19

MANAGING STORE EMPLOYEES

LEARNING OBJECTIVES

- Understanding the essence of managing store employees
- Identifying the ways to train the store employees
- Knowing various methods for training store employees
- Understanding factors that need to be considered while preparing training program
- Analyzing the relationship between managing employees and inventory losses

"Organization doesn't really accomplish anything. Plans don't accomplish anything, either. Theories of management don't much matter. Endeavors succeed or fail because of the people involved. Only by attracting the best people will you accomplish great deeds."

Colin Powell

INTRODUCTION

It has rightly been said that employees training and development is the only reason for success and failure of retail business. Trained employees can work smart and decrease errors and accidents. The right employee training and development at the right time, provides good returns to the retailer in the form of cost cutting, reduction in day to day expenditures and by way of energy savings etc. This unit talks about the essence of training programs and besides explaining various training methods, also suggest the factors that should be considered by a retailer before declaring any training program.

MANAGING HUMAN RESOURCES

The human resource management is an essential part of retailing that consists of inter-related human activities such as recruitment, selection, training, remuneration and supervision. The objective of this exercise is to hire, train and retain employees.

While applying human resource planning process, labour laws, age and sex, diversity and employees' confidentiality should be kept in mind. Diversity in retailing involves two basic issues:

(i) Employees' selection should be fair and free from external pressure, and

(ii) Employees should not be from a particular class or society.

Following issues should be kept in mind during selection of employees:

(i) no recruitment of under age workers

(ii) payment to employees should be made visible

(iii) no biasing in hiring or promotion of retail staff

(iv) to imply with workers' safety guidelines

(v) no business with suppliers that disobey labour laws

IMPORTANCE OF MANAGING EMPLOYEES

The training program has following benefits:

1. Reduced supervision and direction
2. Heightened morale
3. Reduced accidents, errors and omissions
4. Better store management
5. Better store/inter relations
6. Reduced learning time
7. Standardization
8. Improved store's stability and flexibility
9. Fill in manpower needs

OBJECTIVES OF MANAGING EMPLOYEES

A retailer has following objectives while managing and training employees:

1. Optimum capacity utilization
2. Reduce wastages
3. To impart customer education
4. To impart customer handling skills and patience tactics
5. To impart basic knowledge and skills to employees
6. To assist the employee in working more efficiently
7. To broaden the minds of the store employees
8. To place right person at the right job
9. To develop and implement the latest management system

RECRUITMENT OF RETAIL STAFF

Recruitment is a part of selection drive whereby a retailer generates a list of job applicants. This list is generated from various sources like walk in interviews, educational and vocational institutes and placement agencies. Besides this, unsolicited applications, employees' references, ex-employees who are looking for better jobs and advertisement are also used to select retail store employees. Table 19.1 represents the features of some recruitment sources.

Table 19.1
Features of Recruitment Process

Sources of Recruitment	Features
External sources	
Educational and Vocational Institutions	• Schools, colleges and universities • Suitable for entry levels
Advertisements	• Newspapers, journals, magazines and internet • Provides wider choice of applicants • Covers broader area • Understandable and easy to keep record
Placement Agencies	• Private, government and semi-government bodies • Good for applicant screening • Makes selection procedure shorter • Collect payment from both the applicant and the retail company
Unsolicited applications	• Walk-in interviews • Cost effective • Past details should be verified properly
Miscellaneous Sources	• Employees of wholesalers, manufacturers and distribution agents • Reduces training budget • Experienced employees • Less problem in adjustment in stores
Internal Sources	
Employees' References	• Friends, relatives and known • Provides loyal staff • Cost effective • Before recruitment, employee's current position, honesty and judgement of present employees is vital
Current and former Staff	• Promotion within the employees • Good for motivating staff • Cost effective • Saves expenditure on training

Besides this, today job sites like Naukri.com, hot jobs.com, monster jobs.com etc play a big role in recruitment of store employees. It is not only quick but also provides a large database. For entry-level floor jobs, retailers generally rely on educational and vocational institutes, walk-in interviews, recruitment sites and employees' recommendations. For middle-level positions, retailers use placement agencies, newspapers and competitors' turnovers.

During recruitment, the retailers' main stress remain on creating a long list of probable store staff, which will be reduced during selection process. Therefore, while collecting applications, retailers should accept only those applications those meet the minimum eligibility criteria such as educational background and work experience in order to save both money and time involved in the selection procedure.

TRAINING OF RETAIL EMPLOYEES

After selecting required number of employees, big retailers normally send them for one month or more training, depending upon the store size and policies. The purpose of such training is that before handling any task, candidates should know what is expected from them and what is the company's working style. In retailing world, such training is known as pre-training program, which is indoctrination on the firm's history and policies as well as part of the induction program.

FACTS ABOUT TRAINING PROGRAMS

(i) Training period varies according to the store's policies and therefore is different from store to store.

(ii) It can be in-house or out-house.

(iii) Training supervisors / instructors can be internal or external experts.

(iv) Training program can be pre-training (before joining the store) or post joining i.e. on job training.

(v) Attending training program simply will not serve the purpose, its successful completion is a must.

(vi) In case of individual employee's also, training period can vary.

(vii) Effective and successful retaining realize on ongoing activity.

SELECTED TRAINING DECISIONS

Conducting a training program is not an easy task. Several training decisions are to be considered, which are mentioned below:

- When to start a training program?
- What should be the duration?
- Who all should attend?
- Who should conduct the training program?
- Where should training take place?
- What should be the teaching method?
- How should it be taught?
- Should there be an audio-visual effect?
- How to measure its effectiveness?
- How many employees should attend at a time?

METHODS OF TRAINING

Training of store employees is a systematic program to increase the knowledge, skills, abilities and attitude of employees to perform specific jobs in a retail store. There is a long list of methods to train store employees. Some methods are common while some are developed considering the specific needs of the store. Some of the methods that are applicable and widely applied are as follows:

(i) **On the job training:** It is imparted on the job under actual working conditions. It can be provided in one of the following ways:
- Training by supervisor
- Under study system – self study and assessment
- Position rotation

(ii) **Vestibule training**: This method is usually applied in electronics, luxury or luxurious retailing. In this method, training to store staff is given in classrooms through models.

(iii) **Classroom method**: This is a widely used method in Indian retailing. It develops concepts, attitude, theories and problem-solving abilities in one of the following ways:
- Formal lecture method,
- Conferences, seminars or workshops,
- Case study method or
- Role playing

(iv) **Apprenticeship training**: This type of training is given to store's employees as per provision of central / state government laws. It is mandatory in nature.

Training Methods

Many retailing firms spend a considerable amount of money and time to train their sales employees. This becomes necessary in today's competitive environment where sales staff need to be trained for the better consumer services. Some retailing firms divide their training methods as under:

Group Methods	Individual Methods
1. Lecture	1. Personal Counselling
2. Case discussion	2. Correspondence courses
3. Films	3. On the job training
4. Role Playing	4. Product demonstration
5. Video tapes/CDs	5. Self Study system
6. Product demonstration	
7. Business Games & Quizzes	
8. Sensitivity Analysis	
9. Group Presentation	

PRINCIPLES / ESSENTIALS OF A TRAINING PROGRAM

A sound training program must possess the following characteristics or it should be:

- Beneficial for all groups
- Economical
- Expert Training staff
- Flexible
- Interesting
- Motivating
- Multi-parametric
- Preplanned
- Satisfactory
- Systematic
- Time saving

MANAGING STORE EMPLOYEES AND REDUCING INVENTORY LOSSES

The significance of managing store employees cannot and should not be overlooked by the management. If no systematic program of managing is established, the store employees will learn by trial and error on the job, which is rather costlier. The retailer / management should therefore develop a systematic program of managing and training store employees, which will in turn help the management itself.

The major values are discussed below:

1. Reduction in Inventory losses

It has been found that generally store accidents are caused by deficiencies in the people than by deficiencies in equipments and working conditions. Proper training program in the field of safety concerns and job skills contribute towards reduction in the accident rate and inventory losses. Managing store employees qualify them for more responsible jobs.

2. Better and economical use of materials and equipments

An advantageous product of managing is that spoiled work and damages to equipments, shelves, cabinets, merchandise can be kept at minimum by well managed employees.

COMMUNITY RELATIONS

- The manner in which a retailer interacts with the communities around him affects the retail store image. Following points need to be considered for having a good image among public:
- To make certain that disabled and physically challenged customers can enter the store easily
- Supporting donations and charities
- Sponsoring youth activities
- Donating money and/or equipments to schools
- Noting every aspect that support at the company's website
- Running special sales for senior citizens etc

The A,B,C of Human Relations in Retail Management

A ACCEPT genuinely, that Business is people and Retail is about dealing with people i.e.: customers, suppliers and ultimately employees. Employees are the first customers of any retail business! If employees are disgruntled, they will not render service to customers, vendors, and suppliers. I have yet to see a prosperous retailer, or a flourishing outlet, in London, Dubai, or Sao Paulo, whose employees are melancholic!

B BEHAVIOUR of managers should demonstrate conviction of the people factor in the retail management. Mission statements and words must be buffered by action! People are not duffers, just because they do not possess an array of degrees. I have met salesgirls on the floors who are sharper than managers, but due to economic reasons, they could not pursue studies. Such stars cannot be treated like Donald Ducks, for their native intelligences are vibrant. Talent is desperately short in the world, and would continue to be so, so respect and covet your people!

C CUSTOMER-SERVICE is the soul of any retail outlet. If all the employees, from top to bottom, comprehend and believe in this concept passionately, the outlet will be the "talk of the town"! Any retail outlet, ultimately sells services and smiles!

D DEVELOP leaders, everywhere! There is a leader in every salesgirl, merchandiser or manager. (In a recent Hindi movie, A character pronounces, "There is a lion in everyone. It only needs someone to tickle it, to make it roar!") All works get routine after sometime. Then people get frustrated. They either commence job hunting or become disruptive. It is energizing to develop leadership traits in all managers, and promote from within, when opportunities arise.

E ESTABLISH systems, manuals, procedures, business processes for all retail operations in rigorous details. This will help to trim arbitrariness in the store. Manuals also prescribe procedures for standardization of fundamentals across retail stores and branches. Remember: Retail in Detail!

F FORGE teams out of employees. Make each section, floor, category and independent unit, and foster team spirit by giving them collective tasks and team prizes for their achievements. Encourage the teams to spend informal times together i.e., a picnic, a movie, or an outing, to augment bonding.

G GENERATE challenges to keep your highfliers monitoring in top gear. High-energy managers and staff live on hyper-adrenaline energy levels. These high performance managers need to kill a lion daily!

H HELP your employees round the clock. If someone falls sick in the middle of the night, train your managers to land up at the employee's house to take him to the hospital or look after him. Dedicated and devoted teams are the result of the mind-set of being a "Help-Desk" to your employees.

I INVOLVE your top management in key decisions pertaining to new concepts, expansions, diversifications, and promotions of senior staff. Many entrepreneurs tend to monopolize such decisions. This kills the commitment and zeal of the top management. Some retailers tend to be schizophrenic in managing the business personally, for they are enraptured by control; such retailers remain "glorified-grocers", they will never graduate into great retailers!

J JUDGE employees on pure merit! Retailers, who run their businesses professionally, flourish. Avoid favoritism like the plague. In a family business, make your sons/daughters labor their way up the ladder, like a trainee. You would teach them the best lessons of their lives.

K KNOWLEDGE is power in the retail business. Employees should be updated constantly on new technologies, IT systems, selling techniques etc. Product knowledge is the key to excellent customer service. In a retail chain selling electronic products, the sales staff must understand the technical features and assist customers in smart decisions.

L LOSING a retail professional or team, built over the years, due to petty squabbling, ego-clashes, or feeble remuneration, is stupid. Ordinary people, who work selflessly in a store, are the foundation of great retail businesses, it is vital to ensure that trained, committed staff is retained.

M MOTIVATE teams for superior performance through personal encouragement, financial rewards, status enhancing awards, sales contests, bonuses, so that teams feel invigorated and appreciated. Ensure that staff gets an adequate monthly salary to live decently i.e., 70%, if there is an incentive system.

N NEVER condone the use of foul language or uncouth manners on the shop floors. Chewing of gum, winking, scratching etc, are highly obnoxious to customers. Appoint a floor-coach in every outlet, who will focus on etiquette and grooming of the staff.

O OUTPERFORM target culture! Motivate your team so that they do not meet targets, but exceed them. Teams must be willing to do that little incremental, walk than extra mile. Delivering beyond the normal call of duty makes the difference between a merely competent retailer and a great retailer!

P PROFITS are crucial to a retail business. Without profits, no business can survive. However, profits augment if the habit of thinking profits is inculcated down the line. Directors, managers, staff or watchmen, must all think profits! Margins are principally low in retail, hence costs have to be watched like hawks at all levels.

Q QUIET periods, whereby senior managers get away from the daily store pressures, once a quarter and have a "blue-sky" day, debating innovations, will yield many practical ideas for operational efficiencies. It will also cement team members.

R REMUNERTING the team judiciously is the key element of retailing. If a retailer scrounges money by paying your employees below their market value, the latter will desert such a shortsighted employer.

S SALARY reviews against competitors are vital to ensure that staff is remunerated competitively. This will contribute in retaining the team.

T TRAINING and development of the staff on a continuous basis, bringing latest management practices into the retail group and also motivates the staff. Top-team members must be sensitized to deal with the environment, e.g., the recent anger of vegetable vendors against Reliance Fresh in Ranchi.

U UNDERSTAND the customers, via floor staff by spending time with them in the shops. Sales staff on the floors are brilliant sources of information about customer preferences. Then insights are free!

V VERY important it is for top management to interact with the governments in the states and Center to explicate the advantages of large formats of retail for India for employment generation and tax revenues. Retailing in India is nascent, there are social concerns to be addressed by senior managers. This too requires grooming.

W WEE extra benefits like a meal scheme, transportation form and to the residence, when the workplace is far away, make a massive difference to the morale of a team, at negligible costs.

X X-RAYABLE, transparent operations, invariably ensure respect from employees. A transparently managed retail business that pays taxes, adheres to labour laws, pays its employees on time, and stands to its word, lures the bets talent.

Y YOURS is the whole retail world, if you can adhere to even 50% of this list, and build a team, which respects the values enshrined in the organization and the practices of the company.

Z ZEBRA Crossing is sacred! Yes, there is "Management Zebra Crossing" too!! The personal life of employees! Frequently employers have a habit of getting embroiled in the personal lives of their employees, which is avoidable. Employers, particularly family based formats, believe that merely because a person works with them, they have an unbridled right to interfere in one's personal life. Unless the laws of the land are being contravened, employers should respect the "Zebra Line".

***Source:** Idea taken from IMAGES Retail, Nov 2007, Vol. 6, No. 19.*

SUMMARY

No two human beings are alike in their basic mental abilities, understanding capacity, grasping power, stamina to long work, traits, intelligence and appearances. Depending upon these, they behave differently in same circumstances. To deal with them effectively and that to with great care is very essential for accomplishment of store's goals. Managing store employees in retail stores is "train and motivate store employees" in organizational settings to develop teamwork which accomplish individual's as well as store's goals effectively. Retail training programs are used at large scale to teach new and existing employees how best to perform their respective tasks or how to improve the efficiency. Training can range from hours to days, days to weeks, and weeks to months or compliance with affirmative action programs to one/two year programs for executive training on all aspects of the retailing and store operations.

Successful retailers have understood that training to store employees should be a continuous phenomenon. Employees must be informed to use of new equipments, changes in retail laws, and launch of new product lines instead of hiring new employees who are aware of new trends and developments. Further, a training program must be systematically evaluated for effectiveness. Comparisons should be made between the performance of those who have received training and those who have not.

REVIEW QUESTIONS

True and False Questions

1. Trained employees can work smart, reduce errors and accidents.
2. The human resource management is an essential part of retailing that consists of inter-related human activities such as layoff, demotion, transfer, hiring and firing.
3. Diversity in retailing involves two basic issues:
   (*a*) Employees' selection should be fair and free from external pressure, and
   (*b*) Employees should not be from a particular society or class.
4. Recruitment is a part of selection drive whereby a customer generates a list of job applicants.
5. Training period varies according to the store's policies and therefore is different from store to store.
6. Training program cannot be in-house or out-house.
7. Training supervisors can never be external experts.
8. On the job training is imparted on the job under actual working conditions.
9. Vestibule training is not applicable in electronics, luxury or luxurious retailing.
10. Classroom method is a widely used method in Indian retailing.
11. Apprenticeship training is given to store's employees as per provision of central / state government laws.
12. Apprenticeship training is voluntary in nature.
13. A sound training program must possess characteristics such as economical, presence of expert training staff, flexible, interesting, motivating, multi-parametric and pre planned.
14. Human beings are alike in their basic mental abilities, understanding capacity, grasping power, stamina to long work, traits, intelligence and appearances.
15. Managing store employees in retail stores is to train and motivate store employees in organizational settings to develop teamwork which accomplish individual as well as store's goals effectively.
16. Retail training programs are used at large scale to teach new and existing employees how best to perform their respective tasks or how to improve the efficiency.
17. Training can range from hours to days, days to weeks, and weeks to months or compliance with affirmative action programs to one/two year programs for executive training on all aspects of the retailing and store operations.
18. Successful retailers know that training to store employees should be a continuous phenomenon.
19. Employees need not to inform about usage of new equipments, changes in retail laws, and launch of new product lines.
20. Comparisons should be made between the performance of those who have received training and those who have not.

Answers

1. True 2. False 3. True 4. false

5. True	6. False	7. False	8. True
9. False	10. True	11. True	12. False
13. True	14. False	15. True	16. True
17. True	18. True	19. False	20. True

Multiple Choice Questions

1. External source of recruitment is:
   (*a*) Placement Agencies (*b*) Employees references
   (*c*) Current and former staff (*d*) All of the above.
2. The example of internal source of recruitment is:
   (*a*) Unsolicited Applications (*b*) Advertisements.
   (*c*) Employees References (*d*) All of the above.
3. Vestibule training is provided by
   (*a*) Lecture method (*b*) Seminar method
   (*c*) Models (*d*) All of the above
4. Apprenticeship training is .... by law
   (*a*) Mandatory (*b*) Optional
   (*c*) Recommended (*d*) Preferred
5. Sensitivity analysis is used under :
   (*a*) Group method (*b*) Individual method
   (*c*) Direct method (*d*) Law thus mandatory
6. .... is the example of on the job training method
   (*a*) Training by supervisors. (*b*) Under study system.
   (*c*) Position Rotation (*d*) All of the above.
7. The example of classroom training method is ....
   (*a*) Role playing (*b*) Under study system
   (*c*) Position rotation (*d*) Training by supervisor.
8. For a retail training program, instructors can be
   (*a*) only internal (*b*) only external
   (*c*) both internal and external (*d*) from industry only
9. The human resource management is an .... part of retailing
   (a) Internal (b) External
   (c) Essential (*d*) Wasteful
10. Train employes can work .... and .... errors and accidents
    (*a*) Actively, forget (*b*) smoothly, unaffected by
    (*c*) smart, decrease (*d*) fast, increase

Answers

1. (*a*)	2 (*c*)	3. (*c*)	4. (*a*)
5. (*a*)	6. (*d*)	7. (*a*)	8. (*c*)
9. (*c*)	10. (*c*)		

Answers to check your progress

1. What is Job site?
2. Who is loyal staff?
3. What is selection procedure?
4. What are vocational institutes?
5. What is position rotation?
6. What does motivation mean?
7. What is training?
8. What are community relations?
9. What is HRM?
10. What is training budget?
11. What is placement agency?
12. What are unsolicited applications?
13. What is walk in interview?
14. What is role play?
15. What is recruitment?

EXERCISES AND QUESTIONS

Small Answer Questions

1. What issues should be considered during selection of store's employees?
2. Discuss the importance of managing store employees?
3. What are the objectives of a training program?
4. What decisions are taken before deciding a training program?
5. Explain the principles of training programs?
6. How training reduce accidents, errors and omissions?
7. Describe the merits and demerits of vestibule training method?
8. What issues should be considered while recruiting store employees?
9. Differentiate between classroom training and apprenticeship training?
10. Discuss the essence of community relations?

Long Answer Questions

1. What do you mean by training and development? Discuss the essence of a training program? And also explain the various methods available for training store employees?
2. Suppose you are recently promoted as head of personnel department. Besides regular activities, you will also be responsible to train your store employees. Which method you would like to introduce in your organization and why?

RETAIL COMMUNICATION

Unit 20 : Customer Service Strategies
Unit 21 : Retail Sales Promotion
Unit 22 : Retail Communication Mix
Unit 23 : Building Customer Relationships and Competitive Advantage

UNIT 20

CUSTOMER SERVICE STRATEGIES

LEARNING OBJECTIVES

- Understanding the significance of customer service in recent retailing context and explaining the customer's evaluation criteria for measuring service quality
- Illustrating situations leading to satisfactory and unsatisfactory customer experience
- Explaining the concept, role and significance of GAPS model for improving the quality
- Explaining the concept of visitor, customer, consumer and a potential customer to understand the need for good customer service
- Discussing the guidelines to retain customers and essentials of good customer service

"There is only one boss. The customer.
And he can fire everybody in the company from the chairman on down,
simply by spending his money somewhere else."

Sam Walton

"The single most important thing to remember about any enterprise is that
there are no results inside its walls. The result of a business is a satisfied customer."

Peter Drucker

"Quality in a service or product is not what
you put into it. It is what the client or customer gets out of it.

Peter Drucker

"Customers don't expect you to be perfect.
They do expect you to fix things when they go wrong."

Donald Porter

INTRODUCTION

Good customer service has today become an integral part of the retail industry. In retailing, where floor staff has to directly interact with the customers, customer service acts as lifeblood. With sales promotion and lucrative offers you can increase the temporary sales but out of these customers if half or some of the customers do not come back then your store will not survive for long. **Good customer service** is intended to bring back these customers voluntarily and then sending back with smiling faces. Smiling faces means after buying something, they have good feedback about your service. Even in some cases, they recommend your store to others for shopping by sharing their good experiences. Yes this is always possible. It is the word of mouth that multiplies your customer base within a short span of time.

Good floor staff does not mean that you can sell anything to anyone. But it will be your image in the minds of the customers that decides whether or not you can sell something to them. The image is largely influenced by the service provided by the floor staff and the experience of the customers with them. A satisfied customer is bound to tell others about his experiences, as will a dissatisfied customer. The strength of good customer service is to develop a longlasting rapport with customers – a link that individual customer feels that he would like to pursue in the coming time. How you develop such a long term relationship depends on your intention and perseverance. Remember the secret of forming good relationship is the customer service with full dedication and without any greed. By this way, you will be known by what you do, not what you say to customers.

A retailer's ability to device and apply a sound strategy depends on how a retail firm identifies customer needs, expectations and possible gaps that hinder a retailer's ability to minimize or close gap between customers' expectations and customers' perception of the actual service received. When the services offered exceeded the service expected, leads to satisfied customers. However, customers are dissatisfied when the services received by them do not match their expectations. This chapter begins with customer service strategies and besides explaining role of expectations, concept of perceived services discusses the essence of **GAPS** model in recent context.

WHO IS A CUSTOMER?

A customer is someone who pays for goods or services from a store. All the persons coming to your store are 'visitors'. When they buy something and pay for the things they have bought, they become 'customers'. Now, they have purchased these things for their own consumption or for someone else is not clear. While on the other hand, the person who actually enjoys/consumes these things are not as 'consumers'. In short the person who pay the bill is known as customer and the person who uses that thing is known as 'consumer' therefore, in the world of retailing, it has rightly been said 'customers' can be 'consumers' but all 'consumers' necessarily need not 'customers'.

MANAGING THE CUSTOMER

Managing the customers in stores has always been a difficult task. You as a floor staff cannot know what the intention of a customer is? Whether a visitor asking for a particular good, is really interested in buying the thing or just has come for time pass or grab knowledge. But being the member of floor staff, you cannot say 'No' to the customer. Further, customers are from various backgrounds. They have different desires, different tastes, likings and dislikings. The selling behavior which you apply to one customer will not be applicable to all customers.

Some customers are from 'different' background and are interested in your products and have enough purchasing power. But the problem is that they've not visited any mall or are not aware about modern retail store buying. So, they can ask a lot of questions about quality, quantity or after sales services. Even after spending three-four hours, they change their mind of buying things. Here you need not to lose your 'patience' considering 'city' buyers are quick in purchasing decisions. In retail business, the idea of not loosing patience comes under providing good customer service and should be an on-going opportunity. In order to understand the underlying principle behind this assumption and to face the challenge of building customer faithfulness, we divide customers into five categories:

1. **Loyal Customers:** Loyal customers are those customers who have faith in the store and visit store on regular basis. Normally they are satisfied with the store services. Whether the demand is less or more, they like to buy from the same store and also recommend others to visit. If we try to understand loyal customers in terms of customer base of the retail store, we will find it is hardly the twenty percent of store's total customer base, but it makes more than fifty percent of retail store's total sales. These customers are the one who have great influence on the policy making matters. These customers also influence the merchandising buying decision of the store. Hence to retain these loyal customers, store should interact with these customers on regular basis by telephone, e-mail, fax and SMS.
2. **Discount Customers:** These type of customers visit our stores often, but make their decisions on the basis of discounts, offers rebates offered by the store. Sometimes, in absence of any discount offer, they can postpone their buying decision. These customers ensure that inventory is turning over and, as a result, it contributes to retail store's cash flow. This same group, however, can often wind up costing you money because they are more inclined to return product.
3. **Impulse Customers:** These type of customers come to store without the intention of buying the goods. When they come to store even with no desire to buy a particular good but during their stay, they purchase whatever appeals to them. But this type of visitors can be good customers if floor staff attends them properly. Because these customers normally take decisions on the basis of floor

staff recommendations. Obviously, this is the section of our customers that all retailers would like to serve.

4. **Need-Based Customers:** These type of customers come to store with intention of buying some particular goods. When they come to the store, instead of wandering here and there they either go to the specific shelf or ask about that product display. These sort of customers are determined by a specific need. When they come to the store, they make themselves comfortable that their demand will be fulfilled. If not, without wasting further time, they would like to quit the store. Actually this sort of customers come for variety of reasons like on occasion of marriage or for a specific need. For floor staff, normally it becomes difficult to satisfy these visitors because they are always in a hurry and have high expectations from the store. But experience has shown that if these types of customers are taken care of well they in short term can become loyal customers and the source of store's long term growth.
5. **Wandering Customers:** These type of customers come to store without any particular need or desire. They come to store with the intention of timepass or to know the latest trend. It is very difficult to recognize them. Sometime they are well dressed, even belong to well off families. They ask a lot of questions about the goods displayed. But somebody has said that experience is the best teacher. Therefore, after having some experience in the store, to some extent you can recognize them. But again no guarantee that your decision to recognize these wanderers is right. They can be from any community/society. In most of the retail stores, these type of customers is the largest section in terms of numbers of visitors arrived in store.

Note: *This segment of customers may not present a large percentage of store's immediate sales; they represent your store in the community. They come to store for timepass or simply to have knowledge about latest trends or new arrival. You cannot get rid of these customers. But one thing is that they share their experience with others and therefore, are a source of mouth advertisement. As they look for interaction with the floor staff to give the message that they have not come here to shop, time spent with them must be minimized.*

Strategy to be followed

The stores that are serious about its customers and know the value of customers should focus their efforts on loyal customers and merchandise their retail store to impress their impulse customers. The remaining three types of customers are also the visitors to your store, but the resources allocated to them should be in strict manner. The floor staff's role here becomes important that to which segment of customers, it should more concentrate. The art is to recognize these customers and treat them accordingly. Besides this, patience and customer understanding skills are important for decision making process.

CUSTOMERS AND THE STORE

For most stores, understanding customers is the key to success while not understanding them is a recipe for failure. It is so important that the constant drive to satisfy customers is not only a concern for those responsible for carrying out marketing tasks satisfying customers is a concern of everyone in the entire store. Whether someone's job involves direct interaction with customers (e.g., salespeople, delivery drivers, telephone operators) or indirect contact (e.g., finance, accounting), all members of a store must appreciate the role customers play in helping the store meets its objectives. To ensure everyone understands the customer's role, many stores continually preach a "customer is our priority" message in department meetings, store's communication (e.g., internal emails, displays, website postings) and corporate training programs. To drive home the importance of customers, the message often contains examples of how customers impact the company. These examples include:

1. **Source of information and improvement** - Satisfying the needs of customers require stores maintain close contact with them. It is the customer who tells where store is lacking behind as compared to other stores. What should be the appropriate level of customer service? Where they are not satisfied with the store's services. Retailers can get close to customers by conducting marketing research (e.g., surveys) and other feedback methods (e.g., website comments forms) that encourage customers to share their thoughts and feelings. With the information, suggestions and complaints collected, retailers are able to learn what people think of their present marketing efforts and where change is required. Here, experts and specialist of retailing suggest research and feedback methods to have insight into new products and services sought by their customers.
2. **Affects store's policies and decisions** - For most stores, customers not only affect decisions made by the marketing team but they are the key driver for the decisions made throughout the store. For example, customer's reaction to the design of a product, arrangement of goods displayed, interiors and exteriors used can make store to change their layout or some arrangements. Because it is the customer who has to buy the goods if he is not convenient/comfortable when he visits the store, your costly/updated layout will not work. With customers impacting such a significant portion of a company, creating an environment geared to locate, understand and satisfy customers is essential.
3. **Needed to sustain the Store** - Finally, customers are the reason a store is in business. If the customers don't visit the store or hesitate to shop, that store can not run for long time. In the absence of customers, store will be out of competition. Therefore, customers are not only key to revenue and profits but are also key for creating and maintaining jobs within the store.

THE IMPORTANCE OF GOOD CUSTOMERS

For marketers, simply finding customers who are willing to purchase their goods or services is not enough to build a successful marketing strategy. Marketers should look to manage customers in a way that will identify, create and maintain satisfying relationships with customers. By using marketing efforts that are designed to maintain satisfying relationships rather than simply pursuing a quick sale, the likelihood increases that customers will more trust of the marketer and exhibit a higher level of satisfaction with the store. In turn, satisfied customers are more likely to become "good" customers.

For our purposes, we define a "**good**" customer as one who holds the potential to undertake activities that offer long-term value to a store. The activities performed by customers not only include purchasing products, but also:

- offering feedback on store performance,
- making prompt payment,
- informing the store regarding any complaint rather than to public,
- offering suggestions for new products,
- voluntarily promoting the company's products to others.

These activities along with many others (including profit from product sales) represent the value (i.e., benefits for costs spent) a store receives from its customers. In case of "**good**" customers, their potential for providing value should be a signal for marketers to direct additional marketing efforts in building, strengthening and sustaining a relationship with these customers.

The fact that we place the descriptive term "**good**" in front of customers should not be taken lightly. Not all customers who currently have relationships with a store (i.e., existing customers) should be treated on an equal level. Some consistently spend large sums to purchase products from a store, others do not spend large sums but hold the potential to do so, and still others use up a large amount of a store's resources but contribute little revenue. Clearly, there are lines of demarcation between those in the Existing Customer category. As we will see later, identifying this line is critical for marketing success.

CHALLENGE OF MANAGING CUSTOMERS

While on the surface, the process for managing customers may seem to be intuitive and straightforward, in reality, stores struggle to accomplish this. One reason for the struggle is that no two customers are the same. What is appealing to one customer may not necessarily work for another. For one product, customer is ready to pay anything but the other product may not even accept free of cost.

For instance, a marketer may change how it issues coupons to customers by reducing the frequency of issuing coupons by regular mail and instead directing customers to electronic coupons found on its website. The marketer makes this move to encourage customers to visit the website more often with the hope it will lead to cost savings (e.g., sending out traditional coupons by mail requires postage expense) & will allow the marketer to acquire more customer information (e.g., monitor their activities when they visit the website), and also give the marketer the opportunity to sell more products to the customer (e.g., special promotional messages on the website). However, sometimes customers may view electronic coupons as requiring more work on their part compared to coupons delivered through regular mail. In this example, the introduction of a new feature may satisfy some customers while irritating others.

CUSTOMER CONTACT POINTS

One more problem is that customers may interact with stores at different contact points. A contact point is the method, a customer uses to communicate with a store. For instance, consider the different ways customers may interact with a store:

1. **Financial Assistance** – Customer contact may also occur through company's personnel who assist customers with financial issues. For instance, credit personnel help customers arrange the necessary funds to make a purchase while personnel in accounts receivable work with customers who are experiencing payment problems.
2. **Physical Assistance** – Customers seek physical assistance for their needs and wants by visiting retail stores and other outlets and also through face to face discussion with the store's floor staff who visit customers at their place of business or in their home.
3. **In-Person Product Support** – Some in-person assistance is not principally intended to assist with selling but is designed to offer support once a purchase is made. Such services are handled by delivery people and service/repair technicians.
4. **Internet** – The fastest growing contact point is through the Internet. The use of Internet for purchasing (called e-commerce commerce) has exploded and is now the leading method for purchasing certain types of products including electronic goods and books. The Internet is also a key area where customers look for help with their purchases. They send e-mails, chat online in case of any trouble shooting.
5. **Kiosks** – A kiosk is a separate, interactive computer, often equipped with a touch-screen, that offers customers several service options including product information, ability to make a purchase and review of a customer's account. Kiosks are now widely used for airline check-in, retail job applications and banking & insurance.
6. **Telephone/Help line/Toll free Numbers** – Customers seeking to make purchases or have a problem solved may find it more convenient to do so through phone contact. It is not only reliable but very fast method also. In many companies a dedicated department called a 'call center' handles all incoming customer inquiries and complaints.

No matter which contact points customers use, the challenge to satisfy the customers always prevails? As sometimes same customer uses different contact points at different times. Obviously he will be confused by the response received from different employees handling different contact points. The statements given by two persons at various contact points can be conflicting. Hence retailers should develop such system of ***customer service*** where each employee should give same information despite working for different contact points.

CUSTOMER SERVICE STRATEGIES

No doubt that retailing is the most attractive and lucrative sector in the recent era. With increasing per capita income, standard of living and especially the size of middle class, new and new retailers are coming with fresh and unique retailing experience. Our Indian '***kirana stores***' are not only facing competition from domestic players but also from international retailers like Wall-Mart, Spencer's, **Dollar One** shops etc. Therefore, retailers (existing as well as new) besides offering wide and attractive assortments at affordable prices, also offer services those provide the shoppers a memorable shopping experience. Retailers can position themselves by offering services that enhance their purchase experience. There are at least three levels of retail service:

1. **Self Service** – This service level allows consumers to perform most or all of the services associated with retail purchasing. For some consumers, self-service is considered a benefit while others may view it as an inconvenience. Self-service can be seen with:
   (a) **Self-selection services**, such as online purchasing and vending machine purchases, and
   (b) **Self-checkout services** where the consumer may get help selecting the product but they use self-checkout stations to process the purchase including scanning and payment.
2. **Assorted Service** – The majority of retailers offer some level of service to consumers. These retailers carry more shopping merchandise assortment and shoppers require more assistance and information. The assistance may be for product selection, arranging payment plans, delivery methods etc. Besides this, retailers also offer services like credit and merchandise return privileges etc.
3. **Full Service** – The full service retailer attempts to handle nearly all aspects of the purchase to the point where all the consumers select the item they wish to purchase. Retailers that follow a full price strategy often follow the full-service approach as a way of adding value to a customer's purchase.

Critical Success factors for Self service

- Understanding your customer
- Better in-store displays
- By reducing sales staff
- Self selection
- Easy and quick billing
- Proper space to walk and so on

ESSENTIALS OF GOOD CUSTOMER SERVICE

Customers have good and bad experiences each and every time they walk into one's store. If you really want to have good customer service in your store, all you have to do is to ensure that your retail store follows these essentials:

(1) Answer your phone

A good store is one that always answers to your phone calls or queries. Recruit some permanent staff to attend customers' queries over phone. Use answering machine or outsource your complaint and query department. Make certain that your store does not miss any customer's call. Remember these days customers instead of wasting time on answering machines, prefer to talk to a live person.

(2) Doesn't make fake promises

Good stores' employees always say 'Sir/Madam we'll try our level best' instead of 'don't worry we'll do it' and after sometime they forget what they had promised. Being a retailer, you should know that lie has no legs to stand upon. You can befool a customer once or twice but ultimately you'll have to be responsible for his complaint. Therefore, it is better that you should listen to him in the first instance. Remember ***reliability*** is one of the key aspects of retailing. It takes years to build good customer relation but few seconds, a small mistake to loose the customer. For example, if you promise a customer your refrigerator will be delivered at your home on Monday night, make certain that it reaches by Monday night because they will wait for the refrigerator. Therefore, before any commitment, ensure the efficiency and availability of delivery mechanism.

(3) Listen to customers

It has rightly been said that in retailing, it is not the product but the customer who gives you profit. It is the customer payments out of which retail employees get salary. If a customer tells you something or enquire something, pay attention to him. If you don't take him seriously or simply ignore him, he will go to your seniors and then you are forced to **listen** him. Why create such a situation where your customer looses confidence in you and you bear insult from your seniors. Therefore, always listen with full concentration, attention and interest so that the other customer also feels good about it. Also listen to customers' feelings not just words. Show that you are listening to him and ask question wherever necessary.

(4) Handle the complaints

It is the human nature that he is not ready to hear his own complaint made by others and has developed a wrong concept that no one can make all the customers happy. Remember this attitude is the biggest hurdle in building a positive customer relationship. Obviously being a floor staff employee, you can not make all the customers happy at a time. But if you listen to their ***complaints***, you will turn temporary customer into a loyal customer. We should not forget one thing that if one happy customer shares his experience with minimum five, he/she shares the bad with minimum ten people.

(5) Be helpful without considering earning profit always

Some time customers after buying something ask continuously some queries or come for some help, it irritates you. You think you have sold this thing and your duty is over towards that customer. Need is to change this type of attitude. Some time it's seen that for minor repair or some nominal part, shopkeepers ask in response about the expenditure rather your reaction should be **Sir, it's OK**. No need to pay anything. You can go. Then see the magic of mouth advertisement, how this message will reach to a family and then to his neighbours without any media.

(6) Go one step ahead

It simply means to be sensitive to others feelings. Show selflessness & make customers a part of your responsibility. Tell them that they are very important to you. Try to ask their views when and where required. In the world of retailing, it is said that if you want a customer to buy a photograph, make sure he is in the picture. For example, if somebody comes to your store and ask. Where he'll find 40 size shirts' instead of saying like 'straight then right' etc. take that customer to the desired shelf. Remember, customers notice these small gestures. They may not mention you but people appreciate this sort of behaviour. Therefore, recognize the power of customer service and train your floor staff that they should understand them.

Toy 'R' Us bringing baby, toy stores under one roof

Shoppers looking for baby merchandise will now be able to purchase toys as well as Toys 'R' Us Inc. to boost the company's bottom line by combining its stand-alone toy and baby stores under one roof, according to a report from Dow Jones & Co, Inc.

"Mom is time-starved and this gives her the ability to buy everything she needs for her children at one stop," said Jerry Storch, chairman and Chief Executive of Toys 'R' Us, comparing the idea to discount big-box retail chains such as Wal-Mart Stores Inc. Dow Jones said that the New Jersey-based retailer tested the waters over the past year by converting a number of smaller-sized toy stores into combination toy and baby stores and is creating much-larger superstores that sell baby and toy products.

The idea, according to Storch, is to entice busy parents shopping for baby goods at the already popular babies 'R' Us chain to buy playthings as well. The baby and toy stores will have separate entrances and signs. But once inside, consumers can shop both stores freely and check out on either side. The first two superstores have opened in Elizabeth, about a 30-minute drive from Manhattan and in California, followed by stores opening this fall in Florida and Arizona. The Elizabeth location is a former Toys 'R' Us superstore that has been converted.

Source: *www.money.aol.com*

(7) Manage customers creatively

No two customers are alike in their basic mental abilities, personality, intelligence, attitudes, aspirations and appearance. Depending upon these traits, they behave differently. Therefore, to deal with them effectively and creatively, utmost care and art is required. The one behaviour or selling art which is applicable to a particular customer neither will nor work all the time. Therefore, be creative all the times. **Each customer** is an **opportunity** for you and you should not miss that opportunity

In today's complex market environment, service has become a truism and it seems like "everyone's doing it." So, if everyone is doing it, why not jump ahead of the wolf pack by providing even more creative, personalized service to your customers than your competitors can, and then see the magic in the form of increased sales turnover in short period.

SIGNIFICANCE OF CUSTOMER SERVICE

In this era of retailing it is not the pricing that attracts the customers but the customer service, which is voluntarily provide to customers. If customers are happy with the services you are providing, it will result in increased turnover and enhanced goodwill. The benefits of customer service are numerous. But for the better understanding of the concept, some benefits are mentioned. These are as follows:

- Better customer service can beat your competitors
- Builds brand loyalty
- Less Complaints
- Customers are always happy and satisfied
- Customers get value for money
- Customers offer suggestions to improve store's policies and environment
- Reduces expenditure on marketing and advertising
- Drives profitable growth
- Helps retailers create differentiation and value through their experiences
- Improves financial performance
- Improves the image of a store
- Increases client base
- Source of mouth advertisement
- Strengthens competitive advantage
- Visitors become customers and customers become loyal to the stores

CUSTOMER RELATIONSHIP MANAGEMENT (CRM)

CRM (Customer Relationship Management) is a business strategy built around the concept of being customer-centric. The main purpose of CRM is to optimize store's revenue through improved customer satisfaction via improved interactions at each customer touch point. This can be accomplished by a better understanding of customers based on their purchasing patterns and demographics and better information empowerment at all customer touch points whether with employees or other media interfaces.

While CRM is generally used to manage existing customers, it also has application for other customer groups. For instance, **CRM** is used to help identify former customers that may hold potential to become customers again. This is often possible due to the amount of information that is obtained and subsequently retained when former customers were considered existing customers. Additionally, **CRM** can serve an integral role in helping to locate potential customers.

ICT (Information & Communication Technology) plays a vital role in carrying out CRM. A proper technology-based system is needed so that nearly anyone in a store who comes in contact with a customer (e.g., sales force, service force, customer service representatives, accounts receivable, etc.) has access to necessary information and is well prepared to deal with the customer. But CRM is not only about utilizing high-tech products, it also requires a strong organizational commitment that includes extensive training for all employees. But maintaining close and consistent relationships with customers through all contact points which makes good business sense, accomplishing this has often been a challenge. Numerous problems, from technology failures and lack of communication between contact points as well as lack of adequate employee training or outright employee resistance have derailed many **CRM** efforts. So, while CRM is now widely adopted and is becoming an essential tool for most business stores, it still has a long way to go before it is ingrained as an essential business function within most stores.

GUIDELINES FOR GREAT CUSTOMER SERVICE

One of the key aspects of retail service that is most immediately apparent is the relation between customer and sales staff within the outlet. This sort of relation can vary from a passive approach to a highly interactive one. The passive approach is one where customers select their products on their own with floor staff only becoming involved at the point of sale (for example at the cash counters only) While interactive approach is characterized by direct interaction with the customers within the floor area. Helping them, guiding them and providing according to their choice are the essential elements of the approach. Therefore, the practice of interactive approach should not only be present at floor area but in any other sales aspect of retailing. Follow these golden rules of great customer service in retailing:

1. Know the importance of customer

Remember that retail is a business to serve customers' needs and wants. Therefore, you must understand your customers. In case of regular customers, you should know their tastes, liking and disliking. Listen to them carefully. If you pay honest attention, they will let you know what actually they want. What is their budget and for which purpose they need a particular item. This will help you in understanding them and provide them what they are looking for and you will end a deal into cash payment.

2. Be a good listener

Listen more and talk less. Listening to customers and understanding their feelings are essential for floor staff. Always listen with full concentration, attention and interest what services the retailer requires. Also listen to the feelings, not just words. Show understanding and ask relevant questions wherever doubt arises.

3. Avoid arguments

According to Gautam Buddha "Hatred can never be ended by hatred, but can be overcome by love". Misunderstanding cannot be cleared by arguments but by tactics, diplomacy and conciliation. Always remember that argument is a negative exercise, which is harmful for both parties. If you've doubts, discuss it and finish it.

4. Be careful in communication

Spoken words are like arrows, they don't return once they are shot. It takes years to build relations but only few minutes to lose it. Therefore,

(1) Establish formal communication systems including updates and weekly status report.

(2) Educate and inform employees as brokers communicate direct with your firm's personnel by setting up in-house seminars etc.

5. Recognize and predict needs

There is nothing wrong in saying that customers don't buy products but feelings and way outs to problems. Most of the visitors are emotional rather than practical. Their decisions are spontaneous and are influenced by attendants/floor staff. Therefore, being a member of the staff, you should directly interact with the customers. Then you will be able to know their preferences and upcoming needs.

6. Make customers feel important and treasured

Take care of your customers as individuals. Use their name and discover ways to praise them, but be honest and real. Customers value seriousness and it is the foundation stone to create good sense and confidence. Think about ways to make good feelings they should make with you while doing business. Today, customers are very responsive and understand whether or not you really think for them. Say 'thanks' every time when they buy something from your store. Do not miss the opportunity to praise them. While on the floor area, make certain that your body language reflects sincerity. Therefore, your words should match with your actions.

7. Assist customers recognize your systems

You are proud of having world's best systems for retail selling but if the customers don't understand them, it will simply confuse them. Let them know how your system is better than the others. How your retail system works and how it make transactions easy and trouble free.

8. Value the power of saying 'Yes'

Successful retailer is the one who is always ready to serve and help customers. He always thinks and develops ways to help them. Whenever they need your help help them without being selfish all the time. Always look for ways to help your customers. Whenever they have query, you should answer for that query. Be prepared to deal with customers' problems instantly and let them know how much valuable they are for the retail store.

9. Get regular feedback

Don't forget the benefits of getting your feedback. It is an ongoing process of self improvement. Sometimes, it is the customer who teaches us the method of effective selling. Therefore, give confidence and welcome suggestions about how you could pick up. There are several ways in which you can find out what customers think and feel about your services. It's up to you which method you select to collect your feedback.

10. Treat employees well

Remember there may be good material, good environment and good salary but if the man who has to work is not satisfied, result will not be up to the mark. It is the human ability which makes the mare go. Employees are human beings and therefore, they should be treated humanly. Employees actually are the internal and loyal customers to your store and therefore, they need regular positive reception. Do not hesitate to say 'thanks'. They want to know how much their organization care for them. Once they are happy and satisfied with store's policies, they will attend the customers in a better and effective manner.

NEW TRENDS IN CUSTOMER SERVICE

Marketers have seen the customer service process evolve from an area that received only marginal attention into a primary functional area. In response to customers' demands for responsive and reliable service, companies are investing heavily in innovative methods and processes to strengthen their service level[1]. These innovations include:

1. Increased Customer Self-Service

A major trend in customer service is the move by companies to encourage customers to be involved in helping solve their own service issues. This can be seen in retail industries where self-service ranges from customers placing their own grocery products in shopping bags all the way to having customers do their own checkout including scanning products and making payment. Also, as we will soon discuss, customers needing information are being encouraged by companies to first undertake the effort themselves often by visiting special company-provided information areas (see Website and Phone Accessible Knowledge Base below). Only after they have explored these options, customers are encouraged to contact customer service[2].

---

1 *www.knowthis.com*

2 *www.sbinfocanada.about.com*

2. Revenue Generators

Companies that maintain a customer service staff have found that these people not only can help solve customer problems but they may also be in a position to convince customers to purchase more. Many companies are now requiring sales training for their customer service personnel. At a basic level, customer service representatives may be trained to ask if customers are interested in hearing about other products or services. If a customer shows interest then the representative will transfer the customer to a sales associate. At a more advanced level, the representative will shift to a selling role and attempt to get the customer to commit to additional product purchases.

3. Out-Sourcing

One of the most controversial developments impacting customer service is the move by many companies around the world to establish customer service functions outside of either their home country or the country in which their customers reside. Called out-sourcing, companies pursue this strategy to both reduce cost and also increase service coverage. For instance, having multiple customer service outlets around the world allows customers to talk via phone with a service person no matter what time of the day. The ability to move service to another country is only viable in large part due to technological developments. But such moves have raised concerns on two fronts. First, many see this trend as leading to a reduction of customer service jobs within the home country. Second, customer service personnel located off-shore may lack sufficient training and often lack an understanding of the conditions within the customers' local market both of which can affect service levels. At the extreme, a poorly managed move to out-source customer service can lead to a decrease in customer satisfaction which in the long-run could affect sales.

The Hottest International Trends in Retail

Experience Stores: These are the stores where you don't need to buy anything, just try the products and fall in live with them. High-tech manufacturers in categories such as TVs and audio systems are even allowing users to experience products before their formal launch. An 'Apple' experience store is often buzzing with activity, with people trying out all kinds of iPods or dancing, surfing the net and playing video games. The store assistants are called 'trainers' and encourage you to try all the gadgets without asking you to buy anything.

Mass customization: Can you enable buyers to customize and personalize their products, while still offering them the mass production price? If you can, you are in a position to ride the new wave called 'mass customization', which sounds like an oxymoron, but is being touted as a great way to meet consumer needs.

A Customized offering can protect you from comparative shopping, by shifting the focus away from the price to the unique relationship with your customer. Mass customization often starts with a software called a 'configurator' where a buyer can select the features he wants, usually a website. The company then needs to have supply chain and manufacturing processes that can support this strategy. Dell is one of the companies that offered "build to order" facilities for PCs, and this technology does seem to have a strong potential for businesses trying to sell apparel over the web.

Sensory Branding: The idea that brands should engage consumers through a variety of touch points gets taken rather to its extreme through this new trend, where scents and sounds are used to make the brand connection.

Martin Lindstrom's book, "Brand sense" uses research to show that the smell of a new car, or the perfect sound of a closing car door, plays a major role in selecting what model is purchased. So a buyer can be made to smell an artificial odor that's been sprayed into the interior, creating a sense of quality. Singapore Airlines cabin smell in their aircraft is an important aspect of branding. Travel agents can create the holiday mood by making their offices smell like pinacoladas and sun-tan lotion.

Fashion with a conscience: This is about fashion that is made using environmentally friendly production, through business practices that promote free trade and empowering communities and do not buy from sweatshops or units that exploit children. Wearing something with these credentials should make you feel good! Ethical fashion is a movement gaining momentum.

Predictive technology: A robot, Hyperactive Bob, counts cars drawing up and people entering to predict what they will order at fast food outlets. This technology is reported to reduce the time required for service and food wastage. The system is at work at McDonalds and Burger King. So the next time you go for a snack, don't be surprised if they don't ask you what you want, they tell you what you want.

Source: *Winning Edge, May'07*

STRATEGIC ADVANTAGE THROUGH CUSTOMER SERVICE

A retailer's ability to create ***strategic advantage*** depends on the way a firm identifies and understands its customers. Retailers win customers by offering excellent and prompt customer service. Today's retailers due to borderless economies and easy availability of finance can have every item of merchandise that customers probably want, but being a retailer if you either underestimate the consumers' importance or don't treat them well, you can be out of competition very soon. Several studies at academic and industrial levels even show that it costs a lot to acquire a new customer but to retain them.

Today if McDonald's, Haldiram's, Sagar Ratna's, Nirulas, Pizza Hut have become choice of Indian families, it is because of their unique offerings, hygienic preparations, ambience and good customer service. Manufacturers try their level best to provide high quality goods to wholesalers and retailers. But providing high quality service to customers is difficult for retailers. Automatic manufacturing enable manufacturers to produce same quality goods, i.e. consistent quality from item to item. For example, you take Pepsi in New Delhi, Kolkata, Mumbai or in Paris, all Pepsi bottles look alike and typically taste alike. But the quality of retail service differs from area to area, store to store and from salesperson to salesperson even within a store. Retailers try regularly that each member of their staff should perform alike selling behavior but few salesperson become very popular among consumers because of their politeness and amicable personality traits. Customers can touch, look and feel the displayed merchandise but the assistance provided by a salesperson make them enable to shop quickly and more. Following strategies are used to keep customers coming back again and again:

(a) Customization Approach

The customization approach enables a retailer to change the offerings, layout, view, site structure and content to satisfy the needs and wants of different target groups. This approach is based on the philosophy that each customer is precious and plays a vital role in store's success. Knowing that today's customers are becoming more demanding, critics, value-driven spenders, practical thinkers and savvy shoppers, the importance of customization approach has become imperative. Some retailers like ***Domino's Pizza India*** has become the market leader because of its product innovation, customization and by maintaining stringent service standards. More specifically, it has made reputation because of quick home delivery that enables them to serve you its pizza within 30 minutes at your doorstep. So 'thinking locally and acting regionally' is the success mantra for Domino's leadership that is subtly blended with colorful images personified with its '***Hungry Kya***?' positioning. Inspired by western hospitality service programs, Indian leading hotel chains have introduced the concept of guest ambassadors that roam from place to place and from one corridor to another to help customers who need some sort of assistance. Apparel retailers have empowered their cash counter employees to certain limit (for say Rs 750/-) to accept the customers' return who come without bill/store's receipt by simply asking how much they have paid for the item in question and give a refund by taking customer's word for prices.

Customized approach and its successful implementation requires companies to focus on customer equity rather than brand equity, like Vodafone's '***happy to help***' promotional scheme has made Vodafone Essar the most respected telecom company, most creative and most effective advertiser and the best mobile services in the country.

High Quality Service

High Quality Service is the type of service that meets or exceeds customers' expectations. High performance retailers can develop relationships with their customers by offering two benefits:

1. **Financial benefits** that increase customer's satisfaction
2. **Social benefits** that increase the retailer's social experience with the customer

A shopper's real wish

- Let me find a parking place near the store.
- Do not let me pay too much.

- Have the same staff pretend that they care
- Do not make me have to return anything
- Get me in and out as fast as possible
- Don't make me have to wait in line to make my purchase
- Let this experience be some what enjoyable
- Don't make me have to deal with other obnoxious shoppers

Courtesy: *www.authorstream.com*

Customization approach experience lasts longer after the merchandise purchased. It has also emerged as a crucial differentiator in the otherwise fast commodization of goods and services. A homely atmosphere not only turns customers' thinking but also builds a strong linkage with the store. Real providers of **24 X 7** access and the cost cutters to service providers have essentials of warm welcome, seamless connectivity, customer friendly staff, trained employees and most importantly customer education and prompt service. In short, ***customization approach*** not merely creates pleasant experiences but prevent migration of your store's customers to others by building customers loyal. No doubt that providing customized service is a costly affair since it requires well trained store employees, user friendly website and more budgets to spend but is essential to survive in the so called fast changing industry.

(b) Standardization Approach

The standardization approach enables a retailer to maintain the same goods and services and elements (**4 Ps**, i.e. product, price, place and promotion) of marketing mix across all local, regional and global markets (depending upon business operations). It is implemented by strictly following a well defined set of policies, procedures and practices. Strict adherence leads to fewer variations in the quality of goods and results in alike goods at unlike locations. For example, through **standardization**, customers receive the same experience with regard to quality, taste and feel irrespective of location.

There is a possibility that customers are not getting what is provided to them, but the offerings are standardized and served in the same manner at low cost. Store appearance, design, layout, ambience, color, furniture and employees' uniform also play an important role in the standardization approach. Sometimes customers don't require the **assistance** of sales staff, as they are aware about the quality and other related aspects. They simply want to know the location of merchandise in the store so that they can select and pay for them without wasting unnecessary time. In such circumstances, retailers offer good service by displaying the store layout with broad visible signs that enable even the new customers to locate merchandise position quickly.

COST OF CUSTOMER SERVICE

Quality and customer service are the two key elements that play vital role in the success of retail business. Successful retailers usually pay a lot of attention to the efforts dedicated to bring customers close to the store. For example, for several decades Taj Group of Hotels has maintained a special place in the hearts of Indians due to their excellent hospitality and business philosophy.

Retailers/service providers know the power of profound, imaginative understanding of customers and the financial benefits of having loyal customers rather than attracting new ones. Successful retailers always focus on ***customer-driven*** business strategies to build relationships with customers and value of service to customer. In devicing customer service levels, a retailer should take decision about variety, level, alternative, cost, measurement and maintenance of service offered.

The cost of consumer service typically depends on the retailer's offerings in terms of value additions and service provided to them. Are your sales people providing the level of customer service you anticipate? Have you communicated your expectations to them? Also makes a difference how much cost it comes on offering customer service. One store that only does promise but seldom fulfill will be saving more as compared to store whose offerings are customized and can go to any level to retain customers. Good stores give customer a rationale to come back because they know their offerings are not unique it will be easily available at next doorstep. Therefore, how much service should a store provide to and how effectively you communicate to store staff to provide that service has bearing on the cost of services offered? To get the answer of these queries, one should consider following issues:

(*i*) At what level customer service should be offered to match a firm's image?

The customer service level of a chic departmental store is usually higher than a discount store as shoppers expect the store to have more sales persons to provide personal attention besides having a large variety of product and services. This is not applicable and even not expected from a discount store. Addition to this, complimentary services offered would be entirely different. Customers of a chic departmental store expect fancy packs, wrappers, attractive carry bags, huge parking lot, drinking water, elevators, air conditioners and sitting arrangements. While on the other hand, discount customers have no objecting in self service, self parking, hence store service offerings are same but it is the 'level' that makes a difference.

(*ii*) Are customer choices to be offered? If yes, then at what level?

Some stores optionally provide various level of service while some stores have standard services. For example one store welcomes all credit and debit cards while other allows only one specific card. Similarly one store provides the option to pay their bills for consumer electronics purchases with in - one month, - three months, - six months and - one year periods (on 'longer the period, higher the interest' basis). On the other hand, one retailer offers only one month credit payment option.

(*iii*) Should a retailer charge 'something' for customer service to offer?

Good retailers always wish to offer customer service absolutely free of cost but two issues cause him to charge for the services offered. These are (i) costs, and (ii) consumer behaviour/expectation. *For instance*, customer would like to buy gifts, souvenirs from a store that offers free fancy packaging (i.e. customer behaviour factor). Similarly in case of home delivery where substantial fee is charged, customers would like to present themselves at home at the time of delivery of products otherwise it will take several attempts for a retailer to deliver the goods (i.e. cost factor).

In this regard one thing should be noted that offering customer service free of cost seems to be a good marketing and selling preposition in the competitive retailing environment. But a retailer before offering such service should think from two angles:

(*a*) Cost to the store that can be perilous to the store in long run and

(*b*) The competitors' policy

If a retailer has made mind to charge for services offered then utmost care should be taken to decide the 'amount' to be levied. For this, retailer should remember his break even point to make a profit on the services.

(*iv*) How a retailer can measure the benefits of offering customer service against his overhead (cost)?

The primary objective of customer service is to attract the customers' attention towards the store and to build longlasting relationship with them. Therefore, augmented services should be offered only if a retailer believes that it will enhance the store turnover. As there is no evidence that augmented services should be offered at what time and how much should be charged if seems appropriate, it is suggested that retailer in this circumstance should use his past experience and must consider competitors' move. In case if it becomes difficult to bear the expense, some portion of it should be transferred to customers' shoulders.

(*v*) Can a retailer terminate customer service?

Undoubtedly, once the shoppers have become habitual to utilize customer service free of cost, any cutback will bring negative connotations. Retailers' this move can be fatal for the whole store's functioning. Therefore, while withdrawing or lessening service level, retailer should withdraw it for the time being and communicate it to the customers why the services have been withdrawn and how they will be benefited in terms of low prices. Sometimes, some retailers choose middle path by allowing the customers to avail the previously offered services on payment basis whosoever is willing to have.

CUSTOMER EVALUATION OF SERVICE QUALITY

Today, due to increased income of Indian middle class and rapidly increasing standard of living has made Indian consumers choosy and demandable. They evaluate retail service and compare their expectations with the perceived service. If the services perceived fall below their expectations, they become dissatisfied. This lead to boycott of that store and searching for new store where the perceived service meets and exceeds their inherent expectations.

Role of Expectations

It is said that '***customer expectations***' are based on customer's personal trails like age, experience, knowledge, education level, income level, standard of living and so on. Expectations even vary from person to person and store to store. For instance, one person's primary criterion to shop in a store is reasonable and convenient parking facility but for another person (an owner of luxury car), primary criterion is availability of brands in a store irrespective of parking and distance factor. How ***expectations*** vary from store to store. We consider an example: customers expect a specialty store like artificial jewelry store/ kids' toys store/ electronic store to have knowledgeable and impressive sales staff to provide information, assistance and variety as per their choice. On the other hand, when these same set of customers visit a supermarket/hyper store, they expect a store to provide convenient parking, extended store hours, wide merchandise assortment, fresh and latest food items those are displayed, located at convenient points and fully refrigerated. They don't like the store to have store staff who roam near them to ask '***May I help you***' or '***Madam, do you need any help***' etc. They even don't want to have any demonstration about '***how to use***', '***safe to use***' and so on.

Customer Evaluation Criteria

- Alteration facility
- Assistance to social Merchandise
- Cards Acceptance facilities
- Check out time
- Child care facilities
- Convenient store timing
- Credit Facilities
- Display of Merchandise
- Display of signs
- Display of store layout
- Drinking water
- Gift wrapping
- Guarantees
- Help line
- Home Delivery
- Mode of payments
- Parking Facility
- Payment from home
- Repair services.
- Replacement facility
- Shopping facility for aged and physically challenged
- Sitting arrangement (if asked for)
- Store Ambience
- Store Staff
- Try rooms
- Variety of Merchandise
- Warrantees
- Wash rooms
- Way of Packaging

Expectations vary from situation to situation too. For Instance, a customer in a Jewelry store where prices are affordable, expect the store to give welcome, offer drinks and personal attention while same person when enters into a exceptionally high priced shop, would like a store to ignore him. Further, a customer some times may be satisfied with a store offering limited services and dissatisfied with a store offering excellent consumer services. For example, while visiting discount stores and super markets, people usually have low service expectations but if some store besides self service concept, offers assistance in selection and serving things, that store becomes favorite choice for the consumers like McDonald's and Haldiram's food outlets in various parts of the country. Department stores like Vishal Mega Mart, Reliance Fresh, Six to Ten, Sabka Bazaar, Spencer, Birla's More, have more sales staff compared to other retail formats to assist customers and answer their queries. Despite the presence of large number of sales staff, signs and display boards, if a consumer like 'you' or 'me' don't find a sales person while locating a particular item, gets dissatisfied and annoyed very soon.

Customer expectations vary from country to country. In India, shop keepers (businessmen) treat customers as '**God**' (**Atithi Deyo Bhavah**) and are always eager to learn and adopt new ways to provide excellent customer service. On the other hand in Germany retailers never think of offering consumers services. They don't accept debit/ credit cards. No home delivery and become rude to customers who come near store's closing time. Thanks to globalization, with the arrival of foreign retailers, German retailers have started thinking about customer's service and in time to come, Germany may be known for its ***customer delight*** likewise, it is known for its manufacturing capability in the world.

Japanese are even several steps ahead when it comes to offering customer services. Like India, Japanese treat their customers as '***God***' and welcome when they come for return/exchange merchandise.

In most parts of the world including India, where retail store display messages like items once sold will not be returned or 'No Exchange, No return', don't want their customers with sold things having in hands for any purpose once the things are sold.

In United States of America retailers believe that '***customer is always right***'. Even if the customer does not use the products as per instructions, retailers take the responsibility that they are responsible for not telling how to use it properly. It is taught to sales staff whosoever first comes to know about the consumer's complaint, should take overall responsibility to attend and satisfy the customer despite knowing the faculties with different department of the store.

Customer Delight

Offering and delivering '**customer delight**' is the topic of today's retailing. Studies show that in the time to come only those retailers will live in the competition who understand what their customers need and provide them before they ask. Customer service is everything in today's business. The better you understand and care your customers, the greater the **customer delight**. According to **Infosys** (an Indian IT Company). Passion, Passion and Passion is the way for delight and customer knowledge is the road to **customer delight**. Therefore merely customers' satisfaction is not sufficient, but retailers should think beyond that & surprise them, making them to say '**wow**'.

According to a study conducted by Parasuram, Berry and Ziethmal (1991):

- A customer expects competency.
- A customer expects fundamental benefits, not fancies.
- A customer expects performance and not empty promises.

In case of hotels

- A customer wants a clean and secure room to be provided.
- A customer wants the promises to be kept.
- A customer wants to be treated as a guest.

In case of goods and services

- A customer wants assurance – the knowledge level and courtesy of employees and their ability to convey trust and confidence.
- A customer wants empathy – the caring individual attention provided to customers. Salesman putting himself in the customers' shoes.
- A customer wants reliability, which is the ability to perform the promised service, dependably and accurately.
- A customer wants responsiveness – it means the responsiveness to a query or a call, For example, telephonic enquiries. If no one attends the phone for long, it may irritate anyone.
- A customer wants tangibility or the appearance of physical facilities, equipment, personnel and other materials.

Perceived Service

During the last couple of years, relationship marketing has been used within services' marketing, since profitable and long-term marketing can be achieved through efficient customer service. Retailers have realized that to establish long-term customer relationships, the success key is to satisfy the customers. In other words, service' quality as perceived by the customers must meet customers expectations. Following are the five customer service factors that they use to evaluate service quality provided by a retailer:

1. **Faith**: It deals with the trust shown (presented) by a retailer by way of offering guarantees, warranties, exchange and return privileges.
2. **Reliability**: Locating a reliable retailer has always been a difficult task. Reliability stands for a retailer's ability to satisfy all written promises. It includes:
   - Accuracy of bills with regard to quality and quantity ordered.
   - Meeting delivery commitments.
   - Offering discounts as and when promised.
   - No false advertisement (Bait Advertisement)
3. **Recognition** (Empathy): It is the retailer's ability to recognize your details like name, address, choices, likings and disliking. It includes:

- Offering personalized service like remembering your choices, address and other related details.
- Acknowledgements of e-mails, letters, suggestions and complaints.
- Remembering by name

4. **Sense of Responsiveness**: It is the retailer's ability to be responsive towards customers' queries, complaints, doubts and communications. It includes:
   - Call back to customers as and when required
   - Offering quick service
   - Attending complaints
   - Returning e-mails, SMS and other modes of communications.
5. **Tangibility**: It is the retailer's ability to establish a longlasting retail image (retail positioning) in customers' minds. It includes:
   - Store layout and appearance
   - Uniform (dressing) of sales staff
   - Hygienic and suitable store environment
   - Welcome and assistance by store staff
   - Air conditioning in the store
   - Store location and geographic coverage
   - Shopping experiences
   - Type and extent of personal assistance (attention)
   - Merchandise quality, assortment, and fashionability
   - Community services

SITUATIONS LEADING TO SATISFACTORY AND UNSATISFACTORY CUSTOMER EXPERIENCE

To consider how situations lead to satisfactory and unsatisfactory customer experience, we consider a hypothetical example under three various situations named A, B and C as follows:

Problem: "*A customer goes to a store to complaint about electric iron, which is not working properly, purchased only last week. He is not carrying bill as he has misplaced it somewhere*".

In case of store 'A'

Store employee asks the customer to present a bill (receipt) to make certain that the electric iron was actually purchased from the store. Customer's inability to produce receipt leads to unwarranted argument with store employee. Approaching the matter to store manager, who after examining the electric iron to see if it is really not performing well and some paper work, instructs the employee to give refund or replace the iron.

In case of Store 'B'

Store employee asks the customer for a receipt and advice to left the iron for 15 days to have view of the concerned supplier from where the retailer has bought that iron.

In case of Store 'C'

Store employee listens emphatically and says Sir what do you want, refund or replacement? Now customer has to decide what to do.

These three cases approximately have the same outcome - the customer gets a cash refund or a new electric iron. But the customer may be dissatisfied in the first case, worried in the second case and delighted in the third case. In short, in most of the cases, it is the employee who makes customer satisfied, dissatisfied or delighted.

GAPS MODEL FOR IMPROVING THE QUALITY OF SERVICE

The Gaps model that deals with improvement of service quality was first time introduced by Valerie Zenthaml and the Center for Retailing Studies at the Texas A & M University. This model basically provides a roadmap to retailer about minimizing the gap between customers' expectations and the perceived service (the service offered by a retailer) or to close that gap, if possible. The model highlights the probable obstacles that usually hinder a retailer's ability to satisfy customers. As discussed earlier, when customers' expectations are greater than or cross their perceptions of the perceived service, they feel dissatisfied and develop negative thinking about the retailer's services. Therefore, it becomes essential for the retailers to remove this negative thinking (service gap – a gap between what customer expects and what is being provided to him), knowing that words travel faster than light. Following are the four potential gaps that must be understood and acknowledged to improve quality of service offered.

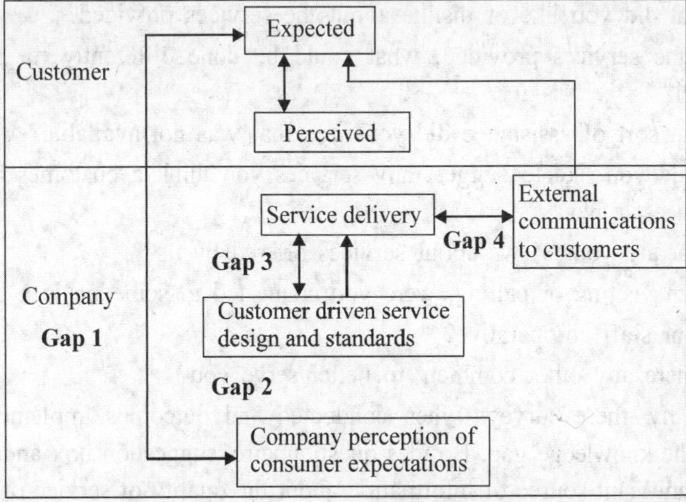

Figure 20.1: Gaps Model of Service Quality

Figure 20.1 illustrates the **GAPS** model for improving the quality of service offered. These four gaps collectively give birth to service gap. The retailer's role is to understand the reasons for these four gaps and to eliminate them to improve the quality of service offered. These are as follows:

Knowledge Gap

This gap arises because of the difference between customer's expectations and the retailer's perception towards customer's expectations. It simply means that the retailer is not aware (whatever the reason may be), what actually customers expect from him. For example, in a departmental store, a retailer tries his level best to provide personal attention to each customer by appointing a number of sales staff, who roam near the customers to help them as and when required. But customers take this service in different way and don't prefer to visit such store considering store staff wandering like police around them. Therefore, a retailer 'facility for personal attention' becomes obstacle for the store as well as the customers. Consequently, retailers must have complete knowledge of customers' expectation from a store. Acquaint of such knowledge becomes simple if a retailer has some provision of interacting with the customers on regular basis.

Some retailers even develop well-structured programs for evaluating the service expectations and perceptions of their customers. For this purpose, retailers use questionnaire method that is filled up by the customers visiting the store. The information received from the customers through structured questionnaire is analyzed and used for policy making or policy alterations. JC Penney (one of America's leading retailer) follow this practice as a part of it annual quality process. In India, it has been observed that few retailers conduct these types of surveys immediately after the transaction is over.

Questionnaire may include following information such as:

(i) What did you like or dislike about the services provided?

(ii) Of the services provided, what could be done differently to improve service level?

(iii) What sort of assistance did you need that was not available?

(iv) Would you like to suggest any services you think a customer needs after our services to you?

(v) What are your views about services offered by us?

(vi) When visiting or calling, were you connected to someone in a timely manner?

(vii) Is our staff co-operative?

(viii) Is there any other comment to better serve you?

Undoubtedly, these surveys when conducted and outcomes implemented, result in minimizing the knowledge gap. Besides questionnaire, suggestion box and complaint box also form significant source of information about the quality of service offered. Retailers often approach suggestions and complaints with a feeling of dread. They don't prefer dealing with unhappy, dissatisfied, angry customers. However, with good quality service, retailers are occasionally left with dissatisfied customers. Customers tend to tell their experiences to other people rather than complaining directly. So, a retailer should try to look at any complaint as a gift-wrapped golden opportunity to put service level right and turn complaints into compliments.

Stores where sales staff is friendly and interact with customers regularly about the service and merchandise offered know a lot about the consumers' service expectations and perceptions. Retailers can facilitate communication routes for floor staff upwards through the organization, they also need to act rapidly to implement improvements suggested as the outcome of surveys, research and communication.

Standard Gap

This gap arises because of the difference between the retailer's perception of customers' expectations and the customer service standards it sets. Besides understanding what customers expect, retailers should develop some service standards. It helps store staff understanding how the top management and store customers define and evaluate a quality task. Customer driven service quality standards are different from the traditional performance standards that most of the retailing firms establish to meet the customers' requirements. Here, standards are set to communicate to customers' expectations and preferences rather than to store concerns such as increasing turnover.

Standard gap exists in retail organizations for a variety of reasons. Managers responsible for setting standards often believe that customers' expectations are irrational or illogical. They may also think that the degree of variability inherent in service confronts standardization and therefore, setting standards only will not work. However, the quality of service offered by store staff is significantly influenced by the standards against which customers are evaluated and compensated.

To close the **standard gap**, retailers besides focusing on high service quality, they should define and describe the role of each employee involved in delivering service. Standards when set and communicated properly, signal to store staff what management expects from them, what are their priorities and which type of performance behavior really counts. When service standards are lacking or when the standards in place do not confront customers' expectations, It leads to dissatisfaction. On the other hand, when standards reflect and confront what customers' expect, the quality of service, customers receive is likely to be enhanced. As services are intangible in nature, therefore, it becomes difficult for the retailers to describe and communicate. Here are some tips for the retailers' top close standards gap:

1. Management should be committed to achieve high levels of service quality.
2. Proper training should be given to all concerned.
3. A proper reward system may enhance staff and management commitment to implement, meet or exceed the set standards.

4. Closing standards' gap can be made easier if new ways of dealing with various service issues are explored.
5. Providing high service quality become easy through the use of technology to standardize processes.

Application of Technology to standardize processes

Retailers can use technology (both hard and soft) to handle day-to-day tasks so that floor staff should concentrate on customers' queries and complaints. Hard technology is usually applied for performing check-in, display and check-out procedures like tag guns, tag pins, bar code equipments, coin counting machines, money counters are used to simplify the routine work while soft technology is the knowledge derived from practical experience and exposures.

Delivery Gap

This gap arises because of the difference between the retailer's service standards and the actual service offered to customers despite the existence of guidelines for treating customers correctly and performing services well. Developing standards and applying them is not enough, standards must be backed by appropriate resources (people, products and technology) and must be evaluated to award and compensate who deserves, on the basis of performance along those standards.

An Insight into GAPS Model

Four Gaps

1. Knowledge Gap	:	It means not knowing what customers' expect.
2. Standards Gap	:	It means not selecting the right service standards.
3. Delivery Gap	:	It means not delivering to service standards.
4. Communication Gap	:	It means not matching performance to promises.

Therefore, even when standards are properly defined and well implemented, if firm fails to provide resources for them, performance will not be up to the mark and definitely will increase delivery gap.

The delivery gap between standards set and those delivered arises because of several reasons like:

- Impractical standards
- Lack of clarity in standards defined
- Improper communication
- Lack of motivation among floor staff
- Absence of regular monitoring of performance analysis practices
- Failure to match market demand and supply
- Problems/conflicts with service intermediaries

In order to close or reduce the service gap and deliver services that exceeds the set standards, retailers can focus on the following areas:

- Providing necessary knowledge and skills to employees concerned
- Explaining standards and staff roles so that they possess and commit to quality
- Regular monitoring and motivation of staff
- Develop spirit of team work to deliver excellent quality
- Appropriate selection and training to concerned staff
- Regular involvement of store staff in setting and modification (if required later on) to get best results.

Communication Gap

This arises because of gap between the actual set of services offered to the customers and the service communicated by the retailer to the customers through their promotional program. In short, ***communication gap*** arises when retailer's promises don't match the performance resulting in adverse effect on the customer gap.

Retailers throughout the globe usually raise the expectations of customers through attractive and bait advertisements. Getting convinced, when customers visit the store and find service quality short of standards, the actual experience disappoint them. Broken promises occur because of several reasons:

(i) Unrealistic promising in advertising or through other communication channels,
(ii) Lack of co-ordination between sales promotion and store operations staff,
(iii) Differences exist between policies and procedures of various store outlets resulting in creating confusion among them, and
(iv) Sometimes the staff whose duty is to promote the service does not understand the realism of service delivery and is likely to make overstated promises that cannot be achieved.

In order to remove or close the ***communication gap***, retailers first try to understand the reasons that create communication gap, once knowing the reasons, retailers should overcome them by developing a clear line of communication between the parties concerned (like intermediaries, promotion and operations staff etc). Any miscommunication between two parties will lead to discrepancy between actual and promised service. Hence the management of a retail store should avoid over-promising in personal selling, advertising or any other way of communication.

SERVICE RECOVERY

The objective of service recovery is to identify customers' objections and complaints and then to address those issues to satisfy the customers to endorse customer retention. Retailers through suggestion boxes, complaint boxes and surveys, collect information to judge the quality of service and merchandise offered. Consequently, they modify their service programs and variety of merchandise wherever need arises to satisfy them. This is a source of building relationships with customers and hence the competitive advantage.

Getting information and rectifing service delivery will not only work but retailers need to apologize for the trouble caused. Most of the retailers follow standard set of policies for handling service problems. If a service delivery is proved to be incorrect / inefficient, pre-decided action is taken. For instance, merchandise sold is found to be defective or expired by date, retailers either replace those things or give cash refund or a credit towards future purchase.

Retailers must know that service recovery is more than handling complaints as it will rebuild the customer's faith (positive feelings) towards the store after a bad experience followed by resolving the root cause of the problem. Complaint handling means only dealings with negative but ***service recovery*** turns negative into positive for customer retention. In some situations, the exact reason for inefficient service delivery is hard to identify. For instance:

- Discrepancy in merchandise title is because of salesperson wrong understanding or customer's wrong explanation
- In case of customer's unnecessary expectations
- The store had to close due to strike (political or otherwise), bad weather or by government order, which cannot be rectified/corrected later on.
- Was it store employee who misbehaved actually

DEVELOPING THE RIGHT CUSTOMER SERVICE LEVEL

No business can offer all the things to all the customers. Retailers must target specific customers and try to satisfy their needs and wants. As a retailer/sales person, one must identify those customers/customers' groups and understand as specifically as possible what they want. The consumer study process for your retail business should not be complex or time consuming. In short, it requires retailers/sales people to know everything what can impact the customers buying decisions that you intend to follow. Once retailer has that information ready, he will be in a better position to capture those customers.

1. CUSTOMER SERVICE COSTS

In the world of retailing, perhaps the most important aspect of customer service leveling is the cost of offering services to the customers. Sometimes cost of providing customer service is exceptionally so high that it becomes difficult for a retailer to stay in the competition because products can not be sold higher than its maximum retail price (MRP). Therefore, retailer's financial books should be carefully examined and a breakeven analysis should be performed regarding the cost of the services and the return on investment. In other words retailers should understand and find out:

- What exactly the cost of providing services is? and
- Is it covered under the selling price of the product in question?

Further, the retailer should take efforts to find out the opportunity lost in terms if loosing customers because of poor customer service levels while developing the break even point[3] (BEP). In case due to financial overburden, company decides to reduce or limit some customer service program, what will be the total financial loss over the life of one customer or group of customers?

2. COMPETITIVE ANALYSIS

The second area to develop the customer service level is to assess the retailer's competition. Competitive analysis basically consists of a set of decisions which leads to the development of an effective strategy. It assumes situation analysis by way of evaluating internal capabilities. The critical examination of strengths, weaknesses, opportunities and threats (SWOT) provides the necessary informational backdrop to the retail planner.

Today, customers not only compare the prices of goods and services offered but compare the service levels of various retailers too. When one competitor offers high service but other does not, customers start wondering why other retailer does not offer the same service level. There must be some substitution (tradeoff) for service levels. Some retailers in order to stay ahead and differentiate themselves from others, offer goods and services at exceptionally low prices. Some retailers offer other low-priced services to stay in competition. This supplementary service offering may be in terms of lower credit rates, free vouchers, free gifts, additional quantity, extended store hours or in any other way.

3. STORE CHARACTERISTICS

This is the third area to develop the right customer service level. Store characteristics itself provide paid impersonal communications to its customers. **Store characteristics** is the combination of the store's physical characteristics such as its location, size, layout, displays, colors, sounds, smells, lighting, temperature and store's offered service level. It communicates information about the store's pricing, its service level and fashionability of its merchandise. For example, customers would like to know is the retailer an off price retailer? or a high end retailer? Because the thumb rule says the higher the retailer's personal attention level, better will be the service offered?

The type of merchandise offered within the store area is an important consideration for customers and competitors. Several types of products themselves demand higher service levels. Consumer electronics and jewelry store have to offer additional customer services because here the salesperson skills can turn customers' negative attitude into positive purchase decision. For service retailers, it becomes essential to pay personal and quick attention to customers' needs and wants. They also need to craft some level of tangibility for the service they offer. It will make customers' belief stronger that they will get proper value of their money spent.

4. INCOME LEVEL OF TARGETED MARKET

The income generated from a particular target market will have deep impact on the level of service offered. People in different income brackets demand different types of

---

3 *Break even point is a point at which there is no loss and no profit i.e. no loss no profit point.*

goods and services. For example, many retailing firms have developed huge and unique stores to serve the high status customers belonging to a particular high status colony. Also, the retailing thumb rule implies, the higher the income of the target segment, the higher the customer service level should be.

Classifying income levels is often a difficult task. The definition of middle class even vary from state to state if we decide the customer classes on the basis of income level, as few states are economically (per capita income wise) ahead from other states. Further, due to geographical differences and connectivity with major metros, cost of living and income level vary from state to state. Despite these difficulties, retailers use income classification to help them understand consumers' spending habits. Customers belonging to lower income group are more likely to eat and dine in their home than other high income groups. These consumers are less likely to buy luxury goods and tend to be more practical to their buying decisions. In short, in their pursuit for value, low income group typically shop at department stores or local *kirana* store instead of super specialty stores or mega marts.

5. CUSTOMERS' WANTS AND NEEDS

In the retail world, it has become customary for the retailers to sell and provide the solutions rather than products and services. Providing solutions mean employing sales people who know how to help customers find shoes that fits, offering good quality product assortments and accepting payments whatever way the customers selects to pay the bills. Research reports have shown that majority of retailers hardly try to improve their customer service levels. Even they have no idea about the issues they should focus on. The way the retail industry is growing with the entry of domestic and international players, understanding customers' needs and wants is the success key for any businessman. But irony of the system is that customer predictability is almost negligible.

Benefits of understanding customers' needs and wants

- Understanding customers' wants and needs help retailers defining new market opportunities, make improvement and income growth in each section of the retailing firm.
- One must understand that each customer is unique and has its own way of thinking. Customers come from various backgrounds and have individual pressures and criteria. Therefore, an astute retailer infers and accepts the buying logic of the customers and serves them the way they want.
- It has found that some of the retail customers conceal their actual motivations. In a lot of cases the causes are unclear to the customers themselves. Most buying decisions are multi-causal and often conflicts abound. For example, a buyer of an air conditioner may desire to have a look of split air conditioner but cooling of window AC. Such customers' desires are unable to understand until the customers are not interviewed.

- Sometimes the reasons why customers prefer a particular product are many. Some buy a product because of the company's goodwill, some buy because of its attractiveness or color or shape or price. Sometimes, customers buy the same product because of its market report. Therefore, minor information governs. A word of caution here—that a retailer should pay attention to the details thoroughly, they may be crucial for retailers as well as customers too. Considering, Rudyard Kipling rightly said that the exact system to understand customers' needs and wants is what called his six honest serving men. "Their names are what, why, where, when, how and who".

These are explained as follows:

What

It basically involves the following:-

- What customers are buying?
- What they want?
- What they expect from a product? and
- What they expect from a store to make them happy?

For instance, customers buy a car for several reasons:

- For few having a car is a standard of living.
- For some people, car is a means of convenience.
- Some buy car because they actually need it and
- Others buy because of time saving traveling mode.

A retailer describes what customers are buying as goods and services – shaving creams, deodorants, cameras, cell phones or face creams. Consumers don't choose face cream for same purpose always. For some, it is the way to look smart and beautiful. For some, it is the fashion of the day, some want to fair look, others want an image of growing personality.

Astute retailers or sales people, sell benefits by educating customers for which customers are willing to pay. Successful retailers and wholesalers select offerings of such demanded benefits that they can resell easily. In other words, successful business people understand the reasons **what** their customers expect from buying the things.

Why

What makes the customers to buy a particular product? What makes customers to visit a particular store again and again? What stops people to not visit other stores despite the product they wanted is not in their favourite store? The reason is logical from customers' point of view.

Knowing customers derives from this elementary premise. Don't argue with customer. For a product, a customer is ready to travel and pay double the cost of it. But on the same side, if the same product is offered to other customer even free of cost, he may not be ready to buy it free of cost. To know ***why*** customers buy is always not an easy task but can be made easier if efforts are made to continuously monitor their choices and actions. If required, customers may be contacted at the places of sale.

When

It is said that customer can come to the store any time. A retailer should be ready when the buyer is, lest an opportunity be forever lost. Customers visit store and buy when they want an offering and have the time and money to purchase it. Purchasing patterns can often be different from an analysis of buyers and their purchases. For instance, wants and needs for many FMCG are tied to customers' rites of passage.

The following buying occasions in an adult's life cycle are typical:

- Buying a new home
- Change in employment or career
- Children start going to school/college/university
- Death of a family member
- Engagement, marriage and anniversary
- Festivals/social activities
- Higher study
- Medical treatment, injury, illness
- Pregnancy, nurturing of children
- Retirement from job
- Shifting to new locality
- Summer/winter vacations

Astute retailers keep track of such buying events and lead over competitors. Some time retailers before the start of few seasons/festivals start accumulating the things so as to serve masses without getting into out-of-stock position. Similarly, manufacturers increase their production and wholesalers too start refilling their warehouses before seasonal demands, like in north India, before diwali, people usually demand for paints, whitewash, new clothes and new utensils.

In metro cities like Hyderabad, Delhi and Mumbai, majority of people prefer to shop on weekends or in the evening. Trend from a single earning hand per family has changed to multi hands. Successful retailers therefore, adjust their trading hours, sales staff, and availability of merchandise according to the demand, days and the locality they are into.

How

Having knowledge of how customers pay their bills, helps in several ways: (1) Retailers can design their offerings to satisfy the exact wants of their buyers (2) Retailers can influence decision makers at crucial steps of the buying process, and (3) Retailers can lay the groundwork for repeat business.

Purchasing decisions and methods are best viewed as processes. Household buying generally begins when a consumer has a desire or a problem that an acquisition might satisfy or solve. Industrial buying generally starts when a user or a routine sets off an individual (requisition) for approval of a procurement.

People are diverse in terms of their buying attitude, selling behavior and perception. Likewise, buying processes[4] depend on the nature of the product to the buyer and on other circumstances. Experience has shown that all buying processes are not uniform. Several steps are common to most of them. The retailer/sales person needs to know only those vital steps where they can affect the ending of the buying decision.

Customers demand some products when they face some emergency or a particular season comes. For example, people think of carrying umbrella with them when it rains. One will arrange for funeral immediately after the death of some near or dear. An unexpected winter calls for immediate demands for woolen clothes, heaters and boilers. Usually easy availability and convenient location decides when these products and services are purchased. And even if customers do have enough time to select goods and services, retailers/sales people who stand ready to offer demanded brands are appropriate to gain preferences and profit when buyers decide where to shop.

Today, customers besides quality and quantity, want options although proximity and convenient availability is the main buying criterion for many routine household products. Successful retailers stock a wide assortment of the same product to the diverse preferences of their customers. Some customers want goods and services as used by their film/sports stars in advertisements/films. Some customers demand manufacturers' advertised brands while resellers' brands are demanded by others. In some product categories, generic brands are becoming popular in recent years. Likewise, many consumers look for special and unique collection/variety. Consequently, the decision of which goods and services to offer is critical to retail success. Having variety of shopping goods in the store becomes essential because today customers compare goods before purchase. In case of specialty goods, those are selected by brand name, in the absence of variety, a prospect may leave without buying and whoever offers them on acceptable terms gains the sale. Astute retailers/sales people look into the behavioral milestones of buyers. For their loyal/bulk customers, they draft separate buying process, indicating names of influencers at each step, elapsed time between steps and any other relevant information.

Where

From a multitude of studies emerge different criteria for deciding where to shop. Most researchers on the subject agrees that store location is a major consideration. Stores usually draw most of their patronage from their surrounding neighbourhood.

---

4 *A business process is nothing but a collection of unified tasks that accomplish a particular goal. For instance, enabling a customer to evaluate and decide what to purchase. It ends with the ownership transfer for exchange of money.*

Savvy store managers make a special effort to understand the shopping related motivations and preferences of local residents. New managers of fast food units, for example, canvass nearby dwellings and introduce themselves to the households. Some supermarkets maintain consumer advisory boards to elicit suggestions and reactions. Other means of communication with customers include informal conversations at the store and suggestion boxes with interviews and awards.

Incidentally, complaints are an excellent guide for making store policies more amenable to customers. Personnel should be instructed to thank patrons for their comments. Prompt consideration, followed by a personal letter from the store manager is highly desirable.

Location is extremely important to "captive" buyers. Exclusively franchised utilities, shops in isolated hotels and cafeterias or automatic vending machines in factories are examples. At the opposite extreme, shoppers escape spatial restrictions by buying from mail-order firms or telephone solicitors.

Other patronage influences vary. They depend on the type of product, type of store and the characteristics of the consumer. The offered assortment's perceived quality, depth, and breadth certainly are very important along with the price. This does not imply that all goods have to be top quality or all prices the lowest. Perceptions are decisive.

If quality seems high, some customers infer that prices are high too regardless of the facts. The important point is to understand customers and to provide what causes them to buy. For example, assurance of repair service weighs heavily with the worrier type of customer. A convenience-minded buyer is concerned with parking space or delivery service.

Of course, shoppers must be told that wanted goods and services are available. Advertising helps disseminate this information. So does a store's reputation for consistent policies of satisfying its customers.

Occasional promotions inject some excitement into the tedium of shopping. Some clients like to socialize, which can absorb much of an employee's time and may even annoy other buyers. Nevertheless, personnel should be friendly and helpful. Also influential, for some customers, is the apparent socio-economic level of other shoppers.

Personal affinity for other customers or for salespeople is a decisive factor in the success of party-selling, e.g., household goods and in-home selling (cosmetics). The choice of where to buy items requiring major outlays (securities and insurance) often revolves around from whom to buy.

In selecting a retail store, many customers consider physical features. Layouts can invite or repel patronage. Motorists who are in a hurry, for instance, are apt to use a gasoline station at which business can be transacted quickly. Altogether, buyers perceive a mix of tangible and intangible factors that comprise a store's atmosphere. Accordingly, they either do or don't feel comfortable about shopping there.

To the casual observer, all supermarkets seem more or less alike, But infact, store managers can regulate many of the above mentioned variables and thereby affect where shoppers buy. According to the recent studies, in several American cities, household buyers perceive supermarkets in their neighborhood as sufficiently different to determine their patronage preference. The four main types of supermarkets offer: (1) High quality at commensurate prices, (2) Lowest price level in the area, (3) Swift completion, (4) Friendly atmosphere. Each can profit by appealing to a different segment of buyers.

Who

Who are the customers? is a question for which, each retailer strives to collect information to the extent possible. Small retailers pride themselves on knowing their customers personally. In the world of whole selling, understanding of each major customer and buying influence is indispensable for the success of business, however, personal familiarity is not viable. Consequently, large retailers/merchandisers in this circumstance, group their various customers on the basis of similar reactions to particular offerings and then device separate marketing program for each segment under question.

Strategies vary from company to company and in some cases even within the company in case of multi departments because customers are volatile and impulsive. The specializing firm finds it difficult and is exposed to sudden changes in their target segment's patronage. Therefore, some companies cater various segments concurrently. Although this strategy seems to be expensive and time consuming but employing different tactics for different segments has been found to be profitable in long term. Otherwise firms are free to scatter their offers to just anybody with the hope that segments will select themselves.

The oldest way for segmentation is geographic. Retail customers usually shop from their neighbouring stores. Wholesalers mostly tend to concentrate regionally. Thorough cultivation of local would-be customers may be competitive and rewarding. Familiarity of local customers and having knowledge of their liking and disliking (though difficult) help longlasting relations with these customers. Segmenting the customers' market is an art. It not only requires strong determination on the part of marketers but all "honest serving men" - what, why, where, when, how and who - can be the success key to effective segmentation. Therefore, following points are worth considering:

1. Whatever the base for segmentation is chosen, each identified segment should have enough buying capacity to make a special effort commercially meaningful.
2. Segmentation undoubtedly is indispensable but understanding customers' needs and wants require in-depth analysis of their buying roles. In a family buying decisions are taken by male members or females, one man is responsible to finalize consumer purchases or two or more have some role to play in it. Is decider a user or not? Are outsiders are influential, may be considered critically.
3. Understanding customers' needs and wants enables a retailer to increase overall sales. If applied wisely, this same know-how can equally serve to reduce costs. Higher sales at lower costs certainly increase store's turnover.

4. Goods and services should be ready when ever consumers demand. Thus, a successful retailer avoids unnecessary inventory blockage or situation of order-canceling in case of exceptionally late delays. Further, logistics cost may be cut down by sending goods where it is more required. Understanding ***who*** comprises appropriate segments and the separate buying roles can lessen the waste of soliciting unqualified or uninterested people to a major extent.
5. The appropriate source for retailers to understand about their potential customers is their individual interaction with them at regular intervals. Be it at place of work, in or outside the store, one should try to collect customers view about the store's offerings, store service and complaints or suggestions (if any).

6. SUPPLIER CUSTOMER SERVICE LEVEL

Offering right customer service level is a good gauge of how well retailers are meeting their customers' immediate needs and wants. In actual, this is your reliability as a good retailer. It measures how often retailers have committed to goods and services when customers demand for them. Retailers should always remember that if they don't have what their customers want, they will go elsewhere and no guarantee that in future they again will return to you or not. In order to develop the ***right customer service level***s for its customers, retailer needs to assess that *what kind of customer service it wants from its supply channel?* In evaluating suppliers, retailers usually compare their supplier against some predetermined factors. Today throughout the globe, many retailers use a supplier rating system that allows them to rate each supplier choice. This method is aptly used by businessmen dealing with several suppliers. Similar type of survey for the first time was successfully acknowledged by Victor H. Pooler and David J. Pooler in their study of 'Retailer's Top Criteria for Choosing a Supplier' as shown below.

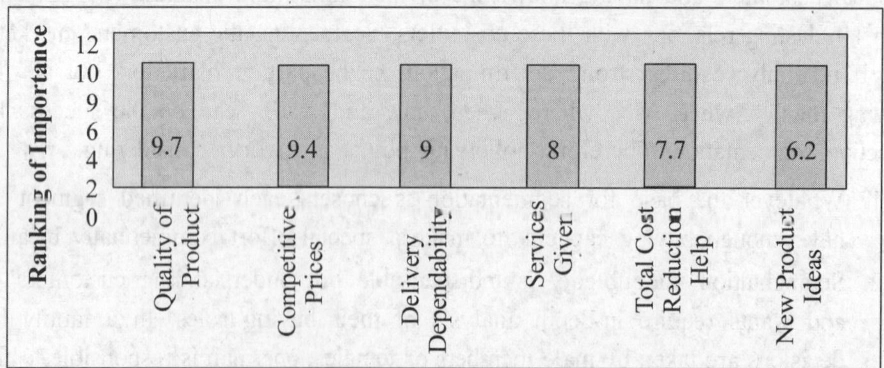

Source: *Victor H. Pooler and David J. Pooler (1997), Retailer's Top Criteria for Choosing a Supplier, New York: Charpman & Hall.*

In a supply chain relationship, the retailer is totally dependent on the supplier to deliver goods and services in right quality, right quantity, right time and at right place. Thus, the success of customer service level not only depends upon the retailer efforts to satisfy consumers' needs and wants but also upon the supplier's performance because if supplier is not providing the goods at right time, how retailer will take care of its customers. Thus, the supply chain becomes an important part of retailer's overall customer service process and to build the retailer-supplier relationship, retailers must be committed to provide good customer service all the time.

HANDLING OBJECTIONS

Sometimes, when a salesperson demonstrates a product with regard to its features, applications, benefits etc., customers may raise various objections regarding the product's attributes, price, place and behaviour, appearance and attitude of the salesperson. These objections, if not addressed promptly, hinder the selling process. The ideal way to respond to these issues is to handle these objections. This task is referred to as 'objection handling'. Following are the instances where Indian consumers usually create objections (whatever the reason may be).

Sometimes, a customer is in a daisy situation whether to buy or not buy the product? In such situation, he unnecessarily argues with the salesperson by lame objections such as '*I like the item but it is too small or big*', or '*it is too heavy*', *I'm looking for some compact size thing*' or '*it seems local*' etc., In this circumstance, the salesperson should handle the customers' objections wisely and provide quick and creative reason to convince him buy the product by eliminating his vague objections. Salesperson here should inform the customer about the demand and performance of product in the market.

Consumers usually raise objections about the 'price' of the product in question. They in the first instance, find it high and unaffordable. In such circumstance, the retail sales person should educate the customer that first the price is competitive, not too high as you think. If it is little bit high that is because of its quality and promise to perform better. In some cases, customer admits that he likes the product but not in position to pay at the moment. Here salesperson should inform him about the credit payment facilities offered by the store.

In certain cases, may be through advertisement or word of mouth, the customer develops wrong perception about the store but when he actually comes to store finds his perception different from what he actually has developed, he starts dancing between the horns of dilemma. In such circumstance, the salesperson should assure the customer about the store's standing, management commitment and merchandise offered.

In India, salespersons face one odd situation where the customers show interest in the product and are convinced with the merchandise offered but they don't want to share why they are not buying the product at the moment. This creates a difficult situation for salesperson to convince the customer about purchase. Here, a salesperson should handle the customer's objections by creating interest in the customer choices by informing him about prevalent special offers (if any), or caution him about the price hike in the time to come and make him convince to buy merchandise.

One unusual situation in direct selling/face-to-face selling comes that customer has made his mind to buy the product but because of salesperson, he postpones the buying decision. Customers may not like the accent, appearance, behaviour or body language of the salesperson resulting in postponement of merchandise buying. In such circumstance, salesperson should emphasize more on merchandise features, benefits and applications to the consumer.

Objection Handling Techniques

- **LAARC**: it deals with Listen, Acknowledge, Assess, Respond and Confirm.
- **Pre-empting**: it means handling objections before they happen.
- **LAIR**: it means Listen, Acknowledge, Identify Objection, Reverse it.
- **3F**: it deals with Feel, Felt and Found philosophy and a classic way of moving them.
- **Pushback**: it means objecting to customers' objections.
- **Humour**: it means responding with humour rather than showing frustration.
- **Writing:** it means write-down objections then cross them off once handled.

EVALUATING A SALESPERSON

No two employees are alike, they think differently, behave differently and perform differently. Some salespersons are hardworking while remaining shirk from work. One despite newly appointed knows the 'ins and outs' of merchandise and services offered but on the other hand, other (old employee) still is ignorant and ask from other salespersons frequently. Therefore, evaluation of salesperson becomes essential to reward who works and deserves. This evaluation in the retail industry is the base of store staff's promotions, demotions, transfers and terminations of salespersons. The salespersons are evaluated under following parameters.

Sales

- Contribution towards sales' goals
- Assistance in developing and promoting a marketing plan
- Assistance towards building a competitive advantage
- Achievement of sales targets

Customer Service

- Customer response towards employee
- Has he provided some exceptional service so that customers recognize him and ask for him?

Merchandise

- Its knowledge with regard to price, quality, features and demonstration
- How efficiently one manages merchandise levels

Job Knowledge

How much employee understands his

- Job profile

- Job responsibilities
- Expectations from him

Quality of Work

- Precision of work performed
- Repetition of tasks
- Neatness of work done
- Consistency of work
- Degree of errors, omissions and accidents

Punctuality, Sincerity and Regularity

- How much punctual, sincere and regular a sales person is?
- Degree to perform under odd circumstances

Problem/Complaint/Objections handling Skills

- How he handles complaints, issues and objections
- His past records with regard to problem solving attitude
- Management and seniors opinion about his conduct of work

Initiation

- The degree to take initiative about accomplishment of tasks without direction and any recognition
- Accomplishing tasks in the best possible manner

Store Maintenance

- It involves maintaining
  - Properties
  - Furniture and fixtures
  - Planogram

Other Tasks

- Accomplishing tasks assigned at short duration
- Performing additional duties whenever assigned or asked for
- Assist in sales promotion programs

CONVERSION RATE

Conversion rate refers to the percentage of shoppers who actually purchase the things from the store. Everyday several shoppers visit stores. Some are window shoppers, some come simply to enjoy and time pass while some come to see the latest trends and grabbing ideas. Some customers come to store, ask about merchandise, payment options, terms and conditions but don't make purchase. Hence, it is expected from salespersons to increase the store's conversion rate. Retailers who train their employees to increase their ***conversion rate*** get competitive advantage over competitors.

Increasing ***conversion rate*** is not in the hands of salespersons only but depends on retailers' promotional programs and quality of service and merchandise offered. It varies from store to store and one outlet to another outlet of the same organization. Conversion rate also vary from one retail format to another retail format. For instance, luxury or jewelry stores have lower conversion rate as compared to grocery stores. Similarly, books stores have less conversion rate as compared to shoe or readymade garments store. Some times, a mall may have more customer traffic throughout the year but in actual its sale is less than a '**destination store**' situated outside the city.

A store suffering with low or continuous falling ***conversion rate*** should take it seriously otherwise very soon it may be out of competition. The conversion rate in actual is a parameter to measure the store's performance. A falling/low conversion rate may be due to several reasons such as:

- Poor product displays
- Wrong /incomplete description to customers
- Absence/shortage of sales staff at the point of sale
- Wrong arguments with shoppers
- Wrong/unfriendly behaviour of store employees
- Not providing proper information about payment options
- Lack of motivation among sales staff

DESTINATION STORE

The destination store, as the name implies, is the retail store where customers make a special visit for the purpose of shopping. The main philosophy behind the destination store lies because of its uniqueness in terms of merchandise assortment, way of presentation, ambience, pricing and customer service. For a retail store, it is not easy to become 'a destination store' in the eyes of the customers.

How to become a Destination Store?

The key to become a destination store lies in the following considerations:

1. **Retail location**: Once a new-comer retailer asks a successful retailer "what is the secret of your success?" He answered that the most important consideration is the 'location'. No doubt, some locations are better than others in some aspects. It includes convenience, cleanliness, proximity to residential area, quality, selection, customer service and handling the customers. For instance, to have a franchisee of 'Agarwal Sweet Corner' in NCR, Delhi, requires you to have a corner shop located either at the end of the road or street.

2. **Service that attracts**: Somebody said, today is the world of retailing, it is not the product but the customer service that gives you the profit. A product is available in different types of stores or shops but if the customer prefers to go to a particular store then the answer is simple – it's the welcome and way of handling that attracts the

customer to visit a particular store. If all retailing factors are equal and same like quality, price, presentation and selection of goods displayed between your retail store and other nearby stores, then you will find it is 'customer service' that makes your store a dream (destination) store. Here, is a list that can be beneficial to make your store customer savvy:

- Proximity to your store;
- Does your store meet what is publicized and presented within the store?
- Does your store invites strangers or casual shoppers from outside?
- Are your windows neatly cleaned and displays kept up regularly?
- Do you have enough parking place?
- Have you heard customers talking about your customer service?
- Convenience.

Each retailer is not fortunate enough to have a good location. Sometimes, you have no shortage of funds and human resources but suitable location is not available in the area where you have planned to open a retail store. Here, you have nothing to do about a bad location except make it convenient to the customers. Convenience here implies 'can a shopper get in and out of the store quickly and easily?' For a retailer, it means, blend of full and self-service system, variety of merchandise assortments, regular fill up of racks and provision of customer complaint handling.

SALES PER HOUR (SPH)

Sale per hour is the commonly used indicator to evaluate the performance of a sales person in a store. It is calculated as under:

$$\text{SPH} = \frac{\text{Total store sales at a given period of time}}{\text{Total trading hours}}$$

SPH may be used to evaluate the performance of an entire work force or in case of individual sales person. SPH vary from store to store and format to format. A sales person SPH in a super market is different from SPH of a departmental store.

USE OF TIME STANDARDS

Evaluating sales persons' performance through time standards is an old and widely used method in the retail industry. It is based on the concept that how much time a sales person spend in a store in a given period of time and is compared with each other to know the dedication of salesperson towards the store under following ways:

(i) Time spent at place of selling
(ii) Time spent away from place of selling
(iii) Absent hours
(iv) Idle hours

The selling time is the time devoted by a sales person in selling activities such as talking to customers, demonstrating, objection handling, preparing sales order/invoices or assisting the customer by roaming around the product/store to make him buy the products.

The time spent away vary from place of selling is the time devoted to non-selling activities such as arranging the merchandise on shelf, refilling the stock, roaming in the warehouse or around the display area to check the merchandise status.

Idle time is the time spent by a salesperson on the sales floor but is not involved in productive work.

Absent time refers to time duration for which a salesperson is not present on the sales floor. It includes time used for:

- Lunch
- Recreation
- Outside visit due to personal reasons etc.

Retailers have proper record of each salesperson's time standards (time spent on each activity). The sum total reveals the fact that how efficiently and productively a sales person spends his time in and outside the selling floor.

NEW TRENDS IN SERVICE STRATEGIES

1. Up selling

Up selling is a business philosophy applied to increase the retail sales turnover. It involves marketing strategies used to convince customers to purchase additional or more profitable products by providing them various lucrative offers or simply educating them to buy additional accessories to perform the product better. ***Up selling*** basically is a marketing stunt where a salesperson calls a customer attention to a costly item and convinces him to buy.

Examples

(i) Convincing a customer to buy 'olive oil', which is usually two or three times costlier that the normal cooking oil.

(ii) Telemarketing people wearing leather jackets with a fur lining for only Rs 500 more and describing its features like made in a pleasant, warm manner and of single leather piece.

(iii) One kg potato, onion or tomato for only Rs 1 after a purchase of Rs 500 or more.

One thing should be noted in this regard that offering incentives is essential for the success of *up selling*. As in *up selling* you compel a person to spend some extra money, will work when you come up with some inherent benefits with the product you are canvassing to buy for. For example, a customer wants to buy one litre 'A' brand mustard oil while buying you suggest to buy two and 'get one absolutely free' offer. After thinking for a while, he goes with the offer. Similarly a customer, who wants small packing of a product, is convinced to buy extra large pack not only for a lower price but with additional quantity (say 20% extra) as a high pressure sales tactic.

Understanding the customer financial background and the psychology behind spending extra money is vital for effective up selling. Tell him the clear picture with respect to extra benefit in terms of additional quantity and amount saved.

2. Cross Selling

Cross selling is a selling technique where a salesperson calls a customer's attention towards an additional product with the main item for which actually the customer has come for. Oxford English Dictionary defines Cross Selling as "*the action or practice of selling among or between established clients, markets, traders etc" or "that of selling an additional product or service to an existing customer*". The primary objective of ***cross selling*** is to increase the store's sales turnover. Other objectives are:

(i) To promote the less selling items.
(ii) To promote a new brand / item.
(iii) To maintain relationship advantage over other stores and to attract new customers.
(iv) To build competitive advantage over other stores.
(v) To promote private brands.

One thing should be noted in this regard that ***cross selling*** is not an easy selling philosophy, as it seems. It involves an element of risk because a wrong preposition under *cross selling* may spoil existing customer relationship and store's image. Therefore, it is imperative to make certain that the additional product or service offered to the client must increase the value to the customers.

Examples:

- Selling accessories to a person who just has bought a new car from your store.
- Offering installation service with air conditioners or coolers.
- Offering Annual Maintenance service Contract (AMC) with the sale of electronic items.
- Convincing customer to get the suit length stitched from the store itself.

SUMMARY

Neither one size shoe does not fit to all feet, nor is one type of customer service suitable for all your customers. Similarly one selling style can not be successful in all cases. As customers come from different backgrounds, floor staff should understand this and react accordingly. If a customer comes to you about a complaint, be very serious about how you handle it. Is the customer upset and angry? First, calm him with words and action and show that you are serious about doing something to correct the problem. Even if it is obvious that he's wrong, sometimes it's better for repeat business to take the loss and compensate the customer. Remember, it is the customer whose contributions enable store to pay salary to store staff. Therefore, when your customer is satisfied that his complaint has been properly addressed, thank him for bringing the problem to your attention. Remember, no amount of advertising can repair the damage done by failing to properly address a customer's concern. Even more damaging to a small business is the "silent complainer": the customer who simply walks out of your shop without saying a word and you never see him again. These silent complainers have friends and their friends have friends and rumors spread like wild fire.

With growing competition and the presence of national and international brands have been forcing retailers of today to incorporate all activities that determine (i) the convenient and one shop shopping, (ii) the ease of completing a transaction and (iii) the customer satisfaction followed by customer delight after the shopping. Such activities and practices followed by retailers' add great value to the goods and services bought by the customers and are the source of creating competitive advantage over competitors. The **GAPS** model in this context plays a vital role to highlight the various obstacles that hinder a retailer's ability to close or bridge the gap between the customers' expectations and the perceived value. Managing customer service is a complex subject, but can be made easier if we consider the following mantras:

1. Be understanding and caring

If your customer asks you for advice on a product, don't try to sell him the item that best enhances your bottom line, sell him the item that's best for your customer. In the long run, your bottom line will thank you for having made this choice.

2. Train and educate your employees from time to time

Educate your floor staff to be equally as concerned about your customers as you are. Instead of showing unnecessary items to customer and not showing what actually he is looking for will force him to change the route of shopping to another store. Hence if you are not understanding what he needs, better to say sir 'I don't know, you come with me, my seniors might help you out'.

3. Stay proactive and keep gathering customer service ideas

After collecting ideas, don't forget to implement these to the extent possible if it is in your reach and limit. Otherwise convey these collected suggestions to seniors. It is a fact that if you regularly implement these ideas, if seem fit, your store will be world class. Because customers whatever find in other stores, want also in the store they visit on regular basis.

4. Admit your mistake

Every human being makes mistakes and can learn from mistakes. Whenever we make a mistake, we should accept it immediately and willingly. Being a floor employee, whenever you make a mistake, never miss to say, "I am sorry", it is all my fault", 'I admit I made a mistake". Always remember, never repeat your mistake.

5. Avoid arguments

According to Gautam Buddha, "Hatred can never be ended by hatred, but can be overcome by love". Misunderstanding cannot be cleared by arguments but by tact, diplomacy and conciliation. Argument is a negative exercise, which is harmful for both parties. If you have doubts, discuss it but don't argue.

6. Smile

Smile is a curved line that can straighten many problems. A smile costs nothing, but it creates much. It enriches those who receive it, without impoverishing those who give it. It happens in a flash and the memory of it may last forever. A smile increases the face value of a person. It only requires only twelve muscles to smile while frowning uses one hundred thirteen facial muscles. A captivating smile is the most charming and the least expensive make-up available to floor staff.

7. Be careful in communication

Spoken words are like arrows, they don't return once they shot. It takes years to build a customer but only a few seconds to loose it. Therefore, choose your words very carefully and tactfully. Never fail to say "I'm sorry, I hurt you, I take my words back" knowing very well those words spoken can't be retrieved.

Last but not the least, be sensitive to other people's feelings. Empathy alone is a very important characteristic of a positive personality. When dealing with people, try to put yourself in their place and ask yourself – "How would I feel or react if I were in his shoes? Or "How would I feel if someone have treated me that way?"

REVIEW QUESTIONS

True and False Questions

1. Good customer service is intended to bring back customers voluntarily and then sending back with smiling faces.
2. A retailer's ability to device and apply a sound strategy depends on how a retail firm identifies customers' needs, expectations and possible gaps between them.
3. The person who pays the bill is known as 'consumer'.
4. The person who uses the purchased thing is known as 'customer'.
5. Is it right to say that 'consumers' can be 'customers' but all 'consumers' cannot be 'customers'.
6. Loyal customers are those customers who don't have faith in the store and come to store on irregular basis.
7. Discount customers visit stores often, but make their decisions on the basis of discounts, offers, rebates/offers offered by the store.
8. Impulse customers come to store with the intention of buying the goods.
9. Need-based customers come to store without the intention of buying some particular goods.
10. Wandering customers come to store with some particular need or desire.
11. Satisfying the needs of customers requires the store to maintain distance with them.
12. Customers have no impact upon store's policies and decisions.
13. Customers are not only the key to revenue and profits but also to create and maintain jobs within the store.
14. A good customer is one who holds the potential to undertake activities that offer short term value to a store.
15. Internet is the fastest growing contact point.
16. Self-Service allows consumers to perform most or all of the services associated with retail purchasing.
17. CRM stands for Competitive Relationship Management.
18. ICT stands for Information and Customer Technology.
19. The customization approach enables a retailer to change the offerings, layout, view, site structure and content to satisfy the needs and wants of different target groups.
20. The standardization approach enables a retailer to maintain the same goods, services and elements of marketing mix across all local, regional and global markets.

21. To close the standard gap, retailers besides focusing on high service quality, should define and describe the role of each employee involved in delivering service.
22. Delivery gap arises because of the difference between the retailer's service standards and the actual service offered to customers despite the existence of guidelines for treating customers correctly and performing services well.
23. Communication gap arises because of the difference between the actual set of services offered to the customers and the service communicated by the retailer to customers.
24. The objective of service recovery is to identify customers' objections and complaints for the purpose of removing them.
25. 'Break even point' is a point at which there is no loss and no revenue.
26. The critical examination of strengths, weaknesses, opportunities and trade is known as SWOT analysis.
27. 3Fs deal with Feel, Felt and Found.
28. Pushback means objecting to customers' objections.
29. Humour means responding with humour rather than showing frustration.
30. Writing means write-down objections then cross them off once handled.

Answers

1. True	2. True	3. False	4. False
5. False	6. False	7. True	8. False
9. False	10. False	11. False	12. False
13. True	14. False	15. True	16. True
17. False	18. False	19. True	20. True
21. True	22. True	23. True	24. True
25. False	26. True	27. True	28. True
29. True	30. True		

Multiple Choice Questions

1. Impulse customer are those who:
   (*a*) have faith in the store
   (*b*) have no intention to buy the goods
   (*c*) take decision on the basis of discounts and rebates.
   (*d*) visit store with the intention of buying the goods.
2. Wandering customers usually
   (*a*) ask a lot of questions
   (*b*) come to store with no intention of buying
   (*c*) make decision on the basis of discounts
   (*d*) have faith in a store.
3. A kiosk is a ....
   (*a*) specially designed software for stores accounting
   (*b*) type of security system
   (*c*) separate, interactive computer for offering service to customers.
   (*d*) financial assistance booth.
4. Customer service results in:
   (*a*) Building Brand Loyalty
   (*b*) Less complaints

(*c*) Strengthens competitive advantage.
(*d*) All of the above.

5. .... plays a vital role in carrying out ....
(*a*) ICT, CRM, (*b*) B2B, B2C
(*c*) CRM, ICT (*d*) Internet, self service
6. The GAPS model was introduced by:
(*a*) Gautier (*b*) FICCI.
(*c*) Grasim, S. Kumar (*d*) Valeric Zenthaml
7. Knowledge gap arises because of difference between customer's expectations, and the retailer's
(*a*) personality (*b*) perception
(*c*) behaviour. (*d*) assessment.
8. .... means not matching performance to promises
(*a*) Knowledge Gap (*b*) Standards Gap
(*c*) Delivery Gap (*d*) Communication Gap.
9. The objective of service recovery is to :
(*a*) identify customer's objections (*b*) identify customer's complaints.
(*c*) both of the above. (*d*) develop spirit of teamwork
10. For becoming destination store retailer should concentrate on:
(*a*) Retail location (*b*) Variety of assortment
(*c*) to reduce sales per hour (*d*) all of the above

Answers

1. (*b*)	2 (*a*)	3. (*c*)	4. (*d*)
5 (*a*)	6. (*d*)	7. (*b*)	8. (*d*)
9. (*c*)	10. (*a*)		

Answers to check your progress

1. What is CRM?
2. What is a kiosk?
3. What do you mean by internet?
4. What does self service mean?
5. What is ICT?
6. What is customer delight?
7. What is MRP?
8. Elaborate SWOT?
9. What is trade off?
10. What is target market?
11. What LAARC implies?
12. What LAIR implies?
13. What is trade off?
14. What BEP stands for?
15. What is conversion rate?
16. What is up-selling?

17. What is cross-selling?
18. Name four consumer gaps?
19. What is idle time?
20. What is tangibility?

Small Answer Questions

1. Customer can be a consumer but consumer cannot be a customer! Explain? Why managing the customers is a tedious task in stores?
2. Explain the importance of CRM? What role CRM lays in modern retailing?
3. Explain the difference between loyal and needful customer?
4. How wandering customers can be vital for an organization? Being a floor staff, what guidelines you would follow to provide great customer service?
5. It has generally seen that floor staff normally looses its patience, despite knowing they are the means of bread and butter for them. What you would like to suggest to floor staff to maintain their patience level?
6. What can be done to improve the behaviour of floor staff if they don't perform well with the customers?
7. Explain few strategies to keep customers coming back again and again?
8. "Service quality as perceived by the customers must meet customers' expectations" Explain this statement?
9. Describe few situations that lead to satisfactory and unsatisfactory customer experience?
10. Being a senior HR executive, how you would evaluate your salespersons?
11. Explain the role of employees in maintaining store loyality?
12. Which of the four gaps do you think is hard nut to crack (minimize/close)?

Long Answer Questions

1. Suppose being a newly appointed manager of a retail store, you want to apply the gaps model to improve the level of service offered with which gap you would start your improvement exercise, and why? In which way you would like to close various gaps?
2. Critically analyze the significance of Gaps model for improving the quality of retail service in recent context?
3. Suppose you are a salesperson working in a Super Bazaar for quite few years. Explain some customers' objections that you face in your day to day life and you would like to share with fresh entrants?

Applied Questions

1. How you would evaluate the loyalty programme of a pharmaceutical retail store with that of a local chemist in the same locality?
2. Select a departmental store each in two different product categories in your city/ location and compare their relationship marketing strategies. Assess the impact of product category issues, market conditions, and customer preferences in both cases.
3. Select a store of your choice in your neighborhood and evaluate its customer service strategy.

Appendix

Exhibit 20.1: Types of Customers

Basic Types	Customers	Recommendations
Defensive	Doesn't trust any salesperson. Resists communication as he has a dislike of others. Generally, uncooperative and will explode at the slightest provocation.	Avoid mistaking their silence for openness to your ideas. Stick to basic facts. Tactfully inject the product's advantages and disadvantages.
Interrupter	Intense, impatient personality. Often interrupts salespersons and has a perpetually "strained" expression. Often driven and successful people who want results fast.	Don't waste time; move quickly and firmly from one sale point to another. Avoid overkill since they know what they want.
Decisive	Confident in their ability to make decisions and stay with them. Open to new ideas but prefer brevity. Highly motivated by self-pride.	No canned presentations. The key is to assist. Don't argue or point out errors in their judgment.
Indecisive	They worry about marketing the wrong decision; therefore, they tend to postpone all decisions. Want salesperson to make decision for them.	Avoid becoming frustrated. Determine the need as early as possible and concentrate on that. Avoid presenting too many alternatives. Start with making decisions on minor points.
Sociable	Friendly, talkative types who are enjoyable. Many have access time on their hands (e.g., retirees). They usually resist the close.	You may have to spend time with these customers. Listen for points in conversation where you can interject the merits of the product. Do not pressure for the close. Subtle friendly close is needed.
Impulsive	Quick to make decision. Impatient just as likely to walk out as they were to walk in.	Close as rapidly as possible. Avoid any useless interaction. Avoid any oversell. Highlight the merits of the product.

Source: *Patrick Dunne and Robert F. Lusch, Retailing (Third Edition), Harcourt Brace College Publications, 1999.pp 445.*

Exhibit 20.2: Criteria for Evaluating Retailer's Promotion Program

Following are the ten questions to assess whether a retailer's promotion is serving the customer:

1. Are multi-payment modes are available?
2. Are sufficient quantities available on sales promotion items?
3. Are the sales people easy to find when required?
4. Are the sales people friendly and courteous?
5. Are the sales people helpful and informative?
6. Do sales people know about the ad and what's being promoted and why?
7. Does the advertising provide all the information the customer needs?
8. Is gift wrapping and packaging facility available?
9. Is the advertising informative and helpful?
10. Is home delivery and credit facility offered?

Courtesy: *www.authorstream.com*

Exhibit 20.3: Do's and Don'ts of Customer Service

The atmosphere you create in your place of business is vital to your retail sales. Customers who come to your store and feel contented and take pleasure in your store are expected to come back not alone but with the friends and family members. Retailers are worried about making their store customer's friendly. Follow these recommendations:

Enhancing your display with lighting

Lighting fixtures include track lighting and accessories such as rope lights. In the absence of 'SAIL' signs, how you would attract customer? Rather it is difficult to bring them in your store. Therefore, it is important to use proper lighting and accessories to make your product 'pop' in the display. Incandescent spots are very successful and effective here. Lighting needs to come from various directions. Try this straightforward trial and see how this works. Customers will automatically get attracted to your store and ultimately to the product.

No doubt, lighting plays a big role in merchandising, but don't stop there. Take the same five pieces of jewelry. This time set each one on a different colored background. You can use towels, clothing, leather, anything handy. Again shine the light over each piece. Do some color enhance the merchandise or detract from its beauty? The right color combinations and the right lighting can do wonders. If you will be putting some merchandise in glass showcases make sure they are lighted and always use background fabric that enhances the merchandise.

Another type of lighting that can lit up your store is the use of colored neon lighting. This is particularly effective if your customer base leans more to the trendy, upscale market.

Enhancing your display with sound

A customer's senses can be stimulated by more than brightly lit displays. Sound can play a major part in creating an appropriate atmosphere in your shop. Mood setting for a Southwest store can be achieved with classical guitar, Indian flute, or lively Gypsy King tapes. Avoid extremes such as gangster rap or sleepy elevator music. The overall tone should be upbeat and pleasing to the ear. Mexican Mariachi and country western music is also very appealing to compliment the day's repertoire

When you establish which music seems to stimulate the most sales, play those tapes every single day. You will probably end up with less than half a dozen that are real winners. Don't worry that you will get tired of the same old songs. Pretty soon you won't even hear the music. You will be too busy capitalizing on the customers' responses.

Another compelling reason to play music in your store is that it does away with a store's "empty" feeling when there are only a few shoppers. The music has already welcomed the customer, so the sound of your voice greeting won't echo off the walls. Avoid at all costs a cold, empty, lonely atmosphere. Shoppers who have already had a really bad day can be revived with proper stimulation.

Enhancing your display with smell

Ever notice what neat tricks grocery stores use to get shoppers to fill those carts? How bout the smell of freshly baked bread and pastries? Umm, doesn't that make you hungry?

Food smells would not be appropriate for a Southwest store, but there are scents that can be used effectively. Some of the most appealing scents come directly from the merchandise. Leather products particularly have distinct olfactory effect. Keeping all your leather items in one department will concentrate and heighten the effect.

Textile products also emit their own pleasant fragrance. This primarily comes from the natural lanolin in sheep's wool. Since this is a more subtle scent, textiles should not be placed near items of dominant odors.

Enhancing your display with touch

Touch is another important sense that is involved in selling Southwest merchandise.

- The richness and depth of wool fiber
- The smoothness of tanned leather
- The coolness of clay pottery
- The coarseness of a horsehair rope
- The gentleness of a feather
- The sleekness of a cowhide rug
- Tightness of woven threads in a tapestry

Don't worry about your goods getting shop worn from all this touching. With the right merchandise at the right price presented in an attractive setting, the goods will be at the cash register before you know it.

After taking all these steps, you can easily make the customer feel like buying? But besides this, you make sure your negatives don't outweigh all the positive effort you already expended. Too many store owners offend their clientele starting right at the front door to make the store environment friendly for all customers.

- No cameras/No videography
- No drinking/No smoking
- No food
- No gum
- No pets
- No shirt, no shoes, no service
- No shopping bags/poly bag
- No strollers
- No toothpicks
- No unattended children

Remember, the more space and freedom and respect you show to a customer, the closer they will bond with you. You and your shop will be a special memory for them and they will return again and again. In all your attempts to make your shop customer friendly, be sure you're not giving the store away. Unfortunately, a small percentage of these clients you have been so nice to are shoppers. Not only have they soaked up your hospitality, they've made off with valuable merchandise. Carefully study and implement these techniques to deter shoplifting.

1. Greet all customers soon after they enter. Even if you're assisting someone, look up, smile and verbally acknowledge the presence of each new person. Shoplifters don't want assistance and don't like attention. If they know you're watching, then hopefully they'll move on to another store.
2. A system of alertness between you and your assistants can also deter shoplifting. A certain gesture, such as touching your eye with your index finger, can signal everyone to watch a particular suspect. If you're reasonably sure a shoplifter has left your store with merchandise, call the police immediately with a description. Do not try to apprehend a shoplifter on your own. It is too dangerous. Not only might you get hurt, you can get sued.
3. Be suspicious of someone who enters frequently but never purchases. Put more pressure on this type of shopper. "Can help you find something

in particular? What style are you looking for? Is there a certain price range you'd like to stay within?" If it is a shoplifter, they'll be nervous about the questioning and you will have politely made your point.

4. Keep expensive merchandise, especially small items, in locked showcases. Keep the keys with you so that you can access the item if you have a truly interested customer. Replace all merchandise promptly if the sale is not made.
5. Keep shelves, counters and rack displays full and orderly. Take immediate notice of gaps or something obviously out of order. Accurate inventory records need to be kept to detect shrinkage not accounted for in sales. If a particular item is routinely short, consider moving it to a safer location in the store.
6. Keep the layout of your store fixtures in a pattern such that you can see down most aisles from your vantage point at the cash register.
7. Place convex mirrors in high comer positions to reveal areas that otherwise might be blocked from your vision.
8. Position your telephone so that you can see your customers plainly while you take a call. Keep conversations as brief as possible so you can get back to making sales.
9. Tell fellow merchants about suspected shoplifters. They will in turn alert you to people they have suspicions about.
10. While customers are in your store do not turn your back on them or go to the stock room. Maintain a vigilant presence at all times while you assist each shopper.

The small courtesies and attention you show to your customers would work together to encourage sales and discourage shoplifters.

Source: *www.elpasosaddleblanket.com*

Exhibit 20.4: New Trends in Customer Service

Marketers have seen the customer service process evolve from an area that received only marginal attention into a primary functional area. In response to customers' demands for responsive and reliable service, companies are investing heavily in innovative methods and processes to strengthen their service level. These innovations include:

1. Increased Customer Self-Service

A major trend in customer service is the move by companies to encourage customers to be involved in helping solve their own service issues. This can be seen in retail industries where self-service ranges from customers placing their own grocery products in shopping bags all the way to having customers do their own checkout including scanning products and making payment. Also, as we will soon discuss, customers needing information are being encouraged by companies to first undertake the effort themselves often by visiting special company-provided information areas (see Website and Phone Accessible Knowledge Base below). Only after they have explored these options are customers encouraged to contact customer service[5].

2. Revenue Generators

Companies that maintain a customer service staff have found that these people not only can help solve customer problems but they may also be in a position to convince customers to purchase more. Many companies are now requiring sales training for their customer service personnel. At a basic level customer service representatives may be trained to ask if customers are interested in hearing about other products or services. If a customer shows interest then the representative will transfer the customer to a sales associate. At a more advanced level the representative will shift to a selling role and attempt to get the customer to commit to additional product purchases.

3. Out-Sourcing

One of the most controversial developments impacting customer service is the move by many companies around the world to establish customer service functions outside of either their home country or the country in which their customers reside. Called out-sourcing, companies pursue this strategy to both reduce cost and also increase service coverage. For instance, having multiple customer service outlets around the world allows customers to talk via phone with a service person no matter what time of day. The ability to move service to another country is only viable in large part due to technological developments. But such moves have raised concerns on two fronts. First, many see this trend as leading to a reduction of customer service jobs within a home country. Second, customer service personnel located off-shore may lack sufficient training and often lack an understanding of the conditions within the customers' local market both of which can affect service levels. At the extreme a poorly managed move to out-source customer service can lead to a decrease in customer satisfaction which in the long-run could affect sales.

5 *www.sbinfocanada.about.com*

Exhibit 20.5: Customer Service Overhaul

We all seem to know how important customer service is-if we are going to be successful in retail. Then why do we keep getting lousy service wherever we go?

Assuming most customers are reasonable people, the answer to the above question is 1. Store staff doesn't know or don't understand what the expected behavior in terms of customer care is or 2. Management gives this issue only a lip service and do not place firm criteria to maintain high customer service levels.

It always boils down to quality of management doesn't it? In both of the above cases, it's management that is squarely responsible. So, before things get even worse, here are the commandments you need to put in place and make sure they are ingrained into everyone's mind:

1. **A Vision of Customer Service Excellence That is Clearly Developed and Communicated**: If you do not set the expectations right from the beginning, you can't blame anyone but yourself.
2. **Recruit, Hire, Train and Promote People with People Skills:** When you are interviewing for new people, look for indications of friendliness, helpful nature and ask questions probing for the level of people skills. When evaluating staff performance, make sure there is enough indication and consideration to their performance in customer service.
3. **Measure Individual Service Performance, Report Results and Celebrate Victories:** What is not measured can not be managed. End of story. Develop a performance chart for each staff member and rate them from 1 to 10 for their Customer Service performance. You'll see a marked improvement almost immediately.
4. **Solve Problems When and Where They Occur immediately:** Customer studies show that as long as a problem is resolved fast and to the customer's benefit, most become very loyal customers for life. Study your policies and procedures and eliminate the fluff and unnecessary steps that take time. To speed up the resolution process, empower your staff to make certain decisions without having to look for management.
5. **Stay Close to Your Customer:** When was the last time you took one of your customers to lunch or even a coffee? I know a lot of you are thinking we don't do that in retail, that's the domain of B2B sales; but unless you know your customer's honest opinion, how are you going to improve your operation? Think about it.

Courtesy: www.dmsretail.com

RETAIL SALES PROMOTION

LEARNING OBJECTIVES

- Understanding the concept of sales promotion
- Knowing sales promotion is necessary or wasteful activity?
- Identifying best techniques of sales promotion
- To Know timing of sales promotion
- Understanding how to maximize sales promotion benefits

"The manufacturer who finds himself up the creek is a short-sighted opportunist who siphons off all his advertising dollars for short-term promotions."

David Ogilvy

INTRODUCTION

In the retail industry, with the dawn of large players like Big Bazaar, Spencer, Shoppers' Stop, Reliance Fresh, Subiksha, Big Apple and Globus more recently, the battle has been to hold customer base. Be it loyalty program or providing 'ease of payment facility' to customers, are introduced to retain existing customer base. The result is that our traditional Indian '*kirana stores*' are facing problems to survive their entities. Their resources are limited and can not use these costly sales promotion techniques. In the race of moving ahead and increase their client base, stores are offering lucrative offers to the customers.

SALES PROMOTION DEFINED

Retail sales promotion is a scheme undertaken by a business to encourage an increase in store's sales, practice or trial of a product or service. In this process, a store persuades the customer to buy a particular product through normally personal selling. Today sales promotion has various forms. Time and again they are innovative and original, and hence a complete list of all existing techniques is nearly not possible.

Retail sales promotion is one of the important aspects of sales promotional mix. (Remaining three parts of the promotional mix are personal selling, publicity, and advertising). A sales promotion can be defined as a paid, non-personal form of communication that offers incentive to potential customers for visiting a store and/or purchase products during a specific period of time. These promotional efforts are intended to have an instant impact on retail sales. Under sales promotion, media and non-media efforts are used for a pre-determined limited time to increase customers' demand, excite market demand or pick up product availability. Sales promotion can be aimed at the customer, floor staff, or any member of distribution channel. Sales promotions embattled at the customer are termed as 'customer sales promotions' and sales promotion aimed at retailers and wholesalers is known as 'trade sales promotion'. Depending upon the sort of promotion effort, it can help increase impulse buying, greater excitement and can also motivate the members of retail chain.

Sales promotion techniques are used in retailing business to stimulate trial purchases. This is generally done when a store wants to catch the attention of new customers. It involves various communications tricks that effort to provide added value or incentives to customers, retailers, wholesalers, or other retail store customers to excite instant sales. These tricks can help to excite product interest, trial or purchase. Some of the commonly conducted sales promotions devices are coupons, demonstrations, contests, premiums, point-of-purchase (POP) displays, rebates and prizes.

OBJECTIVES OF RETAIL SALES PROMOTION PROGRAM

The main objective of any sales program is to increase the store's sales. But today sales promotion has various dimensions. These are explained as follows:

1. **To create awareness about product** – It has been found that most of the sales promotion techniques are highly effective in exposing customers to products for the first time and can serve as key promotional components in the early stages of new product introduction. Additionally, as part of the effort to build product awareness, several sales promotion techniques possess the added advantage of capturing customer information at the time of exposure to the promotion. In this way, sales promotion can act as an effective customer information gathering tool (i.e., sales lead generation), which can then be used as part of follow up marketing efforts[1].
2. **To create interest among customers** – Researches have shown that sales promotions are very successful in creating interest in a product. In actual, creating interest is often considered the most important use of sales promotion. In the retail industry, an appealing sales promotions can significantly increase customer traffic to retail outlets. Internet marketers can use similar approaches to bolster the number of website visitors. Another important way to create interest is to

[1] *www.knowthis.com*

move customers to experience a product. Several sales promotion techniques offer the opportunity for customers to try products for free or at low cost. This exercise can convert visitors into customers.

Figure: 21.1

VLCC: Creating Interest among Customers

Attracting customer through 'sharing experience' is a widely used promotional tactic. Under this strategy company in its advertisements portrays the feelings, experience of their old and loyal customers who have been using the company products and services for long and actually have been benefited. VLCC by this tactics has revolutionized this industry and acquired the status of India's largest health and beauty brand. Today VLCC is the single largest player in the organized sector with a pan-India presence of nearly 150 outlets across 70 cities, 1 in Katmandu, 8 locations in UAE and 1 in Oman. Having served over a million customers since its inception, VLCC, today, has achieved an iconic status across the world and is India's largest and most preferred Slimming, Beauty & Health brand.

Courtesy: *Company Website*

3. **Source of Information** – Usually sales promotion techniques are planned to move customers to some action and are rarely simply informational in nature. However, some sales promotions do offer customers access to product information. For instance, a promotion may allow customers to try a fee-based online service for free for several days. This free access may include receiving product information via email.

4. **To stimulate Customers' demand** – After informing the initial basic knowledge, the most important use of sales promotion is to build demand by convincing customers to make a purchase. Special promotions, especially those that lower the cost of ownership to the customer (e.g., offering heavy discount), can be employed to stimulate sales for a small period.

Figure 21.2
Stimulating Demand for Additional Purchase

Domino's Pizza Inc is famous for its great deals. When it comes to special offers, Domino's believes in spoiling you for choice! And all you've got to do is specify the offer you want when you call your nearest Domino's outlet. They've got new offers every now and then to promote sale and attract not you but your whole family.

Courtesy: *Company Website (www.dominos.co.in)*

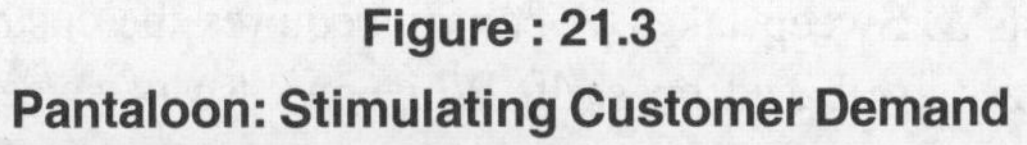

Figure : 21.3
Pantaloon: Stimulating Customer Demand

Convincing customers for bulk purchase is not an easy task. Today's customers are smart and cost conscious. But the task becomes easy if company is able to lure them through attractive offerings. Pantaloon here exactly does so and offers Rs. 100 off on a purchase of 1000 or above. A person who is buying clothing worth Rs. 650 may be easily motivated by store employees or through mass advertising to spend Rs. 350 extra for availing Rs. 100 off offer.

Courtesy: *Company Website*

5. **Brand Building** – Building brand value is one of the main objective of sales promotion. A sales promotion may be done to attract attention towards a new product/brand or some services that has been launched by the retailer and to induce trail purchase. It has been practiced by some retail companies like Pantaloon reward good or "privileged" customers with exclusive promotions schemes, such as email "exceptional deals" and price cut while cash payment.

TYPES OF RETAIL SALES PROMOTION PROGRAMMES

Considering the primary target audience, sales promotion can be classified into three broad categories. These include:

1. **Consumers Directed** - Possibly the most well known methods of sales promotion are those intended to appeal to the final consumer. Consumers are exposed to sales promotions nearly everyday but some buyers are habitual to look for sales promotions schemes before making any purchase decisions. Examples of such techniques are:
   - Checkout end: On checkout end the customer is provided with a coupon or a scratch card based on total quantity purchased.
   - Contests & Sweepstakes: A contest requires the customers to compare and the prizes are based on skill. While in case of sweepstakes, the customer only needs to enter into competition on the basis of the amount paid to a retail store. In these two promotion schemes, only a few lucky customers get the value presented in the promotion scheme.

Contests are particular promotions schemes giving value to winners based on skills they show as compared to others. For example, a bread company may offer free foreign tour to winners of a bread contest. Contest award winners are usually selected by a panel of few judges. While sweepstakes are not skill based but rather depend on fortune. Lucky winners are selected on the basis of random selection. Sometimes, in some situations the probability of winning may be high for those who do purchasing if entry into the sweepstake takes place automatically when a purchase is made. But in majority of cases, anybody is liberated to enter exclusive of the requirement to make a purchase.

- Dangler: It is a sign that affects when a customer walks by it. It can make up the mind of customers to purchase.
- Discounted prices: Some of the Indian budget airline companies such as Air Deccan and Kingfisher send their loyal and regular customers with the latest low-price deals when new flights are released or bonus destinations are announced.

- Free gifts: For example in India, 'Subway' the sandwich chain shop gives a card with six spaces for stickers with each the purchase of each sandwich. When the card is full, the customer is given a sandwich at no extra cost.
- FSI (Free-standing insert): FSI is a coupon booklet that is inserted into the local newspaper for delivery to its readers.
- Glorifier: It is a small sized stage that lifts up a product higher than other products during display time.
- Lipstick Board: It is a board on which stylish messages are written in crayon to attract customers.
- Loss leader: It is the price of a popular product that is reduced for short-term period in order to fuel sales of other non-daily items.
- Loyalty rewards schemes: In this scheme, customers collect some numbers, points, miles or credits for every purchase and then redeem them for rewards during some bill payment or further buying. For example, Pepsi Stuff and Advantage.
- More Merchandising: In this scheme, reward is given in the form of some merchandise addition, for example, charging for one litre but providing for one and half litre.
- Mobile coupons: This is of recent origin. In this scheme, coupons are made available on a cell phone and customers show the offer to the retailer or a salesperson for cash redemption.
- Necker: This is very popular and old scheme of sales promotion. In automobile sector, neckers are vey popular. Necker actually is a coupon that is placed on the 'neck' of a bottle or packaged item in a bin.
- Online couponing: In this scheme, coupons are made available online. Customers print them out and take them to the retail store for exemption or redemption.
- Online interactive sponsorship games: In these games, customers play an interactive game linked with the promoted product. For example, the interactive add of tomato ketchup available on net.
- On-shelf coupon schemes: In this scheme, coupons are available at the store's shelf where the product is presented.

- Price deal: It is a temporary reduction offer in the price of some retail item such as 'happy hour' menu scheme in bars and restaurants.
- Price-packed deal: This sort of packaging deal offers a consumer a certain percentage more of the product for the same price (for example, twenty five percent extra in the same price).
- Vouchers and coupons scheme: Vouchers and coupons are often seen in newspapers and magazines.

> **Note:** *Most of the above mentioned examples relate to retail customers. But it does not mean the promotions are only to excite customers but sales promotions can be aimed at wholesalers and distributors too. The promotion which is meant for customers is known as retail promotion and which is meant for distributors and wholesalers is known as trade sales promotion. For example, joint promotion between a manufacturer and its authorized dealerships for distributing sales promotion material like pamphlet, leaflet and other material like traveling bags, caps and T-shirts, and cash incentive for dealers sales people and their retail store clients.*

2. **Trade Market Directed** – Marketers use sales promotions to target all customers including intermediaries/agents within their channel of distribution. Trade promotions are initially used to lure channel members to carry a marketer's products and once products are stocked, marketers utilize promotions to strengthen the channel relationship. This method is normally adopted during festivals and marriage sessions.

Techniques of Trade sales promotion

Many sales promotions aimed at building relationships with channel partners follow similar designs as those directed to consumers including promotional pricing, contests and free product. In addition to these, several other promotional approaches are specifically designed to appeal to trade partners. These approaches include:

(i) Advertising Support Programs

Sometimes marketers with the offering of promotional support in the shape of physical displays, also offer financial assistance to their retail chain partners in the form of payment of their advertisement bills. These finances are usually directed to retailers who then incorporate the company's products in their advertisement media. In extreme cases, the marketer offers pay the whole cost of advertisement campaign but generally the retailer pays the partial payment, which in the world of retailing is known as co-op advertising funds.

(ii) POP (Point-of-Purchase) Displays

POP displays have become integral part of modern retailing. They help reinforce the store/product image, enhance retail sales through floor communication and provide information to the customer. POP actually is particularly designed materials planned for placement in retail outlets. These displays permit products to be significantly presented, usually in high traffic areas of the retail stores, and thereby raise the likelihood that the product will be noticeable. These displays come in many shapes, though the most popular are those allowing a product to stand alone, such as placed in between a store walkway or sit at the end of a walkway, where it will be exposed to intense customer traffic.

The main function of POP in a retail store is to enhance sales. It has been found that for the retail channel partners, these displays can result in considerable sales increase as compared to sales levels in a normal shelf position of a retail store.

(iii) Short-term Trade Allowances

These allowances are offered to those retail channel partners who agreed to stock the product. Generally these allowances are not only given so that channel members should stock marketer's products but to induce them to promote the products in different ways like offering some attractive shelf space within the store. Sometimes, these allowances may be in the form of price reductions or guarantee to buy back the products if these are not sold in certain period of time.

(iv) Retail sales Incentives/ Push Money

Here sales promotion offers are subject to induce efforts that lead to meet store's promotional objectives, it makes common sense that these should also be applied to those people who actually participate in increasing the sales. These are the persons who help the store in making their dreams come true. Thus retail stores from time to time offer some retail incentives in the form of monetary or non-monetary incentives to those who affect sales. These people are the sales executives or floor employees who directly interact with the customers and sell the goods. Sometimes these incentives are called 'push money' as these offer employees cash or prizes, such as foreign trips to those who meet sales requirements.

(v) Promotional Products

This is among the commonly used methods of sales promotion. This is the way by which company with some purchase of goods, gives some reminders with the company name or stamp which serve as reminders of the actual product. For example, companies often hand out free diaries, calendars, coffee mugs, pens, paper weights, decorative pieces or wall clocks.

(vi) Trade Shows

This is also the common form of promoting retail sales. This includes industry trade show (exhibitions, conferences and conventions). The purpose of organizing trade shows is to bring both industry buyers and sellers together at one platform. Spending money on trade shows is one of the topmost of all sales promotion drives. In fact, FICCI estimates that over Rs. 500 crore is spent annually by marketers to participate in trade shows, exhibitions and conventions.

Marketers are attracted to trade shows since these offer the opportunity to reach a large number of potential buyers in one convenient setting. At these events most sellers attempt to capture the attention of buyers by setting up a display area to present their product offerings and meet with potential customers. These displays can range from a single table covering a small area to erecting specially built display booths that dominate the trade show floor.

3. **B2B Market Directed** – B2B in the line of business stands for 'Business-to-Business' dealings. A small, but important sub-set of sales promotions are targeted to the business-to-business market. While these promotions may not carry the glamour associated with consumer or trade promotions, B2B promotions are used in many industries besides retailing. Actually in B2B sales promotion is

used as a way of moving clients to action. Though, the promotional options available to the B2B marketer are not as broad as those found in the customers or trade markets. For example, in India, most of the B2B marketers do not use coupons as a medium for sales promotion with the exception of companies that sell to both customers and business clients.

The most widely used techniques for B2B promotions are:

- distributing samples
- price reductions
- promotional goods
- trade shows
- trade-in

Besides these options, trade shows are the most widely used means of B2B sales promotion.

B2B Transactions

B2B is an abbreviation for 'Business-to-Business' transactions. This term is often used for the exchange of goods and services between business entity to another rather than between business entity and customers. In B2B transaction, buying and selling take place electronically via Internet. To maintain the confidentiality of B2B transaction, whole system of B2B is protected with passwords so that price information should not be public.

B2C Transactions

B2C is an acronym for 'Business-to-Consumer', describing business transactions taking place between business and consumers. B2C is the modern retailing part of e-commerce under which a site is accessible to the Internet users, who can after looking the shape, size, features etc can place their orders electronically (online). The examples of B2C transactions are:

- Booking a Railway ticket online.
- Placing an order for a pen drive online.

In nut shell, B2C is nothing but the commerce between Business and its Consumers electronically.

RETAIL MARKETING MIX

The various communication devices are used to educate, inform and generate awareness about the merchandise and the services offered by the retailer. These efforts also aim at building store image. The most common modes used for promotion are advertising, sales promotion, personal selling, public relations and publicity. Retailers usually employ a combination of various elements of promotion mix to achieve promotional and business objectives. The degree and the nature of usage of each of the promotion methods depend on the objectives of the retail firm, product, market profile and availability of resources. Small retailers generally depend on point–of–purchase material provided by the companies which provide the merchandise. ***Promotion mix*** employed by the retailers should be compatible with the desired store image, provide scope for modification if need arises and fit within the budget allocation. Therefore, various retail promotion methods can be compared on the basis of degree of control, flexibility, credibility and cost associated with them.

Figure 21.4(a)

Retail Marketing Mix

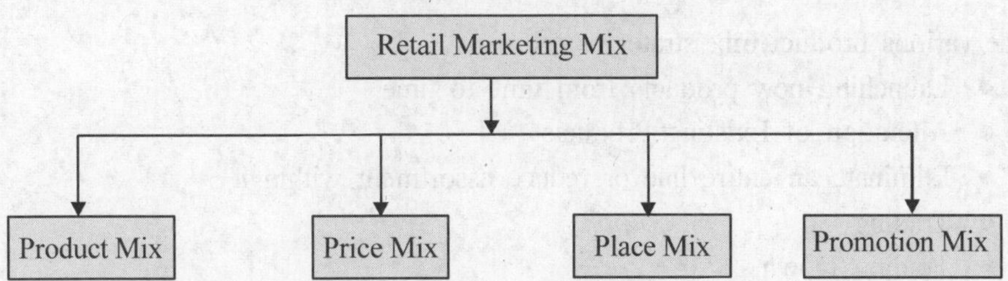

Figure 21.4 (b)

Retail Marketing Mix

The 'Product' Mix

Every organization has a *product mix* that is made up of product lines. The variety of products that a company produces, or that a retailer stocks is known as *'product line'*. It is a broad group of products, intended for similar uses and having similar characteristics. The ***product mix*** is the set of all the products offered for sale by a company. It refers to the length (the number of products in the product line), breadth (the number of product lines that a company offers), depth (the different varieties of product in the product line), and consistency (the relationship between products in their final destination) of product lines. Product mix is sometimes called *'product assortment'*.

The basic components of product mix are:

- Services
- Packaging
- Brand
- Product Item and
- Product line

The various product mix strategies are:

- Launching new products from time to time
- Alteration of Existing Products
- Eliminate an entire line or reduce assortment within it
- Trading Up
- Trading Down
- Product life cycle management

Trading up: It is a business practice of adding a higher-priced product to the existing product line to attract a higher-income market and improving the sales of existing lower-priced products.

Trading down: It is a business practice of adding a lower-priced item to existing product line of prestige products to encourage purchases from people who cannot afford the higher-priced product but would buy if offered at an affordable price.

The ***retail product mix*** is deviced so as to develop an appropriate promotion strategy for the store depending on the target market to be reached. Once the target market is identified and positioning strategy defined, the retailers employ various tools of product mix to reach out to consumers. These efforts also aim at building store image. Retailers usually employ a combination of various elements of product mix to achieve promotional and business objectives. The degree and the nature of usage of each of the promotion methods depend on the objectives of the retail firm, product, market profile, and availability of resources.

Product Mix

Product mix is a combination of products manufactured or traded by the same business house to reinforce their presence in the market, increase market share and increase the turnover for more profitability. Normally the product mix is within the synergy of other products for a medium size organization. However large groups of Industries may have diversified products within core competency. Larsen & Toubro Ltd, Godrej, Reliance in India are some of the examples.

One of the realities of business is that most firms deal with multi-products .This helps a firm diffuse its risk across different product groups/Also it enables the firm to appeal to a much larger group of customers or to different needs of the same customer group .So when Videocon chose to diversify into other consumer durables like music systems ,washing machines and refrigerators, it sought to satisfy the needs of the middle and upper middle income group of consumers.

Likewise, Bajaj Electricals.a household name in India, has almost ninety products in its portfolio ranging from low value items like bulbs to high priced consumer durables like mixers and luminaries and lighting projects .The number of products carried by a firm at a given point of time is called its product mix. This product mix contains product lines and product items. In other words it's a composite of products offered for sale by a firm.

Product Mix Decisions

Often firms take decisions to change their product mix. These decisions are dictated by the above factors and also by the changes occurring in the market place. Like the changing life-styles of Indian consumers led BPL-Sanyo to launch an entire range of white goods like refrigerators , washing machines, and microwave ovens .It also motivate the firm to launch other entertainment electronics. Rahejas, a well-known builders firm in Bombay, took a major decision to convert one of its theatre buildings in the western suburbs of Bombay into a large garments and accessories store for men ,women and children, perhaps the first of its kind in India to have almost all products required by these customer groups Competition from low priced washing powders (mainly Nirma) forced Hindustan Levers to launch different brands of detergent powder at different price levels positioned at different market segments .Customer preferences for herbs, mainly shikakai motivated Lever to launch black Sunsilk Shampoo ,which has shikakai .Also ,low purchasing power. and cultural bias against shampoo market made Hindustan Lever consider smaller packaging mainly sachets , for single use .So, it is the changes or anticipated changes in the market place that motivates a firm to consider changes in its product mix.

Source: *www.citesales.com*

The 'Price' Mix

Price has always been one of the most important variables in retail buying decision. It is the factor which makes or mars a retail organization. It is also the easiest and quickest element to change. Pricing helps an organization to achieve its objective. This is particularly significant for new market entrants who need to first establish a brand and then enjoy increasing profits as the brand gets market acceptability. For a customer, price is the main reason to visit a particular store.

A pricing strategy must be consistent over a period of time and consider retailer's overall positioning, profits, sales and appropriate rate of return on investment. Lowest price does not necessarily neet be the best price, but the lowest responsible price is the best right price. The difference between price and cost is the profit, which can be very high when the salesperson wants to exploit an urgent situation.

To survive in the retail business, retailers need to seek cash flow, profitability and overall growth in order to consolidate their market position. But pricing cannot be determined in isolation. Costs and operating expenses are equally important while establishing the retail price. ***Servicing pricing*** pursues the 'doctrine of pricing of goods', therefore, they are either cost-based or market based. Within this, these pricing can be profit oriented, government controlled, consumer oriented or competition oriented. Pricing needs certain considerations before actually determining it. The market position of the product, consumer perception and stage of the product life cycle, competitor's strategy and overall marketing strategy needs to be considered.

The components of price mix are:

- Organizational objectives
- Competition
- Cost and profit
- Credit terms
- Discount etc
- Fixed and variable costs
- Pricing options
- Pricing policies
- Proposed positioning strategies
- Target group and willingness to pay

The 'Place' Mix

The retailer should keep in mind the fact that his '***product***' should be available near the place of consumption so that the consumers can easily buy it. If the brand preferred by the consumer is not easily available at a convenient location, he may buy some other brand in the same product category. Hence, the retailer has to ensure that the product is available to the target consumers whenever required. There are **two major components** of place: **marketing channels** and **physical distribution** (logistics management). Channel decisions affect considerably the elements of marketing mix and involve a long term commitment of resources. Intermediaries involved in channel network are independent (at times contractual) organizations, hence their needs must be taken into account while evaluating channel alternatives. The success of marketing efforts, to a large extent depends on the sound distribution network. Physical distribution involves transportation, warehousing, material handling, bulk packaging etc. Some of these activities are carried out by intermediaries. A considerable coordination is required among various channels to seek maximum results of marketing operations. Following are the components of a retail price mix:

- Distribution channels
- Intermediary
- Distance Factor
- Inventory Level
- Transportation
- Warehousing and Storage

The 'Promotion' Mix

After deciding upon the budget, retailer should determine the appropriate promotional mix – a combination of advertising, public relations, ***personal selling*** and sales promotion. Small retailers having limited funds may use store displays, hoardings, direct mail, flyers and publicity methods to attract customer traffic, while on the other hand, retailers having no bar on finance, may use print or television media for their sales promotion activities.

The retail promotion mix varies from retailer to retailer and nation to nation depending upon technological advancement, nature of competition and availability of finance etc. Retailers design a promotional mix in compliance with store's objectives such as positioning of the organization, attracting customers, increasing sales turnover, clear out seasonal merchandise, announcing special events and educating public about the organization and its offerings. Retailers generally spend their promotional budget on developing advertisement campaigns and on other sales promotion activities. A retailer has a variety of sales promotion methods to promote its goods and services. Therefore, promotion mix used by the retailer should be compatible with the desired store image, budget allocation and flexible enough to modify whenever need arises. These various promotional vehicles may by compared on the basis of following issues:

- Cost of the method
- Its reach
- Degree of flexibility
- Credibility
- Control over media

Components of Promotion Mix

(a) Sales Promotion
(b) Publicity
(c) Advertising
(d) Public Relations and
(e) Personal selling

These are explained as below:

(a) Sales Promotion

Sales promotion programs are used by a wide range of organizations in both the consumer and business markets, though the frequency and spending levels are much greater for FMCG goods. Sales promotion describes promotional methods using special short-term techniques to persuade customers of a target market to respond or make purchases. As a reward, retailers offer goods at an affordable price or provide with certain gift items.

> **Sales Promotion**
>
> Every retailer wants to increase the sale of his store. He has several ways to achieve this. You might have heard about "Become Millionaire", "win a tour to Malaysia", "Buy one get one free", "fill the card or scratch it to win a prize" etc. You might also have seen gifts like electronic diaries, lunch box, soft drink bottles, shampoo pouch, caps etc. offered free with some products. All are examples of retail sales promotion.

Sales promotions are usually confused with advertising. For instance, a television advertisement mentioning a contest awarding winners with a free trip to a foreign country may give the contest the impression of advertising. While the delivery of the marketer's message through television media is certainly labeled as advertising, what is contained in the message, namely the contest, is considered a sales promotion. The factors that distinguish between the two promotional approaches are:

1. Time period: Whether the sales promotion involves offer for short term or long. and
2. The customer must perform some activity in order to be eligible to receive the reward (e.g., customer must enter contest).

The inclusion of the time framework and an activity requirement are hallmarks of sales promotion.

Here are some examples of popular sales promotions activities:

- 5% cash back
- Buy one get one free
- Discounted prices
- Free finance facility
- Free gifts
- Free samples
- Joint Promotions between retailer and manufacturers
- Offering bonus points on every purchase
- Online lucky number checking
- Vouchers and coupons

(b) Publicity

Publicity refers to any non-paid communication to promote an organization or its products and services in public media. The publicity differs from advertisement in following senses.

(i) In case of advertisement, sponsor bears all the expenses while in publicity, media is not paid for the presentation.

(ii) In advertisement, how the message will be shown, what text will be used and when and where it will be shown, everything by and large is in the control of the concerned company, whose products are to be shown and who is bearing the broadcasting expenses.

Objectives of Publicity:

1. It assists in the launch of new goods and services at mass level.
2. It creates interest in the goods and services category.
3. Publicity helps in reposting a mature product.

Advantages of Publicity

Publicity has the following advantages:

1. The first advantage of publicity is that it is credible because nothing is paid for it and the presentation is entirely based on independent assessment.
2. Publicity appeals to mass audience at a time.
3. It costs nothing to an organization and is widely used means of promoting a product.
4. As publicity is done in newspapers, magazines, journals ands online newspapers etc, large number of general persons can be covered.

Methods of Publicity

There are various methods that can be employed to promote the product and / or its company. But the senior management has to decide what advertising vehicle should be selected on the basis of availability of funds, reach of the media, nature of competition and considering on whom the goods and services are aimed for. These media include:

(i) **Press publicity**: It means releasing news in the media about the company, its offerings etc.

(ii) **Speech**: It implies giving presentations through speeches about the company and its goods and services etc.

(iii) **Special events**: Sometimes, marketers organize some special

Strengths of Publicity

- Wide coverage
- Low cost
- More informative
- Timeliness
- Free form biasness

Weaknesses of Publicity

- Less / no control over message
- No repetition
- Not free always
- Difficult to control and time

events such as conferences, debates, seminars, workshops, awareness camps, games, quizzes, star nights, beauty contests, singing competitions etc.

(iv) **Sponsorships**: Under this mode of publicity, company sponsors some social activities dedicated to public welfare like sponsoring health check up camps, maintaining public parks, children parks, planting trees, blood donation camps, eye check up / operation camps etc.

(c) Advertising

Advertising is multidimensional. It is a form of mass communication, a powerful marketing tool, a component of the economic system, a means of financing the mass media, a social institution, and an art form, an instrument of business management, a field of employment and a profession. **Advertising** may be sign, a symbol, an illustration, an ad message in a magazine or newspaper, a commercial on the radio or on television, a circular dispatched through mail or a pamphlet etc. ***Non – personal*** advertising would mean that it is not on a person-to-person basis. Goods, Services, Ideas for action would mean making a consumer aware about the product of the firm. ***Paid by an identified sponsor*** implies that the advertiser has to pay the media for the services it seeks.

(d) Public Relations

It is essentially an art of persuasion in order to influence people. The process includes human behaviour and manner in which people react to certain situations. It is defined as "the management function which evaluates public attitude, identifies the policies and procedures of an organization for public interest and executes a programme of action (and communication) to earn public understanding and acceptance".

(e) Personal Selling

Personal Selling involves person-to-person communication with the prospect. It is a process of developing relationships, discovering needs, matching the appropriate products with these needs and communicating benefits through informing, reminding, or persuading. ***Personal selling*** is thus, considered as a process that adds value. The salesperson attempts to understand consumer's needs and fit the product to meet those needs.

Figure 21.5

The Changing Role of the Sales Persons

Strategies for Selling	Activities
Business Management	• Manage accounts and Territory strategies as a strategic business unit
	• Invest time and expenses in the most profitable opportunities
	• Sell to meet the clients total system and long term needs. Be a
Client Profit-Planning	• Become part of the clients' plan
Strategies	• Expand to other department

	• Find new uses for your product
	• Services are an important part of the offer at this point.
	• The customers become a client.
	• Perceive, classify and serve customers' needs.
Negotiation Strategies	• The product is adjusted to meet the customers' need.
Persuasion Strategies	• The representative tries to fit the customers into the existing product mix by skillfully overcoming objections.
Communication Strategies	• The representative is a personal communicator, providing product and service information close to the point of the buying decision.

Source: *Adapted From: M. Haven, J. Cribben and H. Keiser, Consultative Selling American Management Association, Inc. New York91970 eds., G.D. Huges and C.H. Singler 'Strategic Sales Management' Addison-Wesley Publishing Co. London,1983.*

Figure 21.6

Situations Conducive for Personal Selling

Undoubtedly, personal selling provides an effective and efficient solution to most of the selling problems. However, its economic efficiency relative to other element of the marketing mix needs to be thoroughly appraised. The most obvious situations where personal selling in an organization comparatively becomes effective and relevant are:

Category	Situations
Market	• A company is selling to a small number of large-size buyers. • A company sells in a small, local market or in government or institutional market. • An indirect channel of distribution is used for selling to merchant-middlemen only. • Desired middle men or agents are not available.
Company	• Purchases are valuable but infrequent. • The company is not in a position to identify and make use of suitable non-personal communication media.
Product	• A product requires personal attention to match specific consumer needs e.g. insurance policy. • Product has no or very poor brand loyalty. • Product requires after sales service. • Product requires demonstration like in most of the industrial products. • When a product is in the introductory state of its life cycle and requires creation of core demand. • When a product is of a high unit value like Xerox machine, computers etc.

PUSH Vs PULL RETAIL SALES PROMOTION

Some experts of the subject are of the view that all the retail promotion schemes can be divided into three categories namely push, pull and mixed. These are discussed as follows:

Push Strategy

Is se *sasta* aur *accha* kahin nahi!

A retail push strategy includes offers that convince trade intermediaries channel members to "push" the underline product through vigorous distribution channels to the ultimate customer via some sales promotion schemes and personal selling efforts. Under push strategy, the retail company promotes the product through a reseller who in turn promotes it to yet another reseller or the ultimate customer. The push strategy is used to convince retailers or wholesalers to stock a brand, provide a brand shelf space, encourage a brand in their advertisement drives, and/or push a brand to its ultimate customers. The usual tactics used in push strategy are: cash rebates, monetary or non-monetary allowances, buy-back schemes, free trial offer, contests, quizzes, promotional reminders, heavy discounts, and displays.

Big Apple moves on to second phase of expansion

Big Apple, a unit of Express Retail Services Pvt Ltd, completed its first phase of retail expansion with the opening of its 65th store at Karol Bagh in New Delhi. Big Apple stores are of an average 2,000 sq.ft format and are owned by the company. After completion of first phase, Big Apple plans to open another 100 stores as a part of IInd phase, and 200 stores in the IIIrd phase of expansion in Delhi and NCR. After covering the National Capital Region, Big Apple will further expand into different geographies like Gujarat and Karnataka, in keeping with its aim to eventually have a pan-India footprint.

Pull Strategy

A retail pull strategy efforts to get customers to pull the product from the manufacturer through its marketing channel. Under this strategy, company focuses its marketing communication efforts directly to customers with the hope that it encourages curiosity and requirement for the product at the end-consumer level. This strategy is often employed if distributors/agents are reluctant to sell a product because it receives as many customers as likely to go to retail outlets and request the product, thus pulling it through the retail channel. The objective of the pull strategy is to attract customers to try a new product, lure customers away from competitors' products, get consumers to weigh on a mature product, hold & reward loyal customers and build longlasting customer relationships. Usual tricks employed in retail pull strategy are: cash refunds, samples, coupons, and heavy rebate, premiums, promotional reminders, advertising specialties, loyalty schemes, rewards, mementoes, contests, quizzes and point-of-purchase (POP) displays. If the pull strategy is well prepared and implemented, it results in extraordinary retail sales. But it depends on the commitment and dedication of retail staff and management.

Figure : 21.7
Building Consumer Demand through Pull Strategy

Store Rs. 99 that offers everything for Rs.99 or less is a discounted store and seems akin to one dollar shop concept. For such stores to become successful, require high spending on advertising and consumer promotion to build up consumer demand for their offerings. Once the strategy is successful, consumers will ask their retailers for the products, the retailers will ask the wholesalers, and the wholesalers will ask the producers.

Mixed Strategy

As the very name implies, this strategy is the combination of above mentioned two strategies. Electronic and car dealers often use such type of strategy. Most of the car dealers near festival season advertise or offer cash discount or cash back offers to customers and dealer incentives which is the combination of both the push and pull strategies.

TIMING OF RETAIL SALES PROMOTION

Sales promotion has always been a controversial matter. Some experts are of the view that it is a wasteful expenditure. According to them, people buy when actually they are in need of some goods. Sales promotion efforts can attract them but cannot be helpful in forced buying decisions. If we talk about the companies' expenditure on marketing efforts, we find that these vary from industry to industry and then size to size. But one thing on which everyone will so agree that it has curved extremely in the last two decades throughout the world and is still rising. This question is awaiting to be answered that what is the exact time of sales promotion. Whether it should be adopted when a store is not doing well or it should run throughout the year? No one is able to give the answer of this question, some retailers and experts believe that sales promotion should be used only in case of decline in sales. They also argue that when a store or a brand or a product is performing well then what's the need for spending money on its promotion part. It is not the promotion effort but the quality and features of the product that attract the clients. What these retailers/marketers do not like is that almost hundred percent of the time sales promotion does not contribute towards its brand equity. In actual it spoils brand image. Intense advertising looks desperate and erodes the perceived value of a product displayed.

While others say if by spending few rupees, your sales increases four or five times then there is no harm in that sales promotion is done whole year or at any time. They view that sales promotion brings immediate payback to store's net sales. Sales promotion is flagrantly regarding making sales will go up very fast at minimum expenditure. This is the reason that MDs of public companies favour it and sometimes apply it to prop up the stock prices. For instance, because of the descending demands on sales of print media such as newspapers and magazines due to internet revolution, retailers have to resort to switching almost all of their marketing rupees to short-term sales promotion to protect circulation statistics and consequently future advertising returns. They also give good reason for the cost of sales promotion by saying that they can sample products which will give them reliable customers in coming future.

In short, it is right to say that experience is the best teacher. It depends on a particular store that sales promotion drive should be a regular exercise or should be adopted once in a while. The only time that sales promotion may be a justifiable long-term means of building a product sales is for a launch, or perhaps a re-launch. Next thing if in your promotion policy, trial is one of your marketing goals, then sampling, free gifts, free items and money-off tactics are legitimate ways of influencing people will give you a go. Nonetheless these are improbable to work without other elements of the retail marketing mix.

HOW TO MAXIMIZE SALES PROMOTION BENEFITS

The keys to maximize sale promotion benefits normally come from two areas namely (1) The creation of perceived value and (2) The strength of the communication.

Perceived value is the value that the consumer places on what you are offering. It is key to offer something which consumers think is worth a lot but which costs you a little. Before the great FM radio popularity in 2004, FM radio had a perceived for Indian retailers. So if you had put FM radio on a magazine, watch, bicycle or other product selling for a rupee or less that looks would look like a fantastic deal to the consumer. Now the perceived value of free FM radio's is much lower, because they are so commonly given away and people may have poor experiences with them.

The strength of communication is especially significant at how effective you are at combining the sales promotion with other parts of the marketing mix. For example, if your sales promotion is at point of-purchase, certain words are most effective at triggering a response: Free is best, Bonus or extra is good, Long-winded explanations are bad, so just get straight to the point. Certain colour combinations work best, with white out of red (think Diwali sales) being the punchiest and most attention grabbing. Fluorescent is also fine, but think about the image of your brand and attitude of your store's employees.

Market Segmentation

It is a key strategic decision that refers to the division of customers into some meaningful buyer groups or into sub-markets. The market segmentation can be done on the basis of variables as socio-economic characteristics of buyer groups (age, income, sex, education, occupation, family size etc) or geographical basis or buyer behaviour or industrial categories. The main benefits of market segmentation is that the retail organizations get alerted to the needs of different buyer groups. Secondly, a retail organization can allocate its marketing efforts and budgets on the basis of the customers' response from each buyer groups.

Case let

India Retail Opportunity Unveils

The shop is the most substantive unraveling of intellectual and information exchange for the retail business in the Indian subcontinent. It presents the business of retail in the region to a global audience with the express aim of facilitating, understanding about and encouraging investment in this massive marketplace.

At India Retail Forum, it is a congregation of some of the best retail brands, companies and minds from across the globe, from diverse retail-related segments, from retail real estate and design and architecture, to visual merchandising, retail support and technology. Indeed, Indian retail has to play a part larger than its definition implies. The industry has a catalyst's role to fulfil in the country's economic destiny, a destiny that is finally finding itself. Economic prosperity also means higher standards of living and higher consumption levels and only an efficient and organized retail sector can ensure and sustain this growing demand of the evolved consumer. The challenges of the newly found growth are tremendous and as they say can make or undo the story. Which is why, The Shop is a market date for all the industry's head honchos, brands, retailers, mall and shopping center developers, real estate firms, architects and designers, and logistics and technology support vendors.

In essence, the shop takes to the world and gets the world to understand and appreciate the fastest-growing consumerist region of modern times.

Q. What message this case let conveys?

COST AND BENEFIT ANALYSIS OF SALES PROMOTION

What the cost of a sales promotion program is for a retail store, depends on the change in store's sale. Before framing a promotion policy, retailer should calculate the cost of the promotion programme and the benefit accrued from its successful completion. If the cost of the discount or gift offered is not in proportion to the margin a retail store receives from each incremental sale, it in long run can make a profitable store into a loss making.

One big cost of promoting at point of sale is that of rewarding everyone who buys your product not just the incremental customers you were aiming for. So you will effectively be paying the people who would have bought your product anyway – another reason why sales promotion is most profitable for launches, as no one was purchasing the product before.

NEW TRENDS IN SALES PROMOTION

With the entry of foreign retail players and the increased use of ICT (Information and Communication Technology), the old and traditional techniques are being replaced by new techniques and experiments. Game is old but rules are new and still changing. The important trends in sales promotion include:

Buy One Get One Free (BOGOF) – The trend of giving one item free with one purchase of one item is becoming very popular not only in urban areas but in rural/sub-urban areas too. For example, if pack of bread is priced at Rs.10 and its actual manufacturing cost is Rs.3 and you two breads for Rs.10, you will be still in profit especially if sales increase due to this BOGOF offer. In retailing this practice is actually known as a premium promotion tactic. The stores use this method because due to increased sales they are able to get benefit because of economies of scale.

Figure: 21.8

Increasing Sales through BOGOF Offers

Today in the world of retailing, "Buy one, get one free" offers are common form of promoting sales. Universally, this mode of sales promotion is known as BOGOF and is regarded as one of the most effective forms of special offers for goods. Initially BOGOF offer was a random, end of season or stock clearance method used by garments' shopkeepers who were left with a large quantity of stock that they were looking to sell quickly. But these days, be it water park, PVR, or places of leisure and enjoyment, everywhere BOGOF offers are being offered.

Customer Relationship Management (CRM) – The concept of CRM is of two fold: it is a part of retail strategy that aims at creating customers for long-term say whole life and on the other hand, CRM is largely technology driven. The main focus of CRM is on customers rather than products it offers. Examples are incentives such as bonus points, collecting numbers are very popular. Besides this, there are several other examples of CRM, from petrol pumps to malls. This increases longlasting relationship with the customers.

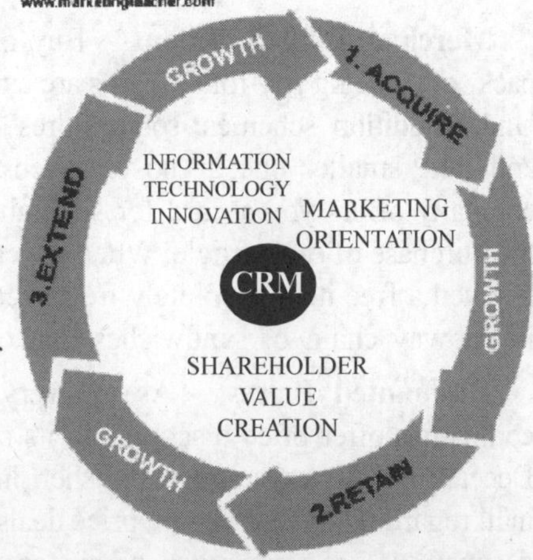

New Media – With the change in technologies, e-retail, online buying, and vending machines are the fashion of the day. SMS, e-mails, websites and mobile phones are used for the purpose of placing orders. For example Nestle a Swiss MNC printed some individual codes on KIT-KAT chocolate packaging, whereby a customer after buying it, would enter the code into a dynamic website to know whether if he had won a prize/gift or not. Customers also had option to check these printed text codes via their cellular phones. In India, some companies have also started use of such techniques as experimental method.

Customers Expectations - The onslaught of sales promotion activity over the last several decades has eroded the value of the short-term requirement to act on sales promotions. Many customers are conditioned to expect a promotion at the time of purchase otherwise they may withhold or even alter their purchase if a promotion is not present. For instance, food shoppers are inundated on a weekly basis with such a wide variety of sales promotions that their loyalty to certain products has been replaced by their loyalty to current value items (i.e., products with a sales promotion). For marketers, the challenge is to balance the advantages of short-term promotions offer versus the potential to erode loyalty to the product.

E-Retailing - Sales promotions are delivered to customers in many ways such as by mail, in-person or within print media. However, the Internet and mobile technologies, such as cell phones, present marketers with a number of new delivery options. For example, the combination of mobile devices and geographic positioning technology will soon permit marketers to target promotions to a customer's physical location. This will allow retailers and other businesses to issue sales promotions such as electronic coupons, to a customer's mobile device when they are near the location where the coupon can be used.

Tracking - As we discussed in our coverage of advertising, tracking customer's response to marketers' promotional activity is critical for measuring success of an advertisement. In sales promotion, tracking is also used. For instance, grocery retailers, whose customers are in possession of loyalty cards have the ability to match customer sales data to coupon use. This information can then be sold to coupon marketers who may use the information to get a better picture of the buying patterns of those responding to the coupon.

Merchandising Additions Buy one litre get 200 ml free with the pack, buy one kg pay for 750 gms are examples of merchandising addition. Under addition schemes, some stores offer schemes like buy big pack and take smaller one at no extra cost. Besides this, sometimes some company offers you a card for six/eight spaces for pasting stickers with the purchase of each article. When the card's spaces are full, the consumer is given a free item absolutely free of cost. In India, the popular example is Subway chain of sandwiches that comes under addition scheme.

Discounted Prices – As the very name implies, under this promotional scheme, companies offer price discounts to its customers. Some of the budget airlines such as Air Deccan, Go Airways and Kingfisher, inform their regular and loyal customers through e-mail regarding any latest low-price deals once new flights are introduced or some additional destinations are announced within or outside India.

Figure 21.9

Building Customer Traffic through Discounted Prices

Courtesy: *Company Website*

Further, some new ways of sales promotion are in practice. We don't give notice to them but they are working and we even have seen them. Have a look on few sales promotion schemes. These are not very popular but some stores are using on mass scale like. **Joint promotions** drives between brands owned by a retail company or with another company's brands. For example, fast food restaurants and soft drink companies like Pepsi and Coca Cola usually run sales promotion programmes where caps, toys, T-shirts, hanging pens and film tickets relating to a specific movie release are offered with promoted meals in the restaurants.

Figure: 21.10

Kingfisher Airline's Discounted Pricing

Kingfisher Airlines is India's first and only 5-Star airline and the only one to offer a premium first class service on domestic routes. Besides being the first and the only airline to offer in-flight entertainment on every seat in the domestic skies, Kingfisher Airlines is the only one to offer LIVE TV with 16 channels of live & exciting content. Kingfisher Airlines has received 30 awards for innovation, customer responsiveness and was voted the ~Best New Airline of the Year~ within months of its launch due to its lucrative offers and attractive pricing policy.

Courtesy: *Company Website*

Free samples – for example, tasting of food and drink at sampling points in supermarkets, trade fairs and exhibitions like 'Good Living', 'Art of Living' annual fairs at Pragati Maiden in New Delhi. For example, Milk Mix (a flavored fizzy drink) was given away to potential consumers at supermarkets, International Trade Fair and at in Delhi.

Besides this, the craze towards some specific cause-related and fair-trade products that raise instant money for the purpose of charity and the less well off farmers and orphanages have become very popular.

SUMMARY

Sales promotion is one of the most valuable and effective promotion strategies adopted by retailers. It refers to communication strategies that are designed to act as a direct inducement, a value addition or some rebate to the customers. Normally, it is designed for immediate increase in retail sales. It provides extensive tactical measures to retailers to manage internal or external impediments to sales or profits. It includes various communication tactics that attempt to provide added value or incentives to customers, agents, wholesalers, retailers or other corporate clients to excite instant sales. These efforts can attempt to excite product curiosity, trial or bulk buying. Whatever the case one thing is sure that now customer is the 'king'. These traditional '*kirana*' stores now cannot sell only those items or brands on which they get maximum commission. Further, the benefit of these sales promotion techniques is that customers have become more cautious about their rights and prices.

CASES

Case Study 1

Marketing to kids - The New legislation

The new regulations will make it illegal for fast food outlets to encourage consumption of their foods with give-away toys or of 'junk food' to be promoted with the use of cartoon characters. Marketing of sweets aimed at children will be curtailed and even some soft drinks will have to re-think their marketing strategies. The Health Department published its second draft of the proposed regulations in July 2007, which the department says is aimed at ensuring honest and responsible labeling and marketing as part of public health attempts to prevent obesity and promote good health[3].

The Advertising Standard Authority believes there is a need for the regulations: "What is important about these regulations is that there are huge international concerns about advertising junk food to children. There is definitely a growing concern about the problem of childhood obesity and advertisements for 'unhealthy' products have been part of the blame", says Lillian Mlambo, ASA communications manager. "If South Africa does not keep up with international concerns, with international norms, we could find ourselves in a difficult position."

Nick Tselentis, legal and regulatory affairs manager of the Consumer Goods Council of South Africa, has prepared a code of practice to guide the industry when it comes to the issue of advertising to children, as well as a suitable amendment to the current code, for the ASA to adopt. However, The ASA does not have the several questions which are currently being considered in a proposal to the Government, which has not yet been completed; including the definition of what is foodstuff and which foods will be governed by this act, as well as the Trademark Act itself.

In certain instances, the regulations will directly contradict the provisions of the Trademark Act, which protects the likes of Simba, Niknaks, Ronald McDonald, The Baker's Man and Chappies. In these instances, for example, it is believed that only a protracted legal battle would decide the future of the brands. That's one of the reasons Yellowwood's Andy Rice says the proposed regulations are nothing more than a 'dumbing down of society'. "These regulations deny any responsibility to adults or their children.

The industry should be sitting up and taking notice because self-regulation is always better than imposed regulation, which usually becomes quite draconian. "Famous Brands, for example, took the view that they will simply stop actively promoting kids meals and this has not affected their sales at all". Alda Heunis of egg Marketing and Communications agrees: "Children ultimately grow up to be adult consumers. Instead of just regulating, one should also be educating."

She adds that obesity amongst children is as much the result of unethical marketing on the part of certain food and snack brands as it is the lack of proper marketing on the part of many health institutions, industries and brands: "where are the Teletubby-branded apples?". She agrees that the marketing of food products has to be done in an ethical manner, but stresses that different elements contribute to childhood obesity, all of which have to be addressed.

Network BBDO Simba Account Manager Lucia Gorgoglione says her client has recognized that its advertising cannot appeal directly to kids anymore by using characters, toys etc and has basically changed its approach: "Our new approach is to encourage moms to buy chips for the family and kids, but to do it responsibly. We encourage them to lead an active life and exercise, then snack in moderation".

But the move is more radical than that. Gorgoglione says Simba are taking steps to re-introduce Simba as a character who looks after the well-being of the family and encourages a healthy lifestyle. "The new legislation is an attempt to look after the consumer's health and well-being as opposed to marketers just pushing sales.... It's very positive and marketers are also supporting this initiative completely". Kellogg's recently agreed to raise the nutrition value of cereals and snacks it markets to children.

The company avoided a lawsuit threatened by parents and nutrition advocacy groups in America who were worried about increasing child obesity. The Kellogg's Global Nutrient Criteria (KGNC) apply to all products currently marketed to children around the world, including SA favorites Coco Pops, Froot Loops and Frosties, so Kellogg South Africa will not need to reformulate cereals or change its advertising strategies. Marketers are embracing the change, but it's still a long road for many brands as they seek the new opportunities hidden within this revolution.

Questions for Discussion:

1 Why the marketing of sweets aimed at children will be curtailed and soft drink companies will have to re-think their marketing strategies?

2 What are the pros and cons of having junk foods? As a retailer, would you want junk food in your store? Why and why not?

3 Describe the three advantages of new legislation that will have an impact on customers' health and well being?

4 "It appears that marketers have adopted a pro-active approach and are already exploring and implementing changes to keep in line with proposed new regulations that will alter the way certain foods are marketed to young children". Explain?

Case Study 2

What keeps a brand on top?

To determine the influence of advertising spend on being a Top Brand and although there are many definitions of what a top brand is, in this context I'm specifically referring to the Markinor/Sunday Times definition of a Top Brand, which comes in two forms: Single, spontaneous questions like 'favourite brand' and 'favourite advertiser' and a neatly-packaged metric called the Brand Relationship Score. Just so that we are all on the same page, the 'Brand Relation Score' is an assemblage of three metrics: spontaneous awareness, level of trust and degree of differentiation.

So how does advertising spend influence Top Brand status? Thanks to Neilson's ADEX data (advertising spent on all media types: TV, Print, Radio, Cinema, direct mail, Outdoor and Internet), we are able to unpack this relationship. Let's start simple, with our 'favourite brand' question. Remember, it's a single, spontaneous question. What did we find when we correlated advertising spend to the Top 10 brands in this category?

As it happens, the correlation is fairly weak, anaemic, even. To link to our 'favourite advertiser', question is stronger, but the power of the almighty advertising brand is not so strong as one would expect even here.

So what's going on? Does advertising spend not influence on my brand's status? It does, of course, but the path is not as simple as we'd hope. The answer lies in the unbundling of the Brand Relationship Score and the appreciation of how the three weighted metrics interact to yield a strong brand. Now of course we can't expect consumers to tell us how these three concepts work together in their minds, although many marketes have tried! Why? Because when we interface with brands, we are all bird-spotters.

Borrowing from Malcolm Gladwell's inimitable thinking on how we make lasting and fundamentals decisions based on the smallest sliver of encounters, the transitory manner in which we interact with brands means that we have become adept brand-spotters. Gladwell describes ornithologists' ability to correctly categorize birds from the briefest of glances as their unconscious detection of the bird's jizz – its essence (derived from US slang giss, meaning 'general impression of size and shape').

This instinctive identification of shapes, colors and angles ofcourse resembles the way in which we are able to live (semi) sanely in the ubiquitous world of brands. So, if we are incessantly thin-slicing brands and making decisions based on almost no conscious thought whatsoever, how can I influence my Brand's jizz and where does my intensity of advertising spend fit into all of this?

Let's begin with ***Top Brands'*** third metric, 'differentiation', since this is a brand's ultimate end-state in order for this thin-slicing to be successful. We need to differentiate our brands effectively enough so that the most miniscule of servings beguiles our consumers. 'Differentiation', as we measure it, means that it would not matter a great deal if that brand could no longer be bought. So how does ad spend influence the perception of differentiation? Unfortunately, we find no relationship whatsoever. This is intuitive, of course, because if moola alone was the answer to differentiation, brands appearing in our single 'favourite brand' question would be closely correlated to spend.

So where do I see a return on my advertising rand? Let's turn our attention to a ***brand's keystone*** – spontaneous awareness. Ofcourse, things like how early your brand is mentioned in response to this question matter, so we up weigh the familiarity frontrunners. Determining the elasticity between the level of advertising expenditure and the level of achieved awareness does not reveal any new news. We found once again that one's likelihood to mention a brand spontaneously was closely correlated to the amount marketers spent on their brand's exposure. The link between spend and awareness is stronger in high-touch industries where our relationship is ongoing, such a telecom or retail banking, as opposed to the automotive industry, for example, where our purchases are much more infrequent.

So what's the link? I can influence the ability of my consumers to summon up my brand in their mind but what's the point if it is interchangeable with other brands? How do I ensure a dazzling jizz? This is where metric number two – the degree of trust and confidence consumers have in our brands – provides the answer. When correlated with differentiation, we found the relationship to be strongly positive, thus the more trust we have in a brand, the more it makes a material difference to our lives if we can't purchase that brand in the future.

And spontaneous awareness, as expected, has an impact on the level of trust in brands because meaning gets infused into brands via advertising. This finding is also supported by something called the 'Zajonc effect', which talks about the fact that the humans don't initially like rare or unfamiliar things. The more we see the same thing, the more we like it and hence trust it. So, trust becomes the adhesive between spend, awareness and differentiation.

The trick in the trust equation is that the yin to advertising's yang is delivery. A brand is a promise made and a promise kept (Interbrand Sampson). Essentially this all culminates into some piercing questions. If the brand war is based on a consumer's coup d'oeil, or the power of glance, how are we ensuring a consistent jizz and in what ways are we measuring and leveraging this?

Just like birders, we infer things from what we learn and what we experience and if trust is the critical factor which binds these two together, are we using this as a strategic filter in the business of brand building?

REVIEW QUESTIONS

True and False Questions

1. Retail sales promotion is a scheme undertaken by a business to encourage an increase in store's sales, practice or trial of a product or service.

2. Retail sales promotion is one of the least important aspects of sales promotional mix.
3. Sales promotion techniques are used in retailing business to stimulate trial purchases.
4. On checkout end the customer is provided a coupon or a scratch card based on total quantity purchased.
5. A contest requires the customers to compare their knowledge and skills.
6. In case of sweepstakes, the customer only needs to enter into the competition on the basis of the amount paid to a retail store.
7. Contests are particular promotions schemes giving value to loosers based on skills they show as compared to others.
8. Dangler is a sign that affects when a customer walks by it and can make up the mind of customers to purchase.
9. Free-standing insert (FSI) is a coupon booklet that is inserted into the local newspaper for delivery to its readers.
10. Glorifier is a large size stage that brings down a product lower than other products during display time.
11. Lipstick board is a board on which stylish messages are written in crayon to attract competitors.
12. Loss leader is the price of a popular product that is reduced for long term period in order to fuel sales of other daily used items.
13. Loyalty rewards schemes collect some numbers, points, miles, or credits for every purchase and then redeem them for rewards during some bill payment or further buying.
14. Under 'more merchandising scheme', reward is given in the form of some merchandise addition.
15. Under mobile coupons scheme, coupons are made available on a cell phone and customers show the offer on a cell phone to the retailer or a salesperson for cash redemption.
16. Necker, a popular and old scheme of sales promotion is not used in automobile sector.
17. Under 'on-line coupon scheme', coupons are made available at the store shelf where customers print them out and take them to the retail store for exemption or redemption.
18. Under online interactive sponsorship games, customers play an interactive game linked with the promoted product.
19. Under on-shelf coupon scheme, coupons are available online where the product is presented.
20. Price deal is a temporary reduction offer in the price of some retail item such as happy hour menu scheme in bars and restaurants.
21. Price-packed deal is a sort of packaging deal that offers a consumer a certain percentage more of the product for fewer prices.

22. Vouchers and coupons are often seen in newspapers and magazines.
23. A promotional product is the commonly used methods of sales promotion by which company with some purchase of goods, gives some reminders with the company name or stamp that serve as reminders of the actual product.
24. B2B stands for business to *bazaar*.
25. B2C stands for *bazaar* to customer.
26. Product, price, place, purity are the basic elements of any retail marketing mix.
27. Pricing helps an organization to achieve its objective.
28. A sales promotion can be defined as a non-paid, personal form of communication that offers incentive to potential customers for visiting a store and/or purchase products during a specific period of time.
29. Publicity refers to any paid communication to promote an organization or its products and services in public media.
30. Personal selling is a process of developing relationships, discovering needs, matching the appropriate products with these needs, and communicating benefits through informing, reminding, or persuading.

Answers

1. True	2. False	3. True	4. True
5. True	6. True	7. False	8. True
9. True	10. False	11. False	12. False
13. True	14. True	15. True	16. False
17. False	18. True	19. False	20. False
21. False	22. True	23. True	24. False
25. False	26. False	27. True	28. False
29. False	30. True		

Multiple Choice Questions

1. A sales promotion can be defined as a .... form of communication.
   (*a*) Paid, personal (*b*) Paid, non-personal
   (*c*) Non-paid, personal (*d*) Non-paid, non-personal.
2. The objective of any sales program is
   (*a*) To increase the store's sales
   (*b*) To create awareness about product
   (*c*) Both of the above.
   (*d*) None of the above.
3. Dangler is used to:
   (*a*) tighten the store's security
   (*b*) make up the mind of customers to purchase.
   (*c*) distract the customers' attention towards display

(*d*) make store's accounting more effective.

4. Neckers are usually popular in:
   (*a*) automobile sector (*b*) pharmaceutical sector
   (*c*) packaged foods (*d*) consumer electronics.
5. POP displays are widely used
   (*a*) to clear the old stock (*b*) to sell seasonal goods.
   (*c*) to prevent store theft (*d*) to enhnance stores sales
6. The most widely used technique for B2B promotion is:
   (*a*) distributing samples (*b*) price reductions.
   (*c*) trade shows (*d*) all of the above
7. Trading up is a practice to:
   (*a*) add higher priced product to the existing line
   (*b*) Increase the prices of goods for some period.
   (*c*) increase the store's product quality.
   (*d*) Increase the store's trading hours.
8. The main strength of publicity is.
   (*a*) Low cost. (*b*) No repetition
   (*c*) Easy to control (*d*) Biased.
9. Trade directed method of sales promotion is normally adopted:
   (*a*) during seasonal changes
   (*b*) during festival and marriage seasons.
   (*c*) during high degree of competition.
   (*d*) during inflated economy.
10. Placing an order for a pen drive online is an example of:
   (*a*) B2B (*b*) B2C
   (*c*) Trade-in (*d*) POP display,

Answers

1. b	2. c	3. b	4. a
5. d	6. d	7. a	8. a
9. b	10. b		

Check Your Progress

1. List some sources of Information?
2. Name common items that are distributed as free gifts?
3. What is advertisement?
4. What is B2B?
5. What is B2C?

6. What is BLC?
7. What is BOGOF?
8. What is cash refund?
9. What is contest?
10. What is CPM?
11. What is CRM?
12. What is dangler?
13. What is FSI?
14. What is gift voucher?
15. What is ICT?
16. What is POP?
17. What is Promotion Mix?
18. What is service pricing?
19. What is trademark?
20. Why glorifier is used?

Short Answers Questions

1. Discuss the term 'joint promotion'?
2. What are the objectives of sales promotion?
3. Explain various types of sales promotion techniques?
4. Discuss the relevance of trade shows in sales promotion?
5. Explain the concept of pull and push sales promotion?
6. Write a short note on new trends in retailing?
7. What do you mean by promotional mix?
8. Is sales promotion necessary for retailing business?
9. Some experts say that sales promotion should not be a continuous exercise? Do you agree with this? Explain few techniques of sales promotion with its merits and demerits?
10. List few promotional vehicles with its merits and demerits?

Long Answers Questions

1. Describe how a retail advertisement campaign can be planned? What are its various steps?
2. Unlike advertisement, publicity is managed not by the advertisement firm but by a third party. Explain? Also tell the process of publicity management?
3. Discuss the concept of joint promotion with its merits and demerits?
4. Discuss the objectives of retail sales promotion?
5. What are the major sales promotion techniques?
6. Discuss the relevance of trade shows in sales promotion?

Applied Questions

1. Critically explain the changing role of personal selling?
2. Do you agree that a sales promotion job requires a degree of mental soundness, and physical stamina to perform routine tasks. Discuss.
3. 'In the changing business environment, it is often referred to that sales persons are in better position than past'. Do you agree with this statement? Justify your answer with proper examples and real corporate illustrations.
4. 'Push strategy is a one-way communication best suited to a company marketing consumer product with a poor brand loyalty'. Discuss.
5. To what extent timing of retail sales promotion influence the retail sales? Explain.

UNIT 22

RETAIL COMMUNICATION MIX

LEARNING OBJECTIVES

- Understanding how a retailer can build brand equity of his store and its underlying products.
- Describing the role of communication in retailing.
- Explaining the methods of communicating with customers.
- Understanding how to plan retail communication process.
- Discussing the procedure for implementing and evaluating retail communication programs.

"Communication is the foundation of all business relationships. To effectively communicate, we must realize that we are all different in the way we perceive the world and use this understanding as a guide to our communication with others."

Anthony Robbins

INTRODUCTION

After understanding how retailers develop their merchandise budget plans, merchandise and price the merchandise, next step is to know how to inform the customers about the products they want to sell. The **communication** program intimates the customers about the presence of a store and its merchandise uniqueness. Communication program invites the customers, attract them and lure them to visit the store. This chapter talks about the role of communication in retailing, various communication methods and describes the procedure of planning, implementing and evaluating a retail communication program.

RETAIL COMMUNICATION MIX

In order to attract customers towards their products and services, retailers adopt various methods (paid and/or unpaid). These methods invite customers to visit their stores and make purchases. All these methods adopted by retailers to communicate to the target audience regarding the presence of a store come under the category of retail communication mix.

Over a period of time, due to change in lifestyle, status of rapidly increasing middle class and scarcity of time to shop has made customers more demanding. Now in India, most of the families have more than one earning hand and have several commitments to attend. Further, increasing distance and traveling hours between workplace and residence compel the customers to visit the store that provide most of the daily used items under one roof. It gave birth to mart, shopping plazas, super bazaar, hyper markets and recently grown mall culture. Now the situation especially in metros is that within one kilometer of area, one may find more than one mall, resulting in tough competition and decreased profit margins. Hence, the significance of continuous communication has been felt amidst retailers backed by heavy expense on sales promotion.

ROLE OF COMMUNICATION IN RETAILING

It takes years to build a brand. Once a retailer has established himself as a brand, it will provide value to both the retailers and the customers. Brands not only convey the name of a retailer but about the retailer's mix and the shopping experience at a particular store. One thing should be noted that in this regard that brand is a name, symbol or logo that indicates the items of merchandise offered by a retailer with the objective of differentiating those items of merchandise from the competitors. But under retailing context, the retailer itself is a brand that indicates particular set of merchandise offered by a retailer. Brands also affect the customers' confidence in making buying decisions. Visiting and buying brands (private/manufacturer) satisfy customers and save their buying time. Brands increase retailers' profit margins. When customers are loyal to a particular store, retailers instead of Every Day Low Pricing (EDLP) policy adopt premium pricing policy and also save their expenses by limiting sales promotion programs. Further, for brands it becomes easy to launch a new product due to brand loyality and established image.

Building Brand Value

Building brand value is a must in recent years especially in retail sector. As in India, new and new brands are entering into competition, they are also making the competition tougher for the existing brands, who are not only facing competition from the traditional '***kirana* store**' but also from the well established global brands. Following are the tasks that a retailer performs to build its brand value for the store's brands or the store itself. These are:

1. **Increasing brand awareness** – Brand awareness is the expansion of a brand to the customers. It is a measure/proportion of target customers that remember a brand name or recognize your brand as yours. It always does not mean that they prefer or buy your brand always but recall it/identify it.
2. **Associations** – Brand awareness is the very first step to build brand value but this task can be accomplished by associations that customers develop with a brand. Association is anything that brings customers close to the brand or linked to customers' memory. For example, in case of Vishal Mega Mart stores,

associations that consumers might have are white-pink color stripes, clean stores, well arranged merchandise, clock room at the entrance. Similarly, in case of Vodafone outlets associations are red color furniture, dog's picture, 'ready to help' slogans, well dressed office staff etc. Experience has shown that these associations greatly affect the consumer buying behaviour and his perception towards brand image. For example, when somebody thinks of having a burger, McDonalds' name comes automatically in his mind. Even you have seen small kids in your families or nearby, how they compel their parents to visit these McDonalds outlet for want of 'free attractive balloons'. The usual practice to develop associations as adopted by Indian brands (retailers) are:

(i) Merchandise Uniqueness: Some retailers want that their customers should remember them as and when they need a particular merchandise category. For example, McDonald would like to have consumers associate its name with burgers, Pizza Hut for pizza, Sagar Ratna for South Indian food, KB's Fairprice shops for cheap grocery, Haldiram's for hygienic food preparations, MDH for spices, Bata for quality shoes etc.

(ii) Pricing policy: Pricing policy also helps in developing association with the brand name. For example, Rs.199, Rs.499, Rs.599.99 in case of BATA shoes, Sony products for high range, Chinese electronics for affordable prices.

(iii) Unique Lifestyle: Some retailers would want to have consumers' associate its name with their particular lifestyle. Like Himalaya Drug Co. presents itself as a safe herbal healthcare science.

(iv) Unique properties: Some retailers associate themselves with the consumers by way of presenting some unique attributes like home delivery convenience etc. For instance, 'Six to Ten' retail stores are famous for their convenient timings. Eureka Forbes' Aquaguard Water Purifier is famous for home demonstrations-cum-delivery.

3. **Continuous Recall**: A powerful brand defines how a firm is unique and set it apart from others. Today, a customer is aware about your brand but tomorrow will he be, is difficult to say? Therefore, being consistent with your branding is essential to firm's recognition. A retailer needs to depict the same message over a period of time through its communication. This consistent reinforcement results in consistent behaviour on the part of consumers. For communicating effectively with customers, a retailer has several options in its **integrated marketing communication** (IMC) programme. IMC is a programme that is composed of all the elements of communications to deliver a precise and consistent message. In short, **IMC** programme is the combination of various communication tools, such as:

- Advertising
- Sales promotion
- Publicity

- Direct marketing
- Public Relations, and
- Personal Selling

METHODS OF COMMUNICATION

If we look into types of communication methods, we will find that in today's world of retailing, there exists clear difference between the two classifications of communication methods. Basically these are divided into two broad categories; (i) Paid and (ii) Unpaid. Under each category there is division with regard to personal and impersonal communications as shown in figure 22.1 as under.

Figure 22.1
Methods of Communication

	Impersonal	Personal
Paid	• Sales Promotions • Advertising • Store Atmosphere • Websites	• Personal Selling • E-Mail
Unpaid	Publicity	• Word of Mouth

(A) PAID IMPERSONAL COMMUNICATIONS

Following methods come under paid impersonal communications.

(I) Sales Promotion

Retail sales promotion is a scheme undertaken by a business to encourage an increase in store's sales, practice or trial of a product or service. In this process, a store persuades the customer to buy a particular product through normal personal selling. Today, sales promotion has various forms. Time and again they are innovative and original, and hence a complete list of all existing techniques is nearly not possible. Sales promotion techniques are used in retailing business to stimulate trial purchases. This is generally done when a store wants to catch the attention of new customers. It involves various communication tricks that are used to provide added value or incentives to customers, retailers, wholesalers, or other retail store customers to excite instant sales.

(II) Advertising

An advertising campaign has a lot of significance to a retail firm. It not only promotes the organization's sales but also may change the fate of a retail firm. A careful consideration of several factors like the nature of competition, consumers' attitude, products' features, availability of funds, reach of advertising media etc are must.

(III) Store Atmosphere and Visual Merchandising

Store atmosphere is the key aspect for communicating the retailer's image to the customers. It is the ambience created within a store to communicate information about the store's offerings that gives an idea about store's pricing policy, varieties and fashionability of its offerings. It helps the retailer in knowing that where and how many racks/shelves should be arranged? Where and at what gap they will be arranged? What item will be placed at which shelf? In short, stratosphere gives all major and minor information about the merchandise arrangement.

Visual Merchandising (VM)

Visual Merchandising (VM) is the art of creating visual displays and arranging merchandise assortments within a store to improve the layout and presentation and to increase traffic and sales which puts the merchandise in spotlight. VM informs the visitors, creates desire and finally augments the selling process. This is an area where the Indian retail industry, particularly, the unorganized stores lack adequate knowledge and expertise. This inadequacy is best reflected in poor product display and communication during various promotional events. For instance, in clothing stores, mannequins are commonly used as a way to promote products and apparel accessories.

(IV) Websites

Website is the most recently developed way of communication with customers. Retailers have been increasingly using websites to build their brand image and to communicate with the consumers about the followings:

- Information about the company
- Lines of businesses
- Store's Offerings
- Special Offers
- Prices
- Store's location - from where customers can buy merchandise
- How to place orders
- Special discounts (if any)
- Store's ranking/position in the industry
- How to contact

(B) PAID PERSONAL COMMUNICATIONS

Personal Selling

As the very name implies, in this sort of communication, sales staff assist customers directly (face to face) and satisfy their needs and wants through exchange of information. Personal attention is the integral part for the success of personal selling. Personal selling can be at a store level or at customers' residence or at their place of work.

E-Mail

Just a few years ago, e-mail communication used to be a method of communication with nears and dears. But due to technological advancement, its credibility and lightening speed has made it an essential lifeline to revolutionize business communication. It basically involves sending messages over the internet. These days, retailers are using this method to communicate following information:

(i) About the company
(ii) Line of businesses
(iii) About new launch
(iv) About new sales promotion programmes
(v) Franchisee information etc.

(C) UNPAID IMPERSONAL COMMUNICATIONS

Publicity

Publicity is one component of promotion which gives some sort of positive or negative image on the basis of activities done by the store. For example, if a retail store gives huge donation for some noble cause, it attracts media's attention and then leads to media coverage. It has been experienced that publicity is more effective in tone for promotion than advertising. However, stores should refrain from getting into controversial areas to avoid any negative publicity which may adversely affect its image amongst the target audience.

Publicity is non-personal communication, which is typically in the form of a news story that is transmitted through the mass media. The purpose of publicity is to draw favourable attention to a company and/or its products without having to pay the media for it. One product that received an incredible amount of publicity was Viagra. Sometimes, a film – especially one that is controversial – can generate a great deal of publicity.

(D) UNPAID PERSONAL COMMUNICATIONS

Word of Mouth Communication

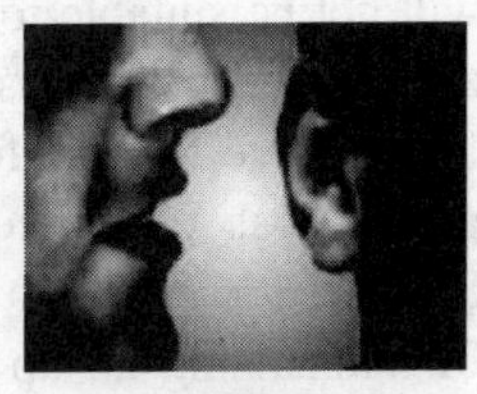

This type of communication belongs to unpaid personal communication. It is basically the reference to pass the message verbally by face to face spoken communication or some sort of telephonic conversation. It includes a variety of sub-categories like blog, viral, buzz, cause, grass root, influencer and social media marketing. Because of personal nature of communication between individuals without paying anything (Rupees), make it unpaid personal communication. It is firmly believed that message transferred in this way travels very fast and has an added layer of confidence.

RETAIL COMMUNICATION PROCESS

As discussed earlier, all means that a retailer adopts to communicate the store's specific message to the customer constitute a retail communication. A retail communication programme should follow a particular process for its success. These are:

1. Planning the Retail Communication Programme

This is the first step in developing a retail communication programme. Each retailer knows that it is not only the matter of gaining profits but also to survive for a long time. Therefore, he decides about communication objective initially aimed for a large traffic flow so that store should get maximum branding and there on, a retailer tries to satisfy the consumers' demand category-wise. Communication objectives are planned for both long and short term.

Long-Term Communication Objectives

These objectives belong to long period, say, over one to three years or even more than that. These objectives, a retailer would not like to change in the short run as it takes years to achieve these goals but once the underlined objectives are achieved, these cannot be overcome by the competitors in the short run. Examples of long-term objectives are: (i) to create a strong brand image for the store, and (ii) to create a strong brand loyalty towards retailer. Hence, it has been said that these are not achieved overnight.

Short Term Communication Objectives

As the name implies, these objectives keep on changing as per the market trend. For instance, during festival season, a retailer wants to attract footfall so he designs his communication strategy that lures the customer to visit the store during particular period of time, say, before Diwali or Christmas, Companies offer lucrative offers for customers.

2. To Device the Communication Strategy

Once the communication objectives are set, a retailer studies the market situation and designs the communication strategy comprising of various constituents like advertising, sales, event management, sales promotion, e-mail promotion, personal selling, etc. On the basis of situation analysis, a blue print of what-to-do, how-to-do is prepared, so as to achieve the communication objective. A retailer knows that one communication vehicle will not be suitable to interact with various target segments. For example, in case one of the retailers' stores is located in small but densely populated area where people would like to have a value for their money, so a retailer would like to communicate his store's products as fair price, every day low pricing (EDLP), cheap & affordable range, etc. Similarly, in case of a store located in a posh area, a retailer would like to plan a strategy of maintaining an up market image and delivering merchandise at pricing that justifies that sort of image.

3. Preparing the Communication Budget

All objectives and strategies of a retailer are achieved through funds only. Without funds, no strategy can take shape and will simply go flat. Therefore, it becomes imperative for a retailer to allocate budget considering the firm's turnover and the affordability. While planning a budget, a retailer should consider not only the short term and long term objectives but implications of investment also. For example, if a retailer spends more money on displays, ambience, interiors and exteriors, he would have shortage of funds to meet its day-to-day requirement (working capital).

4. Implementation of Communication Programme

Implementing the communication programme is one of the critical stages of retail communication process. A retailer must understand that retail market is the fast changing market and the most dynamic place in today's era. Therefore, even after having view of the current market trends and designing the strategy, if need arises, minor changes should be made at the implementation stage itself. An ideal communication programme always should be flexible to amend as and when need arises. Making sincere assumptions in this regard can play vital role towards the success of communication programme.

5. Evaluating the Communication Programme

After implementing the plan of action, a retailer must look into the result of the communication programme. Once implemented, programme starts giving results within a realistic period of time. Now a retailer should plan for the success of such communication program. If the customers are persuaded and excited, it will result in increased customer traffic as well as enhanced sales. However, in case customers are not persuaded, they can completely reject the move taken by the retailer by not visiting the store. The reason may be competitor's communication program which came because of your move. Sometimes, the competitors' campaigns are so successful which don't only minimize the impact of your move but may completely neglect your outcome. Therefore, considering a retailer must have a contingency program in place so that if one becomes unsuccessful, second program should replace the earlier one.

SUMMARY

Sales promotion is one of the most valuable and effective promotion strategies adopted by retailers. It refers to **communication strategies** that are designed to act as a direct inducement, a value addition, or some rebate to the customers. Normally, it is designed for immediate increase in retail sales. It provides extensive tactical measures to retailers to manage internal or external impediments to sales or profits. It includes various **communication** tactics those attempt to provide added value or incentives to customers, agents, wholesalers, retailers or other corporate clients to excite instant sales. These efforts can attempt to excite product curiosity, trial or bulk buying. Whatever the case is, one thing is sure that now customer is the 'king'. These traditional *kirana* stores now cannot sell only those items or brands on which they get maximum commission on selling. Further, the benefit of these **communication** techniques is that customers have become more cautious about their rights and prices.

REVIEW QUESTIONS

True and False Questions

1. Communication program invites the customers, attract them and lure them to visit the store.
2. Is it right to say that it takes very long period to build a brand?
3. EDLP stands for every day legal prices?
4. Is brand awareness an expansion of a brand to the customers?
5. IMC stands for Integral Marketing Channel.
6. Retail sales promotion is a scheme undertaken by a business to discourage an increase in store's sales, practice or trial of a product or service.
7. Sales promotion is generally done when a store wants to catch the attention of new customers.
8. Store atmosphere gives an idea about store's pricing policy, varieties and fashionability of its offerings.
9. Visual Merchandising is the art of creating visual displays and arranging merchandise assortments within a store to improve the layout and presentation.
10. Visual Merchandising informs the visitors, creates desire and finally augments the selling process.
11. Website is the oldest but costlier way of communication with customers.
12. Publicity refers to any paid communication to promote an organization or its products and services in public media.
13. Press publicity means releasing news in the media about the company, its offerings on payment basis.
14. Speech implies giving presentations through lectures about the company and its goods and services
15. Organizing conferences, debates, seminars, workshops, awareness camps, games, quizzes, star nights, beauty contests, singing competitions etc. are the typical examples of special events.

Answers

1. True	2. True	3. False	4. True
5. False	6. False	7. True	8. True
9. True	10. True	11. False	12. False
13. False	14. True	15. True	

Multiple Choice Questions

1. EDLP stands for:
   (*a*) Everyday legal prices (*b*) Everyday linear prices
   (*c*) Everyday low prices (*d*) Everyday local prices
2. Brand awareness is the expansion of a brand to ....
   (*a*) Wholesalers (*b*) Retailers
   (*c*) Media people (*d*) Customers.
3. The very first step to build brand value is ....
   (*a*) brand loyalty (*b*) brand personality
   (*c*) brand hierarchy (*d*) brand awareness
4. Publicity is an example of .... communication.
   (*a*) Paid, Impersonal (*b*) Paid, Personal
   (*c*) Unpaid, Impersonal (*d*) Unpaid, Personal
5. Personal selling and E-mail are examples of:
   (*a*) Paid, Impersonal (*b*) Paid, Personal
   (*c*) Unpaid, Personal (*d*) Unpaid, Impersonal
6. Visual Merchandising (VM) is an art of ....
   (*a*) creating visual displays (*b*) Arranging merchandise in warehouses.
   (*c*) back up merchandise (*d*) Inventory management.
7. IMC program is the combination of:
   (*a*) Advertising and sales promotion.
   (*b*) Publicity and personal selling.
   (*c*) Direct marketing and public relations.
   (*d*) All of the above.
8. Personal selling can take place at:
   (*a*) Store level (*b*) Customer's residence
   (*c*) Customer's place of work (*d*) All of the above.
9. The first step in a typical retail communication process is
   (*a*) Planning the retail communication programme.
   (*b*) To device the communication strategy.
   (*c*) To prepare the communication budget.
   (*d*) Evaluating the communication program.
10. Website is the .... and .... way of communication with customers.
   (*a*) fast, costlier. (*b*) oldest, costlier.
   (*c*) new, cheaper. (*d*) new, fast.

Answers

1. (*c*)	2 (*d*)	3. (*d*)	4. (*c*)
5. (*b*)	6. (*a*)	7. (*d*)	8. (*d*)
9. (*a*)	10. (*d*)		

Answers To 'Check Your Progress'

1. What is EDLP?
2. What is VM?
3. What is FSI?
4. What is POP?
5. What do you mean by communication?
6. What is sponsorship?
7. What is press publicity?
8. What store atmosphere includes?
9. What is IMC?
10. What is Website?

Small Answers Questions

1. Explain the essence of retail communication mix in a retailing firm?
2. Describe the role of communication in retailing?
3. How a retailer can build brand value?
4. Why recall is must in a communication campaign?
5. Differentiate between B2B and B2C?
6. Illustrate the merits and demerits of publicity.
7. What do you mean by Personal Selling?
8. Explain the concept of VM?
9. Discuss the significance of store atmosphere?
10. Explain with example the significance of 'word of mouth'?

Long Answer Questions

1. Critically analyze the various communication methods used by today's retailers to communicate with its customers?
2. Illustrate a retail communication process by considering an example of a retail firm of your choice and describe the issues, steps and measures taken by a retailer while implementing the communication process?

Applied Questions

1. Recall a recent experience of a retail communication for any product or service. What tasks you feel that a retailer performs to build its store's brand value?
2. Choose a product or service and search for atleast retail communications – one each in the category of advertising and publicity. Compare these two and write down their features?
3. Identify two instances of television commercials which seek to inform, educate, remind and persuade its buyers?
4. Explain the ways in which paid, impersonal communication will be different from paid personal communication?
5. Choose at least three product categories where direct marketing will have an added advantage over publicity?

UNIT 23

BUILDING CUSTOMER RELATIONSHIP AND COMPETITIVE ADVANTAGE

LEARNING OBJECTIVES

- Understanding the essence of relationship marketing.
- Explaining what 'value' really means in building and sustaining various relations.
- Describing how customer relationships and channel relationships lead to competitive advantage.
- Understanding the concept of competitive advantage in retailing and the key areas to develop sustainable competitive advantages
- Describing how customer service affects the total retail experience provided to customers

"Good business leaders create a vision, articulate the vision, passionately own the vision, and relentlessly drive it to completion."

Jack Welch

"Leadership is not magnetic personality/that can just as well be a glib tongue. It is not making friends and influencing people /that is flattery. Leadership is lifting a person's vision to higher sights, the raising of a person's performance to a higher standard, the ***building*** *of a personality beyond its normal limitations."*

Peter F. Drucker

INTRODUCTION

Making your store indispensable is a crucial key to retail success. It is a super path to enhance your store, add value and position before your competitors. It adds value to customers' values and benefits a retail organization in the form of increased profitability. To develop and keep a loyal customer base, retailers must develop and sustain relationships with their customers. These continuous relationships provide long term loyal customers. The longer a customer stays with a firm, the more that customer is worth. Loyal customers buy more in small store's time and are least concerned with firm's pricing policy. Above all, acquisition cost is nil in case of loyal customers.

Building competitive advantage is the overall plan or framework of action that guides a retailer and outline the mission, vision, location, aspects of customer loyalty, human resource management, customer services and control mechanism of the retailer. The location of a store, the selection of target market and customer satisfaction by offering unique merchandise is crucial for sustaining competitive advantage. A retailer is better able to create competitive advantage if he has a good understanding of consumer behaviour, distribution and information systems. This chapter covers each step in the development of a comprehensive, integrated strategy to build a sustainable competitive advantage. It also explains how building relationships with loyal customers is more essential rather than inviting new ones.

RETAILING RELATIONSHIPS

In any distribution channel, there are several members from different backgrounds, therefore, cooperation from each member is critical for smooth flow of business. To deal effectively and carefully, good relationships are must for accomplishment of organizational goals. In retailing, these members are manufacturers, wholesalers, retailer and customers. Business dealings are always apt to be pleasing to all members when they have same set of beliefs about the value provided and received, and the payments for that level of value.

If we look from manufacturer, wholesaler and retailer's point of view, 'value' is the set of tactics that make their customer happy. For them, 'value' involves their desire to earn profit and the efforts (sales promotion, rebate, discount etc) to make their customer purchase.

If we look from customer's point of view, ideally '**value**' is the relationship/bond of what the customer gets (goods/services) for what he/she has paid for. To some or most of the customers, 'value' means always getting a low price. In the world of retailing, 'value' for a customer is based on perceived benefits received versus payment made for it. Experience shows that 'value' varies from one set of customers to another. For instance, one group of customers being price sensitive will always prefer low prices, while others are ready to pay as long as they are sure that they are getting right value for their paid money.

Therefore, retailers plan and respond as per customers' liking, disliking and affordability. Following are the reasons to explain why 'value' is so meaningful:

- Value is the reason to select or reject a retailer for a retail customer.
- Value is desired by all set of customers.
- Offering good value is must for any retailer to survive in the long run.
- To beat a customer, 'value' is the centuries' old and successful weapon.

VALUE CHAIN

'Value chain' popularly known as 'value chain analysis' is a chain of activities that provides a given level of 'value' to the customers. It is the sum total of all visible and invisible goods and services attributes offered to a customer. In other words, a typical retail value chain represents the sum total of benefits available to customers through a channel of distribution. It commonly includes retailer's location, parking facility, space, range of merchandise assortment, the brands offered for sale, level of service, pricing policy, mode of payment, ease of bill payment, retailer's image and goodwill, displays etc.

> **Retailing values**
>
> (i) Knowing customers' liking and disliking
> (ii) Identifying target segments
> (iii) Customer relationship management
> (iv) Developing efficient communication network
> (v) Enhanced service quality
> (vi) Low price policy
> (vii) Wide merchandise assortments
> (viii) Preference to customers not to profit
> (ix) Sell that customers want
> (x) Customer loyality
> (xi) Improved brand success

One thing should be noted in this regard that customers are concerned with 'value' not with the steps/processes to offer such value. For instance being a customer of 'Pizza Hut', you are only concerned with the quality and the type of pizza ordered not the way/process how it reaches to your home within half hour.

Each value chain has some visible and invisible elements to shoppers. The visible elements of value chain are store's trading hours, windows, displays, floor staff and computerized bill and payment section.

RETAILER'S RELATIONSHIPS

Retailing is the final stage in a channel of distribution, which comprises of all the efforts and people involved in movement and transfer of ownership of goods and services from manufacturer to the end consumer. Retailer is a person who interacts with both the manufacturer and the customer. He is the link between the manufacturer, wholesaler and the end consumer as shown in the figure below.

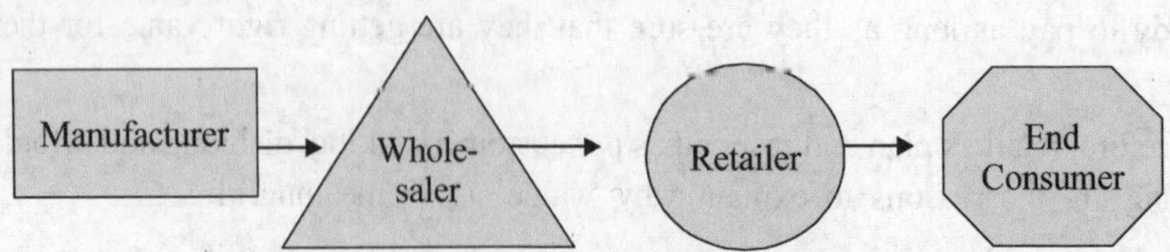

Figure 23.1: Retailer's Relationships

Therefore, the relationships between the retailer and other member of the distribution channel must be understood properly. Today, due to competition, entry of new players etc. has realized retailers to engage in relationship retailing, where they seek to develop and continue long-lasting relationships with customers, as it is evident in retailing that it is not the product but the customer who gives the profit. Therefore, to sustain in retailing industry, retailers must concentrate on developing and maintaining relationships with customers.

Relationship retailing is based on two points:

(i) Retailing experience should have win-win situation for both the retailer and the customer. It means that both should realize the position of gain (for retailer, gain will be appropriate price and sufficient profit, while for a customer, it is the satisfaction and customer service). Otherwise, the retailer will loose a customer and the customer will loose his/her money and precious time.

(ii) To achieve fruits of relationship retailing, it is essential to have updated data base of customers from their past shopping behaviour and their liking and disliking (if any). This is based on the fact that in retailing, it is always difficult to attract new customers rather than making existing customers happy and satisfied.

For a relationship retailing to act properly, it is essential to have healthy relationships with other members of the distribution channel besides customers. All relationships should go hand in hand.

Customer Relationships

Today customers are smart and know what they want. Retailers cannot befool them easily. They are tough critics, selective and practical thinkers. Their purchasing power is good and at the same time, they are ready to spend rather than save. They are loyal till the retailer understands them and provides value for their money. Loyal customers usually buy more, consume less time and are less price-sensitive and share their retailing experience with others. Therefore, retailers have realized that for making customers loyal, they need to become loyal to the customer, as customers are the lifeline of the retail business in real sense.

Seven customer retention strategies

1. Delivering high quality goods and services
2. Know your target group
3. Offering excellent customer service
4. Reward regular/loyal customers
5. Frequent change of displayed goods
6. Understanding of 'customer first, profit next' – concept
7. Listen to customers' feelings

ESSENTIALS OF RELATIONSHIP RETAILING

Before implementing relationship retailing, four essentials should be considered:

(i) The customer base (target market),

(ii) Level of customer service,

(iii) Customer satisfaction, and

(iv) Customer loyalty.

These are explained as follows:

(1) Customer base (target market) – As customers habits, liking, disliking tend to change frequently with the passage of time, retailers must regularly analyze their customer base/target market in terms of changing trends, attitude of loyal customers towards the store.

In India, teenage population is more, death rate is declining due to efficient medical facilities, joint families are breaking up into nuclear families, middle class is fast growing, people from rural areas are migrating to towns and cities, and middle class income is increasing year after year. Thus, market structure is on change, per capita income is higher and market segments are enlarging. People instead of buying from local '*kirana*' stores, prefer visiting to a mall or super bazaar where they can get variety of goods under one roof in varied brands. Therefore, retailers besides attracting and concentrating on new customers must take care of existing ones and loyal customers due to less acquisition cost. Further, a retailer's desire mix of old versus new customers depends on the firm's position in its lifecycle, amount of resources, objectives and its policy towards meeting competition. If a retail firm has growth as its main objective, then besides concentrating on existing and loyal customers, a retailer must focus on new customers too.

(2) Customer service – It is the sum total of all the retail activities those enhance the value, customers receive when they shop and buy merchandise. For relationship retailing to work, retailers must build and maintain a distinctive image among consumers. This image is created and sustained by efficient customer service that strongly affects the total retail experience. Customer service is the level of service that customers expect to receive from any retailer against their payments. Therefore, a retailer should develop a comprehensive customer level strategy that answers what all services are expected and what all services are significant for him. The philosophy behind developing a customer service strategy is that the expected customer service is an essential part of a retail strategy and therefore, it must be provided without any question.

(3) Customer satisfaction – Successful retailers believe that customer satisfaction should be the main motive of each retail business. Customer satisfaction persists when the value offered and customer service provided meet each other or exceed customers' expectations. In case the expectations and level of customer satisfaction do not move hand in hand, there are chances of consumer's complaints or dissatisfaction. Customers want proper value for their money and if their expectations are not met, by human nature, they share their unhappy experience/s with everyone they could. Dissatisfied customer spoils three to five customers but hardly make any customer in case he is satisfied. Therefore, retailers should consider following things in their mind:

(i) Customers' expectations continuously move upward with passage of time,

(ii) What 'customer satisfaction' actually means for a retailer?

(iii) Usually customers change their place of shopping in case they are dissatisfied rather than informing and complaining,

(iv) Review of customer satisfaction programs are must for building long term relationships with them

(v) Don't buy merchandise for your store what you like most, but put yourself in customer's shoes and look from his/her eyes.

Six building and sustaining relationship strategies

1. Communicate frequently with channel partners
2. Reward loyal members of the distribution chain/customers
3. Know the importance of two way communication
4. Payment in time
5. Equitable profit distribution
6. Trust, fairness and reliability in relations

(4) Customer loyalty – The objective of consumer loyalty program is to reward the best consumers in terms of their purchases, faith and in terms of existence. It is the base for developing long-term relationships with the customers. Customer loyalty programs not only reward loyal and best customers but also tend to find defection (the point of dissatisfaction). By studying and analyzing such defections, a retailer can have best picture towards his strength and shortcomings of loyalty programs.

Typical Customer Services

Essentials	Miscellaneous
• Information/education	• Try rooms
• Credit	• Rest rooms
• Delivery	• Parking
• After sales service	• Water
• Packaging	• Trolleys
• Handling complaints	• Home delivery
• Trial purchases	• Baby/aged sitting
• Special offers for regular customers	
• Flexible store hours	
• Ease of bill ordering	

Channel Relationships

Any distribution channel requires continuous cooperation from its members. These members jointly present a value delivery system, comprising all the parties that develop, manufacture, procure, provide and sell merchandise assortments. Each member of the distribution channel is dependent on other's performance and actions. This is teamwork therefore, clarity of jobs is essential at each stage of distribution channel. The fault on the part of any member's action may hamper the whole channel relationships. A channel relationship has following implications for a retailer:

- Consumer buying behavior is because of retailer's image and the merchandise he carries.
- Value delivery system must revolve around the consumers' expectations.
- Channel member costs and way of functioning primarily depends on each member's role and attitude towards the value delivery system.
- Cooperation between members of the value delivery system results in efficiency and better performance.
- Small retailers, due to limited access to the manufacturers, are suggested to explore and use suppliers outside the prevalent distribution channel.

A relationship-oriented technique that has emerged and is becoming common among leading retailers is **'category management'**. It orients retailers/store managers toward the merchandise decisions necessary to maximize the total return on the assets assigned to them.

Community Relations

The manner in which a retailer interacts with the communities around him affects the retail store image. Following points need to be considered for having a good image among public:

- To make certain that disabled and physically challenged customers can enter the store easily
- Supporting donations and charities
- Sponsoring youth activities
- Donating money and/or equipments to schools
- Noting every aspect that support the company's website
- Running special sales for senior citizens etc

BUILDING A SUSTAINABLE COMPETITIVE ADVANTAGE

Any business effort taken by a retailer from time to time can be a reason for competitive advantage but some advantages are sustainable over a long period of time, while others are of trial nature. Sustainable advantages are usually hard nut to crack. A retailer puts its full energy to keep competitors away from the market. By providing, the same quality goods and services and by following the same price policy, any retailer can be in and out of retailing competition. If a retailer is successful due to its wide merchandise assortments, its competitors can be provide wider and deeper merchandise to attract the customers. This phenomenon does not come under the concept of sustainable competitive advantage.

Building a sustainable competitive advantage means besides developing private/ store brands, lucrative offers and customer service, retailers should create certain advantages that enable them to survive against all odds as and when presented by its competitors. Knowing one's competitive advantage is difficult for its competitors. To begin with, even for a retailer, it is difficult to identify its own competitive advantages. Particularly, competitive advantage is your unique skills and inherent resources devoted/dedicated to your business that competitors cannot predict easily. Though competitors continuously try to weaken these advantages, successful retailers sustain these advantages by building strong cover against them. In nutshell, building a sustainable competitive advantage is the path to survive for long.

Retailers throughout the globe basically have seven key areas to develop sustainable competitive advantage:

(1) Customer loyality
(2) Store location
(3) Human resource management
(4) Distribution and information systems
(5) Unique merchandise
(6) Vendor relations
(7) Customer service

These respective areas are explained as follows:

1. Customer Loyalty

Loyal customers are long-term assets for a retail organization. They have emotional bond with a retailer and regularly visit the retailer. From a retailer's point of view, customer loyality means that customers are committed to purchase merchandise and services as and when required from the retailer with resistance of competitors' move. To retain loyal customers is not an easy task. It requires dedicated floor staff, efficient customer service and unique merchandise. For example, loyal customers will continue to shop at 'Subhiksha Mobile' even if 'go mobile' opens a store nearby and offers low price policy and gift packs with every purchase.

2. Store Location

The selection of location for a retail store is one of the most crucial strategic decisions a typical retailer makes. Since most of the retail sales in India take place at stores, utmost care should be taken before taking a site location decision. A good location not only reduces distribution cost to considerable extent but also attracts more customers. No matter what quality merchandise a store offers, customer service or attractive pricing, every retailer has to compete over three success elements: location, location and location. Therefore, before making a decision about a particular location, retailer should go through the detailed locational analysis considering various factors, like financial, political and socio-cultural forces. A retailer should understand that ***store location*** decision is a long-term strategic decision, which is irreversible and cannot be changed once decided upon. A good location reduces day-to-day loading, unloading and distribution cost. Consequently, extreme care and proper planning is essential to select the most suitable location.

Store location decisions ultimately decide the future and overall profitability of the organization. Not only in the retailing organizations but ideal location is required for non-retailing organizations too. Buying a good location does not only assure success, but undoubtedly is must for smooth flow and accomplishment of day-to-day operations like loading and unloading of goods etc. Therefore, it is advisable that utmost planning should be taken care of. Retailer must understand that each individual is a case in itself.

3. Human Resource Management

Human resource management plays a vital role in success of retailing. Despite technological advancements, retailers still rely on people (human resources) to perform the fundamental retail activities such as procurement, displaying merchandise and providing service to customers. Retailers know the importance of hardworking and loyal employees. Committed employees are critical assets to the retailers. Recruiting and retaining good employees have never been an easy task. No two employees are akin in their basic mental abilities, skills, personality, intelligence, energy levels, interests, aspirations etc. Depending upon these, they behave differently in same set of circumstances. Therefore, managing human resource is always a challenging task for a retailer or store manager. But by the way of understanding employees' problems, developing, motivation and by providing appropriate incentives, retailers/store managers can gain competitive advantage.

4. Distribution and Information Systems

All retailers wish that they should supply exactly the same quality, quantity and price what their customers need. They take all possible steps to supply the goods well in time and at prices which are lesser than their competitors. Some retailers instead of using low price policy provide additional facilities (margin) to lure customers such as wide merchandise assortments under one roof, even better customer service and visual presentations.

Retailers achieve these efficiencies by way of developing error free and latest distribution and information systems network. An efficient distribution and information system has two benefits for customers: (i) fewer stock outs, and (2) assortment of merchandise that customers want, where they wish to, for a retailer (store manager, these benefits translate into increased sales, higher inventory turnover, and lower mark downs. For example, Wal-mart being a largest retailer in the world has the largest data warehouse enabling its vendors like Proctor & Gamble to plan merchandise assortments on a store-by-store, format-by-format and category-by-category basis. This is the efficiency of Wal-Mart's distribution and information system that makes its retailers possible to offer low cost merchandise across the globe perhaps the secret of Wal-Mart's success in the world of retailing.

5. Unique Merchandise

Technological advancement, borderless economies and free flow of goods across the countries have enabled a retailer to procure any good and sell it in their stores, whenever and wherever they want, but in order to keep themselves ahead in the retailing race, many retailers get competitive advantage through development of personal/private/store brands. These products are designed, produced and marketed exclusively by the retailer and are sold by that retailer only. For example, if someone want to buy 'Star and Sitara' cosmetics, you can buy it from pantaloon.

6. Vendor Relations

Having good vendor relations is another success key of retailing. Successful retailers develop strong relationships with their vendors and get competitive edge over competitors under following ways:

- By obtaining special selling rights to sell merchandise in a particular region where they have monopoly bird position.
- To obtain special terms/conditions rights that are not available to competitors who lack good vendor relations and
- To obtain popular/fast moving merchandise in short supply/short notice. The longer the relationship exists, the longer the competitive advantage retailers will get.

7. Customer Services

Good customer service has today become an integral part of the retail industry. In retailing, where floor staff has to directly interact with the customers, customer service acts as lifeblood. With the sales promotion and lucrative offers you can increase the temporary sales but out of these customers if half or some of the customers do not come back then your store will not survive for long time. ***Good customer service*** is intended to bring back these customers voluntarily and then sending back with smiling faces. Smiling faces means after buying something, they have good feed back about your store. Even in some cases, they recommend your stores to others for shopping by sharing their good experiences. Yes, this is always possible. It is the mouth advertisement which multiplies your customer base within a short span of time.

Good floor staff does not mean that you can sell anything to anyone, but it will be your image in the minds of the customers that decides whether or not you can sell something to them. The image is largely influenced by the service provided by the floor staff and the experience of the customers with them. A satisfied customer is bound to tell others about his experiences, as will a dissatisfied customer. The strength of ***good customer service*** is to develop a longlasting rapport with customers – a link that individual customer feels that he would like to pursue in the coming time. How you develop such a long term relationship depends on your intention and perseverance. Remember that the secret of forming good relationship is the customer service with full dedication and without any greed. By this way, you will be known by what you do, not what you say to customers.

CUSTOMER SERVICE

In reality, goods and services aren't sold; products and services are bought by customers.

The Single most important thing to remember about any enterprise is that there are no results inside it's walls. The result of a business is a satisfied customer.

—Peter Drucker

A STRATEGIC ADVANTAGE

Leaders in today's rapidly changing business world have determined that there is more to success than catchy advertising campaigns. Whether it's a business, a professional practice, a healthcare facility, or a government agency, success comes to organizations that are dedicated to looking after their customers. Quality alone isn't enough!

High-performance organizations have realized that their proactive approach to employee skills development helps them leverage customer service as a strategic advantage.

In this first module you will :

- Define a vision of customer service.
- Discover customer expectations.
- Recognize the customer experience.
- Enhance customer service skills.

COACHING CUSTOMER SERVICE

Effective customer service coaches focus their attention on monitoring performance, providing feedback and recognizing accomplishments. They direct their attention to every level of customer service delivery, working with superstars as well as low performers to improve their customer service skills.

Organizations that place a high value on attracting new customers, dazzling customers with their superior services and keeping them long term, value the role that coaching plays in developing their workforce.

In this module you will :

- Understand customer service coaching.
- Develop customer service coaching techniques.
- Coach customer service personnel.
- Enhance customer service coaching skills.

CONTACT : HIGH PERFORMANCE ADVOCATES 530 288-0180, WWW. HIGHPERFORMANCEADVOCATES.COM

Source: *http://images.google.co.in / (www.highperformanceadvocates.com)*

CONCEPT OF GROWTH STRATEGY

Growth strategies are basically about decisions related to allocating available resources among different target markets and retail formats, transfering resources from one set of merchandise to others and managing and nurturing a portfolio of business in such a way that the overall organizations objectives are obtained. A retailer has four types of growth strategies to pursue, as shown below.

1. Market Penetration
2. Market Expansion
3. Retail Format Development
4. Diversification

Retail Formats	Target Markets: Existing	Target Markets: New
Existing	Market Penetration	Market Expansion
New	Format Development	Diversification

Figure 23.2. Various typos of Growth Strategies

The horizontal axis indicates the synergies between a retailer's current retail mix and the growth opportunity. 'Retail mix' implies that whether the present format is capable enough to grab the prevalent opportunities or needs to be changed. On the other side, vertical axis represents the synergies between thc retailer's current markets and growth opportunity markets. It implies whether opportunities exist in the retailer's current trading area or not.

1. Market Penetration

A market penetration opportunity exists when a retail company penetrates its existing market with same product range but with attractive offers. Under market penetration, retailers usually try to attract competitors' customers or those who come to store but do not buy merchandise. The underlying objectives are:

(i) To increase/broaden the existing customer base

(ii) To gain competitive edge

(iii) To restructure a market that has reached its maturity stage in its product life cycle

(iv) To increase the usage of merchandise offered by its existing customers – for example, by offering loyality programmes.

2. Market Expansion

A market expansion opportunity exists when a retailer sells the same product range with no/some alteration in the new market. It means that merchandise will remain the same but will be marketed to a new customer group.

How to expand market

(i) By searching a new market to sell, either by exporting or by entering into a totally new market.

(ii) By introducing new product packaging or dimensions with regard to colour and size.

(iii) By using new means of distribution and selling.

(iv) By developing different price policies for different customer groups.

3. Format Development

Retail format opportunity is the name given to a strategy where a business offers a new retail format with some sort of new retail mix to the same target market. For example, Amazon.com began selling electronic items such as CDs, videos, pen drives and other electronic items in addition to books and literature. In India, one example of retail format development opportunity is when 'Big Bazaar', a leading retailer started providing home services like plumber, electrician, furniture, kitchen interiors besides general merchandise. The main advantage of such retail strategy is that instead of developing a new retail format, here retailers offer new goods and services in addition to their regular merchandise that comparatively involves less investment.

4. Diversification

In retailing, diversification is a much used and much talked about set of strategies. A diversification strategy may involve related or unrelated dimensions. Essentially, diversification opportunity involves a substantial change in the business definition – individually or jointly in terms of customer functions, alternative technologies or customer groups. In short, a diversification opportunity is when a retailer introduces a new retail format directed toward a market segment that is so far not served. Diversification may take form of related or unrelated diversification.

Related Vs Unrelated diversification

In **related Diversification**, a retail organization takes up an activity in such a manner that it is related to its existing business line, either in terms of customer groups, alternative technologies or customer functions. These commonalities might entail procuring from the same suppliers, using the same distribution or supply chain system or promoting in the same media to similar target market. For instance, a retail company in the sewing machines business diversifies into consumer electronics and/or kitchenware, which are sold to housewives through a chain of retail stores.

In **unrelated diversification opportunity**, a retail organization adopts a growth strategy, which requires adoption of those activities that are unrelated to the existing business line in any terms. There are several examples of unrelated diversification in Indian retail industry. The classic example of Subhiksha, a general merchandise retail company diversifying into pharmacy and mobile industry.

Why is diversification strategies adopted?

The three basic and important reasons are:

A. To minimize the risk by spreading it over several businesses.

B. To capitalize on organization's strengths or minimizing weaknesses

C. In case where business growth is blocked due to prevalent regulatory and environmental factors.

CASE STUDY

Organizational Dilemma

Durable Fresh is a pioneering and internationally reputed retailing firm in the FMCG industry. It is also one of the largest firms in the country. Every year it attracts employees from internationally reputed institutes and industries by offering luring salary packages, additional performance perks etc. It has advertised for a position of recently. Nearly over 100 candidates applied for the advertised position. **Mr Rajesh**, a MBA from IMM with four years working experience in a medium sized specialty chain store was shortlisted and recruited from among 120 candidates who took tests/group discussion and interviewed. Seeing his performance before interviewed board and at Rajesh's personal request, management of Durable Fresh recommended an enhancement in his salary by Rs 10,000 more than his present salary. With this new salary package and working with reputed brand, Rajesh was very happy. On his achievement, he was congratulated by his nears and dears including his previous colleagues and employer.

Mr Rajesh joined Durable Fresh Limited on 30th June 2007, with great enthusiasm and zeal. In his initial days, he found his **new job** and designation to be quite cool and calm. He was also excited to work with a reputed global brand in the initial years of his career. In the new company, he found most of the staff (at all levels) supportive and friendly. He started thinking that now his career is on the right track and sooner or later he will reach his destination, but his dream did not continue long. After six months of his service, he found strange and unpleasant experience with some of his subordinates and seniors too. He also came to know about number of unpleasant stories about the company, management and the senior-junior relations, high employee turnover, clashes between employees and management and many more. This made him uncomfortable and mentally disturbed for the time being. But Rajesh decided to continue considering everything will go fine in the time to come. In order to please management and with the desire to have visibility in the company, he started contributing to the extent possible, but the management got the impression that Rajesh is comfortable with the company and will not go elsewhere. Now everyone in the company started knowing the importance and contribution of Rajesh for the company. Even in several conferences, debates, seminars and trade fairs, Rajesh represented his company well.

After sometime, the seniors started riding over Rajesh and overloaded him with heterogeneous tasks. His participation, freedom in deciding and implementation was shrinked to nil. He was under-rated and illtreated on a number of occasions in front of his juniors. His colleagues who use to be friendly initially also started assigning their tasks to Rajesh. But with doing justice to his job, Rajesh started neglecting his social and personal family life. Despite overburdened and poor personal relations with his owns, he stayed calm and quiet. In turn, management felt that Rajesh has the potential and art to be overburdened.

Then on, the foggy day of 31st Dec 2007, Managing Director started sweating when he saw the '***one month notice cum resignation letter***' of Mr Rajesh on his table. With the advice of managing director, general manager was not able to convince Rajesh to withdraw his resignation, but to surprise of Rajesh one-month's notice was waived off and his accounts were settled on the first day of 2008. The general manager wanted to appoint a committee to go deep into the matter immediately but dropped the idea later.

Questions for discussion

Q1 What made Rajesh resign from his dream job?

Q2 Why managing director started sweating on seeing Rajesh's resignation?

Q3 What prevented the general manager from appointing a committee?

Q4 Why management of Durable Fresh Limited waived off Rajesh's one-month notice and relieved him immediately?

Q5 Being a management graduate, what suggestions would you like to give to management of Durable Fresh Limited considering the importance of key employees for a corporate?

SUMMARY

Building and sustaining relationships with the members of the distribution channel is vital for the long-term survival of any retail firm. Relationship marketing is an effective way to attract, maintain and enhance relationships within the retail industry. Due to the increased complexities in the retail industry, Indian retailers have understood the significance of '**building and sustaining relationships**' in their retail strategy. Even leading retailers have been improving customer service and channel relationships by empowering personnel, giving then the authority to bend some rules.

To fully comprehend and develop a **competitive advantage** plan, retail managers must have a better understanding of the environment in which they are operating. This chapter explains the key areas retailers must consider to succeed in competition. An understanding of retail formats and managing resources effectively allows the retailer to gain competitive advantage over other retailers. Further, a competitive analysis approach gives a retailer a detailed understanding of the competition they face in their normal course of operations. But having uptodate knowledge of competitor's movements and developing internal strengths (unique merchandise, managing human resources effectively and high level of customer service) give consumers a reason to select his/her store.

REVIEW QUESTIONS

True and False Questions

1. 'Value' is the relationship/bond of what the customer gets to what he/she has to pay for.
2. 'Value' remains constant from one set of customers to another.
3. Value is the reason to select or reject a retailer for a retail customer.
4. Value is the sum total of all visible and invisible goods and services attributes offered to a customer.
5. Retailing is the first stage in a channel of distribution.
6. Retailer is a person who interacts with both the manufacturer and the customer.
7. Loyal customers usually buy more, consume less time and share their retailing experience with others.
8. Customer service is the sum total of all the retail activities that enhance the value, customers receive when they shop and buy merchandise.
9. Customer satisfaction persists when the value offered and customer service provided differs from each other.
10. Customers' expectations continuously move downward with passage of time.
11. The objective of consumer loyalty program is to reward the best consumers in terms of their purchases, faith and in terms of existence.
12. Community relations refer to the various methods companies use to establish and maintain a mutually beneficial relationship with the communities in which they operate.
13. The underlying principal of community relations is that when a company accepts its civic responsibility and takes an active interest in the well-being of its community, then it gains a number of long-term benefits in terms of community support, loyalty, and goodwill.
14. Customer loyalty means feelings or attitudes that incline a customer either to return to a company, shop or outlet to purchase there again, or else to re-purchase a particular product, service or brand.
15. Store location decision is a shot-term strategic decision which is reversible and can be changed as per retailer's convenience.
16. A good location increases day to day loading, unloading and distribution cost.
17. Human resource management is responsible for how people are treated in an organization.
18. Customer service is considered a necessity by most service and retail businesses.

19. Good retailer means listening to customers' wants and needs and providing them the product that they need.
20. Growth strategies means by which an organization plans to achieve its objective to grow in volume and turnover.
21. As a strategy based on selling existing products in an existing market, the purpose of market penetration is maintenance rather than growth.
22. For a market penetration strategy to work, organizations must ensure that they have an adequate supply of products and an effective customer retention program.
23. Customer loyalty is affected by a combination of factors including reliability, responsiveness and price.
24. A market expansion opportunity means that merchandise will remain the same but will be marketed to old customer group only.
25. Diversification is a form of growth marketing strategy for a company.
26. Diversification seeks to increase profitability through greater sales volume obtained from new products and new markets.
27. Product development means improving an existing product or developing new kinds of products.
28. Misperceptions of the value offering arise where customers perceive planned service features as problems or failures rather than positive benefits.
29. Increasing market share within the market by increasing demand for the organization's products ahead of those of its competitors is an example of market penetration.
30. Goodwill is the difference between the value of a business as a going concern and the sum of the value of its assets, if taken separately.

Answers

1. True	2. False	3. True	4. True
5. False	6. True	7. True	8. True
9. False	10. False	11. True	12. True
13. True	14. True	15. False	16. False
17. True	18. True	19. True	20. True
21. True	22. True	23. True	24. False
25. True	26. True	27. True	28. True
29. True	30. True		

Multiple Choice Questions

1. Making a retail store indispensible is a crucial key to
   (*a*) retail failure (*b*) retail criticism
   (*c*) retail success (*d*) retail communication

2. Value is the relationship between.

(*a*) Goods and its performance (*b*) Performance and cost of goods.

(*c*) Image and Good will. (*d*) Wholesaler and retailer.

3. Retailing is the .... stage in a channel of distribution.

(*a*) First (*b*) Middle

(*c*) Last (*d*) Second

4. Under market penetration retailers usually try to attract .... customers:

(*a*) Lost (*b*) Competitors

(*c*) Wandering (*d*) New

5. Under market expansion merchandise is offered to:

(*a*) Old customer group (*b*) New customer group

(*c*) Competitors customers (*d*) Wandering customers

6. Value is the reason to .... a particular retailer.

(*a*) Select (*b*) Reject

(*c*) None of the above (*d*) Both of the above

7. Loyal consumers, usually buy .... and consume ....

(*a*) Less, more time. (*b*) More, less time

(*c*) More, more time (*d*) Less, less time

8. Store location decision is a .... decision.

(*a*) Short term strategic (*b*) Long term strategic

(*c*) Medium term strategic (*d*) Repetitive.

9. A good location reduced following expenses.

(*i*) transportation cost (*ii*) vehicular traffic

(*iii*) Unloading expenses (*iii*) distribution cost

Which one is true?

(*a*) (*i*) and (*ii*) (*b*) (*i*) (*ii*) and (*iii*)

(*c*) All of the above (*d*) (*i*) (*iii*) and (*iv*)

10. Product development means:

(*a*) Improving an existing product. (*b*) Developing new product.

(*c*) None of the above. (*d*) Both of the above.

Answers

1. c	2. a	3. c	4. b
5. b	6. d	7. b	8. b
9. d	10. d		

Check your progress

1. Explain the term competitive advantage?
2. What is human resource?
3. What do you mean by customer loyalty?
4. What makes a merchandise unique?
5. Is customer service essential in retailing?
6. What is CRM?
7. Name few FMCG products?
8. What is shoplifting?
9. What is outsourcing?
10. What is display?

Small Answers Questions

1. Why should a retailer devote special attention to its loyal customers?
2. Device a consumer loyality program for a local '*kirana*' store?
3. Explain the significance of managing human resources in order to get competitive advantage?
4. How a retailer can achieve effectiveness in its distribution and information systems?
5. Explain the types of customers in retailing?
6. Why customers are necessary to run a store?
7. Discuss the customers' contact points with examples?
8. Highlight the essentials of good customer service?
9. Write a short note on new trends in customer service?
10. What role floor staff can play in customer service?
11. Explain the difference between loyal and wandering customer?
12. What is the significance of strategic planning in retailing industry?
13. What is the concept of self service?
14. Explain the term 'potential customer'?
15. Differentiate between Market penetration and Market Expansion?

Long-Answer Questions

1. What do you mean by customer service? What are the benefits of good customer service? Being a floor staff, what guidelines you would follow to provide great customer service?
2. Differentiate between a customer, visitor and a consumer? How loyal customers can help a store to become competitive?

Applied Questions

1. Building a sustainable competitive advantage means besides developing private or store brands, retailers should create certain advantages that enable them to survive against all odds as and when presented by its competitors. Explain with examples wherever necessary?
2. Make a visit to your nearest departmental store and after mapping out the categories/ sub-categories prepare a list of the growth enablers across categories. Follow this up with discussing with store managers/category managers, the broad strategy guidelines and organization structure and key roles responsibility.
3. Visit a few retail chain stores that sell through various formats like online, shop-in-shop, flagship stores formats. Then identify the scope of various diversification and expansion strategies that can be evaluated and implemented after talking to store managers /customer relationship managers.

FUTURE OF RETAILING

UNIT 24

RETAILING THROUGH INTERNET

LEARNING OBJECTIVES

- Understanding how Internet and IT add value to retailing.
- Exploring the reasons why online retailing is becoming fashion of the day.
- To assess the impact of internet on online shoppers.
- Understanding what factors result in success of online retailing.
- Identifying cyber retailing as a new format of retailing.

"If you make customers unhappy in the physical world, they might tell 6 friends each. If you make customers unhappy on the Internet, they each can tell 6,000 friends"

Jeff Bezos

INTRODUCTION

Retailing through Internet was first developed on a large scale in 1980s in European countries. Since then retailing through Internet has established itself as a viable alternative to retail-based shopping experience. One of the most popular and well known internet retailer is Amazon.com, which was launched in 1995. In some countries like USA and France, internet retailing has progressed fastest but in other countries like India and China, it is in the nascent stage. Even UK and Russia have not been able to achieve similar levels of penetration (in terms of percentage) so far. Even India is not expected to achieve significant share until 2010. Overall expectations are that this pace of development is likely to grow and will have a vital impact on store-based retailing. Researchers have shown (Melle Dorger, 2003) that store-based retailers have been slow to react to this emerging trend of retailing, although they are now trying to cope up the declining graph by adopting modern strategies like 'clicks and mortar' strategy to complement their existing stores with internet retailing.

MEANING AND DEFINITION OF INTERNET RETAILING

Internet retailing, which is also known as electronic retailing, e-tailing, cyber-retailing, virtual retailing or e-retailing is the sale of goods /services through electronic media. This electronic media, we all know is Internet (World Wide Web). But these days due to revolution in electronic communications, besides internet, several other Medias like digital television, web-enabled mobile telephones (WAP), tele-conferencing devices etc are also operational. The main advantage of electronic/internet retailing is that it does not require any direct human interactions. Besides this, internet retailing offers same quality, convenience of access, reliability and lower cost. In short, this form of retailing allows the customers to evaluate and purchase goods and services without going to any physical retail store.

Internet Retailing

Internet retailing today is considered as the fastest growing format of the retail industry. It helps the shoppers to acquire information about quality, quantity, colour, price and sizes without traveling and incurring any cost. Two systems are used under internet retailing:

(1) **Passive retail system**: This system is non-interactive and involves all forms of one-way communication such as clubs on television, shopping pages or one-way cable system. This system of retailing includes video catalogues or electronic media, which display the products in use or provide other relevant information.

(2) **Interactive System**: This system is interactive and allows the user a two-way interaction and includes World Wide Web (www) or kiosks for items such as airline or railway ticketing and promotional touch screen booths. Some interactive systems display the goods and services meant for sale and in the case of touch screens, give printouts or allow further enquiries from the database.

Note: *The common feature of both systems is that a credit or a debit card can be used to secure the sale.*

CYBER RETAILERS AS A MODERN RETAILING FORMAT

Today, most of the big sized retailers have their own website, which allows a retailer to conduct a targeted business 24 hours a day and seven days a week. Providing retail business, offers the retailer not only a modern way of getting business but also cost effectiveness. This one time small investment in creating and registering the website on World Wide Web is accessible to everyone irrespective of location, time zone, income level or computer system. Internet also provides the fuel and information about the goods and services through digital images, visual and audio effects. Electronic brochures provide three-dimensional aspects of the goods and services, which a shopper can explore anytime before making the buying decision.

Figure 24.1: Retailing on the Internet

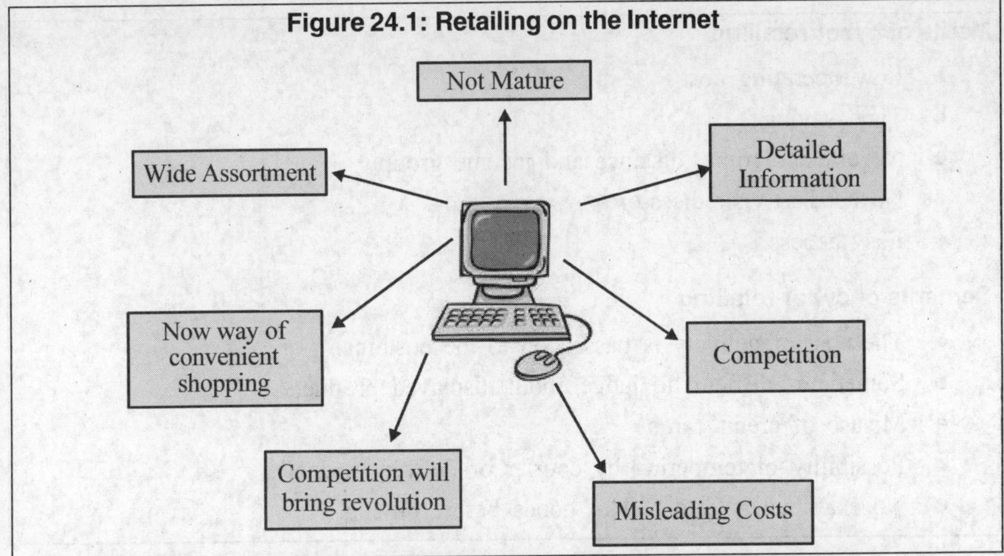

One of the well known and oldest examples is Amazonbooks.com. Amazon is the largest and the maximum accessible bookshop in the world. According to Amazon sources, today 30% of its sales come from cyber retailing only. Dell, a well known computer company, claims to sell more than $ 1 million of its personal computers everyday on the internet. The distinguishing feature of these retailers is that they sell their products through internet and as such do not have any physical store. Under retailing through internet concept, customer visits a website of the store, checks the shown items with regard to its size, colour and related features, having convinced with some items, customer fills up the form and after entering credit/debit card details and postal address completes the transaction. Once the transaction is complete, the goods are delivered directly to the customer at his/her doorstep.

Cyber Retailing

Cyber retailing is variously referred to as virtual retailing or e-tailing. Due to case of access and lower operating costs, the internet is revolutionizing retailing in many fundamental ways like eliminating wholesalers/intermediaries after the concept of manufacturing to retailing.

Merits of cyber retailing

- Low operating cost
- Time saving
- No effect of time, distance and income group
- No need to visit the store
- Easy access

Demerits of cyber retailing

- The cost of delivery is passed on to the customer
- Sometimes difficult to judge about displayed products
- Misuse of credit cards
- Possibility of tempering by courier or delivery agencies
- No examination and feel of goods before buying.

ITEMS OF INTERNET RETAILING

Due to technological revolution, graphical impact, audio and visual displays, any item can be sold through internet. Studies have shown that there are few items that have very poor response when sold through cyber retailing. These are gold, diamonds, automobile components, vehicles and electronic items of daily use. However, the items that have strong demand and make up the vast majority of internet sales are:

Limitations of Web

- Network problem
- Computer literacy
- Fear of transaction
- Availability
- Computer related problems

- Computer parts and accessories
- Computer softwares and hardwares
- Gift items including electronic toys
- Books and magazines
- Travel products and
- Branded apparel

FACTORS AFFECTING INTERNET BUYING DECISIONS

Unlike physical stores, the success of cyber retailing depends on following factors:

- The goodwill of the retailer,
- Merchandise characteristics,
- Website effectiveness,
- Ease to access the website, and
- Consumer attitude towards internet buying.

TRADITIONAL RETAILING Vs CYBER RETAILING

Cyber retailing is entirely different from traditional retailing (traditional retailing here implies mall retailing being the order of the day), since cyber retailing involves a rather different retailing philosophy to their existing operations. Some of the differences are presented below in figure 24.1. The first reason to differentiate this is the site location decision: Site (store) location like traditional retailing is immaterial in cyber retailing. Secondly, the problem of managing inventory is missing in cyber retailing, while on the other hand logistics is of utmost importance because of the need to develop home delivery systems, and bulk sales order processing requires new systems and IT skills. The two-way communication (interactive capacity) also implies that relationship marketing becomes more vital both for building loyality and increasing sales via marketing of related products and services. Further, the human resource is the ultimate reason for the success of physical retail stores and plays no role in cyber retailing.

Figure 24.2
Traditional Retailing Vs Cyber Retailing

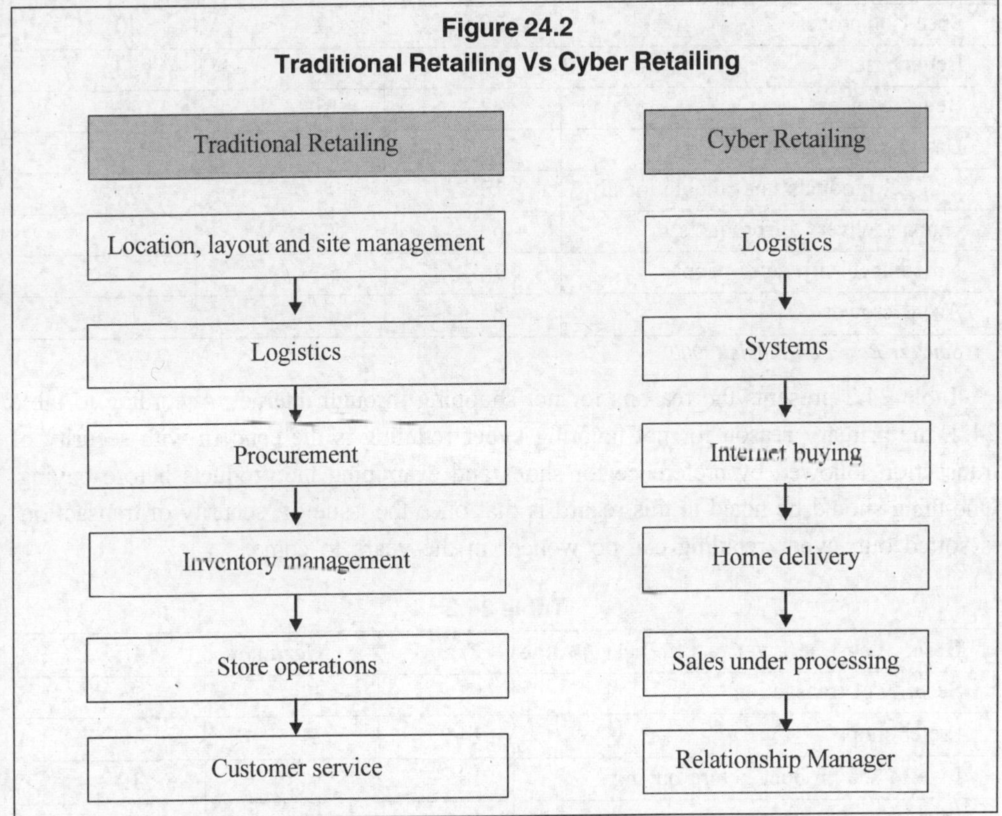

REASONS FOR POPULARITY OF CYBER RETAILING

There is no doubt that internet retailing is becoming popular throughout the globe but the degree of take-up of cyber retailing is increasing in metro cities and in urban areas only. Cyber retailing is mainly done through personal computers having internet connection but other alternatives include cable/digital TV, mobile phones having internet access, internet sticks are also becoming popular. The number of adult internet users is currently estimated to be around 50 million and is expected to reach 1 billion by 2015. In India, internet access is also being available in rural areas but the trend towards internet retailing will take several years to happen. In Europe, cyber retailing is most popular in UK with nearly 45% of UK cyber users claiming to have bought goods including books, computer hardware and software online (Stobie, 2000).

The primary reason for cyber retailing is ease and convenience while other reasons include speed of the process, better prices, better choices, whole day purchase experience and many more. The Table 24.1 provides the main reasons for cyber (online) retailing as per Stobie, 2000 which is not useful for researchers but retailers and policy makers.

Table 24.1

Base: All Web Purchasers	France	Germany	UK
Ease/convenience	42	55	67
Speed of process	39	37	30
Better prices	21	20	32
Better choices	22	15	12
Day or night purchase	9	24	6
Can get products unavailable locally	13	9	9
Global delivery of products	6	7	9
No contact with sales people	7	5	6
Avoid crowds	8	6	1

Source: *Based on Stobie (2000)*

Table 24.2 presents the reasons for not shopping through internet. According to table 24.2, the primary reason for not favoring cyber retailing is the concern with security of transaction followed by preference for shops and examining the products before buying. One thing should be noted in this regard is that once the issue of 'security of transaction' is sorted out, cyber retailing can do wonder in the years to come.

Table 24.2

Base: Web Users yet to Purchase Online	France	Germany	UK
Security of transaction	52	32	25
Prefer shops	14	24	17
Like to see product before buying	18	16	12
Like human contact	10	16	4
Not got around to trying it yet	12	5	11
No need/no interest	8	12	18
Don't own credit card	8	2	7
Not allowed to use PC for that	4	3	11
Only just got access to PC	2	5	8
Private worries	5	6	4

Source: *Based on Stobie (2000)*

Co-buying (co-operative buying) is also an emerging phenomenon that is giving fuel to cyber retailing. The reason behind increasing popularity is that co-buying purchases are cost effective as compared to individual buying. These co-buying sites require internet visitors (shoppers) to agree to a price and if more people also buy the same product within a certain period, the price charged will go down. For instance, *www.adabra.com* and *www.letsbuyit.com* are the famous sites for co-buying.

Table 24.3 presents the areas that electronic retailers must consider to be successful in cyber retailing, while table 24.4 presents the list in rank order listing of sales.

Table 24.3

S. No	Success Factors
1	Strong branding
2	Unique merchandising
3	Complementary merchandise assortments
4	Distribution efficiency
5	Effective use of customer information
6	Strong website design
7	User friendly web links
8	Efficient customer service
9	Customer relationship management

Source: *Alba et al, 1997*

Table 24.4

S No	Rank	Name of the Product
1	Ist	PC hardware and software
2	2nd	Travel
3	3rd	Entertainment
4	4th	Books and music
5	5th	Gifts, flowers and greetings
6	6th	Clothing and footwear
7	7th	Food and beverages

Source: *Idea taken from IGD (1998)*

SUMMARY

Cyber retailing that used to be an European buying trend has spread not only to other developing nations but to the third world also. For retailers, it is the source of new income and enhanced sales in minimum efforts, also customers find it economical and time saving. IT enabled services have enabled retailers to make their merchandise re-ordering system more accurate and rcsponsive to online customers at the same time relieving them from headache of controlling inventory.

Traditional (mall) retailers should consider this development seriously and take proper action to think and device how internet can be useful for them ranging from information only sites to 'clicks and mortar' strategy. The cyber retailing is likely to increase due to fall in prices of computers, easy and affordable access to internet media.

REVIEW QUESTIONS

True and False Questions

1. Retailing through Internet was first developed on a large scale in the year 2001.
2. Amazon.com is the popular online pharmaceutical retailer.
3. 'www' stands for world wide window.
4. WAP stands for world automatic protocol.
5. The term cyber is used for crime and politics.
6. Electronic brochures provide four-dimensional aspects of the goods and services which a shopper can explore any time before having buying decision.
7. Dell is the world famous online book seller.
8. Except books and magazines, almost everything can be purchased online.
9. Inaccuracy and low speed are the disadvantages of online retailing.
10. The primary reason for cyber retailing is ease and convenience.
11. The co-buying purchases are getting popularity because of cost effectiveness as compared to individual buying.
12. Cyber retailing is considered to be an Asian buying trend that has spread not only to other developing nations but to the developed world too.
13. IT enabled services have enabled retailers to make their merchandise re-ordering system more accurate and responsive.
14. The cyber retailing is likely to increase due to fall in prices of computers and easy and affordable access to internet media.
15. Credit cards are used to pay for internet purchasing.

Answers

1. True	2. False	3. False	4. False
5. False	6. False	7. False	8. False
9. False	10. True	11. True	12. False
13. True	14. True	15. True	

Multiple Choice Questions

1. Retailing through Internet was developed in which year?
   (*a*) 1960's (*b*) 1970's
   (*c*) 1980's (*d*) 1990's
2. Amazon. com was launched in which year?
   (*a*) 1990 (*b*) 1992
   (*c*) 1995 (*d*) 1997
3. Which of the following systems are used in Internet retailing:
   (*a*) Active and Passive (*b*) Active and Interactive
   (*c*) Passive and Interactive (*d*) Passive and Submissive.
4. The main demerit of cyber retailing is:
   (*a*) High operating cost (*b*) No need to visit the store.
   (*c*) Easy access. (*d*) Misuse of credit cards
5. Co-buying is generally popular as:
   (*a*) Co-operative buying (*b*) Community buying
   (*c*) Co-ordination buying (*d*) Collective buying
6. The main limitation of web retailing is:
   (*a*) Network problem (*b*) Difficult to operate
   (*c*) Operating cost of internet (*d*) Time saving.
7. Amazon. com deals in:
   (*a*) Toys and shoes (*b*) Pharmaceuticals
   (*c*) Plastic cookwares (*d*) Books
8. WWW stands for
   (*a*) World wide window (*b*) World wide wall
   (*c*) World wide width (*d*) World wide web.
9. Dell is the world famous .... seller.
   (*a*) Book (*b*) Consumer Electronics
   (*c*) Computer (*d*) Health and entertainment equipments.
10. WAP stands for:
    (*a*) World automatic protocol.

(*b*) Wireless automatic planogram.

(*c*) Web-enabled assortment protocol.

(*d*) Wirless application protocol.

Answers

1. (*c*)	2 (*c*)	3. (*c*)	4. (*d*)
5. (*a*)	6. (*a*)	7. (*d*)	8. (*d*)
9. (*c*)	10. (*d*)		

Answers to 'check our progress'

1. What is FDI?
2. What is IT industry?
3. Explain www?
4. Explain virtual retailing?
5. What is WAP?
6. What is website?
7. Explain the term 'Co-buying'?
8. What do you mean by internet?
9. What is Pharma retail?
10. Describe Entertainment?

EXERCISES AND QUESTIONS

Small Answer Questions

1. How internet retailing is different from traditional retailing?
2. What items are most popular on internet buying?
3. In India, what obstacles are faced by internet customers?
4. In India, Internet Retailing is in nascent stage, why?
5. What is Indian Government policy towards retailing in India?
6. What factors contribute to the success of internet retailing?

Long Answer Questions

1. Why cyber (online) retailing is becoming popular day by day? What suggestions you would like to give to traditional retailers to face this impending danger? Also discuss the future of mall retailing considering the growth and development of online retailing throughout the globe?
2. What are your suggestions and guidelines for a multinational retailer who just has decided to enter into Indian retail industry?

Applied Questions

1. Define a modem retail format. How does it differ from a traditional retail format?
2. Make a visit to an online retail store and after buying something, discuss your experience in terms of excitement, learning, merits and demerits of online retailing. Would you suggest others to buy things online?
3. When it has been accepted and proved that online shopping is not only fast but accurate and hassle free, why in India people hesitate to buy things online? What is the main reason that 'people per thousand', who buy online is less than China and other developing countries in India?

Appendix

Exhibit 24.1: Online Retailing in UK

United Kingdom (UK) is one of the leading online retail markets of the world[1]. Online retailing in the UK has grown at its fastest rate since the dotcom bubble burst. The amount of money spent by consumers shopping online increased by 33.4% to £10.9bn last year, retail analysts Verdict Research said[2]. Verdict also sees online sales almost tripling over the next five years. The research group said that faster and cheaper internet access was driving the growth at a time when many High Street retailers were seeing demand wane.

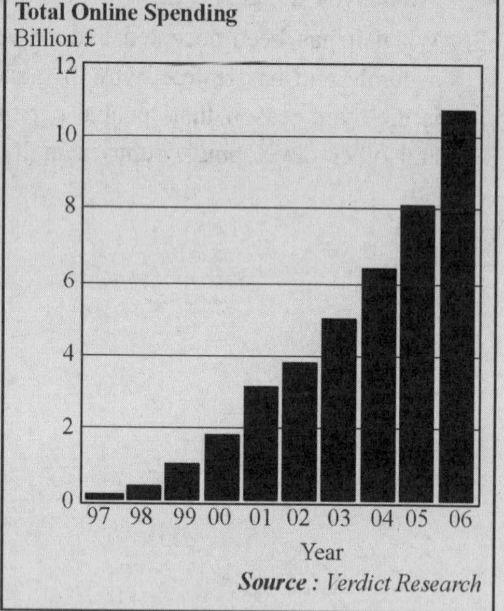

Of 3,000 customers surveyed, two thirds had broadband internet connections and shopped online more often because of it, Verdict said. The company's research covered online spending on goods, and did not include sales of flights, tickets and insurance. Verdict predicts that in 2011, online retailing will be worth about £28.1bn, or about 8.9% of the UK's total retail sales. However, Verdict warned that most of the growth in sales probably would come from existing online shoppers buying more items rather than more people shopping over the internet.

Staying offline

While many UK retailers have scaled up their online operations, including Ikea and Waterstones, Verdict identified three types of retailers that were proving reluctant to increase their online presence. Verdict said that food retailers that were not already providing an online service were staying off because the cost of launching a web operation was too high. Value retailers such as Primark and Matalan have tended not to launch online operations because their business models depend on driving sales in their stores, it added. And small, specialist retailers have been avoiding online sales because their small scale made it difficult to pay for the necessary infrastructure. Despite these pockets of resistance, the outlook remained bright with other industries moving quickly into cyberspace, the analysts said.

"Even with some retailers staying out of the market, online sales in the UK are set to triple in value," Verdict explained. "By 2011, the typical spend of an online shopper will grow to £1,056 per year with the clothing and footwear, DIY and gardening, and food and grocery sectors achieving the fastest growth," it predicted.

Source:

1. *www.nzherald.co.nz*
2. *www.news.bbc.co.uk*

Exhibit 24.2: Seven Best Practices of Online Retailing

As online retailing has matured and customers have become comfortable with the online shopping experience, a series of best practices has begun to emerge. These practices will ensure that your site remains in the forefront of revenue generation while ensuring a positive client experience.

1. **Go to the Buyers** - "Location, location, location" is the old adage, and it holds true for the Internet as well. Search engines and e-commerce brokers such as AOL, MSN and Yahoo! are the malls of the Internet. By forging partnerships with these portals, retailers can quickly and cost-effectively gain access to and capture qualified customers who actively seek your products.
2. **Optimize Home Page Design** - Many retailers commit large amounts of precious "above the fold" home page real estate to branding and corporate messaging. Unless you are a new or niche retailer, this is unnecessary and limits your ability to immediately promote saleable products. Identify the products and categories that you want to sell and place them (or compelling links) on your home page to allow visitors quick access to purchase options. *Bed, Bath & Beyond* does an excellent job of balancing home page layout while including a friendly and useful DHTML product menu navigation system that helps orient visitors and increases the likelihood of quickly finding desired products.
3. **Strong Supporting Images and Content** - It is surprising how many sites provide little explanatory documentation to support and close the sale. Since visitors can't closely inspect, touch and try the product online, retailers must close this gap with thoughtful product descriptions, imagery and sales information. It is not uncommon on retail sites to see colour swatches without a name (is that green or teal?) or to view a product description that simply states, "boot cut blue jeans." Not only does this limit your ability to complete the sale and improve conversion rates; it creates a poor user experience and negatively impacts your company's brand.
4. **Promote Online and Offline Synergies** - *Circuit City* and *Target* have successfully proven the value of tightly integrating "bricks and clicks" and providing seamless cross-channel customer experiences. Cross branding, inventory management and customer focused pick-up and return policies promote trust, purchasing comfort, good will and an excellent customer service experience. This is a situation where the whole is greater than its parts (sometimes, 2 + 2 does equal 5).
5. **Excellent Store Locator** - If you have an engaged and interested customer visiting your site with the sole purpose of locating one of your physical

stores, the experience must be simple, quick and helpful. Too many retail sites provide unorganized and less than helpful lists of store locations. Sites like *Mercedes Benz* lead the pack in providing simple locator tools and excellent results pages that include contact information, maps, directions and local dealer links. If you don't make it easy for your customers to find you, your competitior will.

6. **Excellent Search Engine Capabilities** - Poor search engine results limit sales and negatively impact the customer's experience. According to PricewaterhouseCoopers, 70 percent of visitors use a Website's search engine and 43 percent stated that it is the most important feature on a site. Many retail sites provide good product search engine capability but don't account for misspellings or functionality and service searches. Often, a user searching for "shipping and return" policies receive no results. It is also critical that search engines sort page results effectively and provide multiple search options such as related links and natural language queries. It's important to support the user in the manner they prefer to search for items.

7. **Clear Customer Support Options** - Every customer has a different preference for interacting with retailers. To ensure the completion of a sale and a continued relationship, it is important to provide customer support in the manner each customer desires (e.g. - FAQ's, email, phone, fax, real-time online support and offline store support). Most often, customers won't access these additional services and they add cost to your bottom line. However, these services will create user comfort with the site and reinforce the buying decision. Everything else being equal, if your competitor offers these services and you don't, this could be the deciding factor in retailer's selection.

Courtesy: *http://www.ecommerce-guide.com*

UNIT 25

CAREER OPPORTUNITIES IN RETAIL

LEARNING OBJECTIVES

- Knowing various positions and job assignments in retailing
- Discussing the essentials to join retail industry
- To provide an overview of employment opportunities available in the retailing sector
- Understanding the essentials before joining the retail industry

"What is the recipe for successful achievement? To my mind there are just four essential ingredients: Choose a career you love, give it the best there is in you, seize your opportunities, and be a member of the team."

Benjamin F. Fairless

INTRODUCTION

Retailing being labour intensive, offers positions for everyone regardless of age and eligibility. With hundreds of retailers entering the retail industry every year and with many Indian retailers becoming International, the openings in retail industry are growing rapidly. Not only in marketing and selling but also in other areas such as data maintenance, operations cell, accounts & finance etc, it offers growth opportunities. This chapter is an attempt to know what kind of career options exists in retailing and who is eligible for them.

RETAILING CAREERS

Retailing is one of the fastest growing sectors of the Indian economy. On one hand, retail sales are at their highest records in the retail industry. New technologies and retail formats are emerging from time to time. On the other hand, retailers have been facing several challenges. Retailers have no shortage of funds, technology and resources. But retailers are not getting right person at right job. Sometimes, candidates/job seekers are over qualified and have high expectations, and sometimes new entrants are not eligible for performing basic functions of retailing. Consumer expectations about customer service are high, while retailers find it difficult to provide them personal attention. At the same time, many retailers are not yet sure how to take work from the retail employees.

A person looking for a career in the world of retailing has two broad options: first to start his own retail business or to work for a retailer. In India, it has been observed that most of the people after working with few retail stores start their own retail shops. A person seeking career and business opportunities in retailing may choose 'franchising', which has element of both entrepreneurship and managerial assistance. In retail industry, career opportunities are plenty because of the number of new domestic and international players coming year after year. Malls are mushrooming and traditional 'kirana' stores are taking new shapes. Furthermore, few segments of retailing such as food retailing, luxury retailing, shoe and cloth retailing etc are growing at rapid rates. The increase in number of retail stores, malls, super bazaars, metro malls and mega marts during the last decade, offer significant opportunities for today's youth who is full of talent and passion.

RECRUITMENT OF RETAIL STAFF

Recruitment is a part of selection drive whereby a retailer generates a list of job applicants. This list is generated from various sources like walk in interviews, educational and vocational institutes and placement agencies. Besides this, unsolicited applications, employees' references, ex-employees who are looking for better jobs and advertisement are also used to select retail store employees. Table 25.1 represents the features of some recruitment sources.

Table 25.1
Features of recruitment process

Sources of recruitment **External sources**	**Features**
Educational and Vocational Institutions	❒ Schools, colleges and universities ❒ Suitable for entry levels
Advertisements	❒ Newspapers, journals, magazines and internet ❒ Provides wider choice of applicants ❒ Covers broad area ❒ Understandable and easy to keep record
Placement Agencies	❒ Private, government and semi-government bodies ❒ Good for applicant screening ❒ Makes selection procedure shorter ❒ Collect payment from both the applicant and the retail company
Unsolicited applications	❒ Walk-in interviews ❒ Cost effective ❒ Past details should be verified properly

Miscellaneous Sources	❐ Employees of wholesalers, manufacturers and distribution agents ❐ Reduces training budget ❐ Experienced employees ❐ Less problem in adjusting in stores
Internal Sources	
Employees' References	❐ Friends, relatives and known ❐ Provides loyal staff ❐ Cost effective ❐ Before recruitment, employee's current position, honesty and judgement of present employees is vital
Current and former Staff	❐ Promotion within the employees ❐ Good for motivating staff ❐ Cost effective ❐ Saves expenditure on training

Besides this, today, job sites like Naukri.com, hot jobs.com, monster jobs.com etc play a big role in recruitment of store employees. It is not only quick but also provides a large database. For entry-level floor jobs, retailers generally rely on educational and vocational institutes, walk-in interviews, recruitment sites and employee's recommendations. For middle-level positions, retailers use placement agencies, newspapers and competitors' turnovers.

During recruitment, the retailer's main stress remains on creating a long list of probable store staff, which will be reduced during selection process. Therefore, while collecting applications, retailers should accept only those applications that meet the minimum eligibility criteria such as educational background and working experience in order to save both money and time involved in the selection procedure.

CAREER OPPORTUNITIES IN RETAILING

In retail industry, most college graduates begin their retail careers as corporate staff or departmental floor staff. But for certain positions such as auditor, audit manager, store manager, marketing/sales manager, retail firms look for post graduate students having degree/diploma in concerned field. In India, usually opportunities exist in these three areas:

(1) Store Management
(2) Merchandise Management
(3) Corporate Staff
(4) Floor Staff

1. Store Management

Retailing being a high potential area, requires from its store managers to be sensitive to customers' needs, wants and complaints (if any). Store managers must have the ability to lead and motivate employees to achieve store's goals. Under store management, employees are supposed to perform activities such as: sales planning, customer services, sales supervision, maintenance and repairs, store and merchandise protection, training and development of employees, personnel administration and public relations. Following job options exist under management of stores:

Table 25.2

Opportunities in the Area of Management of Stores

Job Title	Job Assignment
Assistant Store Manager	To help implement merchandising strategies and policies; interview; hire and train sales personnel; take inventory; and order supplies.
Department Manager	Responsible for a department's merchandise displays, analyzing merchandise flow, and the training and direction of the sales staff. To assist buyers in selecting merchandise for branch stores.
Divisional Merchandise Manager	To plan, manage and integrate buying for an entire merchandise division (comprising many departments).
Group Manager	To manage a number of department managers in different merchandise classifications. To train, supervise and evaluate these department managers.
Management Trainee	First position for most college graduates entering retailing. Involves company orientation, classroom and on-the-job training, and close contact with buyers and group managers. Leads to department manager or assistant buyer.
Public Relations Director	To keep public aware of the retailer's positive accomplishments. To measure public attitudes to maintain a favorable image of the company.
Salesperson	To enable customers to make proper choices. To handle minor complaints. To stock some items and setup some displays. To note under stocked items. May also serve as a cashier.
Sales Promotion Manager	To plan and enact special sales, themes, and sales promotion tools (such as contests).
Store Manager	To oversee all store personnels and operations in a given outlet. To coordinate activities with other units in a chain. Responsible for customer service; to implement merchandising and human resource policies.

2. Merchandise Management

Merchandise management involves activities that are involved in acquiring particular goods or services and making them available at the place, time, quantity, quality and prices to enable a retailer to reach its goals while meeting the firm's financial goals. This area attracts two sorts of employees: one involved in buying process and other involved in merchandise planning.

Buyers are responsible for knowing customers' changing needs and wants, styling sizes, emerging trends and monitoring competition. The buyers constantly visit their stores and critically analyze whether the products shown/ displayed are appropriate for the store.

Planners have wide responsibilities to perform than buyers do. Planners' job start with determining how many styles, sizes, colours and individual items to purchase and then allocating merchandise to stores. Planners further continuously monitor store's sales and take decisions such as when to stop/reduce merchandise, if the sales are not sufficient. In such decisions, planners involve buyers and also decide a benchmark such as how much additional merchandise to purchase if it has good demand.

Following job titles exist under managing merchandise:

Table 25.3
Opportunities in the Area of Managing Merchandise

Job Title	Job Assignment
Assistant Buyer	To work under the supervision of a department manager. To assist in managing personnel, controlling inventory and to order supplies.
Catalog Manager	To select merchandise for inclusion in catalogs, work with vendors, order catalogs, and monitor order fulfillment (particularly timely shipments).
Merchandise Administrator	To coordinate and evaluate and work of buyers in several related merchandise classifications (in a division).
Merchandise Analyst	To plan and evaluate merchandise allocation to stores to ensure items are shipped at the right time, in proper amounts, and in the right assortment. To set assortment strategy based on trends. To monitor recorder systems.
Merchandise Manager	To coordinate selling efforts among different departments (merchandise categories). To act as a liason between store managers and buyers. Similar to group manager, but, there are expanded merchandise responsibilities.
Operations Manager	Responsible for receiving, checking, marking and delivering merchandise; customer service; work-room operations; and maintaining the retailer's physical plant.
Warehouser	To store and move goods within a warehouse; to keep inventory records and rotate stock.

3. Corporate Staff

Corporate staff basically belongs to diverse areas such as computer system, loss prevention, finance and control, advertising and sales promotion, real estate etc. Therefore, these areas provide opportunities for individuals having specific skills and interests. Following job titles exist under this head:

Table 25.4

Opportunities for being a member of corporate staff

Job Title	Job Assignment
Accountant (internal)	To record and summarize transactions; to verify reports; to provide financial information, budgets, forecasts and comparison reports.
Advertising Manager	To develop and implement an advertising program; to determine media, copy and message frequency; to recommend ad budget and choice of ad agency.
Auditor (internal)	To analyze data, interpret reports, verify accuracy of data and monitor adherence to the retailer's regular policies and practices.
Commercial Artist	To create illustrations, layouts and types of print to be used in the retailer's ads and catalogs, as well as on private-label packages.
Credit Manager	To supervise the credit process, including credit eligibility, credit terms, late payment fees, and consumer credit complaints.
Data-processing Manager	To oversee daily operations of the computer facility; to generate appropriate accounting, credit, financial, inventory, and sales reports; to recommend hardware and software.
Security Supervisor	Responsible for minimizing pilferage among employees and customers; to recommend security systems and procedures; to manage a retailer's security personnel.
Web Specialist	Involved with firm's Website, from design of pages to oversight of customers' interactions.

Career in Retailing

The retail industry in India is one of the major employers after agriculture. Retail career opportunities are plentiful and offers promising career. Throughout the globe, by any measure, more people are working in retailing than in any other sector of the economy. Further, the sudden spurt in rising middle class, emergence of nuclear family concept, and rapidly increasing per capita income (especially in metros) has made India a favourite destination to invest, resulting in increase in employment.

Indian retail Industry is broadly divided into organized and unorganized forms of retailing. Organized sector constitutes for mere 2% of the total retail trade and provides employment to just 5 lakh people, while unorganized retailing that refers to 'mom and pop' stores or nearby '*kirana* stores', '*baniya* shops', local departmental stores, convenience shops and so on offers employment to over 42 million people. Various segments in Indian retail industry are:

(i) Retail merchandising management
(ii) Fashion and clothing
(iii) Food retailing
(iv) Jewellery and luxury retailing
(v) Retail service and customer selling management
(vi) Entertainment and web retailing
(vii) Retail advertising and marketing management

Retailing being a vertical industry is not synonymous for malls and super bazaars but it offers opportunities for every strata of the population. From illiterate to post graduate, entry to top level management and teenager to aged, retailing has something to offer.

Areas where career opportunities exist:

(i) Selling related jobs
(ii) Managing store operations
(iii) Store management
(iv) Advertising (sales promotion)
(v) Sales distribution, supply chain and logistics management
(vi) Merchandise management
(vii) Information and communication technology
(viii) Accounts/finance
(ix) Store loss prevention
(x) Human resource management, and
(xi) Running an own store (entrepreneurship)

Essentials to join Retail industry

- Friendly and cooperative
- Outgoing
- Reliable and adjustable
- Professional and mature
- Good listener
- Patient

4. Floor Staff

Be it food and beverage retailing, shoe and clothing retailing, or luxury retailing, without the positive contribution of ***floor staff***, selling goods is not only difficult but a hard nut to crack. The retail business industry provides merchandise and services directly to customers, the floor staff is accountable for making certain that customers receive reasonable service and worth goods. They also respond to customers' inquiries, collect ideas and handle complaints. Retail controllers and managers administer the work of floor staff, salespersons, cashiers, customer care executives and store employees. They are responsible for managing merchandise, displaying and refilling whenever the need arises.

While the everyday jobs of retail sales employee, supervisors and managers vary, depending on the store size and type of retail store, as well as with the rank of management. When the size of retail stores and the variety of merchandise and services increases, these employees increasingly concentrate in one division or one aspect of merchandising. Big and large size retail stores have several levels of management. Like other companies, supervisory-level retail managers generally account to their mid-level counterparts who, in turn, account to their top-level managers/supervisors. The stores that are small in size and carry particular merchandise, generally, have less levels of management. In retail industry, supervisory-level retail managers often known as 'departmental heads' provide day-to-day report of each section, such as luxury, grocery, or kids wear.

Departmental Heads

Departmental heads usually are found in large size/chain retail stores. These managers setup and execute store's policies, mission, objectives, and practices for their precise departments; manage activities with other departmental heads; and struggle for horizontal functions within their specific departments. They administer employees who put prices, tags and place them on shelves; clean and systematize racks, shelves, and displays. They check inventory level in store rooms; and scrutinize goods to make certain that none is outdated or expired. Departmental heads also evaluate inventory level and store's sales records, build up merchandising policies, synchronize sales promotions drives, and may greet and help potential customers, promote sales and develop excellent public relations. Salary range: Rs 15,000 to Rs 35,000.

Management Trainee

If you're shortlisted or recruited into a store's placement or management training drive, then this will be your title for six months to one year. You will get exposure of learning merchandising, marketing, finance, business operations, and human resource management. Normally, sales trainees and others who show good performance in various 'departments including floor area get first chance in these programs, though company recruiters hire college students and other outside experienced candidates as well for the openings that linger. Salary range: Rs 4,000 to Rs 10,000.

Working Conditions

The majority of retail sales supervisors and managers have their offices within the retail stores. Though less time is spent in the office completing and managing merchandise orders or arranging work agendas, a large segment of their workday is washed-out on the sales floor area.

Normally, working hours of supervisors and managers differ significantly among retail stores, because work schedules generally depend on customers' needs and requirements. The majority of supervisors and managers work 40-50 hours or more a week; long hours are not unusual. This is predominantly correct during sales, festival days, holidays, busy shopping hours, and when inventory is taken. They are likely to work in late evenings and weekends but by and large are remunerated by getting a weekday off or one day extra salary. Working hours may vary monthly, and managers sometimes must report to work on small notice, particularly when floor staff is absent. Independent retail proprietors can often lay down their own schedules, but working hours must be suitable to customers.

Major Responsibilities:

- Adhere to policies and procedures of the store
- Assist in the flow of merchandise from stock areas to the selling floor in a timely and organized manner.
- Assist in the preparation and completion of accurate physical inventory as requested
- Attend training, education and meetings as required
- Completing opening and closing activities (i.e., opening cash counts, closing deposits, shift administration, etc.) in accordance with Origins policies
- Demonstrate products for customers
- Enforce and maintain the highest visual standards, including displays, signage, lighting and props
- Helps in the planning, research and implementation of cost effective measures to make additional sales
- Implore and correspond merchandise feedback from staff and customers to team leader
- Make certain maximum levels of customer service which will result in augmented productivity
- Present a positive attitude toward the Company, product and staff
- Present a professional appearance and maintain 'Origins' grooming standards and Dress Code
- Provide direction and give feedback to store management regarding staff performance
- Serve as a resource for general product knowledge to all customers and staff members
- Track retail sales against goal using the system provided
- Utilize and maintain customer database for phone calls, product launches, events and appointments

Job Summary

It includes maximization of store's sales through efficient customer service and personal assistance to customers in the selection of proper merchandise without violating store's standards, policies and practices. Floor staff also helps store management in supervising the sales floor area. They also help and participate with the store management in the implementation of store's sales programs, practices, policies and procedures. Floor staff also works with the retail manager to implement store's merchandising principles and the refilling of merchandise whenever necessary.

Next opportunities will come from retail

The rapid growth of the retail sector and its deep penetration in various parts of the country within a very short span of time has now been termed as the **retail revolution** by Indian media. In order to cater to the manpower needs of the retail industry, various retail management courses are being launched by several business schools in India. As the sector is booming in India, a career in retail sector promises good wages and growth potential for the ambitious youngsters. Retail management is associated with retailing business of departmental stores and shopping malls. There is a big demand for the retail management professionals to process all merchandise shipments, to achieve store sales and profitability, administration of stores as well as communication with the clients to satisfy them. Owing to this ever growing demand, the retail industry, especially organized retail, is going to expand on a mammoth scale in the Asian countries especially India. International retailers are viewing India as a potential market due to the rapidly growing customer base and it's ability to assimilate new brands into it's market. Employment opportunities in retail are not confined to malls and factory outlets alone. It is a field intersecting several other industries at various points and thus has multifaceted opportunities to offer, right from designing to sales, scouting the location for an outlet to running a mall.

In recent years, several Indian and international companies like Reliance, Pantaloons, Wal-Mart, Big Bazaar has rooted their presence in the country. The vacancies in retail sector are available from the entry to senior management level. Career in retail sector can be developed as store managers, retail managers, retail buyers, retail design/visual merchandise, merchandise planning and product developers. Several institutes in India including Birla Institute of Management Technology in New Delhi, RPG Institute of Retail Management, Indian Retail School offer various courses associated with retail management.

Every aspect of retailing gives an individual a chance to experiment, an opportunity to grow and to earn profits. Whether it's direct selling or buying and merchandising, retail industry has numerous jobs to offer; to suit the talent and qualifications of the people of various ages and academic backgrounds. Retail manager, store manager, visual merchandiser, pay roll administrator, category manager, buying administrator, product manager, commercial officer, key holder or designer are some of the jobs offered by the retail sector.

Retail industry includes various segments like:

Sales forms an important part of the retail segment and the frontline positions associated with this category are sales supervisor, store stock associate, cashier, stock receiver and sales associate. All these jobs are usually entry level in nature and require personal attributes like passion for competition, being a team player, ability to work with people from various fields, market analytical skills, and persuasive skills

- Some of the store related jobs that are available are - zone/district/regional/area manager, head of store operations
- Prevention of loss is also essential for retailing, for risk management issues pertaining to it like ensuring the safety of the customers and employees, preventing thefts from the stores, managing the finance audit, are covered by it.
- Merchandise category has opportunities like merchandise buyer/planner/ distributor/ analyst /controller. Their duties involve buying and dividing the merchandise into various categories, transferring them to stores,and exercising control.
- Online retailing is gaining momentum in India as most of the firms now offer the facility to purchase their products through online transactions. Many e learning portals are now offering courses in retailing, both real and virtual.
- Unlike the French original meaning of the word 'retail'- "to cut off, shred, paring", the retail industry is knitting the boundaries of global markets dexterously. Grab an opportunity and get into retailing.

Courtesy :

1. http://www.indiaedu.com/career-avenues/career-in-retail-sector.html
2. The Hindu (Online edition), Jan 10, 2007 (http://www.hinduonnet.com)

ESSENTIAL DUTIES AND RESPONSIBILITIES OF FLOOR STAFF

I. Sales/Customer Service:

Selling and floor supervision are the primary responsibilities with customer service being the number one priority.

- Adheres to all corporate dress code policies.
- Adheres to and practices all corporate selling skills programs and assists store management in rolling out and tracking the programs, goals and guidelines for entire sales staff.
- Assists store management in determining work schedules and floor coverage requirements.
- Assists store management in ensuring sales staff is aware of and informs customers of current promotions. Ensures that sales staff invites customers to return to the store by mentioning future testing, special events and pending arrival of new products.
- Assists store management in resolving customer complaints.
- Assists store management to ensure that all sales are accurately processed; this includes how to process all returns, voids, store credits and gift certificates. In absence of the store management, the supervisor will approve the above transactions.
- Assists store management to ensure that sales professionals achieve their individual goals and that customer receives the best service.

- Assists store management to ensure that sales staff prepares merchandise for purchase or delivery by wrapping, bagging and packaging product in accordance with all corporate and store guidelines.
- Attends and participates in all store meetings and corporate promotions.
- Ensures that sales staff understands and participates in all corporate and store sales contests and special programs.
- Ensures that the customer is greeted within 30 seconds of entering the store and that friendly, prompt and courteous service is being offered.
- Identifies customers' needs and answers customers' questions. Assists store management to ensure that all sales staff can answer questions regarding price, location, features, benefits and use of products.
- Maintains an individual clientele book and adheres to all corporate preferred-customer programs. Assists store management in developing other sales staff's clientele and preferred customers.
- Meets or exceeds individual and store-assigned sales and productivity goals.
- Obtains merchandise requested by customers and successfully processes telephone orders, utilizing the Crabtree & Evelyn Telephone Etiquette guidelines.
- Responsible for product knowledge and for assisting store management in the product training of all other sales staff.

II. Day to day business operations

- Displays merchandise in accordance with corporate guidelines.
- Ensures that all advertising and promotional displays are set up properly.
- Ensures that Sales Professionals adhere to and practice all corporate and store policies and procedures.
- Receives and prices product. Assists store management to ensure that the sales staff is stamping, marking and tagging the product correctly.

III. Supervision

- Assists store management in the development and direction of the store sales staff.
- Assists store management to ensure that all sales staff are meeting the standards listed above.
- Opens and closes the store when necessary. Acts as the "lead" in the absence of the Store Manager or Assistant Manager.
- Reports and properly addresses in accordance with store guidelines all sales staff development and performance issues by working with store management as a team to approach issues pro-activity.

IV. Safety/Security

- Ensures that all safety and security programs and policies are adhered to. Reports any health or safety issues to store management and takes appropriate corrective action.

SUMMARY

Retailing is a dynamic field and requires dynamic employees to perform day-to-day activities of a retail store. Person who are young, educated and have potential to grow are in great demand. Broadly, it offers two career options:

(i) to start your own retail business

(ii) to work for a retailer

Both options are full of enthusiasm, challenges and rewards. Further, retail careers offer all individuals the change to prosper and succeed irrespective of the caste, creed and religion. In short, career opportunities in retailing are many and will generate a huge source of employment. This is also evident by the Ernst & Young's report entitled 'the great Indian retail story', which anticipates that the Indian retail industry would offer over 2 million employment opportunities within the year 2010.

REVIEW QUESTIONS

True and False Questions

1. Retailing is a labour intensive industry.
2. Retailing offers positions for everyone regardless of age and eligibility.
3. Retailing is one of the fastest growing sectors of the Indian economy.
4. A person looking for a career in the world of retailing has two broad options: first to start his/her own retail business or to work for a retailer.
5. Recruitment is a part of selection drive whereby a retailer generates a list of job applicants.
6. During recruitment, the retailers' main stress remains on creating a long list of probable store staff, which is reduced during selection process.
7. In retail industry, most college graduates begin their retail careers as entrepreneurs.
8. Merchandise management involves activities that are involved in acquiring particular goods or services and making them available to the customers.
9. Buyers have wide responsibilities to perform than planners.
10. Corporate staff basically belongs to diverse areas such as computer system, loss prevention, finance and control, advertising and sales promotion, real estate etc.
11. Without internet there can't be any online retailing.
12. Retail controllers and managers administer the work of floor staff, salespersons, cashiers, customer care executives and store employees.
13. Departmental heads usually are found in small sized retail stores.
14. The majority of retail sales supervisors and managers have their offices within the retail stores.
15. Selling and floor supervision are the primary responsibilities with customer service being the number one priority for a floor manager.

Answers

1. True 2. True 3. True 4. True

5. True 6. True 7. False 8. False
9. False 10. True 11. True 12. True
13. False 14. True 15. True

Multiple Choice Questions

1. Retailing being labour intensve offers jobs to:
   (*a*) Only experienced. (*b*) Minimum graduate.
   (*c*) Every one (*d*) Who have degree/diploma in retail.
2. Entrepreneurship basically means:
   (*a*) Working with an entrepreneur
   (*b*) beginning careers at low levels in corporate
   (*c*) starting own business
   (*d*) All of the above.
3. Recruitment is part of ....
   (*a*) Training (*b*) Development
   (*c*) Interview (*d*) Selection.
4. The primary responsibility of a store manager is:
   (*a*) To oversee all store employees and their operations.
   (*b*) To coordinate activities with other units
   (*c*) Being responsible for customer service
   (*d*) All of the above
5. Internal auditor is responsible for
   (*a*) to record and summarise transactions
   (*b*) to supervise the credit process
   (*c*) minimising store pilferage
   (*d*) to verify accuracy of data.
6. Floor staff is responsible for:
   (*a*) displaying merchandise
   (*b*) providing financial informations.
   (*c*) recommending securing system
   (*d*) generating appropriate accounting
7. Essentials to join retail sector are:
   (*a*) Friendly and cooperative. (*b*) Reliable and adjustable.
   (*c*) Professional and mature. (*d*) All of the above.
8. Departmental heads are usually found in
   (*a*) small sized retail store. (*b*) large size retail store
   (*c*) mom and pop stores (*d*) kiosks.

9. The salary range for a retail management trainee generally lies between:
   (*a*) Rs. 15000 to Rs. 35,000 (*b*) Rs 2000 to Rs. 4000
   (*c*) above. 10,000 (*d*) Rs. 4000 to Rs. 10,000
10. The retail industry is one of the major employers after ....
   (*a*) Indian civil aviation (*b*) Agriculture.
   (*c*) Pharmaceuticals (*d*) Diamond makers.

Answers

1. (*c*)	2 (*c*)	3. (*d*)	4. (*d*)
5. (*d*)	6. (*a*)	7. (*d*)	8. (*b*)
9. (*d*)	10. (*b*).		

Check your progress

1. What do you mean by 'owning a business'?
2. What is corporate staff?
3. What is 'option' in job?
4. Explain the meaning of 'planner'?
5. What is 'benchmarking'?
6. Who is 'Individual'?
7. Describe the term 'Job title'?
8. What is organized retailing?
9. What is 'segment' in retailing?
10. Explain the term 'Entrepreneurship'?

Short-Answer Questions

1. What are the prerequisites to join the retail industry?
2. Why Indian retail sector has a lot to offer to youth?
3. How franchising offers both the qualities of entrepreneurship and managerial assistance?
4. Briefly explain various sources of recruitment in retail industry?
5. What sort of career opportunities exist in the area of merchandising management?
6. Why it is said that in retailing, career opportunities are temporary in nature.
7. Is it right to say that while working in retail industry, person should leave his emotions, anger and personal views outside the store?
9. What aspects of retailing career appeals to you?
10. What are the merits and demerits in joining retail industry?

Long-Answer Questions

1. What broad options would you like to suggest somebody who is looking for a career in retailing? Explain various career opportunities available in the retailing sector with proper examples wherever necessary?

2. It is still unexplored that technology careers are numerous and varied in the retail industry. Explain?

Applied Questions

1. Why a career in retailing is considered a challenging option with growth potential.
2. Why it is said that retail career has nothing to do much with age groups?
3. Doing business in retailing through 'franchisee route' is the safest and easiest way to begin with. Explain with examples wherever necessary?
4. Make few visits to retail stores in your colony and try to read the state of mind of the employees working over there. Please explain?

Appendix

Exhibit 25.1: Careers in Restaurant Operations

CAREERS IN RESTAURANTS' OPERATIONS

If you are looking for exciting and challenging career opportunities, come to McDonald's. We believe that employees are our biggest assets. In fact there is a reason why we are the world's number one Quick Service Restaurant ... it's our people.

Our selection process is very systematic and comprises of 3 stages:

- **Psychometric Testing and Initial Interview**
- **On the Job Evaluation [OJE]**

  Shortlisted candidates undergo 3 days OJE at a McDonald's restaurant which provides the candidate with an opportunity to look at McDonald's as a potential employer. It also gives McDonald's a chance to observe and assess the candidate's performance.
- **Final Interview**

  Candidates who have passed their OJE are called for the final interview.

We have two entry levels for those who want to make a career in restaurant operations.

LEVEL 1: CREW

Qualifications: If you are 18 years of age, passed your X / XII, smart and ambitious, you can join as Crew trainee or Trainee Host/ess.

Career Path of a Crew Trainee

Crew Trainee >> Crew Member >> Training Squad (TS) >> Floor Manager (FM) >> Shift Running Floor Manager (SRFM) >> Second Assistant Manager >> First Assistant Manager >> Restaurant Manager

Job profile of a Restaurant Manager:

- A Restaurant Manager is responsible for running an independent, multi-crore restaurant
- Training, motivating and leading a team of 50-100 employees
- Independently managing the restaurant's operations in terms of sales, profitability and community relations.
- Delivering 100% Total Customer Satisfaction to every customer - every time

Career Path of Trainee Host/ess

Trainee Host/ess >> Host/ess >> Customer Care Representative (CCR) >> Field Marketing Coordinator (FMC) >> Field Marketing Executive (FME)

LEVEL 2 : TRAINEE MANAGER / CCR

Qualifications: Fresh Graduates or Hotel Management Degree / Diploma Holders

Career Path of a Trainee Manager

Trainee Manager >> Second Assistant Manager >> First Assistant Manager >> Restaurant Manager >> Area Supervisor >> Operations Consultant / Training Consultant >> Operations Manager >> Operations Director

Your Career Growth at McDonald's

How quickly you progress at McDonald's depends entirely on your ability to grasp the skills you need to master. There are specific training courses that you will have to attend which will equip you with the necessary knowledge.

1. **Management Development Programme (MDP):**

   The MDP series is designed to help you become the most effective manager that you can be.

2. **Floor Management Course (FMC)**

   The FMC is geared towards improving the trainee's ability to deliver QS&C as a Floor Manager.

3. **Basic Operations Course (BOC)**

   BOC addresses the 'why's' and 'how-to's' of McDonald's procedures and standards, rather than 'what-to-do's' or 'what-to-know's'. It also deepens the candidates understanding of operational skills, standards and procedures

4. **Basic Management Course (BMC)**

   BMC develops the manager's ability to observe and gather facts, analyze information, and then act and communicate according to McDonald's policies and good business/people practices.

5. **Intermediate Operations Course (IOC)**

   IOC is an opportunity for managers to gain knowledge of recognizing various real-world problems within the restaurant and the different approaches in analyzing and resolving them

6. **Advanced Operations Course (AOC)**
7. **Operations Consultant Course (OCC)**
8. **Training Consultant Course (TCC)**

Courtesy: *Company Website*

Exhibit 25.2: Employment Scenario in Retail

At present, India is employing about 22 million people in retail i.e. at par with USA. The present scenario depicts that there will be a very high demand for talented manpower in the retail business. It is predicted that retail employers in India will need more than two million skilled people in various specialized areas for retail across the country. Retail is challenging, engrossing, dynamic and quality education is required to advance and succeed in the Retail industry today.

Moreover, due to its correlation with other industrial and service sectors, organized retailing is generating a great deal of indirect employment; security, and electrical and mechanical maintenance, property management services, parking, sorting, packaging, etc. If both direct and indirect employment is taken together, organized retailing is bound to create more and better paid, better quality jobs.

This is a large growth opportunity in an organized business that the country will see after a long time. Apart from the direct jobs, every retail job created adds further jobs in the support businesses. The Indian retail industry is structuring itself to meet global demands and the management institutes such as Acumen Academy of Retail are jumping on the bandwagon.

Acute shortage

- Immediate manpower requirement of 1 lakh at front end, 20,000 at back end, 20,000-25,000 percent at supervisory level
- 30% retail industry CEOs are Indian experts from South-East Asia, West Asia and Eastern Europe to address the new sales system and processes.
- Organized retail to require 5 lakh trained manpower in 3 years. Organized retailing, which is set to grow to a 24 billion dollar industry by 2010, will require 500,000 trained manpower to run hypermarkets, super stores and wholesale cash and carry facilities in major Indian cities, a national think-tank has said.

Need for qualified and trained manpower

Qualified and trained manpower is of utmost importance in retail. The need for specialized skills is increasingly felt in the areas of:

Strategic management - strategizing, targeting and positioning, marketing and site selection.

Merchandise management - Vendor selection, inventory management, pricing.

- Store management - Layout, display, customer relationship, and inventory management etc.
- Administrative Management - Human resources, finance, marketing and so on.

Retailing falls under a vertical industry and is not just restricted to malls, as most tend to believe. This industry offers ample opportunity and has room for everyone starting from entry level to senior management level.

Retailing provides employment to the largest section of the population across most industrialized nations. It is an industry that promises a profitable road.

The boom in the retail industry has brought with it many employment opportunities in this arena. People with varied skills and talents are required in this fast emerging industry. A career in retailing is considered as a challenging option with growth potential.

Exhibit 25.3: Primary Areas Where Employment Opportunities Exist

Sales and Sales-Related Jobs

The sales and sales-related retail career area includes positions like sales associate, cashier, store stock associate, and stock receiver. These frontline positions bring retail's core business of serving the customer and generating sales.

The passion for working with all varieties of people, flexibility, level-headedness, problem solving, and teamwork are critical for success in this area.

These positions are typically entry points into retail careers. High-end commission-based sales areas like jewelry, appliances are highly preferred sales jobs. Frontline sales experience is highly valued and many retailers promote from within

Store Operations

Retail professionals in the store operations area oversee overall store operations and profits. They include Head of Store Operations, Regional Manager, and District Manager, and responsibilities in this area may include managing staff functions like loss prevention and/or human resources.

Store Management

The store manager or management team has responsibility ranging from departmental to overall establishment. Managers at all levels supervise and assist sales and other employees.

Additional responsibilities, depending upon store/company size and management level include opening and closing the store, staffing, administration, and financial functions. Promotions to management positions can be earned through experience, or an MBA degree may offer direct entry to management.

Marketing/Advertising

Depending upon company's size, marketing functions may be centralized in one department, divided into different departments (like advertising, sales promotion, art and visual merchandising, and public/press relations), or group in various combinations.

Marketing also conducts focus groups and statistical analysis of customer buying patterns to develop strategies and plans that guide marketing components like ads, websites, store signage etc.

Distribution, Logistics, Supply Chain Management

This retail career area oversees movement and storage of consumer products. Responsibilities include management and facilitation of distribution centers, logistics traffic management, trucking and other transportation operations, and may include import/export shipping and related duties.

Merchandise Buying/Planning

These retail professionals select the merchandise to be sold in the stores by sourcing vendors. They facilitate order follow-up, inventory flow through and allocation of merchandise to stores, attending to issues like flow quantities and timing.

Statistical development and analysis are increasingly woven into this retail career area, where team members also coordinate gross margin planning/analysis responsibilities, develop distribution plans for merchandise categories and subclasses, and balance stock unit ratios by store.

IT and E-Commerce

Technology careers are numerous and varied in the retail industry. From web design to servers and network systems management, inventory systems etc., technology careers are growing in the Retail industry.

Finance

Financial and accounting skills are more than a game in retail, they can be your career! The finance retail career area includes all accounting and treasury functions like accounting for income, paying expenses, compiling and maintaining financial records, money management and cash flow control, banking, investment, and credit lines.

Source: *Adapted from www.acumeneducation.in*

THE ROAD AHEAD IN INDIA

LEARNING OBJECTIVES

- Understanding the emerging retail destinations in India
- Describing how cyber retailing is gaining popularity in Indian retail industry
- Explaining the future of organized retailing in India
- Understanding the government policy towards FDI
- Analyzing the reasons for popularity of internet retailing

"I think one of the big errors people are making right now is thinking that old-style businesses will be obsolete, when actually they will be an important part of this new civilization. Some retail groups are introducing e-commerce and think that the "bricks" are no longer useful. But they will continue to be important"

Carlos Slim Helu

INTRODUCTION

The Indian retail sector is highly fragmented consisting of more than 12 million outlets run by family members. Conventionally, these small 'kirana stores' have been one of the easiest ways to generate self employment as it requires less investment in land, capital and labour. As a result, India is known for highest retail densities in the world at over 6% (12 million retail shops for about 210 million households). India's peers, such as Brazil and China, took 10-15 years to raise the share of their organized retail sectors from 5% when they began to 20% and 38% respectively. India too is moving towards growth and maturity in the retail sector at a fast pace[1]. Organized retailing is projected to grow at the rate of 25-30% annually and is estimated to reach over an astounding Rs 100,000 crore by 2010. Its contribution to total retailing sales is likely to rise to 9% by the end of the decade[2].

---

1 *www.ey.com*
2 *www.coolavenues.com*

OPPORTUNITIES IN ORGANIZED RETAIL MARKET IN INDIA

According to Tata Strategic Management Group (One of the largest management consulting firms in South Asia), the overall retail market in India is likely to grow at a Compound Annual Growth Rate (CAGR) of 5.5% (at constant prices) to 1,677,000 Cr before 2015. The organized retail market is expected to grow much faster at a CAGR of 21.8% (at constant prices) to Rs. 246,000 Crore by 2015 thereby constituting 15% approximately of the overall retail sales. Based on our projections, the top 5 organized retail categories by 2015 would be general merchandise, food, grocery, durables, apparel & food service and home improvement[3].

If we talk about India's peers such as Brazil and China, took more than 10 years to increase the share of their organized retail industry from 5% when they began to 38% and 20% respectively. India too has learnt lesson from its peers and is moving towards expansion and maturity in the retail sector at a high speed[4]. Figure 26.1 depicts India's success story in the retail sector while figure 26.2 reveals the success story of India's retail sector. Further, the Ernst & Young's report entitled '***the great Indian retail story***', which anticipates that the Indian retail industry would offer over 2 million employment opportunities within the year 2010, today, India's retail is amongst the fastest growing sectors in the country. It ranks first ahead of Russia in terms of emerging markets potential in retail and is deemed a 'Priority one' market for international retail.

Figure 26.1

Penetration of organized retail with respect to leading economies

www.ey.com

[3] www.tsmg.com

[4] www.ey.com

Figure 26.2

Success story of India's Retail Sector

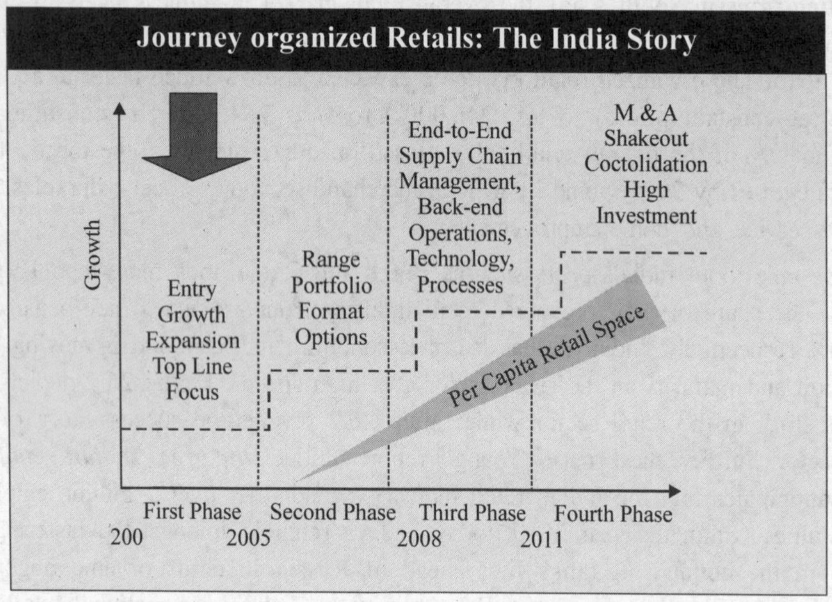

Source: *www.ey.com*

INDIAN RETAIL INVESTMENTS ON THE ANVIL

India's vast middle class with its expanding purchasing power and its rapidly growing retail industry are key attractions for global retail giants wanting to enter newer markets.

- Disney Consumers Products (DCP) is ramping up retail presence by launching several products - apparel accessories, cartoon, station ries, kids section, food, health and beauty.
- Esprit, a premium fashion brand plans to add 50 new outlets to its present network of 34 by 2010 with an investment of about US$ 12.63 million.
- Estee Lauder will be setting up 20 outlets over the next three years.
- Giordano Fashions (India) will establish a chain of single-brand retail.
- Indian Oil Corporation (IOC) is planning to invest US$ 189.103 million in rural areas during the financial year 2009.
- Inorbit Malls (India) Ltd. will be investing around US$ 294.79 million to build eight malls across the country within the next two years.
- Luxury watch brand, Rado, is planning a major expansion drive to double its exclusive stores to 15, covering new Tier-II cities like Jalandhar and Ludhiana.
- Marks & Spencer plans to put in 51 percent foreign direct investment in single-brand retail business.
- Panasonic is planning a US$ 200 million investment in India for setting up new units, brand positioning, and upgrading its facilities by 2011.

- Reebok will open 250 stores in 2009-10 in India, touching the target of 850 by end of this fiscal. Besides consolidating its position in metros and tier-I cities, it is also going for a major expansion in tier-II and tier-III and lower-tier cities.
- Reliance Retail Ltd will start 50–60 'i stores' all over India, in the next 18 months, and also open 150 Reliance Digital stores by 2011–12. Reliance Retail Ltd (RRL) runs from over 600 stores in more than 57 cities across 13 states.
- Religare Enterprises, the integrated financial services firm is planning to set up multi-product, multi-brand retail stores in the personal finance space under the brand name Finmart, with an investment of more than US$ 23.779 million to set up 200 such stores across the country.
- Retail major Subhiksha plans to open 1,250 more outlets by end-2010.
- Singapore-based, US$ 5 billion worth OSIM International Ltd is planning to set up another 100 exclusive brand outlets in India.
- Titan Industries will launch 'Titan Eye +' branded spectacles stores all over India with an investment of US$ 5.05 million for putting up 80 stores in the metro, tier-I and tier-II cities. The company has a plan to roll out 200 stores in three years.
- To expand its presence in the apparel sector in India, Koutons Retail will be investing US$ 70.79 million to open 200 large Koutons Family Stores and add another 1,400 stores in modern retail format to the existing 605 stores within the next 18 months.
- Videocon Retail plans to invest US$ 168.45 million to expand its electronic retail format, 'Next' Retail and Planet M, the mobile, music, entertainment and lifestyle chain, in the next three years.

Source: *www.ibef.org*

EMERGING RETAIL DESTINATIONS

With growth in incomes, increasing size of middle class and Indian's economy position against all odds in the last decade has resulted in retail revolution making the customer in real sense a 'king' or 'queen'. Due to rapidly increasing middle class in terms of size and income has made India a favourite destination for foreign direct investment. All world class brands are available in most of the malls making India a hub of malls. Following are some of the emerging retail destinations that have emerged recently and are growing by leaps and bounds. These are:

1. Luxury Retail Destination:

India's luxury retail market which is in its 'growth stage' is roughly estimated to be around Rs. 2000 crore and the way malls are mushrooming all over the country is expected to grow by 30-40 percent in next decade. Further, the Forbes list of 500 richest people shows the success story of India as a leading destination. Yet, the luxury retailing is limited to metro Tier I, & Tier II cities, but the advent of 'small shoppers' is believed to add a thrust to this leading destination.

By the next four to five years, India is expected to become a manufacturing hub for global luxury brands, according to a FICCI-Yes Bank report on luxury brands. The report states that India has the most rapidly growing High-Networth Individuals (HNI) population in the world and the income level of consumers is expected to grow three times by 2025. The active age group (25–45 years) is likely to rise to one third of the population. The report further states that the manufacturing business of luxury items in India can cross US$ 500 million with global brands like Louis Vuitton and Frette looking at India as a manufacturing base[5].

According to a survey done by AT Kearney, the Indian luxury retail market is estimated to touch US$ 30 billion by 2015. Estimated to be the 12th largest in the world, it has been growing at the rate of 25 percent annually. In the kids' retail sector, brands like Monalisa, Zapp, Disney and Swiss kidswear brand Milou are coming to India. French furniture brand Gautier and Marks & Spencer will be launching a special range for kids in India.

According to research firm KSA Technopak, the branded segment comprises US$ 701.7 million of the total kids' apparel market-size of over US$ 3 billion. Industry experts say kids' retailing will touch annual growth of 30–35 percent.

2. Entertainment Destination

Technological advances, changing demographics, shifts in consumer preferences and stress in personal and workplace life have brought up structural changes in Indian's entertainment and leisure industry. In fact, entertainment industry has been changing very fast due to retailing of movies, amusement parks and music products.

PVR being a pioneer in the field of Cineplex, had a turnover of Rs 41 crores in 2001-02, which is expected to rise to about Rs 500 crores in 2008-09. PVR Limited raised Rs 100 crores through private equity from ICICI venture as part of funding to PVR expansion plan. This represents the most significant investment in the Indian entertainment industry. Further, the way the theme parks, music outlets, cyber cafes, resorts, clubs are mushrooming all over the country, will lead India as the next hub for entertainments.

3. Retail Banking

Changing consumer demographics, increasingly affluent with bulging middle class and the youngest population in the world has given birth to retail banking in India. Today, baking market has transformed into a 'buyer's market' from a 'seller's market'

Retail banking response to the change

- 'Bank' customer has replaced 'Branch' customer
- Customer oriented strategies

[5] *www.ibef.org*

- Differentiation/Segmentation of customers
- Emergence of "Any where Any time" Banking concept
- Fastest withdrawal and deposits
- Focus on understanding customer ease
- Improved processes/Bundled product offerings
- Stress on building and sustaining relationships

There are two emerging retail destinations in real sense that need not to prove their success stories but these are other destinations that are in burgeoning stage but will become the trend of the day in the years to come. These are:

(i) Real Estate Retailing
(ii) Petro-retailing
(iii) Catering Retailing
(iv) Pharma Retailing and so on.

GOVERNMENT POLICY FOR RETAILING IN INDIA

List of key Government bodies to look after FDI matters

1. District Industries Centers
2. Investment Promotion and Infrastructure Development Cell
3. Licensing Committee (LC)
4. Project Approval Board (PAB)
5. Foreign Investment Promotion Board (1991)
6. Foreign Investment Promotion Council (1996)
7. Foreign Investment Implementation Authority (1999)
8. Investment Commission (2004)

Indian government policy with regard to development of retail industry has been liberal and motivating. The Indian traders/ retailers register their outlets/shops with concerned authorities in various states and by honoring sales tax and other obligations of the state concerned, they can run their retail business. As such, there is no constraint on the entry of any domestic business house into retail sector. Therefore India has more than 12 million 'kirana' stores making India a hub of retail shops. With the rising disposable income of Indian middle class and 8-10 % annual GDP growth has attracted global players to enter and explore the opportunities in Indian untapped retail market. Considering the future of 12 million of shopkeepers, policy makers and even some state governments in consultation with centre have been planning to restrict foreign players in the Indian retail sector, which is in its nascent stage. Therefore, the decision of allowing FDI in retailing has been a controversial subject for last decade. FDI is allowed in several sectors of the economy by the central government but FDI in retailing is still restricted and not allowed in full swing.

FDI in retailing

As allotment of land is a subject matter for states, central government is concerned with FDI approvals in the sector. Due to political compulsion and the opposition from the Left parties, the government has banned FDI in retailing since 1997. At present, foreign investors can only enter the retailing sector through franchising agreements. Till January 2006, the retailers entered the market through the franchisee route, but in January 2006, the Indian government decided to have up to 51% stake in local (domestic) subsidiary. Currently, multiple brands are not allowed but the government has proposed 49% FDI in multi-brand segment.

Guidelines for FDI approval

1. The government has permitted FDI 51% in "***single brand***" segment or in joint venture for the retail of its exclusive product. Therefore, so far foreign players in India are entering through franchisee route only.
2. No incentives are required to attract FDI because indigenous market size and potential of market is already large and ample inducers exist like increasing size of middle class, increasing disposable income of Indian youth.
3. Following sectors are prohibited for FDI
   (i) Multi-brands
   (ii) Atomic and nuclear energy
   (iii) Lottery business
   (iv) Gambling and betting
4. State governments are not supposed to provide any land and power subsidies.
5. 100% FDI is permitted in wholesale trading which involves building a large distribution infrastructure to assist local retailers and manufacturers.
6. Further there is no need to give costly breaks and import duty exemption.
7. In addition to above mentioned restrictions, Indian government has permitted FDI in these sectors, to the maximum limit of 100%, through the automatic route:
   I. Power trading
   II. Petroleum infrastructure
   III. Processing and warehousing of coffee and rubber
   IV. Coal Mining and Diamond

This decision of Indian government is not welcomed by some political parties especially the leftist one; gates have been opened for global players interested in these areas after fulfillment of concerned formalities.

Note: *With prior permission, FDI upto 51% in retail of 'single brand' products is allowed and they are subjected to the condition that goods to be sold under same name globally are branded during manufacturing.*

POLICY AND REGULATORY ENVIRONMENT

For Joint Ventures

Foreign players can enter into agreements with Indian retailers and set up base in India but the share of the multinational is restricted to forty nine percent in this route.

For Manufacturing

International retailers can setup manufacturing units for their products in India. Entry through this route entails the company the rights to retail the products in India through individual retailing outlets.

For Distribution

A foreign player can setup distribution offices, branches in India and provide goods and services to the local retailers. There is also no restriction for franchisee outlets under this route. The Indian labour laws are committed to ensure higher liberalization with the Government permitting flexibilities in the rules in emerging retail hubs like Bangaluru and Hyderabad. Fundamental instituted laws like restricted working hours, compulsory closing of the store atleast once a week are being modified to suit the demands and requirements of today's retailing without adversely impacting the labour benefits. Further, Indian government is also taking efforts to ensure that licensing and clearance mechanism should not deter the retail growth. Considering European model, single window clearance mechanism is being put into practice to reduce the entry and establishment timelines for new players in the market and facilitate easy procedures in issuance of necessary approvals.

In order to facilitate easy access to retail space for international investors, the government is serious to take a calibrated approach by reforming land laws and the real estate regulatory environment. Considering, Central government is releasing large tracts of unused land for retail development in the Delhi NCR region and Mumbai. It is expected to be followed by the other state governments also with monetary benefit from the access to impressive revenues from land sales and tax collection from retail developments. To resolve the problems related to lease rentals and pro-tenancy laws, which considerably discourage international players, are being followed by the Government, with initiatives like setting up Special Economic Zones (SEZs), allotment of Government controlled land etc. Introduction of Value Added Tax (VAT) in most of the Indian states and territories and many industry verticals to resolve the multiple taxation issue and maintain uniform prices across regions is one of the outcomes of government's commitment to make India as Asian retail hub.

The Agricultural Produce Marketing Committee Act (APMCA), which curtails direct sourcing of agricultural produce (grocery, food grains) is proposed to be amended soon, with a Draft Model Act being legislated by the government. The new act promotes direct marketing to corporate investors, setting up of farmers/consumers market and contract farming. Contract farming is already being pursued in certain states with players like Reliance and Pepsi Co. forging alliances with local farmers for direct procurement of raw materials. The Government is encouraging the contract farming practice, as it benefits both the farmers and the corporate retailers, with the former gaining access to better prices and the latter to a steady supply source. The Government is currently considering modernizing and developing eight strategically located "*Mandis*" with cold storage, sorting and grading facilities made available as a part of the infrastructure services[6].

---

[6] *www.ibef.org*

Figure 26.3

Indicative List of Foreign Players' Entry to India

Entry Route	Expected Players
Franchisee	• Pizza Hut • Domino's Pizza • Marks & Spencer • Nike, Tommy Hilfiger • Subway
Manufacturing	• Bata • United Colors of Benetton
Distribution	• Hugo Boss, Mango swarovski
Cash and Carry Wholesale trading	• Metro • ShopRite
Joint Ventures	• McDonald's • Reebok

Source: *Idea taken from Retail Market and Opportunities, www.ibef.org*

RETAILING: THE ROAD AHEAD

Retailing in India can be traced to the emergence of local '*kirana*' stores serving to the needs of near consumers. The year 1980 saw some change in retail when India started to open up economy. In the textile sector, companies like Raymond's, Vimal,

Figure 26.4

Organised Retail Market in India (Rs. Cr.)

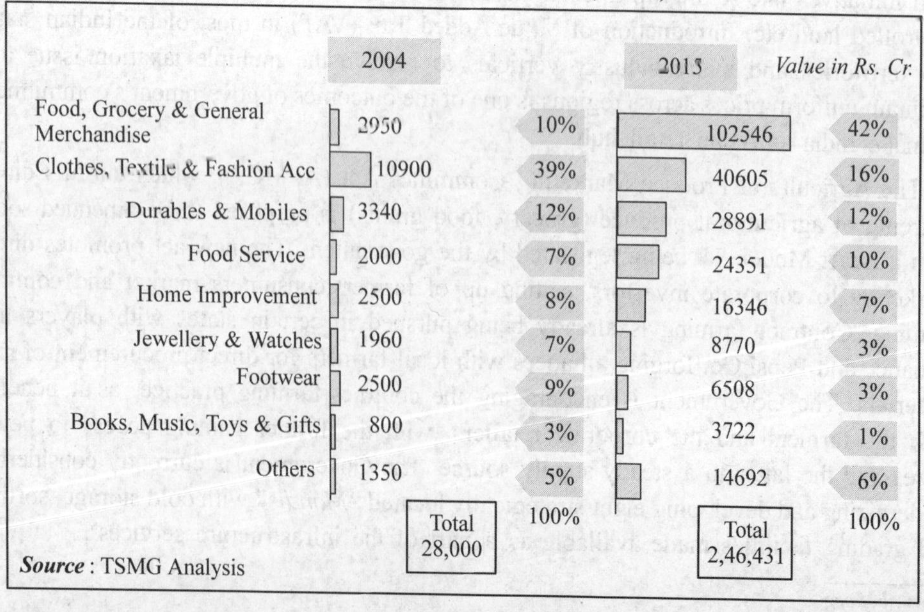

	2004		2015	*Value in Rs. Cr.*
Food, Grocery & General Merchandise	2950	10%	102546	42%
Clothes, Textile & Fashion Acc	10900	39%	40605	16%
Durables & Mobiles	3340	12%	28891	12%
Food Service	2000	7%	24351	10%
Home Improvement	2500	8%	16346	7%
Jewellery & Watches	1960	7%	8770	3%
Footwear	2500	9%	6508	3%
Books, Music, Toys & Gifts	800	3%	3722	1%
Others	1350	5%	14692	6%
	Total 28,000	100%	Total 2,46,431	100%

Source : TSMG Analysis

Grasim, S.Kumar's and Bombay Dyeing initially opened their retail outlets in major Indian cities. Getting inspiration, later on HMT and Titan created an organized retailing by opening series of showrooms with after sales service concept. In 1991, with a fresh wave of new entrants because of LPG (Liberalization, Privatization and Globalization) drive, retailing spreaded to Indian cities and towns. Food World, Subhiksha, Nilgiris, Music World, Cross World and Fountain head were the main to open their outlets throughout the country year 1995 onwards, Indian retail industry saw emergence of shopping centers and malls with facilities like parking, home delivery and payment through plastic money. Figure 26.4 shows the current and future size of retail industry in India. It shows that the size of organized retailing which was 28,000 crore in 2004 will reach 2, 48,431 crore by the end 2015.

Despite some uncertain chunks, everyone can expect the immense potential of the boom in the Indian retail sector. Given the increasing size and the purchasing power of the Indian consumer, the road ahead can only get smoother and it is only a matter of time before the domestic retail industry is on par with its western counterparts[7].

THE FUTURE EXPECTATIONS

As India is targeting for its GDP to grow by 8–10% per year, it requires raising rate of investment as well as generating demand for the increased products and services produced. Exporting is the first way to raise that demand and encouraging private consumption and expenditure is another way. But, if we allow FDI, it can do both the above mentioned tasks – the retail business firms can adopt successful managerial practices and ICT advanced techniques to cut wastages, errors and omissions and may set up integrated supply chains for replacing the present disorganized and fragmented market. As per the McKinsey report, India approximately wastes Rs 50,000 crores in food chain management every year. The rapidly growing economy, favourable demographic pattern, changing standard of living and untapped rural markets are the reasons to allow FDI.

Even according to AT Kearney report 2007, India is one of the leading retail destinations in the world. The report estimated India's total retail market at US $300 billion, which is expected to grow at a compounded 30-40 percent over the coming five to seven years. The share of organized retail segment which is currently 3.5 percent is likely to grow to 15-20 % over the next decade. 100 million square feet of mall space will be ready for organized retail by the end of 2010. IT enabled services and efficient supply chain management practices will play crucial role to get competitive advantage over competitors.

IMPLICATIONS FOR INDIAN RETAILERS

The way new formats are emerging and old retail practices are becoming obsolete, it seems that the fast changing global trends have important implications for Indian retailers. The Indian consumer is becoming demanding and still value conscious. Fast emerging earning middle class is keen to spend money, but remains cost conscious, evaluating

7 *www.coolavenues.com*

every rupee spent on shopping. Consequently, it is imperative for Indian retailers to offer price advantage via operational efficiency and sourcing to attract customers and by building strong private labels. Existing and new entrants need to achieve sale target fast for driving efficiencies in procurement, warehousing, supply chain and marketing.

Shortage of skilled manpower and tie up with real estate developers will be the critical drivers to build competitive advantage. There are a few hundred malls under various stages of development throughout the country; unorganized retailers (kirana owners) should think how they can be the part of organized retail. Given the rising demand for retail real estate, retailers will need to take a long-term view on rentals and look at the alternative options like ownership or very long-term leases. Retailers that invest in training will be able to ensure availability of quality manpower in the rapidly growing market[8]. However, to take advantage of the golden opportunity, a retailer needs to be aggressive in its viewpoint and build sale quickly.

Further, to overcome inherent complications of retailing such as rapid price changes, constant threat of product obsolescence and low margins, Indian retailers must learn both the art and science of retailing by critically analyzing and understanding how retailers in other parts of the world are organizing, and managing with new threats in a fast changing global environment. To face competition with global competitors, Indian retailers should develop and use modern retail formats to boost up shopping experience, and try to differentiate the regional variations in consumer attitudes to retailing.

Figure 26.5

Implications for Indian Retailers

Factors Description Implications	**Factors Description Implications**	**Factors Description Implications**
Barriers to FDI	▪ FDI not permitted in pure retailing ▪ Franchisee arrangement allowed	▪ Absence of global players ▪ Limited exposure to best practices
Lack of Industry Status	▪ Government does not recognize the industry	▪ Restricted availability of finance ▪ Restricts growth and scaling up
Structural Impediments	▪ Lack of urbanization ▪ Poor transportation infrastructure ▪ Consumer habit of buying fresh foods Administered pricing	▪ Lack of awareness of Indian consumers ▪ Restricted retail growth ▪ Growth of small, one store formats with unmatchable cost structure ▪ Wastage of almost 20%-25% of farm produce

High Cost of Real Estate	▪ Pro-tenant rent laws ▪ Non-availability of government land, zoning restrictions ▪ Lack of clear ownership titles, high stamp duty (10%)	▪ Difficult to find good real estate in terms of location and size ▪ High land cost owing to constrained supply ▪ Disorganized nature of transactions
Supply Chain Bottlenecks	▪ Several segments like food and apparel reserved for SSIs ▪ Distribution, logistics constraints – restrictions of purchase and movement of food grains, absence of cold chain infrastructure ▪ Long intermediation chain	▪ Limited product range ▪ Makes scaling up difficult ▪ High cost and complexity of sourcing & planning ▪ Lack of value addition and increase in costs by almost 15%
Complex Taxation System	▪ Differential sales tax rates across states ▪ Multi-point octroi ▪ Sales tax avoidance by smaller stores	▪ Added cost and complexity of distribution ▪ Cost advantage for smaller stores through tax evasion
Multiple Legislations	▪ Stringent labor laws governing hours of work, minimum wage payments ▪ Multiple licenses/clearances required	▪ Limits flexibility in operations ▪ Irritant value in establishing chain operations ▪ adds to overall costs
Customer Preferences	▪ Local consumption habits ▪ Need for variety ▪ Cultural issues	▪ Leads to product proliferation ▪ Need to stock larger number of SKUs at store level ▪ Increases complexity in sourcing & planning ▪ Increases the cost of store management
Availability of Talent	▪ Highly educated class does not consider retailing a profession of choice	▪ Lack of trained personnel ▪ Higher trial and error in managing retail operations ▪ Increase in personnel costs
Manufacturers' Backlash	▪ Lack of proper training ▪ No increase in margins	▪ Manufacturers refuse to dis-intermediate and pass on intermediary margins to retailers

Source: *Market Participants, Fitch & www.indianretailobserver.com*

Hence, the future of retail will depend on the right kind of retail mix supported by right policies, right economic environment, right infrastructure, and the right people. Unless these things happen, retail in India would not be benefited. In this e-age where customer is king and queen, retailers can not deny the customers from experiencing the product. Food retailers have realized this aspect as a matter of survival or otherwise. It is, therefore, expected that time will come soon in India when other category retail chains allow people to see, realize and sense their offerings unlike other retail categories.

SUMMARY

Retail in India is at crossroads of an intensive development spree. With the entry of large Indian houses and the foreign players, completion is becoming tough. The reason for such unprecedented growth can be largely attributed to the high economic growth that the country has been experiencing for past one decade. New and new retail destinations are emerging. Petro-retailing, Pharma-retailing and retail banking are the examples of such innovations. Cyber retailing that used to be a European buying trend has spread not only to other developing nations like India but to the third world also. For retailers, it is the source of new income and enhanced sales in minimum efforts, customers find it economical and time saving.

Traditional (mall) retailers should consider this development seriously and take proper action to think and device how internet can be useful for them ranging from information only sites to 'clicks and mortar' strategy. The cyber retailing and other emerging retail destinations are likely to increase due to fall in prices of computers and easy and affordable access to internet media. Further, government policy towards FDI in retail will give path to other global retailers who otherwise directly cannot enter in Indian retail sector. It is believed that if these trends continue, organized retail in India could well emerge as a next sunrise industry.

REVIEW QUESTIONS

True and False Questions

1. The Indian retail sector is highly fragmented consisting of more than 120 million outlets run by family members.
2. Marks and Spencer is an Indian enterprise.
3. Religare is UK's most popular enterprise.
4. Luxury retailing is limited to metros, Tier I, and Tier II cities.
5. HNI stands for High -Networth Individuals.
6. FDI means Foreign Direct Investigation.
7. FICCI is India's leading retail industry.
8. PVR is a pioneer in the field of online retailing.
9. Today retail market has transformed into a 'seller's market' from a 'buyer's market'.

10. In India, FDI in retail is strictly prohibited due to opposition from left parties.
11. Retailing in India can be traced to the emergence of local '*kirana*' stores.
12. LPG stands for Liberalization, Privatization and Government.
13. Shortage of skilled manpower and tie-up with real estate developers are the critical drivers to build competitive advantage.
14. In India, luxury retailing is as popular as *kirana* retailing.
15. Indian youth is considered to be the main driver of retail success.

Answers

1. False	2. False	3. False	4. True
5. True	6. False	7. False	8. False
9. False	10. False	11. True	12. False
13. True	14. False	15. True	

Multiple Choice Questions

1. TSMG is:
   (*a*) world's biggest online retailer. (*b*) world's famous furniture retailer.
   (*c*) management consulting firm (*d*) security instrument provider.
2. Which of the following is not a global retailer:
   (*a*) Marks and Spencer. (*b*) Primark
   (*c*) SRL Religare (*d*) Subway.
3. F.I.P.B. stand for
   (*a*) Foreign Investment Promotion Board
   (*b*) Foreign Intellectual Property Board
   (*c*) Foreign Internet Provider Bureau
   (*d*) Foreign Income Promotion Board.
4. Luxury retailing usually is not found in ....
   (*a*) Rural Areas (*b*) Tier I cities.
   (*c*) Tier II cities. (*d*) Tier I and II cities
5. As per Mckinsey report, India approximately wastes Rs. .... in food chain management every year.
   (*a*) Rs. 7300 crores (*b*) Rs. 15,000 crores
   (*c*) Rs. 25,000 crores (*d*) Rs. 50,000 crores
6. IT enabled services and efficient SCM are necessary to get competitive advantage over ....
   (*a*) retailers (*b*) wholesalers
   (*c*) manufacturers (*d*) competitors.
7. SEZs are:
   (*a*) Special electronics zones. (*b*) Significant electronics zones.
   (*c*) Special economic zones. (*d*) Staple elevator zones.
8. The objective of introducing VAT system is to
   (*a*) Provide relief to retailers by tax deduction.

(*b*) impose tax on retailers unearth income
(*c*) generate income source for retailers as well as government
(*d*) resolve multiple taxation issue.

9. India has more than .... million kirana store.
(*a*) 8 (*b*) 12
(*c*) 16 (*d*) 20

10. Two emerging retail destinations are:
(*a*) Grocery and food (*b*) Internet and kiosk.
(*c*) Real estate and Pharma (*d*) Automobile and FMCG

Answers

1. (*c*)	2 (*c*)	3. (*a*)	4. (*a*)
5. (*d*)	6. (*d*)	7. (*c*)	8. (*d*)
9. (*b*)	10. (*c*).		

Check our progress

1. What is FDI?
2. What is IT industry?
3. Explain customer loyality?
4. What is HNI?
5. What is JV?
6. What is LPG?
7. What comes under GDP?
8. What is *kirana* store?
9. Explain the term 'Co-buying'?
10. What is real estate industry?
11. What is talent?
12. What is APMCA?
13. Describe Entertainment?

Small Answer Questions

1. Explain the opportunities that exist in Indian retail industry?
2. Briefly explain the future prospects of Indian *kirana* stores?
3. Explain few emerging retail destinations in India?
4. Write short note on Indian government policy on inviting FDI in retail?
5. Explain the implications of emerging new formats on Indian retailers?
6. Why Indian retail industry is said to be at crossroads of an intensive development spree?
7. Discuss the impact of Pharmaceutical retail on local chemist stores?
8. Critically explain the concept of entertainment retail?

9. What impact FDI will have on traditional *kirana* stores?
10. Do you think that India will loose its traditional *kirana* setup in the coming future?

Long Questions

1. What are your suggestions and guidelines for a multinational retailer who just has decided to enter into Indian retail industry?
2. Explain the Indian government policy on FDI in retail? What guidelines are laid for approval of FDI? Like third parties, do you believe India should ban on FDI atleast in retail that can spoil the future of more than 12 million *kirana* stores? Comment.

Applied Questions

1. Visit few local *kirana* stores and gather retailers' views on emergence of 'mall shopping' culture on their fate?
2. Why left parties always oppose when it comes to FDI in retail?
3. Visit a pharma retail chain shop and a local chemist shop. What typical changes you observe that can differentiate them from each other?

APPENDIX

Exhibit 26.1: Future of Mom & Pop Stores

MOM & POP STORES SHALL RULE 84% OF RETAIL TILL '13

Allaying fears of ***mom & pop*** store owners, a study by the Indian Council for Research on International Economic Relations (**ICRIER**) has found that the unorganized sector will retain around 84% of the retail market till the year 2013. The share of the unorganized sector will come down with the advent of large-format stores, but any negative impact will wear off with time, the think tank has indicated in the largest study so far on retail sector in India.

ICRIER was commissioned the study early last year after the Prime Minister's Office (PMO) directed the commerce and industry ministry to get an assessment done on the impact of organized and big retail on the smaller 'mom & pop' stores. Pointing out that organized retail does not have an adverse impact on intermediaries; the study found that unless retail trade is modernized, bottlenecks would continue. Another key recommendation is that the government should rationalize licensing norms to encourage growth of organized retail.

The ICRIER study does not talk about the role of foreign direct investment in the retail sector, but is only an assessment of the impact of organized and modern retail on mom & pop neighborhood stores. Around 2,000 ***mom & pop stores*** and 1,000 consumers across the country were surveyed for the study.

One of the most important findings of the study is that 'mom & pop' stores have so far been able to adjust to the emergence of organized retail and malls. Comparing regions in the south (where organized retail has been around for long) with those in the north (where organized retail is a very recent phenomenon), ICRIER has concluded that the impact of modern retail on the profitability of small stores wear offs with time.

This finding is interesting since large players, particularly Reliance Industries' fresh fruit and vegetable outlets have been a target of protestors alleging such stores snatch the livelihood of small traders and kirana stores. ICRIER has also found that none of the small stores are affected by organized retail to the extent that they want to move out of this business. Even a large majority of the next generation of those owning mom & pop stores have said that they want to remain in this business despite the advent of organized retail. Then, even customers appear to favour the existence of big guys, saying they would like both organized retail and mom & pop stores to co-exist since they derive value from both. Very few of those surveyed wanted one of the two formats to go.

Source: *www.india-reports.com*

Exhibit 26.2: Emerging Grocery Retail

GROCERY IS THE ONLY RETAIL HIT WITH BUYERS

Retailers trying to move up the value chain with *'private labels'* – also known as store brands, had run into a roadblock in India. Other than groceries, consumers were not very keen to go for store brands for high-end products, even if the products were similar and could be bought cheaper. Giant retail chains like the Future Group (Big Bazaar and Pantaloons), Reliance, Tata, AV Birla and Videocon are now betting on specialty retail stores to increase the 'ticket price' - the average revenue earned per sale.

And there is money waiting to be made. According to a report by consultancy CLSA, the retail industry in India is about to touch $350 billion (over Rs 15 lakh crore) by 2010. Currently, the organized sector comprises just four percent of the overall retail market in the country. Specialty retail is likely to grow at 25 percent.

Take an example of Reliance though its groceries arm, Reliance Fresh, has been a hit among customers, other variants have not done as well. No, it is kicking off its specialty store plan with an eyewear and optical chain. The company will launch the first outlet of its optical chain store, Vision Express, by September this year. Reliance has entered into a joint venture with Pearle Europe and the first store would be launched in Bangaluru. Reliance Retail at present has multi-brand apparel retail stores under the brand name Reliance Trends. The company also has a jewelry retail chain, Reliance Jewels. The optical chain would comprise independent stores and stores within Reliance Retail's other formats such as Hypermart, Super and wellness.

Other chains are also jostling for entry, with plans for special stores targeting everything from home furnishing to shoes and fashion accessories. Organized retail has been hit hard this year, with inflation reducing footfalls by over 10 percent, while operating margins are being shaved by rising costs, especially transport. High real estate costs have also slowed expansion plans, besides rendering many mega stores unviable. By splitting the business into smaller, tightly focussed stores, retail chains are hoping to improve margins.

Kishore Biyani's Future Group has launched the exclusive home furnishing stores, Home Stores, and the electronic durables outlets, e-zone, across the country. Similarly, Aditya Birla Nuovo has opened its specialty stores under the Peter England brand in tier I cities. Tata has launched Croma, a multi-brand durables retail format that has 40 outlets in various parts of the country. Tatas have invested Rs 120 crore in the venture so far. Videocon has also joined the retail bandwagon through the launch of its consumer durables retailing chain, NEXT, across the country. Welspun Retail, the retail arm of Welspun group also plans to increase the number of its WelHome and Spaces stores across the country.

Source: *Mail Today, Vol. 1, No. 236, Wednesday July 9, 2008.*

Exhibit 26.3: Retailing Institutes in India

POST-GRADUATE INSTITUTES OFFERING SPECIALIZED COURSES IN RETAIL MANAGEMENT

Most of the institutes (B-Schools), colleges and universities have been offering 'Retail Management' subjects under their graduate and post graduate programmes. Besides this these, 20 Indian institutes offer specialized courses in retail management under their post graduate programmes.

1. Birla Institute of Management Technology, New Delhi
2. Ebony Retail Academy, New Delhi
3. Foreign Trade Development Centre – Centre for Retail Management, Delhi & Jaipur
4. Global Retail School, Multiple centres across India
5. Indian Institute of Jewelry, Mumbai
6. Indian Institute of Retail, New Delhi
7. Indian Retail School, New Delhi
8. Indian School of Business, Hyderabad
9. Institute of Management Studies, Mumbai
10. Institute of Technology and Management, Mumbai
11. International Institute of Retail Management, New Delhi
12. K J Somaiya Institute of Management Studies & Research, Mumbai
13. Mudra Institute of Communications, Ahmedabad.
14. National Institute of Fashion Technology (NIFT), New Delhi
15. Pearl Academy of Fashion, New Delhi
16. PG Institute of Retail Management, Mumbai & Chennai
17. Retail Academy of India, Distance Learning programmes
18. SP Jain Institute of Management and Research, Mumbai
19. The Retail Academy, Ahmedabad
20. Welingkar Institute of Management, Mumbai

Exhibit 26.4: Retailing Chains Caught In Wave of Bankruptcy

The consumer spending slump and tightening credit markets are unleashing a widening wave of bankruptcies in American retailing, prompting store closings that are expected to redefine the contours of suburban malls and downtown shopping districts across the United States.

Since last autumn, eight mostly mid-sized chains – as diverse as the furniture store Levitz and the electronics seller Sharper Image – have filed for bankruptcy protection. The trouble is quickly spreading to bigger companies like Linens'n Things, the bedding and furniture retailer with 500 stores in 47 states. It may file for bankruptcy in near future.

Even retailers that can avoid bankruptcy are shutting down their stores to preserve cash through what could be a long economic downturn. Foot locker said it would close 140 stores, Ann Taylor will start to shutter 117, and the jeweler Zales will close 100 in a year. The surging cost of necessities has led to a national belt-tightening among consumers. Figures released on Monday showed that spending on food and gasoline is crowding out other purchases, leaving people with less to spend on furniture, clothing and electronics. Consequently, chains specializing in those goods are proving vulnerable.

"You have the makings of a wave of significant bankruptcies," said Al Koch, who helped bring Kmart out of bankruptcy in 2003 as the company's interim chief financial officer. "For years, no deal was too ugly to finance," he said. "But now, nobody will throw money at these companies." Because retailers rely on a broad network of suppliers, their bankruptcies are rippling across the economy. The cash-short chains are leaving behind tens of millions of dollars in unpaid bills to shipping companies, furniture manufacturers, mall owners and advertising agencies. Many are unlikely to be paid in full – spreading in economic pain. When it filed for bankruptcy, Sharper Image owed $6.6 million to United Parcel Service. The furniture chain Levitz owed Sealy $1.4 million. When Domain, the furniture retailer filed for bankruptcy, it owed On Time Express, a 90-employee transportation and logistics company in Tempe, Ariz., about $30,000.

"We'll be lucky to see pennies on the dollar, if we see anything," said Ross Musil, the chief financial officer of On Time Express. "It's a big loss." Most of the ailing companies have filed for re-organization, not liquidation. But in contrast with previous recessions, many are unlikely to emerge from bankruptcy, lawyers and industry experts said. As Sally Henry, a partner in the bankruptcy law practice at Skadden, Arps, Slate, Meagher & Flom and the author of several books on bankruptcies, puts it: "It's no longer re-organization or even liquidation for these companies. In many cases, it's evaporation."

Source: *http://tpwireservice.com*

INDIAN RETAIL INVESTMENTS ON THE ANVIL

India's vast middle class with its expanding purchasing power and its rapidly growing retail industry are key attractions for global retail giants wanting to enter newer markets.

- Disney Consumers Products (DCP) is ramping up retail presence by launching several products - apparel accessories, cartoon, stationeries, kids section, food, health and beauty.
- Esprit, a premium fashion brand plans to add 25 new outlets to its present network of 34 by 2008 with an investment of about US$ 12.63 million.
- Estee Lauder will be setting up 20 outlets over the next three years.
- Giordano Fashions (India) will establish a chain of single-brand retail.
- Indian Oil Corporation (IOC) is planning to invest US$ 189.103 million in rural areas during the financial year 2009.
- Inorbit Malls (India) Ltd. will be investing around US$ 294.79 million to build eight malls across the country within the next two years.
- Luxury watch brand, Rado, is planning a major expansion drive to double its exclusive stores to 15, covering new Tier-II cities like Jalandhar and Ludhiana.
- Marks & Spencer plans to put in 51 per cent foreign direct investment in single-brand retail business.
- Panasonic is planning a US$ 200 million investment in India, for setting up new units, brand positioning, and upgrading its facilities, by 2011.
- Reebok will open 230 stores in 2008-09 in India, touching the target of 850 by end of this fiscal. Besides consolidating its position in metros and tier-I cities, it is also going for a major expansion in tier-II and tier-III and lower-tier cities.
- Reliance Retail Ltd will start 50–60 'i stores' all over India, in the next 18 months, and also open 150 Reliance Digital stores by 2011–12. Reliance Retail Ltd (RRL) runs from over 600 stores in more than 57 cities, across 13 states.
- Religare Enterprises, the integrated financial services firm is planning to set up multi-product, multi-brand retail stores in the personal finance space under the brand name Finmart, with an investment of more than US$ 23.779 million to set up 200 such stores across the country.
- Retail major Subhiksha plans to open 1,000 more outlets by end-2008.
- Singapore-based, US$ 5 billion worth OSIM International Ltd is planning to set up another 100 exclusive brand outlets in India.
- Titan Industries will launch 'Titan Eye +' branded spectacles stores all over India with an investment of US$ 5.05 million for putting up 80 stores in the metro, tier-I and tier-II cities. The company has a plan to rollout 200 stores in three years.
- To expand its presence in the apparel sector in India, Koutons Retail will be investing US$ 70.79 million to open 200 large Koutons Family Stores and add another 1,400 stores in modern retail format to the existing 605 stores, within the next 18 months.
- Videocon Retail plans to invest US$ 168.45 million to expand its electronic retail format, Next Retail, and Planet M, the mobile, music, entertainment and lifestyle chain, in the next three years.

Source: *www.ibef.org*

1. Problems in Handling Complaints
2. Indian Toy Industry Vs Cheap Chinese Import
3. Tata Ace: The Making of the Small Truck
4. The Prospective Rural Market
5. Customer Empowerment through Empowering Employees
6. Retailing Restructuring through Formats (A Case of Reliance Retail Limited)
7. Maximizing Revenues through Joint Ventures (A Case of Bharti-Wal-Mart' Retail)
8. What's in a Name: Small Brands Big Savings?
9. Subhiksha – A Movement against Needless Spending
10. Retailing Recruitment
11. Appropriateness & Effectiveness of Corrective Training in Retail
12. Marks And Spencer: The United Kingdom's Retail Leader

CASE SDUDY # 1

PROBLEMS IN HANDLING COMPLAINTS

Pioneer Electronics Store, one of the leading electronic stores in Hyderabad sells batteries, all shapes and sizes, all voltages and prices. One particular battery sells for Rs 300 for a package of three. Mohit a salesperson at Pioneer electronic store sold a package of these batteries to a customer on Monday this week. He paid cash for them and left the store, headed for home. The next day, on Tuesday morning, the customer returned to the store, having battery packet in hand, and told Rohan (different salesperson as Mohit was on leave) that he had purchased these batteries the day before, and they are not working. Rohan tested the batteries and found the batteries really dead.

Customer started shouting *'you wasted my time'*, *'you are fraud'*, and so on. It put Rohan in trouble. He was dancing between horns of dilemma. In the last five years at Pioneer store, he never heard of such complaint. But he was quite because the batteries looked like new. How do we resolve such customer complaint? To begin with there is no way to determine that the batteries the customer has in hand is indeed the batteries he bought last day. Since most batteries show no external sign of wear, for all practical purposes they may all have been the older set, the set that the new one replaced. Second, the nature of batteries is such that the customer may be accidentally drained them himself, and now wants to become smart and pass the responsibility to the store. In either case, the salesperson Rohan standing in front of the customer who claims he was sold defective batteries, and now wants the situation resolved as soon as possible.

Suppose, you face the same complaint while working as same sort of sales store:

1. How would you examine the case from store's point of view and customer's point of view?
2. Suggest a solution that has win-win solution for both the parties concerned?

CASE STUDY # 2

INDIAN TOY INDUSTRY VS CHEAP CHINESE IMPORT

Chinese exports are competing with goods produced by industries in several countries including India. Many of India's small-scale industries are under threat or facing stiff competition of cheap imports from China. These industries manufacture a wide range of consumer products (electrical goods, batteries, toys, watches, pharmaceuticals) and intermediates (chemicals.) Indian toy industry has also been facing stiff competition from the cheap Chinese imports in soft and hard toys. Many Indian toy retailers have reduced their selling prices by downsizing the floor staff. Kinder Garden (an Indian toy retail chain), on the other hand, has instructed its marketing and sales promotion staff to make frequent calls to its retail and wholesale buyers along with personal visits. The selling staff is promised to take a share of the additional profit that comes due to their personal efforts. Appropriate commission on sharing basis will be offered for sale figures over and above routine targets. Company opines it a fantastic way to satisfy the management's desire to increase its market share without huge spending. Further, company also plans to promote the efficient employees.

Questions for discussion:

1. What role personal selling can play in Toy Industry? Do you think the strategy of motivation by additional commission and promotion will actually fruitful?
2. Do you believe that promoting efficient employees will satisfy management's desire to increase market share?

CASE STUDY # 3

TATA ACE: THE MAKING OF THE SMALL TRUCK

In May 2005, Tata Motors Ltd commercially launched a long awaited, mini truck -India's first indigenously developed sub-one tonne capacity vehicle. TATA decided to manufacture the 'Ace' after a research that found that Indian customers wanted a last mile-distribution vehicle that had low maintenance costs, higher driver safety, and better driving comfort on Indian roads. Understanding the customer real requirements, the company developed and launched the Ace, which created a new segment in the market for four-wheel commercial vehicles — the small commercial vehicle (SCV) segment, which was earlier the province of three-wheel cargo carriers like Mahindra, Bajaj and Vikram. The inner and outer design was developed to achieve higher top speeds than that of the other three-wheelers. The cargo bed was also made larger. The product was designed with low turning radius to easily steer the narrow lanes and by lanes of towns and villages. The muscular, car-like features ensured comfort in ride and handling.

The overall look, style, fitting and finishing differentiated the vehicle from the existing three wheelers and at the same time, gave social prestige to the owner as well as the driver of the vehicle. The mini truck was advertised using the symbol of a baby elephant with the tagline *"small is big"*. Tata Ace was launched with a 15%-20% higher price tag than that of a comparable model of a three wheeler. Positioned as a replacement for the three-wheelers that predominated as small commercial vehicles in India, the Ace create a new product category and enabled Tata Motors to access a new market segment.

Despite being priced higher than the three-wheeler alternatives, the Ace received huge response from the commercial market. One reason for the success of the vehicle was that customers felt that it looked and performed better than the existing alternatives. Besides this, Tata's own brand name and success of other Tata's automobile products, such as Indica and Tata 407, fueled confidence in Indian dealers and customers. To fulfill the repair and service needs of Ace, the company augmented the service network by training automobile garages that were branded as Tata-certified service points. Within less than two years of its launch of Ace, the company rolled out 1 lacs trucks, surpassing the company's optimistic targets.

Market experts expected the Ace to face stiff competition in the coming days. After witnessing the successful response to the vehicle, all the major Indian three-wheeler manufacturers and light commercial vehicle (LCV) makers announced their plans to roll out sub-one tonne, four-wheel vehicles for the SCV segment.

Questions for discussion:

1. What will be different with Ace if, in the future, competitors launch such mini trucks?
2. You are contacted by Mahindra and Mahindra (M&M) to help them develop a design for entering the four-wheel vehicle market where presently Tata's Ace has the dominant market position. As lead consultant to M&M, what would you do?

CASE STUDY # 4

THE PROSPECTIVE RURAL MARKET

Rural marketing is on high demand these days as number of the companies has started seeking to enter in rural areas now due to number of the reasons one of them is saturation in uraban areas. But because of some backward living-hood the personal selling efforts become a challenging role to play. The word of mouth is an important message carrier in rural areas. Infect the opinion leaders are the most influencing part of promotion strategy of rural promotion efforts.

The Indian established Industries have the advantages, which MNC don't enjoy in this regard. The strong Indian brands have strong market so the consumer demand-pull and efficient and dedicated dealer network which have been created over a period of time. The rural market has a grip of strong country shops, which affect the sale of various products in rural market. The companies are trying to trigger growth in rural areas. They are identifying the fact that rural people are now in the better position with disposable income.

Some actual aspects for Indian marketers

In India more than 65-70% area is covered by in rural areas. Which can provide a great opportunity for Indian companies? As we know that, rural markets have acquired significance, as the overall growth of the economy has resulted into substantial increase in the purchasing power of the rural societies.

Hurdles for Indian Rural market

The concept of rural markets in India is still in sprouting form, and the field poses a numbers of challenges. Circulation costs and non-availability of retail outlets are major problems faced by the marketers. The success of a brand in the Indian rural market is as unpredictable natural aspects like rain, dry, storm etc.

The main problems in rural marketing are: -

- Understanding the mind set of rural consumers
- Pitiable Infrastructure
- Logistics
- Channel Management
- Promotional activities

Thus, looking at the hurdles and the prospects as well the strategies, which rural markets offer to the marketers and the manufacturers, it can be said that the future is very bright for those companies who can understand the variations of rural markets and make use of them to their best advantage. A radical change in attitudes of marketers towards the positive and growing rural markets.

Questions for discussion:

1. Why Indian companies are eyeing at rural areas?
2. What benefits, you think a company will get if it decides to go rural?
3. What are the actual problems in rural markets?

CASE STUDY # 5

CUSTOMER EMPOWERMENT THROUGH EMPOWERING EMPLOYEES

Giving great customer service can be a very difficult task. This is a true statement. However, it isn't impossible. Treat your customers as you would want to be treated in the same situation and you will find the key to giving quality service to your customers. Great customer service means happy customers, the kinds who remain loyal to your company for their entire lives and demand that every person they know patronize your business. They're your best advocates, giving your company the word-of-mouth advertising and buzz you couldn't buy with a thousand ads. But happy customers don't just materialize out of thin air. Happy customers are made by happy employees.

Of course, empowering your employees means giving up some of your control and actually trusting the people you pay to be the face of your business, an idea that many business owners despise. It also means instilling a sense of pride and ownership in the company in those same people, and those factors go a long way toward making them want to go that extra mile when it comes to serving the customers.

Empowering customer service representatives requires that you assume you have hired competent, intelligent people who want to do an excellent job. It is important to recognize that they need your support and confidence in order for them to do an excellent job. Arming them with the training, education, support, and tools to do their job effectively ensures their success and the success of your company.

When a customer calls to complain, they are typically angry, upset, and frustrated. Resolving their issue on the first call is critical to retaining them as a long-term customer and this requires that your customer service representatives have the authority to make decisions on the company's behalf. You have to trust them to make appropriate decisions within the guidelines prescribed. Representatives need to feel and act like business-owners and assume accountability for outcomes.

Empowering customer service representatives is a key to success in today's world. Time constraints are driving customers to seek immediate resolution to issues. Retaining current customers is a company's top most priority and the customer service experience contributes heavily to that goal. Give your representatives the tools, training, and support they need to succeed. You'll find that everyone benefits when you trust them to do their jobs effectively!

Questions for discussion:

1. Do you think that loyal employees make customers loyal easily?
2. What do you mean by empowering employees?
3. Describe the benefits of loyal and happy customers?

CASE SDUDY # 6

RETAILING RESTRUCTURING THROUGH FORMATS (A CASE OF RELIANCE RETAIL LIMITED)

About Reliance Retail

Reliance Retail Limited (RRL), a 100% subsidiary of Reliance Industries Limited (RIL)[1] is one of the latest and fastest growing business houses of the country. It started rolling its stores in November 2006 and today has opened 750 stores in 15 different formats in 70 cities of the country in the last two years of its operation. RRL is a multi-format retailer that operates Reliance Fresh – a neighborhood store concept, Reliance Digital – a Consumer Durables and Information Technology concept, Reliance Mart - a Hyper Market concept, Reliance Trends - an apparel specialty concept, Reliance Wellness – a health, wellness & beauty concept , Reliance 'i' Store- an Apple specialty store concept, Reliance Footprint -a footwear concept, Reliance Jewels – a jewellery concept, Reliance Time - Out books, music & entertainment concept, Reliance Super - a Minimart concept and Reliance AutoZone – an automotive specialty concept[2].

The first of their format is Reliance Fresh, a convenience store. These stores, range from 2,000 to 5,000 sq feet, provide customers with a variety of fresh fruits, vegetables, staple foods and other products in a world class ambience. They aggressively partnered farmers by following a farm-to-folk strategy to ensure fresh fruits and vegetables at affordable prices. They chose Hyderabad to test waters, as the city offers real estate at a price that does not quite pinch. They selected the cream crowd from pioneers in organized retailers to head the organization. With such a strong foothold, they ventured and their cash counters clicked Rs 3.5 to Rs 6.5 lakh per day and some outlets at prime locations are averaging Rs 5 lakh per day[3]. After doing well in grocery segment, now it plans to expand it across the electronic goods, farm implements and inputs, distribution of energy products and services, distribution of travel and financial services, entertainment and leisure experiences, health and well-being products and services and educational products and services[4].

---

[1] *Reliance Industries Limited (RIL) is India's largest private sector company on all major financial parameters. It is the first and only private sector company from India to feature in the Fortune Global 500 list of 'World's Largest Corporations' and ranks amongst the world's Top 200 companies in terms of profits. RIL is amongst the 25 fastest climbers ranked by Fortune. RIL also features in the Forbes Global list of world's 400 best big companies and in FT Global 500 list of world's largest companies.*

[2] *http://www.valuenotes.com/press/pr_reliance_22Apr08.pdf*

[3] *http://www.chillibreeze.com/articles_various/Reliance-Industries.asp*

[4] *http://www.naukrihub.com/best-workplaces/retail-employers/reliance-retail.html*

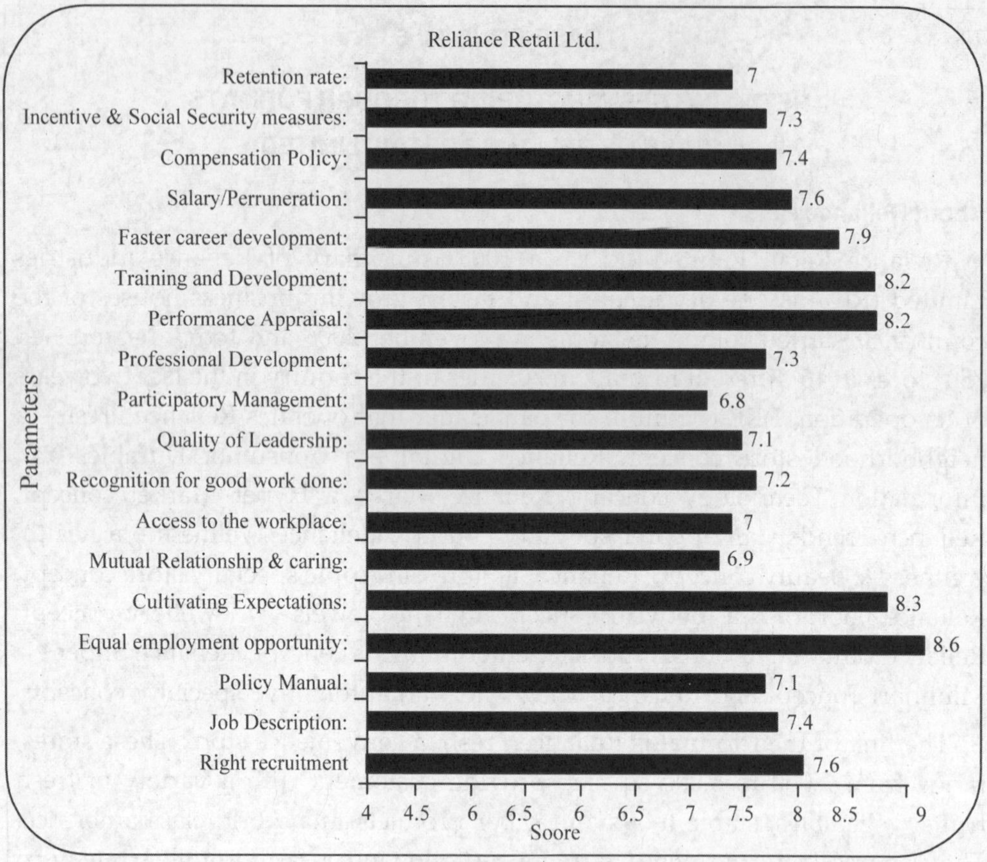

Reliance Retail Ltd.

Parameters	Score
Retention rate:	7
Incentive & Social Security measures:	7.3
Compensation Policy:	7.4
Salary/Perruneration:	7.6
Faster career development:	7.9
Training and Development:	8.2
Performance Appraisal:	8.2
Professional Development:	7.3
Participatory Management:	6.8
Quality of Leadership:	7.1
Recognition for good work done:	7.2
Access to the workplace:	7
Mutual Relationship & caring:	6.9
Cultivating Expectations:	8.3
Equal employment opportunity:	8.6
Policy Manual:	7.1
Job Description:	7.4
Right recruitment	7.6

4 4.5 6 6.5 6 6.5 7 7.5 8 8.5 9

Soore

Source: *Company Website & www.naukrihub.com*

In order to revolutionize the retailing industry in India, it is aggressively working on introducing a pan-India network of retail outlets in multiple formats. A world class shopping environment, state of art technology, a seamless supply chain infrastructure, a host of unique value-added services and above all, unmatched customer experience, is what this initiative is all about. The retail initiative of Reliance will be without a parallel in size and spread and make India proud. Ensuring better returns to Indian farmers and manufacturers and greater value for the Indian consumer, both in quality and quantity, will be an integral feature of this project. By creating value at all levels, we will actively endeavour to contribute to India's growth. The project will boast of a seamless supply chain infrastructure, unprecedented even by world standards. Through multiple formats and a wide range of categories, Reliance is aiming to touch almost every Indian customer and supplier.

RIL's Retail Project is through its following subsidiary companies:

Subsidiaries of Reliance Retail

1. Abcus Retail Private Limited	2. Reliance Integrated Agri Solutions Limited
3. Advantage Retail Private Limited	4. Reliance Leisures Limited
5. Bigdeal Retail Private Limited	6. Reliance Lifestyle Holdings Limited
7. Delight Proteins Limited	8. Reliance Loyalty & Analylitics Limited
9. Reliance Agri Products Distribution Limited	10. Reliance Retail Finance Limited
11. Reliance AutoZone Limited	12. Reliance Retail Insurance Broking Limited
13. Reliance Brands Limited	14. Reliance Retail Limited
15. Reliance Commercial Trading Private Limited	16. Reliance Retail Securities and Broking Company Limited
17. Reliance Dairy Foods Limited	18. Reliance Retail Travel & Forex Services Limited
19. Reliance Digital Media Limited	20. Reliance Supply Chain Solutions Limited
21. Reliance F&B Services Limited	22. Reliance Trade Services Centre Limited
23. Reliance Financial Distribution and Advisory Services Limited	24. Reliance Trends Limited
25. Reliance Food Processing Solutions Limited	26. Reliance Universal Ventures Limited
27. Reliance Footprint Limited	28. Reliance Wellness Limited
29. Reliance Fresh Limited	30. Reliance digital Retail Limited
31. Reliance Gems and Jewels Limited	32. RESQ Limited
33. Reliance Home Store Limited	34. Retail Concepts and Services (India) Limited
35. Reliance Hypermarket Limited	36. Strategic Manpower Solutions Limited

Strategic Alliances

RIL owns 98.74% stake in the retail business and we understand that Reliance Retail is the parent company and each format has been housed in a separate subsidiary. For the FY ended March 08, Reliance Retail had total assets of Rs 48bn and sales revenues of Rs 22bn and loss of Rs 974m. Reliance Retail operates through a number of subsidiaries. The top 5 subsidiaries w.r.t sales in FY 2008 are,

- Reliance Dairy Foods with sales Rs 658 mn
- Reliance Digital reported sales of Rs 400 mn
- Reliance Fresh sales of Rs 3.5 bn
- Reliance Hypermart - Rs 291 mn
- Reliance Wellness Stores - Rs 284 mn

Reliance Retail is structured in such a way that Logistics is handled by Reliance Supply Chain Solutions, Manpower by Strategic Manpower Solutions, Food Processing by

Reliance Agri Products Distributions and Reliance Food Processing Solutions. The only profit making subsidiary of Reliance Retail is the financial arm Reliance Retail Finance [Issues Credit Cards and Loyalty Points to Reliance customers]. Other subsidiaries are Reliance Financial Distribution & Advisory, Reliance Retail Insurance & Broking and Reliance Retail Travel & Forex Services.

Future Plans

Reliance Retail, promoted by Reliance Industries, has opened 700 stores in 14 different formats in 60 cities of the country in the last two years of its operation. Its food and grocery chain Reliance Fresh has 600 stores across the country with over 4 million sq ft. Considering competition; it has been planning to open 75 'i' stores[5] by 2009 end and 150 Reliance Digital[6] stores by 2011-12. Company believes on an average Rs 7 crore from 'i' store format and Rs 70 crore per annum from Reliance digital will come in the first year of its operaton. The company is looking to have 1,000-1,200 square feet of area under 'i' store and 20,000-30,000 square feet under Reliance Digital. Presently, the company has 'i' store in Bangalore, Hyderabad, Mumbai and Jaipur and Reliance Digital stores in Hyderabad, Bangalore, Mumbai, Gurgaon and Ghaziabad[7].

Restructuring of Reliance Retail

Despite showing consumers' acceptance and increasing sales, Reliance Fresh has embarked upon operational restructuring. According to sources, the company is mulling converting its 216 partly franchised stores into company-owned outlets with franchisees possibly brought on the company payrolls. The reason for the change is difficulties in manpower scheduling. Reliance Retail is also evaluating other models, such as one under which the franchisee might continue on a revenue-sharing model despite being on the company's rolls[8].

The switchover is bound to have an impact on the retail market since the franchise model is seen as a popular move to co-opt shopkeepers, neutralizing the charge that big retailers will eventually displace small retailers. In fact, Bharti Retail, the Sunil Bharti Mittal group's retail venture with US retail giant Wal-Mart, has also expressed its intent to co-opt '*kirana*' stores by implementing a franchise model for its convenience stores. The Aditya Birla group and Tata Woolworths are also likely to focus on the franchise model for their proposed stores.

Reliance Industries has stunned India's Retail Sector by announcing a gigantic investment of over Indian Rupees 25,000 Crores (roughly equivalent to USD $ 5.5 Billion) in their proposed **Reliance Retail** greenfield project in India.

6 *Reliance Digital is a consumer durable and IT arm of Reliance Retail Ltd, which offers home appliance, consumer electronics, IT and telecom products.*

7 *www.financialexpress.com viewed on July 16, 2008*

8 *www.financialexpress.com, Posted on July 28, 2007*

In the series of launching new formats, 'Reliance Wellness' outlets are being launched in the country. They would offer pre-emptive, curative, health and beauty solutions with world class products to customers. Customers could take 'Reliance One[9] loyalty card' free of cost to save points on purchases in any of the Reliance retail stores and redeem them[10].

Reliance New Formats

In Dec, 2007 Reliance Retail limited (RIL) announced the launch of a new specialty store 'Reliance TimeOut' on Cunningham Road in Bangalore today. This store houses Books, Music, Stationery, Toys and Gifts. After the successful launch of Reliance Fresh, Reliance Mart, Reliance Digital, Reliance Trendz, Reliance Footprint, Reliance Wellness and Reliance Jewels, this is the 8th format of stores from Reliance Retail to be launched in India. Spread over 21,000 sq feet and with over 56,000 products, it offers the customers an extensive range of merchandise in Books, Music, Stationery, Toys and Gifts. Reliance TimeOut is all set to revolutionize this business with its unique combination of wide product range and an exciting customer experience[11].

In Books, Reliance TimeOut has over 30,000 titles, sourced from National & International publishers. In Music and Movies, Reliance TimeOut has over 12,000 titles sourced from leading international and national music companies. Searching for your favourite music and books is efficiently handled by a search engine and complemented by knowledgeable and energetic staff, so that customers can easily find what they want in a store of this size. The Stationery section with over 7000 products is a wonderland for children, students and working people. For the first time in India, Professional Artists too have an exciting range of products to buy their art supplies from.

The Toy section with over 3,000 toys in an environment that is a lot of fun for the children will definitely make every outing to Reliance TimeOut great fun for the family. The store also has over 4,000 products in gifts, watches, sunglasses and fragrances. Reliance TimeOut is truly a wonderful space to simply take time out!

Source: *Company Website and www.indiaprwire.com*

After the successful launch of consumer-good super market Reliance Fresh and Consumer Electronic and Digital, Reliance Mart (1,50,000-3,00,00 sq. ft.), is the company's hypermarket format, RRL plans to set up a series of 500 hypermarkets across the country by 2010. Beginning is with Jamnagar's

---

[9] *Reliance one, a pre-paid facility which allows customers to start using it right from the point of purchase, is valid across all the nine different formats of Reliance Retail stores. Building on the success of Reliance One, the company is also seeking to become "the distributor of choice" for all financial services companies with an all-India footprint at every product level.*

[10] *www.hindu.com , dated Oct 26, 2007*

hypermarket in Gujarat and in the NCR with a planning to open 30 such marts by the end of this year includes six in National Capital Delhi, five each in Punjab and Andhra Pradesh, three in Gujarat and two in Bangalore. It will offer a range of 95,000 types of items includes consumer durable products (clothing, stationery, toys, medicines, home furnishings, footwear etc), FMCG, IT, automotive accessories, apparel accessories, fine jewelry and fashion jewelry under one roof. According to company sources, Reliance hypermarket concept will be the best in the market. Company would ensure that their products would be cheapest on the consumers wallet and would match the lowest price in the market with the best quality as benchmark. Reliance is also planning to provide some innovative and unique services to the shoppers such as tailoring, shoe repair, watch repair, a photo shop, gifting services and laundry services all within the store under one roof. The facility of owned fresh bakery service will be all time available under brand name of "hot off the oven". To fulfill its dream, Reliance has been looking for deserving lands across the country to fulfill its dream project.

Vimal, a well-known fabric brand of Reliance Industries Ltd. will also relaunch its products that will have a store within its hypermarkets and will offer custom-tailoring services. Besides this, Reliance Retail is building a vigorous and state of the art supply chain infrastructure in parallel to cover the entire country along with setting up its own cold storage chain discretely. Company has planned to generate direct employment for half-a-million people and indirect employment to two million in couple of years.

Reliance Retail Ltd (RRL) is planning to set up a joint venture firm with British food retailer Marks and Spencer[11] (M&S) with an initial investment of 29 million pounds (Rs.2.3 billion). M&S will hold 51 percent stake in the JV, while the remaining will be held by RRL. The new firm will be named Marks and Spencer Reliance India Pvt Ltd. The proposal is awaiting approval from the Foreign Investment Promotion Board (FIPB) of India. Though the initial investment will touch 29 million pounds (in cash or in kind), both firms have agreed to go for further funding as and when required[12].

Sales Promotion

To encourage the customers, Reliance hypermarkets will keep on offering versatile offers to all its customers such as 'Reliance One', a common membership and loyalty programme across all its formats, which follows the philosophy of

---

[11] *Marks & Spencer (M&S) Group is a British retailer, with 840 stores in more than 30 countries around the world: 600 domestic and 240 international. It is also the biggest clothing and food retailer of UK and as of 2008, the 43rd largest retailer in the world.*

[12] *www.nerve.in/news*

'Earn Anywhere, Spend Anywhere'. 'Reliance Hypermarket' will also provide easy and attractive finance options, including zero percent financing for the purchases on some selected products[13].

Conclusion

Indian Retail industry is gradually inching its way to become the next boom industry. The whole concept of shopping has altered in terms of format and consumer buying behaviour, ushering in a revolution in retail shopping. India has entered in modern retailing as seen in sprawling shopping centers, multi-storied malls and huge complexes those offer shopping, entertainment and food all under one roof. The way the Reliance retail has been progressing, entering into new formats, signing with foreign players, it seems in the years to come, Reliance Retail will be associated with common people in one or other way. For the RRL to achieve further growth considering the entry of national and international players like Wall-Mart, the spread of organized retailing has to spread in rural India too and whosoever will take the first step obviously is going to have the lion's share in Indian retail industry.

Questions for discussion:

1. Why it is said that for the retail sector to achieve further growth, the spread of organized retailing has to become a national phenomenon?
2. Explore the need for innovations, customer-centric strategies and launching new formats in the retailing & FMCG segment? Do you think that the decision of reliance retail in entering into new formats months after months will benefit RRL in the long run?
3. Critically analyze and discuss the issues concerned with Reliance Industries Limited decision to restructure its retail arm despite knowing shortage of skilled labour and entry of national and international business houses?

---

[13] *www.newstrackindia.com dated August 16, 2007*

CASE STUDY # 7

MAXIMISING REVENUES THROUGH JOINT VENTURES (A CASE OF BHARTI-WAL-MART' RETAIL)

About Bharti Enterprises

Bharti Enterprises commonly known as Bharti-Airtel is one of India's first private telecom service provider and leading telecom company providing world-class services built on modern edge technologies. It has been a revolutionary force in the Indian telecom industry and today enjoys a strong nationwide presence in all the 23 telecom circles. Besides telecom, Bharti has its presence in other business groups like agri-business, insurance and retail.

Under the stewardship of Sunil Mittal, Bharti Group has grown successfully in partnership with several other leading global companies like - Singapore Telecom, Warburg Pincus, Vodafone, and British Telecom. Bharti AXA, a financial services JV with AXA of France, Beetal communication and media devices, and Bharti Del Monte India, a JV with Del Monte to offer fresh and processed vegetables and fruits in the domestic as well as global markets. Recently Bharti has entered into the retail sector with its subsidiary Bharti Retail.

About Wal-Mart

Wal-Mart Stores, Inc. is basically an USA based public corporation having a chain of large, discount department stores. Founded by Sam Walton in 1962, incorporated in 1969, has become the world's biggest public corporation by revenue. It is also known for the largest private employer in the world and the fourth largest utility or commercial employer, followed by British National Health Service, and the Indian Railways. With an estimated 20% of the retail grocery and consumables business, Wal-Mart today is the largest grocery retailer and to seller in the United States. According to moneycnn.com, Wal-Mart is also the most powerful company in the capitalist world.

Bharti-Wal-Mart Joint Venture

On November 27, 2006, Bharti signed a Memorandum of Understanding (MoU) with Wal-Mart Stores Inc – world's leading luxury and discount chain store, to explore business opportunities in the fast emerging Indian retail industry under Mittal-Mart's name. This 50:50 joint venture is established for cash 'n' carry and back end supply chain operations and have plan to launch its first wholesale facility by the end of year 2008. Each such store will be spread over an area of 50,000-1,00,000 sq. ft.. With the name of Bharti-Wal-Mart, it will be selling groceries, vegetables, fruits, staples, stationery, clothing, consumer durables, footwear and allied products. In the next seven years 10 more facilities are expected to be opened in other parts of the country and will employ approximately 5,000 people. Moreover, venture plans to open such stores only in tier-II and tier-III cities not in the metroes and big cities. According to Rajan Mittal, MD Bharti Enterprises, Joint Venture would cater to all the retailers and not just Bharti Enterprises' upcoming stores. The basic idea behind is to give customers the lowest price everyday.

Bharti Enterprises opened its first store on April 16th, 2008 in Ludhiana with the name 'Easy Day'. The store has products of daily usage, ranging from personal care products, stationery, household articles, hosiery items, daily-need groceries including staples, processed foods, bakery, dairy products, meat, poultry and fresh produce to sell. The company is also planning to open three more such stores by the middle of the year. Company plans to employ local manpower that would be trained by Bharti Academy of Retail.

Experts' views on joint venture

Retail experts opined that both the partners in the joint venture have their own strengths and would supplement each other. According to Viswanathan Vasudevan (Singapore based equity analyst at Aquarius Investment Advisors Pte,) "It is a great fit for Wal-Mart as Bharti knows the rules of the game and will save Wal-Mart a lot of time and energy to overcome the system". According to Gajendra Nagpal, Director, Unicorn Investments "This joint venture is a winning combination. Wal-Mart's logistics skill and Bharti's execution capability will create a potent force in the Indian market."

Though the partners in joint ventures have not clearly disclosed the amount of investment, retail industry sources expect that Bharti-Wal-Mart venture would make an initial investment of US$ 100 million, which could further increase to US$ 1.46 billion. To implement Wal-Mart's operations in India, Wal-Mart Inc has appointed their two experienced executives, Andy Guttery and Lance Rettig.

Retail Industry experts believe that the largest competitor for Bharti-Wal-Mart venture will be Reliance Retail that has planned to establish 10,000 stores by the end of 2010. Pantaloon Retail (India) limited, a retail arm of Kishore Biyani's Future Group is expected to give tough competition with its more than 100 Big Bazaars across India. On the other hand, some optimists believe that the foray of global retail giants like Wal-Mart, Tesco Plc (Tesco) and Carrefour SA would present new techniques of doing retail business and successful international practices in Indian retailing. However, it is believed that the success of this joint venture would depend on how successfully Wal-Mart will build cost efficient and sustainable competitive advantage over its competitors.

Some experts believe that for Wal-Mart, it will not be easy to achieve economies of scale in the grocery, food retailing and especially consumer products where there is very less scope of intermediation. They opined that the Wal-Mart's business model was not successful in all foreign markets. For example, Wal-Mart had to withdraw its retail operations in South Korea and Germany. What will be the result is difficult to predict under clouds of uncertainty. Let it leave to the future. One thing is obvious that the gap between organized and unorganized retailing will reduce and it is the customer who will be benefited in terms of quantity and quality.

Questions for Discussion:

1. How do you see the impact of Bharti-Wal-Mart tie up on Indian retail industry?
2. If big business tycoons like Bharti, Birla and Reliance will enter into organized retailing, what consequences it would have on our 12 million *'kirana'* stores?
3. Being a retail graduate what you would suggest to Wal-Mart and other new entrants about retailing success considering Wal-Mart's retail operations withdrawal issue of South Korea and Germany? What future this joint venture will have?

CASE STUDY # 8

WHAT'S IN A NAME: SMALL BRANDS BIG SAVINGS?

"Good business is business
with profits to both sides"

Anonymous

India's top retail chains have suddenly become the new champions of the also-rans in the Great Shopping Scrum. And if the sheer marketing muscle of Big Bazaar, Piramyd, Subhiksha and Adani Retail now behind these tiny home care and ready-to-fry food players is any criterion, the meek may still inherit the earth. Kishore Biyani's Big Bazaar will be the first off the mark with a formal new strategy to take local brands national. In less than a month from now, Big Bazaar will be unveiling a list of small town brands ready to hit big time*. Similarly, Reliance Retail, which made foray in apparel retailing through Reliance Trends, has introduced 22 in-house brands in the men, women and kids segment.

What's in a Name?

- In-house brands are created and merchandised by the retail chains.
- Due to the absence of advertising and distribution costs, these products can be 10-40 per cent cheaper than the big, national brands.
- These products are available across a range of categories, including apparel, accessories, home care items, food items, consumer durables, electronic items and kitchen appliances.

In UK, supermarkets like Tesco and ASDA are capitalizing on the growth of own-brand non-food goods, especially in the clothing sector. With a steady flow of cheap imports from China and the Far East, supermarkets and retail groups such as Primark is also planning to continue offering low-cost own-brand clothing and other non-food items, in their bids to expand their own-brand portfolios. The growth in own brands has shifted the power in the retail supply structure to the retailer, instead of the brand owner. Retailers now control category price setting and are more adept at promoting their own goods in store. By offering their own brand labels they can reap higher profit margins and with the huge quantities they purchase, they can bargain hard with their suppliers. The own-brand market appears to be highly resilient to economic changes, so the outlook appears very positive. Over the 5 years to 2011, sales are forecast to rise ahead of inflation, as retailers continue to diversify into new areas and consumers become more accustomed to purchasing own-brand goods. Further, as consumers become ever more accepting of own-brand goods, they will naturally be developed in new and emerging markets.

* *The Economic Times, December 9, 2005.*

In USA, store brands now account for one of every five items sold everyday in supermarkets, drug chains and mass merchandisers. They represent more than $50 billion of current business at retail and are achieving new levels of growth every year. For American consumers, store brands are brands like any other brand. In a landmark nationwide study by The Gallup Organization, 75% of consumers defined 'store' brands as "brands" and ascribed to them the same degree of positive product qualities and characteristics - such as guarantee of satisfaction, packaging, value, taste and performance - that they attribute to national brands. Moreover, more than 90% of all consumers polled were familiar with store brands, and 83% said that they purchase these products on a regular basis. (www.plma.com).

It's no surprise that store brands are held in such high esteem. They are a boon to consumers' pocketbooks. U.S. shoppers who reached for the store brand of their favorite grocery products rather than the national brand, enjoyed an estimated $15.8 billion in annual savings, based on industry sales data. The difference is the so-called "marketing tax," which consists of advertising and promotional costs incurred by national brand makers that are passed onto consumers in the form of higher prices at the shelf.

Store brands are important to retailers, too. Throughout Europe, retailers use store brands to increase business as well as to win the loyalty of their customers. Whether a store brand carries the retailer's own name or is part of a wholesaler's private label program, store brands give retailers a way to differentiate themselves from the competition. Store brands enhance the retailer's image and strengthen its relationship with consumers. Retailers know that consumers can buy a national brand anywhere, but they can only buy their store brand at their stores.

If you're brand loyalist with an unanswering faith in the products you purchase, be it apparel, food or toiletries, this story is not for you. But if the recent financial upheaval has compromised your budget and you want to bypass the big brands for less expensive products, without foregoing the quality, read on. Several renowned retail chains have created brands which are sold from their own outlets along with the other national brands – but are upto 40 per cent cheaper. So while they may not be objects of social envy, they will certainly be easy on your wallet and the quality is almost intact. "During financially tough times, people don't mind picking up an in-house brand, particularly in the FMCG category.

While the FMCG section provides rich pickings, even apparel and electronic goods are being retailed at lesser prices. So you have Shopper's Stop, Ebony, Reliance Fresh, Big Bazaar, Westside, Spencer's, Subhiksha and Lifestyle Furnishing, a bevy of in-house brands or private labels across product categories ranging from apparel accessories, food, skin care and oral hygiene to home care, kitchen appliances, consumer durables and even electronic items, all these are available at huge discounts to national brands (see table below).

Comparison: In-house Bands versus National Brands

Products	Retail Chain	In-House Brand	Price (Rs)	National Brand	Price (Rs)	You save (Rs)
APPAREL						
Kurta (Women)	Ebony	ETC	499	Biba	799	300
Formal Shirt (Men)	Big Bazaar	Knighthood	499	Provogue	1,395	896
ACCESSORIES						
Sunglasses	Shopper's stop	Life	695	Fastrack	1,595	900
Footwear	Lifestyle	Roselle	495	Catwalk	795	300
TOILETRIES						
Handwash(1 litre)	Big Bazaar	Caremate	130	Dettol	150	20
Shampoo (100 ml)	Subhiksha	Tatva	30	Clinic Plus	42	12
FOOD ITEMS						
Tea (500 gm)	Reliance Fresh	Reliance Value	98	Taj Mahal	146	48
Ketchup (1 Kg)	Big Bazaar	Tasty Treat	59	Maggi	91	32
Jam (500 gm)	Spencer's	Smart Choice	60	Kissan	76	16
Noodles (320 gm)	Reliance Fresh	Reliance Select	29	Maggi	40	11
ELECTRONIC ITEMS						
Air Conditioner (1 Tonne)	Koryo	Big Bazaar	11,990	LG	13,490	1,500
Microwave (20 litre)	Great	Spencer's	2,990	Onida	5,490	2,500

Source: *Mail Today, December 15, 2008 pp 30*

What are In-house/store brand products?

Store brand products encompass all merchandise sold under a retail store's private label. That label can be the store's own name or a brand name created exclusively by the retailer for that store. In some cases, a store may belong to a wholesale buying group that owns labels which are available to the members of the group. These wholesaler-owned labels are referred to as 'controlled' labels.

Why do retailers develop in-house (own) brands?

The basic reason behind developing store brands is to *differentiate themselves from other retailers.* Though the classic copycat branding strategy does help as a tool against manufacturer brands, it does not help differentiate the store against other retailers. *For example,* Wal-Mart's Equate brand of dental rinse compares itself on the front of the package to its branded competitor, Plax. The drug store chains CVS and Walgreens also have similar copycat store-branded mouthwashes.

In fact, in the consumers' mind, often the only thing separating one retailer store brand from the other is the name on the label. To escape this commoditization, retailers are investing in premium store brands.

1. *Retailers want to generate higher profits.* Copycat private labels have to sell at a considerable discount versus leading manufacturing brands. Although the profit *margin percentage* that the retailer earns is higher on its copycat store brand than on leading manufacturer brands, profit *dollars* may actually be lower. This is because copycat private labels sell at a considerable discount: A 30% profit margin on the sale of a store brand priced at $1 generates less profit than a 20% profit margin on the sale of a manufacturer brand at $1.75. (www.marketingprofs.com).

What products are sold as store brands?

Major supermarkets, drug chains and mass merchandisers today offer consumers as store brands almost any product that is manufactured and distributed. These include full lines of fresh, frozen and refrigerated food, canned and dry foods, snacks, ethnic specialties, pet foods, health and beauty care, over-the-counter drugs, cosmetics, household and laundry products, lawn and garden chemicals, paints, hardware, auto aftercare, stationery, and house wares (www.plma.com).

What are the benefits of buying store brands?

For the consumer, store brands represent choice and the opportunity to regularly purchase quality food and non-food products at considerable savings compared to buying national brands, without relying on coupons or promotional pricing. Moreover, store brands are made of the same or comparable ingredients as the national brands and because the store's name or symbol is on the package, the consumer is assured that the product is manufactured to the store's quality standards and specifications.

Retail Advice

If you're not brand conscious, switching from big names to in-house brands is a good way to boost your budget.

Who makes store brands?

Manufacturers of store brand products fall into four classifications:

- Large national brand manufacturers that utilize their expertise and excess plant capacity to supply store brands
- Small, quality manufacturers who specialize in particular product lines and concentrate on producing store brands almost exclusively. Often these companies are owned by corporations that also produce national brands
- Major retailers and wholesalers those own manufacturing facilities and provide store brand products for themselves.
- Regional brand manufacturers these produce private label products for specific markets.

FUTURE BETS ON IN-HOUSE BRANDS FOR GROWTH

Future Group, the country's largest retailer, announced that it targets to earn Rs 10,000 crore from the business of its own brands in FMCG, household consumer durable and electronics and apparel categories by 2012. "Having achieved stupendous success in some of our consumer brands, such as Tasty Treat, Fresh & Pure, DJ&C, Koreo, we felt that it was the right time to extend it to broader categories such as health & beauty, dairy, apparel, accessories etc. Hence, we have drawn up an ambitious plan of achieving Rs 10,000 crore in the next four to five years. Through our consumer brands, we will be able to offer our consumers, best of the products at much more reasonable prices," Future Group CEO Kishore Biyani said.

The group has decided to invest around Rs 200 crore by 2012 for marketing on the consumer brands, which will also be available at regular retail stores. Its retail formats are Big Bazaar, Pantaloons, Food Bazaar, Central, Home Town and eZone. The business from the consumer brands is expected to be around one-third of the group's total turnover in the next four to five years. This initiative is designed to consolidate the group's position in the business consumer brands by creating more brands.

Source: *The Economic Times, November 21, 2008*

"In food, private labels are 25-40 per cent cheaper than national brands, whereas in apparel, they are 15-20 percent cheaper". This means one can save around Rs 500 by buying a STOP formal shirt, a Shopper's Stop Product, compared to a popular pan-Indian brand. In beverages like tea, one can save Rs 50 if he/she opts for Reliance Select rather than your favourite brand. Home brands in electronic items (Koryo and Sensai by Big Bazaar and Great by Spencer's) are Rs 1,000-3,000 cheaper than the national brands. While retailers vouch for the quality of their merchandise, it is advisable to check the products before one buys.

To compensate for the random incidences of qualitative inferiority, the companies claim that they offer guarantees, and have exchange and after-sales services for their in-house brands. "Exchange options are open for almost all categories of products except inner wear or perishable products". As with normal brands, the exchange should be carried out within a certain time frame. We don't have any specific exchange or return policy on our private labels," says Samar Singh Sheikhawat, VP (marketing), Spencer's Retail.

But what accounts for the price difference between an in-house brand and a national brand? This is easily explained by the absence of advertising and distribution costs in case of a home brand. This cost is included in the selling price of a national brand. For instance, in apparels, a national brands spends upto 35 per cent on manufacturing, about 7-20 per cent on advertising, 6 per cent on distribution and the remaining on sundry costs, besides a margin of upto 15 per cent. In case of the retail chain brand, only the production cost is incurred and no money is spent on advertising and distribution.In the FMCG category, where the manufacturing cost goes up to 65 per cent, the retailer only spends on production while retaining the same margin. This results in lower prices. While price may be reason enough to try out these product, one might also end up forming new brand loyalties.

What Experts Say

Needless to say, the prices of the private labels are attractive, but what about the quality? "Our in-house brands are technically and qualitatively as good as the other brands, or even better. If one is not finicky about flaunting a particular brand, one should pick up these labels," .....

Salil Nair, Chief of Operation, Shopper's Stop Ltd.

Personal Experience about In-house Brands

I bought two-in-house shirts from different retail outlets a While one turned out to be superior in terms of quality, the other was disappointing. I don't differentiate between a private label and a national brand, but the quality does matter, he adds.

Prashant Kapoor, a resident of Ashok Vihar, Delhi.

Questions for Discussion:

1. Illustrate the strategy behind the decision of major retail giants to opt for store-owned brands and the merits and demerits of such a strategy?
2. Explore the need for innovations and customer-centric strategies while developing in-house brands especially in the grocery and FMCG businesses?
3. Examine and appreciate the new innovative business practices emerging in the Indian retail industry? Also gain insight into the challenges faced by national and international brands, if any?

CASE STUDY # 9

SUBHIKSHA – A MOVEMENT AGAINST NEEDLESS SPENDING

Much before the retail revolution had begun to sweep India at the turn of the new millennium and much before many had heard of the concept of retail chains, there was a brand from Chennai, slowly gearing up to become a powerhouse in Indian Retail. Started as a single store entity in South Chennai and the promise of consistently low prices on everything as its rock solid foundation, the 'Subhiksha' brand today has grown to over 1600 stores across the length and breadth of India. Its name inspires trust and its consumers rely on it through all times to deliver larger savings as compared to any other retail chain or stand alone mom and pop stores. It is the only retailer from India to feature in the world's top 50 local dynamos list, as per a recent study conducted by the global firm Boston Consultancy Group (BCG). Today Subhiksha because of its customer centric policies enjoys a large share of every organized retail market that it operates in.

About Subhiksha

Subhiksha is India's largest supermarket, pharmacy and telecom chain. Started in 1997 as a single store entity in South Chennai, it is now present nationally with 1600 outlets and spread across more than 90 cities. ICICI Venture Capital has a 21% stake in Subhiksha. Derived from the Sanskrit word, *Subhiksham* or "giver of all things good", Subhiksha was founded by Mr. R. Subramanian who did his B.Tech from IIT and PGDBM (MBA) from IIM, Ahmedabad has many first to his credit like starting asset securitization in early 90s, IPO financing in 94 and debentures trading. His vision to deliver consistently better value to Indian consumers has guided Subhiksha to deliver savings to all consumers on each and every item that they need in their daily lives, 365 days a year, without any compromise on quality of goods purchased. Subhiksha now has the pan Indian presence with stores across Delhi, UP, Punjab, Haryana, Gujarat, Maharashtra, AP, Karnataka and TN. Today, it is a multi-locational, professionally managed and vibrant a organization that is poised to change the lives of millions of Indians, faster than ever before Subhiksha now has even opened Specialized Mobile shops called *Subhiksha Mobile* where mobiles are sold at a discounted price.

Fast Facts

Type	:	Discount department store
Founded	:	Flag of India Chennai, India (1997)
Locations	:	1600 stores
Key people	:	R. Subramaniam
Industry	:	Retail
Employees	:	25,000
Website	:	www.subhiksha.in

Subhiksha's range of fresh fruits and vegetables is sourced directly from farms on city outskirts and made available to consumers at very reasonable prices. It provides medicines to consumers at a flat 10% discount. It is also India's largest mobile retailer and offers handsets, accessories and charge cards from all leading brands including Nokia, Motorola, Sony Ericsson, LG, Samsung, etc. at the lowest prices. What is exemplary about the Subhiksha brand is that it has spawned a completely indigenous business model that is ideal for the Indian market as opposed to blindly aping what is done in the west – a fact recognized even by global retailing giants. Its strategy of multiple neighbourhood stores, no-frills formats and genuinely low prices as opposed to gimmicky promotions or limited time offers has today found acceptance amongst millions of middle class consumers. Today, it is not just India's largest supermarket chain but also its biggest telecom retailer. Whether consumers are looking for the best quality rice and *daals* for their monthly grocery or trying to find the best price for their favourite mobile or wanting to sample the latest alphosos from Ratangiri or grapes from Nasik, there is Subhiksha that consistently springs to mind. Even Reader Digest recognized Subhiksha as the most trusted retail brand in their 2008 survey of India's most trusted brands (www.rd-india.com).

SCOUTING FOR 'VIABLE LOCATIONS'

Falling retail volumes and high rentals have forced value retail chain Subhiksha to scout for viable locations to relocate its store. Slamming rumors of their shops shutting down across India, the head of Subhiksha said that the group was only 'relocating' some stores, and not shutting them. The move was only to reduce their operating costs, he added. However, many stores in Delhi and Mumbai, where the south-based retailer had extended aggressively, are currently shut, or have minimal stocks. Subhiksha denies any store closures and opines to relocate 10% of their stores across the country. The purpose is to save around 90 crore, which is the cost of generating about two percent of its sale by way of taking advantage of falling rentals. Through relocation, the company would be saving on its rental costs. In addition, it is also taking a re-look at other elements, including marketing costs.

Source: *Mail Today, December 12, 2008, pp 37.*

On the entry of MNCs and Reliance in the retail market

With the entry of Reliance, AV Birla, and Wal-Mart coming to India, everybody was worried about Subhiksha's future because Wal-Mart is also going to be run by people like them. When this issue was discussed between media people and Mr. Subramanian, he pointed out that one should not worry about anybody's entry. There is a huge potential for growth in India. There is potential for another ten people to come in. Ultimately, the share of the unorganized *kirana* will come down and the share of organized sector will go up because of the efficacy in buying and distributing. Also, this is an extremely low margin business. Ultimately, everybody has to sell within the cost. It is not that we are geniuses; we have been in the business for ten years, and we have made enough mistakes and learnt from them.

THE SUBHIKSHA PROMISE

Lowest Prices & Great Savings Everyday!

Subhiksha offers all goods at sharply discounted prices so that consumers can genuinely save in every transaction. Unlike other stores, the low prices at Subhiksha are not limited to few goods or to a few specific days. Customers can get the same discounted prices on all items and on all days, irrespective of the fact whether they make a small or a big purchase. In fact, the discounts and customer savings at Subhiksha are 4-5 times that offered by other small and big retailers.

Wide Selection of Goods

Subhiksha offers consumers a wide selection to choose from:

Supermarket

Quality groceries, packaged foods, cosmetics and toiletries, household provisions etc., sourced from the best brands in India - all available at the lowest prices.

Fruits and vegetables

A large range of fresh fruits and vegetables is sourced directly from farms on city outskirts and made available to consumers at very reasonable prices. Consumers get the freshest produce at the best prices.

Pharmacy

All medicines are made available to consumers at a flat 10% discount. This is especially helpful for elderly consumers and those who are on continuous medication.

Telecom

Subhiksha is now India's largest mobile retailer and offers handsets, accessories and charge cards from all leading brands including Nokia, Motorola, Sony Ericsson, LG, Samsung, etc., at the lowest prices. You do not just get genuine company warranty but also amazing exchange offers on old phones, spot finance offers and much more.

Guaranteed Delivery

Subhiksha guarantees to deliver the exact product you have selected. In case you have received a different product, or if the product was damaged in transit, please contact us within the stipulated time period and we will ensure that we replace it or refund you for it. Please note, we will deliver goods within the committed time period, but there could be occasional delays. We will contact you, in case deliveries are expected to get delayed.

Our Simple Return Policy

If you have purchased something at Subhiksha and are not satisfied with its quality, then you can return the same to us; no questions will be asked, as long as it is in its original packaging and accompanied by its invoice. We will even make the return process simpler for you - just contact our call centre number or nearest Subhiksha outlet from where the stock was delivered to you and we'll arrange to pick up the product from your home. Alternately, you could drop it off at the nearest Subhiksha store.

Real Customer Support

For any information you can contact our call centre at 60607777. Be assured that when you call us, you can talk to someone who will be able to help resolve your problems.

Source: *Company's Website*

Subhiksha's Future Plans

Recent reports have indicated that Subhiksha is in an extremely cash-strapped situation. The store had to even stop its fruits and vegetables. But according to Subramanian, this part of the business was only secondary and not the core as a result of which it did not align with Subhiksha's market strategy. The company also plans of entering the consumer durables space. He further added that other retailers in this industry too have started to renegotiate on their existing deals, Subhiksha is not an exception to it. Currently Subhiksha has around 1600 stores in India. The company does not have any plans to reduce this number but plans to add 400 more stores to touch 2000 mark. Turnover for the previous financial year was Rs 2,300 crore. It is expected to cross Rs. 3000 crore in FY 2009. The company had dropped earlier plans of raising money through an initial public offer (IPO) due to current market circumstances. Instead, the company is looking to merge with another listed company, Blue Green Constructions and Investment Limited. Blue green is a non-banking finance company (NBFC) listed on the Madras Stock Exchange (MSE). The merger will be complete over the next two to three months wherein the Subhiksha shareholders will hold 75 per cent of Blue green. Around 2.5 crore was paid to acquire 40 per cent stake in Blue green recently.

Conclusion

Even in inflationary times when other retailers have upped their prices, Subhiksha continues to deliver the same savings and still lower prices on all its merchandise to consumers. And this is winning it even more accolades and trust from its consumers. The future looks bright as the company plans to take its total store count to 3000 by 2010. And its biggest dream to have an outlet within 1-2 km from every Indian household is finally coming true.

Questions for Discussion:

1. Chennai has around 15,000 domestic mom and pop stores. In contrast, Mr. R. Subramanian decided to start his new venture from Chennai which was considered to be over populated by retail stores. What do you think were the reasons that motivated R. Subramanian to start retailing business in Chennai?
2. Do you think that reason given by R. Subramanian in response to slamming rumors of their stores shutting down across India is viable in the given circumstances or he presently is not accepting the media's reports about store closures?
3. Subhiksha stores are a step ahead of small *kirana* stores but do not offer any shopping add-ons. Considering the vibrant changes in the retail industry, do you think that Subhiksha's business model is sustainable. Explain?

CASE STUDY # 10

RETAILING RECRUITMENT

Sidak Reliance Retail Limited was registered under Companies Act, 1956 in the year 1992. The company is basically into grocery and kitchen appliances. It is a chain of department stores in India, currently with more than 480 stores. Taking the advantage of European and other Asian nations' success stories, company opened its outlets in almost all major cities of the country. Due to effective management and policy of offering quality merchandise at reasonable prices, company has been enjoying the status of market leader for the past 16 years. Today, it is the biggest and the fastest growing chain of department store and aims to have 600 by 2010.

Analysts observed that its heavy investment in manufacturing and infrastructure indicated that Sidak Reliance was bullish on the prospects of its food and grocery business. Sidak Reliance developed new product lines in its foods business drawing on its competencies in brand building, R&D, packaging, and distribution. However, market analysts were not sure whether Sidak Reliance would achieve success in packaged food categories that it had entered. According to a consultant at Mudra Advisory, apart from the ready to eat category, Sidak Reliance Foods was likely to face hurdles in every other food category and especially so in the biscuits and confectionery category due to intense competition. However, more recent reports suggested that even in the ready to eat category, the competition was heating up. Entering the foods business was a strategic decision for Sidak Reliance. While it's core business, grocery was under pressure owing to several factors like entry of countless players and emerging concept of online shopping. Being a cash-rich company, Sidak Reliance planned to deploy its surplus in the packaged food business, where it saw huge business potential.

But due to entry of domestic and foreign players in large numbers under grocery section, company started facing competition especially since mid 2007. There has been tremendous competition to the company's products from other companies which were ventured into the field of grocery and consumer durables in the last five to seven years. As a result of stiff competition with domestic as well as foreign players, profit margin of the company has been steeply declining year after year to the extent that in the financial year 2007-08 company made a net loss of Rs 124 crore against consistent profit throughout from the day of its inception. In the year 2006-07, company made net profit of Rs. 65 crore. During its hay days, company has been promoting employees due to constant growth and profit and in most cases even those employees who do not even have any formal qualification in retail management and capability to sell things have been promoted to senior level positions.

The personnel policies of the company somehow have not been well defined as a result of which every new chief executive has been changing it from time to time so much so that present chief executive decided two years back to induct professionally qualified people at the lowest rank of executives. The situation created a very high sense of uncertainty in those managers who have come from ranks without any formal degree in retailing, on the other side professionally qualified sales employees find lack of direction from seniors which have led to high degree of frustration in them. Because of the above mentioned reasons is total demoralization among the employees at all levels resulting into poor performance and lack of concern for the corporation.

Questions for Discussion:

1. What are your views about the recruitment/promotion policies of the company?
2. What can be done to increase the morale of the employees in present circumstances?
3. What type of training and development program should be imparted for both the professionally qualified and non-professionally qualified personnel?

CASE STUDY # 11

APPRORIATNESS & EFFECTIVENESS OF CORRECTIVE TRAINING IN RETAIL

"An inventor is simply a person who doesn't take his education too seriously. You see, from the time a person is six years old until he graduates from college he has to take three or four examinations a year. If he flunks once, he is out. But an inventor is almost always failing. He tries and fails maybe a thousand times. It he succeeds once then he's in. These two things are diametrically opposite. We often say that the biggest job we have is to teach a newly hired employee how to fail intelligently. We have to ***train*** him to experiment over and over and to keep on trying and failing until he learns what will work."

Charles F. Kettering (American engineer, inventor of the electric starter)

Vineet Sharma, a graduate in retailing management has been working in sales department of a retail store, franchisee of a supermarket chain for past nine months. You being a senior employee have been his supervisor for the past six months. Recently, you have been asked by the management to find out the contributions of each employee in the sales department and monitor carefully whether they are meeting the targets set by the management; communicated and defined at the time of their appointments. Few days back you have completed your performance appraisal and with the exception of Vineet, all seem to be meeting the targets set by you. Along with plentiful errors, Vineet's work was also found to be 'below performance' – he often meets 25 per cent less than the other sales staff of his scale.

TRAINING AND DEVELOPMENT

It is a subsystem of an organization to ensure that randomness is reduced and learning or behavioural change takes place in structured format.

Traditional Approach – Most of the organizations earlier never used to believe in training. They were holding the traditional view that managers are born and not made. There were also some views that training is a very costly affair and not worth, organizations used to believe more in executive pinching. But now the scenario seems to be changing.

The ***modern approach*** of training and development is that Indian Organizations have realized the importance of corporate training. Training is now considered as more of a retention tool than a cost. The training system in Indian Industry has changed to create a smarter workforce and yield best results.

As you look into Vineet's performance appraisal sheets again, you start wondering whether some sort of corrective training is needed for employees like him.

Questions for Discussion:

1. What the case is all about?
2. Being a supervisor, what do you think, may be the reason for Vineet's poor performance?
3. If you find Vineet has been incorrectly trained, how do you go about introducing a corrective training programme?
4. Please discuss the issue of poor performance with Vineet?

CASE STUDY # 12

MARKS AND SPENCER: THE UNITED KINGDOM'S RETAIL LEADER

Introduction

United Kingdom has often been called a country of shopkeepers, and Marks & Spencer (M&S) is undoubtedly the shopkeeping leader. Marks & Spencer are one of the UK's leading retailers, with over 15 million people visiting their stores each week. They offer stylish, high quality, great value clothing and

home products, as well as outstanding quality foods, all responsibly sourced from suppliers we trust. They employ 65,000 people and have over 600 UK stores, as well as a flourishing international business. Globally, it is also the 43rd largest retailer in the world. Most of its domestic stores sell both clothing and food, and since the turn of the century, it has started expanding into other ranges such as furniture and technology. Today, it serves more then 10 million customers a week in more than 600 UK stores. The group has a turnover in excess of £8 thousand million. Also, up until late 2008, the Company also traded in 35 countries worldwide. This includes M&S' largest store at Marble Arch, Marks & Spencer London, which has around 170,000 square feet of sales floor. "It's a truly unique business, a business with fundamental strengths borne of hard work and dedication, and supported by one of the most loyal teams of people of any retailer. It is also listed on the London Stock Exchange and is a constituent of the FTSE 100 Index.

By working closely with local partners in each of their international markets, M&S has been able to tailor its services to the needs of different consumer groups, constantly adapting and improving their offer in each of the countries in which it operate. Above all, M&S wants its customers to trust and respect for its quality, value and service in each and every one of their stores. And it aims to continually exceed expectations wherever its customers choose to shop with it. Marks & Spencer also offers online shopping facility to serve remote and distant customers who have no time to visit physically and shop.

History

M&S was founded by Michael Marks, an immigrant from Minsk (now in Belarus), in 1884 as a single market stall in Leeds. After Thomas Spencer joined the company in 1894 it was known as 'Marks and Spencer'. The site of the first stall is marked with a green and gold commemorative clock in Leeds Kirkgate Market. One of the original Penny Bazaars - in the Grainger Market, Newcastle upon Tyne - remains open to this day, and is now the smallest Marks & Spencer store in operation. Marks and Spencer, known colloquially as "Marks and Sparks" or "M and S", made its reputation in the 20th century on a policy of only selling British-made goods. It entered into long term relationships with British manufacturers, and sold clothes and food under the "St Michael" brand (trademark registered in 1928), a name which honours its co-founder Michael Marks. It also accepted the return of unwanted items, giving full cash refund if the receipt was shown, no matter how long ago the product was purchased. It has now adopted a 90-day returns policy. By 1950, all goods were sold under the St Michael label. Simon Marks, son of Michael Marks, died in 1964, after 56 years' service to the Company. Israel Sieff took over as Chairman. A cautious international expansion began with the introduction of Asian food in 1974. M&S opened stores in continental Europe in 1975 and in Ireland four years later. In 1988 the company acquired Brooks Brothers, an American clothing company and Kings Super Markets, a US food chain. Both were subsequently sold off in 2001 and 2006 respectively. Today M&S is not only a name but a success story for the retailers of today and tomorrow.

> **Self check-out**
>
> M&S was the first retailer in UK to introduce self checkout tills in the food-halls of a small number of trial stores back in 2002. Self Checkout was implemented in the GM (general merchandise) sections in 3 trial stores in 2006 and rollout to flagship stores is in progress.

Company's Plan

Company plans to grow M&S into a world class retailer that's customer-focused, fast-moving and flexible. They work hard to ensure the highest quality products, service and shopping environments in all of their stores at reasonable prices.

They focus on five key growth areas:

1. Continue to invest in and grow their core UK retail business, by introducing new goods and services.
2. Strengthen their UK property portfolio.
3. Drive their M&S Direct business.

4. Expand their International business.
5. Integrate Plan A* (our 'eco plan') into every aspect of how we do business, so that we grow in a sustainable way.

M&S brand values – **quality, value, service, innovation and trust** – are more important than ever. Their commitment to these values sets company apart from their competitors, and enables them to offer its customers something truly special.

Financial Performance

This is a fact that since its inception, M&S has been improving on its financial grounds and has shown consistent growth in its profits as reflected in its annual reports.

Year ended	Turnover tax (£ M)	Profit before (£ M)	Net profit (£ M)	Basic eps (p)
March 2008	9,022.0	1,129.1	821	49.2
March 2007	8,588.1	936.7	659.9	39.1
March 2006	7,797.7	745.7	520.6	36.4
March 2005	7,490.5	505.1	355.0	29.1
March 2004	8,301.5	781.6	452.3	24.2
March 2003	8,019.1	677.5	480.5	20.7
March 2002	8,135.4	335.9	153	5.4
March 2001	8,075.7	145.5	2.8	0.0
March 2000	8,195.5	417.5	258.7	9.0
March 1999	8,224.0	546.1	372.1	13.0
March 1998	8,243.3	1,155.0	815.9	28.6
March 1997	7,841.9	1,129.1	746.6	26.7
March 1996	7,233.7	965.8	652.6	455.8

Source: *http://en.wikipedia.org/wiki/Marks_&_Spencer*

Revenue

	UK Retail	**International Retail**
2008	**£8,309.1m**	**£712.9m**
2007	£7,977.5m	£610.6m
Total	**+4.2%**	**+16.8%**
Like-for-like	**-0.5%**	**+6.6%**

We're doing this because it's what you want us to do. It's also the right thing to do. We're calling it Plan A because we believe it's now the only way to do business and one thing more, there is no plan B."

* According to M&S "Plan A is five-year, 100-point 'eco' plan to tackle some of the biggest challenges facing our business and our world. It will see us working with our customers and our suppliers to combat climate change, reduce waste, safeguard natural resources, trade ethically and build a healthier nation.

Total revenues were up 5.1% driven by new space in UK and strong performance in International business. UK revenues were up 4.2% in total with like-for-like decline of 0.5%. The performance in the first half of the year was strong, despite the unseasonable weather and significant disruption from modernization programme. However, in the second half of the year the deterioration in the economic environment and consumer spending had an adverse impact on performance. During the year, M&S added 4.8% of space (on a weighted average basis), 8.7% in food and 3.0% in general merchandise. While International revenues were up 16.8% with good performances in both owned and franchised stores, up 15.5% and 18.7% respectively. This was driven by both strong like-for-like performance and 38 new store openings.

Operating profit

	UK Retail	International Retail
2008	**£972.9m**	**£116.4m**
2007	£956.5m	£87.5m
Total	**+1.7%**	**+33.0%**

Operating profit before property disposals and exceptional items was £1,089.3m, up by 4.3%. In the UK, operating profit before property disposals and exceptional items was up 1.7% at £972.9m. The UK gross margin was 0.4 percentage points down on the year at 43.0%, mostly due to a greater proportion of food sales in the overall mix. General merchandise gross margin was level on the year at 52.6%, with further improvement in primary margin being offset by higher markdowns. Food gross margin was 0.1 percentage point lower than last year at 33.9% due to higher waste and the growth in franchised, Simply Food stores which generate a lower gross margin. The net operating margin for franchised stores is above that achieved by owned Simply Food stores. UK operating costs were up 4.3% to £2,630.0m. A breakdown of UK operating costs is shown below:

	52 weeks ended		
	29 March 2008 £m	**31 March 2007 £m**	**% increase/ (decrease)**
Retail staffing	**834.8**	819.5	+ 1.9
Retail occupancy	**841.4**	750.4	+ 12.1
Distribution	**383.8**	329.7	+ 16.4
Marketing and related	**144.6**	137.5	+ 5.2
Support	**408.9**	394.6	+ 3.5
Total before bonus	**2,613.2**	2,431.7	+ 7.5
Bonus	**16.8**	91.0	– 81.5
Total including bonus	**2,630.0**	2,522.7	+ 4.3

Despite the step up in space growth, retail staffing costs were well controlled, in response to the more difficult trading environment experienced over the year. Our mystery shop scores, which measure the quality of service in stores, continue to be very strong. The increase in retail occupancy costs reflects both space growth and the increased depreciation related to the modernization programme. Increase in distribution costs reflects growth in both general merchandise and food volumes, as well as furniture order deliveries. Growth in marketing expenditure reflects higher in-store marketing costs due to new store openings and modernizations. Support costs, which include non-store related overheads, were well controlled.

Company is planning to pay a bonus of £16.8m for 2007-08 (last year £91.0m). The level of bonus payment reflects performance against original operating plan. The UK operating profit includes a contribution of £28.3m (last year £19.5m) from the Group's continuing economic interest in M&S Money. International operating profit before property disposals was £116.4m, up by 33.0%, reflecting the strong sales performance of the business. Owned store operating profits decreased by 2.0% to £44.5m, largely due to the Republic of Ireland where operating results were affected by new store opening costs, and start up losses relating to Taiwan. Franchise operating profits grew by 70.8% to £71.9m reflecting strong sales and margin performance.

Capital expenditure

Investing in the business continues to be a key part of our strategy. Capital expenditure for the year was £1,054.5m compared with £792.4m last year.

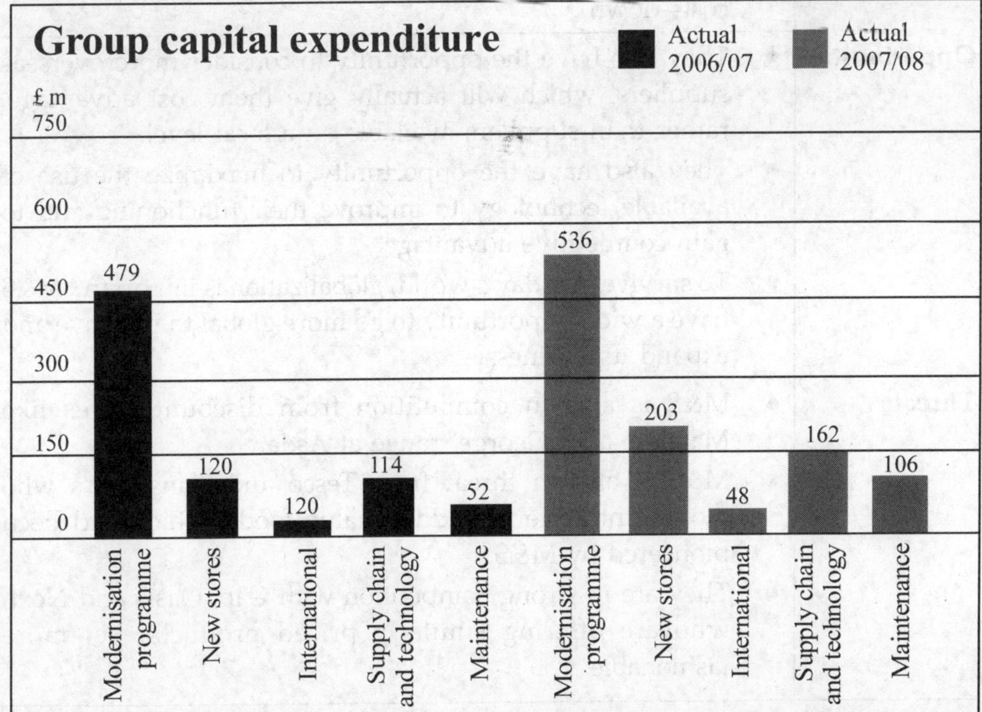

Source: *Company's Website (www.marksandspencer.com)*

SWOT Analysis

Marks & Spencer's SWOT Analysis	
Strength	• M&S was renowned for their attention to detail in terms of supplier control, merchandise and store layout. • Provide highest standards of quality • Suppliers use the most modern and efficient production techniques • The success of M&S under Simon Marks was often attributed his understanding of customer preferences and trends
Weaknesses	• Stocked generic clothing range with wide appeal to the public: buyers often had to make choices, which would outlast the fashion and trends seen in other high street retailers • They always used British suppliers believing that it would give them highest quality with low costs but actually sometimes made them weak to challenge its competitors • This lagging behind in case of introducing latest fashionable clothing to keep pace with the environment actually made them vulnerable to their competitors. • Some competitors are using overseas suppliers to keep the costs down
Opportunities	• They also have the opportunity to consider more overseas suppliers, which will actually give them cost advantage, rather than suppliers available on a local level. • They also have the opportunity to maximize the use of available technology to improve their functioning and to gain competitive advantage. • To survive in today's world, globalization is important. M&S have a wide opportunity to go more global to improve and expand its business.
Threats	• M&S is also in competition from discount stores like Matalan, and 'George' range at Asda. • M&S is also in threat from Tesco and Seinsbury's who moved into offering added value foods, which had been pioneered by M&S. • They are in strong competition with Gap, Oasis and Next, who are offering similarly priced products, yet more fashionable.

Source: *Adapted from www.bizcovering.com*

Products

M&S is the number one provider of womens wear and lingerie in UK, and is rapidly growing its market share in menswear, kidswear and home, due in part to their growing online business. Overall, their clothing and homeware sales account for 49% of their overall business. The other 51% of their business is in food, where they sell everything from fresh produce and groceries, to partly-prepared meals and ready to eat meals. Now more than ever, they're also known for their green credentials as a result of their five year 'eco' plan, Plan 'A', which will see them, amongst other things, become carbon neutral and send no waste to landfill by 2012.

Womens wear

The Company markets its women wear under the following brand names:

- Autograph
- Autograph Weekend
- Plus Collection
- Petite Collection
- Limited Collection (Larger stores only)
- Limited Collection Maternity (Larger stores only)
- Per Una
- Per Una Petite (Only available online)
- Classic Collection
- Bridal (Only Available Online and in selected stores)
- Long & Tall (Only Available Online)

Menswear

The Company markets its menswear under the following brand names:

- Blue Harbour - Britain's largest men's casual brand, includes the sub-brands Heritage, Luxury and North Coast
- Autograph - Smart-casual clothing exclusively designed for M&S by designers such as Nigel Hall and Jeffery West.
- Collezione - Formal, Italian inspired clothing.
- Stormwear - Water-repellent clothing, includes denim, shorts, chinos, coats, footwear and suits.
- Big & Tall - Larger sized clothing only available from marksandspencer.com or in-store ordering.

Technology

In 2006, the Company launched a range of technology products. A total of 36 stores now offer this range. Additional services offered include television installation and technical help.

Wine

In 2006 and 2007, Marks and Spencer entered over 100 of its own wines into two wine competitions, *The Decanter World Wine Awards* and The International Wine Challenge. Both years, almost every wine won an award, ranging from the 2005 Secano Pinot Noir, Leyda Valley, Chile (Best Pinot Noir in the world for under £10) to the Rosada Cava (Commended).

List of M&S Stores Overseas

Bahrain	Indonesia	Russia
Bermuda	Jersey	Saudi Arabia
Bulgaria	Kuwait	Singapore
China	Latvia	Serbia
Croatia	Libya	Slovakia
Cyprus	Lithuania	Slovenia
Czech Republic	Malaysia	South Korea
Gibraltar	Malta	Spain
Greece	Montenegro	Switzerland
Guernsey	Oman	Thailand
Hong Kong	Philippines	Turkey
Hungary	Poland	Ukraine
India	Qatar	United Arab Emirates (UAE)
Republic of Ireland	Romania	

Conclusion

Undoubtedly, today Marks & Spencer is one of the largest retail stores in UK. Its food business, specializing in high quality convenience fresh foods such as sandwiches and home dinners, occupies a prominent position in the UK food retailing sector. To gain the benefits of retail revolution throughout the world, M&S is not only opening its store outlets throughout the world but is continuously updating its product range with new products developed in conjunction with leading manufacturers of short-life food products. The M&S system calculates an optimal layout by determining how many shelf-facings are needed for each SKU in each store. At the same time, the system maintains a consistent look but considers specific fixtures and store layouts. Further, by implementing automated space plaiing, M&S has greatly increased the productivity of its centralized space planning team and gained control over store layout and product presentation. It can now do weekly plans with 20 plannogrammers – and it does a much better job. Product placement at M&S is now more efficient and uniform throughout the chains and customers can more easily find specific products. This is of particular importance to M&S as many of its customers shop in more than one of its stores, particularly in clusters of high density. The main achievements are as follows:

- Because M&S is so well known, it spends little on advertising, decorates its stores austerely, offers very little personal service and provides no dressing rooms or public bathrooms.
- Being so already dominant, M&S would have to add new products or appeal to new market segments to maintain its growth rate.
- But the company admits that the percentage has slipped to about four-fifths and will likely fall further as its British suppliers move more of their production abroad.
- Domestic and international marketing principles are the same, however, environmental differences often cause managers either to overlook important variables to misinterpret information.
- Its attempt to move into higher-priced clothing into a more fashion conscious market has not been very successful.
- Its marble arch store in London is in the Guinness Book of World Records as the store that takes in more revenue per square foot than any other in the world.
- M&S has been successful in appealing to the nationalism of its British clientele by promoting heavily the fact that nearly all the clothing it sells originates in United Kingdom.
- Soft goods (clothes and household textiles) account for about 58 per cent of the company's sales and food lines account for about 42 per cent.
- The goods are perceived as having excellent value, quality and so there is a little need to discount prices for sales.

Questions for Discussion

1. What is Marks and Spencer's core competence?
2. Can M&S sustain in both food and clothing?
3. Identify the main strengths and weaknesses of M&S Plc?
4. How would Marks and Spencer become successful in the international arena?

Courtesy:

1. *Company's Official Website (www.marksandspencer.com)*
2. *www.groceryheadquarters.com*
3. *http://en.wikipedia.org/wiki/Marks_&_Spencer*

GLOSSARY

Advertisement: Advertising is multidimensional. It is a form of mass communication, a powerful marketing tool, a component of the economic system, a means of financing the mass media, a social institution, and an art form, an instrument of business management, a field of employment and a profession.

Assets: Any item or property with a monetary value that a retail store owns.

Atmosphere: Store atmosphere deals with the physical characteristics that are used to develop an image and draw customers like vending machines, catalogs, website presentations, outlook etc. A retailer's image depends heavily on the atmosphere it establishes.

Bait Advertising: It is an illegal practice in which a retailer lures a customer by advertising goods and services at exceptionally attractive prices and once a customer comes to the store, staff tries to convince the customer to buy an expensive substitute that is available. The retailer does not show any intention to sell the advertised item.

Brand Extensions: The process of leveraging a brand name by bringing more products under its fold.

Buying Power: It is the customers' ability to buy goods and services.

Cash Generator: A strategy for a category to achieve high cash sales and frequency of sales.

Catalogue Retailing: It is a form of retailing in which retail outlets communicate about their merchandise through a catalogue.

Category: It is defined as "the logical groupings of products for example on lines of consumer taste preferences and product characteristics where a reasonable substitution is seeked by consumer."

Category Management: It is the process of managing a retail business with the objective of maximizing sales and profits of a category rather than the performance of individual brands so on.

Chain: When a retailer has several outlets under same ownership. Here all the outlets are engaged with centralized purchasing and decision making.

Chain Retailer: A chain store is a group of two or more outlets carrying the same sort of merchandise assortment, owned and controlled jointly and usually supplied from one or more central warehouses.

Channel of Distribution: The route that the title to a product takes from the producer to the ultimate user.

Cross-category Analysis: An assessment across two or more categories to explore their relative strengths and weaknesses.

Check Out: a place within a store where customers before going outside the store, stop and pay for the goods bought.

Combination Stores: These basically are food-based retailers that combine their supermarket and general merchandise sales at one place.

Consumer Behavior: It involves the consumer's perception towards some retailing decisions such as what to buy, when to buy, how to buy, and from where to buy?

Consumer: The person who actually consumes the merchandise produced.

Consumer Cooperatives: These are retail outlets owned and managed by its customer members. A group of interested customers (members) start retail operations by investing money receive stock certificates, elect members to run day to day activities and share the profits on the basis of investment made or certificates held.

Contest: A contest requires the customers to compare and the prizes are based on skill.

Convenience Store: There are small retailers that offer a limited variety of merchandise at small scale but convenient locations ranging from 2,000 – 3,000 sq. ft. These outlets /stores are modern versions of the traditional '*kirana*' stores.

Conventional Supermarket: It is a departmentalized grocery store with a wide range of dairy products and household items such as soft and hard drinks (wherever allowed to be sold), household cleaning products, shampoos, soaps, clothes, medicines and plastic items.

Cross Selling: It is a selling technique where salesperson calls a customer's attention towards an additional product with the main item for which actually the customer has come for.

Customer: The person who does the buying.

Demographics: Information about population in terms of age, sex, income, household size etc.

Department store: It is merely a large general store that is operated by departments and groups of departments.

Destination store: The destination store, as the name implies, is the retail store where customers make a special visit for the purpose of shopping. The main philosophy behind the destination store lies because of its uniqueness in terms of merchandise assortment, way of presentation, ambience, pricing and customer service.

Direct distribution: A distribution system in which the ultimate buyer acquires the title directly from the manufacturer of the product.

Direct Selling: It is a retail format where salesperson makes a personal contact with the ultimate consumers at his home or at his/her place of work. In this format, usually salesperson invites some friends or neighbors at his home, office or club and demonstrates the product after formal lecture/briefing.

Discounters: Discounters typically operate with very low pricing policy by strictly controlling operating costs such as expenses incurred on store layout, cost of land, e-retailing and by offering limited/very few services to their shoppers.

Downsizing: a practice where loss making stores are closed or sold by the retailer.

EDLP (Every Day Low pricing): It is a practice in retailing where goods and services are offered to customers at consistently low prices throughout the year.

Electronic Shopping: Electronic Shopping is variously referred to as virtual retailing or e-tailing. Due to case of access and lower operating costs, the internet is revolutionizing retailing in many fundamental ways like eliminating wholesalers/intermediaries after the concept of manufacturing to retailing.

Excitement Creator: A strategy for a category which stimulates interests in consumers through impulse appeal, for example it may be a lifestyle opportunity or seasonal offering.

Exclusive Distribution: A distribution system that involves territorial protection for authorised dealers.

Factory Outlet: A Factory retail outlet is a retail store, owned and managed by a retail firm (usually manufacturer) for the purpose of selling defected items, close outs, irregular, cancelled orders and season-end items. These are off-price retail stores and are commonly known as factory Outlets.

Finished Goods: The goods that are ready to consume.

Fixed Assets: Assets that require long period to convert to cash.

Flextime: A job scheduling system in a retail store where employees choose the time to work.

Forward Integration: An expansion strategy aimed at acquiring a greater consume base through acquisition of complementary marketing channels/entities.

Franchisee: The owner or controller of an individual store in a franchisee agreement.

Franchising: A selling arrangement between two parties where franchiser is a wholesaler or a manufacturer who allows a retail franchisee (the store owner) to conduct a given form of business under a common name and given pattern of business.

Franchising: It is a contractual agreement between a franchisor and a franchisee that allows the franchisee to operate a retail outlet using its name and format developed and supported by the franchisor.

Frequency: The number of times a potential customer is exposed to an advertisement.

Gap Analysis: It enables a retail store to compare present performance against its potential performance and helps in determining the areas in which productivity needs to be improved.

General Store: A store that sells daily used items, including foodstuff.

General Merchandise Retailers: These retailers usually sell all non-food items such as house wares, furniture, consumer electronics, toiletries, toys, greeting cards, plastic wares, hardware, Jewelry items, shoes, kitchen appliances, clothes, readymade garments, bakery, music world, gift items, cell phones, home appliances, cooking wares, furniture, sports and food courts

Human Resource Management: It is the management of a retailer's employees at different levels.

Hyper Market: A hypermarket usually is a very large retail unit offering merchandise at low prices and combines various department stores. In India, hypermarkets have a floor area of more than 50,000 sq. ft. These have their own multi-level spacious car parking facility for their customers and employees. In fact, hypermarkets are giants that offer long range of merchandise in varied quantity and quality under one roof.

Image Enhancer: A strategy for a category which seeks to enhance the image the retailer wants to create in the minds of the consumer.

Impact: The effect of an advertisement on the minds of the audience.

Independent Retailer: A small retailer who runs his own store. The independent retailers are found in all lines of trade and in all communities.

Independent: Retailer owing a single retail store.

Indirect Distribution: A distribution system that uses middlemen i.e. wholesalers and retailers to reach the ultimate buyer.

Intensive Distribution: A distribution strategy that strives to have the firm represented in the maximum number of outlets.

Internet: An electronic media where computers are attached with each other that use a common protocol and are associated with satellite and telecommunication lines.

Kiosk: A small selling space offering a limited merchandise assortment.

Knowledge Gap: This gap arises because of the difference between customer's expectations and the retailer's perception towards customer's expectations. It simply means that the retailer is not aware (whatever the reason may be), what actually customers expect from him.

Leased Department: A leased department which is also known as shop-in-shops or store-in-store, is a section of a department in a retail store in the form of specialty/discount store given to any outside party on monthly rental basis. The person who provides the store space to outside party is known as lessor, and the person who takes the shop/store space is known as lessee.

Lifestyle: It refers to how people live, how they spend their time and money, what activities they pursue, and their attitudes and opinions about the world they live in. In short, it is the way of living and spending money & time.

Logistics: Transportation means to distribute goods and services.

Loyalty Program: A program set up to reward customers with incentives such as discounts on purchases, free food, gifts, free pases, free coupans or trips for their repeated business.

Mall: A shopping centre with a pedestrian focus where customers park in outlying areas/basement and walk to the store for shop.

Manufacturer: Is a person who is indulged in producing goods and services.

Margin: It is simply a 'profit'.

Markdown: The percentage reduction in the initial retail price.

Market Area: A market place from where a store gets its consumer base.

Market Share: A retailer's sales divided by the sales of all competitors within the same market.

Media Coverage: The numerical number of potential customers in a retailer's market who could be exposes to an ad.

Membership Club Retailing: Warehouse club stores usually sell merchandise in fixed quantities at low prices. These stores require that their customers should take their membership and visit their stores. The products offered are food items, grocery, and clothing with an array of consumer electronic items that vary from season to season. Customer service is nominal due to low price policy.

Merchandising: It is a phenomenon of buying goods and services and making them available to customers/public with ease.

Merger: It is a business phenomenon where two identities merge with each other in a way where one looses its identity and other being financially sound, remains in business.

Mission: It is a long term view of what a store is striving to become in future with present resources.

Monopolistic Competition: A market situation where many sellers offer differentiated products to a large number of customers.

Multi Channel Retailer: Retailer that sells merchandise or services through several channels at a time.

Multiple Store: A retail chain.

Needs: The basic psychological forces that motivates customers to act.

Negotiation: it is an interaction between two parties to reach at an agreement or common point.

Net Profit: A financial measure of overall performance of a retail firm; revenues (store's sales) minus expenses and losses for the period.

Objectives: These are defined as ends, which a retail store seeks to achieve by its existence and operation.

Outlet: It is a shop or a branch or a store.

Parasite Store: A parasite store is a small store/outlet, which neither have neither its own floor area nor its own customer traffic. The size, nature and timing of these stores, depend on people/visitors who are drawn to that location for their own reason.

Personal Selling: It involves oral communication with one or more prospective customers for the purpose of making sales. The level of personal selling utilized by a retailer depends upon the image of the company.

Planogram: It is the store's layout that has description of store's products by the way of drawings, diagrams or other visual objects.

Point of Purchase (POP): POP actually is particularly designed materials planned for placement in retail outlets. These displays permit products to be significantly presented, usually in high traffic areas of the retail stores, and thereby raise the likelihood the product will be noticeable.

Print-of-sale (POS) system: POS is a process of recording the details of customers' payments, their purchases and adjusting inventory levels.

Procurement: The process of obtaining goods and services for further sales. This is a buying and receiving step and includes ordering, receiving and displaying merchandise in a retail store. This also includes how much merchandise should be kept for display and in warehouse.

Profit Generator: A strategy for category to achieve profits higher than any other category.

Publicity: Publicity refers to any non-paid communication to promote an organization or its products and services in public media.

Public Relation: Public relation generally means any type of communication that fosters a favorable image for the retailer among its consumers. It may be personal or non personal, paid or unpaid, sponsored or non-sponsored.

Reorder Level: A level at which fresh merchandise is to be ordered.

Reserve Stock: The merchandise that is kept aside for the purpose of safety stock and generally is not meant for sale.

Retail Chain: It is a group of store run and controlled by the same organizatio0n or company.

Retailing: The business activity of selling goods, services or a combination of both to the end consumer.

Retailing Formats: The process of identifying, evaluating and choosing a particular layout in term of size, location, look for selling a range of merchandise logically grouped under categories so on.

Safety Stock: It is the extra quantity of merchandise that is used at the time of sudden shortage.

Sales Promotion: A period when some products are offered at extra discount through extra publicity and intense marketing. It can be defined as a paid, non-personal form of communication that offers incentive to potential customers for visiting a store and/or purchase products during a specific period of time.

Self Service: A store facility where shoppers can pick the displayed items from the shelves and take with them after paying the amount.

Specialty Store: A specialty store concentrate on a narrow product line, with deep assortments in that product line, such as apparel and accessories, furniture, consumer electronics etc. The specialty stores have very clearly defined target market and therefore provide a top level of consumer service and sales expertise in the concerned category.

Standard Gap: This gap arises because of the difference between the retailer's perception of customers' expectations and the customer service standards it sets. Besides understanding what customers expect, retailers should develop some service standards.

Store Layout: It is the disposition of the various facilities and services of the store within the area of the site selected previously.

Store Maintenance: A process whereby all the store's facilities are continuously monitored for its proper functioning.

Strategic Vision: It is a road map of the future of a retail store.

Supply Chain: It is a path taken by a product from production stage to product consumption.

Survey: A method to collect customers' views.

Sweepstake: Unlike contests, the customer only needs to enter into competition on the basis of the amount paid to a retail store.

Territory: The geographical area a sales person is assigned.

Trade Selling: Long-term, business relationship with a stable group of customers like wholesalers or retailers.

Trade Shows: This is also the common form of promoting retail sales. This includes industry trade show (exhibitions, conferences, and conventions). The purpose of organizing trade shows is to bring both industry buyers and sellers together at one platform.

Traditional Departmental Store: A Traditional department store is a large retail outlet that offers a large variety and deep assortment and is organized into separate departments for the purpose of selling, display and promotion, customer service and control.

Threat: Environmental forces that can affect the retailer's business if no provisions are made.

Transporter: A person who provides truck-facility to carry goods.

Upper Wear: The garments that are worn on the upper part of the human body.

Up Selling: Up selling is a business philosophy applied to increase the retail sales turnover. It involves marketing strategies used to convince customers to purchase additional or more profitable products by providing him various lucrative offers or simply educating him to buy additional accessories to perform the product better.

Variety Store: A store that sells variety of goods and services.

Vending Machine: Vending machines are automatic machines that serve the purpose of selling general merchandise like soft drinks, burgers, snacks etc. to customers in the absence of any retailer.

Vertical Integration: The strategy by the manufacturer, which involves acquiring ownership rights down the channel of distribution.

Vertical Marketing System (VMS): It is a system in which almost all the members of distribution channel such as manufacturers, wholesalers and retailers work together to satisfy human needs and wants by facilitating the smooth flow of goods and services from manufacturer to ultimate consumer.

Visual Merchandising: An arrangement of displaying store goods.

Volume: The amount of merchandise being sold.

Wholesaler: A trader who usually sells goods in bulk to retailers.

World Wide Web (WWW): World Wide Web or Internet retailing today is considered as the fastest growing format of the retail industry. It helps the shoppers to acquire information about quality, quantity, color, price and sizes without traveling and incurring any cost.

SUBJECT INDEX

C

F

G

H

I

J

K

Q

R

S

T

U

V

W

Z

NAME INDEX

J

K

L

M

N

O

P

V

W